Praise for *The ADHD Book of Lists, Second Edition*

"Sandra Rief is a pioneer in the development and application of educational strategies for youth with ADHD across the age span. This new and improved volume is a welcome addition to my resource library. Reasoned, reasonable, well-organized, easy to follow and understand and, most importantly, consistent with the science of ADHD, Sandra's new book is a must for all classroom and special educators."

—Sam Goldstein, Ph.D., ABPdN, editor in chief, *Journal of Attention Disorders* and co-editor in chief, *Encyclopedia of Child Behavior and Development*

"Sandra Rief has once again compiled an incredible collection of tools and resources to not only empower older students to manage their own ADHD behaviors, but also provides teachers and parents of children from preschool through high school the facts and proactive strategies necessary to turn successful children with ADHD into successful adults with ADHD."

—Silvia L. DeRuvo, M.A., special education specialist, WestEd Learning Innovations; author, *Teaching Adolescents with ADHD* and *The Essential Guide to RTI*

"*The ADHD Book of Lists* stands out as a comprehensive and easy-to-read compendium of information and practical strategies. A master teacher and a leader in the field, Sandra Rief, has written a book to turn to again and again for those teaching or living with children and teens with ADHD. In this book you will find important tidbits from the latest research, reviews of tried-and-true techniques, and creative, new strategies to try out immediately. It will be one of my go-to books!"

—Joyce Cooper-Kahn, Ph.D., clinical child psychologist; co-author, *Late, Lost and Unprepared: A Parents' Guide to Executive Functioning* and *Boosting Executive Skills in the Classroom: A Practical Guide for Educators*

"*The ADHD Book of Lists* provides educators and parents with an easily understandable overview of the disorder, and information on evidence based treatment strategies to cope with its symptoms and behaviors. This book is necessary reading and a vital tool for anyone trying to understand ADHD and how to successfully manage it."

—Dr. Elizabeth Laugeson, Psy.D., assistant clinical professor, UCLA Semel Institute; author, *The Science of Making Friends: Helping Socially Challenged Teens and Young Adults*

"Sandra Rief has brought together her expert knowledge of ADHD with her extensive experience in teaching children with ADHD. Her book is comprehensive about children with ADHD and the educational techniques that are available to meet their needs. The revised edition provides the latest information about the condition such as how it is now defined in DSM-5."

—Mark L. Wolraich, M.D., Shaun Walters Professor of Pediatrics and Edith Kinney Gaylord Presidential Professor, University of Oklahoma Health Sciences Center, OU Child Study Center

"*The ADHD Book of Lists* first written and published by Sandra Rief 10 years ago has been an incredible resource to parents of ADHD children, physicians, mental health providers, and particularly educators. It includes a great overview of the many aspects of ADHD, and how ADHD impacts behavior, learning, and maturation into adulthood. It has provided, by using a "book of lists" format, a thorough yet practical approach to all the issues that arise in these children and adolescents. And in this revised edition, Sandra takes it to a new level, particularly how the new DSM-5 guidelines open up new concepts in the understanding and care of ADHD. This invaluable resource should be utilized by all those caring for ADHD children."

—Harlan R. Gephart, MD, Clinical Professor of Pediatrics,
University of Washington, Seattle

Jossey-Bass Teacher provides educators with practical knowledge and tools to create a positive and lifelong impact on student learning. We offer classroom-tested and research-based teaching resources for a variety of grade levels and subject areas. Whether you are an aspiring, new, or veteran teacher, we want to help you make every teaching day your best.

From ready-to-use classroom activities to the latest teaching framework, our value-packed books provide insightful, practical, and comprehensive materials on the topics that matter most to K-12 teachers. We hope to become your trusted source for the best ideas from the most experienced and respected experts in the field.

For more information about our resources, authors, and events, please visit us at: www.josseybasseducation.com.

You may also find us on Facebook, Twitter, and Pinterest.

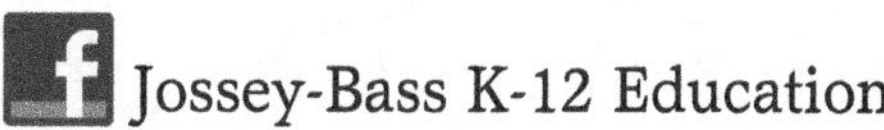

Pinterest jbeducation

The ADHD Book of Lists

The ADHD Book of Lists

A Practical Guide for Helping Children and Teens with Attention Deficit Disorders

Second Edition

Sandra F. Rief

Illustrated by Ariel Rief

JOSSEY-BASS™
A Wiley Brand

Published by Jossey-Bass
A Wiley Brand
One Montgomery Street, Suite 1000, San Francisco, CA 94104-4594—www.josseybass.com

Jossey-Bass books and products are available through most bookstores. To contact Jossey-Bass directly call our Customer Care Department within the U.S. at 800-956-7739, outside the U.S. at 317-572-3986, or fax 317-572-4002.

Wiley publishes in a variety of print and electronic formats and by print-on-demand. Some material included with standard print versions of this book may not be included in e-books or in print-on-demand. If this book refers to media such as a CD or DVD that is not included in the version you purchased, you may download this material at http://booksupport.wiley.com. For more information about Wiley products, visit www.wiley.com.

Library of Congress Cataloging-in-Publication Data
Rief, Sandra F.
The ADHD book of lists : a practical guide for helping children and teens with attention deficit disorders / Sandra F. Rief.—Second edition.
pages cm
Includes bibliographical references and index.
ISBN 978-1-118-93775-4 (paperback), ISBN 978-1-118-93777-8 (ePDF), ISBN 978-1-118-93776-1 (ePub)
1. Attention-deficit-disordered children—Education—United States—Handbooks, manuals, etc. 2. Hyperactive children—Education—United States—Handbooks, manuals, etc. I. Title.
LC4713.4.R53 2015
371.94—dc23

2015014589

Cover design: Wiley
Cover image: © Top Row (left to right): Thinkstock/Jupiterimages; Thinkstock/Andrei Malov
Center Row (left to right): Thinkstock/AKIRA/amanaimagesRF; Thinkstock/Nanette_Grebe
Bottom Row (left to right): iStockphoto.com/SanneBerg; Thinkstock/Jani Bryson; carlosalvarez/iStockphoto.com; Thinkstock/Fuse

Printed in the United States of America

SECOND EDITION

PB Printing V007323_052418

Contents

Section 2 Minimizing and Managing Behavior Problems

Section 3 Instructional Strategies, Accommodations, and Supports

Section 4 Study Skills, Organization, and Other Executive Function Strategies

Section 5 Academic Difficulties, Strategies, and Supports in Reading, Writing, and Math

Section 6 Educational Rights and Systems of Support at School

Section 7 Understanding, Supporting, and Improving Outcomes for Children and Teens with ADHD

Acknowledgments

My deepest thanks and appreciation to the following people:

- My precious, wonderful family (that has grown and blossomed since the first edition of this book): Itzik, Gil, Sharon, Daniella, Raquel, Jackie, Jason, Maya, Jonah, Ezra, Ariel, and Anna. I love you all so much.
- All of my former students and the other children who have touched my heart and challenged me throughout the years to keep learning and seeking the best ways to help them
- The special families who have shared with me their struggles and triumphs and have been such an inspiration to me
- All the outstanding, dedicated educators I have had the great fortune to work with and meet over the years; thank you for sharing with me your creative strategies, ideas, and insights
- The extraordinary parents (especially the wonderful volunteers in CHADD and other organizations worldwide) whose tireless efforts have raised awareness about ADHD and as a result, significantly improved the care and education of our children
- Tracy Gallagher, my wonderful editor at Jossey-Bass, for your help and guidance on this new edition, as well as the rest of the J-B team; it is always such a pleasure to work with you
- All of the researchers and practitioners in the different fields dedicated to helping children and families with ADHD, LD, and other disabilities, from whom I have learned so much
- Ariel Rief, my wonderful son, illustrator of this book and the 2003 first edition, who always takes the time to help me and others
- Itzik Rief, Julie Heimburge, Abigail Roldan, Janet Poulos, Amanda Gerber, Alison Finberg, and Earl Chen for creating and sharing some of the charts found in the appendix of this book

About the Author

Sandra Rief, MA, is an internationally known speaker, educational consultant, and author who specializes in practical and effective strategies for helping students with ADHD and learning disabilities (LD) succeed in school. She has written several books and presented numerous seminars, workshops, and keynote speeches nationally and internationally on this topic. Sandra has trained thousands of teachers in the United States and throughout the world on best practices for helping students with ADHD and has worked with many schools in their efforts to provide interventions and supports for students with learning, attention, and behavioral challenges.

Among some of the books she has authored (published by Jossey-Bass/Wiley) are *How to Reach & Teach Children with ADD/ADHD: Practical Techniques, Strategies, and Interventions, Second Edition* (2005); *The ADD/ADHD Checklist: An Easy Reference for Parents and Teachers, Second Edition* (2008); *The Dyslexia Checklist: A Practical Reference for Parents and Teachers* (coauthored with J. Stern, 2010); *How to Reach & Teach All Children in the Inclusive Classroom: Practical Strategies, Lessons, and Activities, Second Edition* (coauthored with J. Heimburge, 2006); and *How to Reach & Teach All Children through Balanced Literacy* (coauthored with J. Heimburge, 2007). Sandra also wrote these laminated guides (published by National Professional Resources, Inc.): *ADHD & LD: Classroom Strategies at Your Fingertips* (2009); *Dyslexia: Strategies, Supports & Interventions* (2010); *Section 504: Classroom Accommodations* (2010); and *Executive Function: Practical Applications in the Classroom* (2015).

Sandra developed and presented these acclaimed educational DVDs: *ADHD & LD: Powerful Teaching Strategies and Accommodations (with RTI); How to Help Your Child Succeed in School: Strategies and Guidance for Parents of Children with ADHD and/or Learning Disabilities; ADHD: Inclusive Instruction and Collaborative Practices;* and together with Linda Fisher and Nancy Fetzer, *Successful Classrooms: Effective Teaching Strategies for Raising Achievement in Reading and Writing* and *Successful Schools: How to Raise Achievement & Support "At-Risk" Students.*

Sandra is a former award-winning special education teacher with San Diego City Schools (California Resource Specialist of the Year), with a few decades of experience teaching in public schools. Presently, Sandra is an instructor for continuing education and distance learning courses offered through a few universities on instructional and behavioral strategies and interventions for reaching and teaching students with ADHD, LD, and other mild to moderate disabilities. She received her BA and MA degrees from the University of Illinois. For more information, visit her website at www.sandrarief.com.

About This Book

Every elementary school teacher most likely has at least one or two students with ADHD in his or her classroom. Middle and high school teachers may teach several students who have ADHD each day. It is important that educators understand the nature of the disorder, its impact on school functioning, and the most effective strategies for reaching and teaching these students.

To make well-informed decisions on how to best help their son or daughter, parents of children with ADHD must learn as much as they can about the disorder and research-validated treatments. They must also be equipped with the skills and strategies that help in managing their child's ADHD symptoms and often challenging behaviors.

The purpose of this book is to help parents and teachers gain insights into and better understanding of children and teenagers with ADHD as well as the kinds of intervention, practical strategies, and supports that will help them succeed. Although the book is written primarily for parents and educators, many others (physicians, mental health professionals, relatives, for example) should find the information and tools useful as well.

I have had the privilege of presenting seminars and speaking at conferences on ADHD in several countries (Brazil, Canada, Costa Rica, Israel, Colombia, South Africa, Spain, Guatemala, China, Singapore, Philippines, Iceland, and Sweden). ADHD most definitely is not just an "American" disorder; it is one that significantly affects the lives of children and families in countries around the world. Teachers, parents, and clinicians everywhere share the same challenges and frustrations in getting the proper treatment and education for children with ADHD and are seeking the best strategies and interventions that will help them. Fortunately, our understanding of ADHD keeps developing over time, and there is much that can be done to help children, teens, and adults with this disorder.

This new edition of my original *ADHD Book of Lists,* first published in 2003, has been completely updated with the most current information on the disorder and interventions. I also included additional new lists on various topics: managing children's difficulty with emotional control and regulation, working memory weaknesses and supports, Response to Intervention (RTI), ADHD coaching, ADHD and gifted (dual exceptionalities), and research-based instructional approaches and intervention resources.

This book contains ninety lists and is designed to be an easy-to-use reference; it also has an appendix full of management forms, charts, and tools. The appendix contains illustrations that can be used as visual cues and prompts of behavioral expectations or other graphic reminders. Appendix materials are also available online at www.wiley.com/go/adhdbol2. The password is the last five digits of the book's ISBN, which is 37754. By accessing the appendix materials online, the illustrations are able to be printed in larger size and some charts can be customized to your needs.

Throughout the book are also numerous resources you may wish to explore for further ideas and information.

The lists are divided into seven sections.

Section 1 provides information about the disorder (the neurobiological differences, likely causes, executive function impairment) as well as diagnosis, treatment, common coexisting conditions, and more. We have learned a lot in the twelve years since the first edition of this book. The information in this section explains our new understanding of ADHD, which has evolved as a result of the tremendous amount of brain research and genetic studies in the past decade.

Section 2 addresses behavior: preventing or minimizing behavioral problems at home, in the classroom, and other environments; behavior-modification techniques and incentive systems (group and individual); increasing children's focused attention, on-task behavior, listening, and compliance; managing challenging behaviors (impulsive, hyperactive, argumentative, oppositional); and social skills interventions.

Section 3 explains the difference between accommodations and modifications and shares lots of instructional strategies teachers can implement to engage the attention and participation of students, keep them on task, increase work production, accommodate learning style differences and sensory needs, and more.

Section 4 provides numerous practical strategies for parents and teachers to help children and teens with executive function impairments. There are lists that explain working memory weaknesses and the difficulties that students with ADHD commonly have with organization, time management, and homework. There are hundreds of strategies and recommended resources provided in these lists that address how to improve those important skills and compensate for weaknesses.

Section 5 describes the common academic weaknesses that students with ADHD (and learning disabilities) often have in reading, math, and written language. The lists throughout this section provide numerous practical strategies, supports, accommodations, and resources for building skills and circumventing weaknesses in reading, writing, and mathematics.

Section 6 addresses the educational rights of students with ADHD under federal laws IDEA and Section 504. Since the first edition of this book, there have been significant changes in these laws as per the reauthorization of IDEA by Congress in 2004 and the 2008 amendments that were made to the Americans with Disabilities Act (ADA), which affected, in turn, Section 504. Lists throughout section 6 explain these laws, the special education process and IEPs, the difference between 504 plans and IEPs, and systems of support that parents and teachers should find within their schools (RTI and others).

Section 7 covers a lot of other important topics necessary for the success of children and teens with ADHD: teamwork, collaboration, and communication; advocacy; the benefits of exercise, outdoor "green time," music, mindfulness, and other healthy, fun, and therapeutic ways to help manage ADHD; a very extensive list of websites and resources; and much more.

It is my hope that readers will find this book to be a valuable resource in teaching, parenting, or treating children and teens with ADHD—one that you will refer to frequently. I do want to point out that I am aware that with so many strategies and suggestions provided throughout this book, it can be overwhelming. Parents and teachers are advised that it is best to choose a few reasonable and doable new strategies or interventions and then evaluate how well they seem to be working. Introduce other strategies into your repertoire a few at a time as you feel comfortable doing so. Trying to implement too many new things at once is hard to follow through with and is often counterproductive. Fortunately, there are always things to try if something doesn't work or stops working. There is always plan B, C, D, and so forth.

I wish you success and all the best. Please feel free to contact me at www.sandrarief.com.

A Note from the Author

The official term for the disorder at this time is attention-deficit/hyperactivity disorder, which is abbreviated as ADHD. You may see it in print as ADHD or AD/HD (with a slash). The term ADD is also used by many people either interchangeably with ADHD or when referring to individuals with the predominantly inattentive presentation or type of the disorder—those who do not have the "H" characteristics associated with hyperactivity.

Throughout this book, I use only *ADHD,* which is inclusive of all types or presentations of the disorder:

- Predominantly inattentive
- Predominantly hyperactive-impulsive
- Combined (inattentive and hyperactive-impulsive)

See *List 1.3* for a thorough explanation of these three presentations of ADHD.

For your convenience, I have provided numerous cross-references to related lists throughout the book. These are indicated by the list numbers in parentheses following individual items or topics. You will find that these cross-references are useful for finding related topics in *The ADHD Book of Lists*.

In memory of my beloved son, Benjamin, and to all of the children who face struggles in their young lives each day with loving, trusting hearts, hope, and courage

The ADHD Book of Lists

Section 1

Understanding, Diagnosing, and Treating ADHD

Contents

Please note that a lot of the content of these lists has been adapted and updated from my other books, published by Jossey-Bass/Wiley, which you may be interested in exploring for further information, tools, and strategies:

Rief, S. (2003). *The ADHD book of lists: A practical guide for helping children and teens with attention deficit disorders*. San Francisco: Jossey-Bass.

Rief, S. (2005). *How to reach & teach children with ADD/ADHD: Practical techniques, strategies and interventions* (2nd ed.). San Francisco: Jossey-Bass.

Rief, S. (2008). *The ADD/ADHD checklist: A practical reference for parents and teachers* (2nd ed.). San Francisco: Jossey-Bass.

1.1 ADHD: Definitions and Descriptions

Some of the definitions and descriptions of attention-deficit/hyperactivity disorder (ADHD) have been changed or refined as a result of all that we have learned in recent years from neuroscience, brain imaging, and clinical studies, and likely will continue to do so in the future. Until recently, ADHD was classified as a neurobehavioral disorder, characterized by the three core symptoms of inattention, impulsivity, and sometimes hyperactivity.

It is now recognized that ADHD is a far more complex disorder, involving impairment in a whole range of abilities related to self-regulation and executive functioning (*Lists 1.2, 1.4*). This more recent understanding of ADHD is reflected in some of the following descriptions, as shared by leading ADHD authorities Dr. Russell A. Barkley, Dr. Thomas E. Brown, Dr. Sam Goldstein, and others. Some of the following descriptions are from Children and Adults with Attention-Deficit/Hyperactivity Disorder (CHADD), as well as the National Institute of Mental Health (NIMH), and other expert sources.

What Is ADHD?

- ADHD (attention-deficit/hyperactivity disorder) is the term now used for a condition that has had several names over the past hundred years.
- ADHD is a chronic neurobiological disorder affecting children and adults that causes difficulty with self-control and goal-directed behavior.
- ADHD is one of the most common and most studied neurodevelopmental disorders of childhood. It is usually first diagnosed in childhood or adolescence and often lasts into adulthood.
- ADHD is a neurobiological disorder characterized by chronic and developmentally inappropriate degrees of inattention, impulsivity, and in some cases hyperactivity, and is so pervasive and persistent that it interferes with a person's daily life at home, school, work, or other settings
- ADHD is a disorder of self-regulation and executive functions.
- ADHD is a brain-based disorder involving a wide range of executive dysfunctions that arises out of differences in the central nervous system—both in structural and neurochemical areas.
- ADHD is a neurobiological disorder characterized by a pattern of behavior, present in multiple settings, that can result in performance issues in social, educational, or work environments.
- ADHD represents a condition that leads individuals to fall to the bottom of a normal distribution in their capacity to demonstrate and develop self-control and self-regulatory skills.
- ADHD is a developmental impairment of the brain's self-management system. It involves a wide range of executive functions linked to complex brain operations that are not limited to observable behaviors.
- ADHD is a performance disorder—a problem of being able to produce or act on what one knows.
- ADHD is a neurological inefficiency in the area of the brain that controls impulses and is the center of executive functions.
- ADHD is a dimensional disorder of human behaviors that all people exhibit at times to certain degrees. Those with ADHD display the symptoms to a significant degree that is maladaptive and developmentally inappropriate compared to others at that age.

- ADHD is a common although highly varied condition. One element for this variation is the frequent co-occurrence of other conditions.
- ADHD is a medical condition caused predominantly by genetic factors that result in certain neurological differences. It comes in various forms.

Lists throughout this book, particularly *Lists 1.2, 1.4, and 1.7,* will clarify what these definitions mean and explain our understanding at this time about ADHD, executive functions, and the neurodevelopmental brain differences previously referred to.

Descriptions of ADHD: Explaining It to Children

As noted, ADHD is a disorder of executive functions. Of the executive functions (*List 1.2*), the primary one is inhibition—a person's "behavioral brakes." Poor inhibition is seen in the inability to resist or ignore distractions (inattention), to delay gratification, be able to stop long enough to think about possible consequences before acting or reacting (impulsivity), and slow down or stop physical activity (hyperactivity).

One way to explain ADHD to children is through the analogy of a race car with poor brakes.

- Dr. Edward (Ned) Hallowell (n.d.) tells children with ADHD: "You have an amazing brain with a Ferrari engine. It's very powerful. You are a champion in the making. But there's one problem . . . you have bicycle brakes." He then explains that he is a brake specialist and together they are going to strengthen those brakes so in time the child will be able to slow down or stop when he or she needs to and win races instead of spinning out at the curve.
- Dr. Patricia Quinn and Judith Stern (2009) tell children to imagine a sleek sports car speeding around the curves of a track. But, the race car has no brakes. It can't slow down or stop when it wants to and may get off the track or even crash. They explain that with ADHD, they may be like that racing car—with a good engine (lots of thinking power), a strong body, but brakes that don't work very well. The poor brakes cause problems being able to keep still, stay focused, or stop themselves from doing something, even when they know they should.

Sources and Resources

American Academy of Child & Adolescent Psychiatry. (n.d.). Frequently asked questions. ADHD Resource Center. Retrieved from www.aacap.org/cs/ADHD.ResourceCenter/adhd_faqs

Barkley, Russell A. (2005). *ADHD and the nature of self-control.* New York: Guilford Press.

Barkley, Russell A. (2013). *Taking charge of ADHD: The complete authoritative guide for parents* (3rd ed.). New York: Guilford Press.

Brown, Thomas E. (2000). *Attention deficit disorders and co-morbidities in children, adolescents, and adults.* Washington, DC: American Psychiatric Press.

Brown, Thomas E. (2013). *A new understanding of ADHD in children and adults.* London: Routledge.

Centers for Disease Control and Prevention. (n.d.). Attention-deficit/hyperactivity disorder. Retrieved from www.cdc.gov/ncbddd/adhd/

Hallowell, Ned. (n.d.). Explaining ADHD to a child. Kids in the House: The Ultimate Parenting Resource. Retrieved from www.kidsinthehouse.com/special-needs/add-and-adhd/parenting-tips/explaining-adhd-child

National Institute of Mental Health. (n.d.). Attention deficit hyperactivity disorder. Retrieved from www.nimh.nih.gov/health/topics/attention-deficit-hyperactivity-disorder-adhd/

National Resource Center on AD/HD. (2008). The disorder named ADHD. *What We Know, 1*. Retrieved from http://help4adhd.org/documents/WWK1.pdf

National Resource Center on AD/HD. (n.d.). What is ADHD or ADD? Retrieved from http://help4adhd.org/en/about/what

Quinn, Patricia O., & Stern, Judith M. (2009). *Putting on the brakes: Understanding and taking control of your ADD or ADHD* (2nd ed.). Washington, DC: Magination Press.

1.2 ADHD and the "Executive Functions"

Based on extensive research, ADHD is now recognized as a disorder in the development of executive functions—a person's self-management and self-regulatory abilities. The current belief is that impairment of executive functions is the underlying problem causing the symptoms associated with ADHD. People with ADHD experience a wide range of executive dysfunction issues that can vary from person to person. What are the executive functions, and how is executive function (EF) impairment related to ADHD?

Definitions of Executive Function (EF)

EFs have been described in many ways:

- The management functions (overseers) of the brain or the management system of the brain
- Cognitive control skills
- The self-directed actions individuals use to help maintain control of themselves and accomplish goals
- The range of central control processes in the brain that activate, organize, focus, integrate, and manage other brain functions and cognitive skills
- The higher-order cognitive processes involved in the self-regulation of behavior
- A term used to describe the complex nature of cognitive processes involved in identifying, setting, maintaining through, and meeting goals despite distractions and problems along the way
- Cognitive processes or brain functions that enable a person to engage in problem-solving and goal-directed behaviors
- The brain's control center that orchestrates resources in memory, language, and attention to achieve a goal
- Broad set of cognitive skills used to organize, self-monitor, control, and direct our behavior toward purposeful goals
- The neuropsychological processes needed to sustain problem-solving toward a goal

EF Analogies and Metaphors

- *Conductor of a symphony orchestra*. Thomas E. Brown and others use this popular analogy of EFs having a role like that of the conductor of a symphony orchestra—responsible for integrating and managing all of the different components for a successful performance. If the conductor fails to do his or her job well, even with very skilled musicians, the performance will be poor.
- *Chief executive officer (CEO)*. Many experts explain the role of executive functions as being similar to that of a successful corporate CEO: analyzing a task, planning, prioritizing, being flexible, making mid-course corrections as needed, being able to assess risk, able to delay immediate gratification to achieve long-term goals, keeping an eye on the big picture, making informed decisions, and completing tasks in a timely way (Silver, 2010; Willis, 2011).
- *Iceberg*. Chris Zeigler Dendy (2002, 2011), Dr. Martin Kutscher (2010), and others share the analogy when describing ADHD as an iceberg with the visible core symptoms (inattention, impulsivity, hyperactivity) just the tip. Looming under the surface

are often the most challenging aspects of ADHD: the executive function impairment and co-occurring conditions.

- *Air traffic control center*. Just like air traffic control coordinates all of the different planes coming and going, the executive functions involve managing a lot of information, resisting distractions, inhibitory control, mental flexibility, and so forth. (Center on the Developing Child, Harvard University, n.d.).

EF Components

It has not as yet been determined exactly what constitutes all of the executive functions. However, most experts agree they involve the following:

- *Inhibition* (impulse control, ability to stop, put on the brakes, and think before making a response, being able to resist temptations and distractions); this is considered by many to be the main executive function because inhibitory control is necessary for all of the other EFs to adequately develop
- *Working memory* (holding information in mind long enough to act on it, to complete a task or do something else simultaneously, a mental desk top for holding information active while working with other information)
- *Planning and prioritizing* (thinking through what needs to be done, structuring an efficient approach to accomplish those tasks, and making good decisions about what to focus on)
- *Organization* (imposing order and structure to manage information, efficiently communicate one's thoughts, carry out goal-directed behavior)
- *Arousal and activation* (being able to arouse effort and motivation to start or initiate tasks and activities, particularly those that are not intrinsically motivating)
- *Sustaining attention* (maintaining alertness and focus, resisting distractions, especially when the task is tedious or not of interest)
- *Emotional self-control* (modulating or self-regulating one's frustrations and emotions)
- *Time awareness* (being aware of how much time has passed, how long things take, keeping track of time and planning and acting accordingly)
- *Goal-directed persistence* (perseverance, maintaining the effort and motivation to follow through with actions needed to achieve goals)
- *Shifting and flexibility* (adaptability and making adjustments when needed, mentally shifting information around, making transitions, ending one task to move to the next)
- *Self-monitoring and metacognition* (being aware of and self-checking one's own behavior, thought processes, strategies, and comprehension; evaluating one's own performance, strategy monitoring, and revising)
- *Self-talk and private speech* (using your inner voice, mentally talking to yourself to control and guide your behavior, work through a problem)

EF Dysfunction in ADHD

- Research has found that children and teens with ADHD lag in their development of EF skills by approximately 30 percent compared to other children their age. So, expect that a ten-year-old with ADHD will have the EF maturity of a seven-year-old, and a fifteen-year-old to have the EF skills of a ten- or eleven-year-old. It is very important for teachers and parents to be aware of this developmental delay in executive skills and adjust their expectations for self-regulation and self-management accordingly.

- EF weaknesses can be expected to cause some academic and work-related challenges to varying degrees (mild to severe), irrespective of one's intelligence.
- The frontal lobes (particularly the prefrontal cortex and extended neural networks) are the primary center of executive functions. This region of the brain has been found to be underactive, smaller, and less mature in people with ADHD than in those without ADHD (*Lists 1.4, 1.7*).
- For all people, the prefrontal cortex (PFC) matures and develops gradually from childhood into adulthood (the late twenties), with most rapid development occurring during school years. The PFC is the last part of the brain to fully mature, and for those with ADHD, it is delayed in development by a few years.
- It is not just the prefrontal cortex that is involved in executive functions. The brain's executive system is complex as other regions of the brain and neural networks interact with the PFC. (*Lists 1.4, 1.7*).
- Kutscher (2010) explains that the ability to modulate our behavior comes largely from our frontal and prefrontal lobes. In ADHD, the frontal lobe brakes and other executive functions are "asleep on the job".

Models Explaining Executive Function Impairment in ADHD

Russell Barkley and Thomas Brown, two world-renowned researchers and authorities on ADHD, have been key leaders in the field and their work and teachings have fundamentally changed our understanding of ADHD to being that of a disorder of executive functioning—our self-management system. Both Barkley and Brown have developed their own conceptual models of ADHD as a disorder of executive functions, which are best understood by going directly to their books, websites, and other resources, some of which are provided in the "Sources and Resources" section of this list.

Barkley's Model of EF and ADHD

According to Barkley, each of the executive functions is actually a type of self-regulation—a special form of self-directed action that people do to themselves (usually mentally and not visible to others). These self-directed actions are what people do in order to modify their own behavior so that they are more likely to attain a goal or change some future consequence to improve their welfare.

Barkley says that there are five or six things people do to themselves for self-regulation:

- Self-direct their attention (self-awareness)
- Visualize their past to themselves
- Talk to themselves in their minds
- Inhibit and modify their emotional reactions to events
- Restrain themselves (self-discipline)
- Play with information in their mind (take it apart, manipulate it in various ways, and recombine it to form new arrangements)

See Barkley (2005, 2011a, 2011b, 2012, 2013) in the "Sources and Resources" section of this list and his website at www.russellbarkley.org/.

Brown's Model of EF and ADHD

Brown's conceptual model is that of six clusters of executive functions that are impaired in ADHD. These symptoms of impairment often appear and work together in various combinations in people with ADHD.

- *Activation.* Organizing, prioritizing, and activating work
- *Focus.* Focusing, sustaining, and shifting attention to task
- *Effort.* Regulating alertness, sustaining effort, and processing speed
- *Emotion.* Managing frustration and modulating emotions
- *Memory.* Using working memory and accessing recall
- *Action.* Monitoring and self-regulating action

See Brown (2005, 2008, 2013) in the "Sources and Resources" section of this list and his website at www.drthomasebrown.com.

Both doctors have also developed executive function assessment tools: Barkley Deficits in Executive Functioning Scale—Children and Adolescents (BDEFS-CA) and Brown ADD Rating Scales for Children, Adolescents and Adults. See these, along with the Behavior Rating Inventory for Executive Function (BRIEF) in *List 1.15*.

Other Interesting Information about Executive Functions

- Executive dysfunction is not exclusive to ADHD. EF impairment to some degree is also common in learning disabilities, autism spectrum disorders, obsessive-compulsive disorder, bipolar, and some other developmental or psychiatric disorders, and can also be acquired by damage to the prefrontal cortex, such as by traumatic brain injury or strokes.
- Studies have shown that self-discipline has a bigger effect on academic performance than does intellectual talent (Duckworth & Seligman, 2005; Tangney, Baumeister, & Boone, 2004).
- A growing body of research has demonstrated that children's EFs (along with their skills in modulating emotion) are central to school readiness in early childhood (Raver & Blair, 2014).
- EFs may be a better predictor of school readiness than one's IQ or entry level reading or math skills (Diamond, Barnett, Thomas, & Munro, 2007).
- There is growing evidence that because of neuroplasticity, a person's self-regulation and executive skills can be strengthened with practice.
- Tools of the Mind is one early childhood school program that has been studied by researchers and has shown impressive results. In this program, teachers spend most of each day promoting EF skills with their preschool and kindergarten children (Diamond, Barnett, Thomas, & Munro, 2007). See www.toolsofthemind.org and *Lists 2.15 and 7.4*.

School-Related EF Difficulties

EF weaknesses interfere with most all aspects of school success and result in a number of challenges. Weak executive skills are the reason that students with ADHD often struggle with the following:

- *Controlled attention* (focusing and resisting distractions, maintaining on-task behavior, and shifting attention as needed)
- *Time awareness and time management* (significantly underestimating how much time is needed to perform tasks, missing deadlines and due dates or scrambling last minute to complete homework and projects, tardiness to class, chronic lateness)
- *Organization* (messy papers, notebooks, desks, and lockers; unprepared with needed materials and supplies; losing homework and belongings; lack of organized flow and sequence on essays and other assignments)
- *Planning and follow-through* (failing to think through systematically all of the steps or components of a task, experiencing great difficulty with long-term assignments and projects)
- *Self-control and inhibition* (blurting out in class, curbing inappropriate behavior or speech, not putting on the brakes long enough to think things through or get things done)
- *Memory and forgetfulness* (not following all parts of the directions, not turning in homework even when they have it in their notebook or backpack completed, poor recall of information)
- *Work production* (requiring a high degree of positive feedback, cues, and structural supports and incentives to keep on task and motivated, far more than needed by other students)
- *Handling negative emotions* (having low frustration tolerance, getting stuck on things that are bothering them, overreacting when upset, dealing with anger, and other feelings)
- *Homework, independent classwork, study, and test-taking skills*
- *Making many careless errors* (not checking work, not noticing details such as punctuation marks, math processing signs, and decimal points)
- *Reading comprehension, written expression, mathematical problem solving* (and other complex or lengthy academic tasks that require a heavy working memory load, planning and organization of thoughts and information, and self-monitoring or self-correction throughout the process)
- *Processing speed* (being very slow, taking a lot longer than average time to process information or complete tasks and assignments)

See *Lists 1.5, 4.1, 4.4, 5.1, 5.6, and 5.13* for related executive dysfunction symptoms and manifestations.

What Parents and Teachers Should Keep in Mind

- EF weaknesses cause academic challenges to some degree (mild to severe), irrespective of one's intellectual and academic capabilities. Every individual with ADHD will be affected differently in EF areas of strength and weakness.

- Many highly intelligent, gifted children and teens with ADHD (even those who manage to get good grades) struggle in their daily functioning because of their EF impairment (*List 7.10*).
- Most students with ADHD will need supportive strategies and some accommodations to compensate for their deficit in EF, whether they are part of a formal plan (IEP or 504 accommodation plan) or not (*Lists 6.3, 6.4, 6.5*).
- Every aspect of schooling involves a high level of EF. From the beginning of a school day to the end, a student is employing EF in order to get to school on time, respond appropriately to peers and adults, follow directions, initiate work, recall and organize information, find and organize materials, comprehend and complete assignments, and meet deadlines.
- When students have executive dysfunctions, support from teachers and parents and efforts to teach and strengthen EF skills are critical for school success. There are many proactive strategies and interventions that can be helpful—supporting the development of their executive functions as well as compensate for their weaknesses.
- Many students with ADHD manage to do well in elementary school because of the high degree of support provided by teachers and parents (who often take on the role of the younger child's prefrontal cortex). But by middle and high school, the executive demands for organizing, planning, time management, problem solving, and other EF skills can become overwhelming. As students with ADHD move up in the grades, the expectations for self-management and independence are often unrealistic, and many teens who did well in elementary school fall apart at this time.
- Dendy (2011) reminds us that, unfortunately, kids with ADHD and EF deficits are often mistaken for being lazy "because it can seem as if he or she has chosen not to get started on or complete work; and they are often admonished to try harder. In reality, these children and teens may work very hard, but because of attention and executive function deficits, their productivity does not match their greater level of effort" (p.39).

What Parents, Teachers, and Other Supportive Adults Can Do to Help

Numerous strategies, supports, and accommodations for helping students with ADHD compensate for their EF impairments and strengthen skill development are found throughout this book. The following points describe a few general ways to help:

- Environmental structuring to provide a great deal of external structure, such as visual and auditory cues, prompts, reminders, and clear organization of the classroom and home environment (*Lists 2.1, 2.2, 2.3, 2.6, 2.12, 2.13, 2.15, 2.16, 3.2, 3.3, 3.4, 3.7, 4.1, 4.2, 4.5, 4.6, 4.7, 4.8, 4.9, 4.10, 7.4, 7.5, 7.8,* and examples in appendix).
- Explicit teaching of executive skills to model and provide a high degree of guided and independent practice with clear feedback and reinforcement. Executive skills such as planning, organizing, time management, goal setting, and self-monitoring need to be taught with lots of practice opportunities. The same applies for explicitly teaching of learning strategies and study skills that are typically affected by EF weaknesses, such as note taking, test-taking strategies, and memorization (*Lists 4.1, 4.2, 4.3, 4.5, 4.6, 4.7, 4.8, 4.9, 4.10*).

- Management techniques and strategies that enable procedures, routines, and transitions to become smooth and automatic; clear rules and expectations that are effectively taught, practiced, and reinforced at the point of performance—each environment, task, or activity where and when those rules and expectations are expected to be used (*Lists 2.1, 2.2, 2.4, 2.6, 2.8, 2.10, 2.12, 2.13, 2.15, 2.16, 2.17*)
- Supports and accommodations to compensate for memory weaknesses, such as use of checklists, recorded messages, visual aids, tools of technology (*Lists 3.5, 4.1, 4.2, 4.5, 4.6, 4.7, 4.8, 4.9, 4.10*)
- Academic assistance or intervention in areas affected by working memory or other EF weaknesses (*Lists 4.1, 4.2, 4.3, 4.5, 4.6, 4.7, 4.8, 4.9, 4.10, 5.3, 5.4, 5.5, 5.7, 5.8, 5.9, 5.11, 5.12, 5.13, 5.14, 7.6*)
- Reenergize the brain by providing frequent breaks in activities (brain breaks) and physical exercise to avoid cognitive fatigue (*Lists 2.12, 2.13, 3.2, 3.3, 3.4, 3.6, 3.7, 4.9, 7.7*)
- Strategies and supports for focusing attention, initiating tasks, and maintaining on-task behavior (*Lists 2.12, 3.2, 3.3, 3.4, 3.5*)
- Supports and strategies for dealing with frustrations, regulating emotions, and for teaching, practicing, and motivating use of self-control (*Lists 2.9, 2.13, 2.15, 2.16*)
- Supports and accommodations as needed for organization, time management, classroom work production, and homework difficulties, particularly for long-term projects and assignments (*Lists 4.5, 4.6, 4.7, 4.8, 4.9, 4.10*)

Sources and Resources

ADHD Partnership, Fairfax County Public Schools, VA. (2008). Powerpoint: Executive function deficits. Free download retrieved from http://adhdpartnership.com/

Barkley, Russell A. (2005). *ADHD and the nature of self-control.* New York: Guilford Press.

Barkley, Russell A. (2011, January 20). The importance of executive function in understanding and managing ADHD. CHADD and the National Resource Center on ADHD. *Ask the Expert Chat Series.* http://www.chadd.org/Portals/0/AM/Images/Support/Ask%20The%20Expert/2011_January_Barkley.pdf

Barkley, Russell A. (2012a). *Executive functions: What they are, how they work and why they evolved.* New York: Guilford Press.

Barkley, Russell A. (2012b). Fact sheet: The important role of executive functioning and self-regulation in ADHD. Retrieved from www.russellbarkley.org/factsheets/ADHD_EF_and_SR.pdf

Barkley, Russell A. (2013). *Taking charge of ADHD: The complete, authoritative guide for parents* (3rd ed.). New York: Guilford Press.Bertin, Mark (2012, May 15). ADHD goes to school. Huff Post Parents Blog. *Huffington Post.* Retrieved from www.huffingtonpost.com/mark-bertin-md/adhd_b_1517445.html

Brown, Thomas. (2005). *Attention deficit disorder: The unfocused mind in children and adults.* New Haven, CT: Yale University Press.

Brown, Thomas E. (2008). Executive functions: Describing six aspects of a complex syndrome. *Attention Magazine, 15*(1), 12–17.

Brown, Thomas E. (2013). *A new understanding of ADHD in children and adults: Executive function impairments.* New York: Routledge.

Center on the Developing Child, Harvard University. (n.d.). *Key concepts: Executive functions.* Retrieved from http://developingchild.harvard.edu/key_concepts/executive_function/

Cooper-Kahn, Joyce, & Dietzel, Laurie. (2008). *Late, lost, and unprepared: A parent's guide to helping children with executive functioning.* Bethesda, MD: Woodbine House.

Dawson, P., & Guare, Richard. (2010). *Executive skills in children and adolescents: A practical guide to assessment and intervention* (2nd ed.). New York: Guilford Press.

Dawson, Peg, & Guare, Richard. (2009). *Smart but scattered.* New York: Guilford Press.

Dendy, Chris A. Ziegler. (2002). 5 components of executive function. *Attention* (February), *26–31*

Dendy, Chris A. Zeigler. (2011). *Teaching teens with ADD, ADHD & executive function deficits* (2nd ed.). Bethesda, MD: Woodbine House.

Diamond, A., Barnett, W. S., Thomas, J., & Munro, S. (2007). Preschool program improves cognitive control. *Science, 318*(5855), 1387–1388. Retrieved from www.ncbi.nlm.nih.gov/pmc/articles/PMC2174918/

Duckworth, Angela A., & Seligman, Martin E. P. (2005). Self-discipline outdoes IQ in predicting academic performance of adolescents. *Psychological Science, 16*, 939–944.

Horowitz, Sheldon H. (n.d.). What's the relationship between ADHD and executive function? National Center for Learning Disabilities. Retrieved from www.ncld.org/types-learning-disabilities/executive-function-disorders/relationship-adhd-attention-deficit

Katz, Mark. (2014). Executive function: What does it mean? Why is it important? How can we help? *The Special Edge: Student Behavior*, *27*(3), 8–10.

Kaufman, Christopher. (2010). *Executive function in the classroom.* Baltimore, MD: Paul H. Brookes.

Kutscher, Martin L. (2010). *ADHD: Living without brakes.* Philadelphia: Jessica Kingsley.

Mauro, Terri. (2013). Executive function. About.com. Retrieved from http://specialchildren.about.com/od/behaviorissues/g/executive.htm

Meltzer, Lynn. (2010). *Promoting executive function in the classroom.* New York: Guilford Press.

Moyes, Rebecca A. (2014). *Executive function "dysfunction": Strategies for educators and parents.* London: Jessica Kingsley.

National Center for Learning Disabilities (NCLD) Editorial Team. (n.d.). Executive function fact sheet: What is executive function? Retrieved from www.ncld.org/types-learning-disabilities/executive-function-disorders/what-is-executive-function

Oregon Developmental Disabilities Coalition. (n.d.). *Executive functioning: Skills, deficits, and strategies.* Retrieved from http://oregonddcoalition.org

Raver, C. Cybele, & Blair, Clancy. (2014). At the crossroads of education and developmental neuroscience: Perspectives on executive function. *Perspectives on Language and Literacy*, *40*(2), 27–29.

Rief, Sandra. (2011). *Executive function: Practical applications in the classroom.* Port Chester, NY: National Professional Resources.

Silver, Larry. (2010). Not your father's ADHD. *ADDitude Magazine, 10*(3), 47–48.

Tangney, J. P., Baumeister, R. F., & Boone, A. L. (2004). High self-control predicts good adjustment, better grades, and interpersonal success. *Journal of Personality, 72*(2), 271–324.

Tools of the Mind. (n.d.). What is self-regulation? Retrieved from www.toolsofthemind.org/philosophy/self-regulation/

Wikipedia. (n.d.). Executive dysfunction. Retrieved from http://en.wikipedia.org/wiki/Executive_dysfunction

Willis, J. (2011, June 13). Understanding how the brain thinks. *Edutopia* blog. Retrieved from www.edutopia.org/blog/understanding-how-the-brain-thinks-judy-willis-md

1.3 The Official Diagnostic Criteria for ADHD (*DSM-5*)

- The cornerstone of an ADHD diagnosis is meeting the criteria as described in the most current edition at this time of the *Diagnostic and Statistical Manual of Mental Health Disorders,* published by the American Psychiatric Association. The *DSM* is the source for diagnosing ADHD as well as other developmental and mental health disorders. The *DSM* has been updated and revised over the years, with different editions. The fifth edition (*DSM-5*) is the most current at this time, published in 2013 and replacing *DSM-IV* and text-revised *DSM-IV-TR*.
- Although much remains the same in *DSM-5,* there were some significant changes to the diagnostic criteria in the fifth edition, which are explained in "Changes to the DSM."
- For a diagnosis of ADHD, a person must show a persistent pattern of inattention and/or hyperactivity-impulsivity that interferes with functioning or development.
- When evaluating for ADHD, the doctor, mental health professional, or other qualified clinician must collect and interpret data from multiple sources, settings, and methods to determine if *DSM-5* criteria are met.

DSM-5 Criteria

- The *DSM-5* (as in previous editions) lists nine specific symptoms under the category of inattention and nine specific symptoms under the hyperactive-impulsive category.
- To be diagnosed with ADHD, the evaluator must determine that the person often presents with a significant number of symptoms in either the *inattentive* category or the *hyperactive-impulsive* category or in *both* categories.
- Children through age sixteen must often display six out of nine symptoms (in either one or in both of the categories). For individuals seventeen years old and above, only five symptoms out of the nine must be present.

Nine Inattentive Symptoms

- Often fails to give close attention to details or makes careless mistakes in schoolwork, at work, or with other activities
- Often has trouble holding attention on tasks or play activities
- Often does not seem to listen when spoken to directly
- Often does not follow through on instructions and fails to finish schoolwork, chores, or duties in the workplace (for example, loses focus, gets sidetracked). *Note:* This is not because of oppositional behavior or failure to understand instructions.
- Often has trouble organizing tasks and activities
- Often avoids, dislikes, or is reluctant to do tasks that require mental effort over a long period of time (such as schoolwork or homework)
- Often loses things necessary for tasks and activities (for example, school materials, pencils, books, tools, wallets, keys, paperwork, eyeglasses, mobile telephones)
- Is often easily distracted
- Is often forgetful in daily activities

Nine Hyperactive-Impulsive Symptoms

- Often fidgets with or taps hands or feet or squirms in seat
- Often leaves seat in situations when remaining seated is expected
- Often runs about or climbs in situations when it is not appropriate (adolescents or adults may be limited to feeling restless)
- Often unable to play or take part in leisure activities quietly
- Is often on the go, acting as if driven by a motor
- Often talks excessively
- Often blurts out an answer before a question has been completed
- Often has trouble waiting his or her turn
- Often interrupts or intrudes on others (for example, butts into conversations or games)

Three Presentations of ADHD

Based on the specific symptoms, three types or what are now called *presentations* of ADHD can occur:

- *Predominantly inattentive presentation.* If enough symptoms of inattention but not hyperactivity-impulsivity were present for the past six months
- *Predominantly hyperactive-impulsive presentation.* If enough symptoms of hyperactivity-impulsivity but not inattention were present for the past six months
- *Combined inattentive and hyperactive-impulsive presentation.* If enough symptoms in the category of inattention and in the category of hyperactivity-impulsivity were present for the past six months

Note: Because symptoms can change over time, the presentation may change over time as well. For example, a young child may be diagnosed with predominantly hyperactive-impulsive ADHD and later be reclassified as having the combined presentation of the disorder as inattentive symptoms become more significantly out of norm compared to other children the same age.

Other Criteria That Must Be Met

- Several symptoms need to be present in two or more settings (for example, at both home and school or other settings).
- The symptoms are inappropriate for their developmental level (compared to others their age).
- Symptoms are to the degree that they interfere with or reduce the quality of their functioning (for example, school, social, or work functioning).
- Other disorders (such as anxiety or depression) or conditions do not better account for these symptoms.

Changes in the *DSM* Criteria

- In the previous editions of the *DSM*, the criteria was designed to help clinicians diagnose ADHD in children. As the research has proven that ADHD is not just a childhood disorder, it became clear that the criteria did not reflect adequately the experiences of adults with the disorder. *DSM-5* adapted the criteria to more effectively diagnose adults, as well as children.

- ADHD is no longer in the "Disruptive Behavior Disorders" section of the *DSM*. It is now found in the "Neurodevelopmental Disorders" section.
- As symptoms tend to be reduced with age, *DSM-5* accounts for this by reducing the number of required symptoms for diagnosis in individuals over seventeen to five out of nine (rather than six out of nine).
- The age of onset changed in the criteria, reflecting our understanding that not all symptoms are evident at a young age. Now symptoms need to occur by age twelve, instead of the previous requirement that symptoms must occur before seven years old. (See *List 1.12* about the common later onset of symptoms in girls.)
- The impairment criteria and wording changed. It used to be a requirement that symptoms must cause *impairment* in at least two settings. This has been changed to "... clear evidence that the symptoms *interfere with, or reduce the quality of*, social, academic, or occupational functioning."
- Although the nine symptoms in each category stayed the same, *DSM-5* added additional descriptions to the symptoms—including what the symptoms may look like in teens and adults. Examples in *DSM-IV* were only of what symptoms may look like in children.
- Instead of being referred to as the three *types* of ADHD, the wording is now three *presentations* of ADHD.
- Now people with Autism Spectrum Disorder can also be diagnosed with ADHD. It is now recognized that Autism Spectrum Disorder can be a coexisting disorder with ADHD (*List 1.8*).
- There is now a severity level of ADHD (mild, moderate, severe) that is to be specified under the new *DSM-5* criteria.

See *List 1.15* for information about the diagnostic process for ADHD in determining if *DSM-5* criteria is met.

References

American Psychiatric Association. (2013). *Diagnostic and statistical manual of mental disorders* (5th ed.). Washington, DC: American Psychiatric Association.

American Psychiatric Association. (2013). DSM-5 Attention-deficit/hyperactivity disorder fact sheet. Retrieved from http://www.dsm5.org/documents/adhd%20fact%20sheet.

Centers for Disease Control and Prevention. (n.d.). Attention-deficit/hyperactivity disorder: symptoms and diagnosis. Retrieved from www.cdc.gov/ncbddd/adhd/diagnosis.html

National Resource Center on AD/HD. (2014). ADHD awareness month: ADHD and the *DSM-5*. Retrieved from www.adhdawarenessmonth.org/wp-content/uploads/ADHD-and-the-DSM-5-Fact-Sheet1.pdf

Rabiner, David. (June 2013). New diagnostic criteria for ADHD: Subtle but important changes. *Attention Research Update*. Retrieved from www.helpforadd.com/2013/june.htm

1.4 What Is Currently Known and Unknown about ADHD

We Know ...

- ADHD has been the focus of a tremendous amount of research, particularly during the past three decades. Literally thousands of studies and scientific articles have been published (nationally and internationally) on ADHD.
- ADHD is very common not just in the United States but throughout the world. On average it affects 5 percent of school-age children around the world and 4 percent of adults. In the United States, prevalency rate of ADHD in school-age children is estimated to range between 5 and 11 percent (*List 1.6*).
- There is no quick fix or cure for ADHD, but it is treatable and manageable.
- ADHD is not a myth. It has been recognized as a very real, valid, and significant disorder by the US Surgeon General, the National Institutes of Health, the US Department of Education, the Centers for Disease Control and Prevention, and all of the major medical and mental health associations.
- Proper diagnosis and treatment can substantially decrease ADHD symptoms and impairment in functioning (*Lists 1.15, 1.19, 1.20, 1.22*).
- ADHD is a neurobiological disorder that is a result of different factors—the most common cause by far being genetic in origin (1.7).
- Regardless of the underlying cause, there are on average differences in both the size and function of certain areas of the brain in individuals with ADHD (Wolraich, & DuPaul, 2010).
- ADHD exists across all populations, regardless of race, ethnicity, gender, nationality, culture, and socioeconomic level.
- ADHD symptoms range from mild to severe.
- There are different types or presentations of ADHD with a variety of characteristics. No one has all of the symptoms or displays the disorder in the exact same way (*Lists 1.3, 1.5*).
- Approximately 75 percent of individuals with ADHD have additional coexisting disorders or conditions. People with ADHD commonly have other mental health disorders, for example, oppositional defiant disorder, anxiety disorder, or depression; developmental disorders, such as dyslexia or other learning disabilities; and other conditions, such as sleep disorders (*List 1.8*).
- Many children, teens, and adults with ADHD slip through the cracks without being identified or receiving the intervention and treatment they need. This is particularly true of racial and ethnic minorities and girls.
- ADHD is diagnosed at least two to three times more frequently in boys than girls, although many more girls may actually have ADHD. Because they often have less disruptive symptoms associated with hyperactivity and impulsivity, girls are more likely to be overlooked (*List 1.12*).
- The challenging behaviors that children with ADHD exhibit stem from neurobiological differences. Their behaviors are not willful or deliberate. Children with ADHD are often not even aware of their behaviors and their impact on others (*List 1.7*).

- The prognosis for ADHD can be alarming if it is not treated. Without interventions, those with this disorder are at risk for serious problems in many domains: social, emotional, behavioral, academic, health, safety, employment, and others (*List 1.6*).
- Children with ADHD are more likely than their peers to be suspended or expelled from school, retained a grade or drop out of school, have trouble socially and emotionally, and experience rejection, ridicule, and punishment (*List 1.6*).
- ADHD is typically a lifelong disorder. The majority of children with ADHD (approximately 80 percent) continue to have the disorder into adolescence, and 50 to 65 percent will continue to exhibit symptoms into adulthood. In the past, ADHD was believed to be a childhood disorder. We now know that this is not the case (*Lists 1.6, 1.11, 7.5*).
- Although ADHD is most commonly diagnosed in school-age children, it can be and is diagnosed reliably in younger children and adults (*Lists 1.3, 1.15, 7.4*).
- The prognosis for ADHD when treated is positive and hopeful. Most children who are diagnosed and provided with the help they need are able to manage the disorder. Parents should be optimistic because ADHD does not limit their child's potential. Countless highly successful adults in every profession and walk of life have ADHD.
- ADHD has been recognized by clinical science and documented in the literature since 1902 (having been renamed several times). Some of the previous names for the disorder were *minimal brain dysfunction, hyperactive child syndrome,* and *ADD* with or without hyperactivity.
- Children with ADHD can usually be taught effectively in general education classrooms with proper management strategies, supports, and accommodations, and engaging, motivating instruction.
- ADHD is not the result of poor parenting.
- ADHD is not laziness, willful misbehavior, or a character flaw.
- Medication therapy and behavioral therapy are effective treatments for ADHD (*Lists 1.19, 1.20, 1.22*).
- Medications used to treat ADHD are proven to work effectively for reducing the symptoms and impairment in 70 to 95 percent of children diagnosed with ADHD. They are effective in adults as well (*Lists 1.19, 1.20*).
- Behavioral interventions and programs, such as a token economy or a daily report card system between home and school, are beneficial for students with ADHD (*Lists 1.22, 2.8, 2.9*). *Note:* See other lists in section 2, as well, and examples of daily report cards for children and teens in the appendix.
- A number of other conditions, disorders, or factors (for example, learning, medical and health, social, emotional) may cause symptoms that look like but are not ADHD (*List 1.9*).
- A number of factors can intensify the problems of someone with ADHD or lead to significant improvement, such as the structure in the environment, support systems in place, or level of stress.
- ADHD can be managed best by a multimodal treatment and a team approach. We know that it takes a team effort of parents, school personnel, and health and mental health professionals to be most effective in helping children and teens with ADHD. Other supports and interventions such as exercise and ADHD coaching also are helpful in managing ADHD (*Lists 1.23, 2.17, 7.1, 7.3, 7.6, 7.7*).

- No single intervention effectively manages ADHD for most people with the disorder. Various treatments or supports are typically needed, and these change at different times in the person's life. It takes vigilance and ongoing monitoring of the interventions in place for their effectiveness.
- The teaching techniques and strategies that are necessary for the success of children with ADHD are good teaching practices and typically helpful to all students.
- There are many resources available for children, teens, and adults with ADHD as well as those living with and working with individuals with ADHD. (See lists throughout this book.)
- There is need for better diagnosis, education, and treatment of this disorder that affects so many lives.
- We are learning more and more each day through the efforts of the many researchers, practitioners (educators, mental health professionals, physicians), and others committed to improving the lives of individuals with ADHD.

We Do Not Yet Know Enough About ...

Further and future research will hopefully shed light on the following:

- All of the causes. We have learned a lot, particularly since the 1990s about delayed maturation and underactivity in some regions of the brain. There is still much to be learned, for example, the precise areas of the brain affected, the reasons for any alteration or differences in the brain, which genes are affected, and possible environmental causes.
- How to prevent ADHD or minimize the risk factors and negative effects
- Diagnosing and treating the disorder in certain populations (very young children, females, adults, and racial and ethnic minorities), as the majority of research in past decades was studying ADHD in school-age Caucasian boys.
- More conclusive tests for diagnosing ADHD
- More targeted treatment options
- Long-term treatment effects
- The inattentive type of ADHD
- What may prove to be the best, most effective treatments and strategies for helping individuals with ADHD

Note: Still in its infancy at this stage, a different, distinct attention disorder that resembles the inattentive presentation of ADHD is being observed by researchers. It is currently called *sluggish cognitive tempo (SGT),* although Russell Barkley advocates for a change of name to *concentration deficit disorder (CDD).*

The symptoms of this possible other disorder or different subtype of ADHD include excessive daydreaming, easily confused, stares a lot, slow moving or sluggish, persistent difficulty concentrating, appears spacey, lacks energy, and is drowsy, easily fatigued, slow to complete tasks, withdrawn, and doesn't process information as quickly or accurately as others.

Early research is finding that this group of children does not have the self-regulation difficulties associated with ADHD.

Evidence to date indicates that SCT is a distinct disorder of attention from ADHD, yet one that may overlap with it in about half of all cases (Barkley, 2014).

Much more research needs to be done. SGT or CDD is not something that many professionals in the field have even heard about at this time. Currently, there is not a separate disorder or classification and it is not found in the *DSM-5*. It is currently being studied by scientists, so we undoubtedly will be learning and hearing much more about this in the future.

Reputable, leading scientists, such as Barkley and Dr. Rosemary Tannock, have written about this and are reliable sources of information (Barkley, 2013, 2014; Tannock, 2014).

Sources and Resources

Barkley, Russell A. (2013). *Taking charge of ADHD: The complete, authoritative guide for parents* (3rd ed.). New York: Guilford Press.

Barkley, Russell A. (2014) Sluggish cognitive tempo (concentration deficit disorder): Current status, future directions, and a plea to change the name. *J Abnorm Child Psychol*, 2014 Jan., *42* (1), 117–125.

Tannock, Rosemary. (2014). The other ADHD. *ADDitude Magazine, 14*(4), 42–43.

Wolraich, Mark L., & DuPaul, George J. (2010). *ADHD diagnosis and management: A practical guide for the clinic and the classroom*. Baltimore, MD: Paul H. Brookes.

See CHADD www.chadd.org and National Resource Center on AD/HD http://help4adhd.org/ for up-to-date information as per the research in the field, as well as some of the other sources that are found in the "Sources and Resources" sections at the end of the other lists throughout section 1.

1.5 Signs and Symptoms of ADHD

In making a diagnosis of ADHD, a qualified clinician does so based on the criteria set forth in the fifth edition of the *Diagnostic and Statistical Manual of Mental Disorders* (*DSM-5*), published in 2013 by the American Psychiatric Association, which is described in detail in *List 1.3*.

The *DSM-5* lists nine specific symptoms under the *inattention* category and nine specific symptoms under the *hyperactive-impulsive* category. Part of the diagnostic criteria for ADHD is that the child, teen, or adult often displays a significant number of symptoms of *either* the inattentive *or* the hyperactive-impulsive categories *or* in both categories.

Following are behaviors or observable symptoms that are common in children and teens with ADHD. The eighteen symptoms that are found in the *DSM-5* criteria are *italicized*. Additional symptoms associated with ADHD are also included, but they are not italicized.

All people exhibit these behaviors at times. If a child or teen frequently exhibits several of these symptoms and they are affecting his or her functioning and causing him or her problems (e.g., at school or socially), it is a red flag that an evaluation for ADHD is appropriate. The evaluation determines if all of the *DSM-5* criteria have been met in order to receive the diagnosis of ADHD (*Lists 1.3, 1.15*).

Symptoms of Inattention and Associated Problems

- *Easily distracted by extraneous stimuli* (for example, sights, sounds, movement in the environment)
- *Does not seem to listen when spoken to directly*
- Difficulty remembering and following instructions
- *Difficulty sustaining attention in tasks and play activities*
- Difficulty concentrating and is easily pulled off task
- Difficulty sustaining sufficient level of alertness and effort needed to get through nonpreferred tasks (homework, chores) or any that are tedious, lengthy, or perceived as boring
- *Forgetful in daily activities*
- *Does not follow through on instructions and fails to finish schoolwork, chores, or duties in the workplace (not because of oppositional behavior or failure to understand instructions)*
- Tunes out; may appear spacey
- Daydreams (thoughts are elsewhere)
- Requires a lot of adult prompts and refocusing to complete tasks
- Appears confused
- Easily overwhelmed
- Difficulty initiating or getting started on tasks
- Has many incomplete assignments and unfinished tasks
- *Avoids, dislikes, or is reluctant to engage in tasks requiring sustained mental effort (such as schoolwork or homework)*
- Difficulty working independently; needs a high degree of supervision and redirecting attention to task at hand

- Gets bored easily
- Poor listening and communication: not following directions, pulled off topic in conversations, not focusing on the speaker
- *Fails to pay attention to details and makes many careless mistakes*
- Many errors with academic tasks requiring attention to details and accuracy (such as math computation, spelling, and written mechanics)
- Unaware of mistakes and errors made
- Difficulty staying focused while reading as seen by losing his or her place, missing words and details, spotty comprehension, and needing to reread the material (sometimes a few times)
- Poor study skills, such as test-taking and note-taking skills
- Off topic in writing—losing train of thought
- Many written errors in capitalization and punctuation; difficulty editing own work for such errors
- Numerous computational errors in math because of inattention to operational signs (plus, minus, multiplication, division), decimal points, and so forth
- Slow, minimal written work production and output (taking often two to three times longer or more than classmates to complete homework or class assignments)
- Appears to have slower speed of processing information (for example, responding to teacher questions or keeping up with class discussions)
- Inconsistent performance—one day is able to perform a task, the next day cannot
- *Loses things necessary for tasks or activities (for example, toys, school assignments, pencils, books, or tools)*
- *Difficulty organizing tasks and activities (for example, planning, scheduling, preparing)*
- Fails to record assignments and bring home necessary materials for homework
- Missing verbal and nonverbal cues, which affects social skills
- Lack of or minimal class participation

Predominantly Inattentive ADHD

- As described in *List 1.3,* there are three types or presentations of ADHD. The predominantly inattentive ADHD is what some people prefer to call ADD because those diagnosed with it do not have the hyperactive symptoms. They may show some but not a significant amount of symptoms in the hyperactive-impulsive category.
- These children and teens often slip through the cracks and are not as easily identified or understood. Because they do not exhibit the disruptive behaviors associated with ADHD, it is easy to overlook these students and misinterpret their behaviors and symptoms as "not trying" or "being lazy." Many girls have the predominantly inattentive presentation of the disorder (*List 1.12*).
- Most people display any of these behaviors at times and in different situations to a certain degree. Those who truly have the disorder have a history of frequently exhibiting many of these behaviors (far above the normal range developmentally when compared to their peers), in multiple settings (such as home, school, social, work), and to the degree that they interfere with or reduce the quality of their functioning (*List 1.3*).

- Be aware that people with ADHD who have significant attention difficulties are often able to be focused and sustain attention for long periods of time when they play video games or are engaged in other high-interest, stimulating, and rapidly changing activities. In fact, many hyper-focus on such activities and have a hard time disengaging from them.

Symptoms of Hyperactivity and Impulsivity and Associated Problems

The nine italicized symptoms are found in the *DSM-5* criteria (*List 1.3*).

- Much difficulty in situations that require waiting patiently
- Difficulty with raising one's hand and waiting to be called on
- *Interrupts or intrudes on others* (for example, butts into conversations or games)
- *Blurts out answers before questions have been completed*
- *Has difficulty waiting for his or her turn in games and activities*
- Cannot keep hands and feet to self
- Knows the rules and consequences but repeatedly makes the same errors or infractions of rules
- Gets in trouble because he or she cannot stop and think before acting (responds first, thinks later)
- Difficulty standing in lines
- Does not think or worry about consequences, so tends to be fearless or gravitate to high-risk behavior
- Accident prone and breaks things
- Difficulty inhibiting what he or she says, making tactless comments; says whatever pops into his or her head and talks back to authority figures
- Begins tasks without waiting for directions (before listening to the full directions or taking the time to read written directions)
- Hurries through tasks, particularly boring ones, and consequently makes numerous careless errors
- Gets easily bored and impatient
- Does not take time to correct or edit work
- Disrupts, bothers others
- *On the go or acts as if driven by a motor*
- Highly energetic, almost nonstop motion
- Engages in physically dangerous activities (for example, jumping from heights, riding bike into the street without looking); hence, a high frequency of injuries
- *Leaves seat in classroom or in other situations in which remaining seated is expected*
- *Fidgets with hands or feet or squirms in seat*
- Cannot sit still in chair (is in and out of chair, rocks and tips chair over, sits on knees, or stands by desk)
- Inability to sit still long enough to perform required tasks
- *Runs about or climbs excessively in situations in which it is inappropriate (in adolescents or adults, may be limited to subjective feelings of restlessness)*

- A high degree of unnecessary movement (pacing, tapping feet, leg bouncing, pencil tapping, drumming fingers)
- Seems to need something in hands; finds or reaches for nearby objects to play with or put in mouth
- Is not where he or she is supposed to be (for example, roams around the classroom)
- *Talks excessively*
- *Difficulty playing or engaging in leisure activities quietly*
- Intrudes in other people's space; difficulty staying within own boundaries
- Overall difficulty regulating motor activity
- Cannot wait or delay gratification; wants things immediately
- Constantly drawn to something more interesting or stimulating in the environment
- Hits when upset or grabs things away from others (not inhibiting responses or thinking of consequences)
- Becomes overstimulated and excitable and has difficulty calming oneself or settling down
- Appears to live in the moment, acting without foresight or hindsight
- Easily pulled off task, affecting work performance and class participation
- A greater challenge to motivate and discipline (not responding as well to typical rewards or punishments effective for most students)

Predominantly Hyperactive-Impulsive ADHD

- Individuals with this presentation of ADHD have a significant number of hyperactive-impulsive symptoms. They may have some but not a significant number of inattentive symptoms that are developmentally inappropriate.
- Hyperactive-impulsive ADHD (without the inattention) is most commonly diagnosed in early childhood. Children receiving this diagnosis are often reclassified as having the combined type or presentation of ADHD when they get older, and the inattentive symptoms emerge more and become developmentally significant.
- Although all people will exhibit these behaviors at times to a certain degree, for those with ADHD, the symptoms far exceed that which is normal developmentally (in frequency, level, and intensity) and are evident and problematic in multiple settings.

Note: The combined presentation of ADHD (having a significant number of symptoms in both categories) is most common.

Other Common Difficulties Experienced by Children and Teens with ADHD

In addition to symptoms related to inattention, hyperactivity, and impulsivity, other challenges related to executive function and self-regulation weaknesses, as well as common coexisting conditions (such as learning disabilities), are often evident in individuals with ADHD.

Social and Emotional

- A high degree of emotionality (for example, temper outbursts, quick to anger, gets upset, irritable, moody)
- Easily upset or frustrated and has a hard time coping with or managing feelings
- Overly reactive—easily provoked to fighting and uses inappropriate means of resolving conflicts
- Difficulty with transitions and changes in routine or activity
- Displays aggressive behavior
- Receives a lot of negative attention and interaction from peers and adults
- Difficulty working in cooperative groups or getting along with peers in work or play situations
- Gets along better with younger children
- Immature social skills
- See *Lists 1.2, 2.15, 2.16, 2.17)*.

Organization and Time Management

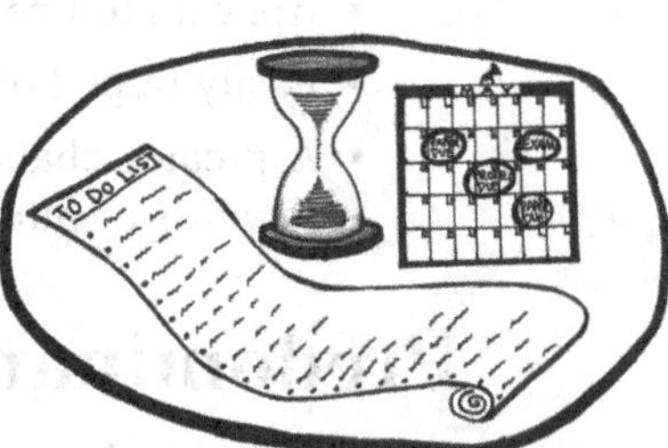

- Disorganized—frequently misplaces or loses belongings; desks, backpacks, lockers, and rooms extremely messy and chaotic
- Unprepared with materials and books needed for schoolwork and homework
- Poorly organized work, such as writing assignments
- Little or no awareness of time; chronic lateness, often underestimates length of time a task will require to complete or how long it takes to get somewhere
- Procrastinates
- Great difficulty with long-term assignments and projects—scrambling last minute to complete important assignments
- Misses deadlines and due dates
- See *Lists 1.2, 4.4*.

Other Executive Skills

- Forgetfulness (such as not remembering to turn in homework even when completed)
- Difficulty with tasks requiring a heavy memory load
- Poor planning for assignments and projects
- Difficulty prioritizing
- See *Lists 1.2, 4.1*.

Learning, Language, Academic, Other

- Learning and school performance difficulties; not achieving or performing to level that is expected given his or her apparent ability
- Language and communication problems (for example, not sticking to topic, not fluent verbally)

- Inefficient learning strategies
- Poor handwriting and fine-motor skills
- Problem-solving difficulties
- Variability of performance and output (one day can do the task, the next day cannot)
- If learning disabilities such as dyslexia coexist, then difficulty with basic reading skills (word recognition and fluency, writing, spelling, and other academic difficulties) will be more significant.
- See *Lists 4.3, 5.1, 5.6, 5.13.*

Note: See lists throughout this book describing executive function difficulties, social, emotional, and academic challenges, symptoms in girls, and other lists that provide more information on this topic. Also, coexisting conditions each have their own set of signs and symptoms. *List 1.11* describes more symptoms across the lifespan. Every individual with ADHD has his or her own profile of specific weaknesses or symptoms as well as numerous strengths (*List 1.10*).

See information in *List 1.4* regarding sluggish cognitive tempo (SCT).

Source and Resource

American Psychiatric Association. (2013). *Diagnostic and statistical manual of mental disorders (DSM)* (5th ed.). Washington, DC: Author.

1.6 ADHD Statistics: Prevalence and Risk Factors

ADHD places those who have this disorder at risk for a host of serious consequences, which raises the urgency for early identification, diagnosis, and proper treatment. Numerous studies have shown the increased risk of negative outcomes associated with those who have ADHD. Compared with peers of the same age, youth with ADHD experience the following:

- More serious accidents, hospitalizations, and significantly higher medical costs
- More school failure and dropout
- More delinquency and altercations with the law
- More engagement in antisocial activities
- More teen pregnancy and sexually transmitted diseases
- Earlier experimentation with and higher use of alcohol, tobacco, and illicit drugs
- More trouble socially and emotionally
- More rejection, ridicule, and punishment
- More underachievement and underperformance at school or work

Prevalence of ADHD

The number of people estimated to have ADHD varies, depending on the source, which can be confusing. Here are some of the reported prevalence rates:

- The American Psychiatric Association states in the *DSM-5* that 5 percent of children have ADHD (American Psychiatric Association, 2013). However, studies in the United States have estimated higher rates in community samples (CDC, n.d.; CHADD, n.d.-a, n.d.-b).
- The prevalence of ADHD in children ranges from 5 to 11 percent, depending on the age group (CDC, n.d.-a; CHADD, n.d.-b).
- Approximately 11 percent of children four to seventeen years of age (6.4 million) have ever been diagnosed with ADHD as of 2011, according to the results surveys that asked parents whether their child received an ADHD diagnosis from a health care provider (CDC, n.d-a.).
- Based on the CDC analysis of data from the National Survey of Children's Health, which has been collected every four years since 2003, the percentage of children diagnosed with ADHD increased from 7.8 percent in 2003 to 9.5 percent in 2007 and to 11.0 percent in 2011 (CDC, n.d.-a,).
- The worldwide prevalence of ADHD for children is approximately 5 percent, based on a review of over one hundred studies comprising subjects from all world regions (Polanczyk et al., 2007).
- ADHD is found in about 5.8 percent of all children worldwide, about 7.8 percent of US children. (Barkley, 2013).
- Studies throughout the world have reported the occurrence of ADHD in school-age children as being between 5 and 12 percent. This means that on average there are at least one to three children in every class with ADHD (Centre for ADHD Awareness, Canada, n.d.).

- There is variation geographically across the country (different states and communities) with regard to the number of children diagnosed with ADHD, which can be seen at the CDC website (www.cdc.gov/ncbddd/adhd/data.html).
- The prevalence of ADHD in US adults is 4.4 percent, according to a study by the National Institute of Mental Health (Kessler et al., 2006).

More Statistics

- The CDC survey (CDC, n.d.; Visser et al., 2014) also showed that the percentage of children four to seventeen years of age taking medication for ADHD, as reported by parents, increased by 28 percent between 2007 and 2011. See other interesting results from the data of this large-scale survey at www.cdc.gov/ncbddd/adhd/data.html and www.cdc.gov/ncbddd/adhd/features/key-findings-adhd72013.html.
- The steady increase in prevalence of ADHD and medication use for treating ADHD is unclear, but mostly attributed to greater awareness about the disorder among parents, health care professionals, and teachers, resulting in more evaluations and treatment in recent years; however, other factors likely are involved as well. Dr. Stephen Hinshaw and Dr. Richard Scheffler explore the science-based evidence and various factors for the rise in ADHD diagnosis and medication use in their book *The ADHD Explosion*, listed in the resources below.
- Up to 80 percent of school-age children with ADHD will continue to have the disorder in adolescence and between 50 and 65 percent or more will have it into adulthood (Barkley, 2013).

Statistics Regarding Risks Associated with ADHD

- Having ADHD increases the risk for other disorders as well. At least 75 percent of children and teens with ADHD have at least one other coexisting disorder (CHADD, n.d.-a). Over 50 percent also have a third coexisting disorder (Barkley, 2013).
- The most prevalent co-occurring disorder with ADHD is oppositional defiance disorder (ODD), appearing 41 percent of the time (CHADD, n.d.-a). See *Lists 1.8 and 2.14* for more on ODD.
- Compared to individuals without the disorder, people with ADHD have more than six times a greater risk of developing a substance use disorder (Teplin, 2012).
- Individuals with ADHD are at increased risk for cigarette smoking compared to their peers who do not have ADHD, and those with ADHD start smoking at an earlier age compared to the general population (Kollins, 2012).

According to Russell Barkley (2013), one of the world's leading ADHD experts and researchers, the following statistics are also found:

- Up to 58 percent of youth with ADHD may be retained in a grade in school at least once.
- As many as 35 percent fail to complete high school.
- For half of children with ADHD, social relationships are seriously impaired.
- More than 25 percent of ADHD youth are expelled from high school because of serious misconduct.

- More than 30 percent of youth with ADHD have engaged in theft.
- More than 40 percent of youth with ADHD drift into early tobacco and alcohol use.
- Adolescents and young adults with a diagnosis of ADHD have nearly four to five times as many traffic citations for speeding, two to three times as many auto accidents, and accidents that are two to three times more expensive in damages or likely to cause bodily injuries as young drivers without ADHD.
- As many as 20 to 30 percent of those diagnosed with ADHD may be experimenting with or abusing substances, such as alcohol, nicotine, and marijuana.

Note: Compared to the general population as a whole, people with ADHD are at greater risk than others for negative outcomes (as described). However, provided with supports and effective treatments and intervention, risks for children with ADHD are reduced substantially. Parents should maintain a positive mind-set and be optimistic about their child's future.

See *Lists 1.4, 1.7, and 1.12* for more related topics.

Sources and Resources

Akinbami, L. J., Liu, X., Pastor, P. N., & Reuben, C. A. (2011). Attention deficit hyperactivity disorder among children aged 5–17 years in the United States, 1998–2009. Retrieved from www.cdc.gov/nchs/data/databriefs/db70.htm

American Psychiatric Association. (2013). *Diagnostic and statistical manual of mental disorders (DSM)* (5th ed.). Washington, DC: Author.

Barkley, Russell A. (2013). *Taking charge of ADHD: The complete, authoritative guide for parents* (3rd ed.). New York: Guilford Press.

Centers for Disease Control and Prevention (CDC). (n.d.-a). Attention-deficit/hyperactivity disorder data and statistics. Retrieved from www.cdc.gov/ncbddd/adhd/data.html; reporting findings from *Key Findings: Trends in the Parent-Report of Health Care Provider-Diagnosis and Medication Treatment for ADHD: United States, 2003.2011.*

Centers for Disease Control and Prevention (CDC). (n.d.-b). Key findings: Trends in the parent-report of health care provider-diagnosis and medication treatment for ADHD: United States, 2003–2011. Retrieved from http://www.cdc.gov/ncbddd/adhd/features/key-findings-adhd72013.html

Centre for ADHD Awareness, Canada (CADDAC). (n.d.). What is attention-deficit hyperactivity disorder? Retrieved from www.caddac.ca/cms/page.php?67

Children and Adults with Attention-Deficit/Hyperactivity Disorder (CHADD). Understanding ADHD: Coexisting disorders. (n.d.-a). Retrieved from www.chadd.org/Understanding-ADHD/Parents-Caregivers-of-Children-with-ADHD/Coexisting-Disorders.aspx

Children and Adults with Attention-Deficit/Hyperactivity Disorder (CHADD). (n.d.-b). Understanding ADHD: Symptoms and causes. Retrieved from www.chadd.org/Understanding-ADHD/Parents-Caregivers-of-Children-with-ADHD/Symptoms-and-Causes.aspx

Hinshaw, Stephen P., & Scheffler, Richard M. (2014). *The ADHD explosion: Myths, medication, money, and today's push for performance*. New York: Oxford University Press.

Kessler, R. C., et al. (2006). The US National Comorbidity Survey Replication (NCS-R): Design and field procedures. *International Journal of Methods in Psychiatric Research, 13*(2), 69–92.

Kollins, Scott. (2012). Where there's smoke there's ... ADHD: What the science says. Children and Adults with Attention Deficit-Hyperactivity Disorder (CHADD): *Attention Magazine*, *19* (5), 14–17.

National Resource Center on AD/HD. (2014, January). Statistical prevalence of ADHD. Retrieved from www.help4adhd.org/en/about/statistics.

Polanczyk, G., de Lima, M. S., Horta, B. L., Biederman, J., & Rohde, L. A. (2007). The worldwide prevalence of ADHD: A systematic review and metaregression analysis. *American Journal of Psychiatry, 164*(6), 942–948.

Teplin, David. (2012). Adult ADHD and substance use disorders: What's the deal? *Attention Magazine, 19*(5), 10–12.

Visser, S., Danielson, M., Bitsko, R., et al. (2014). Trends in the parent-report of health care provider-diagnosis and medication treatment for ADHD disorder: United States, 2003–2011. *Journal of the American Academy of Child & Adolescent Psychiatry, 53*(1), 34–46. doi: 10.1016/j.jaac.2013.09.001.

1.7 Causes of ADHD

ADHD has been researched extensively in the United States and a number of countries throughout the world. Sophisticated brain-imaging technologies and genetic research in recent years, has dramatically increased our knowledge of the probable causes of ADHD.

We now know there are multiple causes, although we certainly do not know all of them. Based on hundreds of well-designed and controlled scientific studies, the evidence clearly suggests that ADHD is the result of brain differences: abnormalities in size, maturation, and levels of activity in the regions of the brain involved in executive functions and self-regulation.

Heredity is the main known cause of ADHD, accounting for most cases. In other cases, there are problems and factors that occur prenatally, during birth, or in childhood that might interfere with a child's brain development and be contributing causes of ADHD.

Heredity

- Based on the evidence, heredity is the most common cause of ADHD, accounting for approximately 75 to 80 percent of children with this disorder (Barkley, 1998, 2013a).
- ADHD is known to run in families, as found by numerous studies (twin studies with identical and fraternal twins, adopted children, family studies, molecular genetic studies). For example, in studies of identical twins, if one has ADHD there is as high as a 75 to 90 percent chance that the other twin will have ADHD as well (Barkley, 2013a).
- It is believed that a genetic predisposition to the disorder is inherited. Children with ADHD will frequently have a parent, sibling, grandparent, or other close relative with ADHD—or whose history indicates they had similar problems and symptoms during childhood.
- ADHD is a complex disorder, which is undoubtedly the result of multiple interacting genes in most cases (National Resource Center on AD/HD, 2008).
- Genetic research involving several methods have so far identified at least nine genes that link to ADHD—at least three involving the regulation of dopamine levels (two dopamine receptor genes and a dopamine transporter gene) (Barkley, 2013a).
- Other genes have also been identified that affect brain growth, how nerve cells migrate during development to arrive at their normal sites, and the way in which nerve cells connect to each other (Barkley, 2013a).
- The genetic contribution to ADHD has been thought to reflect differences in certain brain structures, brain chemistry, as well as the interaction of the two (Goldstein, 2007).
- Research suggests that certain genes or alterations in some genes may be inherited and influence the development or maturation of certain areas of the brain or affect the regulation or efficiency of certain brain chemicals. Other researchers suggest that children who carry certain genes may be more vulnerable than other children to various environmental factors associated with ADHD symptoms.

What Are These Brain Differences Associated with ADHD?

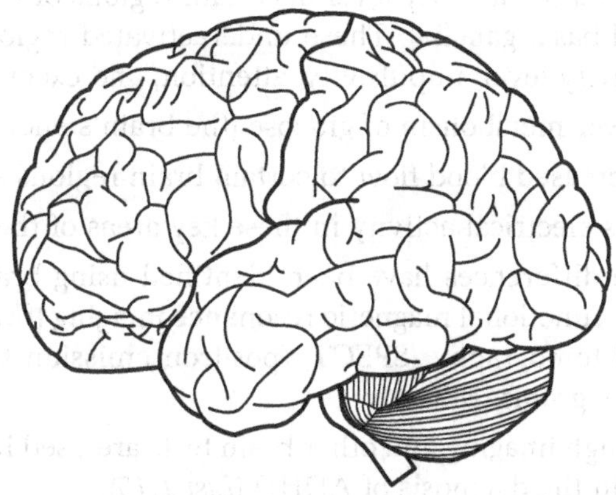

Delayed Brain Maturation and Structural Differences

Recent research has shown delayed maturation in specific areas of the brain to play a significant part in ADHD. According to Thomas Brown (2013c):

> Those with ADHD have been shown to differ in the rate of maturation of specific areas of the cortex, in the thickness of cortical tissue, in characteristics of the parietal and cerebellar regions, as well as in the basal ganglia, and in the white matter tracts that connect and provide critically important communication between various regions of the brain. Recent research has also shown that those with ADHD tend to have different patterns in functional connectivity, patterns of oscillations that allow different regions of the brain to exchange information.

- Dr. Philip Shaw and other researchers at the National Institutes of Mental Health used brain imaging technology to study the brain maturation of hundreds of children and teens with and without ADHD and reported their findings in 2007. They found that in youth with ADHD, the brain matures in a normal pattern, but there is approximately a three-year delay in some regions compared to other children, particularly in the frontal cortex (American Psychological Association, 2008; Shaw et al., 2007).
- Neuroimaging studies have found that on average, children with ADHD have about a 5 percent reduction in total volume and a 10 to 12 percent reduction in the size of four or five key brain regions involved in higher-order control of behavior (Nigg, 2006).
- Russell Barkley (2013a) reports that a team of international scientists published a review of research studies measuring the gray matter volume of the brain, which showed that those with ADHD have significantly smaller brain sizes, particularly in the caudate region (part of the basal ganglia). They also found, interestingly, that these differences in brain volume improved with age and with the length of time children take stimulant medication (implying that medication may actually facilitate maturation in brain size).

Diminished Activity and Lower Metabolism in Certain Brain Regions

- Numerous studies measuring electrical activity, blood flow, and brain activity have found differences between those with ADHD and those without ADHD:
  - Decreased activity level in certain regions of the brain (mainly the frontal region and basal ganglia). These underactivated regions are responsible for controlling activity level, impulsivity, attention, and executive functions.
  - Lower metabolism of glucose (the brain's energy source) in the frontal region
  - Decreased blood flow to certain brain regions associated with ADHD
  - Less electrical activity in these key areas of the brain
- These differences have been identified using brain activity and imaging tests and scans: functional magnetic resonance imaging (fMRIs), single photon emission computed tomography (SPECT), positron emission tomography (PET), and electroencephalograms (EEGs).
- Although imaging and other brain tests are used in researching ADHD, they are not used in the diagnosis of ADHD (*List 1.15*).

Brain Chemical (Neurotransmitter) Inefficiency

- There is significant evidence that those with ADHD have a deficiency or inefficiency in brain chemicals (neurotransmitters) operating in certain brain regions associated with ADHD. The two main neurotransmitters involved in ADHD are dopamine and norepinephrine. Other brain chemicals also play a part in the disorder and are being studied.
- Dopamine is involved in regulating, among other things, attention, inhibition, motivation, motor activity, and emotional responses. It plays a major role in ADHD. As noted, genetic research has found that some of the dopamine receptor and transporter genes are altered or not working properly.
- Neurotransmitters are the chemical messengers of the brain. The neurons in the brain are not connected. They have a synapse or tiny gap between them where nerve impulses are sent from one neuron to another. The neurotransmitters help carry messages between two neurons by being released into the synapse and then being recycled or reloaded once the message gets across. It is believed that with ADHD, those essential brain chemicals may not be efficiently releasing and staying long enough in the synapse in order to do their job of getting the message across effectively in those key regions and circuits of the brain.
- Research indicates that individuals with ADHD may have disturbances in their dopamine signaling systems.
- Brown (2013b) explains that the problem with ADHD is not one of a generalized chemical deficiency or imbalance. "The primary problem is related to chemicals manufactured, released, and then reloaded at the level of synapses, the trillions of infinitesimal junctions between certain networks of neurons that manage critical activities within the brain's management system" (p. 8).

Other Causes of ADHD

Maternal or Childhood Exposure to Certain Toxins

- Certain substances the pregnant mother consumes or exposes the developing fetus to are believed to increase risk factors and be a cause for ADHD in some children.

This includes fetal exposure to alcohol, tobacco, and high levels of lead. Mothers who smoke cigarettes and those who drink alcohol while pregnant increase the risk that their child will have ADHD.

- Children who carry certain genes may be more vulnerable when exposed to environmental toxins than other children.
- Of concern to many people are the unknown effects of all the chemicals in our environment and other toxins. Most are as yet not studied. It is reasonable to assume that some may be identified in future research that affect brain development or brain processes in children and possibly contribute to ADHD or other disorders.

Birth Complications, Illnesses, and Brain Injury

These are other factors that raise the risk for and may lead to the development of ADHD:

- Premature birth and significantly low birth weight
- Trauma or head injury to the frontal part of the brain
- Certain illnesses that affect the brain, such as encephalitis

Other Environmental Factors

- It is generally believed in the scientific community that environmental factors influence the severity of ADHD symptoms, but are not the cause of ADHD.
- "Research does not support the popularly held views that AD/HD arises from excessive sugar intake, excessive television viewing, poor child management by parents, or social and environmental factors such as poverty or family chaos. Of course, many things, including these, might aggravate symptoms, especially in certain individuals" (National Resource Center on AD/HD, n.d.).

See *List 1.4* for related information.

Sources and Resources

American Psychological Association. (2008). ADHD: Delay or deviation? *Monitor on Psychology, 39*(2). Retrieved from www.apa.org/monitor/feb08/adhd.aspx

Barkley, Russell A. (1998). Attention-deficit hyperactivity disorder: A psychological model of ADHD. *Scientific American,* pp. 66–71. Retrieved from www.sciam.com/1998/0998 issuebarkley.html

Barkley, Russell A. (2013a). *Taking charge of ADHD: The complete, authoritative guide for parents* (3rd ed.). New York: Guilford Press.

Barkley, Russell A. (2013b). Understanding and improving your ADHD child's behavior. *ADDitude Magazine* webinar. Podcast and transcript retrieved from www.additudemag.com/RCLP/sub/10265.html.

Brown, Thomas E. (2013a). *A new understanding of ADHD in children and adults: Executive function impairments.* New York: Routledge.

Brown, Thomas E. (2013b). Ten myths about ADHD and why they are wrong. *Attention Magazine, 20*(3), 6–9.

Brown, Thomas E. (2013c). Understanding attention deficit: The new ADHD. Retrieved from http://www.additudemag.com/slideshow/28/slide-1.html

Goldstein, Sam. (2007). Research briefs: The genetics of AD/HD. *Attention Magazine, 14*(1), 37–39.

National Resource Center on AD/HD. (2008). The disorder named AD/HD. *What We Know, 1*. Retrieved from www.help4adhd.org/documents/WWK1.pdf

National Resource Center on AD/HD. (n.d.). About AD/HD: Causes and brain chemistry. Retrieved from www.help4adhd.org/en/about/causes

Nigg, Joel T. (2006). *What causes ADHD: Understanding what goes wrong and why*. New York: Guilford Press.

Shaw, Philip, et al. (2007). Attention-deficit/hyperactivity disorder is characterized by a delay in cortical maturation. *Proceedings of the National Academy of Sciences, 104*(50), 19663–19664.

1.8 ADHD and Coexisting Disorders

ADHD is often accompanied by one or more other conditions or disorders: psychiatric, psychological, developmental, or medical. Because symptoms of these various disorders commonly overlap, diagnosis and treatment can be complex. The word *comorbidity* is the medical term for having coexisting disorders (co-occurring and presenting at the same time as ADHD).

- As many as two-thirds of children with ADHD have at least one other coexisting condition such as learning disabilities, oppositional defiant disorder, anxiety disorder, conduct disorder, Tourette syndrome, or depression (MTA Cooperative Group, 1999; National Resource Center on AD/HD, 2003).
- Coexisting disorders can cause significant impairment above and beyond the problems caused by ADHD.
- Coexisting conditions make diagnosis, intervention, and management more complicated.
- In order to effectively treat the child or teen, an accurate diagnosis must first be made. That is why it is so important for the clinician to be skilled and knowledgeable about ADHD and coexisting conditions. It will be important to tease out what may be ADHD and what may be something else.
- There are also conditions that produce similar symptoms that mimic ADHD (*List 1.9*).
- Determining the proper diagnosis requires that the clinician is thorough in obtaining information and data about the child from multiple sources and perspectives and carefully reviews the history and behaviors. Effective intervention will require treatment for the ADHD and the other conditions.
- It can take time for all of the pieces of the puzzle to come together, and parents, teachers, and clinicians need to monitor the child's development and any emerging concerns.
- As Dr. Ari Tuckman (2010) points out, "Overlapping symptoms can make it more difficult to get the diagnosis right, but a skilled clinician can tease them apart. It's worth the extra effort to get an accurate diagnosis, because treatment can only be as good as the diagnosis it's based on" (p.19).
- In addition to disorders that may coexist with ADHD, there are also a number of conditions, disorders, or other factors that cause a person to look like they may have ADHD—for example, that cause behaviors or symptoms such as inattention or hyperactivity (*List 1.9*). There are children and adults who are misdiagnosed as having ADHD when in fact they do not have this disorder.
- The most common conditions comorbid with ADHD in childhood are oppositional defiant disorder (ODD) and conduct disorder (CD). In adulthood the most common comorbid conditions with ADHD are depression and anxiety (Goldstein, 2009).

Common Coexisting Conditions and Disorders

- The prevalence of specific coexisting conditions and disorders accompanying ADHD varies depending on the sources. Most sources indicate the following ranges:
  - *Oppositional defiant disorder (ODD).* From 40 to 65 percent of children and teens have this disorder (National Resource Center on AD/HD, 2003). It occurs eleven

times more frequently in children with ADHD than in the general population (Barkley, 2013).

- *Anxiety disorder*. Approximately 25 to 30 percent of children and 25 to 40 percent of adults have this disorder (National Resource Center on AD/HD, 2003).
- *Conduct disorder*. Approximately 10 to 25 percent of children, 25 to 50 percent of adolescents, and 20 to 25 percent of adults have this disorder (National Resource Center on AD/HD, 2003).
- *Bipolar*. Up to 20 percent of people with ADHD may manifest bipolar disorder (National Resource Center on AD/HD, 2003).
- *Depression*. Approximately 10 to 30 percent in children and up to 47 percent in adolescents and adults have this disorder (National Resource Center on AD/HD, 2003, 2008a).
- *Tics, Tourette syndrome*. About 7 percent of those with ADHD have tics or Tourette syndrome, but 60 percent of Tourette syndrome patients also have ADHD (National Resource Center on AD/HD, 2008c).
- *Learning disabilities*. A range from 20 to 60 percent, with most sources estimating that between one-quarter and one-half of children with ADHD have a coexisting learning disability.
- *Obsessive-compulsive disorder*. Up to one-third of people with ADHD may have OCD (Goodman, 2010; Kutscher, 2010).
- *Sleep disorders*. One-quarter to one-half of parents of children with ADHD report that their children suffer from a sleep problem, especially problems with falling asleep and staying asleep (National Resource Center on AD/HD, 2008d).

Other Disorders and Conditions

- Nearly 20 to 30 percent of children and teens with ADHD also have some form of challenge in the area of language, and 25 to 50 percent of students who have speech-language disability also have ADHD (Spencer, 2013).
- Autism spectrum disorder (ASD) is now recognized as a possible coexisting disorder with ADHD and was added to the *DSM-5* as such (*List 1.3*).
- ASD symptoms are more common in children with ADHD than in the general population. In some studies nearly 50 percent of youth with autism spectrum disorders meet diagnostic criteria for ADHD (Goldstein, 2010).

Note: The website of the National Resource Center on AD/HD (www.help4adhd.org) is a good source of up-to-date and reliable information about coexisting disorders with ADHD.

Identifying and Treating Coexisting Disorders

- Most children with ADHD have school-related achievement, performance, or social problems. It is important that they receive the educational supports and interventions they need.
- Because a high percentage of children with ADHD also have learning disabilities, such as dyslexia, the school district should evaluate the student when a possible learning disability is suspected. Parents are advised to request an evaluation if concerned that their child may have coexisting LDs (*Lists 6.1, 6.2, 6.3, 6.4*).

Note: Information regarding dyslexia and dysgraphia (two common learning disabilities) are found in *Lists 5.1, 5.6, and 5.11*.

- Parents, educators, and medical and mental health care providers should be alert to signs of other mental health disorders that may exist or emerge, often in the adolescent years, especially when current strategies and treatments being used with the ADHD child or teen are no longer working effectively.
- Anxiety disorder and depression can easily go unrecognized and overlooked. There is a high rate of these internalized disorders, particularly among teenage girls (*List 1.12*).
- Early identification of ADHD and implementing appropriate interventions can help significantly in all respects, reducing the risk for future problems developing and increasing overall successful outcomes.

About Oppositional Defiant Disorder (ODD) and Conduct Disorder (CD)

These two behavioral disorders are believed to probably lie on a continuum. ODD emerges first and can develop into conduct disorder (with more serious and problematic symptoms and behaviors) over time.

Oppositional Defiant Disorder

ODD usually starts before age eight, but no later than early adolescence (CDC, 2011). To be diagnosed with ODD, a child presents with many of these behaviors or symptoms:

- Often loses temper
- Often argues with adults
- Often actively defies or refuses to comply with adults' requests or rules
- Often deliberately annoys people
- Often blames others for his or her mistakes or misbehavior
- Is often touchy or easily annoyed by others
- Is often angry and resentful
- Is often spiteful or vindictive

The symptoms show a pattern of negative, defiant, disobedient, and hostile behavior toward authority figures that is exhibited more frequently than in other children of the same age, lasting at least six months, and resulting in significant difficulties in school, at home, and with peers (National Resource Center on AD/HD, 2008b).

CD is a behavioral pattern characterized by aggression toward others and serious violations of rules, laws, and social norms. It involves serious behaviors associated with juvenile delinquency, such as destruction of property, lying, stealing, and skipping school. It also may include aggression toward people or animals (CDC, 2011; National Resource Center on AD/HD, 2008b).

Theory about ADHD and Comorbidity

- Thomas Brown (2009) suggests that ADHD is not just one more among other mental health disorders, but instead it may be foundational in the sense that a person with

ADHD-related impairments of executive functioning is more vulnerable to other psychiatric disorders.

- Sam Goldstein (2009, p. 32) describes this as well: "As a condition reflecting impaired self-regulation or poor executive functioning, the core deficits of ADHD likely act as catalysts increasing the risk of the development of other problems and fueling the severity of these problems when they occur."

Sources and Resources

Barkley, Russell. (2013). *Taking charge of ADHD: The complete, authoritative guide for parents* (3rd ed.). New York: Guilford Press.

Brown, Thomas E. (2009). AD/HD and co-occurring conditions. *Attention Magazine, 16*(1), 10–15.

Centers for Disease Control and Prevention (CDC). (2011). ADHD: Other concerns and conditions. Retrieved from www.cdc.gov/ncbddd/adhd/conditions.html

Goldstein, Sam. (2009). Comorbidity in AD/HD. *Attention Magazine, 16*(1), 32–33.

Goldstein, Sam. (2010). AD/HD and autism spectrum disorders. *Attention Magazine, 17*(1), 32–34.

Goodman, Bryan (2010). Compulsively impulsive/impulsively compulsive. *Attention Magazine, 17*(1), 20–23.

Kutscher, Martin L. (2010). *ADHD: Living without brakes*. London: Jessica Kingsley.

MTA Cooperative Group. (1999). A 14-month randomized clinical trial of treatment strategies for attention deficit hyperactivity disorder. *Archives of General Psychiatry, 56*, 12.

National Resource Center on AD/HD. (2003). ADHD and coexisting disorders. *What We Know, 5*. Retrieved from www.help4adhd.org/documents/WWK5.pdf

National Resource Center on AD/HD. (2008a). ADHD and coexisting conditions: Depression. *What We Know, 5C*. Retrieved from http://help4adhd.org/documents/WWK5c.pdf

National Resource Center on AD/HD. (2008b). ADHD and coexisting conditions: Disruptive behavior disorders. *What We Know, 5B*. Retrieved from www.help4adhd.org/documents/WWK5B.pdf

National Resource Center on AD/HD. (2008c). ADHD and coexisting conditions: Tics and Tourette syndrome. *What We Know, 5A*. Retrieved from http://help4adhd.org/documents/WWK5a.pdf

National Resource Center on AD/HD. (2008d). ADHD, sleep, and sleep disorders. *What We Know, 5D*. Retrieved from http://help4adhd.org/documents/WWK5D.pdf

Pierce, Karen. (2003). Attention-deficit/hyperactivity disorder and comorbidity. *Primary Psychiatry, 10*(4), 69–76.

Spencer, Linda E. (2013). Helping students with ADHD and language disability. *Attention Magazine, 20*(2), 10–12.

Tuckman, Ari. (2010). Along for the ride: Conditions that co-exist with AD/HD. *Attention Magazine, 17*(1), 15–19.

1.9 ADHD Look-Alikes

Not everyone who displays symptoms of ADHD has the disorder. There are a number of other conditions and factors (medical, psychological, learning, psychiatric, emotional, social, and environmental) that can cause inattentive, hyperactive, and impulsive behaviors. The following list identifies some disorders or conditions that might coexist with ADHD or that may produce some symptoms that look like or mimic ADHD:

- Learning disabilities
- Sensory impairments (hearing, vision, or motor problems)
- Substance use and abuse (of alcohol and drugs)
- Oppositional defiant disorder (ODD)
- Conduct disorder
- Allergies
- Posttraumatic stress disorder (PTSD)
- Anxiety disorder
- Depression
- Obsessive-compulsive disorder
- Sleep disorder
- Bipolar disorder
- Thyroid problems
- Rare genetic disorders (for example, Fragile X syndrome)
- Seizure disorders
- Sluggish cognitive tempo
- Lead poisoning
- Hypoglycemia
- Anemia
- Fetal alcohol syndrome/fetal alcohol effects
- Chronic illness
- Language disorders
- Auditory processing disorders
- Visual processing disorders
- Tourette syndrome
- Autism spectrum disorder
- Developmental delays
- Sensory integration dysfunction
- Low intellectual ability
- High intellectual ability or giftedness
- Chronic ear infections
- Severe emotional disturbance
- Side effects of medications being taken (such as antiseizure medication, asthma medication)

Emotional and environmental factors that have nothing to do with ADHD can also cause a child or teen to be distracted, unable to concentrate, and have acting-out or aggressive behaviors, for example, if the child or teen is living in high-stress situations such as the following:

- Experiencing or witnessing abuse or violence
- Family stresses (for example, divorce and custody battles, death of a loved one, financial difficulties)
- Bullying or peer pressure and other social issues
- A chaotic, unpredictable, unstable, or neglectful home life with inappropriate expectations placed on the child

Inattention and disruptive classroom behaviors can be school related (having nothing to do with ADHD). Students may display those behaviors if they are in a school environment with these characteristics:

- A pervasive negative climate
- Poor instruction and low academic expectations
- Nonstimulating and unmotivating curriculum
- Ineffective classroom management

Source and Resource

Porter, Eloise. (2012). Misdiagnosis: Conditions that mimic ADHD. Retrieved from www.healthline.com/health/adhd/adhd-misdiagnosis#1

1.10 Positive Traits and Strengths

So many children, teens, and adults with ADHD are very bright and talented. It is important to recognize and appreciate the numerous strengths and positive traits that are so common in individuals with ADHD. Parents and teachers need to highlight and focus on the positive with children and do whatever is possible to nurture their interests, strengths, and talents.

Kids and adults with ADHD often have these characteristics:

- Energetic
- Spontaneous
- Creative
- Persistent
- Innovative
- Imaginative
- Tenacious
- Big-hearted
- Accepting and forgiving
- Enterprising
- Ready for action
- Independent thinking
- Inquisitive
- Adventurous
- Resilient
- Resourceful
- Risk taking
- Entrepreneurial
- Inventive
- Observant
- Empathetic
- Charming
- Full of ideas and spunk
- Intelligent
- Enthusiastic
- Outgoing, gregarious
- Optimistic
- Charismatic
- Good sense of humor
- Playful
- Passionate
- Willing to take a chance and try new things
- Good at improvising
- Able to find novel solutions

- Good in crisis situations and thinking on their feet
- Talented in certain skills and areas (artistic, musical, athletic)

And they typically

- Know how to live in and enjoy the present
- Make and create fun
- Are never boring

1.11 Developmental Course of ADHD across the Life Span

It is now known that ADHD is not just a childhood disorder. In approximately 80 percent of cases, a child with ADHD will continue to have the disorder as a teenager, and the majority of children with ADHD will have it into adulthood (*Lists 1.4, 1.6*).

Infancy and Toddler Stages

ADHD is typically diagnosed in school-age children. However, there is evidence that even in infancy, toddler, and early childhood years there are indicators that a child may be at risk for eventually being diagnosed with ADHD (or another developmental disorder). "Difficult temperaments" characterize many infants and toddlers who may later experience childhood problems and be diagnosed with ADHD or some other disorder.

The following are signs to watch for in infancy that may be symptomatic of possible future difficulties:

- Irritability
- Shrill, frequent crying
- Overactive and restless
- Sleep problems
- Fussy eater
- Difficulty adapting well to changes in the environment
- Difficulty nursing and feeding
- Colicky
- Hard to please
- Hard to establish and maintain on a schedule

In the toddler years, early indicators may include the following:

- Excessively active
- Picky eater
- Sleep problems
- Fussiness and irritability
- Higher degree of crying, temper tantrums, and noncompliant behavior than is typical for children that age
- Poorly adapting to changes
- Clumsiness and being accident prone
- Speech and language problems

What to Do?

It is recommended that when children in these very early years show signs of a difficult temperament and possible developmental disorders, early intervention should be initiated in order to reduce the risk of future problems developing. This would involve doing the following:

- Parents receiving guidance on positive strategies and supports to implement in the home (for example, behavioral, learning, language, motor, environmental)
- Parents sharing their concerns with their child's pediatrician and inquiring about Child Find, which is a mandate in the federal law, Individuals with Disabilities Education Act (IDEA) (*List 6.4*). Child Find requires states to identify, locate, and evaluate all children suspected of having a disability, from birth through age twenty-one.

Preschool and Kindergarten Years

- *See List 7.4* for information and strategies specific to children of preschool and kindergarten age range.
- When a young child is in social and educational environments with other children for half-day or full-day programs, more signs and symptoms of possible ADHD, learning disabilities, or other developmental disorders may become evident.
- Parents, teachers, pediatricians, and day-care providers should be alert to children in this age group who exhibit a number of the following difficulties that are more excessive and problematic when compared to other children that age.

Symptoms and Indicators in Preschool and Kindergarten

- Very short attention span (much more apparent than in the average child that age)
- Trouble sitting and staying with the group (such as circle time with class on the rug)
- Can't listen for more than a brief amount of time to stories
- Uncooperative and noncompliant behaviors
- Excessively active
- Overly reactive (cries easily, frequent and intense temper tantrums)
- Poor self-control when frustrated or angry
- Highly impulsive
- Aggressiveness
- Clumsy or accident prone
- Fearless behavior
- Trouble adapting to changes of routine or new environments
- Difficulty following class rules and teacher directions
- Has trouble following one- or two-step directions
- Jumps from one task to another—can't stick with any for more than a brief amount of time
- Not interested in playing with other children or has great difficulty doing so
- Difficulty holding and using a crayon, pencil, or scissors
- Avoids writing or any fine-motor task
- Argumentative
- Moodiness
- Persistently demanding
- Speech and language difficulties (understanding or expressing self in language)

- Motor-skill problems
- Seems overly sensitive to noise or touch
- Seems to get easily overstimulated and has trouble calming

According to Russell Barkley (2013), at least 40 to 80 percent of preschool children with ADHD (especially boys) may be seriously defiant or oppositional. Unfortunately, many preschool children with ADHD are asked to leave their preschools (kicked out) because the school does not know how to manage the child's behaviors.

What to Do?

- Parents should share their concerns with their child's pediatrician and may want to consult with a developmental pediatrician or a child psychiatrist. A qualified clinician may evaluate the child for possible ADHD and other disorders if indicated and refer for other evaluations such as speech-language or occupational therapy.
- Young children can be diagnosed with ADHD, and there are guidelines by the American Academy of Pediatrics for primary care clinicians to diagnose and treat ADHD in children ages four to five (*List 1.15*). The first line of treatment for children of this age group is behavior therapy. Research shows that many preschool children improve symptoms with behavior therapy alone (which typically involves parent training and teacher training of effective behavioral management strategies) (*Lists 1.19, 1.22*).
- Parents should work with the preschool or kindergarten teacher in identifying problems, implementing strategies, and obtaining any needed help.
- The state's Child Find mandate applies even in private preschools. Children showing signs of a possible disorder should be referred for screening (whatever the state policy and local procedures are for Child Find and early intervention programs).
- It is very important for parents to seek support, guidance, and information—beginning the journey of learning about ADHD and how to best help their child.
- See *List 7.4* for information about ADHD in young children (ages three to five).

Elementary School Years

- ADHD is typically diagnosed in the elementary school years when the expectations for academic and behavioral and social performance (following rules, sitting quietly, paying attention, working cooperatively and productively, and so on) become problematic.
- Elementary school children with ADHD have been the subject of a great deal of research—the bulk of research worldwide on ADHD. All of the information and lists in this book are relevant to children in this age range.

Middle School Years

For many youngsters, these are very difficult and painful years:

- There is rapid growth and development, causing many to feel awkward and unattractive in their changing bodies.
- The overriding concern is to fit in with peers and be accepted.
- Children are trying to gain more independence, so they challenge their parents' authority.

- They must also cope with the expectations of multiple teachers and harder academic and self-management demands (being an independent learner, more organized and responsible, and having mastered their basic skills).

In addition, middle-schoolers with ADHD may have the following:

- All the usual struggles as their peers who do not have ADHD, but theirs present a much greater challenge—affecting their social and school success
- Most of the same challenges as the elementary school child with ADHD and often the executive function–related difficulties become more problematic at this time
- Developed antisocial symptoms by this age and may have existing ODD or CD

What to Do?

See List 7.5 for more information and strategies to help this age group of preteens with ADHD; other lists throughout this book provide numerous strategies, supports, and interventions that help.

High School and Teen Years

During this period, teens with ADHD generally have a change in their symptoms. For example, the overt hyperactivity is now manifested as restlessness and fidgetiness. Executive function impairments often become a more significant problem because of the high executive skill demands and expectations placed on teens (*Lists 1.2, 7.5*). By teenage years, coexisting disorders (*List 1.8*) are common, as are engaging in behaviors that can have serious consequences (*List 1.6*).

Adolescence is a period that can be challenging for all kids (and their parents and teachers). Similar to preteens, teenagers assert their independence, trying to establish their identity, face numerous social pressures, and also are coping with their physical changes and lots of other stressors.

The following signs and symptoms are commonly seen in teens with ADHD:

- Time-awareness and time-management issues (lateness, procrastination)
- Forgetfulness
- Disorganization
- Difficulty waking up and falling asleep
- Easily bored (and falls asleep in class)
- Impulsive (the many behaviors related to poor self-control and not considering future consequences of actions)
- Difficulty paying attention and staying on task
- Immaturity (social, emotional, behavioral)
- Poor planning and goal-directed behavior
- Irritability
- High rate of noncompliance and oppositional behavior
- Restlessness and fidgetiness (tapping pencils, pacing, squirming in seat)
- Gravitates to high-risk behaviors and associates with peers with similar problems and behaviors
- Argumentative, talks back to authority figures

- Emotionally reactive
- Higher-than-average amount of speeding tickets, traffic violations, and accidents
- Academic difficulties
- Significant problems in school keeping up with projects and managing the work load
- Behavior and social problems in out-of-school functions and activities

See additional symptoms related to impulsivity, inattention, and executive function weaknesses often seen in teenagers with ADHD (*Lists 1.2, 1.5, 4.1, 4.4*). Studies show that by adolescence, over half of those with ADHD may have a history of failure in academic performance and marked difficulties in social relationships (*List 1.6*).

A common issue and source of conflict in homes is that teens with ADHD require far more supervision, monitoring, and help from parents than others their age at a developmental stage in which they desire additional freedom and independence (National Resource Center on AD/HD, 2008).

What to Do?

- See *List 7.5* for more information and strategies specific to adolescents a with ADHD.
- If the teen has not yet been diagnosed, it is very important to have a comprehensive evaluation by a skilled clinician who is experienced with diagnosing and treating adolescents with ADHD and coexisting conditions (*Lists 1.8, 1.14, 1.15*).
- See the many other lists throughout this book for strategies, supports, and interventions that are beneficial for teens with ADHD, including ADHD coaching (*List 7.6*).

Adults

It has only been in recent years that ADHD in adulthood has been studied, and that attention has been focused on the diagnosis and treatment of the disorder in this population.

- Approximately 50 to 65 percent of children diagnosed with ADHD continue to have ADHD as adults.
- ADHD is a disorder that persists across the lifespan.

Many adults with ADHD were never diagnosed as children and spent their lives struggling, mislabeled, and misunderstood. Many parents realize that they themselves have the disorder when their child is evaluated and diagnosed with ADHD. Now that it is recognized that ADHD is an adult disorder as well, *DSM-5* diagnostic criteria has changed (*List 1.3*). Now many adults are benefiting from diagnosis and treatment.

In addition to symptoms related to inattention, impulsivity, more subtle hyperactivity (restlessness), and executive function difficulties (*Lists 1.2, 1.3, 1.5*), common symptoms in adults include the following:

- Chronic time-management difficulties (procrastination, lateness)
- Pattern of short-lived interests
- Poor memory and forgetfulness
- Emotional volatility
- Excessively impatient
- Undertakes many projects simultaneously

- Difficulty staying focused in conversations
- Drawn to situations of high intensity

Adults with ADHD, especially if untreated over the years, commonly have additional coexisting disorders and problems, such as the following:

- Antisocial behavior
- Educational underattainment
- Vocational underattainment
- Depression
- Anxiety
- Substance abuse
- Low frustration tolerance
- High levels of stress
- Long-term relationship problems
- Employment difficulties
- Frequent moves and job changes
- Sleep-arousal problems
- Money-management problems (such as impulsive purchases, poor budgeting)
- See *List 1.6*.

What to Do?

- As with children and teens, effective intervention starts with a thorough evaluation that identifies coexisting conditions as well as ADHD and then to learn about treatment options, strategies, and supports from reputable sources.
- See the many excellent resources available geared for helping adults with ADHD, such as the national organizations Attention Deficit Disorder Association (ADDA) (www.add.org), Children and Adults with Attention-Deficit/Hyperactivity Disorder (CHADD) (www.chadd.org), and other resources in *List 7.12*.

Points to Keep in Mind

- Even though ADHD generally persists from childhood throughout adulthood, it does not have to limit one's future. There are countless adults with ADHD who are highly successful in every profession and walk of life.
- Many people with ADHD are able to use their strengths and talents to excel in their chosen careers and hobbies.
- It is a fact that individuals with ADHD have a much greater likelihood than others in the general population for a host of negative outcomes, and that is why this disorder must be taken very seriously. But it certainly does not mean that those negative outcomes will occur—particularly if the child or teen is receiving treatment and has a team of support.
- With diagnosis and intervention, ADHD can be managed properly, significantly minimizing the risk factors. This is a time of good fortune for those with ADHD. We understand so much more than in the past about how to help—the strategies, supports, and treatments that enable those with ADHD (children, teens, and adults) to succeed.

Sources and Resources

Barkley, Russell A. (2013). *Taking charge of ADHD: The complete, authoritative guide for parents* (3rd ed.). New York: Guilford Press.

National Resource Center on AD/HD. (2008). ADHD and teens: Information for parents. *What We Know, 20B*. Retrieved from http://help4adhd.org/documents/WWK20B.pdf

Rief, Sandra. (2001). *Ready ... start ... school: Nurturing and guiding your child through preschool and kindergarten*. Paramus, NJ: Prentice Hall.

See CHADD (www.chadd.org), National Resource Center on AD/HD (http://help4adhd.org), and ADDA (www.add.org) for information on ADHD across the lifespan.

There are excellent webinars available through *ADDitude Magazine* (www.additudemag.com/webinars/), CHADD (http://www.chadd.org/Support/Ask-the-Expert-Online-Chats.aspx), and the National Resource Center on AD/HD (www.help4adhd.org), and other sources with expert speakers presenting on topics related to ADHD as it presents in various age groups (preschoolers, teenagers, adults).

There are also several books that are specific to certain age groups, such as this first book of evidence-supported early intervention with children ages two to five years who have or are at risk for ADHD:

DuPaul, George J., & Kern, Lee. (2011). *Young children with ADHD: Early identification and intervention*. Washington, DC: American Psychological Association.

See other sources and recommended resources for specific age groups in *Lists 7.4 and 7.5*.

1.12 Girls with ADHD

- Girls with ADHD often go undiagnosed and untreated because they frequently do not have the typical hyperactive and disruptive symptoms seen in boys that signal a problem and lead to a referral.
- Girls tend to be teacher pleasers and often put a lot of effort into trying to hide their problems, which is another reason their ADHD is often undetected.
- Many girls are labeled and written off as being "space cadets," "ditzy," or "scattered."
- The unrecognized struggles of girls with ADHD and their need for proper diagnosis and treatment places them at high risk for a number of serious negative outcomes (academic and learning problems; social, behavioral, and emotional problems; demoralization; low self-esteem; and more).
- Many girls don't receive an evaluation for ADHD because parents, teachers, and physicians are often unaware that ADHD symptoms manifest differently in girls than boys. When they are evaluated (often in their preteens and teen years), girls may be misdiagnosed or a coexisting condition (commonly anxiety disorder or depression) may be identified, missing the primary disorder of ADHD that existed first.
- Girls being evaluated for ADHD also may have been undiagnosed because the *DSM* criteria until very recently required that significant symptoms be evident by age seven. We now know that symptoms may emerge later, particularly in girls. Fortunately, the new *DSM-5* criteria has acknowledged this later onset of symptoms and changed the criteria so that now symptoms must occur by age twelve, instead of seven (*List 1.3*).
- Most of the research on ADHD over the years has been on boys or has had very few girls participating in the studies.
- In recent years, much more attention has been paid to gender differences, thanks to the work, leadership, and advocacy of Patricia Quinn, Dr. Kathleen Nadeau, Dr. Ellen Littman, and others. The scientific community is now looking at gender issues in ADHD. There have been some significant studies on ADHD in females, such as by the research teams of Dr. Joseph Biederman and Stephen Hinshaw. Much more research still needs to be done to understand the impact of ADHD in females and the best ways to help girls and women with this disorder.

What We Have Learned

According to Nadeau (2000a, 2000b, 2004a, 2004b), Quinn (2008, 2009, 2012), Littman (2000, 2012), Nadeau, Littman, and Quinn (2000, 2015), and Quinn and Nadeau (2000, 2004), girls with ADHD present symptoms in these ways:

- Commonly have the inattentive presentation (type) of ADHD
- Often have impaired social skills
- Often experience academic difficulties and underachievement
- Often experience peer rejection (generally more so than boys with ADHD and are more devastated by rejection from their peers)
- Often unleash frustrations at home that were kept hidden at school; parents may see behaviors in their daughter such as temper tantrums and meltdowns that would never be exhibited at school
- Have a greater likelihood of anxiety and depression

- Often feel a sense of shame
- Have more internalized and less externalized (observable) symptoms
- Have verbal expression and processing problems that are more problematic than they are in boys because so many of girls' interactions rely heavily on verbal communication and demands
- Experience a lot of difficulty with executive function impairment (disorganization, prioritization, poor time management, working memory difficulties, and so forth)
- Tend to experience a lot of worry, stress, and dread from concerns about the following:
  - Not feeling liked and accepted by other girls
  - Not being able to keep up with all that is expected of them
  - Fear of failure and embarrassment at school

Girls with the inattentive presentation (type) of ADHD often present with these characteristics:

- Shy, timid, withdrawn
- Introverted
- Passive daydreamers
- Reluctant to participate in class
- Quick to give up when frustrated
- Often overwhelmed
- Disorganized
- Forgetful
- Self-critical
- Exhibiting anxiety-related behaviors (pulling hair, biting nails, picking at cuticles)

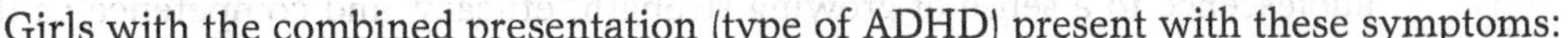

Girls with the combined presentation (type of ADHD) present with these symptoms:

- Stand out, because their behavior is significantly out of norm for other girls that age
- Show hyperactive and impulsive symptoms that often look different than is commonly seen in boys
- Begin to have social problems as early as preschool
- Are at greater risk for consequences stemming from poor self-control combined with lower self-esteem; impulsivity in girls can lead to high-risk activities, such as smoking, drinking, drugs, sexual promiscuity, engaging in unprotected sex, or binge eating (*List 1.6*)
- Are at a much higher risk for self-harm—suicide attempts and self-injury (Hinshaw et al., 2012)

Girls with hyperactivity and impulsivity often present with these symptoms:

- Hyperverbal and hypersocial (cannot stop talking, chatting, commenting on everything)
- Much giggling, "silly," and immature behavior
- Emotional over-reactivity (lots of drama)
- Disruptive behavior (as is also seen in boys with ADHD)

We also know that for girls the following often occurs:

- Symptoms get worse at puberty with hormonal changes.
- Premenstrual syndrome, for example, presents additional problems, worsening ADHD symptoms by adding to irritability, low frustration, mood swings, and emotionality.
- They often work exceptionally hard (compulsively so) to achieve academic success and cover up their difficulties.
- Low self-esteem is evident and begins at a young age.
- They commonly develop anxiety disorder or depression by their teen years.
- They tend toward addictive behaviors offering immediate gratification in terms of self-medication and peer acceptance (Littman, 2012).
- Female social rules place a greater value on cooperating, listening, caretaking, and maintaining relationships. According to Giler (2001), ADHD females appear to have specific problems in five areas that may cause them to struggle socially:
  - Appearing uninterested because of poor listening skills
  - Displaying poor management or expression of anger or moods
  - Bragging or being outspoken and appearing self-involved
  - Forgetting appointments or being late
  - Failing to show interest by not remembering or checking with their friends about their feelings, relationships, or reactions to events that have occurred in their friends' lives

With regard to teenage girls with ADHD, Nadeau (2004b) reminds us that "high school years can be very challenging and to meet these challenges, girls with ADHD need support from peers, parents, and schools, combined with appropriate medical and psychological treatment, depending on their particular needs and issues. With the right supports and interventions, these girls can make the crucial transition from the chaos and self-doubt of adolescence to a sense of growing strength, efficacy, and competence as they enter their young adult years."

Research on Girls with ADHD

- Biederman and colleagues (1999) conducted the first major research study on girls with ADHD, shedding new light on the subject. Dendy (2011) summarized the results of more recent research conducted by Biederman and his research team, which followed a group of almost two hundred girls (about half with ADHD) for eleven years. The Biederman et al. (2010) results showed that girls with ADHD were two and a half times more likely to have a learning disability, sixteen times more likely to have repeated a grade, and ten times as likely to be in special education classes, although their IQ and academic achievement test scores were not much lower than those of their non-ADHD peers.
- Quinn (2008) reports that girls with ADHD are four to five times more likely to be diagnosed with a major depression and three times more likely to be treated for depression prior to their ADHD diagnosis.

Note: For more in-depth information about the issues and treatment of girls with ADHD, see the excellent books and other publications by Nadeau, Littman, and Quinn (some of which are listed in the "Sources and Resources" section) as well as the ADDvance website (www.ADDvance.com), founded by Quinn and Nadeau and dedicated to helping girls and women with ADHD.

Sources and Resources

Biederman, J., Faraone, S., Mick, E., et al. (1999). Clinical correlates of ADHD in females: Findings from a large group of girls ascertained from pediatric and psychiatric referral services. *Journal of the American Academy of Child and Adolescent Psychiatry, 38*(8), 966–975.

Biederman, Joseph, et al. (2010). Adult psychiatric outcomes of girls with attention deficit hyperactivity disorder: 11-year follow-up in a longitudinal case-control study. *American Journal of Psychiatry, 167*(4), 409–417.

Dendy, Chris A. Zeigler (2011). *Teaching teens with ADD, ADHD and executive function deficits*. Bethesda: Woodbine House.

Giler, Janet Z. (2001). Are girls with AD/HD socially adept? *Attention Magazine, 7*(4), 28–31.

Hinshaw, Stephen P., et al. (2012). Prospective follow-up of girls with attention-deficit/hyperactivity disorder into early adulthood: Continuing impairment includes elevated risk for suicide attempts and self-injury. *Journal of Consulting and Clinical Psychology, 80*(6), 1041–1051.

Littman, Ellen. (2000). We understand far too little about girls with ADHD. *ADDvance, 3*(6), 17–21.

Littman, Ellen. (2012). The secret lives of girls with ADHD. *Attention Magazine, 19*(6), 18-21.

Nadeau, Kathleen. (2000a). Elementary school girls with AD/HD. *Attention Magazine, 7*(1) 44–49.

Nadeau, Kathleen. (2000b). Middle school girls with AD/HD. *Attention Magazine, 7*(2) 61–71.

Nadeau, Kathleen G. (2004a). Helping your daughter with ADD (ADHD) to feel good about herself. Retrieved from http://addvance.com/help/women/daughter.html

Nadeau, Kathleen G. (2004b). High school girls with AD/HD. Retrieved from http://addvance.com/help/women/high_school.html

Nadeau, Kathleen, Littman, Ellen, & Quinn, Patricia O. (2000). *Understanding girls with AD/HD*. Silver Spring, MD: Advantage Books.

Nadeau, Kathleen, Littman, Ellen, & Quinn, Patricia. (2015). *Understanding girls with AD/HD Updated and Revised: How they feel and why they do what they do.* (2nd ed.) Silver Spring, MD: Advantage Books.

Note: This is the new edition to the original groundbreaking book by Nadeau, Littman, and Quinn and is a must source about the needs and issues of girls with attentional problems: why they are often undiagnosed, how they are different from boys, and what their special needs are in school, in their social world, and at home. It also contains age-related checklists from preschool to high school and a girl's self-report scale to help parents and professionals better identify and help girls with ADHD.

Quinn, Patricia O. (2008). AD/HD in women and girls. *Attention Magazine, 15*(6), 20.

Quinn, Patricia O. (2009). Women and girls with AD/HD. *Attention Magazine, 16*(5), 10–11.

Quinn, Patricia. (2012). How girls and women can win with ADHD. *ADDitude Magazine* webinar. Retrieved from http://www.additudemag.com/RCLP/sub/9796.html

Quinn, Patricia, & Nadeau, Kathleen. (2000). Understanding preschool girls with AD/HD. *Attention Magazine, 6*(5), 42–45.

Quinn, Patricia, & Nadeau, Kathleen. (2004). ADD (ADHD) checklist for girls. Retrieved from http://addvance.com/help/women/girl_checklist.html

Books Specifically for Girls with ADHD

Quinn, Patricia. (2009). *Attention Magazine, girls! A guide to learn about your AD/HD*. Washington, DC: Magination Press. (for ages 8–13)

Roberts, Barbara. (2010). *The adventures of Phoebe Flower*. Silver Spring, MD: Advantage Books. (for ages 8–11).

Walker, Beth (2004). *The girls' guide to AD/HD*. Bethesda, MD: Woodbine House. (for teenage girls)

For Information on Women with ADHD

There are also numerous resources that are very beneficial for women with ADHD. Some of the leading authors and authorities on women with ADHD are Patricia Quinn, Kathleen Nadeau, Ellen Littman, Sari Solden, Terry Matlen, and Zoë Kessler. The national organizations of Children and Adults with Attention-Deficit/Hyperactivity Disorder (CHADD) (www.chadd.org) and Attention Deficit Disorder Organization (ADDA) (www.add.org) are great sources of information on females with ADHD as well as *ADDitude Magazine* (www.additudemag.com).

1.13 ADHD and Its Effects on the Family

It is important to be aware of the challenges that exist in the home when one or more children have ADHD because this disorder has a significant impact on the entire family. Unfortunately, teachers and others are generally unaware or underestimate the struggles these families face. Typically, families with members who have ADHD must cope with a much higher degree of stress than in the average family for these reasons:

- There are generally major issues surrounding homework as well as morning and evening routines (getting ready for school and bedtime).
- It is common for parents to disagree about treatment, discipline, management, structure, and other issues.
- Parents may blame one another for the child's problems or be highly critical of one another in their parenting role. This discord causes a great deal of marital stress and a higher rate of separation and divorce than is typical.
- Often it is the mother who must cope with the brunt of the issues throughout the day, which is physically and emotionally exhausting.
- As any parent of a toddler knows, having a child who needs constant supervision and monitoring is very time-consuming and interferes with the ability to get things done as planned (for example, housework and other chores).
- A child with ADHD who also has serious oppositional, defiant, and aggressive behaviors can be a major source of parenting stress that affects the whole family.
- Parents of children who have ADHD are constantly faced with needing to defend their parenting choices as well as their child. They must listen to negative press about this disorder and reject popular opinion in order to provide their child with necessary interventions and treatment.
- Parents must deal with criticism and advice from relatives, friends, and acquaintances regarding how they should discipline and parent their child. This causes a lot of parental self-doubt and adds to the stress they are already living with day in and day out.
- Frequently the family must deal with such social issues as the exclusion of the child from out-of-school activities. It is painful when your child is not invited to birthday parties or has difficulty finding someone to play with and keeping friends.
- Siblings are often resentful or even jealous of the central role their sibling with ADHD plays in the family's schedule, routines, and activities as well as the extra time and special treatment this child receives. In addition, siblings are acutely aware of and feel hurt and embarrassed when their brother or sister has acquired a negative reputation in the neighborhood and school.
- Parents of children with ADHD may feel unsupported from extended family and also experience social isolation.
- Parents have a much higher degree of responsibility in working with the school and being proactive in the management of their child than is typical for most parents. Furthermore, they must educate themselves about ADHD, research-validated treatments, their child's educational rights under the law, and other things in order to successfully advocate their child's needs.

Important Points to Keep in Mind

- It is likely that more than one family member (a parent or sibling) also has ADHD.
- In many cases, other family members who have ADHD were never diagnosed and have been struggling to cope with their own difficulties without proper treatment and support. That is why the clinicians who specialize in treating children with ADHD say it is important to view treatment in the context of the family. Learning about the family (for example, the ways the members communicate and their disciplinary practices) helps in designing a treatment plan that is most effective for the child.
- Commonly a parent may recognize for the first time that he or she has been suffering with undiagnosed ADHD for years when a son or daughter is diagnosed with the disorder. This realization can result in a positive change in the family dynamics.
- Without question, families of children with ADHD need support and understanding. Fortunately, there are many supports now available to parents. See *Lists 7.3, 7.9, and 7.11* for more related information on this topic.

1.14 Pursuing an Evaluation for ADHD: Tips for Parents

Many symptoms associated with ADHD are common in and of themselves (*List 1.5*). They do not mean the child has a disorder. But when your child is exhibiting inattentive, hyperactive, or impulsive behaviors that seem to be much more excessive than you see in other children and that are causing problems for your child at home, school, and elsewhere, you may wish to pursue an evaluation.

- It is common for parents to become concerned about their child's problematic behaviors once the child starts school and faces the demands of an academic environment. For many children, it is not until third or fourth grade that they start to struggle in school as the academic demands get much harder, and expectations for on-task behavior, work production, and self-control intensify.
- Some children have significant behavior problems and ADHD symptoms that are evident from early childhood, with lots of difficulty functioning in preschool and kindergarten (*Lists 1.11, 7.4*).
- Other children with ADHD do not have hyperactive and disruptive behaviors that raise concerns and get the attention of teachers and parents. There are many children with ADHD who manage to function adequately in an elementary school setting with the high degree of support and structure provided by parents and teachers, but fall apart in middle school and high school with the increased academic demands and expectations for self-management (*Lists 1.11, 7.5*).
- You may have had teachers, relatives, friends, or others express concerns or share observations that indicate your child may have ADHD.
- When you decide to seek an evaluation for your child, it is a very important step for you and your family (*List 1.15*).

Finding a Professional to Evaluate Your Child

- Parents are advised to share concerns with their child's pediatrician or other primary care physician and let the doctor know you want your child evaluated and why. You may request a referral to a specialist or the primary care doctor may inform you that he or she can do the evaluation.
- Parents need to be proactive and not be embarrassed to ask the doctor about his or her experience evaluating for ADHD and what will be involved in the diagnostic process. You may want to ask as well about possible treatment approaches if your child does have ADHD *(List 7.2)*.
- If you feel you are being hurried and not listened to carefully or your concerns are brushed off and questions are not satisfactorily answered, you should probably find a different professional to evaluate your child.
- In finding the professional, it helps to have recommendations. You may wish to speak with other parents of children who have ADHD (for example, through the local chapter of CHADD—Children and Adults with Attention Deficit/Hyperactivity Disorder) regarding recommended professionals in the community. These parents often know which professionals have expertise in diagnosing and treating ADHD. School nurses and school psychologists are also excellent resources and knowledgeable in most cases about health care providers in the community who have expertise in diagnosing ADHD and coexisting conditions (*List 7.9*).

- Local university medical hospitals or children's hospitals are often good resources you may want to explore as well.

A School-Based Evaluation

- It is always important to communicate with your child's teachers regarding any of your concerns. You likely have been doing so prior to reaching this decision to pursue an evaluation for ADHD. If not, the first step should be to set up an appointment and have a conference with the teacher.
- The next step is often a school multidisciplinary team meeting to discuss your child, concerns, and strategize a plan of support and intervention. This team goes by various names such as student support team (SST), student assistance team (SAT), child study team (CST), and others. It may also be the Response to Intervention (RTI) team in your child's school (*Lists 6.1, 6.2*).
- At the meeting, share your concerns and ask for input regarding your child's performance from teachers and other staff who know your son or daughter and observe his or her functioning in the classroom and other settings.
- The SST meeting is especially helpful when considering an evaluation for ADHD because the school can share with you its role in the assessment and obtain your written permission to begin gathering relevant data from school for the evaluation (*Lists 1.16, 1.18*). It is more likely that efforts will be coordinated when a school team is informed and involved.
- A plan of support (strategies and other school interventions) should be developed to address some of the difficulties your child is experiencing at school if not already in place. Your school may follow an RTI process for doing so (*List 6.1*).
- For any appropriate clinical ADHD evaluation, the school will be called on to supply the necessary data (such as records, reports, observations, behavior rating scales, work samples) to the physician or other licensed medical or mental health professional conducting the evaluation. The teacher and other various members of the school's SST may be involved in gathering and providing this data (*List 1.16*).
- Parents have the right to request an evaluation at any time (even if your school follows the RTI model and asks for other interventions to be implemented first). For more on pursuing an evaluation to determine eligibility for special education and related services under federal law IDEA or for a Section 504 accommodation plan, see *Lists 6.3, 6.4, and 6.5*.
- If your child is experiencing problems with learning and appears to be underachieving, be aware that a high percentage of children who have ADHD also have a coexisting learning disability, such as dyslexia, and should be evaluated. Others also are developmentally delayed in their language skills or motor skills and should be evaluated by the school district for possible speech-language therapy, occupational therapy, adapted physical education, or other special services (*Lists 3.6, 5.1, 5.6, 6.1, 6.3, 6.4, 6.5, 7.2*).
- Some schools take a very active role in the diagnosis of ADHD and perform a comprehensive evaluation (*List 1.18*).

1.15 Diagnosing ADHD in Children and Teens

The diagnosis of ADHD is not a simple process. There is no single laboratory test or measure to determine if a person has ADHD, and no particular piece of information alone can confirm or deny the existence of ADHD. Nevertheless, ADHD can be diagnosed reliably. Perhaps in future years, we may see the use of genetic testing, brain imaging, or other more conclusive tools and methods recommended to be used for diagnostic purposes, but currently this is not the case.

The Diagnosis

- The cornerstone of an ADHD diagnosis is meeting the criteria described in the most current edition of the *Diagnostic and Statistical Manual of Mental Health Disorders*, fifth edition (*DSM-5*), published by the American Psychiatric Association in 2013 (*List 1.3*), which replaced the previous editions (American Psychiatric Association, 1994, 2000).
- The diagnosis is made by gathering and synthesizing information obtained from a variety of sources in order to determine if there is enough evidence to conclude that the child meets all of the criteria for having ADHD. Basically, the clinician needs to determine the following:
  - The child has a significant number of specific symptoms of inattention, hyperactivity-impulsivity, or both.
  - The symptoms are to a degree that are out of norm for what is developmentally appropriate (compared to other children that age).
  - The symptoms are evident in at least two settings (typically home and school) and negatively affecting the child's life. They are serious enough to interfere with successful functioning (such as social, behavioral, academic).
  - The child does not have another disorder or condition that better accounts for these symptoms

See *List 1.3* for more specifics regarding *DSM-5* criteria.

- An appropriate evaluation for ADHD takes substantial time and effort. It is not sufficient for a child to be seen by a community physician for a brief office visit. An ADHD evaluation cannot be done without gathering and analyzing the necessary diagnostic data from a variety of sources.
- The clinician needs to gather data from parents or guardians, teachers, and others involved in the child's care to determine that ADHD diagnostic criteria have been met.
- If the school has not been communicated with and has not provided the evaluator information about the student's current functioning, and teacher input and observations have not been provided, then an appropriate assessment for ADHD cannot be made (*Lists 1.16, 1.17, 1.18, 7.1*).
- A diagnostic evaluation for ADHD also should include instruments (rating scales or questionnaires) completed by parents, teachers, and sometimes others who interact frequently with the child.
- Evaluation of the child should include screening or assessment when indicated for conditions that mimic (produce similar-looking symptoms) or may coexist with ADHD (*Lists 1.8, 1.9*).

In 2011, the American Academy of Pediatrics (AAP) published guidelines for primary care doctors for the diagnosis, evaluation, and treatment of ADHD. These guidelines were revised and updated from the initial guidelines of 2000. The current guidelines (AAP, 2011) for primary care physicians state the following:

- Doctors should evaluate children four through eighteen years of age for ADHD if they present with academic or behavioral problems and symptoms of inattention, hyperactivity, or impulsivity.
- To make a diagnosis of ADHD, all *DSM* criteria must be met.
- Any alternative cause for the symptoms (other than ADHD) should be ruled out, and the evaluation should include, if indicated, assessment for other conditions that might coexist with ADHD (emotional, behavioral, developmental, physical).

Who Is Qualified to Diagnose ADHD?

- A number of professionals have the qualifications to assess children for ADHD: child psychiatrists, pediatricians, neurologists, psychologists, social workers, family practitioners, and other licensed medical and mental health professionals.
- Specialists in childhood medical and mental health, such as child psychiatrists, child psychologists, child neurologists, and developmental or behavioral pediatricians, have the most training and are recommended for complex cases.
- A key qualification is the professional's knowledge and experience evaluating children and teens for ADHD. If the child is being evaluated by his or her pediatrician, that doctor should be following the American Academy of Pediatrics ADHD guidelines and *DSM-5* diagnostic criteria. Not all primary care doctors are aware of or follow these, and if not, parents should seek another professional to evaluate their child (*Lists 1.3, 1.14*).

Components of a Comprehensive Evaluation for ADHD

Clinical Interview

- This is the single most important feature of the evaluation process, during which the clinician spends a significant amount of time speaking with parents to obtain the following information:
  - The child's medical history (for example, fetal development, birth, illnesses, injuries), developmental history (approximate dates of milestones reached in language, motor, self-help, learning skills), and school history
  - The family history (of medical, psychiatric, psychological problems and diagnoses of parents and other family members—particularly looking for known or possible ADHD and coexisting conditions in parents, siblings, grandparents, or other relatives)
  - Information about any significant family circumstances or stressors (which may be causing some of the symptoms), such as death or serious illness in the family, parental separation or divorce, and so forth
  - Parents' perceptions, insights, and observations regarding, for example, the following:
    - The child's difficulties in learning, behavior, health, and social relationships

    - The child's strengths, interests, and motivators
    - Responses to discipline and disciplinary techniques used in the home
    - How the child responds when upset, angry, or frustrated
    - How the child gets along with siblings, neighborhood children, and others
    - The child's feelings (worries, fears, frustrations)
- The interview also involves talking with and observing the child (at what length the evaluator interviews the child or teen, and questions that will be asked vary, of course, depending on the child's age).
- An interview with the teacher is also recommended. By directly speaking with the teacher, the evaluator will be able to obtain a much better picture of the child's functioning and performance at school (academic, behavioral, social-emotional) and teacher's observations of the child compared to other students in the classroom.
- Questionnaires (such as Russell Barkley's home and school situations questionnaires) or rating forms that may have been sent to parents and teachers prior to the evaluation may be reviewed with further questions asked of parents, the child, or teachers during the interview process.
- It is helpful if prior to the evaluation, parents be prepared before meeting with the evaluator by having the information readily available (particularly the child's history).

Behavior Rating Scales

- These are very useful in determining the degree to which various ADHD-related behaviors or symptoms are observed in different key environments (for example, home and school). In addition to information from teachers and parents, rating scales may be filled out by others who spend time with the child, such as the school counselor, special education teacher, child care provider, or other relative.
- The evaluation typically involves filling out one or more rating scales. A variety of scales and questionnaires can be used as part of the ADHD process for obtaining information from parents and teachers. Those that provide information specific to the *DSM-5* diagnostic criteria for ADHD include the Vanderbilt Parent and Teacher Assessment Scales, Conners Parent and Teacher Rating Scales, Attention Deficit Disorders Evaluation Scale (ADDeS), Swanson, Nolan, and Pelham (SNAP-IV-C), the ADHD Rating Scale-IV, and others.

More about Rating Scales

- There are other broad band rating scales that may be used in addition to but not instead of the ADHD rating scales that may pick up on anxiety, depression, and other possible mental health disorders.
- There are also scales for executive functioning that the clinician may use for obtaining additional information, such as the Comprehensive Executive Function Inventory (CEFI; Naglieri & Goldstein), Behavior Rating Inventory of Executive Function (BRIEF), Barkley Deficits in Executive Functioning Scale—Children and Adolescents (BDEFS-CA), and Brown Attention Deficit Disorder Scales (BADDS).
- Rating scales list a number of items that teachers or parents rate according to the frequency they observe the child exhibiting those specific behaviors or problems. Sometimes the ratings range from "never" to "almost always" or from "not at all" to "very much." Some rating scales are numerical (ranging from 1–5 or 0–4). The scales

are standardized and enable the evaluator to compare a child's behavioral symptoms with those of other children of that age or developmental level.

- In some of the instruments, various situations in the home or school are described, and parents or teachers rate if they see the child presenting difficulty in any of those situations and to what degree (mild to severe).
- Teachers may be asked to rate the student in comparison to others in the class on the existence or degree of disruptive behavior, moodiness, oppositional behavior, distractability, organization skills, forgetfulness, on-task behavior, activity level, aggressiveness, ability to display self-control, paying attention, and so forth.

Physical Exam

- A clinical evaluation for ADHD generally includes a routine examination to rule out other possible medical conditions that could produce ADHD symptoms or that may require medical management.
- The routine exam may include measuring the child (height, weight, head circumference), vision or hearing screening to rule out poor vision or chronic ear infections, screen for gross motor skills, or neurological signs of a developmental disorder.
- Based on the child's physical exam, as well as medical history (through interview and questionnaire), a physician may look for evidence of other possible causes for the symptoms or additional issues that may need to be addressed, such as sleep disturbances, allergies, bed-wetting, or anxiety.
- Other medical tests (blood work or imaging scans such as CT, SPECT, PET, EEGs) are not done in an evaluation for ADHD.
- It is the doctor's responsibility to determine the need for additional medical testing or referral to other specialists if indicated.

Observations

- Directly observing the child's functioning in a variety of settings can provide helpful diagnostic information. Most useful are observations in natural settings where the child spends much of his or her time, such as school. How a child behaves and performs in an office visit is not indicative of how that same child performs and behaves in a classroom, on the playground, in the school cafeteria, or other natural setting. School personnel may provide this information (*Lists 1.16, 1.18*).

Note: School personnel may not share *any* information unless the required release of information forms have been filled out and are on file—which grants the school permission to do so.

Academic and Intelligence Testing

- An evaluator should have at least a general indication of a child's academic achievement levels and performance, as well as a rough estimate of his or her cognitive (thinking and reasoning) ability. Some means of obtaining this information is through a review of the student's report cards, standardized test scores, classroom work samples, or curriculum-based assessment, or through informal screening measures. Information can also be gleaned from the child, teacher, and parent interview.
- If there is indication of possible learning disabilities, a request for a psychoeducational evaluation is appropriate and recommended. This evaluation assesses

cognitive and processing abilities, academic achievement levels, and information about how the child learns. Parents may request this evaluation from the school, which is the beginning of the individualized education program (IEP) process. See *Lists 1.16, 5.1, 5.6, 6.1, 6.2, 6.3, 6.4, and 7.2* for information related to this topic.

Performance Tests

- Additional tests are sometimes used by some evaluators to obtain more information about how a child functions on various performance measures. Some clinicians use computerized tests that measure the child's ability to inhibit making impulsive responses and to sustain attention to tasks. These tests, however, are not standard practice or routinely done in ADHD assessments. They are not necessary for making the diagnosis.

More Tips and Information

- A thorough history is critical in making an accurate diagnosis of ADHD, which is obtained through the interview, use of questionnaires, and a review of medical and school records. With regard to the school history, a great deal of useful data is located in the student's school records, which might include past report cards, IEPs, district and state achievement testing and other school evaluations (such as psycho-educational, speech and language), referrals to the school team, and so forth. Parents may provide some of this information or the school.
- See *List 1.14* for recommendations of steps parents should take in pursuing an evaluation for their child and finding a suitable professional to do so.
- See *Lists 1.16, 1.17, and 1.18* for information about the school's role in the diagnostic process and what teachers should be prepared to share with the professional who is diagnosing the child for ADHD.

A proper diagnosis is the most important step in getting the necessary help and intervention a child with ADHD needs in order to achieve success and minimize risks of any negative outcomes. Parents are advised not to wait and see when they have concerns, especially if the child is struggling in learning, behavior, or social skill competence.

Sources and Resources

American Academy of Pediatrics (AAP). (2011). ADHD: Clinical practice guidelines for the diagnosis, evaluation, and treatment of attention-deficit/hyperactivity disorder in children and adolescents. *Pediatrics, 128*(5), 1007–1022.

American Psychiatric Association. (1994). *Diagnostic and statistical manual of mental disorders* (4th ed.) *(DSM-IV)*. Washington, DC: American Psychiatric Association.

American Psychiatric Association. (2000). *Diagnostic and statistical manual of mental disorders* (4th ed., text rev.) *(DSM-IV-TR)*. Washington, DC: American Psychiatric Association.

American Psychiatric Association. (2013). *Diagnostic and statistical manual of mental disorders* (5th ed.) *(DSM-5)*. Washington, DC: American Psychiatric Association.

Centers for Disease Control and Prevention (CDC). (n.d.). Diagnosing ADHD in children. Retrieved from www.cdc.gov/ncbddd/adhd/diagnosis.html

Children and Adults with Attention-Deficit/Hyperactivity Disorder (CHADD) and the National Resource Center on AD/HD (www.help4adhd.org/) offer online information regarding ADHD diagnosis, available at these links:

www.chadd.org/Understanding-ADHD/Parents-Caregivers-of-Children-with-ADHD/Evaluation-and-Treatment.aspx

http://help4adhd.org/en/treatment/guides

http://help4adhd.org/en/treatment/guides/keycomponents

www.chadd.org/Understanding-ADHD/Parents-Caregivers-of-Children-with-ADHD/Evaluation-and-Treatment/Professionals-Who-Diagnose-and-Treat-ADHD.aspx

University of Maryland Medical Center. (n.d.). Diagnosing ADHD in children. Retrieved from http://umm.edu/health/medical/reports/articles/attention-deficit-hyperactivity-disorder

The following are resources on practical advice for parents regarding what to expect in the diagnostic process for a comprehensive evaluation, how to prepare, and the struggles many families have in obtaining the diagnosis of ADHD (with coexisting conditions):

Barkley, Russell A. (2013). *Taking charge of ADHD: The complete, authoritative guide for parents* (3rd ed.). New York: Guilford Press.

Barrow, Karen. (2014). What's up, doc? *ADDitude Magazine, 14*(3), 36–39.

Carpenter, Deborah. (2007). The diagnostic puzzle. *ADDitude Magazine, 7*(3), 32–35.

Engler, Natalie. (2006). The AD/HD road map. *ADDitude Magazine, 6*(2), 39–42.

McCarthy, Laura Flynn. (2009). Knowing. *ADDitude Magazine, 10*(1), 35–39.

1.16 The School's Role and Responsibilities in the Diagnosis of ADHD

Information about Current School Functioning

- As described in *List 1.15,* the diagnosis of ADHD is dependent on gathering sufficient information from multiple sources to get a clear picture of how ADHD symptoms are affecting a child's functioning in more than one setting. School is a key setting—where the child spends much of his or her life.
- No one is in a better position than the teacher to report on the child's school performance compared to other students of that age and grade. This includes the teacher's observations and objective information indicating the student's academic productivity and social, emotional, and behavioral functioning.
- The teacher should be prepared to share information regarding the student's ability to exhibit self-control, stay focused and on task, interact with peers and adults, initiate and follow through on assignments, and other behaviors.
- In an appropriate evaluation for ADHD, teachers will be asked to report their observations about the student through standardized behavior rating scales, questionnaires, narrative statements, phone interviews, or other measures.
- Other indicators of a student's current school performance (academic and behavioral) may be helpful as well—for example, disciplinary referrals (among the records of guidance counselors or administrators) and work samples.
- Direct observations of the student's performance in the classroom and other settings (such as the playground or cafeteria) also provide useful evidence of problems the child may be exhibiting (with work production, social interactions, disruptive or off-task behavior, and disorganization) compared to peers. Evaluators should have observational data from the school, which of course are more beneficial than just observing the child in the unnatural environment of a doctor's office.

Information about the School History

- Data indicating the existence of symptoms in previous school years, when those symptoms started to become apparent, and difficulties the student experienced in prior grades can be obtained from the school records and interviewing the parents or school personnel.
- A great deal of useful data is located in the student's records, which might include past report cards, district and state achievement testing, other evaluations (psycho-educational, speech and language), referrals to the school's multidisciplinary team, or any school-based support or intervention plans that may have been generated by the SST (*List 6.2*), RTI (*List 6.1*), or IEP (*List 6.4*) team.

Points to Keep in Mind

- In addition to the presence of symptoms, the evaluator must determine that the symptoms are causing the student difficulties and interfering with the child's functioning (for example, with social success and interpersonal relationships, academic productivity, or disruptive behavior problems), and to what degree. Teachers and other school personnel who interact and observe the child on a daily basis are best able to provide this information (*Lists 1.3, 1.15*).

- Parents have a right to expect the school to be supportive and responsive in the diagnostic process. Schools need to provide information requested by the child's physician or mental health professional conducting a clinical evaluation for ADHD (*List 1.18*).
- It will be necessary for parents to sign a release-of-information form before school personnel can communicate with other professionals outside of school or provide documentation and data regarding the child. Make sure this is on file with the school district before sharing information requested by a doctor or other evaluator.
- School personnel should be prompt and thorough in providing any information requested for an evaluation (such as behavioral rating scales).
- It is also helpful (and may be requested) that the teacher write a paragraph or two indicating how he or she views the child in relation to other students in the classroom (regarding behavior, social skills, work production and output, and so on).
- It is highly recommended that schools provide information to the physician in a manner that takes into account the physician's limited time. A one- or maximum of two-page summary of the child's school history and current performance is helpful (*Lists 1.17, 1.18*).
- Teachers should be willing to speak and confer with whomever is conducting the evaluation if they are asked to do so. It is beneficial (but rare) for physicians to call to speak directly with teachers (*List 1.15*).
- If a student is receiving a clinical evaluation for ADHD and the school is not requested to send information, and no attempt is made to communicate with or obtain input from the school, it is an *inappropriate evaluation* for ADHD. See *Lists 1.3, 1.14, and 1.15*.
- School personnel need to be alert and aware of the high rate of coexisting conditions and disorders with ADHD (*List 1.8*). Often those students who exhibit very significant behavioral challenges have ADHD and another coexisting mental health disorder needing treatment. It is important for the school to communicate about all issues with parents and help facilitate referrals to appropriate community agencies and medical or mental health-care professionals, when indicated.
- The school is responsible for determining educational impairment of a suspected or known disability. Schools have the responsibility of initiating and following through with a comprehensive evaluation if the student is suspected of having ADHD or any other disability impairing educational performance. (This includes behavioral, not just academic, performance.) If the student meets eligibility criteria, the school is then responsible for providing supports and services under either of the two federal laws: IDEA or Section 504 of the Rehabilitation Act of 1973 (*Lists 6.3, 6.4, 6.5*).
- Approximately 25 to 50% of students with ADHD also have coexisting learning disabilities. If a student with ADHD is struggling academically (for example, in learning to read or write), the school should consider the probability of learning disabilities (such as dyslexia or dysgraphia) and provide a more comprehensive psycho-educational evaluation to determine his or her learning needs (*Lists 5.1, 5.6, 6.1, 6.3, 6.4*).
- See *List 1.17* for tips on what teachers should do if they suspect a student has ADHD and would like to recommend evaluation.
- *See List 1.18* for information regarding a school-based evaluation for ADHD, which is conducted in some school districts (not all).
- See *Lists 6.1 and 6.2* on the RTI and SST processes in schools, which are problem-solving team approaches and means of identifying students in need of support and providing appropriate intervention.

1.17 If You Suspect a Student Has ADHD: Recommendations for Teachers and Other School Personnel

- When you observe a student displaying inattentive, hyperactive, and impulsive behavior in the classroom, you should automatically attempt to deal with those behaviors by using strategies known to help with those issues. These strategies include, for example, environmental structuring, cueing and prompting, organization and study skills assistance, and behavior-modification techniques. Obviously this is simply good teaching practice because all students who display the need should be provided with behavioral and academic help and support.
- Of course, teachers should communicate with parents about difficulties the student may be experiencing.
- It is also good practice if concerned about a student to keep records on strategies and interventions you are using in your attempt to help the student, anecdotal records regarding the student's behaviors and classroom performance, work samples, as well as any phone contacts, conferences, or other communication you have had with parents.

- Consult informally with appropriate support staff (such as school counselor, school nurse, psychologist, or special education teacher). Share your concerns and ask for advice and assistance as needed.
- You may also want to communicate with the previous year's teacher(s) to see if your areas of concern were also of issue the prior year, and if so, find out what strategies and interventions were used successfully or unsuccessfully by that teacher.
- Most schools use a student support team (SST) or Response to Intervention (RTI) team process for the next step (*Lists 6.1, 6.2*). This team process may go by other names such as student intervention team, instructional support team, or others.
- The SST or RTI team, which generally includes school professionals (teacher, administrator, support staff) and parents of the student meet to share and identify problems the student is experiencing as well as other relevant information and data. They strategize and try to problem solve together.
- Information about the child's strengths and interests are also presented as well as concerns.
- There is team effort in designing a plan of targeted actions to address difficulties the student is having at school (academic, behavioral, social, or other). *See List 6.1*, which describes tier 1 and tier 2 interventions under an RTI model.
- If ADHD symptoms and resulting problems are evident, and the school feels an ADHD evaluation should be recommended, it may do so at this time (or in a follow-up meeting) with parents.
- The team may share information or resources about ADHD (such as literature or websites) and inform parents about the diagnostic process (clinical or school-based screening or assessment), if interested. See *Lists 1.15 and 1.18*.

Caution and Tips for Teachers

- It is important that school professionals are careful how they express to parents their concerns that a child might have ADHD because there are liabilities that may be incurred if it is not communicated properly. For example, school districts do not want teachers telling parents that their child needs to have a medical evaluation because the district may be asked to pay for it. It is, however, an astute and helpful teacher who alerts parents to problems that lead to the successful diagnosis and treatment of many children with ADHD. So, teachers do have a professional obligation to alert parents.
- It is generally best to discuss with parents the possibility that their child may have a medical reason or disorder causing the problems he or she is experiencing through a team forum. At minimum, one other school professional (the school nurse, guidance counselor, administrator, or school psychologist, for example) should join the classroom teacher in doing so.
- Do not tell parents that you think their child has ADHD or make statements that sound as if you have concluded the child must have this disorder.
- Do not attempt to diagnose ADHD. You are not qualified to do so.
- Do not tell parents that their child *needs* to be evaluated for ADHD.
- Never tell parents that their child needs medication for ADHD.
- Share with parents the positives about the student (strengths, talents, character traits, behaviors), not just your concerns.
- Emphasize the difficulties (learning, academic, social) the symptoms or behaviors are causing *their child,* not the problems they are causing *you*.
- Be very explicit in describing objectively the behaviors of concern, and ask parents if they have seen any of the same behaviors at home.
- Following are some possible statements to use in communicating with parents:
  - "These are the behaviors I have been observing that have been causing your child difficulty at school and affecting his learning and relationships with the other children."
  - "Sometimes there are physiological reasons or medical causes for these kinds of difficulties (with paying attention, self-control, impulsive behavior, being highly active and restless . . .)."
  - "You may want to share these concerns with your child's doctor or consider an evaluation."

It is usually okay to make a statement such as, "I have had students in the past with similar behaviors and some of them were diagnosed with ADHD. The only way to know if that's the case for your child would be through a professional evaluation."

1.18 School-Based Assessment for ADHD

- In some school districts, a school-based evaluation is conducted for ADHD—for educational purposes and interventions.
- Schools that do such evaluations generally follow certain procedures and steps, which are completed in stages.

Referral

- The evaluation begins with referral and information documented about presenting concerns.

Screening

- The teacher shares information briefly about the student's performance in the classroom and some strategies that have been tried so far.
- The teacher can complete an ADHD behavior rating scale using some initial screening methods to measure the number of presenting symptoms of inattention, hyperactivity, and impulsivity (*List 1.15*).
- If there are a sufficient number of presenting ADHD symptoms on the rating form, a comprehensive assessment would be initiated.

Comprehensive Assessment

This involves multiple measures, such as the following:

- Parent interview for obtaining information about the child's developmental, medical, and academic history, family history, eliciting parents' input regarding the child's functioning, when they started noticing symptoms, and the degree to which they are affecting the child's life
- Teacher interview to obtain information about the student's academic, behavioral, and social functioning at school; the teacher may be asked to share information such as how and to what degree the symptoms and behaviors are causing the student impairment and interfering with success, the most problematic times and environments (for example, transition times, the playground), the child's strengths, interests, and motivators, the interventions that have been tried, and their degree of success
- Behavior rating scales and other scales or questionnaires filled out by parents, teachers, and others who know the child well or who observe and interact with the child frequently, such as a school counselor or special education teacher
- Direct observation of the student in the classroom (by someone other than the classroom teacher) and in other school settings (such as the playground or cafeteria)
- Review of cumulative school records (including report card grades and teacher comments, standardized assessment, diagnostic reports, school behavioral referrals)
- Academic measures, such as curriculum-based assessment, observation of student independent work performance, checking for number of assignments missing or incomplete
- Vision and hearing screening may be done at school.
- Other assessments, as indicated

Interpreting the Data and Next Steps

- Once the data is gathered it needs to be reviewed and interpreted—looking to see if *DSM-5* diagnostic criteria have been met for ADHD.
- For educational purposes, such as eligibility for a 504 accommodation plan, that is often sufficient. The ADHD screening and assessment procedures previously described are sufficient for determining if a student has "a physical or mental condition that significantly limits a major life activity," which would meet the criteria under Section 504 to offer reasonable accommodations (*Lists 6.3, 6.5*).
- ADHD is a clinical diagnosis. In some school districts, the school psychologist or other professional is qualified to make the diagnosis for the purpose of determining eligibility for special education and related services under the special education law IDEA (*Lists 6.3, 6.4*).
- Other school districts require a physician's statement in writing that the child has ADHD in order to be considered eligible for special education under OHI—other health impaired—criteria (*Lists 6.3, 6.4*). The school's assessment data and summary is sent to the physician, who then makes the official ADHD diagnosis.
- The physician may also be asked to describe how the symptoms, which led to the diagnosis, might adversely affect the student's educational performance.
- If the school team (which includes parents) determines that the ADHD symptoms are having an adverse impact on the student's educational performance, the student would qualify under the federal law IDEA to special education and related services (*Lists 6.3, 6.4*).
- See *Lists 1.15, 1.16, and 1.17* for more related information.

Sources and Resources

DuPaul, George J. (n.d.). ADHD identification and assessment: Basic guidelines for educators. National Association of School Psychologists (NASP). S8-17–S8-19. Retrieved from www.nasponline.org/resources/principals/nasp_adhd.pdf

Dendy, Chris A. Zeigler, Durheim, Mary, & Teeter Ellison, Anne. (2006). *CHADD educator's manual on ADHD*. Landover, MD: CHADD. (Section on stages of a comprehensive assessment of ADHD in the schools)

1.19 Multimodal Treatment for ADHD

Once a child is diagnosed with ADHD, there are many ways to help the child and family. ADHD is not something that can be cured, but it can be treated and managed effectively. A multifaceted or multimodal treatment approach is the most effective. It is important to keep the following points in mind:

- Parents are the primary case managers for their children. Once they receive the diagnosis, parents need to start the journey of becoming an ADHD expert—learning all they can about the disorder and research-based treatment options. Parents who become educated about ADHD are able to make the best-informed decisions regarding their child's care and management.
- Most positive outcomes for youngsters with ADHD are achieved when parents, teachers, other involved school professionals, and treating medical and mental health providers have good communication and collaborate well (*Lists 7.1, 7.3, 7.8*).
- All parties involved in the care and education of the child with ADHD should be working together in establishing target outcomes (goals), formulating plans to reach the goals, and monitoring the effectiveness of the interventions being used.
- The two research-validated interventions known to be most effective at this time are *medication* and *psychosocial (or behavioral) therapy*. One, the other, or combination of both are the main treatments for ADHD. The scientific evidence clearly shows these are the treatments that make the biggest difference with regard to improvement of symptoms and degree of impairment. These interventions have been extensively tested with controlled studies and proven effective in managing ADHD (*Lists 1.4, 1.20, 1.22*).
- Educational supports and interventions are a critical component in the success of students with ADHD as well, which are described in lists throughout this book.
- There are additional complementary supports and interventions to enhance the plan and benefit the individual with ADHD (*Lists 1.23, 7.6, 7.7*).
- ADHD is recognized as a chronic condition (such as asthma) and follows a chronic care plan of action (AAP and NICHQ, 2002). This means looking at the long-term picture. Various supports and treatments may be needed throughout one's lifetime or employed at different times in life as needed (for example, treatment from medical and mental health professionals, various school interventions, out-of-school tutoring or coaching). In addition, because of the long-term management involved, the treatment plan requires vigilance on the part of parents, educators, and health providers in monitoring and following up on the effectiveness of the plan and adjusting as needed.

Multimodal Intervention

Parent Training

This is a key and crucial component of ADHD treatment. Parents must learn and be provided with the following information to help them help their child:

- Accurate and reliable information about ADHD in order to understand the impact and developmental course of the disorder, the treatment options, and available resources
- A new set of skills for managing their child's challenging behaviors

- Training in effective behavioral techniques and how to structure the home environment and other aspects of their child's life
- How to best navigate the educational and health care systems

Note: The Parent to Parent training program offered through CHADD is highly recommended. See www.chadd.org.

Medication Therapy (Pharmacological Intervention)

Pharmacological treatment is the use of medication to manage ADHD symptoms. Stimulant medications have been proven effective in treating approximately 70 to 90 percent of children with ADHD (Barkley, 2013; Brown, 2005). These medications work to increase the action of the neurotransmitters (brain chemicals) available in certain brain regions and circuits that are not working efficiently in individuals with ADHD. Some FDA-approved nonstimulant medications are also used successfully in ADHD treatment. Appropriate medical treatment requires well-managed and carefully monitored use of medication(s) for ADHD. When there are coexisting disorders, various medications may be prescribed in the treatment of those other conditions as well. *See Lists 1.4, 1.7, 1.8, 1.20, and 1.21.*

Behavior Therapy

- Behavior modification and specific behavioral strategies implemented at home and school are very important interventions for managing ADHD. This involves parents and teachers learning skills and strategies to manage the challenging behaviors of children with ADHD, such as how to provide clear, consistent structure and follow-through, effective use of rewards (to increase desired behaviors) and negative consequences (to decrease unwanted, undesirable behaviors).
- Behavior therapy provides specific techniques and interventions adults can implement, such as a token economy system or home-school daily report cards, and help in recognizing and adjusting the antecedents or triggers to problem behavior. Among the research-validated behavioral interventions for children with ADHD is the use of daily report cards (DRCs). See *List 2.9* for detailed information about implementing DRCs and other individualized behavioral interventions, examples of DRCs and other management forms in the appendix, and the many behavioral supports and strategies for parents and teachers found in lists throughout section 2.
- The research-based behavioral interventions for children with ADHD include those learned through parent training and implemented at home, those provided at school by teachers and other school personnel, and ones that the child learns to improve peer relationships. See *Lists 1.22 and 2.17.*

Educational Interventions

- *Differentiated instruction.* Teachers who recognize that one size does not fit all embrace the challenge of using multiple approaches in teaching the curriculum and enabling students to demonstrate their learning (*Lists 3.7, 3.8*).
- *Accommodations.* Teachers should provide accommodations (environmental, academic, instructional, behavioral) as needed to enable students to achieve success, whether they are done informally or as per a student's IEP or Section 504 accommodation plan (*Lists 6.4, 6.5* and lists throughout sections 2, 3, 4, 5, and 7 and lists throughout this book).

- *Special education and related services.* Some students with ADHD qualify for special education and receive an IEP and related services provided through the school district (*Lists 6.3, 6.4*).
- *Other school interventions.* Various supports and safety nets may be available at the school that students in general education are able to access, such as homework or organizational assistance, mentoring, peer or adult tutoring, school counseling, and RTI tier 1 and tier 2 academic and behavioral interventions (*List 6.1*).
- *Tutoring or academic supports.* Parents may pursue private tutoring or other academic interventions to help their child in specific areas of academic weakness, such as reading.

Other Psychosocial Interventions

- *Family counseling.* The whole family is often affected by issues relating to children with ADHD. Family therapy can address concerns that affect parents and siblings and improve family relationships.
- *Individual counseling.* Counseling can teach the child coping techniques, problem-solving strategies, and how to deal with stress or anger.
- *Social skills training.* This training is usually provided in small groups with curriculum addressing specific skills that children with ADHD tend to have difficulties with in their interpersonal relationships. The children then practice the skills they have learned in natural settings, receiving feedback and reinforcement (*List 2.17*).
- *Psychotherapy for teens and adults.* This counseling helps the person with ADHD who has a history of school, work, personal, or relationship problems talk about his or her feelings and deal with self-defeating patterns of behavior.
- *Vocational counseling.* This can be a helpful intervention for teens and adults.

Other Helpful Interventions

- *ADHD coaching.* This is a service that many teens and adults find beneficial in learning and applying strategies to be more focused and productive and to help them with organization and time management. Coaching generally assists with scheduling, breaking work tasks down into reasonable short-term goals, checking in regularly (for example, over the phone, Skype, or by text or e-mail), and keeping the ADHD client on target with his or her individual short- and long-term goals (*List 7.6*).
- *Support groups and opportunities to share with others and network.* Support organizations such as CHADD and the Attention Deficit Disorder Association (ADDA) are highly recommended resources. CHADD has local chapters throughout the United States, and such groups are an excellent source of information and support. Online chat groups and other vehicles to interact with others with similar concerns and experiences can also be very helpful (*Lists 7.9, 7.12*).
- *Exercise.* It is important for children and teens with ADHD to engage in sports, dance, or other physical activities. There are numerous benefits of exercise, such as enhancing mood, alertness, and self-regulation, having an outlet for their need to move, and others (social, recreational, self-image) derived from the challenge and gaining of new skills and competencies (*List 7.7*).
- *Develop and nurture their strengths and interests.* Very important to the child's happiness and successful future is to enable them to participate in activities such as arts and crafts, music, dance, sports, performing arts, scouts, or other areas of interest.

This is a very important part of a multimodal and therapeutic plan for children with ADHD—to help them find their strengths, and have areas in their life in which they shine (*List 7.7*).

- *Healthy diet and lifestyle*. Environmental factors can worsen ADHD symptoms. All children and teens (including those with ADHD) should be health conscious and have a well-balanced diet, high in nutrition (plenty of protein, fruits, vegetables). Nutritionists point out that a balanced diet can help control behavioral swings related to surges in blood sugar or hunger. Getting a good night's sleep is also very important but often problematic for many children and teens with ADHD. More outdoor activities as opposed to indoor ones (glued to a screen of some type) are good choices for everyone and may be even more important for those with ADHD (*List 7.7*).

Complementary Interventions

- There are some complementary treatments that may also be beneficial for some children, teens, and adults in a multimodal treatment plan, (such as mindfulness practices, neurofeedback and other brain training technology, and some dietary factors). See *Lists 1.23* and *7.7* for more on this topic.

Additional Points to Keep in Mind

- The intervention plan should be designed not just to focus on areas of weakness but also to help the child or teen recognize and build on his or her strengths (*List 1.10*).
- Parents need to become well-educated about evidence-based treatments for ADHD as well as their legal rights in the educational system. This is necessary in order to advocate effectively for their child in both the educational and health care systems.
- Children, especially teens, should be included as active partners in their treatment program so that they will be willing participants and cooperate. They need to understand the disorder, the reason for various interventions, and how those treatments are intended to have a positive effect on their daily lives.

Sources and Resources

American Academy of Pediatrics. (2011). ADHD: Clinical practice guideline for the diagnosis, evaluation, and treatment of attention-deficit/hyperactivity disorder in children and adolescents. *Pediatrics, 128*(5),1007–1022.

American Academy of Pediatrics and National Initiative for Children's Healthcare Quality. (2002). *Caring for children with ADHD: A resource toolkit for clinicians*. Chicago: American Academy of Pediatrics.

Barkley, Russell A. (2006). *Attention-deficit/hyperactivity disorder: A handbook for diagnosis and treatment* (3rd ed.). New York: Guilford Press.

Barkley, Russell A. (2013). *Taking charge of ADHD: The complee, authoritative guide for parents* (3rd ed.). New York: Guilford Press.

Brown, Thomas E. (2005). *Attention deficit disorder: The unfocused mind in children and adults*. New Haven: Yale University Press.

Centers for Disease Control and Prevention. (n.d.). ADHD treatment. Retrieved from www.cdc.gov/ncbddd/adhd/treatment.html

National Resource Center on AD/HD. (2011). Managing medication for children and adolescents with ADHD. *What We Know, 3*. Retrieved from www.help4adhd.org/en/treatment/medication/WWK3

National Resource Center on AD/HD. (2004). Psychosocial treatment for children and adolescents with ADHD. *What We Know, 7*. Retrieved from www.help4adhd.org/documents/WWK7.pdf

Teeter, Phyllis Anne. (2000). *Interventions for ADHD: Treatment in developmental context*. New York: Guilford Press.

Wolraich, Mark L., & DuPaul, George J. (2010). *ADHD diagnosis and management: A practical guide for the clinic and the classroom*. Baltimore, MD: Paul H. Brookes.

1.20 Medication Treatment for Managing ADHD

- Medications have been used safely for decades to treat ADHD. They do not cure the disorder but do help in controlling and reducing the symptoms. The most commonly used medications for treating ADHD are stimulants.
- There continues to be much attention (media sensationalism and public controversy) regarding the use of stimulant medication in treating children with ADHD. A great deal of misinformation exists, which makes it difficult for parents trying to make an informed decision.
- Parents need to consult with their physician or other medical professionals about any medication issues, questions, or concerns. This list of information is meant only as a general reference.

Stimulant Medications in the Treatment of ADHD

- Stimulant medications (the methylphenidates) have been regularly used since the 1960s in the treatment of children and adolescents with ADHD (although it was not called ADHD at that time). Stimulants have been studied more extensively than any other psychoactive drug prescribed for children. Hundreds of controlled scientific studies demonstrating their effectiveness in treating children with ADHD have been conducted.
- Stimulants have been used safely with millions of children for at least fifty to sixty years.
- Stimulants have been proven to work for 70 to 90 percent of children with ADHD. They are also effective in adults. There are very few people with ADHD who do not respond to stimulant medications, and the results can be very dramatic.
- Because the scientific evidence so strongly supports the effectiveness of stimulants in managing the symptoms and reducing impairment, they are recommended as the first choice of medications used in treating children with ADHD.
- There are two main classes of stimulants: the *methylphenidate* formulas (for example, Ritalin, Concerta, Methylin, Daytrana) and the *amphetamine* formulas (Adderall, Dexedrine, Vyvanse).

How Stimulants Are Believed to Work

- Researchers suspect that stimulant medications act to normalize biochemistry in the parts of the brain involved in ADHD (primarily the prefrontal cortex and related brain areas).
- Stimulants increase (or stimulate) the production of neurotransmitters, which are the brain chemicals, to a more normalized level in these key brain regions.
- The brain chemicals involved are dopamine and norepinephrine. Scientists believe that medications that increase the availability of these neurotransmitters help nerve-to-nerve communication, thereby boosting the signal between neurons.
- The stimulants are thought to be working within the system involved in the release of these brain chemicals into the synapse (the gap between two neurons), and their

reuptake or reabsorption out of the synapse. Stimulants are believed to help in keeping the proper level of these neurotransmitters in the synapse long enough to do the job of transmitting messages from one neuron to the next efficiently.

- Stimulants (while in the bloodstream) work to activate the areas of the brain that are underactive and not working efficiently in those with ADHD. These are the regions responsible for attention, inhibition of behavior, regulation of activity level, and executive functions.
- *See Lists 1.2, 1.4, and 1.7* for more on this topic of brain differences in individuals with ADHD.

Stimulant Medications Prescribed for Treating ADHD

There are several stimulant medications. In the following list, the italicized name is the generic name, and the names in parentheses are the brand names. Also, SR stands for "sustained release," LA is "long acting," and ER and XR mean "extended release."

The Stimulants

- *Methylphenidate* (Ritalin, Ritalin LA, Ritalin SR, Concerta, Metadate CD, Metadate ER, Methylin, Methylin ER, Quillivant XR, Daytrana patch)
- *Dexmethylphenidate* (Focalin, Focalin XR)
- *Dextroamphetamine* (Dexedrine, Dexedrine Spansule, DextroStat, ProCentra)
- *Mixed amphetamine salts* (Adderall, Adderall XR)
- *Lisdexamfetamine dimesylate* (Vyvanse)

- Methylphenidates are among the most carefully studied drugs on the market. Thousands of children have been involved in research evaluating their use in the treatment of ADHD.
- Each of the stimulants has a high response rate. A child who does not respond well (in symptom improvement) to one stimulant medication will often respond well to another.
- Physicians have a number of possibilities of stimulants to choose from. The initial choice is generally a matter of doctor and parent preference. Some of the stimulant medications come in tablets or capsules to swallow whole, some are chewable or can be dissolved in liquid, others can be sprinkled on food like applesauce. Daytrana is a patch adhered to the skin, and ProCentra is a liquid.
- The different stimulant prescriptions vary in their onset (when they begin working), how they are released into the body (immediately or over an extended or sustained period), and how long the effects last (from a few hours to as many as twelve hours).
- The short-acting and immediate release formulas of the stimulants (such as Ritalin or Methylin) do the following:
  - Start to work about twenty to thirty minutes from the time the medication is taken
  - Metabolize quickly and are effective for approximately three to four hours
  - Reach their peak effect within one to three hours
  - Generally require an additional dosage to be administered at school

- May require a third dose (often a smaller one) to enable the child to function more successfully in the late afternoon and evening hours
- May be prescribed as an additional booster dose later in the day when a longer-acting stimulant wears off (to provide symptom relief in the late afternoon and evening)

- The longer-acting, extended release stimulants have a time-release delivery system. They work differently. These medications:
  - Take longer for the effect to begin
  - Vary from approximately five to eight hours of coverage for some of the medications to lasting as long as ten to twelve hours for others
  - Provide a smoother, sustained level of the drug throughout the day
  - Minimize fluctuations (peak and trough) in blood levels
  - Minimize rebound phenomena (a worsening of symptoms as the effects of the drug wear off)
  - Eliminate the need for a midday dose at school, which is very beneficial for many children and teens, particularly those who are forgetful or embarrassed to take medication at school

About Stimulant Medications

- They take effect quickly (generally within thirty to sixty minutes).
- For some children, their initial prescription and dosage will work well. But many others require adjustments in dosage or trying others among the stimulant medications and formulas to get the best effect.
- For most children with ADHD taking a stimulant medication, once the optimal dosage has been found, they experience improvement (often very significant) in behavior and symptoms.
- Stimulants are found to improve the core symptoms (hyperactivity, impulsivity, inattention) and many of the secondary or associated problems these children experience (for example, oppositional behavior, difficult interpersonal relationships, and lack of work production and school performance).
- On a therapeutic dosage of stimulant medication, there are many positive effects that often occur: reduced disruptive behavior, emotionality, improved ability to get started on and complete assignments, paying attention, staying focused, producing work, following directions, interacting with others, tolerating frustration, as well as improved handwriting and academic accuracy.
- If a child isn't showing improved symptoms when treated with a stimulant medication, the physician will typically prescribe a different stimulant (among the several on the market)—which often does produce a positive response.

Side Effects of Stimulant Medications

- The side effects that are most common are appetite suppression, weight loss, and mild sleep disturbances. Some children may also experience headaches, stomachaches, irritability, moodiness, agitation, an emergence of tics, and a rebound effect (a worsening of symptoms as the medication wears off, such as irritability, less compliance, more activity).

- A small number of children develop or unmask latent tics (involuntary muscle movements) in the form of facial grimaces, sniffing, coughing, snorting, or other vocal sounds. *Note:* These are rare and in most cases tics do not continue if the medication is stopped.
- Most side effects from stimulant medications are mild, diminish over time, and respond to changes in dosage or the particular stimulant prescribed.
- Stimulant medication may cause some minimal growth suppression (one to three pounds lighter, one-quarter to one-half inch shorter), most notably during the first couple of years taking the medicine. However, research also indicates that by the third year of taking the medication, growth patterns tend to normalize, and most children will ultimately achieve normal height and weight as young adults.

The Titration Process

- Medication treatment begins with a titration phase: a trial period when the physician is trying to determine the appropriate medication and dosage. The correct dosage of a stimulant is determined not by the child's weight or age, but according to how efficiently his or her body metabolizes the medication, which varies in every child or teen.
- The titration process involves the following steps:
  - Starting with a very low dosage and raising it gradually while observing the effects
  - Close monitoring of symptoms and behavioral changes (at home and school) while progressively changing the dosages and sometimes adjusting the timing of medication administered
  - Trying to achieve the most improvement in symptoms and optimal effects from the medication with a minimum of side effects
- Parents and teachers must communicate with the physician and provide the feedback necessary for the doctor to determine the child's response to the medication so that benefits are being achieved at each dosage level and side effects are minimized (*List 1.21*).

Nonstimulants

- *Atomoxetine* (brand name Strattera) is the first nonstimulant approved by the Food and Drug Administration and was released in 2002.
- *Atomoxetine* works differently from stimulants. It is a selective norepinephrine reuptake inhibitor, believed to work by blocking the reuptake or recycling of norepinephrine and increasing the availability of this brain chemical in the affected areas of the brain. Whereas stimulants mostly work to improve the level of dopamine, Strattera works on increasing the norepinephrine level and activity.
- *Atomoxetine* has demonstrated effectiveness for improving ADHD symptoms in children and adults and may also help with oppositional and defiant behavior and anxiety.
- *Atomoxetine* has the advantage of providing smooth, continuous coverage for twenty-four hours. It can help functioning around the clock. It also is easier to reorder the medication because it is not a controlled substance.

- *Atomoxetine* takes weeks of daily use before it shows its benefits. Most common side effects are upset stomach (nausea, vomiting), sleep problems, fatigue, nervousness, and dry mouth.

Other Medications

- *Antihypertensives* (alpha agonists) are another type of drugs that are sometimes used in the treatment of ADHD. They include *guanfacine* (Tenex) and extended release *guanfacine* (Intuniv) and *clonidine* (Catapres) and extended release *clonidine* (Kapvay). Intuniv and Kapvay are more commonly prescribed for children.
- These medications may improve oppositional, defiant behavior, anxiety, aggression, and tics as well as ADHD symptoms.
- *Antidepressants.* Certain antidepressants have also been found effective in treating ADHD, particularly if a child is not responding to the stimulant or nonstimulant or shows signs of depression, anxiety, or tics, as well as ADHD. They are not, however, FDA approved as an ADHD medication.
- These antidepressants include the tricyclic antidepressants: *imipramine* (Tofranil), *amitriptyline* (Elavil), *desipramine* (Norpramin), *nortriptyline* (Pamelor and Aventyl) and the atypical antidepressant *bupropion hydrochloride* (Wellbutrin).
- The tricyclic antidepressants take some time to build up in the bloodstream and reach a therapeutic level.
- Besides helping improve symptoms of hyperactivity and impulsivity, they also help with insomnia, mood swings, anxiety, depression, tics, sleep disturbances, and emotionality.
- Some side effects of the tricyclic antidepressants are fatigue, stomachache, dry mouth, rash, dizziness, accelerated heart rate, and possible risk of cardiac arrhythmias.

Note: These are not all the possible side effects for the various medications in this list. Parents need to discuss risks and side effects of any medication with their doctor and other medical resources.

Additional Information

- Every child has a unique response to medication, and it takes fine-tuning and patience to get it right.
- It is important that the medical professional parents choose to treat their child is very knowledgeable about ADHD and the various medications used in treatment for this disorder.
- Children with ADHD and coexisting disorders require more complex medical treatment, which may involve use of a combination of medications. Generally a specialist, such as a child and adolescent psychiatrist, with expertise in treating these complex cases is recommended.
- All medications can have adverse side effects. Parents need to be well informed of the risks versus benefits in any medical treatment.
- Dr. Kalikow (2013) offers this advice to parents in making a decision whether or not to try medication:
  - Start with a good evaluation by a trusted professional.

- Consider how your child might benefit from medicine.
- Get accurate information regarding the side effects.
- Don't feel rushed to make a decision. You have time to do your research and consider your decision.
- Know that your decision is reversible. If your child does not benefit from a trial of medicine, or experiences intolerable side effects, the medicine can be stopped.

- There are excellent resources about medication treatment for ADHD, including those listed below. Consult with your physician or other medical professionals.

Sources and Resources

Adesman, Andrew. (n.d.). ADHD medication guide. North Shore-Long Island Jewish Health System. Retrieved from http://adhdmedicationguide.com/

American Academy of Child and Adolescent Psychiatry (www.aacap.org)

American Academy of Pediatrics (www.aap.org)

Barkley, Russell A. (2013). *Taking charge of ADHD: The complete, authoritative guide for parents* (3rd ed.). New York: Guilford Press.

Dodson, William. (n.d.). ADHD medications explained. Retrieved from www.additudemag.com/adhd/article/9875.html

Elliott, Glen R., & Kelly, Kate. (2007). AD/HD medications: An overview. *Attention Magazine, 14*(4), 18–21.

Kalikow, Kevin T. (2013). ADHD and the decision to medicate. *Attention Magazine, 20*(1), 12–14.

McCarthy, Laura Flynn. (2007). Top 10 questions about meds ... answered. *ADDitude Magazine, 7*(3), 36–38.

Medline Plus. (n.d.). Drugs, supplements, and herbal information. National Institutes of Health, National Library of Medicine. Retrieved from www.nlm.nih.gov/medlineplus/druginformation.html

National Resource Center on AD/HD. (2008a). Managing medication for children and adolescents with ADHD. *What We Know, 3*. Retrieved from www.help4adhd.org/documents/WWK3.pdf

National Resource Center on AD/HD. (2008b). Medications used in the treatment of AD/HD. Retrieved from www.help4adhd.org/documents/MedChart.pdf

Physicians' Desk Reference (www.pdrhealth.com)

Rodriguez, Diana. (2014). Medications to treat ADHD. Everyday Health. Retrieved from www.everydayhealth.com/adhd/adhd-drugs.aspx

Silver, Larry. (2011). ADHD treatment. *ADDitude Magazine, 11*(4), 44–46.

WebMD (www.webmd.com/drugs/index-drugs.aspx)

Wilens, Timothy E. (2014). The role of medication in managing children's ADHD symptoms. *Ask the Expert* webinar. National Resource Center on AD/HD. http://www.chadd.org/Support/Ask-the-Expert-Online-Chats/Ask-the-Expert-Chat-Transcripts.aspx and click for the slides and You Tube link.

Wilens, Timothy E. (2008). *Straight talk about psychiatric medications for kids* (3rd ed.). New York: Guilford Press.

Wolraich, Mark L., & DuPaul, George J. (2010). *ADHD diagnosis and management: A practical guide for the clinic and the classroom*. Baltimore, MD: Paul H. Brookes.

1.21 If a Child or Teen Is Taking Medication: Advice for School Staff and Parents

What Teachers Need to Know

- Parents do not easily make the decision to try their child on medication. They often are fearful of the long-term effects. In addition, they are frequently made to feel guilty by well-meaning relatives, friends, or acquaintances who are uneducated about proven treatments or biased against the use of medication because of misinformation.
- The school's role is to support any student receiving medication treatment and cooperate fully. School personnel need to communicate their observations so the doctor can determine the child's response to the medication. These observations and frequent feedback to the doctor are necessary particularly in the titration process when a new medication is started. This is critical for the physician to determine the right medication and dosage—one that is providing the desired symptom improvement with minimal side effects. During the titration stage, in which medication dosage (and sometimes timing) is increased every few days until the optimal dosage is determined, teachers will be asked for their feedback each time the dosage is adjusted.
- The teacher is an integral part of the therapeutic team because of his or her unique ability to observe the child's performance and functioning (academically, socially, and behaviorally) on medication during most of the day. Teachers will need to monitor and observe students on medication carefully and report changes observed, such as in these areas:
  - Work production (starting on and completing assignments)
  - Attention and on-task behavior
  - Listening and following directions
  - Focus and concentration
  - Restlessness and activity level
  - Impulsive behavior and self-control
  - Interpersonal relationships
- All students on medication for ADHD (regardless of how long they may be on the medication) need to be monitored for the effects of the medication during school hours. This is necessary to ensure that the child or teen is benefiting from the medication. For these students, teachers should also be prepared to share their feedback on the student's functioning (which will occur much less frequently than during titration periods).
- Physicians (or their office personnel) should be initiating contact with the school for feedback on how the treatment plan is working. Generally this is done through follow-up behavioral rating scales or other observational forms teachers are asked to complete.
- The doctor's office may send the teacher rating forms directly or parents may deliver the rating scales or medication forms to the school.
- Generally it is the school nurse who acts as the liaison between the parent and teacher in helping to manage the medication at school as appropriate. Coordination and communication between all parties involved is important for optimal results.

- Medications, dosages, and times to be administered are often changed or adjusted until the right combination is found for the child. It is important to communicate with parents and report noticeable changes in a student's behaviors. Sometimes parents do not disclose to the school that their child has started taking medication (or has had a change of medication or dosage) and are waiting to hear if the teacher notices any difference.
- Children metabolize medication at different rates. To ensure that the medication is providing coverage throughout the school day, take note of changes of behavior or problems occurring at certain times of the day (for example, in the afternoon).
- Teachers need to let parents (and school nurse, if available) know about any concerns that may be side effects of a medication. Children taking ADHD medications should be showing improved functioning and behavior and not experience a change in personality or appear sedated or lethargic. If so, the dosage may be too high or the child needs a different medication. It is important to share these observations so that the parent can let the physician know.
- Stimulant medications suppress appetite, and students with ADHD who take stimulants may not be eating much breakfast or lunch. They may get hungry at different times and would benefit from being allowed a snack if needed.
- Most students with ADHD who are prescribed medication are now taking the longer-acting, sustained release medications (*List 1.20*). This has helped significantly in terms of school responsibility and management of ADHD medications. Most schools no longer have a line of students in the office at lunch time to be administered their second dose of medication as was seen in the past (when other medication options were not available).
- There are still students who do take the short-acting stimulant medications. For those students, in which a dosage must be taken during school hours, it is important that the medication be given on time (as prescribed by the doctor).
- Be aware that some children experience a rebound effect when the medication wears off. When the next prescribed dose is not given on time, these children may be found crying, fighting, or otherwise in trouble on the playground or cafeteria, and disruptive on returning to the classroom. It takes approximately thirty minutes for the next dose of medication to take effect. Careful timing to avoid this rebound effect helps considerably.
- Students with ADHD have a hard time remembering to go to the office at the designated time for medication because of the very nature of ADHD and executive function impairment. It is the responsibility of the teacher or other school staff to help remind them discretely. Strategies for doing so may include a beeper watch or vibrating alarm, private signals from the teacher, pairing the medication time with a natural transition at that time (for example, on the way to the cafeteria), coded verbal reminders, as well as a sticker chart where the medication is dispensed, rewarding the child for remembering.
- Schools have specific policies and procedures for administering medication, for example, a signed consent form on file, medication in the original, labeled prescription container stored in a locked place, maintaining careful records of the dosage, time of dispensing, and person administering the medication.
- It helps if parents are reminded well before the school's supply of medication runs out so they have plenty of time to renew the prescription and deliver it to school.

- Teachers should see symptom improvement if a child is being treated with medication for his or her ADHD. However, medical treatment is just one leg of multimodal intervention for children and teens with ADHD (*List 1.19*). Educational interventions are critical to school success, and include the array of classroom supports and strategies (behavioral, instructional, academic) and other school-based interventions discussed throughout this book.

What Parents Need to Know

- If a child is taking medication, it is important that the child receives it as prescribed in the morning—on time and consistently—under parent supervision.
- Close monitoring and management of the medication is crucial. If it is administered inconsistently, the child is better off without it.
- Because appetite suppression is a common side effect, it is best to seek advice from the doctor regarding how to manage this, for example, planning for breakfast and other meals at times your child is most likely to have an appetite.
- When a child is on a long-acting medication, and the school isn't involved in administering a midday dose, some parents may be tempted not to inform the school that the child is taking a medication for ADHD. This is not advised. It is best to inform the school of any medical treatment for the disorder and not keep it a secret.
- It requires teamwork and close communication among the home, school, and physician for a child to receive the most benefits from medication treatment. Parents should be prepared to lead this communication effort to make sure that the doctor receives the necessary feedback from the school regarding their child's functioning on medication (*Lists 7.1, 7.2, 7.3*).
- Follow-up visits with the child's doctor are necessary for monitoring the medication's effectiveness.
- For appropriate medical care, the doctor needs to obtain feedback from you *and the school* when your child is on medication.
- As discussed in *List 1.20,* when a child is started on medication therapy, there is always a trial period when the physician is trying to determine the most effective medication and dosage. Some children are fortunate to quickly have that determined to give them significant symptom improvement. Others will take longer, and some will not benefit from or be able to tolerate the medication. However, in 70 to 90 percent of children with ADHD, medication is found to be effective. Parents should be prepared that this process will likely take some time to get it right and therefore should be patient. If one of the medications doesn't seem to work, chances are that another one will.
- Because the commonly prescribed stimulants are classified by the Drug Enforcement Administration as schedule II medications, there are strict laws regarding how they are prescribed and dispensed. The FDA has restrictions that pharmacists must follow. This makes it more difficult for refilling prescriptions. For example, the medication cannot be called in, and doctors can only write a prescription for one month at a time.
- It is important that parents pay close attention and communicate with the school nurse to make sure the school has the medication on hand if it is a short-acting stimulant prescription.

- See *Lists 1.4, 1.7, and 1.20* for research evidence regarding the effectiveness of medication therapy in the treatment of ADHD and about how medications are believed to work within the brain to relieve symptoms and improve functioning.
- Children should be counseled about their medication and why they are taking it. They should be aware that the medication is not in control of their behavior—they are, but that medication helps them (pay attention, get school and homework done, put on the brakes so they can make better choices, and so forth). There are various resources available that can help children better understand ADHD and why they are taking medication to treat it. Some wonderful books geared for children and teens that explain ADHD in kid-friendly, age-appropriate ways are shown in the "Sources and Resources" section of this list.
- Parents must educate themselves about medication treatment as well as the other multimodal interventions that are effective in managing ADHD (*Lists 1.19, 1.22, 1.23, 7.6, 7.7*).With regard to medication questions, parents should talk to their physician and ask all the questions they need as well as check other reliable resources, such as those in *List 7.12* and at the end of *List 1.20*.

Sources and Resources

Dendy, Chris A. Zeigler, & Zeigler, Alex. (2003). *A bird's eye view of life with ADD and ADHD: Advice from young survivors*. Cedar Bluff, AL: Cherish the Children.

Quinn, Patricia, & Stern, Judith. (2009) *Putting on the brakes* (2nd ed.). Washington DC: Magination Press.

Nadeau, Kathleen, & Dixon, Ellen. (2005). *Learning to slow down and pay attention*. Washington DC: Magination Press.

1.22 Behavior Therapy (Psychosocial Interventions) for Managing ADHD

- Behavior therapy is one of the two research-validated interventions proven most effective in the management of ADHD. Medication alone may be sufficient in reducing symptoms of ADHD and problematic behavior for some children. Behavioral therapy combined with medication therapy is often the optimal intervention for many children with ADHD, providing the greatest improvement in the child's functioning, behavior, and relationships. For any child not receiving medication, behavior therapy is essential to treat and manage the disorder.
- According to the American Academy of Pediatrics guidelines for treating ADHD in children (AAP, 2011), primary care physicians should prescribe behavior therapy as the first line of treatment for preschool-age children (four through five years of age), and for children ages six through eleven, the physician should prescribe FDA-approved medications for ADHD or evidence-based behavior therapy (administered by parents and the teacher) as treatment for ADHD—preferably both.
- Behavior therapy requires training of the parent and teacher in behavior modification techniques and the commitment of the adult to implement strategies learned. This is not easy; it takes time and effort, but the benefits are worth it.
- Behavior therapy helps adults improve children's behavior by learning behavioral principles and strategies to implement in managing problem behavior, with professional guidance.
- Behavior treatments work by teaching new skills to parents, teachers, and the children for handling problems and interacting with others. Adults teach the child or adolescent new ways of behaving by changing the ways they themselves respond to the child's or teen's behaviors (National Resource Center on AD/HD, 2004b).
- Behavioral and psychosocial interventions for ADHD may include the following:
  - Proactive parenting and classroom management and effective discipline practices at home and school (*Lists 2.1, 2.2*)
  - Parents and teachers using behavior modification techniques effectively (*Lists 2.8, 2.9*)
  - Communicating in ways to increase compliance—that is, helping the child listen to and follow parent and teacher directions (*List 2.4*)
  - Structuring the environment and being aware of antecedents or triggers to misbehavior to prevent problems at home and school (*Lists 2.3, 2.11*)
  - Using strategies to best deal with the challenging behaviors associated with ADHD in school environments and inside and outside the home (*Lists 2.6, 2.10, 2.13, 2.14, 2.15, 2.16*)
  - Classroom and schoolwide behavioral and social-emotional learning programs and supports (*Lists 2.15, 2.17*)
  - Improving the child's peer interactions and social skills (*List 2.17*)
  - Use of well-designed behavioral programs such as daily charts and school-to-home report cards, token economy programs, and individual behavioral contracts (*List 2.9* with examples in the appendix). *Note:* There are some of the behavioral charts from the appendix that can be accessed online and customized before printing.

General Principles of Behavior Modification

- Behavior modification techniques are a cornerstone of behavioral intervention for ADHD.
- It is based on the three-part A-B-Cs of behavior: A—antecedent, B—behavior, C—consequence. In general, the antecedent (A) is the situation, event, or stimulus that triggers the behavior (B). The consequence (C) is what occurs immediately after the behavior (B) is demonstrated. The consequence will either increase or decrease the likelihood of that behavior occurring again.
- Behavior modification is based heavily on learning how to recognize and adjust the antecedents or triggers that set off behavioral problems and thereby reduce or avoid them. It also works by learning to effectively use consequences to increase those positive behaviors we want to continue and encourage and decrease those negative, undesirable behaviors we want to reduce or eliminate.
- Techniques of behavior modification use incentive systems (such as points or token systems). Rewards are very important in improving behavior. They are particularly necessary for children with ADHD, who require more external motivation than other children typically need. Children and teens with ADHD also need more frequent rewards because their internal controls are less mature and they have trouble delaying gratification (*List 2.7*).
- Negative consequences or punishments are also effective and important in changing behavior, particularly use of time-out procedures and loss of privileges when they are implemented correctly and judiciously (*Lists 2.1, 2.2*).

Home-Based Behavioral Treatment

- Parents of children with ADHD must become far more knowledgeable and skilled in behavior management principles and techniques than other parents. They need training in how to cope with and handle the daily challenges and behavioral difficulties resulting from the child's disorder.
- Parent training is key to understanding the disorder and how to best manage it. Parent training programs incorporate techniques to improve parent-child interactions, decrease noncompliance, reduce behavior problems, and facilitate family communication patterns (Teeter, 2000).
- Parents learn preventive strategies (adjusting or manipulating the antecedents to misbehavior), instructive strategies (directed at providing the child with different and more appropriate ways to accomplish a goal), and consequence-based strategies, including effective use of rewards and punishments (Wolraich & DuPaul, 2010).
- Parent education can be conducted in group format or with individual sets of parents in training sessions over a series of weeks.
- Behavior modification training is typically for parents managing the behaviors of preschool and elementary school children. With adolescents, other techniques and skills such as behavioral contracting and problem solving are taught to parents and the teen (Wolraich & DuPaul, 2010).
- Parent trainings are generally provided in eight or more weekly or biweekly sessions, with specific strategies parents are to implement as homework between sessions.

- Parents typically learn strategies such as establishing daily routines, organizing and structuring for success at home, praising and giving positive attention for appropriate behaviors, giving effective directions and commands to increase compliance and cooperation, effective use of rewards and negative consequences, avoiding power struggles and conflicts, use of incentive systems (daily charts, point and token systems, school-home note systems).
- In order to effectively change their child's behavior, parents must also understand how behavioral principles operate on their own behavior. For example, frustrated parents often respond to children's misbehavior by giving consequences that actually increase rather than decrease that problem behavior's occurrence.
- CHADD offers a unique educational program called Parent to Parent (P2P), which is given in the community, online, and on demand, and is facilitated by a P2P trainer. (See www.chadd.org and information in *Lists 7.1 and 7.9*.)
- See Russell Barkley's book *Taking Charge of ADHD* (3rd ed.) (2013b) for an excellent summary of his recommended steps in parent training and his program for clinicians in *Defiant Children: A Clinician Manual for Assessment and Parent Training* (3rd ed.) (2013a).
- Some other model programs for parent training:
  - COPE (Community Parent Education Program) (Cunningham, Bremner, Secord, & Harrison, 2009)
  - Triple P (Positive Parenting Program) (www.triplep.net/glo-en/home/)
  - Incredible Years Parenting Program (http://incredibleyears.com/programs/parent/)
  - Parent-Child Interaction Therapy (www.pcit.org/)

School-Based Behavioral Treatment

There are a number of school-based behavioral approaches that have been found effective in decreasing problem behavior in children.

- School-based behavioral interventions are implemented by the teacher in most cases and involve the following actions:
  - Proactive classroom management (*List 2.1*)
  - Creating an ADHD-friendly classroom environment (*List 2.3*)
  - Preventing behavior problems during transitions and other challenging times of the school day (*List 2.10*)
  - Using class (group) behavior management systems (*List 2.8*)
  - Implementing individualized behavioral programs, supports, and interventions, such as daily report cards and behavioral contracts (*List 2.9*)
  - Implementing targeted strategies to help students with inattentive, off-task, impulsive, or hyperactive behaviors (*Lists 2.12, 2.13*)
  - Effectively managing students' anger, frustration, and poor self-regulation (*List 2.15*)
- School districts throughout the United States are shifting their focus toward promoting positive behavior and away from reacting to negative behavior in a systematic and structured whole-school effort. This involves modeling and teaching in all classrooms and schoolwide the rules and expected behaviors, creating a supportive and

consistent environment for all students, and employing a number of early intervention strategies (*The Special Edge* editors, 2014).

- Many schools are now implementing a multitiered system of support (MTSS), which is a continuum of increasingly intense supports for students. Schools that use an RTI model and a Positive Behavioral Interventions and Supports (PBIS) model, which are both MTSS models, are well designed to provide effective behavioral treatment to students in need. See *List 6.1* on RTI and *Lists 2.9 and 2.17* on PBIS.
- PBIS schools, for example, teach and reinforce prosocial behaviors as a tier 1 intervention for all students, and provide more targeted and intense supports (tier 2 and tier 3) as needed by individual students, with close monitoring of student responses to the interventions to ensure that all students receive the level of help they need.
- An effective program for preschool is Teaching Pyramid, developed at Vanderbilt University Center for Social and Emotional Learning (http://csefel.vanderbilt.edu). It promotes the healthy social-emotional development of young children (*Lists 2.17, 7.4*).
- For an outstanding program and model proven highly effective in transforming public schools in communities with high levels of needs, see Turnaround (http://turnaroundusa.org/). Turnaround creates a partnership with schools that accomplishes the following:
  - Builds a high-capacity student support system that gets all children, including those with intense needs, help either in school or in partnership with a community-based mental health provider
  - Trains all teachers in proven classroom strategies that foster a safe, engaging learning environment and strong student-teacher relationships
  - Works with school leaders to drive schoolwide improvement, aligned to Common Core State Standards and district guidelines, and creates a high-performing culture that involves the entire school community
- Another very useful school-based behavioral intervention is a functional behavior assessment (FBA), which is a procedure to gather and analyze data to determine the ABCs of the student's problem behavior. Then, based on that information, a behavioral intervention plan (BIP) is designed. Strategies address the antecedents (such as adjustments made in the environment, skill, performance demand, or teacher-student interactions) in order to prevent problems. The plan also addresses the consequences to the problem behavior (changing the responses or reactions to the behavior) and teach the student more appropriate replacement behaviors to use instead of what they are doing. See *List 6.6* for more on FBAs and BIPs.

Child-Based Behavioral Treatment

- Child-based interventions focus on peer relationships. They usually occur in group settings, such as classrooms, small groups at school, in office clinics, and summer camps (National Resource Center on AD/HD, 2004).
- Child-based treatments involve coaching, modeling, role-playing, feedback, rewards, and consequences. They all involve a lot of practice of skills taught in natural settings in which the child is interacting with peers (*List 2.17*).
- Research-validated child-based interventions involve teaching, practicing, and reinforcing prosocial skills and behaviors. They do not include play therapy and talk therapy approaches.

Note: A leading authority on psycho-social (behavioral) interventions for children with ADHD is Dr. William Pelham, Jr. It is recommended to listen to or read the transcript for his CHADD Ask the Expert chat (with the link below) and view the free resources that Pelham and his team developed, available online at http://ccf.buffalo.edu/resources_downloads.php

Sources and Resources

Abramowitz, Ann. (2005). Classroom interventions for AD/HD. *Attention Magazine,* pp. 27–30.

ADHD and You. (n.d.). Behavior therapy. Retrieved from www.adhdandyou.com/adhd-caregiver/behavior-therapy.aspx

American Academy of Pediatrics (AAP). (2011). ADHD: Clinical practice guidelines for the diagnosis, evaluation, and treatment of attention-deficit/hyperactivity disorder in children and adolescents. *Pediatrics, 128*(5), 1007–1022.

Barkley, R. A. (2013a). *Defiant children: A clinician's manual for assessment and parent training* (3rd ed.). New York: Guilford Press.

Barkley, Russell A. (2013b). *Taking charge of ADHD: The complete, authoritative guide for parents* (3rd ed.). New York: Guilford Press.

Centers for Disease Control and Prevention. (n.d.). ADHD treatment. Retrieved from www.cdc.gov/ncbddd/adhd/treatment.html

Cunningham, C. E. (2005). COPE: Large group, community based, family-centered parent training. In R. A. Barkley (Ed.), *Attention deficit hyperactivity: A handbook for diagnosis and treatment*. New York: Guilford Press.

Cunningham, C. E., Bremner, R., Secord, M., & Harrison, R. (2009). *COPE, The Community Parent Education Program: Large group community based workshops for parents of 3 to 18 year olds.* Hamilton, ON, Canada: COPE Works.

Goldstein, Sam. (2008). Educators as environmental engineers: Psychosocial interventions for AD/HD in schools. *Attention , 15*(4), 44–45.

Health Central. (n.d.). Understanding ADHD. Retrieved from www.healthcentral.com/adhd/understanding-adhd-000030_4.145_2.html

McCarthy, Laura Flynn. (n.d.). Behavior therapy for ADHD children: More carrot, less stick. *ADDitude Magazine*. Retrieved from www.additudemag.com/adhd/article/3577.html

National Resource Center on AD/HD. (2004a). Psychosocial treatment for children and adolescents with ADHD. *What We Know, 7.* Retrieved from www.help4adhd.org/documents/WWK7.pdf

National Resource Center on AD/HD. (2004b). Behavioral treatment for children and teenagers with ADHD. *What We Know, 7 short.* Retrieved from www.help4adhd.org/documents/WWK7s.pdf

Park, Ju Hee, Alber-Morgan, Sheila R., & Fleming, Courtney. (2011). Collaborating with parents to implement behavioral interventions for children with challenging behaviors. *Teaching Exceptional Children, 43*(3), 22–30.

Pelham, William E., Jr. (Nov. 2014) CHADD Ask the Expert: Behavior Management and Combined Treatment for Children with ADHD. Transcript available at: http://www.chadd.org/Support/Ask-the-Expert-Online-Chats/Ask-the-Expert-Chat-Transcripts.aspx

Rabiner, David. (n.d.). Behavioral treatment for ADHD/ADD: A general overview. Retrieved from http://helpforadd.com/add-behavioral-treatment

The Special Edge editors. (2014). Early intervention: Supporting student success. *The Special Edge: Student Behavior, 27*(3), 3–16.

Teeter, Phyllis Anne. (2000) *Interventions for ADHD: Treatment in developmental context.* New York: Guilford Press.

Wolraich, Mark L., & DuPaul, George J. (2010). *ADHD diagnosis and management: A practical guide for the clinic and the classroom.* Baltimore, MD: Paul H. Brookes.

1.23 Alternative and Complementary Treatments

Based on decades of research and scientific evidence, medication and behavior therapy are proven most effective in the treatment of ADHD and are, therefore, the primary treatments recommended by the experts and the major national professional organizations and associations. There are many other treatments parents may also hear about that supposedly cure or significantly help children with ADHD. It can be quite enticing to parents who hear that a certain nonmedical product or treatment can improve their child's behaviors and symptoms.

- Complementary treatments are those that are used *in addition to* the standard treatment of FDA-approved ADHD medication and behavioral therapy for added benefit and improved functioning. There are several complementary interventions that may be helpful for individual children and teens and could be part of his or her multimodal treatment plan.
- Complementary interventions that are recommended by experts include a well-balanced diet, exercise and some of the other healthy, therapeutic ways to help manage symptoms and feel good, such as meditation and mindfulness practices, and outdoor green time (*List 7.7*), and interventions such as ADHD coaching (*List 7.6*), academic tutoring, or study skills training as needed.
- Alternative treatments, however, are those that are used *instead of* the proven ADHD treatments of medication therapy or behavior therapy and most likely will not have a significant positive effect on the child's symptoms and functioning.
- Many parents are reluctant or opposed to treating their child with medication. The many advertisements in magazines, TV, radio, or the Internet making claims about various products or treatments that cure ADHD symptoms can sound very convincing and believable.
- Parents need to be cautious and informed consumers when considering alternative treatments. Be aware of the following:
  - Most make their claims based on a small sample of people supposedly studied.
  - Most tend to use testimonials in their advertisement of the product and do not have reputable scientific evidence to support its effectiveness or back up their claims.
  - Although they may cite a few studies as evidence, these studies are not controlled research that meets the scientific standards for evaluating treatment effectiveness. This would require, among other things, proper controls and random assignment of test subjects, measurement techniques enabling the scientific community to evaluate the findings, peer reviews by other professionals prior to publication of results in scientific journals, and replicated studies by other teams of researchers to see if they achieve similar results.
  - Various so-called natural products may be harmful because they have not been through rigorous scientific testing for safety.
  - Any treatment that is advertised as miraculous or groundbreaking is generally bogus.
  - Some of these treatments have been discredited, some lack the scientific evidence to back up their claims, and some show promise but warrant further study and for now remain unproven.

- It is very important to talk to your doctor about any alternative or complementary treatment you are considering for your child.
- A number of alternative treatments have been claimed to be effective in treating ADHD. Those without scientific evidence or that have been disproven include: supplements of megavitamins and antioxidants, chiropractic adjustment and bone realignment, optometric vision training, antimotion sickness medication, vestibular stimulation, herbal remedies, treatment for Candida yeast infection, and others.

Other Complementary Treatments That May Have Benefit for Children and Teens with ADHD

Neurofeedback (EEG Biofeedback)

- Neurofeedback, also called EEG (electroencephalogram) biofeedback, has been used as a complementary or alternative treatment for ADHD for a number of years.
- "Neurofeedback is based on findings that many individuals with ADHD show low levels of arousal in frontal brain areas, with excess of theta waves and deficit of beta waves. Supporters of this treatment suggest that the brain can be trained to increase the levels of arousal (increase beta waves and reduce theta waves) and thereby reduce ADHD symptoms" (National Resource Center on AD/HD, 2008b).
- Brain exercises take place during a series of treatment sessions in which the child wears headgear lined with electrodes and performs video games and computerized tasks while brain wave activity in the frontal lobe (the part of the brain that is under-aroused in those with ADHD) is measured. The treatment is supposed to increase the activation of brain waves in that part of the brain and train patients to eventually produce the brain wave patterns associated with focus on their own.
- During neurofeedback, the brain is observed from moment to moment through an EEG. The information is shown back to the person through a video game that reflects the brain wave activity.
- Neurofeedback is intended to train the child with ADHD to increase and decrease various types of brain wave activity associated with ADHD (such as sustained attention).
- Neurofeedback has been controversial because of limited scientific support from controlled studies and random assignment of subjects.
- In recent years there has been more controlled research support with emerging evidence that neurofeedback may be beneficial in reducing symptoms of ADHD. Dr. Rabiner (2014) reports on two recent studies (Duric et al., 2012; Meisel et al., 2014) that he says provides strong new support.
- Although there is not yet sufficient scientific proof, and research is not conclusive, there is growing support and a number of experts in the field believe that neurofeedback does hold promise (particularly as a complementary treatment, when used along with medication).
- Neurofeedback for ADHD generally involves about forty to eighty sessions, in thirty-minute time frames, and is an intensive, expensive treatment.

- For more on this topic, see the National Resource Center on AD/HD information on neurofeedback (EEG biofeedback) and ADHD (http://help4adhd.org/documents/WWK6A.pdf) and other sources and resources provided in the "Sources and Resources" section of this list.

Other Brain Training Technology Interventions

In recent years various software programs and technologies have been developed to help train and strengthen certain cognitive skills that are weak in children with ADHD. These programs are based on the principles of neuroplasticity—that the brain and our cognitive functioning are not fixed but are malleable and changeable (like plastic) and can improve through systematic, intensive training.

Although still in its infancy, and much more research is needed to validate their positive effects, these types of programs show promise as possible useful complementary interventions. The following describe some brain-training programs that are being used at this time.

Cogmed Working Memory Training Program

- Cogmed (www.cogmed.com) is a well-known and well-researched computer-based program. The software is downloaded on the child's home or school computer. For five weeks, five days a week, an hour a day, the child completes exercises in a video game format.
- The video games, which are programmed to become increasingly harder, require the child to use cognitive skills involving working memory, for example, recalling a series of numbers in reverse order.
- This program was developed from research on Swedish cognitive neuroscientist Dr. Torkel Klingberg, a cofounder of Cogmed. RoboMemo is another name for the Cogmed program.
- Cogmed is used by a range of licensed professionals, including clinical psychologists and psychiatrists as well as educators and is used at home with coaching support from a trainer who calls once a week to check in, troubleshoot, and encourage the child. (*ADDitude Magazine* editors, 2008b, Gilbert, n.d.; Jackson, n.d.).

Activate by C8 Sciences

- The Activate program (www.c8sciences.com) also uses video games, combined with physical exercise, engaging the functions of the brain that are deficient in children with ADHD, such as attention, following directions, and response inhibition. It is available for home or school use (Barrow, 2013).
- Play Attention (www.playattention.com) is another computer-based program involving games. This differs in that it has an armband users wear that measures attention brain activity. Children can activate the cognitive games by applying full attention to get started. Then they can actually move game characters by focusing their attention. If they lose attention, the game will stop until they fully apply themselves again. It is played one hour a week at home, and there are telephone training and support.

iFocus Jungle Rangers

- Jungle Rangers (www.focuseducation.com) is at the core of iFocus, an interactive kids computer game called Jungle Rangers. Playing the game involves cognitive exercises to improve an aspect of attention or working memory.

Brainology by Mindset Works

- Brainology (www.mindsetworks.com/) is web-based interactive program that teaches students "growth mind-sets"—to see their abilities as malleable and to view mistakes and setbacks as learning experiences. Students participate in a series of lessons guided by middle-school-age animated characters and a brain scientist character that teaches them about the functions of the human brain, how thinking occurs, and how learning and memory work. It also teaches students about how they can change their own brains for better learning and school success (Katz, 2008).

Interactive Metronome Training

- Interactive metronome training is a relatively new intervention for individuals with ADHD. It is a computerized version of a simple metronome that produces a rhythmic beat that individuals attempt to match with hand or foot tapping. Auditory feedback is provided, which indicates how well the individual is matching the beat. It is suggested that improvement in matching the beat over repeated sessions reflects gains in motor planning and timing skills (National Resource Center on AD/HD, 2008a).

Regarding Brain Training Programs

- All of these programs are intended as adjunct, complementary interventions to be used in addition to, not instead of, medication or behavior therapy to target skills that may not be adequately addressed with standard ADHD treatment.
- Parents and educators are advised to do their own research before purchasing or using any of these programs.

Dietary Factors and Interventions

- The popular belief that ADHD is because of too much sugar has been studied extensively. Research, however, since the mid-1980s shows that there is no significant link between sugar and ADHD (Barkley, 2013). Common sense would suggest that reducing sugar consumption would be a healthy choice for all children as well as adults.
- "Several dietary factors have been researched in association with ADHD, including sensitivities to certain food chemicals, deficiencies in fatty acids (compounds that make up fats and oils) and zinc, and sensitivity to sugar. No clear evidence has emerged, however, that implicates any of these nutritional factors as risk factors for developing ADHD" (University of Maryland, 2013).
- A substantial amount of research testing the theory that chemical food additives and preservatives may cause ADHD has not produced evidence that normal children develop ADHD by consuming such substances or that children with ADHD are made considerably worse by eating them (Barkley, 2013).
- The conclusion of the scientific community based on research to date is that artificial food dyes are not a major factor in ADHD, although a small subset of people

diagnosed with ADHD who also have food hypersensitivities may respond well to a diet eliminating food dyes or other irritating foods (Hughes, 2011).

- Food sensitivities do not appear to be a specific problem for most patients with ADHD, but more recent studies suggest a small effect for all children regardless of whether or not they have ADHD (Goodman, 2008).
- Because some children may have food sensitivities, such as to gluten, eggs, nuts, soy, or dairy, parents who suspect their child may be sensitive to certain foods may want to experiment with an elimination diet of those suspected culprits to see if behavior improves when doing so. According to Dr. Sandy Newmark (2012), eliminating certain foods from the diet can significantly help some children with ADHD. He also says that this approach should be part of a program that is used in conjunction with ADHD medication and other interventions. It is advised that parents consult with their child's physician before trying an elimination diet.
- There are dietary approaches that are beneficial for children and teens with ADHD and are recommended by many doctors and other experts.

A Well-Balanced Diet

This is important of course for all children. Because ADHD medications may cause loss of appetite, some children may not be eating enough of the foods that provide them with all of the nutrients they need. Parents should speak with their physician or a nutritionist in this regard.

Proteins

- Protein is digested more slowly than carbohydrates and stabilizes blood sugars. Proteins can prevent surges in blood sugar, which may increase hyperactivity (Barrow, 2008).
- Foods rich in protein are used to make neurotransmitters, the chemicals released by our brain cells to communicate with each other. Protein in the morning for breakfast is highly recommended (*ADDitude Magazine* editors, 2008a).
- A child who eats some protein at breakfast will have more stable blood sugar levels in the morning compared with children who eat only carbohydrates and fat, which should help a child focus in the classroom (Newmark, 2013).

Omega-3 Fatty Acids

- Omega-3 fatty acids are important in brain and nerve cell function and increase the level of dopamine in the brain. It seems to improve mental focus in people (*ADDitude Magazine* editors, 2008a; Barrow, 2008).
- There may be some evidence supporting Omega-3 fatty acid supplements as beneficial for individuals with ADHD (Barrow).
- We must get Omega-3s from food and supplements regularly because our bodies are unable to synthesize them on their own. Edward (Ned) Hallowell (2013) recommends that if you use a fish oil, make sure it is pharmaceutical grade and free of contaminants.
- Again, consult with your doctor first before adding a supplement.

Vitamins and Minerals

- Deficiencies of several minerals (zinc, iron, and magnesium) can worsen symptoms of inattention, impulsivity, and hyperactivity. Zinc is involved in the regulation of dopamine (*ADDitude Magazine* editors, 2008a). If concerned, consult with your child's doctor. Do not take zinc supplements without supervision of a doctor.

- Iron is necessary for producing dopamine. A small study indicated that low levels of iron correlate with inattention (*ADDitude Magazine* editors, 2010). If you suspect your child has low levels of iron, talk with your doctor. The safest way to increase your child's iron level is through diet, not supplements.
- Vitamin C helps regulate the synapse action of dopamine, a key neurotransmitter needed in treating ADHD (Hallowell, 2013). Hallowell advises that it is best to get vitamin C from food. Because vitamin C may affect how ADHD medication is being absorbed, consult with your child's physician in this matter.
- A daily multivitamin that contains the recommended daily allowance of key vitamins and minerals may be the best way to ensure that a child is getting sufficient nutrients. This is a regular, simple multivitamin—not megavitamins (which may be harmful).

Note: Again, parents are advised to consult with their physician and other resources before embarking on any alternative or complementary treatments.

Sources and Resources

For reliable information regarding alternative and complementary interventions, go to these websites: National Resource Center on AD/HD (www.help4adhg.org) and National Institutes of Health, National Center for Complementary and Alternative Medicine (http://nccam.nih.gov).

ADDitude Magazine editors. (2008a). Special report: Diet matters. *ADDitude Magazine, 9*(2), 41.

ADDitude Magazine editors. (2008b). Special report on working memory: Programmed for success. *ADDitude Magazine, 8*(3), 46.

ADDitude Magazine editors. (2010). Alternative therapies—Diet dos; The right stuff. *ADDitude Magazine, 11*(2), 43–44.

Barkley, Russell A. (2013). *Taking charge of ADHD: The complete, authoritative guide for parents* (3rd ed.). New York: Guilford Press.

Barrow, Karen. (2008). Facts about fish oil. *ADDitude Magazine, 8*(3), 44–45.

Barrow, Karen. (2013). The mind-body correction. *ADDitude Magazine, 14*(2), 51.

Duric, Nezla S., Assmus, Jørg, Gundersen, Doris, & Elgen, Irene B. (2012). Neurofeedback for the treatment of children and adolescents with ADHD: A randomized and controlled clinical trial using parental reports. *BMC Psychiatry, 12,* 107.

Ellison, Katherine. (2013). Is neurofeedback for you? *ADDitude Magazine, 14*(2), 46–48.

Gilbert, Paul. (n.d.). More attention, less deficit: Brain training. *ADDitude Magazine*. Retrieved from www.additudemag.com/adhd/article/10076.html

Goodman, Bryan. (2008). Ask the expert: Chats with L. Eugene Arnold. *Attention Magazine, 15*(6), 10–12.

Goodman, Bryan. (2010). Five popular approaches to treating ADHD. *Attention Magazine, 17*(3), 14–15.

Hallowell, Ned. (2013). Fight back with food. *ADDitude Magazine, 14*(2) 44–45.

Hughes, Ruth. (2011). Research briefs: Artificial food dyes and ADHD. *Attention Magazine, 18*(3), 12–14.

Jackson, Maggie. (n.d.).Treat ADHD symptoms with brain training. Retrieved from: http://www.additudemag.com/adhd/article/5539.html

Katz, Mark. (2008). Promising practices. Brainology: Using lessons from basic neuroscience. *Attention Magazine, 15*(5), 8–9.

Meisel, V., Servera, M., Garcia-Banda, G., Cardo, E., Moreno, I. (2014). Neurofeedback and standardized pharmacological intervention in ADHD: A randomized controlled trial with six-month follow up. *Biological Psychology, 95*, 116–125.

Michaels, Pamela V. (2008). Special report on neurofeedback: Train the brain. *ADDitude Magazine, 8*(3), 42–43.

Michaels, Pamela. (n.d.). Alternative ADHD treatment: Neurofeedback. *ADDitude Magazine*. Retrieved from www.additudemag.com/adhd/article/3330.html

National Resource Center on AD/HD. (2008a). Complementary and alternative treatments. *What We Know, 6*. Retrieved from www.help4adhd.org/documents/WWK6.pdf

National Resource Center on AD/HD. (2008b). Complementary and alternative treatments: Neurofeedback (EEG biofeedback) and ADHD. *What We Know, 6A*. Retrieved from http://help4adhd.org/documents/WWK6A.pdf

National Resource Center on AD/HD. (2008c). Deciding on a treatment for ADHD. *What We Know, 6 short*. Retrieved from www.help4adhd.org/documents/WWK6s.pdf

Newmark, Sandy. (2012). How to test food sensitivities with an elimination diet. *ADDitude Magazine* (Winter). Retrieved from www.additudemag.com/adhd/article/9807.html

Newmark, Sandy. (2013) Alternative therapies. *ADDitude Magazine, 14*(1), 20.

Rabiner, David. (2014, April). Strong new support for neurofeedback treatment for ADHD. *Attention Research Update*. Retrieved from www.helpforadd.com/2014/april.htm

Stevens, Laura. (n.d.). ADHD and iron: Can nutritional supplements improve symptoms? *ADDitude Magazine*. Retrieved from www.additudemag.com/adhd/article/3993.html

University of Maryland Medical Center. (2013). Attention-deficit hyperactivity disorder (Other treatment approaches section). Retrieved from http://umm.edu/health/medical/reports/articles/attention-deficit-hyperactivity-disorder

Wolraich, Mark L., & DuPaul, George J. (2010). *ADHD diagnosis & management: A practical guide for the clinic and the classroom*. Baltimore, MD: Paul H. Brookes.

Section 2

Minimizing and Managing Behavior Problems

Strategies, Supports, and Interventions

Contents

Please note that a lot of the content of these lists has been adapted and updated from my other books, published by Jossey-Bass/Wiley, which you may be interested in exploring for further information, tools, and strategies:

Rief, S. (2003). *The ADHD book of lists: A practical guide for helping children and teens with attention deficit disorders*. San Francisco: Jossey-Bass.

Rief, S. (2005). *How to reach & teach children with ADD/ADHD: Practical techniques, strategies and interventions* (2nd ed.). San Francisco: Jossey-Bass.

Rief, S. (2008). *The ADD/ADHD checklist: A practical reference for parents and teachers* (2nd ed.). San Francisco: Jossey-Bass.

Rief, Sandra, & Heimburge, Julie. (2006). *How to reach & teach all children in the inclusive classroom* (2nd ed.). San Francisco: Jossey-Bass.

2.1 Proactive Classroom Management

The best classroom management involves anticipating potential problems and avoiding them through careful planning and prevention.

Create a Positive Classroom Environment

Ensure the following in your classroom:

- It is structured and well organized (clear schedule, routines, rules, careful planning of seating and physical space).
- It is calm and predictable.
- It has clearly defined, taught, and practiced procedures that become automatic routines of classroom operation.
- It focuses on the use of positive reinforcement for appropriate behavior.
- It has clear rules and behavioral guidelines, backed up with fair corrective consequences that are enforced predictably and consistently.
- It is respectful and supportive.
- It is warm, welcoming, and inclusive.
- It is flexible and accommodates the needs of individual students.
- It has high academic and behavioral expectations.
- It builds on students' skills of self-management (while supporting those who struggle in this area).
- It is emotionally as well as physically safe; students are not fearful of making mistakes or looking or sounding foolish and, consequently, are willing to risk participation.

See *List 2.3* for numerous strategies for engineering the classroom environment for the success of all students, particularly those with ADHD.

Establish Rules and Behavioral Expectations

- Limit to a few (four or five) well-defined rules and behavioral standards.
- Make sure they address observable behaviors—for example, "Keep hands, feet, and objects to yourself." "Be on time and prepared for class."
- Define concretely what the behaviors should look like and sound like.
- Discuss, model, role-play, and practice those desired behaviors and expectations.
- Post rules to be highly visible in the classroom and refer to them frequently.

- Reward students for rule-following behavior with praise and other positive reinforcement.
- Remind students of your expectations with established visual or auditory prompts and signals.

Teach Procedures and Routines

- Smooth classroom management is dependent on the teaching of specific and consistent procedures and routines.
- Decide on your specific classroom procedures and write those down for clarity. Use the "Classroom Procedures: What Do You Expect Students to Do When … ?" form in the appendix (A-1).
- Teach, model, role-play, and practice procedures until they become so well established and automatic that they are routine. Plan procedures for the start of the school day or class period all the way through dismissal at the end of class or day. See example of a morning routine in the appendix (A-25).
- Monitor, give lots of feedback, review, and reteach as needed throughout the year.
- Reward students for following the procedures quickly and quietly.
- Use auditory cues such as timers, chimes, or other noisemakers to signal the start of routines (cleanup, line up) or songs, chants, or rhymes during the length of time for the procedure or routine.
- Provide visual cues such as projecting a digital countdown timer set for a minute or two or a picture that graphically indicates the procedure or routine students are to follow.

Use Your Proximity and Movement

- Circulate and move around the room frequently.
- Use your physical movement, proximity, and positioning for managing disruptive students. Seat them closer to you or in a location that you can reach quickly and easily to be able to make eye contact and provide discrete cues and warnings, such as placing a hand on shoulder, pointing to or placing a visual reminder on their desk, or whispering a reminder or directive to the student.
- Walk or stand near students prone to misbehaving.
- Create a floor plan for desks and other furniture that enables easy access to all students and paths for walking by and among students without obstruction.

Use Signals and Visual Prompts

- Establish visual and auditory signals for getting students to stop what they are doing and give you their attention. For example, you could flash the lights, use a rainstick or chimes, call out a signal word or phrase that students are trained to respond to, or start a clapping pattern such as AABBB that students join on hearing until you stop clapping and speak.
- Consider teaching and using American Sign Language in the classroom for nonverbal signaling such things as "I have a question." "I have an answer." "I have a

comment." "May I use the restroom?" See Rick Morris's classroom posters for these ASL signs at http://newmanagement.com/main/sign_language.html.

- Use pictures or icons of behavioral expectations and point to or tap on picture prompts as a reminder—for example, to keep your hands to yourself. You can also use an actual photo that you have taken of the student engaged in the appropriate behavior as the visual reminder of expected behavior. See examples of several illustrations that can be used for behavioral promptsin the appendix. *Note:* The same icon-size illustrations of behavioral expectations are also available online at www.wiley.com/go/adhdbol2. By accessing the appendix materials online, the illustrations are able to be printed in larger size as well. See password and download information at the beginning of the appendix.

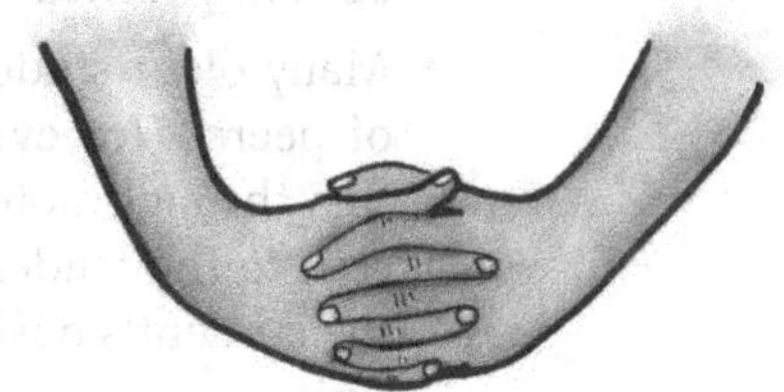

- Set up a private signal with a student to use for warning or redirecting discretely, such as a particular word you say to the student (any word, such as *eyeballs*) or a hand signal such as tugging on your ear that you use once you make eye contact with that student.
- Establish a private signal that the student can use to indicate he or she needs a break and assign a brief task or errand that will enable the student to have a short break.
- Provide students with some form of nonverbal signal to cue "I need help!" when they are working independently, such as a card to prop up on *their* desk.
- Post a time on the board or set a timer to signal when work time has started and will end.
- See *Lists 2.3, 2.4, 2.12, 2.13, 2.15, 4.2, 4.3, 4.4, and 7.4* for more on this topic.

Provide Positive Attention and Reward Appropriate Behavior

- Increase the immediacy and frequency of positive feedback and encouragement—particularly to students with ADHD.
- Focus your attention on students when engaged in appropriate behavior rather than when caught in a rule violation. Remind yourself to notice when students are following class rules and behavioral expectations. Reward for doing so with praise and in other ways such as giving points or other tokens toward earning a privilege.
- Give at least four times more positive attention and praise to students than negative or corrective feedback. Students with ADHD typically receive far more than their fair share of reprimands and criticism. They need a much heavier dose of positive feedback and recognition for what they are doing right.
- Monitor and call attention to students appropriately engaged and describe what they are doing correctly. "I see Karen and Alicia have followed directions. They took out their pencil and math books and cleared everything else off their desks. Thank you, girls." Or "Michael is standing in line quietly with his hands and feet to himself. Michael is ready for recess."
- Provide sincere praise that is descriptive and specific about the behavior exhibited. For example, "Sarah, you were prepared for class and contributed interesting ideas

in our discussion. Thank you." "Nick, I see the effort you put into that assignment. Well done." "Brian, great job cooperating with your group and finishing the assignment on time." Or "James, I appreciate that you remembered to raise your hand and wait until I called on you."

- Additional positive reinforcement can follow praise, for example, "Anna, I noticed how well you followed group rules and were cooperative with your teammates. You earned your team four points today."
- Many older students would be humiliated if teachers praised them openly in front of peers. However, they still need and appreciate the positive feedback. Provide this through notes, quiet statements before or after class, or electronic messages sent to the student. Jot down a positive comment on a sticky note and place it on the student's desk or use another nonverbal signal such as thumbs up or a nod and smile.
- Establish positive reinforcement systems for classroom management. There are several varieties of class (group) incentive systems that teachers may choose to use to best fit their style of teaching, comfort level, and the interest of their students (*List 2.8*).
- The best incentives in a classroom are generally those involving activity rewards. Students are motivated to earn time or opportunity to participate in activities of their choice, such as games or time to work on special projects.
- Together with the class, create a menu of possible rewards that can be earned.
- See *List 2.7* for several ideas of possible rewards for the classroom.

Accommodate the Need to Move

- Alternate frequently between seatwork and other activities that allow for movement.
- Assign tasks that will give movement opportunities to students in need of a break, such as passing out papers, cleaning the board, or running an errand to the office.
- Build in brain breaks particularly after sustained work periods or being seated a lengthy period of time. Have students stand up and stretch, do some jumping jacks, jog or dance near their desks, follow the moves of a brain break video on YouTube, or other brief physical activity for a short amount of time. See several resources, video clips, and ideas for classroom brain breaks at www.pinterest.com/sandrarief/brain-breaks-classroom-games/.
- Students with ADHD particularly need to have the chance during the day to release their energy and have physical activity. Avoid using loss of recess time as a consequence for misbehavior or incomplete work.
- For students who have difficulty sitting, provide options such as moving between two assigned seats (seat A and seat B) or standing up in the back of the room to do their work, such as at a podium, easel, or tall table.

Other Important Strategies and Tips

- Model respectful language, tone of voice, and body language.
- Position yourself at the door and greet students as they enter the room. Begin instruction promptly.

- Minimize instructional lag time—when students are unoccupied and waiting to find out what they are expected to do next.
- Prepare for and provide procedures, structure, and supervision for transitional times of the day. These change-of-activity times tend to be the most problematic (*List 2.10*).
- Post the schedule and refer to it frequently. Inform students in advance whenever possible if changes in the schedule will occur. A desk copy of a student's individual schedule is helpful, particularly if the student receives special education and related services.
- Give choices. For example, "Would you rather do the work at your desk or at the back table?"
- Watch for warning signs of the student becoming overly stimulated, upset, frustrated, agitated, restless—and intervene at once. For example, provide warning signals; try to divert their attention and redirect; change the activity, task, or expectations; remind the student about rewards and consequences; and lend direct support.
- Use contingency management: students must do the less desirable task or activity first in order to get, do, or participate in something they want. Say, for example, "When you finish ... you may then ...." Or "First ... needs to be done, and then you may ...." Or "You may ... as long as you ...."
- Effective classroom management goes hand in hand with good teaching and instruction. Students generally demonstrate appropriate behavior when there is engaging, motivating instruction and learning activities (*Lists 3.2, 3.3, 3.4, 3.7, 3.8*).
- Students with ADHD are often penalized for their difficulties with work production by missing out on PE, art, music, media, and other "specials" when they have not completed their classwork. Avoid doing this when possible. Find ways to provide more support and assistance to help them get caught up with their work.
- The key to effective classroom management is building positive relationships and rapport with students and making a connection on a personal level. This requires teachers to be understanding, flexible, patient, and empathetic. Students typically work hard and want to cooperate and please adults whom they like, trust, and respect.
- Smile, laugh, and communicate through your daily interactions that you sincerely care about and expect the best from all of your students and would never give up on any of them.
- Try to identify the triggers or antecedents to students' misbehaviors (*List 2.11*) and avoid problems when possible through careful planning and environmental engineering (*List 2.3*).
- See related *Lists 2.3, 2.4, 2.7, 2.8, 2.9,2.10, 2.11, 2.12, and 2.13.*
- For more ideas and strategies for classroom management, see www.pinterest.com/sandrarief/class-behavior-management.

Address Misbehavior

Effective behavior management requires a focus on establishing the structure and climate for success, effectively teaching behavioral expectations, and motivating students to cooperate through the abundance of positive reinforcements available in the classroom. However, in addition to positive consequences, negative or corrective consequences are necessary components of effective behavior management. *Note:* Response-cost techniques are found to be highly effective in behavior modification with students who have ADHD (*Lists 2.8, 2.9*).

- Choose to ignore minor inappropriate behavior that is not intentional. Not every behavior warrants teacher intervention. This is particularly important for students with ADHD.
- Back up behavioral limits with fair and reasonable consequences for misbehavior.
- Enforce with speed, consistency, and predictability and in a calm, unemotional manner.
- Handle inappropriate behavior as simply and promptly as possible.
- Deliver consequences using as few words as possible and in a calm, matter-of-fact voice. Act without lecturing or scolding. Discussions about behavior can occur later and privately when possible.
- Prior to a negative consequence (punishment), teachers may use gentle verbal reminders and warnings, such as these:
    - "Steve, remember to raise your hand, please."
    - "Anna, the rule is . . . . That's a warning."
    - "Vincent, where are you supposed to be right now?"
    - "Jared, next time ask permission before you . . . ."
- Teachers may also provide visual cues of expected behaviors, such as tapping on a picture prompt at the child's desk of a student seated appropriately and busy working.

- Prior to implementing a negative consequence, a direct command can also be issued: "Susan, get busy doing problems 1 to 10 now." "Brianna, I need you in your seat and facing forward."
- There are a number of corrective consequences or punishments that can be used, such as the following:
    - Last person to line up or be dismissed
    - Loss of time from participation in a desired activity
    - Brief delay (a minute or two of having to wait before participating in a desired activity or dismissal)
    - Restriction or removal of privilege or desired materials for a period of time
    - Playground restriction from certain games or areas
    - Undesirable task or chore assigned
    - Filling out a think-about-it (problem-solving) sheet or behavioral improvement form, recording behavioral infractions in a log or notebook
    - Being "fined" or losing points or tokens of some kind
    - Restitution or fixing the problem: If the student makes a mess, he has the responsibility of cleaning it up. If the student was disrespectful, she must apologize verbally or in writing.
    - Time-out

- Teacher-student conference
- Parent contact (phone call, e-mail, note home, conference)

There are various forms of time-out or time away from class participation and the chance to earn positive reinforcement:

- Head down at desk (could involve counting to a certain number)
- Being moved a few feet away from the group temporarily—for example, to sit in a chair rather than on the rug during circle time but still within view of the group
- Time-out location in the classroom, away from the view of other students and without the opportunity for positive reinforcement
- Time-out in a neighboring buddy class that has been arranged to exchange students for this purpose
- Time-out in another school location that has supervision. Teachers need to be aware that time-out in other locations may actually be rewarding to the student and not serve the intended purpose.

Source and Resource

Dendy, Chris A. Zeigler, Durheim, Mary, & Ellison, Anne Teeter (Editors). (2006). *CHADD educator's manual on AD/HD*. Lanham, MD: CHADD. Note: Chapter 5 on "Creating a Positive Learning Environment" was authored by Sandra Rief.

2.2 Proactive Parenting: Positive Discipline and Behavior-Management Strategies

Discipline means teaching responsible behavior. Children must learn appropriate, prosocial behavior in order to live and interact successfully with others. Of course, this is a key responsibility of parenting.

Basic Guidelines

The following are basic guidelines for positive discipline and effective behavior management for the home.

- Provide structure, routine, and predictability.
- Set limits and let your child know you mean business.
- Establish a few specific, important rules and expectations that are clearly understood by all members of the household.
- Your responses to your child's behaviors and misbehaviors should be predictable, not random.
- Establish clear-cut consequences in advance with your child that are logical, reasonable, and fair. Enforce them with consistency.
- Use contingencies in establishing boundaries. This basically involves the age-old "Grandma's rule"—"First you eat your vegetables, then you get dessert." Examples:
  - "As soon as you ... , you may ...."
  - "Once you have ... , you will then be able to ...."
  - "You have done your homework. Now you get to go play."
- Children with ADHD receive far more than average negative attention from parents and teachers because misbehavior captures our attention. Notice and pay attention to your child when he or she is behaving appropriately.
- Make it a goal to catch your child being good at least four times more frequently than when you need to respond to misbehavior.
- Be specific in acknowledging and praising:
  - "I really appreciate how you cleaned up without being reminded."
  - "I noticed how well you were sharing and taking turns when you played with Bobby."
- Always reward or give positive attention to the behaviors you want to increase or continue to occur.
- Immediately reinforce desired behavior with a positive consequence by giving something your child likes (praise, smiles, hugs, privileges, points or tokens earned toward a reward) following the behavior.
- Establish rewards and punishments that are easy to do and as simple as possible.
- Children with ADHD require more external motivation than other children because their internal controls are less mature. Therefore, they will need more frequent, immediate, and potent rewards for their effort.
- Realize that children with ADHD have trouble delaying gratification and cannot wait very long for reinforcers. Working toward a long-range goal or payoff is not

going to be effective. It is better to use more frequent, smaller rewards, but ones that are still motivating.

- Token economy systems are effective for children with ADHD. It is worth the effort to learn how to implement such a system at home. It involves the following:
  - Rewarding the child with tokens of some kind (poker chips or points) for demonstrating positive behaviors.
  - These behaviors would include things they would usually be expected to do, such as being ready for the school bus on time, clearing the table after dinner, feeding the dog or other chores, remembering to bring home all books and the assignment calendar for homework.
- A menu of rewards is created with the child, which includes material things (toy, book, ice cream) and privileges (screen time, special activity) the child values. *See List 2.7.* A point value is assigned for each of the items on the list. The child can purchase the reward from the tokens earned.
- Rewards will have to be changed frequently as well. Children with ADHD will not stay interested in the same rewards; they respond best to novelty. Therefore, a menu with a choice of privileges and small-ticket items that are meaningful to the child should be available.
- With a token economy system, the child can also be fined (lose tokens) for targeted behaviors (each incident of fighting with sibling, talking back). It is crucial in such a system to ensure that the child is earning far more tokens or points than he or she is losing or it simply will not work.
- Daily report cards, contracts, or behavior-monitoring forms of some kind between home and school are necessary for many children and teens with ADHD. See the appendix for several examples and *Lists 1.22 and 2.9*. These management forms and charts are also available online at the publisher's website (see information at the beginning of the appendix), and can be downloaded and printed. Some of the charts are able to be customized for personal use.
- Negative consequences are also effective in changing behavior; however, use far more positives than negatives.
- When punishments are required, they should not be harsh. The purpose is to teach your child through its use and enforcement.
- Consequences should be enforced as soon as possible following the infraction of rules—usually one warning, not several.
- The best consequences are those that are logically related to the offense and natural results of the child's actions.
- Some effective punishments include these:
  - Ignoring (particularly attention-getting behaviors)
  - Verbal reprimands (not yelling and screaming)
  - Removal of privileges (for example, TV or other screen time)
  - Response costs (receiving a fine or penalty such as removal of some points or tokens earned in a token economy system)
  - Time-out (isolation for a brief amount of time)
- When delivering consequences, do so in a calm but firm voice. State the consequence without lecturing. Be direct and to the point.

- If using a time-out, choose a location that is boring for your child as well as safe but away from the reinforcement of other people and activities. It should be clear to your child what behaviors will result in time-out. Typically, a reasonable amount of time is one minute per year of age. Set a timer. There are several parenting books that share more specific guidance on implementing time-outs or other punishments. Dr. Russell Barkley's book *Taking Charge of ADHD* is one excellent source recommended for parents of children with ADHD.
- Punishments must have a clear beginning and ending that you are able to control.
- When punishing, be careful to focus on the behavior that is inappropriate. Do not attack the child as "being bad" or criticize his or her character.
- Anticipate and plan in advance (with your spouse or partner) how to handle challenging behaviors. Avoid responding and punishing when you are very angry. You do not want to dole out a punishment you will regret later because it is too harsh, inappropriate, or impossible to enforce.

Preventive Strategies

- Remind through gentle warnings:
    - "The rule is . . . ."
    - "Next time . . . ."
    - "Remember to . . . ."
- Use "do" statements rather than "don't" statements. (Say "Walk in the house" rather than "Don't run in the house.")
- Learn to communicate more effectively (*List 2.4*).
- Talk about, acknowledge, and label feelings—your child's and your own.
- Organize and arrange the home environment in a way that will optimize the chances for success and avoid conflict (*Lists 2.3, 4.5, 4.9*).
- Set up routines (morning routines, mealtime routines, homework routines, bedtime routines) and adhere to them as closely as possible.
- Remove items or objects you do not want your impulsive and hyperactive child to play with or touch. Childproof the house.
- Avoid fatigue—your child's and your own.
- Be observant. Notice when your child is becoming agitated, overly stimulated, or angry and intervene. Try redirecting your child's attention and focus on something else (*Lists 2.6, 2.12, 2.13, 2.14, 2.16, 7.4*).
- Only give your child chores and responsibilities that he or she is developmentally able to handle, not necessarily what other kids of his or her age or siblings can do.
- Provide the supports to enable your child to follow through with chores and responsibilities. Remember that forgetfulness, procrastination, and disorganization are part of ADHD. Your child will need reminders, help getting started, and so forth.
- Provide physical outlets. Your child needs to release energy and participate in active games and physical activities (*Lists 1.23, 7.7*).
- Maintain flexibility and a sense of humor!
- You need to monitor and supervise your child with ADHD much closer than most parents need to do.

- Prepare your child for changes in the home, such as redecorating, visitors or house guests, and changes in parent work schedules. Talk about the change and avoid surprises.
- Purchase toys, books, and games that are developmentally appropriate for your child and not too frustrating.
- Avoid competitive activities or prepare your child for games and activities that involve competition. Walk your child through the rules of the game and what to do if he or she loses. Praise and reward your child for displaying self-control and demonstrating good sportsmanship.
- Provide your child with training in social skills (*List 2.17*).
- Provide a limited number of choices. Do not allow your child to dump out all of his or her toys or browse through all the books before choosing one for you to read with him or her. Allow your child to choose from only a few at one time.
- Be aware of siblings who are teasing and provoking your ADHD child and intervene.

Points to Keep in Mind

- Try to keep calm and avoid discipline that is reactive (not thought out in advance).
- Prioritize and focus on what is important. You cannot make an issue out of everything.
- No matter how exhausted or frustrated you are, maintain your authority as a parent and follow through on what you need to do. Try to do so without losing control of your own emotions.
- Plan ahead which behaviors you will work toward increasing and how you will reward (positively reinforce those behaviors).
- It is far more difficult to manage the behaviors of children with ADHD than most other children. Be willing to seek professional help to find more effective strategies and guidance. Find a mental health professional with expertise in treating children with ADHD and coexisting conditions.
- Parents of children with ADHD must become far more skilled in behavior management than other parents in order to know how to cope with and handle the daily challenges and behavioral difficulties resulting from their child's disorder. This is a key component of behavior therapy for children with ADHD (*Lists 1.19, 1.22*). There are numerous resources available.
- See related *Lists 2.3, 2.4, 2.5, 2.6, 2.7, 2.9, 2.11, 2.12, 2.13, 2.14, 2.16, and 2.17.*

2.3 Creating an ADHD-Friendly Environment

There are many ways to help children and teens with ADHD function better at home and school by engineering the environment to accommodate their needs and self-regulation difficulties. This involves taking into consideration the structure, organization, tools, cues, and other things that can be added to or adjusted in the classroom or home environment to make it more ADHD-friendly.

Environmental Supports and Accommodations in the Classroom

Environmental considerations are essential for classroom management and accommodating individual learning styles. See *List 2.11* for some of the environmental factors that can be problematic for children with ADHD and trigger unwanted behavior.

Student Seating

- Physically arrange the classroom with options for seating. More optimal desk formations for students with ADHD are single-desk options instead of two-person desks or tables, U-shapes, E-shapes, and straight or staggered rows rather than table formations with desk clusters facing each other.
- Students with ADHD are usually best seated in these ways:
  - Close to the center of instruction
  - Surrounded by positive role models and well-focused, on-task students
  - Within teacher cueing and prompting distance
  - With their desks positioned so the teacher can easily make eye contact with them and be able to communicate and redirect discretely
  - Away from high traffic areas and distracters such as noisy heaters or air conditioners, learning centers, doors, windows, and pencil sharpeners
- The key to furniture arrangement is the ability to easily access (with as few steps as possible) each student without obstruction. The best classroom management strategy is teacher proximity: moving among students to monitor, cue, and give feedback.
- Be open, flexible, and willing to make changes in seating when needed.
- Provide alternatives for students with ADHD to sitting in a hard desk chair. Doing so often increases their productivity and is a reasonable accommodation.
  - Allow the student to work on the carpet or beanbag chair if he or she is more comfortable and productive than at a desk, with papers attached to a clipboard.
  - Establish some standing work stations: a high table or podium, an easel, or other surface at which a student can do work standing up rather than seated. Place these in the back of the room where they will not obstruct other students' vision.
  - Consider assigning two desks to a student with ADHD, with the option of doing his or her work at desk A or desk B. This allows for the need to get up and move locations, but within boundaries.
  - Try seat cushions such as the Disc O'Sit or the Move 'N Sit Cushion, which accommodate a child's need for squirming and wiggling in the chair. Your school's occupational therapist has access to such tools or may provide suggestions. You

might also buy inexpensive inflatable beach balls and blow them up partially as an alternative seat cushion.

- Experiment with other kinds of seats such as a round therapeutic ball, a T-stool, such as the Stabili-T-Stool by Abilitations, the Kids Kore Wobble Chair or Teen Kore Active Chair.

Space, Materials, and Minimizing Environmental Distractions

- Students with ADHD are often spilling into or intruding in others' space. Designate physical boundaries within which the student is to stay. For example, use a strip of colored duct tape on the carpet, floor, or tables. The student is asked to not move his or her desk, chair, or body past the line.
- Store materials in clearly labeled bins, shelves, tubs, trays, or folders.
- Reduce clutter and visual distractions, such as unnecessary writing on the board or things hanging from the ceiling over students' heads.
- Be aware of noises in the classroom that can be auditory distractions and find ways to mask or minimize those sounds. Some students are highly sensitive to environmental sounds such as clocks ticking, air conditioners running, or buzzing fluorescent lights.
- Establish rules and procedures for movement within the classroom (such as when it is okay to get up, get a drink, or sharpen pencils) to reduce distractions.
- Permit students to use ear plugs or headsets to block out noise during seatwork, test taking, or other appropriate times of the day.
- If the room is not carpeted, insert old tennis balls on the tips of each chair leg to reduce the noise when chairs are moved. Tips for chairs and desk legs can also be purchased at hardware stores.
- Provide office areas or study carrels for seating options during certain times of the day (such as independent seatwork time) as needed. They are set apart from the other desks and designed to reduce distractions. It is important that they are not viewed as punitive locations or meant for students with special needs only. The class should know they may be used by any student who feels more productive working in an office area.
- Purchase or construct privacy boards to place on tables during test taking or at other times to block out visual distractions and limit the visual field. You can construct desk-size, collapsible privacy boards with three pieces of heavy chipboard and duct tape.
- Turn off the classroom lights at various times of the day for calming, particularly after physical education, recess, and lunch.
- Create an area of the classroom that a student can go to for a few minutes when needed for calming and regrouping. *List 2.15* describes such areas, and are often referred to as some pleasant location, for example, *Hawaii* or *Tahiti*.
- See several examples of organized, structured classroom environments and alternative seats and tools beneficial for students with ADHD at www.pinterest.com/sandrarief/class-organization-time-mgmt/.

Visual and Auditory Cues to the Environment

- Use color cues such as volume control or noise meter charts. At different times of the day or during certain instructional periods the teacher clips a clothespin on the chart or sets a dial to the noise level permissible at that time, for example, on red (no voice), yellow (partner voice), green (group voice), blue (sharing voice). Teachers can also remind students verbally, "We are in the yellow zone now."
- There are many variations of these volume control charts. Some use levels by number, for example: 0 = no talking, no sound; 1 = whisper; 2 = only people near you can hear you; 3 = entire class can hear you; 4 = outside voice. For more examples, see www.pinterest.com/sandrarief/class-behavior-management/.
- Use private visual cues you set up for communicating either with individual students or the whole class. For example, teach and use hand signs or gestures for such messages as "please don't interrupt," "wait your turn," "make a good choice," "get back on task."
- Provide a lot of visual prompts, models, and displays—visual depictions of procedures, routines, and behavioral expectations.
- Use auditory tools such as timers, bells, chimes, a harmonica, and other devices to obtain students' attention. Different sounds and noisemakers can be used to signal transitions or specific procedural expectations such as moving from students' seats to sitting on the carpet area or lining up to leave the classroom.

- Use visual timers, such as Time Timer (www.timetimer.com/) or the many different online timers at www.online-stopwatch.com/classroom-timers/, which can be projected in the classroom.
- See more on this topic in in *Lists 2.1, 2.12, 2.13, 2.15, 3.4, 3.7, 4.1,and 4.6* and several examples of visual prompts in the appendix.

Using Music

- Music in the classroom can be used for several purposes. Certain kinds of music may help with focus and concentration, and soothing, quiet music after recess, physical education, and lunch can calm a group of students.
- For some students, music acts as a filter to other environmental noises and helps block out auditory distractions.
- Music can be used to add structure and time limits during transitions (for example, to clean up and be finished by the end of the song).
- It is very beneficial for energizing the class, such as playing a lively, upbeat tune in the afternoon when students are feeling sluggish. There are many YouTube videos that make excellent brain break energizers for the classroom. Several can be found at www.pinterest.com/sandrarief/brain-breaks-classroom-games/.

- Music can be played quietly during work periods to motivate and stimulate thinking and increase productivity.
- Try a variety of music including classical music, show tunes, environmental sounds of nature (such as a rain forest or the ocean).
- Music at sixty beats per minute, the rate our heart beats when relaxed, may have some therapeutic effects and enhance learning. Some evidence may suggest that such music in the background is prime for learning, relaxation, and using long-term memory. If interested in playing music at sixty beats per minute in the classroom, try Baroque music or music by Gary Lamb at www.musicintheclassroom.com.
- There are several good resources to find recommended music for different purposes in the classroom. Eric Jensen, a leader in brain-based learning, has excellent suggestions about use of music in the classroom: www.jensenlearning.com/news/the-perfect-music-for-brain-based-learning/brain-based-learning.

Environmental Supports and Modifications at Home

Designing and Organizing the Home Environment

- A key environmental support in the home is to create organizational structure for children's bedrooms, homework areas, and other parts of the house.
- Set up a central communication area—a place where the family's master calendar or schedule and message boards are located and all family members can easily reach and access them.
- Create a launching pad area for placing important items needed in the morning when leaving to school and work. This area would likely be located near the front door or door going out to the garage. It may have hooks for hanging backpacks, a shelf or cubbies for other bags and items, and a basket for placing car and house keys.
- Provide the tools and materials to keep your child's room organized, designed for ease in locating, using, and cleaning up his or her belongings.
- Design your child's homework space with easy access to necessary supplies and materials.
- Use color strategically to organize.
- See *Lists 4.5 and 4.9* for organizing your child's supplies, materials, and homework area.
- There are many examples of great ideas for home organization (homework areas, central control centers, and much more) with pictures to see what they look like on Pinterest. See several wonderful examples at www.pinterest.com/sandrarief/home-organization-homework-areas/.
- If possible, design an area of the house, such as the basement, where rambunctious behavior is tolerated.
- Establish in your home specific locations that will be used for homework, time-out (if you use as a discipline technique), and the Internet (if you wish to be able to monitor your child's access and its use).
- We all need a time and place for quiet, and it is helpful if there is an area in the home that anyone can escape to in order to settle down and regroup. Design, if

possible, an area in your home that is more removed and peaceful. For example, with quiet, calming colors (blues, aqua, light green, and pale tones are recommended as opposed to bold colors). If you have an aquarium in your home, that might be a good spot; watching the fish swim around can be calming.

- Many children with ADHD are skilled at and love to construct, build things, and take them apart and do arts and crafts and other hands-on activities. These activities should be encouraged, although they can be messy. Supply the necessary materials, tools, and storage containers.
- If your child tends to be accident prone or destructive, make purchases with this in mind and place furniture and items strategically.

Use Visual and Auditory Supports

- Post calendars and use master schedules. Write each family member's name and activities in different colors.
- Write down and post all chores in a visible place.
- Remember to use as many visuals as possible. Pointing to a picture of a routine or poster of expectations is a better way to remind your child and reduce conflicts than talking about it or nagging.
- Place sticky notes on mirrors, doors, and other visible places as reminders.
- Experiment with the use of timers or playing a particular song as an auditory cue, for example, to get ready for dinner or time to go upstairs for bedtime routine.
- Find ways to reduce the noise level at home—especially during homework, study times, and before bedtime if possible. A good quality headset can also be very helpful.
- Although some people need it completely quiet in order to study, others (including many with ADHD) have great difficulty studying in complete quiet because all the sounds in the environment that most other people never notice (household appliances, electronics, traffic, and other outside noises) are distracting. If this is the case for your child, music in the background may help filter out those annoying, distracting sounds and help your child better focus.
- For study purposes, instrumental music (no lyrics) tends to be best as well as using a recorded playlist of music so as not to be drawn off task looking for songs to play.
- Although classical music has often been the most recommended type of music for studying, there are several other options. Pandora (free online) radio stations have various lyric-free music stations recommended for studying by Kelly Roell on About.com. See the article, "The 6 Best Genre Pandora Stations for Studying" (http://testprep.about.com/od/Study_Skills/a/Pandora_Stations_Study.htm), which shares information regarding Pandora radio stations of instrumental hip-hop, instrumental folk, film scores, solo piano, and a whole combination of instrumentals (from classical to current songs, from solo instruments to full orchestra).
- Music during homework time may energize and motivate your child and increase his or her productivity. When a high degree of concentration (as in studying) isn't required for the homework completion, listening to the radio or the music they like with lyrics may work fine. It is a matter of experimenting to find what works best, with the bottom line being your child's productivity.

- Playing quiet, slow tempo music before bedtime and at times when you need to add calm and peace in your home environment can be helpful.
- See additional suggestions for studying in the "Using Music" section of this list.
- See *List 4.9* for more environmental supports to enhance productivity during homework.

Other Environmental and Sensory Supports

- We all have our own learning styles and preferences. Some of us do not like to work at a desk and are more comfortable and productive sitting on the carpet or propped up against a back rest, writing with paper attached to a clipboard or on a laptop. Have your child experiment with doing homework using different types of seating options: round therapeutic balls, T-stools, swivel chairs, and the kind of computer seat that is meant to be knelt on may be helpful alternatives to a hard chair. Also, seat cushions such as Move 'N Sit Jr. and Disc O'Sit Jr. are inflatable dynamic seat cushions that may be able to accommodate your child's need to squirm and wiggle in the chair. These are available at Therapro (www.therapro.com) and other companies. See other recommendations of alternative chairs in the "Environmental Supports and Accommodations in the Classroom" section of this list.
- If your child and other family members do not have allergies to fragrances, you might want to experiment with aromatherapy. Various scents are believed to have certain effects. For example, the scents of peppermint, spearmint, lemon, orange, and pine are believed to enhance alertness or attention. Perhaps your child may be more attentive when doing homework with one of those scents in the environment.
- See *Lists 2.2, 2.12, 3.7, 4.1, 4.5, and 4.9* for related topics.

Source and Resource

Roell, Kelly. (n.d.). The 6 best genre Pandora stations for studying. About.com. Retrieved from http://testprep.about.com/od/Study_Skills/a/Pandora_Stations_Study.htm

2.4 Tips for Giving Directions and Increasing Compliance

Strategies and Tips for Parents

Get Their Attention

- First, get your child's attention directly before giving directions. This means face-to-face and direct eye contact, not just calling out what you expect your child to do.
- Physically cue your child prior to giving directions, if needed; for example, gently turn your child's face to look at you.
- Do not attempt to give directions to your child if you are competing with the distractions of TV, video games, or when he or she is using the iPad or other electronic device. Pause or turn those devices off first.

Communicate Clearly and Effectively

- Keep verbal directions clear, brief, and to the point. Eliminate unnecessary talking and elaboration. State what you want with as few words as possible, for example, "Please come to the table now."
- Always check for understanding of directions. Have your child repeat or rephrase what you asked him or her to do.
- Show your child what you want him or her to do. Model and walk through the steps.
- Break down tasks into smaller steps that you want to get done. Give one step at a time.
- Use a visual chart of tasks or chores depicting the steps or sequence of what your child is expected to do. With young children, for example, make a morning routine chart showing pictures of (1) clothing, (2) cereal bowl, (3) a hairbrush and toothbrush. A clothespin is attached to the side of the chart that your child moves down to the next picture when completing each task or step in the routine.
- Avoid multiple-step directions. Working memory weaknesses make it difficult for children with ADHD to hold on to information while carrying out tasks. Giving one direction at a time is better (*Lists 4.1, 4.2*).
- If multiple-step directions are needed, a visual such as a checklist or card depicting the steps (1, 2, 3) in pictures or words must be provided to follow.
- Do not state your direction in the form of a question such as, "Would you get in your pajamas, please?" "Are you ready to turn off the lights?" Instead, make a direct statement, for example, "Lights off in ten minutes." "Get in your pajamas now."
- Try using more "do" rather than "don't" directives, such as "Put your bottom on the chair" rather than "Stop standing on the chair" or "Hang up your wet towel, please" instead of "Don't leave your wet towel on the ground."
- Write down the task you want done (in words or pictures) and give that written direction or task card to your child. It serves as an easy reference and reduces the potential for conflict that arises from telling your child to do things he or she prefers

not to do. For example, chore cards (setting or clearing the table or feeding the family pet) can be made that depict in words or pictures the steps for that chore. You just hand the card to your child.

- Do not use vague language that is open to interpretation and lacks enough precise information such as "Clean your room." "Get ready." "Be nice to your brother." Be specific in defining just what you mean. Define your expectations for a clean room, such as (1) All dirty clothes in hamper. (2) Make bed. (3) Put toys away in storage bins.
- What you may perceive as noncompliance when your child does not listen to you may actually be a matter of poor communication on your part.

Follow Up, Reinforce, and Motivate

- Be sure to give immediate praise when your child follows directions. "Thank you for being cooperative." "I really appreciate how you listened and quickly did what I asked you to do. Great job!"
- Reward your child for following directions, as appropriate—for example, "You did a great job straightening up your room. You get to (choose a game, have a snack) or you just earned five points on your chart."
- Keep direct commands to a minimum. Be sure commands that you issue are ones you plan to enforce. Once you give a command, do not repeat what you said without waiting five to ten seconds (or a bit longer) for your child to comply. If your child does not begin to comply, firmly but calmly state the directive or command again. This time use the words: "You need to...." If your child still does not comply, provide a mild negative consequence, such as loss of some TV or screen time, brief time-out, or loss of some points or tokens.
- Try turning chores and tasks into more pleasant experiences by making a game of it. Beat-the-clock challenges can be motivating, such as "Let's see if you can finish picking up your toys before the timer goes off, or put the blocks back in the basket by the time I count to ten or get dressed by the end of the song. Ready ... Set ... Go!"
- You may need to work alongside your child on a task together to get started. Once you have provided the necessary support and guidance, it is important that your child work independently to the best of his or her ability.

Keep in Mind

- Children with ADHD do have trouble following directions. In your frustration with being ignored, you may interpret your child's noncompliance with your directive as being deliberate when it is often not the case. Remember that it is characteristic of children with ADHD to have difficulty with these issues:
  - Stopping and disengaging from activities that they are in the middle of (especially something fun that they enjoy doing)
  - Forgetfulness (because of working memory weaknesses)
  - Getting started (initiating tasks)
  - Getting motivated
  - Performing and following through without prompting and cueing
- Even though other children their age are easily able to perform certain tasks independently, your child developmentally is likely not able to do so. Sometimes the

failure to comply with your instructions is because sufficient structure or assistance was not provided.

- However, many children with ADHD are oppositional and noncompliant. Approximately 40 to 60 percent of children with ADHD have or will develop oppositional defiant disorder (ODD). If your son or daughter has very challenging behaviors in this regard, seek a mental health professional with expertise in diagnosing and treating children and teens with ADHD and ODD.
  - See *List 2.14* for strategies and interventions that are more specific to addressing the challenges of children and teens with argumentative, oppositional behavior. To increase the likelihood of compliance and cooperative behavior and for more related strategies, see *Lists 2.13, 2.16, 4.2, and 4.4.*
  - There are a number of excellent resources that share strategies for helping children better listen and follow directions, as well as resources and expert guidance for parents struggling to manage the oppositional, noncompliant behaviors of their children. See the "Sources and Resources" section at the end of this list for some suggestions.

Strategies and Tips for Teachers

Attention First

- Use an attention-getting strategy. There are many means of doing so with auditory signals, such as chimes or other sound makers, and verbal and visual cues that indicate students are to stop immediately whatever they are doing and give you their attention (*Lists 2.1, 2.3, 2.12, 4.2*).
- Do not talk over students' voices. Wait until it is quiet and you have students' attention before giving instructions.
- You may need to physically cue certain students for their focus prior to giving directions, such as by placing your hand lightly on their back or touching their arm.
- Be sure to face students when you talk.
- See *List 4.2* on getting students' attention

Clear Expectations and Communication

- Give concise, clear verbal directions. Avoid unnecessary talk.
- Let students know that they are not to start the task until signaled to do so (usually with the word "Go!" or "Begin!"). Michael Linsin of Smart Classroom Management (see the "Sources and Resources" section of this list) recommends a silent pause for a moment before giving the "go" signal.
- Following directions should be a class rule that is clearly defined, taught, and repeatedly practiced. Whole Brain Teaching's class rule 1 is "Follow directions quickly!" See the many techniques Whole Brain Teaching (Biffle, 2013) uses for teaching and reinforcing this important rule. One of them involves after every direction is given by the teacher (which are always single and short), at a teacher cue "Teach!" students are trained to reply "OK!" and turn to their neighbor or partner to repeat what the teacher said.
- Write assignments and directions on the board in a consistent spot and leave them there for reference.

- Model what to do by showing the class and walking through the steps, using gestures when appropriate.
- Provide multisensory instructions—visual cues and graphics along with simple verbal explanations.
- Avoid multiple-step instructions. Whenever possible, provide one instruction at a time or at most two.
- If multiple-step directions are used, always clearly delineate the steps and sequence (1, 2, 3) of the directions in writing or pictures that are posted in a clear location.
- Break down tasks into smaller steps, simplifying directions for each phase of the task or assignment. Model each step explicitly.
- Always check for understanding of directions by having individual students volunteer to repeat or rephrase your directions to the whole class.
- Use partners and pair-shares for clarification of directions: "Tell your partner what we are going to be doing on page 247."
- Describe the behavior you want started and be specific—for example, "Desks cleared except for paper and a pencil" or "Books open to page 21, please."
- Read written directions to the class and have students color-highlight, circle, or underline key words in the directions.
- Make sure to give complete directions to students, including what you expect them to do if they have any questions and when they are finished with the task or assignment. Provide these in written or visual format as reference as well as verbally.

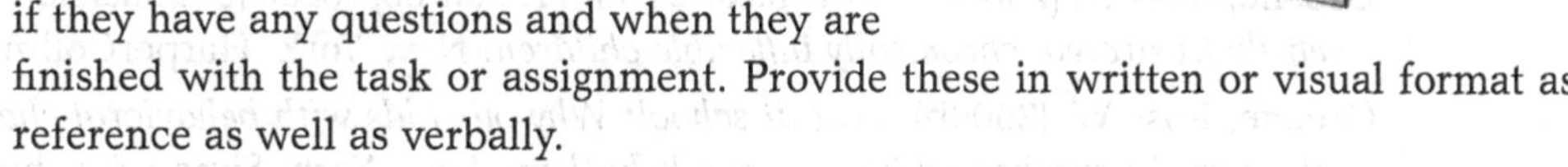

Feedback, Follow-Through, and Motivation

- Give praise and positive feedback when students are following directions or making a good attempt to do so.
- Provide follow-up after you give directions. Monitor that students have followed your directions and praise them for doing so. "I see table 3 is ready. They all have their reading logs, pencils, and books on the table, and are ready to begin. Nice job, table 3." You may also provide points or other reinforcement for following directions quickly.
- It is important to check in on students with ADHD to make sure they have begun the task correctly.

What Else to Keep in Mind

- What may be misinterpreted in students as noncompliant behavior—deliberately disobeying an adult—is often due to the adult's poorly stated directions, such as being vague or giving a string or chain of multiple directions that the student didn't understand or promptly forgot.

- Keep in mind that students with ADHD will often need more assistance, guidance, and incentives for following directions because they tend to have difficulty with these actions:
    - Transitions and changes of activity, particularly disengaging from a fun activity they are involved in when given a direction to do something else
    - Waiting for a full direction or remembering what to do (because of impulsivity and working memory difficulties)
    - With other executive function–related challenges listed in the "Strategies and Tips for Parents" section
- *See List 2.4* for strategies in managing argumentative, oppositional behavior and other related lists (*Lists 2.12, 2.13, 4.2, 4.4, 4.7*).

Sources and Resources

Barkley, Russell. (2013). *Taking charge of ADHD: The complete, authoritative guide for parents* (3rd ed.). New York: Guilford Press.

Barkley, Russell A., & Benton, Christine M. (2013). *Your defiant child: Eight steps to better behavior* (2nd ed.). New York: Guilford Press.

Biffle, Chris. (2013). *Whole brain teaching for challenging kids*. San Bernardino, CA: Whole Brain Teaching.

Clark, Lynn. (2013). *SOS: Help for parents* (3rd ed.). Bowling Green, KY: SOS Programs & Parents Press.

Forehand, R., & McMahon, R. (1981). *Helping the noncompliant child*. New York: Guildford Press.

Greene, Ross W. (2009a). *The explosive child: A new approach for understanding and parenting easily frustrated, chronically inflexible children*. New York: HarperCollins.

Greene, Ross W. (2009b). *Lost at school: Why our kids with behavioral challenges are falling through the cracks and how we can help them*. New York: Simon & Schuster.

Linsin, Michael. (2009). How to get students to follow directions. *Smart Classroom Management*. Retrieved from www.smartclassroommanagement.com/2009/12/19/how-to-get-students-to-follow-directions/

Linsin, Michael. (2014). A fun way to get your students to follow directions. *Smart Classroom Management*. Retrieved from www.smartclassroommanagement.com/2014/01/18/a-fun-way-to-get-your-students-to-follow-directions/

Taylor, John F. (2011). *From defiance to cooperation*. New York: Random House.

Walker, Hill M., & Walker, Janet Eaton. (1991). *Coping with noncompliance in the classroom*. Austin, TX: Pro-Ed Publishers.

2.5 Target Behaviors for Students with ADHD

Students with ADHD need positive behavioral supports and visual prompts to cue and remind them of expected behaviors. The following sections describe possible target behaviors or goals teachers and parents may use when tailoring behavior charts, forms, or intervention plans for a child or teen with ADHD. Those for school are appropriate for use with daily report cards and various monitoring forms, such as those in the appendix or described in *Lists 1.22 and 2.9*. Teachers may select from the variations and optional wording of target behaviors. There are also examples of behaviors parents may want to target for home-based charts. Notice that all target behaviors are stated in positive terms—what you want the student *to be doing*, instead of what you want the child *to stop doing*.

Note: In the appendix (A-27 through A-29) are some illustrations (icons) that are representative of behavioral expectations. Enlarge or shrink to size and use the illustrations together with the target behaviors. They are appropriate for customizing behavioral charts, monitoring forms, and for use as visual prompts (desk copy or chart size). The appendix material (graphics and charts) are also available online and can be downloaded and printed. See the publisher's link and password on the first page of the appendix to access the online materials.

School Target Behaviors

For task initiation, resisting distractions, staying on task, and showing effortful work production on in-class assignments:

- Starts work with *x* or fewer reminders
- Started on assignments promptly
- Stays on task with *x* or fewer reminders
- Completes work or reasonable amount
- Completed work on time
- Turns in completed assignment
- On task; working productively
- On task (no more than *x* warnings)
- Remains on task until work is completed (no more than one prompt or reminder)
- Stayed on task
- Used class time effectively
- Used class time wisely
- Used class time productively
- Shows good effort on tasks
- Uses time allotted for assignments
- Completes assignment(s) by the end of the work period
- Completes 80 percent of assignments on time
- Completes assignment(s) with 80 percent accuracy
- Completes all steps in morning routine with no more than one reminder
- Completes all steps in end-of-day routine with no more than one reminder
- Starts seatwork right away (no more than one prompt or reminder)

- Gets started on assignments right away (within two minutes)
- Completed morning routine (according to checklist or chart)
- Completed assignments (according to checklist)
- Stayed on task with little redirection
- Stays on task when other students are being disruptive, provocative, or disciplined

For Preparedness, Organization, Time Management, Homework

- Turned in completed homework
- Turns in homework assignments on time
- Turns in at least *x* percent of homework on time
- On time and ready.
- On time to class (less than *x* incidents of tardiness)
- Ready to work (has needed materials, books)
- Came to class prepared (with homework and materials)
- Has needed materials and supplies
- Assignments recorded in planner or assignment sheet
- Records assignments (as per teacher check)
- Desk and notebook neat
- Organized work area
- Maintains personal belongings in a responsible manner
- Organized materials
- Organizes materials according to checklist
- Organizes desk and work space (according to checklist)

For Showing Self-Control, Inhibiting Impulsive-Hyperactive Behaviors

- Works quietly
- Talks quietly
- Works without disturbing others
- Participates in class discussions (stays on topic, no interrupting, disagrees politely)
- Keeps hands, feet, and objects to self (no more than one reminder)
- Asks permission before handling other people's property
- Raises hand for permission to speak
- Refrains from blurting
- Refrains from interrupting
- Raises hand and waits for permission to speak (with no more than *x* warnings)
- Waits for permission to leave seat (or assigned area)

- Raises hand for permission to leave seat
- Stays seated (no more than *x* warnings)
- Stays in assigned seat or location (no more than *x* warnings)
- Sits appropriately in assigned area (no more than one reminder or prompt)
- Stays with group
- Stays in class (does not leave room without permission)
- Enters room quietly and goes to right place (no more than one reminder)
- Participates and stays with group
- Remains in assigned desk or classroom location during any instructional activity
- Remains in assigned areas of the building and grounds during the day
- Listens quietly
- Listens without interrupting
- Waits patiently without interruptions (no more than *x* warnings)
- Uses appropriate voice volume
- Talks in a normal volume
- Allows classmates to do their work without bothering
- Refrains from taking or destroying objects in school or other people's belongings
- Waits turn without interrupting
- Refrains from blurting (No more than one calling out or blurting response per period)
- Makes transitions without difficulty
- Transitions quickly and quietly
- Kept personal space

For Following Directions, Cooperation, and Appropriate Interactions with Adults

- Follows teacher directions (with two or less reminders)
- Follows directions (no more than *x* warnings)
- Followed directions quickly
- Accepted redirection
- Participates in activities without complaining
- Participates appropriately
- Respects adults (polite, no arguing or talking back)
- Appropriate interaction with adults (words and manners)
- Polite to teacher and other adults
- Works cooperatively
- Participates appropriately in lessons and activities
- Asks for help appropriately
- Shows respect to teachers and other adults

- Follows directions given by a staff member
- Follows class rules (no more than *x* violations)
- Responds to adult requests and directions with no more than two prompts or reminders
- Receives a positive report from visiting teachers and specialists
- Gets teacher's attention appropriately
- Accepts directions from staff without argument
- Refrains from arguing about behavior points
- Appears attentive and listening (eyes on speaker, not talking)

For Following Rules outside of the Classroom

- Follows cafeteria rules (no more than one rule infraction or reminder)
- Follows playground rules
- Followed bus rules
- Follows rules in hallways
- Follows rules in bathroom
- Follows rules in _____ (music class, PE)
- Follows rules of game(s)
- Follows rules in line (with no more than one reminder)
- No referrals from lunch, recess, or the bus

For Cooperative Behavior and Appropriate Social Interactions with Peers

- Uses appropriate language (no put downs or teasing)
- Solves problems peacefully
- Plays cooperatively
- Gets along with peers (no complaints of teasing, name calling, threatening, touching others or their belongings)
- Uses appropriate language (no foul or rude language)
- Refrains from language that is threatening or insulting
- Refrains from fighting or using provocative gestures
- Engages in appropriate social interactions and treats self and others with respect
- Gets along with peers (no fighting, teasing, or put-downs)
- Follows cooperative group rules
- Follows the rules of games
- Waits turn when playing games
- Refrains from arguing or bossiness with peers
- Keeps hands and feet to self
- Shows good sportsmanship
- Accepts losing games appropriately

- Shares appropriately
- Shares with classmates (no more than one prompt or reminder)
- Takes turns appropriately
- Cooperates with partner
- No more than *x* reminders to ... (for example, stop teasing, bossing, touching)
- Fewer than *x* incidents of . . .
- Participates in group activities
- Shows effort to solve problems before seeking adult help

Home Target Behaviors

For Homework and Organization

- Brings home all needed books, materials, and assignment calendar
- Has assignment calendar or planner filled out accurately and completely
- Begins homework according to schedule with no more than two reminders
- Began homework according to schedule without arguing
- Shows effort on homework
- Turns in homework assignments
- Completes homework (or works on homework until parent determines child worked sufficient amount of time with effort)
- Has materials needed for homework

For Following Rules and Routines

- Completes morning routine of checklist by ... (indicate time)
- Is ready for school and out the door on time
- Follows home rules (no more than *x* violations)
- Completes bedtime routine of checklist by ... (indicate time)
- Goes to bed by the time the timer goes off (with no more than two reminders)
- Goes to bed with no more than *x* reminders
- Follows directions with no more than two reminders
- Followed directions within *x* minutes
- Takes care of belongings
- Uses materials and possessions appropriately
- Waits without interrupting while parent is on the phone (no more than one reminder)

For Cooperative, Respectful Behavior with Parents or Other Adults

- Refrains from arguing when told "no"
- Fewer than *x* incidents of talking back, cursing, or other rude language
- *X* or fewer incidents of interrupting parent while on the phone

For Home-School Collaboration

- Brings home daily report card (home-school note) from school
- Positive report from … (teacher, bus driver, babysitter, coach)
- No more than one incident of … reported by….
- Received no negative reports or phone calls or text messages from school

Appropriate Behavior with Siblings and Other Children

- Gets along with siblings (no more than *x* reminders or redirections)
- Gets along with siblings (*x* or fewer fights or arguments)
- Solves problems peacefully without fighting
- Showed good sportsmanship when playing
- Hands, feet, and objects to self (fewer than *x* incidents of hitting, pushing, kicking, or grabbing)
- Takes turns, shares, and plays cooperatively
- Gets along with siblings and playmates (fewer than *x* incidents of put-downs, name-calling, or teasing)

For Chores and Responsibilities

- Practices piano with no more than two warnings
- Has all needed items for (sports, music, dance, or other activity) ready when needed
- Completes chores according to checklist or task card
- Begins chores according to schedule without arguing
- Begins chores according to schedule with no more than two reminders

Sources and Resources

Some of the target behaviors in this list are from the following sources developed by William Pelham Jr. and the Center for Children and Families, University at Buffalo, for use in daily report cards. These excellent resources contain guidance for teachers and parents in designing effective DRCs and include many other possible target goals for home and school in addition to those shared in the list.

Home daily report card (http://ccf.buffalo.edu/pdf/Home_Daily_Report_Card.pdf)

School daily report card (http://ccf.buffalo.edu/pdf/school_daily_report_card.pdf)

2.6 Preventing Behavior Problems Outside of the Home

Many parents of children with ADHD dread having to take their son or daughter shopping with them or to other places outside of the home where behavior issues often emerge. The behavioral controls expected in some of these environments can be more than a child with ADHD is able to handle. Following are some recommendations for preventing or at least reducing potential behavior problems that can occur outside of the home:

- Anticipate and prepare for potential problems.
- Teach, model, and practice appropriate behaviors and manners that you expect your child to display outside of the home—for example, following directions, cleaning up after yourself, walking instead of running inside a building, and saying "please" and "thank you."
- Give your child advance notice before leaving the house. Avoid catching him or her off guard and provide enough time for getting ready.
- Talk about what to expect.
- Before going into public places (stores, doctor's office, restaurants, church or temple, movie theaters) or visiting other people's homes:
  - Talk to your child about behavioral expectations.
  - State the rules simply.
  - Have your child repeat the rules back to you.
  - Give written directions if appropriate.
- Establish rewards that your child will be able to receive if he or she behaves appropriately and follows the rules. Remind your child of the contingency: "If you . . . , you will be able to earn . . . ."
- Try not to put your child in situations that are too taxing on his or her self-control and attention span. Avoid places that you know will be too stimulating or difficult to supervise and manage the behavior.
- If your child is on medication, consider scheduling activities to coincide with the optimal effects of the medication.
- Avoid taking your child out when he or she is tired and needs a nap or some quiet time.
- Let your child know the negative consequences if he or she behaves inappropriately. Be prepared to enforce them. Mean what you say!
- A token economy system can be very useful in out-of-the-home situations for behavior management. Let your child know that he or she will earn *x* number of tokens or points as an incentive for demonstrating self-control and cooperative behavior when you are out together, and inappropriate behavior will result in the loss of tokens or points.
- When entering a public place such as a department store with your child, scout around for some location that is removed and isolated and can be used for a time-out if necessary.
- Remove your child immediately from the situation when he or she is behaving inappropriately or showing signs of losing control.

- Supervise. Supervise. Supervise. For example, when taking your child to someone else's home, keep aware of where your child is and what he or she is doing—ready to redirect or intervene if necessary.
- Be prepared with a bag of tricks. Knowing the nature of ADHD—that children bore easily, have difficulty waiting, and need to be kept busy—do not leave the house without being equipped. Bring toys, games, books, tablet or other electronic devices with headsets or earbuds, a pad of paper and colored pencils, and so forth that can occupy your child and keep him or her entertained. Keep the bag of tricks replenished to maintain novelty and interest.
- If your hyperactive or impulsive child will be expected to sit quietly (such as in church or synagogue or a movie theater), provide a quiet fidget toy. This keeps his or her hands busy and can help regulate behavior. Try giving a piece of Wikki Stix (a piece of twine with a nontoxic wax covering, available at www.wikkistix.com) or some other item to fidget with silently. See *List 2.12* for some examples and resources for purchasing fidget toys and ideas for a busy box of quiet toys and items suggested in the ADHD Momma blog listed in this list's "Sources and Resources" section.
- Give your child feedback when you are with him or her outside of the home: "I'm proud of how well you are.... It looks like you'll probably earn the reward we talked about."
- If your child is beginning to lose control, prompt him or her to use previously taught self-regulation techniques—for example, "Let's calm down. Take three deep breaths. Now count to ten slowly." Or self-talk, such as repeating to himself or herself, "I need to calm down ... put on the brakes," or "I am calm and in control."
- Talk with your child about the natural consequences of inappropriate behavior: friends or their parents will not want to invite him or her to their house; other children will get angry and not want to play.
- Teach and practice appropriate social skills (*List 2.17*).
- Russell Barkley (2013) has excellent advice with clear steps detailing what to do before, during, and after behavior problems occur in public places. This includes specific locations that may be used for time-out in grocery and department stores, church, restaurants, and other places where behavior problems are common.
- For parents who use Dr. Thomas Phelan's *1-2-3 Magic* approach, the technique involves counting up to three (sometimes four) and immediately punishing with a time-out if the behavior doesn't stop by the final count. Using this technique: when your child is misbehaving, without lecturing or raising your voice, say, "That's 1." If your child continues with the misbehavior, calmly and unemotionally say, "That's 2." If your child still does not stop, say, "That's 3, take 5." This means the child takes a time-out for five minutes. This approach works only if parents use it consistently for stopping inappropriate behaviors. Phelan also gives suggestions for using this method in public places.

Sources and Resources

Barkley, Russell A. (2013). *Taking charge of ADHD: The complete, authoritative guide for parents* (3rd. ed.). New York: Guilford Press.

Choi, Jenn. (2012, June 19). The busy box: How to teach productive waiting. Retrieved from http://adhdmomma.com/2012/06/the-busy-box-how-to-teach-productive-waiting.html.

Phelan, Thomas W. (2010). *1-2-3 magic: Effective discipline for children* (4th ed., pp. 2–12). Chicago: ParentMagic.

2.7 Rewards and Positive Reinforcement for Home and School

Rewards for Home

It is important to catch your child being good, that is, demonstrating appropriate behavior. Be particularly generous with praise, attention, and social reinforcers during that time.

Social Rewards

- Positive attention from parents—preferably your undivided attention for even a short amount of time
- Parents' physical signs of affection (hugs, kisses, cuddles)
- Smiles, thumbs-up, high fives, winks
- Playful attention (piggyback rides, sharing jokes)
- Relaxed time together (talking, playing, doing an activity together)
- Specific, sincere praise and recognition:
  - "That sure was grown up (or mature) of you when … "
  - "That was great the way you … "
  - "I'm so proud of how you … "
  - "That was so helpful when you … Thank you!"
  - "I can really tell you worked hard on … "
  - "Let's make a copy of this for Grandma … "
  - "Let's hang this up somewhere special … "
  - "Great job on how you … "
  - "I can't wait to tell Dad how you … "
  - "I knew you could do it!"
  - "You are making such great progress. I can tell you've really been practicing."
- Most all children and teens (particularly those with ADHD) need additional incentives. Any privileges, items, and activities your child finds of value and would be motivated to work toward earning could be used as rewards. It is recommended to create a reward menu together with your child and be sure to change that menu as often as necessary to maintain your child's interest.

Activity Rewards and Privileges

- Playing a special indoor or outdoor game
- An outing to a park, restaurant, zoo, arcade, or a beach or camping trip, for example
- Extended bedtime
- Earning extra time (for watching TV, Internet access, use of electronic device, playing games, riding bikes, listening to music, talking on the phone)
- Special time alone with a parent (out for breakfast, shopping, ice cream, ball game, building something)
- Freedom from chore(s)

- Craft project
- Drawing or painting
- Selecting a meal or restaurant for lunch or dinner
- Baking cupcakes, cookies, or another treat
- Extra story or reading time with a parent
- Going to the theater, a sporting event, or another special outing
- Extended curfew
- Participating in a school activity that costs money, such as a dance or ski trip
- Participating in sports activity or lessons of choice (for example, skating, bowling, martial arts, tennis)
- Going shopping
- Gym membership
- Driving privileges (the parent drives to a place of the child's choice or gives the car keys to a teen with a driver's license)
- Playing musical instruments
- Gymnastics or dance
- Club participation
- Going to hair or nail salon
- Going to a movie or watching one at home
- Playing computer, video, or other electronic games
- Spending time with a special person (grandparent or a favorite aunt or uncle, for instance)
- Staying overnight at a friend or relative's house
- Inviting a friend over to play, stay for lunch or dinner, sleep over, or come with on a family outing

Note: Some of these activities can also be considered social reinforcers.

Material Rewards

- Toys
- Arts or crafts supplies
- Collectibles
- Snacks
- Books or magazines
- Games
- Music purchases
- DVDs
- Clothing or accessories
- Puzzles
- Pets
- Tickets to movies or events
- Sports equipment

- Gift cards or certificates
- Wanted items for the child's room
- Money
- Electronics (various types)
- Any purchase of choice (within price range).

Note: Some reinforcers may be used for daily rewards or privileges, such as needing to earn their screen time (TV, Internet access); some for weekly rewards (a movie rental or special activity on the weekend); others rewards can be used for a privilege or item the child is working toward earning or saving up to purchase.

Rewards for School

The following lists possible rewards that may be used with classroom (group) and individual behavior management programs. *See Lists 2.8 and 2.9* and the appendix for information and examples of how to implement such behavioral programs and techniques with students.

For any social activity or material reward to be effective in motivating a child, it must have meaning and value to that student. A menu can be created with student input of possible rewards for the whole class or individual students. When you use incentive programs, you will need to discover through an inventory that students fill out or questioning verbally to determine what students find motivating. Students with ADHD typically need to change the rewards frequently (or be provided a menu of different reward options to choose from) in order to maintain interest.

Social Rewards

- Specific praise from teacher, such as "You are really improving." "I see the effort you put into that project. Excellent work!"
- Nonverbal positive teacher attention (smiles, thumbs up, gentle pat on back, shaking the student's hand)
- Written praise and acknowledgment (notes written on student's papers, sticky note with positive comments placed on student's desk, and notes mailed or texted to student)
- Positive phone calls or electronic messages directly to student
- Positive notes, e-mail, phone calls, or electronic messages to parents
- Positive attention and recognition from classmates (compliments, applause, silent cheering, high fives, fist bumps)
- A certificate given to a student recognizing his or her accomplishment or success
- Earning a class privilege of social status, such as being a team captain or class messenger
- Recognition at awards assemblies
- Name being called on the school intercom or at a school assembly recognizing something positive the student accomplished
- Posting the student's name and photo on a wall or bulletin board
- Recognition of the student in the school's newsletters or websites
- Being named "Star of the Day" or "Student of the Week"

- Choice of seating for the period, day, or week
- An object symbolizing success, such as a trophy or stuffed animal, placed on student's desk for the day.

Note: Some of the activity rewards in the next section are also social reinforcers.

Activity Rewards and Privileges

- Playing a game, studying, or working on an activity with a friend
- First in line for dismissal at lunch, recess, or the end of the day
- Early dismissal of one to two minutes for lunch, recess, or passing to the next class
- Special activity: a field trip, party, assembly, movie, dance, or school performance
- Lunchtime activities or privileges: a choice of seating or eating in a special location or table, passing to go to the front of cafeteria line, extended lunch period, eating with principal or other staff member
- Lunch in the class with the teacher and other students who earn the privilege (usually biweekly or monthly); those students bring their own lunch, but the teacher supplies juice or a dessert, such as popsicles
- Music or a video played as well as a game or other fun activity when they finish eating
- Earning time in class to catch up on work with teacher or peer assistance if needed
- Extra time or access to the gym, library or media center, music room, or playground
- Responsibilities or privileges that are desirable: tutoring or mentoring a younger student, ball monitor, sharpening pencils, taking care of the class pet, assistant to the teacher or other staff member, operating audiovisual equipment, taking attendance
- Opportunities to access and use special material and tools such as art supplies, craft materials, the computer to make PowerPoint presentations or do an Internet search, use of other electronic equipment or certain sports equipment not generally available
- Selecting a book to be read to the class
- Special seat, chair, or desk for the day or choice of where to sit for the period or day
- Listening to music of choice
- Reading the morning announcements
- A special game of choice in class, at recess, or during PE
- An ice cream, popcorn, or pizza party for the class or group of students who have achieved a certain goal
- Getting awarded a "no homework" pass for the evening, a "good for removing two or three items from an assignment" coupon, "one late assignment accepted as on time," or "removing one bad grade from the daily recorded assignments" coupon
- Earned time for a physical break, such as running a few laps, dancing to a song, or playing an outdoor game
- Free or earned time (individual or class) for activities of choice such as games, listening to music, drawing, cartooning, yoga or dance, working on special projects, or accessing learning or interest centers
- Decorating a bulletin board or a corner of the room

- Sharing a joke in class
- Listening to an audio book or music with headphones
- Recording a story (just audio or audiovisual) for the class to listen to
- Time for free reading, including books of choice or magazines
- Work on school projects, such as painting a school mural or gardening
- Extra PE, music, art, or computer time
- Leading a class game
- Special parking spot for the day or week for students who drive to school
- Being allowed to help a staff member (secretary, custodian, librarian) for a certain period of time
- Permission to chew gum in class
- Teacher agrees to do something out of character and silly (dress up, tell a personal, funny story)
- Games played as a full class, in team competitions, in small groups, or with partners are among the very best classroom incentives. Game format for practicing and reinforcing academic skills are a great way to motivate students and make learning fun. Jeopardy, math card or dice games, and Whole Brain Teaching's Mind Soccer (www.wholebrainteaching.com) are great examples of possible games.

Material Rewards

- School supplies (special pencils, pens, erasers, folders)
- Stickers, stars, badges, and certificates
- Food (various treats—preferably healthy snacks)
- Cold drinks
- Magazines and books
- Class or school fake money used for purchases in the class or school store
- Tickets, points, or other tokens redeemable at auctions or lotteries or in class or school stores
- Items of choice from a treasure chest (small toys, school supplies, trinkets)
- Free tickets for school dances, concerts, plays, and sporting events
- Coupons from businesses in the community for discounts toward purchases or free items

Level Systems for Activity Reward Time

Some classrooms (usually special education classes) find a level system effective.

- Each student in the class earns points for specified behaviors throughout the day, for example, in proper location, on task, respect for property, appropriate language and verbal interactions, ignores inappropriate behaviors of classmates, and appropriate physical interactions.
- Depending on the number of points earned, the student has access to different levels of rewards at the end of the day (or at the end of the week).

- For example, earning 85 percent or higher of the possible points would enable that student access to the highest level of choices. During activity time, these students would have the choice of most desirable activities, materials, places to sit or play, and other privileges.
- Students earning lower percentages of possible points also have reinforcing activity time, but their choices are more limited.

2.8 Class (Group) Behavior Management Systems

Effective behavior management involves systems and methods in place to motivate students to comply with rules and behavioral expectations. There are many approaches for doing so. Some use strictly a positive reinforcement system. Other systems are based primarily on rewarding appropriate behavior but also incorporate some type of penalty (response cost) for targeted misbehaviors. This list shares examples of both kinds of group incentive systems.

Teachers typically need to change their systems from time to time when effectiveness wears off or at least tweak the system and add new incentives to keep students motivated. It is helpful to have a toolbox of different methods to experiment with that will match teachers' comfort level. Any system implemented needs to be one that teachers find easy to use and manage. The better the whole-class incentive system works, the less teachers will find they need to devise individualized behavior programs for students with ADHD and others with behavioral challenges.

Positive-Only Group Reinforcement Systems

Praise and Positive Attention

- Students are encouraged and cued by the teacher to praise themselves with a pat on the back, stand up and take a bow, or other means.
- Most effective is when positive attention and recognition is given by peers to each other, such as when prompted by the teacher to have the student being recognized get high fives or fist bumps from classmates or having the class give the student a silent cheer or round of applause (clapping index fingers together in a circular motion).

Table or Team Points

- Points are given for specific behaviors, for example, cooperation and teamwork, staying on task, all assignments turned in, area cleaned up, or transitioning by the allotted time. Table points may be used noncompetitively or competitively. For the noncompetitive method, tables or teams are rewarded whenever that table or team reaches a goal, such as having earned a certain number of points or completing their group behavior chart. They don't compete against other tables or teams.
- The more commonly used technique is competitive. Points are awarded to tables or teams demonstrating the target behaviors. "Table 4, good job of cooperating and helping your teammates. You just earned a point." At the end of the day or week, the table or team with the most points earns the reward or privilege (or the top two tables win the reward).

Daily or Weekly Target Goals

- Another strategy that many teachers use effectively is to identify a behavior in class that is in need of improvement (out of seat without permission, talking or calling out without raising hand, not turning in homework). The one behavior that is selected is the target for improvement by the whole class. That behavior is monitored daily and calculated precisely. If they achieve the goal, there is a reward for the class of some type. For example, the goal may be fewer than ten occasions of anyone blurting out or talking without permission during math class, or 90 percent of homework turned in on time for the week, or smooth morning routine with everyone in seat and prepared by the time bell rings four out of five days. Whatever the goal is, it should be a clear but reasonable goal that can be achieved if students are motivated to do their best to comply. It should target an existing problematic behavior to focus on improving (most likely not eliminating).

Tokens in a Jar

- Teachers (usually in primary grade classrooms) catch students engaged in appropriate behaviors. They call attention to the positive behavior (of an individual student, group of students, or something the whole class did well). Then, the teacher reinforces the positive behavior by putting a marble (or other kind of object) in a jar. When the jar is filled, the whole class earns a reward (for example, a popcorn party). *Note:* Some teachers use a scoop of uncooked kernels of popcorn that are later popped or something similar. This is a particularly effective technique for rewarding quick and smooth transitions.

Chart Moves

- A particular goal (or two) is set, such as all students are in their seats with materials ready by the morning bell; no observed incidents of a particular problematic behavior occurring in a certain time frame (such as in the morning, after lunch). Each time the class meets that goal, a move is made on the chart such as connecting to the next dot (on a dot-to-dot chart) or moving a Velcroed object to the next space on the wall chart). See "Race to the Goal" in the appendix (A-10).

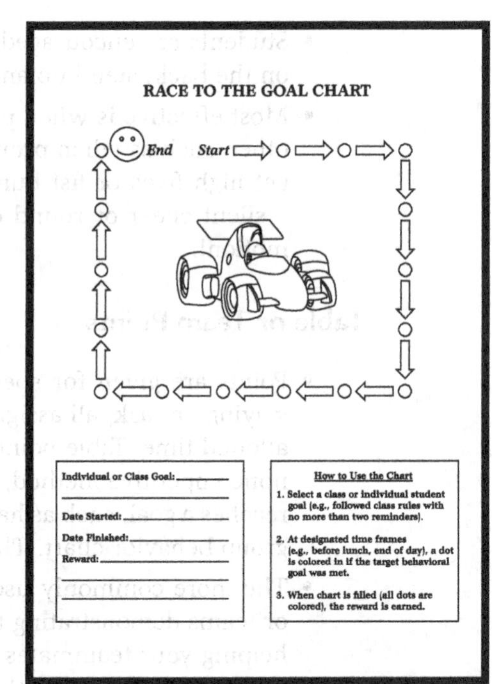

Raffles or Lotteries

- Students earn tickets of some kind (tickets, cooperation cards) for positive behaviors. When passed out to individual students, they are accompanied with praise for the specific behavior being rewarded.
- Students write their names on the back of the card or tear off the corresponding number if a raffle ticket, which is placed in the container for a drawing.
- Those students whose cards or tickets are drawn during the raffle are provided with the reward.

Individual Stamp Cards

- Each student has an index card attached to his or her desk.
- The teacher awards a stamp (as a point) on the card for rewarding cooperative, respectful, on-task behavior. This can be for individual behavior and whole-class positive behaviors.
- Students at the end of the week who have acquired a designated number of stamps receive the reward, which is typically participation in a desired activity.
- See this method's variation shared by Angela Watson with her use of a bead system instead of a stamp card. Each student has a pipe cleaner attached to the desk, and the tokens she passes out to students are beads to place on the pipe cleaner. When beads are counted on Fridays, the reward of best choices of activities or centers goes to those students with the most beads, and students with less beads have more restricted choices. See http://thecornerstoneforteachers.com/free-resources/behavior-management/bead-system.

Unsolicited Compliment Rewards

- With this system, any time the class receives an unsolicited compliment, those compliments are tallied up and a certain number of tallies earns the class a reward. This is done in many different ways. It typically involves use of a chart of some type that is filled in (for example, a sticker on the chart, a box to color in, a marker to move, a link on a chain) for every compliment the class receives that comes without being solicited. These compliments may come from a visitor, administrator, or anyone who enters the room and praises the class. They can also come from any positive report from a substitute teacher or other staff member for in-class or out-of-class behavior.
- Another variation is establishing a system in which students are encouraged to be looking for things they appreciate about their classmates. When they observe something they want to positively acknowledge, thank, recognize, or praise in a peer, they fill out a premade form (of which the teacher has a large supply). It can be something simple like: "I really appreciate the way you ... " or "I thought it was so nice when you . . . ."
- First, model and talk about what kinds of things should be written on positive notes. For example, "I thought it was so nice when you helped Amanda clean up her work area." The class can decide on a means of distributing these forms and tallying up the number given during the day or week.
- Again, the class can be working for a target number of positive notes written and received that when reached will earn the whole class a reward. In the process, it also builds relationships and a positive climate in the classroom.

Note: If using a system like this, it is critical that *all* students receive positive comments from peers, not just more popular classmates. It is very important to be inclusive of everyone.

Lottery Grid and Class Bingo Board

- Draw a large grid on a board with letters going across on one axis and numbers on the other. On popsicle sticks write coordinates for all of the grid spaces (A1, B2, etc.). Students are rewarded for good behavior at the teacher's discretion by getting to pull a stick from a container without seeing the coordinates written on it. Then, that place on the grid is marked. When a row is completed (as in Bingo) horizontally, vertically, or diagonally, the class earns a reward. This can also be done using a one hundred chart, with numbers one to one hundred on individual cards or sticks to be drawn.

- Another variation is for the teacher to make tally marks on the board for reinforcing positive behaviors. For every *x* number of tally marks earned by the class, a number stick is drawn and that space is colored in or covered on the Bingo board or lottery grid.

Mystery Motivator

- There are various means of motivating students through their love of a mystery or surprise. One example is to have a secret reward of some kind written on a slip of paper and sealed in a "mystery" envelope. When students meet a certain behavioral goal to a criterion level, such as 90 percent homework turned in during the week, they earn the reward designated in the mystery envelope.
- Another example is to have six mystery envelopes with slips of paper inside. When the class earns a certain number of points or reaches a certain goal, someone is called up to roll a dice. Whichever number comes up is the number on the envelope to be opened that identifies the class reward.

Note: There are several variations of all of these techniques. A good source of seeing how different teachers have adapted the methods can be found at www.pinterest.com/sandrarief/class-behavior-management/.

Reinforcement Systems That Also May Involve Fines or Deductions

Token Economy System

- Students have the chance to earn tokens of some kind, such as points, tickets, poker chips, or class money. These tokens are redeemable at a class store, auction, or raffle at a later time.
- A menu of rewards is developed with corresponding price values attached. Rewards may include small school supplies, other items for students at that grade level such as free homework assignment coupons, and various privileges. Students can spend their earned tokens, points, or money at designated times during class auctions or shopping at the class store. See *List 2.7* for sample rewards and "Coupon for One Free Homework Assignment" in the appendix for sample homework coupons.

COUPON FOR ONE FREE HOMEWORK ASSIGNMENT

____
STUDENT NAME

has been awarded with a coupon for one free homework assignment for__________.

This student can use this coupon for any one homework assignment.

____
DATE

Great job!

____
TEACHER

- Token economy systems can be used strictly for positive reinforcement (earning tokens), but they can also include being penalized or fined as well. For example, with systems in which students earn money, they can also be deducted. Students would earn a certain amount for everyday expected behaviors (attendance, being to class on time, turning in homework). They may also be fined. At the end of the week or time frame, whatever is the amount of currency they banked is spent at a class store.

Note: Teachers must award generously and frequently for positive behaviors so that students with ADHD are not overly fined, which would result in frustration and loss of motivation.

Group Response Cost

- Response cost techniques are another means of improving and shaping behavior. They work differently than the described positive reinforcement systems. Instead of giving tokens or points for demonstrating the appropriate behavior, students work to keep the tokens or points that they are given up front, and which they can lose for specified misbehaviors.
- There are many variations of response cost systems. Some are shared here for the whole class; others can be implemented as individualized interventions and will be discussed in *List 2.9*. The key is that students are working to keep what they have already been given, which can be a bigger motivator for many children. For example, at the beginning of the day or week, the teacher may automatically give *x* number of minutes free time or special activity time to the class to be used at the end of the day or week. Specific misbehaviors that occur during the day will result in a one-minute (or thirty-second) loss of time from the free minutes given. The number of remaining minutes is awarded at the end of the day or week. The teacher has the discretion to add bonus minutes during the day for good behavior to increase the motivation. *Note:* It is very important to provide just the amount of reward time earned and not go over or under.
- Another example is for the teacher to list numbers, for example, ten to one, on the board, and for every occurrence of the target misbehavior the class is working to improve (for example, out of seat without permission), a number is erased—beginning with ten, then nine, and so forth. If they still have any remaining numbers at the end of class period or day, the class earns a privilege; if they do lose them all, there is a loss of privilege or other consequence.
- See the "Response Cost Chart" in the appendix and *Lists 2.9 and 2.13* for more on response cost strategies.

Good Behavior Game (GBG)

- This class game is a research-validated approach for decreasing disruptive behaviors in the classroom. Basically, the steps involve the following:
  - The class is divided into two or three heterogeneous teams, with team numbers listed on the board. Students are taught clearly that when the good behavior game (GBG) is played, the teacher will be closely monitoring for disruptive behavior and defines those specific behaviors (generally out of seat without permission, talking without permission).

- During game time, a timer is set and any incident of disruptive behavior by any student in the team that occurs during that time period results in a check mark recorded under the team name. At the end of the game's time frame, any team with under *x* number of check marks (typically four or fewer) earns a reward.
- Initially the game is played for periods of ten minutes a few times a week and rewards are tangible and immediate. Gradually the time frame is extended, and reward times are provided at the end of the day or week.
- It is recommended to schedule the GBG for no more than a total of one to two hours during the day.
- The PAX Good Behavior Game is included in the US National Registry of Evidence-Based Programs and Practices (www.nrepp.samhsa.gov). Students differentiate between PAX (positive behaviors) and "spleems" (unwanted behaviors). Rewards earned by teams at the end of game time with three or fewer spleems are brief, fun activities such as a minute of dancing around or throwing wadded up paper balls at each other.

For more information, see Sources and Resources below under the category of Good Behavior Game.

Electronic Feedback Point System—Class Dojo

- Class Dojo (www.classdojo.com) is a popular free app for the classroom. The program enables teachers to track behavior and provide immediate reinforcement (feedback points) to individual students, groups, or the whole class electronically in real time. This is done with one click via the teacher's smartphone, iPad, laptop, or other device. Class Dojo can run on an interactive whiteboard, a computer connected to a projector, or even just a smartphone, tablet, or other device with Internet connection. The teacher can provide on-the-spot positive points for these six behaviors: participating, on task, helping others, persistence, teamwork, working hard. Feedback points can also be provided for these negative behaviors: bullying, off task, disrespect, no homework, talking out of turn, and unprepared.
- Students are each assigned or choose avatars as the visual for their name and displayed on the interactive whiteboard. When the button for the positive or negative behavior is clicked on by the student's name, the plus or minus point and the behavior for which the point was earned is projected and entered next to the student's avatar, along with a beep sound. So, students receive instant auditory and visual feedback, along with reinforcement.
- Many teachers find this to be an effective behavior management system. It has, however, raised controversy and concerns because of the public nature—for example, that all students' scores are displayed for everyone to see.

Scoreboards, Positive or Negative Points

- Make a T-chart on the board labeled in the two columns with something positive and negative. For example, smiley face–frowny face, Way to Go!–Oops! or On Target–Off Target.
- The teacher places tally marks or points in each column based on the students' appropriate and inappropriate behavior. Points or tallies can be given throughout a class period, the whole day, or certain time frames, such as before recess or after

lunch until dismissal. Positive and negative points are recorded at the teacher's discretion.

- If there are more points in the positive column by the end of the time frame, the class earns a small reward (such as a short class game, minutes toward free time, or slight reduction in homework assigned). If there are more points in the negative column, either a small, minor consequence is provided or simply the reward is not earned.
- Whole Brain Teaching's Scoreboard method (www.wholebrainteaching.com) uses this technique in a very well-designed, motivating way that is simple, flexible, entertaining, and involves different levels used throughout the course of the school year. Some of the highlights of the Whole Brain Teaching (WBT) Scoreboard system:
  - A scoreboard T-chart with smiley and frowny faces for positive and negative behaviors. Points or tallies are given in each column for one of the class rules—"keeping the scorekeeper (teacher) happy."
  - According to the Whole Brain Teaching method, there should never be more than three points difference in the columns at all times in order to maintain students' motivation. See the WBT website (www.wholebrainteaching.com/) and Biffle (2013) for more information on how this system is implemented with added levels of motivation throughout the year.
- Another variation of this method is teacher-student points. It works the same way with the teacher putting tally marks in the student column when they are on task and following rules. When off task, loud, or not following directions, tally marks are placed in the teacher column. At the end of the day, whichever side has more points earns five minutes. If students win, they get to put the five minutes toward Friday afternoon's choice time. If the teacher has more points, she keeps the five minutes for more instructional time. See Downeast Teach Blogspot (2013) in the "Sources and Resources" section for more on this technique.

What to Do about Students Whose Behavior Interferes with Group Success on Class Incentive Systems

- When teachers implement class incentive systems they need to know how to address individual students whose behaviors tend to ruin it for the group. For example, a team with a student who has ADHD may be less likely to want that student in their group because the student's ADHD-related behaviors interfere with the group's receiving rewards.
- One way to help in this regard is to provide the opportunity for individual students to be a class hero. Individual students can earn the class the reward of group points or moves on the class chart by meeting their own particular goals. So, an ADHD child's efforts and success in his or her own (individual) behavior program contributes to the advancement of the whole class in meeting that goal and receiving a reward.
- Sometimes it may be necessary to group a student with just one partner rather than a few classmates.
- Another strategy is to group students together who have an "I don't care about this" attitude and who tend to be rebellious and may deliberately sabotage the system

for others. Their behaviors can't hurt the rest of the class's efforts, just their own. See Whole Brain Teaching's Level 5 of the Scoreboard method regarding this strategy.

Points to Keep in Mind

- The best incentives in a classroom are those involving activity reinforcers. Students are motivated throughout the day to earn time to participate in rewarding activities.
- Students with ADHD need the opportunity to earn the reward of participation more frequently than most classmates. They often are penalized for their difficulties with work production, having to miss rewarding activities in order to complete unfinished assignments.
- When this is the case, more support and accommodations may be needed to help ADHD students get caught up with their work.

Sources and Resources

Information about the Good Behavior Game

Blueprints Programs (www.blueprintsprograms.com)

Evidence-Based Programs (http://evidencebasedprograms.org/1366.2/good-behavior-game)

Intervention Central (www.interventioncentral.org/behavioral-interventions/schoolwide-classroommgmt/good-behavior-game)

Katz, Mark. (2004). Promising practices: The good behavior game. *Attention Magazine, 11*(2), 12–13.

The Pax Good Behavior Game (http://goodbehaviorgame.org/)

Information about the Scoreboard, Teacher Point, and Student Point Methods

Biffle, Chris. (2013). *Whole brain teaching for challenging kids.* San Bernardino, CA: Whole Brain Teaching.

Downeast Teach Blogspot. (2013, Feb. 21). The simplest classroom management system ever. Retrieved from http://downeastteach.blogspot.com/2013_02_01_archive.html

Electronic Feedback Points

Class Dojo (www.classdojo.com)

See more behavioral resources appropriate for the classroom in *List 7.12*.

2.9 Individualized Behavior Supports and Interventions

Students with ADHD require far closer monitoring, a higher rate and frequency of feedback, and more powerful incentives to modify their behavior than most children need. So, in addition to classroom (group) behavior management approaches and incentive systems (*List 2.8*), children with ADHD generally need teachers and parents to implement individualized behavioral interventions such as described in the following sections.

Goal Sheets

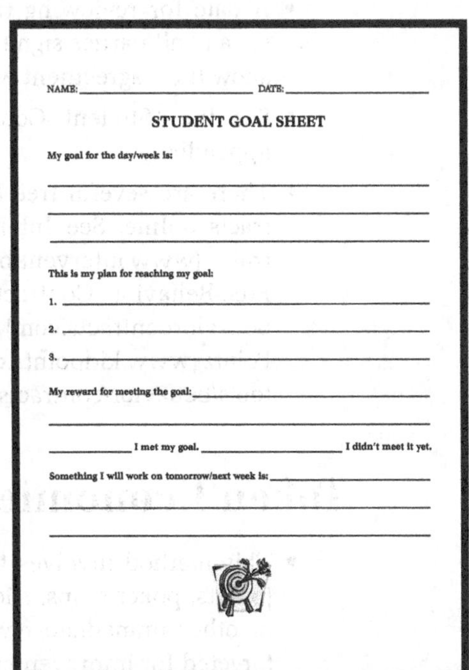
NAME: ______________ DATE: ______________

STUDENT GOAL SHEET

My goal for the day/week is:

____

This is my plan for reaching my goal:

1. ______________
2. ______________
3. ______________

My reward for meeting the goal: ______________

______ I met my goal. ______ I didn't meet it yet.

Something I will work on tomorrow/next week is: ______________

- The child or teen identifies one goal to work on for the day or week, such as "organize my desk or locker," "no fights," "get caught up with my incomplete math assignments."
- The goal sheet includes the student's name, date, and a single goal, such as "My goal that I will work on is ______________."
- The student also plans the specific steps he or she will take to reach the goal. For example, "Some steps I will take to reach my goal are ______________" or "This is my plan for reaching my goal ______________."
- The teacher, other adult, or older peer mentor meets briefly in the morning with the student to discuss the goal and offer encouragement. At the end of the day, they meet again and reward success.
- Some goal sheets may also include a statement of what the adult or peer buddy will do to support the student in achieving the goal.
- The goal sheet is signed by the student and sometimes the adult or older peer mentor.

See the "Student Goal Sheet" in the appendix.

Contingency Contracts

- This is a written agreement among the teacher, student, and parent (or other parties). The contract includes a clear description of the behavior(s) that the student agrees to perform, for example, "I, ______________, agree to do the following: ______________." The contract specifies what the reward will be if the student fulfills his or her end of the agreement successfully and the date the contract ends.

- Some contracts include the criteria for successful performance, such as "at least *x* days a week" or with "*x* percent accuracy." Contracts may also include a penalty clause that indicates not only the reward but also what the consequences will be for failing to meet the terms of the agreement.
- A date for reviewing the contract is set and all parties sign the contract to show their agreement with the terms.
- See the "Student Contract" in the appendix.
- There are several free behavior contracts online. See Intervention Central (www.interventioncentral.org), Free-Behavior Contracts (www.freebehaviorcontracts.com), and Kid Pointz (www.kidpointz.com/behavior-tools/behavior-contracts).

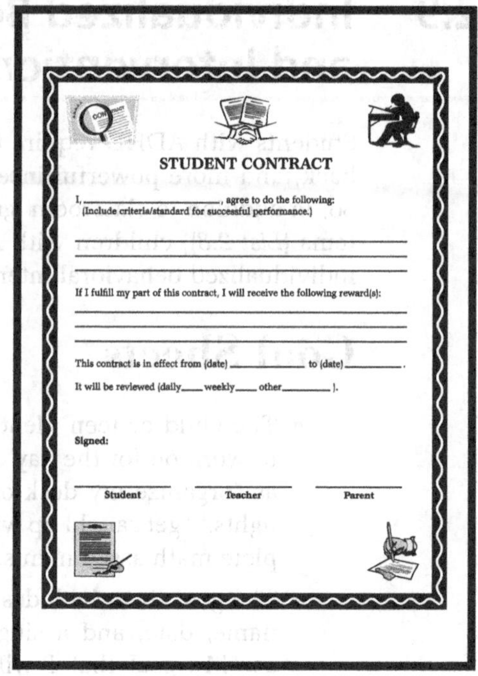

STUDENT CONTRACT

I, ________________, agree to do the following:
(Include criteria/standard for successful performance.)

____

If I fulfill my part of this contract, I will receive the following reward(s):

____

This contract is in effect from (date) __________ to (date) __________.

It will be reviewed (daily____ weekly____ other________).

Signed:

Student　　Teacher　　Parent

Token Economies and Token Programs

- This method involves the child or teen being able to earn tokens of some kind (points, poker chips, stickers on a chart, marbles in a jar, classroom "fake" money, or other immediate reward) for demonstrating positive behaviors that are being targeted for improvement. These tokens are later cashed in for rewards selected by the child.
- Various reward options are assigned a value and are purchased with the tokens. The greater the number of tokens (which can be saved and accumulated), the bigger and more valuable rewards that can be obtained. See *List 2.7* for reward suggestions.
- Class Dojo (www.classdojo.com), described in *List 2.8*, is a very motivating, free program that teachers are finding effective in managing student behavior by awarding points for target behaviors to individual students with a click of a smartphone, laptop, or tablet. These electronic points provide instant feedback.

Note: Token programs can be positive only—with the child only earning tokens, but not losing them. Token economies more typically involve both earning and losing points or tokens (response cost), which is described under "response costs" as well as in List 2.8.

Daily Report Cards

- Sometimes called daily behavior forms or reports, home-school notes, or other similar names, use of a daily report card (DRC) is a research-validated intervention for children and teens with ADHD.
- DRCs are excellent tools for tracking school performance and motivating a student to improve specific behaviors that are interfering with his or her success. They are

highly effective for communicating between home and school and monitoring a child's daily performance.

- DRCs can be powerful motivators for students when parents and teachers are willing and able to consistently follow through with positive reinforcement for the child's successful performance on the DRC goals. Any means to forge a partnership between home and school and work together on improving specific behavioral goals is very beneficial for students with ADHD.
- Basically, DRCs involve selecting and clearly defining one or a few target behaviors or goals to be the focus for improvement. The teacher is responsible for observing and rating daily how the child performed on each target behavior and sending home the DRC at the end of the day.
- Parents are responsible for asking to see the DRC every day and reinforcing school behavior and performance at home. "Good days" in school (as indicated by meeting the criteria of the DRC) earn the child designated rewards or privileges at home that evening. A good week (for example, at least three out of five good days initially and then four out of five days) may also earn the child or teen extra privileges on the weekend.
- Using this system, parents will provide the consequences at home based on the student's school performance as indicated on the DRC. Rewards at home are provided on days the DRC goal was met, such as TV or other screen time, a favorite snack, or other privilege. A negative consequence (loss of screen time or phone privileges, no dessert or other mild punishment) may be provided on days the child was not successful. It is important that any reward that is reserved for successful days at school be provided only on the days the child earned it.
- It is the child or teen's responsibility to bring the DRC home every day after school. To increase this likelihood, parents may want to provide a mild punishment for not doing so.
- Another option for implementing this system is to tie it to a token economy. Russell Barkley (1996) describes how this would work. Parents give or deduct tokens such as poker chips based on the ratings on the daily report. For example, if the DRC rating is on a scale of one to five, every rating of one (the highest score) earns the child five poker chips, a rating of two earns three chips, and a three rating earns the child just one chip. Then the child loses chips for ratings of poor and very poor performance. For example, there would be a five-chip loss for each rating of a five on the DRC.
- DRCs can involve school rewards as well as home rewards. For example, a small school reward such as a sticker or computer time can be given to the child at school on a good day. For a good week, the student can earn a special reward at school on Fridays.
- If the DRC is likely to get lost coming to and from school daily, then perhaps just a card that simply indicates "yes-no" or "met goal-didn't meet goal" can be sent home or a daily e-mail, text, or phone message for parent notification, and the actual DRC remains at school.
- If the family is not able to follow through with monitoring and reinforcement on a consistent and daily basis, it is best to do so at school. In this case, the school needs to be responsible for providing the daily reward when the student was successful, but parents should be asked to reward the child on the weekend if it was a good week. This is manageable in most all homes.

Creating a Daily Report Card

- There are many variations of DRCs. Some forms or charts are given daily, others are rated daily but have room to record for each day of the week. See samples of DRCs in the appendix (charts A-2 through A-8). DRCs involve the following components:
  - Selecting the few goals to be achieved and then defining those goals precisely. See *List 2.5* for numerous options of target goals.
  - Collecting data on how frequently the selected behaviors occur to determine a baseline.
  - Setting criteria for success that is reasonable and achievable (for example, 25 percent improvement from the current performance) and gradually raising the criteria.
- A chart is made with time frames broken down by periods of the day, subject areas, or whatever other intervals fit the student's daily schedule and are reasonable for the teacher to monitor consistently.
- Along the other axis of the chart are the designated target behaviors—for example, "has all necessary materials," "on task; working productively," "cooperating with classmates," "following directions," or others as in *List 2.5*.
- Be clear when defining with the child the target behaviors and what you will be evaluating. For example, "on task" might be defined as "no more than *x* number of warnings or redirections during that time interval," or "worked all or most of the time frame without bothering others," or "completed at least 80 percent of the assignment."
- At the end of each time frame, the teacher marks a simple yes-no, plus-minus sign, thumbs up–thumbs down sign, smiley-frowny face, or other such symbol, or circles the number of points (0, 1, 2, 3) earned according to the specific criteria.
- The student's number of points (or yeses, smiley faces) are tallied at the end of the day to determine the net number earned that day and the student's overall performance. (Did the student meet the criteria for success?)
- Rewards are provided accordingly (at home, school, or both) based on the child's performance on the DRC.
- There are different options for rewarding students with a DRC. One option is provision of the reward contingent on the student successfully achieving a goal for the day or week, such as having earned *x* number of points or smiley faces or a percentage (such as at least 70 percent) of the points possible. If tied to a token economy as previously described, each rating number would be rewarded at home in tokens given or deducted.
- Another option is to use a leveled provision of rewards for daily or weekly report cards. If the child earns, for example, 50 percent to 74 percent of the possible plus marks (or "yes" marks) he or she may choose one thing from the reward menu. For scores of 75 percent to 89 percent, it earns the child a choice of two things from the menu, and 90 percent to 100 percent of positive marks earns the child a choice of three things from the menu. See the website of the Center for Children & Families, University of Buffalo, State University of New York (http://wings.buffalo.edu/psychology/adhd) and their ADHD resources (http://ccf.buffalo.edu/resources_downloads.php). There is excellent information that is provided there on setting up, implementing, and troubleshooting DRCs for parents and teachers.

- See Jim Wright's free guide and apps for creating behavior report cards at www.interventioncental.org.
- There are sample DRCs in the appendix (A2 through A8) for students of different ages. Some are geared for elementary and others for middle and high school students. All appendix materials are also available online. Some of the charts and DRCs are able to be customized before printing for use with individual children.

Check-In Check-Out

- Positive Behavioral Interventions and Supports (PBIS) uses a targeted behavioral intervention called "check-in check-out" (CICO). The program involves individual students in need of a daily point card to check in with a designated adult at the start of school day to retrieve their daily point card.
- The CICO form is like a DRC, with a few target behaviors listed on one axis of the form and the subjects or class periods throughout the day listed on the other axis. All students receive the same CICO form and behaviors being evaluated. These are the school rules or schoolwide behavioral expectations, for example, be safe (keep hands, feet, and objects to self), be respectful (use kind words and actions), be your personal best (follow directions, working in class).
- At the end of each time interval the teacher provides specific feedback and circles the number of points received for each of the behaviors (for example, 2 = excellent!, 1 = good, and 0 = not yet). The goal or criteria for success is also specified on the form, which is how many points or percentage of points received out of the total possible.
- Rewards are also provided for students achieving the goal (meeting the criteria for success).
- CICO is basically the same as using a DRC. What makes the CICO program unique is that it is a schoolwide intervention for all students in need of such a targeted intervention program. At the end of the school day, all students in the CICO program leave class a few minutes early to go to the designated adult in the school with their CICO forms for check-out. The adult reviews the CICO form with the student briefly, provides encouragement, and records the score. Then the report or other home report is completed and sent home for parent signature. The teachers receive data on their individual students' performance (in a graph form). Signed forms are to be returned to the CICO staff member the next day on checking in.
- There are several examples of CICO forms used in PBIS schools and can be found at www.pbis.org and PBIS state network websites.

Other Behavior Charts and Monitoring Forms

- There are many other behavioral forms and charts that can be used for school and home behaviors. Behavior charts for preschool and elementary age children may include sticker charts or ones in which the child gets to color a square or advance forward with a move on the chart when earned. There are also dot-to-dot charts, such as the example in the appendix ("Connect the Dots Chart"), and a variety of others.

- There are a wealth of free behavioral charts online that can be used by parents and teachers, for example, Chart Jungle (www.chartjungle.com), free printable behavior charts (www.freeprintablebehaviorcharts.com), and Kid Pointz (www.kidpointz.com).

Direct Behavior Ratings

- See www.directbehaviorratings.org from the University of Connecticut for excellent tools and information on using direct behavior ratings (DBRs) for home-school notes and DRCs, as a means of self-monitoring behavior, and providing information to communicate about a child's behavior.

With All Positive Incentive Programs

- Focus on improving no more than a few clearly defined target behaviors.
- Expectations for improvement must be realistic and achievable for the individual child.
- It is important that reinforcement is provided consistently and as promised. A well-coordinated system between home and school is the most effective.
- It is very important that the child experiences success when beginning these behavioral programs. It is much better to start off with very easy-to-accomplish goals than setting the bar too high and failing.
- It is recommended to design a reward menu together with the child and include some tangible items, activities, and special privileges for which the child would be motivated to work. A price or value is attached to each item on the menu. The more desirable and bigger the reward, the more tokens or points must be accumulated to earn it.
- In order to be an incentive for behavioral change, the reward choices must be powerful enough to motivate the child or teen with ADHD. Rewards are very individualized and must have meaning and value to the individual child or teen.
- Rewards can be very simple yet creative and motivating, such as adding pieces to a jigsaw puzzle. The reward for meeting the goal for the day or class period may be to add one or more pieces to the puzzle. When the whole puzzle is assembled, the bigger reward is earned.
- It helps to change the rewards the child may choose from in order to maintain interest in the program. Add new options to the reward menu from time to time (*List 2.7*).
- For school rewards, any daily reward when earned needs to be something simple and easy for a teacher to provide, such as a sticker or a few minutes time for a

preferred activity. For weekly rewards, typically the teacher, counselor, or other adult provides the reward for students who met their behavioral goal for the week on Fridays.

Other Individualized Behavioral Interventions

Response Costs

- Response costs refer to when there is a loss of points or privileges for specific misbehaviors. When implemented correctly and not overused, response costs are an effective disciplinary technique for children and teens with ADHD. However, some children are so emotionally reactive or fragile that any loss of earned points or tokens will result in a meltdown, in which case, it may not be the best approach.
- If a token program is being used that is a combination of positive reinforcement and response cost, there must be far more opportunities for points or tokens to be earned than taken away. Otherwise the child will likely become discouraged and give up. The response cost must never become punitive. The student should never lose all points for one infraction or ever be allowed to accumulate negative points.
- Response costs methods for the whole classroom are described in *List 2.8*. Some individualized approaches include techniques such as the one described on the "Response Cost Chart" in the appendix.
- With the response cost method, teachers can use points, plastic chips, or any other token. The child is given a certain number of tokens during a certain time frame or period, and it is very clear to the student which behavior(s) will result in loss of a token (talking back, being out of seat, hitting, for example). A token is removed or point deducted for each incident of the misbehavior. The student is rewarded if any tokens remain at the end of the time period. It is optional if a mild negative consequence is provided for losing all of the tokens.
- An example of an individualized response cost technique for a kindergarten or first grade child in circle time on the rug is to give the child three tokens of some kind at the start of circle time that he or she is trying to keep. Specific disruptive or inappropriate behaviors costs the child one of his or her tokens. If at the end of circle time there is still one remaining token, the child earns a small reward or privilege.
- See *List 2.13* for more on response cost strategies.

Self-Monitoring

Self-monitoring is an important self-regulation intervention. Using a self-monitoring strategy, the child or teen pays more attention to his or her own behavior. This self-awareness often leads to improved performance. DuPaul and Stoner (2003) share the benefits and cite evidence of self-monitoring as an effective self-management intervention for students with ADHD.

Rafferty (2010) and McConnell (1999) recommend the following steps when teaching students to self-monitor their own behavior in the classroom:

1. Identify the target behavior, which is generally worded in positive terms (such as "on task") rather than negative terms ("off task").
2. Define the target behavior, for example, worked without bothering others, on task, completed my assignment, in my seat.

3. Collect baseline data—typically through frequency count or time sampling procedures.
4. Determine if it is an appropriate behavior to remediate by teaching the student to self-monitor. Appropriate behaviors include those that occur frequently, the student is able to control and knows how to, yet has difficulty performing the behavior.
5. Schedule a conference with the student.
6. Design procedures and all materials. This may include a monitoring card broken down into intervals. When cued at intervals (by a timer that goes off, prerecorded beeps that are emitted at set intervals or intermittently, or through some silent but vibrating device that the student can feel, such as a wristwatch or cell phone) the timer goes off. These are the tools typically used for self-monitoring on-task behavior.
7. Teach the student how to use the self-monitoring procedures and provide opportunities to rehearse, practice, model, and review procedures taught.
8. Implement the self-monitoring strategy while providing the student with frequent encouragement and feedback.
9. Monitor student progress.
10. Follow up. Gradually fade use of the self-monitoring procedure as the student gains competence in demonstrating the target behavior and reinstitute if the behavior reoccurs.

Common Self-Monitoring Techniques

- The student is given a sheet or card for self-monitoring with spaces for recording if he or she was or was not performing the target behavior (for example, "I am on task") when signaled to do so.
- During an activity, such as working on a writing or math assignment, there is some auditory signal or cue that when it is heard, the student records either a plus sign or minus sign or other marks such as smiley-frowny, or yes-no. The tone can be a timer or some electronic device set to emit a tone either randomly or at set time intervals (every x number of minutes).

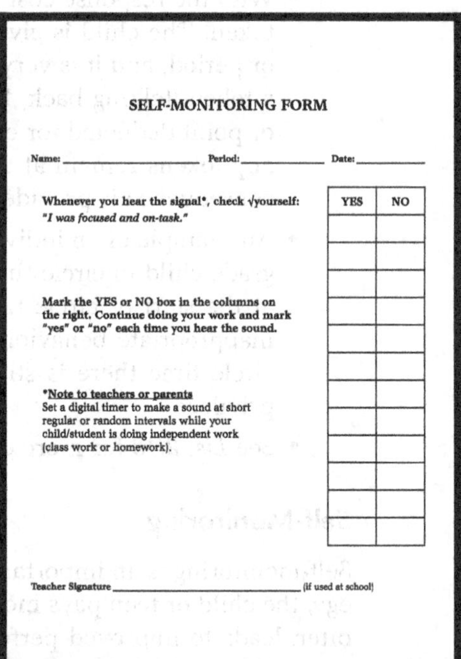

SELF-MONITORING FORM

Name: ____________ Period: ____________ Date: ____________

Whenever you hear the signal*, check √yourself: *"I was focused and on-task."*

YES	NO

Mark the YES or NO box in the columns on the right. Continue doing your work and mark "yes" or "no" each time you hear the sound.

*Note to teachers or parents
Set a digital timer to make a sound at short regular or random intervals while your child/student is doing independent work (class work or homework).

Teacher Signature ______________________ (if used at school)

- If an individual student is using this technique, and the beep or tone that goes off may be distracting to the rest of the class, headsets can be worn. If the whole class or a group is using this self-monitoring strategy, whenever the recorded sound or timer is heard, all students record on their individual sheets. See the "Self-Monitoring Form" for this technique in the appendix.
- Rather than auditory cues, other means can be used to signal when the student is to self-evaluate his or her performance. For example, the student can use a vibrating watch set at time intervals (see WatchMinder.com) or his or her cell phone set on vibration.

- Graphs are frequently used for self-monitoring behaviors such as the number of problems completed correctly, pages read per day, or other such target goals.
- Another self-monitoring technique involves the student evaluating his or her performance using a rating form (usually 0–4) for one or more behaviors (similar to a DRC). The teacher does the same. At the end of the day the teacher's rating is compared to the student's rating. This technique in and of itself is a helpful reality check for many students that may bring about improved performance. An incentive may be added by rewarding the student when his or her rating matches the teacher's or is very close. See the "Self-Monitoring Form" for this technique in the appendix.
- The Bull's Eye Game, which is part of Whole Brain Teaching, uses the following self-monitoring strategy, which Chris Biffle describes in his book (2013) and website (www.WholeBrainTeaching.com). The technique basically involves drawing a bull's-eye target with five rings numbered zero to five, with the smallest, inside circle numbered five. The teacher and student agree to a target behavior goal (such as following the teacher's directions or raising your hand for permission to speak). Then the behavioral goal is modeled and rehearsed. The teacher and student take turns role-modeling both the appropriate and inappropriate behavior until the behavioral goal is clearly understood. Then the game is explained: Several times a day the teacher and student will meet briefly to evaluate the student's performance. The teacher will write down the score (five being a perfect bull's-eye), but not show it to the student. The student then tells the teacher what he or she thinks was the teacher's written score and the reason why. If the teacher and student's scores match, the student earns two points; if off by only one, then one point is earned. If there was more than two points difference, the student doesn't earn any points. At the end of the day the student uses earned points to buy stickers; the size and quality of the sticker depends on the number of points earned.
- See samples of self-monitoring forms in the Appendix, and of the Student-Generated Progress Report, which also involves self-evaluation

Social Stories

- This is a common intervention for children with autism spectrum disorder but it is effective for those with ADHD as well. It basically involves using or creating a simple story that describes explicitly a situation or skill in simple words or pictures. It describes the steps of what the child will be expected to do or how to behave in a certain event, environment, or activity that is problematic for that student (eating in the cafeteria, walking in the hallways, or behaving appropriately in an assembly, for example). The social story is reviewed with the student before he or she performs that activity or enters into the environment or situation that is problematic.
- Carol Gray developed this technique. See her website (www.thegraycenter.org) and other resources on social stories in the "Sources and Resources" section of this list.

Functional Behavioral Assessments and Behavioral Intervention Plans (FBAs and BIPs)

- Functional behavioral assessment (FBA) is the process of determining why a student with a disability engages in challenging behavior, the conditions under which a behavior usually occurs, and the probable consequences that are maintaining the behavior. The FBA process uses a variety of techniques and strategies to identify the purposes or functions of the behavior.

- IEP teams use the information from the FBA to develop a BIP to directly address the problem behavior. Behavioral intervention plans (BIPs) are very explicit about how they will go about changing the target behavior. See *List 6.6* for more detailed information about FBAs and BIPs.

Points to Keep in Mind about Behavioral Supports and Interventions at School

- The information and recommended supports and interventions in this list are very useful for implementing in conjunction with IEPs, BIPs, and 504 or SST action plans (*Lists 6.2, 6.3, 6.4, 6.5, 6.6*).
- Any behavioral program implemented, including use of any behavior chart, monitoring form, and incentive system, will need to be reviewed on a frequent basis to evaluate its effectiveness in improving the target behaviors. The plans or programs will need to be tweaked or modified as needed.
- My other books and website (www.sandrarief.com) also have additional strategies and management tools (charts and forms) for individualized behavioral interventions and supports.
- See the "Sources and Resources" section for behavior support and intervention in *List 7.12*.

Sources and Resources

Barkley, Russell A. (1996). Using a daily school-behavior report card. *The ADHD Report*, *4*(6), 1–14.

Biffle, Chris. (2013). *Whole brain teaching for challenging kids*. San Bernardino, CA: Whole Brain Teaching.

Buck, G. H., Polloway, E. A., Kirkpatrick, M. A., Patton, J. R., et al. (2000). Developing behavioral intervention plans: A sequential approach. Retrieved from www.ldonline.org/article/6031.

Chafouleas, S. M., Riley-Tillman, T. C., & Christ, T. J. (2009). Direct behavior rating (DBR): An emerging method for assessing social behavior within a tiered intervention system. *Assessment for Effective Intervention*, *34*, 201–213.

Chafouleas, Sandra M., Riley-Tillman, Chris, T., & Jaffery, Rose. (2011). *DBR: An overview*. University of Connecticut. www.directbehaviorratings.org

Crone, D. A., Hawken, L. S., & Horner, R. H. (2010). *Responding to problem behavior in schools: The behavior education program* (2nd ed.). New York: Guilford Press.

DuPaul, George J., & Stoner, Gary. (2003). *ADHD in the schools* (2nd ed.). New York: Guilford Press.

Goldstein, Sam & Brooks, Robert (eds.), (2007). *Understanding and managing children's classroom behavior (2nd ed.)*. Hoboken, NJ: John Wiley & Sons. Note: Chapter 13 on "Strategies for Self-regulation" was authored by Sandra Rief.

Gray, C. (n.d.). Social stories. Retrieved from www.thegraycenter.org/social-stories

Grey Olltwit Educational Software. (n.d.). Social stories. www.greyolltwit.com/social-stories-2.html

Harris, K. R., Friedlander, B. D., Saddler, B., Frizzelle, R., & Graham, S. (2005). Self-monitoring of attention versus self-monitoring of academic performance: Effects among students with ADHD in the general education classroom. *The Journal of Special Education*, *39*, 145–156.

Horner, R., Sugai, G., Todd, A., Dickey, C. R., Anderson, C., & Scott, T. (n.d.). Check-in check-out: A targeted intervention. Retrieved from www.pbis.org/common/pbisresources/presentations/05BEPCICO.ppt#13

Intervention Central (www.interventioncentral.org) has many free resources including free apps for behavioral interventions, such as the behavior rating scales report card maker and the behavior intervention planner.

McConnell, Mary E. (1999). Self-monitoring, cueing, recording, and managing: Teaching students to manage their own behavior. *TEACHING Exceptional Children*, *33*(2), 14–21.

Rafferty, Lisa A. (2010). Step-by-step: Teaching students to self-monitor. *TEACHING Exceptional Children*, *43*(2), 50–58.

Rhode, G., Jenson, W. R., & Reavis, H. K. (1995). *The tough kid book*. Longmont, CO: Sopris West.

Rief at Pinterest. Several strategies for managing the behavior of children with ADHD can be found on Sandra's Pinterest boards under the categories of: ADD/ADHD for parents, ADD/ADHD for teachers, class and behavior management, self regulation, PBIS schoolwide positive behavior school, and parenting. See https://www.pinterest.com/sandrarief/

Wright, J. (n.d.). Classroom behavior report card resource book. Intervention Central (www.interventioncentral.org) and Jim Wright Online (www.jimwrightonline.com/pdfdocs/tbrc/tbrcmanual.pdf)

2.10 Preventing Behavior Problems During Transitions and "Challenging Times" of The School Day

Transitions take place frequently during a school day and account for a significant amount of instructional time wasted when students do not transition quickly. Effective classroom management requires routines and procedures that students learn and practice repeatedly for smooth transitions. Students with ADHD have the greatest behavioral difficulties in the classroom during transition times of the day and changes of activity, as well as settings outside the classroom that have less structure and supervision, such as the playground, cafeteria, hallways, and bathrooms.

Classroom Transitions

- Entering the classroom routines and procedures are essential for starting the school day or class period calmly and efficiently.
- Be prepared before school or the class period begins with the opening activity and prepared materials.
- Communicate clearly when activities will begin and when they will end and give specific instructions about how students are to switch to the next activity.
- Clearly teach, model, and have students repeatedly practice transition procedures. This includes activities such as quick and quiet movement from their desks to the carpet or other central area, putting away and taking out materials, lining up, and moving to the next learning station.
- Use signals for transitions to alert students that an activity is coming to an end and they need to finish whatever they are doing.
- Train students to respond to specific auditory signals (a musical sound or novel noise, a clap pattern, a word or phrase) and visual signals (hand signals, flashing lights, or a color cue). These signals get their attention and aid the transition during changes of activity.
- Get creative finding tools for the classroom that make unusual auditory signals—for example, timers and children's or pets' toys that make various noises, musical instruments, such as chimes, a harmonica, a triangle, or xylophone.
- Give students a signal a few minutes prior to the end of an activity so they are alerted to finish what they are working on and be prepared for directions for the next activity. You may also want to provide incremental warnings, such as a ten-minute, five-minute, and then a one-minute warning.
- Primary grade teachers typically use songs or chants for transitions such as cleaning up and lining up.
- When an activity ends, obtain all students' attention and give clear directions for transitioning to the new task, which includes materials needed for the next activity and where and how students will move if going to a different location. Then signal to begin.
- Closely monitor and provide feedback during and after transitions.
- Use songs that you have recorded and play them during certain procedures and transitions. You can use songs of various lengths (two or three minutes) depending on how long you expect it to take for students to perform that procedure or transition (line up

to leave room, come to circle on the rug, or get materials out for the next activity, for example). Use a specific song or part of a song during transitions to motivate and cue students to what they need to do and how much time they have to do it.

- Set the timer or play the song and reward students for a quick, quiet transition. If they are ready for the next activity when the timer goes off or song ends, praise and reinforce. This can be done for the whole class (with, say, marbles in a jar, moves on a class chart, or class points earned) or by rewarding successful tables or teams of students or individuals with tickets, points, or other tokens.
- Visual timers are helpful for alerting students as to how much time they have remaining. Some recommended visual timers are Time Timer (www.timetimer.com), Time Tracker (www.learningresources.com), and the many online timers that can be projected on the board with Internet connection, such as those from www.online-stopwatch.com.
- Provide direct teacher guidance and prompting to students who need more assistance.
- Reward smooth transitions. Many teachers use individual or table points to reward students or rows or table clusters of students who are ready for the next activity. The reward is typically something simple like being the first row or table to line up for recess, lunch, or dismissal.
- Be organized in advance with prepared materials for the next activity to prevent misbehavior.
- Prepare for changes in routine such as assemblies, substitute teachers, and field trips through discussion and modeling expectations. Avoid catching students off guard.
- Maintain a visual schedule that is reviewed and referred to frequently. Point out any changes in the schedule. Using a visual schedule, move a clothespin or other pointer to the next activity on the schedule.

Transition from Out-of-Classroom Activities to the Classroom

- It is helpful for teachers to meet their students after lunch, physical education, recess, and other activities outside of the classroom and walk them quietly back to the classroom.
- Provide and structure clear expectations for classroom entry procedures.
- Greet students at the door as they enter the classroom and direct to the assigned task to begin immediately.
- Set a goal for the class—for example, that everyone enters class after lunch or recess and is quiet and ready to work by a certain time. On successful days of meeting that goal, the class is rewarded with a token, class point, or chart move.

- Use relaxation and imagery activities or exercises for calming after recess, lunch, and physical education. Playing slow-tempo quiet music and assigning a silent, calm activity such as journaling or reading to students at these times is also effective.

- Establish clear procedures and expectations for when students are permitted to leave the classroom for any reason, such as to go to the bathroom, bring something to the office, or retrieve an item from their locker.

Out-of-Classroom School Settings

- It is important to have schoolwide rules and behavioral expectations for all out-of-classroom settings and activities, such as assemblies, passing in hallways, moving up and down stairwells, the cafeteria, playground, bus line, and office. All staff members should be calmly and consistently reinforcing schoolwide rules and procedures in every school environment through positive and negative consequences. This is very supportive of students with ADHD, who best learn and demonstrate appropriate behavior at the point of performance.
- Schoolwide incentives and reinforcers (for example, "caught being good tickets" redeemable for school prizes) are helpful in teaching and motivating appropriate behaviors outside of the classroom.
- Provide plenty of practice and rehearsing of behavioral expectations in all school environments. PBIS schools do an outstanding job of teaching and reinforcing behavioral expectations to all students in all school settings. See their website (www .pbis.org) for recommended schoolwide practices to prevent behavior problems (*List 2.17*).
- Special contracts or some type of individualized behavior plan with incentives for appropriate behavior may need to be arranged for the playground, cafeteria, bus, or other settings (*List 2.9*).
- Assign a buddy or peer helper to assist students who have self-management difficulties during these transitional periods and out-of-classroom times.
- For students who have behavioral difficulty on the bus, create an individual contract or include safe bus behavior as a target goal on a DRC (with the cooperative efforts of the school, bus driver, and parent) (*List 2.9*).
- If you are using a DRC or other monitoring form, a student who has had no reports of behavioral referrals in out-of-classroom settings for the day can get bonus points on his or her card. See examples of DRCs (A-2 through A-8) in the appendix.
- Provide more equipment and choices of activities during recess to avoid boredom and keep all students engaged. Some ideas are hula hoops, jump ropes, board games, and supervised games.
- Schools should identify and positively target those students in need of extra support, assistance, and careful monitoring outside of the classroom, such as walking with the student during passing periods.
- Increase supervision in all environments outside of the classroom: the playground, cafeteria, bathrooms, hallways, and stairwells during passing periods, lunch, recess, and school arrival and dismissal. For example, station teachers at the end of hallways between periods.
- Consider allowing certain students to transition a minute or so before or after the rest of the group or some alternate time.
- It is helpful to have organized clubs and choices for students before and after school and during the break before and after lunch.
- For students who don't return to class promptly, use of a timer (beat the clock) with incentives for doing so may help.

- One of the biggest transitions students face is the move from one grade level to the next, particularly the change from elementary to middle school and middle school to high school. It is very helpful to prepare students, especially those with ADHD, by visiting the new school, meeting with counselors and teachers, practicing the locker combination, receiving the schedule of classes in advance, and practicing the walk from class to class.

2.11 Common Triggers to Misbehavior

Many behavioral problems can be prevented or significantly reduced by anticipating the triggers (also known as *antecedents*). These are the conditions or events that immediately precede the misbehavior. Functional behavioral assessments as described in *List 6.6* are conducted for some students with IEPs and try to determine the factors that may be triggering the behaviors of concern. This information is used when writing a behavioral intervention plan (BIP) for that student.

Following are various conditions or triggers that parents and teachers should keep in mind in order to be proactive in trying to minimize behavior problems. By environmental engineering, adding supports and incentives, adjusting the performance demand and other factors, we can help children and teens with ADHD have greater behavioral success.

Environmentally Based

- Uncomfortable conditions (too noisy, crowded, hot, or cold)
- When there is a lack of
  - Structure
  - Organization
  - Predictability
  - Interesting materials
  - Clear schedule
  - Visual supports
  - Space

Physically Based

- When the child is ill or physically uncomfortable (overly tired, hungry, thirsty)
- Overstimulated
- Bored and understimulated
- Restless, inactive for too long
- Medication related:
  - When wearing off
  - Change of prescription or dosage
  - Too high or too low a dosage

Related to Specific Activity or Event

- Losing a game
- Visiting certain people's homes
- Assemblies
- Certain classes (music, physical education, math)
- Change of routine or schedule without warning
- Cooperative learning groups and sharing of materials

- Practicing the piano
- Tasks perceived as boring, lengthy, frustrating, repetitive
- Certain chores
- Homework
- Teased by siblings

Related to a Performance or Skill Demand

- To remain seated
- To read independently
- To write a paragraph
- To wait patiently
- To hurry and complete a task
- To refrain from talking
- To refrain from touching things
- Any expectation that is a struggle for that child or teen

Related to a Specific Time

- The hour before school
- First class period
- Before or after lunch
- Transition times of day
- Later afternoon
- Evenings
- Monday mornings

Other

- When given no choices or options
- When embarrassed in front of peers
- When having difficulty communicating
- When given no assistance or access to help on difficult tasks
- When recently teased or bullied by other children

2.12 Strategies for Attention, Focus, and On-Task Behaviors

What Teachers Can Do to Help

Environmental Factors and Accommodations

- Provide preferential seating: up front, within cueing distance of the teacher, near well-focused classmates, and away from as many distractions as possible, such as doors, windows, and high-traffic areas of the room.
- Provide options for a less distracting work area through the use of study carrels, office areas, partitions, and privacy boards. These should not be used if they are viewed by the students in the class as punitive measures or as accommodations for students with special needs only.
- Be aware of and reduce environmental distractions, such as unnecessary writing on the board, clutter on tables, squeaky table and chair legs, buzzing fluorescent lights.
- Allow the use of earphones or earplugs for distractible students at certain times of the day, for example, during seatwork time. Keep a few sets available for students to access as well as requiring the use of headsets when working on classroom computers or listening centers.
- See *List 2.3* for many more environmental strategies and accommodations.

Management Factors and Accommodations

- Use clear auditory and visual cues to gain attention of all students, such as flashing lights, ringing chimes, or another distinctive sound maker that alerts the class to stop, look, and listen.
- Train students to respond to a verbal cue, such as Whole Brain Teaching's call and response of "Class! Yes!" and variations (http://wholebrainteaching.com).
- Teach hand signals for nonverbal cueing and communication. See wonderful examples and free downloadables of classroom American Sign Language (ASL) hand signals used for class management at Rick Morris's website (www.newmanagement.com).
- Increase visual, auditory, and physical prompts to gain attention and help refocus inattentive, distractible students:
  - Place hand on student's shoulder, arm, or back.
  - Use private, prearranged visual signals (for example, when you point to and tap your chin, you mean, "Watch my face and pay attention").
  - Attach a cue card to the student's desk showing pictures depicting behavioral expectations, such as raise hand, stay seated, and keep on task). Tap on the card, prompting the student to demonstrate the appropriate behaviors. See the end of the appendix for examples of picture icons that can be used for a prompt card.

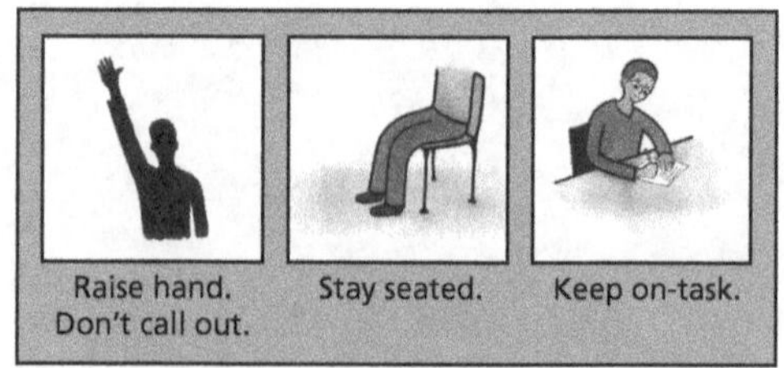

- Use eye contact, your movement, and voice modulation to get and maintain students' attention.
- Increase proximity—standing near or sitting close by distractible students.
- Clear students' desks of distracters, allowing only essential items for the current task on the desk.
- Provide students with access to fidget toys—something to hold or manipulate while seated and listening, as long as it stays within their hands and is not bothering others. When students fiddle with objects when they are supposed to be listening, the tendency is for teachers to remove the object, thinking it is a distraction and the student is not paying attention. For students with ADHD, fidgeting is a means of self-regulating, and can help in their ability to pay attention. Examples of fidget items are a small squishy ball, silly putty, a piece of Wikki Stix (www.wikkistix.com), or a key chain with a little object on it that the child can attach to his or her belt loop as a discrete fidget tool. Companies that sell sensory toys and other resources to occupational therapists are good sources of such products. A few of these companies are www.childtherapytoys.com, www.sensorycomfort.com, www.theraproducts.com, and www.headsupnow.com. See the "What Parents Can Do to Help" section in this list for more fidget strategies.
- Provide lots of movement and brain breaks to reenergize and facilitate focus.
- Monitor closely and provide students with frequent check-ins and reinforcement for on-task behavior.
- Practice self-monitoring. During times of the day or class period when students are expected to be working and on task, the student is given a sheet or card with two columns and spaces for recording "I was on task" or "I was not on task" when signaled to do so. The signal can be tactile (a vibrating watch) or auditory (a timer or other electronic device that makes a beep or tone when set to go off, for example, every two or three minutes). When hearing the tone, the student marks the monitoring sheet or card in one of the two columns (on task–not on task). See *List 2.9* for more on this topic and the "Self-Monitoring Form" for this technique in the appendix.

Instructional Factors and Accommodations

- Make lessons fun, interesting, and relevant to engage students' attention.
- Use multisensory strategies (for example, color, gesture, manipulatives, graphics, demonstrations, music).
- Significantly increase opportunities for active student involvement in the lesson and use questioning techniques that engage all students.
- Be an enthusiastic, animated presenter. Use techniques to capture and hold the attention of students and incorporate variety and novelty into lesson presentations.
- Address students' learning style differences and preferences. Provide auditory, visual, and tactile-kinesthetic input when presenting lessons and let students demonstrate their learning through a variety of methods: role-play, hands-on or experiential, performances, multimedia, artistic, and written expression (3.7).
- Add color to increase focus on work, such as a colored poster board under the student's work on the desk or strip of a colored plastic overlay on the page.

- For a host of instructional strategies to obtain attention, engage their participation, and accommodate learning needs of distractible, inattentive students, see lists in sections 3, 4, and 5.
- Use class management incentive systems with positive reinforcement for attentive, on-task behavior (*Lists 2.5, 2.7, 2.8, 2.12*).
- Use an individual management incentive system with students for whom the group reinforcement system is not sufficient. Include paying attention and being on task as target behaviors on individual student contracts, behavior charts, or daily and weekly report cards (*Lists 2.5, 2.9*).
- Recognize and call positive attention to on-task, focused students: "Thank you, Nick, for having your book open to the right page and following along." "See how nicely Sarah is sitting up and looking at the board."
- Establish mini-work production goals that are reasonable and realistic for the student. For example, to complete the first two rows of the math problems with at least 80 percent accuracy by the end of the period or to write three complete sentences before the timer goes off. Reward when successfully meeting the goal (*Lists 2.1, 2.7, 2.9*).
- Provide note-taking assistance. Give an advance copy of your outline or provide a copy of another student's class notes from your lessons. This should be a supplement, with the student still taking some of his or her own notes. Jotting things down while listening can be a helpful strategy for focus and attention. However, students who have difficulty listening and writing quickly at the same time often struggle with note taking and fail to listen well or record the important information presented. They would benefit from having either a partial outline to fill in during lectures or a copy later of someone else's notes that are more fleshed out, readable, and useful for studying (*List 5.12*).

- Incorporate learning games and activities in your teaching repertoire that require listening, attention, and focus. Brain-break games such as "Simon Says" and "Freeze" require attention and inhibition, and playing such games are opportunities to practice those skills.
- Use a Whisperphone with students who have difficulty staying focused during silent reading. This is a plastic, curved, tubular tool that can be very helpful. The student is able to read aloud in a soft whisper while holding the device like a phone. Because of its hollow shape, they are able to hear their voice while reading loud and clear without disturbing others.
- Teach students the strategy of SLANT, developed by the University of Kansas Center for Research on Learning: S—Sit up straight; L—Lean forward (writing position); A—Activate your thinking; N—Note important points; T—Track the talker (keep your eyes on whoever is doing the informing).
- See the "shiny light bulb" strategy in my book *How to Reach & Teach Children with ADD/ADHD* for helping students increase their awareness and ability to self-regulate their attention level.

- See other strategies to support students with attention difficulties in lists throughout this book, for example, *List 2.3* for environmental and sensory strategies to enhance attention or accommodate attention difficulties and *List 4.5* for structuring materials to support attention and focus.

What Parents Can Do to Help

- ADHD medication is a research-validated intervention that has been proven effective in helping children improve their attention, focus, and on-task behavior (*Lists 1.4, 1.19, 1.20*).
- Structuring and organizing the environment, increasing motivation through incentive systems and behavior modification techniques are also helpful and important interventions.
- Provide visual reminders, such as a checklist, clothespin chart, or sticky notes listing in words or pictures, of your child's responsibilities and routines (for example, morning routine, chores, bedtime routine). Post these in strategic locations.
- Some people need it to be very quiet in order to focus, but for many people with ADHD, trying to concentrate in silence is more distracting and difficult. If your child prefers music, experiment with listening to the radio or recorded music of different kinds. Familiar songs they hear on the radio and know the lyrics to may be better for some and aid focus. Others will have greater focus listening to instrumental, classical music, or a recording of sounds of nature. Experiment with headsets (to either block out noise if your child needs it quiet or for listening to music while working if more productive doing so. See *List 7.7* for more on this topic.
- Some children work best when they are isolated (alone in their bedroom or other location); others need to have people around and work better in a more central location, such as the kitchen. It helps them stay alert with the stimulation of things going on and background or white noise. Again, experiment with best locations for your child's focus and productivity for homework areas in the house. Having a few homework locations is also beneficial for many children. See *Lists 2.3 and 4.9*.
- Martial arts such as Tae Kwon Do and Tai Chi have benefits in building concentration and focus as well as help practice self-control (*List 7.7*).
- Chewing gum may be helpful in staying alert and better able to focus.
- Strengthen attention skills through card and board games, chess, and puzzles.
- Read aloud to your child and engage in discussion and questioning about the book. This is another excellent way to strengthen attention as well as build your child's vocabulary and reading comprehension skills (*Lists 5.3,5.4, 5.5*).
- Attention and focus is strengthened when practicing skills through many activities (reading, learning to play an instrument, sports).
- Fidgeting helps many people with ADHD to activate their brains when in a state of understimulation. They literally need to fidget to focus. There is an excellent book by this title (*Fidget to Focus*) with useful information and strategies.
- Provide your child with a fidget toy, such as a koosh ball, pencil with an object attached at the top, some kind of bracelet, or other object that can be quietly and discretely touched and manipulated to help them better focus. See additional fidget strategies and tips listed earlier in this list for teachers under Management Factors and Accommodations.

- Try using a timer when your child is working with mini-goals of what to complete before the timer goes off. Reward for doing so. Your child may better focus and stay on task if you can motivate her to beat the clock.
- Provide controlled breaks during homework. Schedule breaks either after working a certain amount of time (for example, after every *x* number of minutes of work production or after completing each assignment). Breaks between tasks should be short, such as dancing to one or two songs, shooting baskets for five minutes, playing with your pet, text messaging friends, eating a snack.
- Parents may want to explore some of the technologies and brain-training programs that are designed to help improve attention, focus, and other cognitive skills, such as Cogmed (www.cogmed.com)—an online working memory and attention training program— and Play Attention (www.playattention.com)—a program based on neurofeedback. There are various apps for helping with attention, focus, and work production. Learning Works for Kids (www.learningworksforkids.com) provides a review of several apps and online programs that they have evaluated and rated for children and teens with ADHD (*Lists 1.23, 4.1*).
- There are some sensory-integration programs that may be of interest based on activities for strengthening neural pathways, such as The Alert Program (www.alertprogram.com), Brain Gym (www.braingym.com), and Learning Breakthrough (www.learningbreakthrough.com).
- Suggested strategies for teachers also apply and may be implemented in the home, as well, and lists throughout this book provide many other strategies and supports to aid children with attention difficulties.

Sources and Resources

The Learning Strategy Series, The University of Kansas Center for Research on Learning. (2002). Strategic instruction model (SIM). Retrieved from http://coedpages.uncc.edu/gcampbe1/5279/slant.pdf

Rotz, Roland, & Wright, Sarah. (2005). *Fidget to focus*. New York: iUniverse.

2.13 Strategies for Impulsive and Hyperactive Behaviors

Impaired ability for inhibition (being able to resist impulses and stop and think before acting) causes many difficulties for children and teens with ADHD. It is important to remember that the impulsive and hyperactive behaviors common in children with ADHD are not deliberate but a result of a lack in brain-based self-regulation and self-control weaknesses. Problems commonly stem from poor ability to delay gratification, stop long enough to consider past and future consequences before acting, and control emotions, impulses, and the urge to move.

Ways Parents and Teachers Can Help Children and Teens with ADHD

Management Tips

- Be explicit about your expectations and remind the child about positive and negative consequences.
- Post rules and schedules so they are clearly displayed and referred to frequently. Provide a desk copy of the rules and schedule as well. Refer to them frequently.
- Review and rehearse behavioral expectations right before entering into activities or situations in which self-control is required. For example, remind them of appropriate hallway behavior while standing in line waiting to be dismissed to the next class or review what the rules are (and consequences) right before going to the auditorium for an assembly or taking your child with you shopping.
- Provide visual cues such as a small picture card taped to their desk of a stop sign or of a raised hand or a child sitting appropriately in a chair that you can point to or tap on as a quiet cue or a sticky note reminder placed on the student's desk.

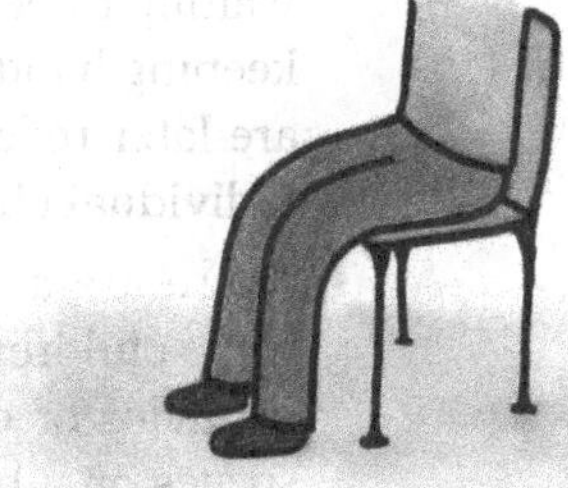

- Use private signals (a gesture, hand signal, cue word) to discretely remind the child of expectations and to stop and make a good choice.
- Provide the child with frequent movement breaks throughout the day.
- Anticipate problems and situations that are challenges for a child with poor impulse control: long waits, group work, taking turns, sharing with siblings or playmates, activities or environments with minimal supervision or structure, going to places that require sitting quietly when over- or understimulated. Plan ahead and use proactive strategies to avoid problems in these situations.
- Start the day when possible with some morning exercise.
- Remove access to items the child misuses, permitting use of the item when the child demonstrates that he or she can handle it properly.
- Prepare and alert the child for transitions (having to stop one activity to start another) and for changes in routine. See *Lists 2.6 and 2.10*.
- Increase supervision and closer monitoring of the child's behavior in activities and situations requiring self-control.

- Use a verbal signal to stop, such as "Brakes!" "Please ... Freeze!" or a silly or nonsense word of some kind.
- Teach, model, and practice thoughtful (not impulsive) decision making, for example, talking things through, identifying and weighing pros and cons, choosing a good option.

- Deliver consequences (such as a brief time-out or loss of a privilege) calmly, consistently, predictably, frequently, and swiftly.
- Use strategies to curb interrupting, such as a specific hand signal indicating wait to speak or wait your turn as well as teaching the child to observe when others are talking and listen for the break or silence after someone talks as the signal that it is his or her turn to speak.
- See *Lists 2.1, 2.2, 2.3, 2.4, and 7.8* for more on this topic.

Feedback and Reinforcement

- Notice the child when demonstrating self-control. Acknowledge the appropriate behavior and praise: "Thank you for waiting quietly and patiently." "That was great self-control—not hitting your little brother when he pushed you. I'm proud of you!" A tangible reward such as points earned or other tokens, class, or home privileges can also be earned. Set up behavior charts and token systems—and award points, stickers, or other tokens for demonstrating self-control such as raising hand and waiting to be called on, remaining in one's place unless given permission to move, keeping hands and feet to self, taking turns and sharing appropriately. These tokens are later redeemable for tangible rewards and privileges that are motivating to the individual child (*Lists 2.5, 2.7, 2.8, 2.9*).
- There are a number of positive-only reinforcement systems that may be best for some children. In these systems, the child either earns the token for the appropriate behavior or does not. When a certain number of tokens have been earned or the spaces on a behavior chart are filled, the reward (prize or privilege) is provided.
- *A token economy sys*tem involving a combination of positive reinforcement (earning of tokens) and response cost (the penalty of being fined or losing tokens) can be very effective for children with ADHD if implemented well. This strategy will work only if the opportunity for earning tokens outweighs the loss of tokens so the child won't be discouraged and lose motivation. Some children can't handle the loss of any tokens earned and would respond better to a different approach.
- Various response cost systems can be beneficial for children with poor inhibition.
  - The way it may work in the classroom is for the individual student (or group) to start off with a certain number of tokens or points given up front at the beginning of the day, class period, or other time interval. A student, for example, may have an index card at her desk with ten points on it at the beginning of class or a younger child may have three Velcro dots attached to his desk in the morning and again after lunch, or a teacher may have five magnets or tally marks on the board for each group or table team. One or more specific behaviors are targeted

for the student(s) that are problematic, such as blurting out, hitting or pushing, being off task or out of seat without permission. During the day, period, or other time interval, a token is removed for each incident of the targeted inappropriate behavior. If any of the given tokens are still remaining at the end of the time interval (one Velcro dot left on desk, one magnet still remaining on the metal chart), the child (or group) succeeded in earning the designated privilege or reward. But, if all points or tokens were lost or removed, the child or group will not receive the privilege and may receive a mild consequence such as no access to certain materials or fewer minutes of participation in an activity.

- Parents may use this technique by filling a jar or other clear container to the top with marbles, poker chips, or other tokens. The child is fined or loses a token for each occurrence of a particular misbehavior or more (talking back, hitting or pushing sibling, not stopping when told to do so and complying with parent directions). If the marbles or other tokens remaining at the end of the week are above a line marked on the jar, the child is rewarded. If below the line, the child loses the opportunity for the weekend reward or privilege. See *Lists 1.22, 2.8 and 2.9*.

Self-Regulation Strategies and Supports

- Teach and practice self-regulation strategies such as deep breathing, counting to ten before responding, using self-talk such as "I'm calm and in control" or "I can handle this."
- Teach and practice a self-control strategy that encourages stopping and thinking before acting. For example, use visual cues such as a stoplight poster that shows in *red*—STOP and take a deep breath; *yellow*—Think. What are my Options and possible consequences? *green*—Proceed. Make a good choice and go with it. There are several variations of this strategy and the wording for the stoplight colors and stop acronym.
- Provide fidget toys such as a pencil with something attached on top that can be manipulated, a stress ball, piece of clay or Play-Doh, or other object.
- Play games that help children develop and practice self-control, such as "Red Light, Green Light," "Freeze or Statues," "Simon Says," and others that require the child to inhibit impulses (*List 7.4*).
- See *Lists 2.9, 2.12, 2.14, 2.15, 2.16, and 7.7* for more self-regulation strategies.

More Strategies for Teachers

- Use instructional methods that provide for frequent opportunities to talk, such as think-pair-shares (*Lists 3.3, 4.3, 5.3, 5.4, 5.8, 5.14*).
- Teach a few classroom rules and give students so much rehearsal and practice hearing and stating the rules that they can recite by memory each one automatically when prompted to do so.
- Seat the ADHD student next to and pair for activities with classmates who are good behavioral models and tend to be patient and supportive.
- Provide lots of movement opportunities (stretching, brief exercise, and brain breaks between tasks or activities) and design lessons that involve active learning (*Lists 2.1, 2.3, 3.3, 3.5, 3.7, 3.8, 5.3, 5.4, 5.10, 5.14*).

- Increase the distance between desks when possible and avoid seating arrangements that are challenges for students with poor self-control.
- Be tolerant of the student's need to move (squirm, fidget with things, tap pencils). These behaviors may be annoying but don't warrant a punishment. Use tools to accommodate this need and find strategies to help minimize the disruptions, for example, encourage the student to tap the pencil on his leg or soft pad, provide an inflatable seat cushion or round therapeutic ball with wiggle room, allow student to work in the back of the room while standing (*Lists 2.3, 3.7*).
- Use a voice volume scale (for example, 0 = silence up to 4 = outside voice) and indicate on a voice volume chart the voice level permissible during different activities.
- Limit the materials on the student's desk when working to only what is needed for the task.
- Avoid loss of recess as a consequence for misbehavior. Find alternatives or if needed, limit recess choices of activity. Instead of sitting out recess on a bench, the student can be directed to walk or jog back and forth from one end of the playground to another for *x* amount of minutes or number of times before playing.
- Teach, practice, provide visual cues, and have all adults in the building reinforce the same clear rules and expectations for all school settings (hallways, cafeteria, playground, bus stop, office). See examples of how this is implemented in PBIS schools (www.pbis.org) and at www.pinterest.com/sandrarief/pbis-schoolwide-positive-behavior-support/.
- Use questioning strategies during whole-group activities that build in think time before responding, such as having students jot down their best-guess answer and then calling on volunteers, or make a habit of waiting (at least five to ten seconds) to call on students after posing a question, or have students first turn to their neighbor and share before a large-group share (*List 3.3*).
- Consider using a clear visual sign for when students are not allowed to interrupt you, such as wearing a hat or big colorful necklace while working with small groups in guided reading instruction. In addition, provide clear guidelines on what students may do or who they may go to if they have questions during that time.
- Teach students to self-monitor during a class period or for part of the day one of their problem behaviors, such as blurting out, interrupting, or being out of their seat without permission. The student is responsible for marking tally marks on an index card each time the teacher needs to remind, redirect, or reprimand the student for that behavior. Together with another adult, have the student record her total at the end of the day or period and set a goal for improvement.
- Provide clear expectations for working in groups, a specific list of group rules, such as stay with your group, participate, be on task, be respectful of others.
- For cooperative group activities, pass out four or five poker chips to each student in the group. The rule is that students are to place one of their chips in the center of the table when they want a turn to talk. This technique during group work helps minimize some students monopolizing the discussion and students talking without listening to others.
- Have students repeat or restate directions in their own words before beginning tasks and assignments.
- Use *what* questions when redirecting, such as "What are you supposed to be doing right now?" "What would be a good choice right now?"

- The free management program called Class Dojo (www.classdojo.com) can provide immediate electronic reinforcement (feedback points) for behaviors in class to individual students or the full class (*Lists 2.8 and 2.9*).

More Strategies for Home

- Use timers for setting limits, such as how much longer they have to play before picking up their toys or get to watch TV or have other screen time before they need to stop and come to the table for dinner or get ready for bedtime routine. It reduces nagging and arguments.
- Prepare for play dates to limit your child's likelihood for social problems (*List 2.17*).
- Teach your child strategies for what to do when you are on the phone or otherwise engaged and cannot be interrupted, such as jotting down what they need to say so they won't forget or using a quiet signal to get your attention.
- Prepare for times your child needs to wait quietly (driving on errands, going to appointments). For children with ADHD these are difficult situations without anything to keep themselves occupied and entertained. Keep a bag of quiet, motivating toys or items of interest in your car for your child to keep busy when going places, as well as books and electronic devices with headsets (*List 2.6*).
- Make sure your child gets exercise after school and preferably outdoor play time (*List 7.7*).
- Indoor exercise equipment (treadmill, exercise bike, trampoline, mounted mini-basketball hoop) are also helpful to have in your home, especially if they are limited in their outdoor play time.
- Set up somewhere in your home a safe area where more rambunctious behavior is allowed as well as making it clear which areas are off limits.
- Teach your child polite words to use if they need to interrupt, such as "Excuse me, may I ask you something?" or "I'm sorry for interrupting, but . . . ."
- Notice, acknowledge, praise, and reward your child frequently for appropriate behavior. Keep in mind that you should provide positive attention and feedback four times more often than you reprimand your child or give critical, negative feedback (*List 2.2*).
- Keep a disability perspective and remind yourself that your child's behaviors are not deliberate but because of a neurobiological immaturity in his or her ability to self-regulate. Your child's lack of self-control and resulting behaviors not only are a challenge to deal with but also can be embarrassing. When managing or responding to your child's impulsive-hyperactive behaviors, doing what you feel is beneficial for your son or daughter is what matters—not what other people think about your parenting choices.

2.14 Tough Kids: Coping and Dealing with Challenging Behaviors

Some children and teens with ADHD present with behaviors that are very challenging to teachers and parents—particularly argumentative, noncompliant, and oppositional behaviors. The following tips can help defuse conflict and avoid getting pulled into a power-struggle situation:

- Provide the structure, clarity of expectations, consistency, and positive discipline that all children need—particularly those with ADHD. Rules, boundaries, and consequences (positive and negative) are necessary (*Lists 2.1, 2.2*).
- Use the proactive strategies that can prevent and minimize behavioral problems in *Lists 2.1, 2.2, 2.3, 2.4, 2.6, 2.10, 2.12, and 2.13*.
- Reward appropriate behaviors and provide effective behavioral techniques such as self-monitoring, behavioral contracts, incentive programs, and others (*Lists 2.8, 2.9*).
- Minimize the triggers to the child's frustration, anger, and meltdowns, and promote effective strategies for helping children manage strong emotions because of their self-regulation weaknesses (*Lists 2.15, 2.16*).
- Employ strategies to communicate in ways that are most likely to improve a child's listening and compliance (*List 2.4*).
- Make a conscious effort to pay attention to, compliment, and reinforce children when behaving appropriately, and try to provide at least four times more positive interactions and feedback than negative. This is not always easy to do, but it is very important. 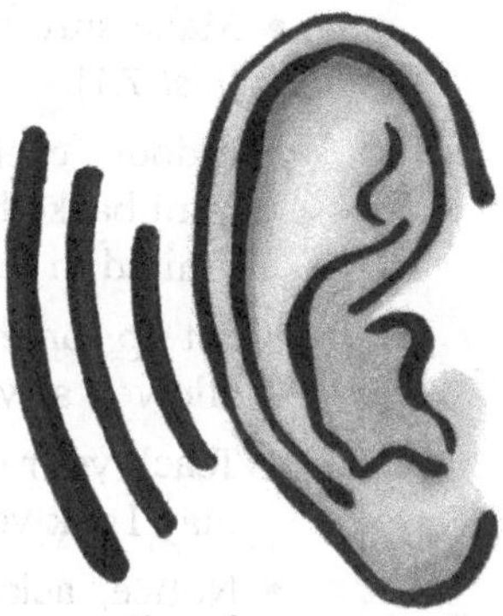
- Children and teens with ADHD seek stimulation. An emotional response is very stimulating. You do not want your highly charged response to be rewarding and, therefore, reinforce the misbehavior. Take whatever steps you need to first gain your composure before responding, such as taking a few deep breaths and cueing yourself to calm down. We want our kids to learn to think before reacting and need to demonstrate our own ability to do so.
- Relax your body and facial muscles. Watch your body language (crossed arms, hands on hips, finger pointing). Speak slowly, softly, respectfully, and in a matter-of-fact manner.
- Communicate your confidence in the child's ability to make good choices and your hope that he or she will choose to cooperate.
- Be aware that oppositional defiant disorder (ODD) commonly coexists with ADHD (*List 1.8*). Children with ODD have a strong need for power and control. If the child knows how to provoke you to the point where you lose control, your response will be rewarding and reinforcing the inappropriate behavior because your child will have effectively gained power and control over you.
- "Oppositional kids have radar for adult hostility. If they pick up your anger, they are going to match it" (Flippin, 2005, p. 43).

- Do not feel compelled to give an immediate response in dealing with situations until you are in a calm, thinking state. You might say, "I'm upset right now and need time to collect my thoughts. I'll get back to you." Then walk away.
- Realize that you cannot control anyone else's behavior but your own: your attitude, body language, tone and volume of voice, strategies, consistency and follow-through, and the nature of the interaction.
- Supervise and monitor the child in situations in which problems can be anticipated, giving verbal and nonverbal cues and redirection as needed.
- Use charts, schedules, and timers—creating less room for argument and getting drawn into a power struggle when you need the child to start or stop activities.
- Disengage from power struggles. Remember that you cannot be forced into an argument or power struggle. You only enter into one only if you choose to do so (it takes two). Say calmly, for example, "I am not willing to argue about this now. I will be free to discuss it later if you wish (and give a specific time, such as after dinner, after class, during lunch period)."
- Affirm and acknowledge the child or teen's feelings: "I understand why that would make you angry." "I can see you are upset."
- Set up signals and cues to serve as warnings and private communication, giving the opportunity to save face in front of others.
- Avoid *why* questions, for example, "Why did you do that?"
- Use *what* questions, for example, "What are you supposed to be doing right now?" "What do you want?" "What is your plan to solve the problem?" "What can I do to help you?" "What would you like to see happen?" "What are you risking by doing that?"
- Use "when ... then" contingencies ("When you put away your toys, then you can go outside and play") rather than "if you don't ... you won't ... " statements ("If you don't pick up your toys, you can't go outside and play").
- Remind the child of the rules and consequences (positive and negative).
- Send "I messages": "I feel ... when you ... because ...." or "I want [or need] you to ...."
- Use words that tend to deescalate a conflict, such as "I wonder ... ?" "What if ... ?" "Maybe ... ?"
- Avoid nagging, scolding, lecturing, or threatening.
- Use the broken record technique: respond by repeating your directions with the same words in a calm, neutral voice. Use the words *however* and *nevertheless*—for example, "I understand you are feeling ... However ... " or "That may be ... Nevertheless ...."
- Other effective words to defuse power struggles include *and* statements, such as "I know you don't want to ... *and* what was our agreement?" and *regardless*—"Yes, I know you think it is unfair ... regardless ...."
- Avoid being judgmental in your interactions.
- Do not take the behavior personally.
- Avoid giving direct demands or commands. Only do so when necessary.
- Avoid an audience when interacting with the child when there is a conflict.
- Do not take the bait.

- Do not try to rationalize, defend yourself, or try to convince the child that you are right when the child or teen is trying to engage you in conflict. Walk away (Adams, 2002).
- Provide lots of opportunities to make choices, have leadership responsibilities, and other means of having some power (the biggest motivator for many children and teens with oppositional behavior).
- Let go of your own anger and keep in mind that this child's behaviors are generally more a result of lagging skills and neurological immaturity than behavior intended to deliberately push your buttons and make you angry.
- The tougher the child or teen, the greater your efforts must be to find ways to build and strengthen a positive, mutually respectful relationship.
- Take time to actively listen to the child or teen: be attentive, listen carefully without interjecting your opinions. Ask a lot of open, reflective, and clarifying questions, rephrasing and restating what was said.
- Provide a two or three choice option: "I can't make you ... But your choices are either ... or ... " (or choices of A, B, or C).
- It is okay to call for a break. Go to a different location or do something away from each other for a while to calm down and have a chance to think.
- Taylor (2007) suggests scheduling pit stops when things get tense. This is just a private conversation in a quiet area where nobody will interrupt.
- Discuss, problem solve, and negotiate win-win solutions after you both have had time to cool down.
- Martin (2013) recommends a strategy for parents of calling for a break to do something to defuse the conflict and change the dynamic, such as pop popcorn together and sit on the couch to talk or as he describes, "I'll get the chips, you get the salsa. I'll meet you outside on the deck."
- Show the child that you are listening to his or her point of view, for example, "I never thought of it that way before. Let me think about that."
- Seek the child's ideas or solutions to problems.
- See the excellent problem-solving resources by Ross Greene and Myrna Shure, and Russell Barkley's books on parenting children with ADHD and challenging behaviors in the "Sources and Resources" section.
- Use Whole Brain Teaching's strategy of "the agreement bridge," which was inspired by Green's (2009) book (www.wholebrainteaching.com).
- Use daily report cards (*Lists 1.22, 2.9*) with goals addressing a few of the child's challenging behaviors and reinforce at home based on the student's school performance.
- Communicate and work as a team (parents, teachers, counselors, doctors) and anyone involved in the child's intervention plan.

About Oppositional Defiant Disorder

Because there is such a high rate of ODD in children and teens with ADHD, parents and teachers need to be aware of the symptoms. Treatment for ADHD (medical and behavioral) can significantly help. Parents are advised to seek help from professionals with expertise in ADHD and coexisting mental health disorders. Teachers need support and assistance from the administration, the guidance counselor, the school psychologist, and other school professionals.

According to the National Resource Center on AD/HD (2008):

- Approximately one-third to one-half of all children with ADHD may have coexisting ODD.
- In some cases, children with ADHD may eventually develop conduct disorder (CD), a more serious pattern of antisocial behaviors.
- It is very important for children with symptoms of ADHD and ODD to be assessed and both disorders treated.
- Medications (stimulants as well as nonstimulants) used for the treatment of ADHD are an important component in the treatment of ADHD and coexisting ODD (*Lists 1.19, 1.20*).
- Home interventions known to be effective or show promise in treating and managing ODD include parent training programs, which are typically programs over a certain number of weeks with periodic booster sessions that teach parents effective behavior management and communication strategies, as well as collaborative problem solving and family therapy (*Lists 1.19, 1.22, 2.2, 2.4, 2.6, 2.9*).

See the National Resource Center on AD/HD website at www.help4adhd.org for the most *reliable source of information on ADHD* and coexisting conditions, such as ODD.

Sources and Resources

Adams, Marilyn. (2002). Solutions to oppositional defiant disorder. *Attention Magazine, 8*(6), 28–33.

Barkley, Russell A. (2013). *Taking charge of ADHD: The complete, authoritative guide for parents* (3rd ed.). New York: Guilford Press.

Barkley, Russell A., & Benton, Christine, M. (2013). *Your defiant child: Eight steps to better behavior* (2nd ed.). New York: Guilford Press.

Barkley, Russell A., Robin, Arthur L., & Benton, Christine, M. (2013). *Your defiant teen: Ten steps to resolve conflict and rebuild your relationship* (2nd ed.). New York: Guilford Press.

Biffle, Chris. (2013) *Whole brain teaching for challenging kids*. Whole Brain Teaching. Retrieved from www.wholebrainteaching.com

Flippin, Royce. (2005). Making peace with your defiant child. *ADDitude Magazine, 5*(6), 41–43.

Greene, Ross W. (2008). *Lost at school: Why our kids with behavioral challenges are falling through the cracks and how we can help them.* New York: Scribner

Greene, Ross W. (2009). *The explosive child: A new approach for understanding and parenting easily frustrated, chronically inflexible children.* New York: HarperCollins.

Martin, Kirk. (2013). How to stay calm when your child acts up: Strategies for the difficult child. *ADDitude Magazine webinar*. Retrieved from www.additudemag.com/webinars

National Resource Center on AD/HD. (2008). ADHD and coexisting conditions: Disruptive behavior disorders. *What We Know, 5B*. Retrieved from www.help4adhd.org/documents/WWK5B.pdf

Rief at Pinterest. Several strategies for parents and teachers in helping to manage children's challenging behavior can be found on Sandra's Pinterest boards at https://www.pinterest.com/sandrarief/

Shure, Myrna, & DiGeronimo, Theresa F. (1996). *Raising a thinking child: Helping your young child to resolve everyday conflicts and get along with others.* New York: Gallery Books.

Shure, Myrna B. (2011). *Thinking parent, thinking child: How to turn your most challenging everyday problems into solutions.* Champaign, IL: Research Press.

Shure, Myrna B., & Israeloff, Roberta. (2001). *Raising a thinking preteen: The "I can problem solve" program for 8- to 12-year-olds.* New York: Holt Paperbacks.

Taylor, John K. (2007). Discipline without regret. *ADDitude Magazine, 8*(2), 27–28.

2.15 Managing Student Anger, Frustration, and Poor Emotional Regulation

Students with ADHD often have difficulty reining in their emotions and reacting without thinking. They commonly have a low frustration tolerance and are prone to anger and outbursts because of their neurological immaturity and poor ability to regulate their emotions. Here are strategies teachers can employ to help avoid and manage a student's escalation of emotions from spinning out of control.

Prevention Strategies

- Be aware of the triggers or antecedents that cause the student to become frustrated, agitated, and upset (*List 2.11*) so you can make whatever adjustments or accommodations are needed to alleviate those feelings.
- Frustration and anxiety can often be eliminated or significantly reduced by adjusting the task demand (shortening the assignment, giving more time to complete the task, or providing peer or teacher assistance), and modifying the environment (such as providing seating options). Avoid situations or conditions that make the student anxious and can provoke emotional reactions.
- Provide the calm, consistent, predictable, and respectful environment as described in *List 2.1*.
- Alert the student about changes in routine and provide warnings and preparation for transitions (*List 2.10*).
- Take steps to prevent the student from becoming overstimulated and employ calming techniques in the classroom (*Lists 2.3, 2.10, 2.13, 7.7*).
- Always watch for warning signs of students becoming frustrated, agitated, or overly stimulated and have strategies and plans in place for preventing escalation.
- Offer choices, such as where the student will do his or her work or which part of an assignment to do first.

It is often helpful to provide a place that a student can access briefly as a preventive (not punitive) measure before behaviors escalate to a higher level. This might be a designated location outside of the room, such as the nurse's or counselor's office, that the student may go to when needed. Elementary classrooms may be designed with an area students use specifically for this purpose. To that end, keep the following points in mind:

- Consider creating a calming area in the room that is equipped with some items such as a fish tank or lava lamp, stuffed animal, soothing music to listen to with headsets, stress ball, pillows, or perhaps a rocking chair.
- Such an area is designed as a take-a-break or cool-down spot. Some teachers give these room locations names such as *Hawaii, Tahiti*, or some other name that the class agrees is a pleasant, relaxing reference. Such an area is also sometimes referred to as *Alaska*—and going to Alaska means to be able to chill out.
- Students can be taught to go directly to this spot when they feel they need to or are directed to or prompted to visit the cool or calm down area for a short amount of time when feeling agitated or angry ("Would you like to go to Hawaii for a few minutes?").
- Establish a prearranged signal with the student to request use of this area discretely.

Note: This is not the same as a time-out, which is a negative, corrective consequence that must be time away from anything rewarding.

- Physical activities relieve stress and can change a person's negative emotional state. You may want to assign a task to the student that would involve something physical when you see warning signs of agitation or frustration.
- Competition can trigger anxiety and fear of failure, which in turn can lead to anger and meltdowns. Use more strategies that encourage students to compete against their own best efforts and work on beating their own records.
- Help the student recognize his or her own physical signs of getting upset (tensed muscles, tight jaw, clenched fists, feeling flushed or hot) and the need to request a break to calm down.
- In order to be able to prompt or cue students to use effective strategies for managing their emotions, they first need to be taught. Teach and model positive strategies for anger management, calming and stress reduction, peer mediation and conflict resolution, dealing with disappointments and frustration, social skills, and problem solving (*Lists 2.9, 2.13, 2.17, 7.7*).
- If we want students to use their words when angry, give them suggested statements and specific language they might use to express their feelings.
- Teach positive self-talk to repeat to themselves (aloud softly or silently) when they feel frustrated or upset, such as "I can deal with this." "This is going to be OK. I can do it." "I am calm and in control."
- Problem-solving strategies are among the most important things we can teach our students. Teach problem solving and practice the skills in every possible situation and opportunity that arises. There are excellent programs and methods that educators can use for teaching problem solving, such as *I Can Problem Solve* by Myrna Shure and collaborative problem solving (CBS) strategies that Ross Greene describes in his books and other resources (see the "Sources and Resources" section in this list (*List 2.14*).
- Consider using a self-regulation curriculum for helping students with poor emotional control, such as these:
  - *Zones of Regulation* (www.Zonesofregulation.com) by Kuypers (2011), which uses a traffic light analogy
  - *Hunter and His Amazing Remote Control* by Copeland (1998), which uses a remote control analogy
  - *The Alert Program* (www.alertprogram.com) by Williams and Shellenberger (1996), which uses an engine analogy
  - *The Incredible Five-Point Scale* by Buron and Curtis (2007)

Strategies to Aid Calming and Avoid Escalation

- When a student is showing signs that he or she is beginning to lose control, intervene at once by doing the following:
  - Provide a cue or prompt, such as standing near student, placing a gentle hand on shoulder, or pointing to a picture card of steps to take to calm down.
  - Use a prearranged private signal, a word, gesture, or visual prompt of some kind as a reminder to settle down.

- Divert the child's attention, if possible.
- Give the student an alternative task or independent activity to do for a while, such as an easy worksheet, a puzzle, maze, or coloring.
- Redirect to a different location, situation, or activity. For example, the student can be asked to run an errand, bring a note to a neighboring class or the office, pass out materials, sort papers, or sharpen a can of pencils. The student can also be redirected to the designated cool-down location.
- Cue the student to use relaxation and self-regulation techniques such as visualization, deep breathing, counting slowly forward or backward, self-talk, or progressive muscle relaxation as described in *List 7.7.*These strategies must have been previously taught and practiced sufficiently before the student can be prompted to use them.
- Remind the student about rewards and consequences.
- Provide the student time and a means to regroup, regain control, and avoid the escalation of behaviors.

- Be very careful of *your* response and behavior when interacting with the student. Watch your voice level, words, and body language. Speak softly, slowly, and calmly. Uncross your arms.
- Affirm and acknowledge the student's feelings ("You seem angry." "I see you're upset." "I understand that you are disappointed." "I can see why you would be frustrated.") or what he or she wanted ("You were hoping....").
- Offer choices. "Would you rather work at your desk or at the back table?" "What would be better for you ... or ... ?" "Would you like to ... or ... ?"
- Use statements of empathy, understanding, reassurance, and concern.
- Talk to an angry student in private—away from an audience.
- Alert administrators, the school counselor, or the nurse if the student arrives at school angry or exhibits behaviors that clearly predict he or she will need intervention early. Perhaps the student can have a chance to talk to the counselor or other designated support person, or someone can follow the child into class and stay there a while until settled down.
- Try the clock-watch strategy for calming described by Harmin (1998), which requires the following steps: (1) stand up near their desk, (2) take a deep breath, (3) face the wall clock and watch it go around one or two minutes, (4) then sit down and get back to work.

- When agitated or angry, encourage the student to express his or her feelings through drawing or writing.
- Breathing slowly is calming. Take a deep breath and hold (for about three to five seconds) then slowly release. Repeat a few or several times. Ask the student to breathe together with you or someone else.
- Arrange with the student to be excused from the room with a pass to a designated location for a certain amount of time to relax and calm down.

- Give the student something physical to do (carrying heavy boxes, stacking chairs, or brief exercise outside of the classroom if someone can supervise, such as running a lap or quickly going up and down the stairs a few times).
- Call for a quick brain break time with the whole class. Play one of the YouTube songs with dance motions. This may change the emotional state of the student without being singled out as needing it.
- Provide the student with a fidget toy to hold and manipulate.
- Certain scents and aromas can be relaxing and calming and help change a person's mood. You may want to experiment with letting an agitated student smell a sticker or something scented.
- If the student escalates into a full meltdown, follow the school's protocol for dealing with such situations.
- Discuss and problem solve after the student is calm—not when emotions are running high.
- See *List 2.16* for strategies on this topic for parents.
- See other related *Lists 2.1, 2.3, 2.6, 2.10, 2.11, 2.13, 2.14, 2.16, and 3.7.*

Sources and Resources

Buron, Kari Dunn, & Curtis, Mitzi B. (2007). *The incredible 5-point scale: Assisting students in understanding social interactions and controlling their emotional responses* (2nd ed.). Shawnee Mission, KS: AAPC Publishing.

Copeland, Lori A. (1998). *Hunter and his amazing remote control: A fun hands-on way to teach self-control to ADD/ADHD children.* Chapin, SC: YouthLight.

Greene, Ross W. (2008). *Lost at school: Why our kids with behavioral challenges are falling through the cracks and how we can help them.* [Kindle ed.]. New York: Scribner.

Greene, Ross W. (2009). *The explosive child.* New York: HarperCollins.

Harmin, Merrill. (1998). *Strategies to inspire active learning.* White Plains, NY: Inspiring Strategies Institute.

Katz, Mark. (2012). Promising practices: The zones of regulation: A curriculum designed to foster self-regulation and emotional control. *Attention Magazine, 19*(5), 7–8.

Kuypers, Leah. (2011). *The zones of regulation: A curriculum designed to foster self-regulation and emotional control.* San Jose, CA: Social Thinking Publishing. Retrieved from www.Zonesofregulation.com

Rabiner, David. (2014, Jan.). An innovative approach for helping "explosive and inflexible children." *Attention Research Update.* Retrieved from http://cpsconnection.com

Shure, Myrna B. (1992). *I can problem-solve: An interpersonal cognitive problem-solving program.* Champaign, IL: Research Press.

Williams, Mary Sue, & Shellenberger, Shelley. (1996). *How does your engine run: Leader's guide to the alert program.* Albuquerque, NM: Therapy Works. Retrieved from www.alertprogram.com/

2.16 Managing Your Child's Difficulty with Emotional Control

Children with ADHD are delayed in their development of self-regulation, including emotional control. You can expect that your child may have much more difficulty than other children coping with frustration and anger. Parents can help their child through preventive measures and strategies to avoid escalating emotions into full-blown meltdowns.

Prevention Strategies

- Know your child's triggers—the situations and conditions that typically lead to frustration, anxiety, overstimulation, and anger (*List 2.11*). Then take steps to remove or minimize these triggers. Make adjustments as needed in the task demand, environment, or expectation, for example:
  - Shorten tasks or break them into a series of manageable steps.
  - Provide more support with chores, homework, or other tedious tasks (*List 4.9*).
  - Help your child with organization and time management (*Lists 4.5, 4.7*).
  - Add more structure and visual cues at home (*List 2.3*).
  - Communicate positively and effectively with your child (*List 2.4*).
  - Avoid situations in which your child is expected to sit quietly for any length of time or otherwise tax his or her limits of self-control.
  - Prepare your child for changes of routine
  - Employ all of the proactive strategies to prevent problem behavior at home and outside of the home (*Lists 2.2, 2.6*).
  - Ensure that your child has the school accommodations that address his or her areas of difficulty—minimize his or her stress and frustration. Homework accommodations are key to preventing many tears and nightly conflicts (*Lists 4.9, 4.10, 5.12*).
- Offer your child choices. "Would you rather ... or ... ?"
- Discuss potential disappointments in advance and ways to deal with it. For example, "Last time we tried to find that game you wanted, the store was all out. I remember how disappointed you were and upset you got. What will we do if you are disappointed today" (Brady, 2005)?
- Have your child do something involving movement and physical activity when you see warning signs of frustration or agitation. Exercise is a positive mood changer.
- Help your child learn how to label or name his or her feelings.
- Talk to your child about situations that cause frustration or anxiety and together think of strategies to use in those situations. Practice and rehearse strategies your child thinks may work.
- Create an area of your home that is a good place for anyone in the family to go to for calming. This is different than a location for time-out, which is meant to be time away from anything rewarding. Instead, this area may have headsets with calming music to listen to, soft pillows, and something to look at such as fish in an aquarium or a window facing your backyard (*Lists 2.2, 2.3,2.13, 2.14, 2.16*).

- Teach your child the following:
  - To recognize his or her physical signs of getting angry (tight jaw and other muscles, clenched fists, feeling hot or flushed, knot in stomach) and steps to calm down when feeling these signs.
  - To use words to express his or her feelings. Your child may have language difficulties and need help with doing so and would benefit from your modeling. You can teach some appropriate words or phrases to use when angry and guide your child through questioning to express how he or she is feeling.
  - Positive self-talk statements to repeat, such as "I am calm and in control." "I can handle this."
  - Self-calming, anger-management, or stress-reduction strategies such as deep breathing, counting slowly forward or backward, and visualization (*List 7.7*).
- Problem solve. This is a critical skill that requires a lot of practice: identifying the problem, brainstorming possible solutions, evaluating pros and cons of the possible solutions, choosing one of the best options, reviewing its effectiveness, and trying another if it does not workg. Greene's collaborative problem-solving (CPS) approach is widely used with success. It has been found helpful in reducing children's rage and explosive episodes. See www.ccps.info and Lives in the Balance (www.livesinthebalance.org/) for more information, as well as his book and others listed in the "Sources and Resources" section at the end of *List 2.15*.
- There are resources for teaching your child self-regulation strategies, such as *Zones of Regulation*, *Hunter and His Amazing Remote Control*, *The Alert Program*, and *The Incredible 5-Point Scale*. See the "Sources and Resources" section at the end of this list and at the end of *List 2.15* for information on these.

Strategies to Aid Calming and Avoid Escalation

- Monitor your child's emotional level. You may want to use a visual like a thermometer or scale showing levels of emotion and ask your child how he or she is feeling according to the scale or thermometer. For example, an anger or frustration thermometer on a one-to-five or one-to-ten scale with low numbers and a cool color (blue or green) for "I'm calm, happy, all is well" moving up to the highest levels (orange then red) for intense feelings and ready to explode.
- When your child is showing signs of becoming overly stimulated, frustrated, or upset, intervene at once, for example, by doing the following:
  - Signal to calm down with a prearranged gesture or cue word.
  - Try to divert your child's attention and redirect to something else (watch a TV show, play the piano, shoot baskets, take the dog for a walk).
  - Change the expectations, setting, or activity.
  - Cue your child to start using one of the self-calming strategies that your child has been taught and practiced. Coach your child through using the technique ("OK. Breathe slowly with me… ").
  - Remind your child about rewards and consequences.
  - Offer your child assistance and direct support.
- Watch your own words, tone of voice, and body language. Speak softly and slowly. Uncross your arms and relax your facial muscles. Position yourself at the same level as your child. (Sit down if your child is seated.)

- Affirm and acknowledge your child's feelings: "I see you're upset." "I understand that would make you mad." "I can see why you would be disappointed."
- Show that you recognize what your child wanted or his or her intent: "You were hoping ... " "You were expecting ... and ... ."
- Be empathetic, understanding, and reassuring.
- Use strategies involving an image your child can visualize. Novotni (2009) suggests asking your child to imagine that there is a candle painted on his or her palm and blowing out the imaginary flame as a calming technique. She also recommends the child to hold an imaginary remote control and press the buttons to lower the emotions. The Copeland (1998) book uses the remote control analogy with buttons for channel changer, pause, fast forward, slow motion, coach, zapper, and way to go! You can say, for example, "Hit your pause (or slow motion) button," then have your child employ one of the calming strategies, such as breathing or counting backward.
- Exercise helps. Running, dancing, martial arts, or any sport or exercise is beneficial for elevating one's mood and can prevent strong emotions from escalating out of control. Pushing and pulling, carrying something heavy, rocking or swinging, hitting a punching bag, or pounding on clay can be helpful.
- Have a basket or box ready at home or the car filled with fidget toys or small items your child can play with when beginning to get restless or agitated and needing a break (*List 2.6*).
- Certain scents or aromas such as vanilla and lavender may have a relaxing, calming effect on your child. You may want to experiment with use of fragrances to help change your child's mood.
- Discuss, problem solve, and negotiate solutions if there was a conflict when you both have had time to cool down and are in a calm, thinking mode.
- See recommended strategies for teachers on managing student anger, frustration, and poor emotional regulation (*List 2.15*).

Sources and Resources

Brady, Carol. (2005). Helping your little tyrant avoid outbursts. *ADDitude Magazine*, *6*(2), 56–57.

Copeland, Lori A. (1998). *Hunter and his amazing remote control: A fun, hands-on way to teach self-control to ADD/ADHD children*. Chapin, SC: YouthLight.

Greene, Ross. (2010). Parenting difficult children. *Attention Magazine*, *17*(3), 10–12.

Katz, Mark. (2006). Promising practices: Preventing explosive behavior in children. *Attention Magazine*, *13*(5), 14.

Novotni, Michele. (2009, Spring). 7 quick fixes for ADHD meltdowns. *ADDitude Magazine*. Retrieved from www.additudemag.com/adhd/article/5762.html

2.17 ADHD and Social Skills Interventions

Children and teens with ADHD frequently have difficulty with peer relationships, which can be a source of great pain and low self-esteem for the child and family. Although usually aware of the social skills they should exhibit, children with ADHD often struggle applying those skills. Because of their developmental delay in self-regulation, it is common for children and teens with ADHD to behave immaturely and display social skills more typical of a younger child.

- Common struggles of children and teens with ADHD that negatively affect their interactions and social acceptance are as follows:
  - Poor self-control and inhibition—causing difficulties with taking turns, sharing, saying something impulsively that is hurtful or inappropriate
  - Poor social problem-solving skills and over-reactivity—being easily provoked to fighting, arguing, name calling, and inappropriate means of resolving conflicts
  - Poor self-awareness and underdeveloped sense of the future—being unaware of their behaviors and how they affect others and not considering the consequences of their actions
  - Difficulty controlling or regulating their emotions, noise level, and activity level
  - Poor communication skills (such as listening to others and refraining from interrupting)
- There are different reasons for social skills challenges. It could be that the child lacks knowledge and has not yet acquired the skill, in which case instruction is necessary to teach the skill. Other times the child has learned the skill and knows what to do, but fails to perform the skill with consistency or at an acceptable level. Another reason for social skill difficulties can be because of internal or external factors such as inattention, impulsivity, or hyperactivity interfering with the ability to perform the skill even though it has been learned (National Association of School Psychologists, 2002).
- For performance deficits, intervention includes prompting, cueing, and reminding them about the appropriate behavior and consequences, lots of practice of the skills with feedback, and reinforcing in motivating ways their use of good social skills in activities and environments where they have problems (for example, the playground, at the bus stop, in the cafeteria, and when playing competitive games with siblings or friends).

School Interventions and Recommendations for Educators

- Every day teachers informally model and teach students positive social behaviors. By setting behavioral standards and enforcing expectations for respectful, cooperative behavior, most students learn and practice social skills daily. Teachers infuse social skills training into daily instruction when they explicitly model, coach, prompt, monitor, and positively reinforce such skills as sharing and taking turns, listening without interrupting, participating in conversations without dominating them, encouraging and complimenting others, disagreeing and expressing opinions appropriately, and employ general manners of using respectful, polite, verbal and body language.

- Within the classroom, there is no better place and structure for teaching and practicing appropriate social skills than in the context of cooperative learning groups. Research has proven cooperative learning to be effective not only in increasing student learning but also in developing positive and supportive relationships, student acceptance, and the ability to see other points of view.
- Schoolwide programs that teach and reinforce positive, prosocial behavior in all school settings are highly effective. See the national website of OSEP Technical Assistance Center on Positive Behavioral Interventions and Supports (www.pbis.org) for developing a comprehensive schoolwide system and a model that is successfully being used in schools throughout the United States. PBIS is proven to improve behavioral and social skills of students as well as many other benefits, including academic. More information is also found through PBIS state networks at www.pbisnetworks.org and links to individual states.
- The PBIS schoolwide model of behavioral supports and interventions involves teaching a clear set of positive expectations and behaviors with procedures for teaching expected behavior, a continuum of procedures for encouraging expected behavior and for discouraging inappropriate behavior, and ongoing monitoring and evaluation (Lewis-Palmer, 2007).
- PBIS, similar to RTI (*List 6.1*), is a three-tiered model that offers tier 1 (school- and classroom-wide primary prevention strategies), tier 2 (secondary prevention and supports for targeted groups and at-risk students), and tier 3 (specialized, individualized interventions for students with high needs and levels of risk). Social skills instruction is part of the intervention at all levels. Tier 1 support involves explicit modeling, teaching, and practicing of social skills with all staff involved in prompting, cueing, and reinforcing skills throughout the school in every setting and in a variety of ways that increase student motivation. Lessons and interventions that take place in the classroom are for the whole class or groups. Tier 2 intervention is more targeted with social skills lessons and interventions for groups and individual students. Tier 3 intervention and social skills lessons for students with significant social skill challenges are customized for individual students, monitored carefully and intensified as needed.
- Many schools are implementing schoolwide character education programs or social-emotional learning programs that focus on teaching and reinforcing prosocial values such as trustworthiness, honesty, dependability, courtesy, sportsmanship, responsibility, friendship, respect, empathy, integrity, persistence, and initiative. Lessons are taught and these targeted virtues or values are reinforced in every classroom and school setting. All staff members, for example, are given a certain amount of "I got caught" tickets to distribute to any student they happen to observe on campus exhibiting the target social skill of the week or month. Tickets earned go into a school raffle with prizes for winning students.
- Some schools provide social skills training through cognitive-behavioral curricula. Systematic lessons and units are taught by the classroom teacher to the whole class or by another staff member such as the school counselor. Social skills training can be taught to the whole class or with small groups of students as an intervention in sessions outside of the classroom.

- In any context or format that social skills are taught, do the following:
  - Explain the need or rationale for learning the skill and define the skill clearly. This can be done through discussion and reinforced by visual displays such as posters and photos.
  - Demonstrate appropriate and inappropriate skills through positive and negative examples.
  - Have students role-play and rehearse the appropriate skill with adult and peer feedback.
  - Ask students to look for and observe the skill being displayed in different settings.
  - Provide many opportunities to practice the skill being taught in authentic, real-world activities, and encourage students to self-monitor their use of the targeted skill.
- Increase student awareness of appropriate skills by modeling, giving positive attention, and reinforcing student displays of prosocial behavior both in and out of the classroom setting.
- Some specific social skills that may be targeted for explicitly teaching, monitoring, coaching, and positively reinforcing include the following:
  - How to disagree respectfully
  - How to give and receive praise and compliments
  - How to share and take turns
  - How to play a game and accept losing appropriately
- Provide corrective feedback in a manner that is not judgmental or embarrassing.
- Help children weak in social skills by carefully pairing them with positive role models and assigning them to groups who will be tolerant and supportive.
- Teachers and other school staff may need to help facilitate the fostering of friendships for students who tend to be socially isolated or rejected. Having at least one friend at school is very important, and teachers should look for opportunities to engage the child in fun activities with compatible peers.
- Many schoolwide interventions can be employed to increase the social functioning and interpersonal relationships of students. Among them are training in conflict resolution, peer mediation, and antibullying programs.
- Specific social behaviors can be the target for improvement in designing DRCs and goal cards for individual students. See *List 2.9* and DRC examples in the appendix (charts A2 through A8).
- There are evidence-based commercial social skills curricula available, such as *ACCEPTS: The Walker Social Skills Curriculum* (Walker, McConnell, Holmes, Todis, Walker, & Golden, 1983), *Skillstreaming the Elementary School Child* (McGinnis & Goldstein, 1997), *Stop and Think Social Skills Program* (Knoff), and *Second Step* (Committee for Children, 2008).
- See recommendations of the National Association of School Psychologists (2002) for school social skills interventions and evidence-based curriculum and the additional resources noted in the "Sources and Resources" section of this list.

Interventions in Settings Outside of School and Recommendations for Parents

- Often a child with ADHD is not socially accepted because of poor skills in playing games and sports so other children do not want to play with or have the child on their team. It is a helpful intervention for parents to build their child's skills and competencies in playing sports and games to raise their status with other children. Provide opportunities to learn and practice the strategies, rules, and skills of those sports and games, and general sportsmanship so that their peers will want to include them in their play.
- Parents often need to intervene in finding compatible playmates for their ADHD child and orchestrating opportunities through monitored play dates and social activities.
- When having other children to the house to play (and just one other child at a time is generally preferable), parents can help reduce the chance of conflict by being prepared with enough activities to keep them busy, keeping the time together short, not having available certain toys that their child doesn't like to share with others, providing snacks, and monitoring from a distance in order to intervene if problems arise.
- Parents often need to be their child's friendship coach. Russell Barkley (2013) recommends that parents set up a home reward token program focusing on one or two social behaviors to work on over a week or two, which are posted on a chart. The child is reminded about the rewards and consequences (earning or losing a point or token) for demonstrating the target skills when interacting with other children. Then, as the child is playing with others, parents monitor discretely, and when observing their child's use of the appropriate skills, find an opportunity (when the playmate is not aware) to praise and reward with the token. When coaching, Mikami (2011) suggests that parents keep feedback brief, for example, "Nice job of letting your friend go first," and specific ("If you lose you can say 'good game' to the winner").
- Parents may try bringing to their child's attention the inappropriateness of some of his or her social behaviors and the negative impact they have on maintaining friendships. It is best to do so at more teachable moments and never when emotions are running high. Parents may wish to discuss with their child why other children get angry with him or her and why they may be having trouble keeping friends. Perhaps practice or role-play appropriate ways to behave for some of the child's problem areas—for example, being a good sport when losing a game, taking turns, being cooperative rather than bossy.
- Some communities have centers or clinics specializing in multimodal treatment approaches for children and teens with ADHD and offer a variety of services and supports for both children and their parents. For example, children may be participating in a social skills training group in one room, while parents are in a different room in a parent training session with a facilitator and group of other parents.
- Social skills training groups can be implemented in a variety of settings, such as clinics, summer treatment programs, learning centers, as well as schools. They typically meet once or twice a week for a limited time, such as up to twelve weeks.
- Social skills programs are designed to systematically teach specific skills within a small group (children and teens generally of same age range).

- Most effective programs use social skills curriculum (see curricular resources below) and training sessions that involve these steps:
  - The trainer provides a brief introduction to the skill, including examples and nonexamples, role-play, and rehearsal.
  - The bulk of the session involves actually playing an indoor or outdoor game or other activity.
  - Children are prompted and coached on the use of the skill.
  - There is a short debriefing with feedback and reinforcement for demonstrating the use of the targeted skill.
- Any social skill taught should be generalizable across settings. This requires that the skills be practiced and reinforced at school, at home, and in other environments where the child spends time interacting with others.
- Other interventions that positively affect social skill competence are teaching strategies for self-regulation of behavior. This may include training in anger management, self-monitoring, and problem-solving techniques (for example, identifying the problem, brainstorming possible solutions, selecting a solution to implement, and evaluating how that worked).
- Parents of children and teens with ADHD need to be part of the intervention plan to improve their child's social skills and interpersonal relationships. This includes training and skill building these skills:
  - Behavior modification techniques, and positive discipline (*List 2.2, 2.6, 2.7, 2.9*)
  - Dealing with challenging behaviors effectively (*Lists 2.13, 2.14, 2.16*)
  - Communicating with effective messages, directions, and commands (*List 2.4*)
  - Working together with the school on joint goals and reinforcement of positive behaviors (*Lists 7.1, 7.3*)
- There are some highly effective summer camps and summer treatment programs designed for children with ADHD that have a high focus on teaching, practicing, and reinforcing social skills throughout the day while participating in fun activities and interactions with the other children. For information about such programs and a listing of some camps and summer programs, see www.additudemag.com/directory.asp.
- Medication is a helpful intervention—improving symptoms that interfere with social success. Research suggests that medication enables children with ADHD to benefit more from the psychosocial interventions they receive.
- Parents should keep this advice in mind (National Resource Center on AD/HD, n.d.):

> It is important to emphasize that simply inserting a child with ADHD in a setting where there is interaction with other children—such as Scouts, Little League or other sports, day care, or playing in the neighborhood without supervision—is not effective treatment for peer problems. Treatment for peer problems is quite complex and involves combining careful instruction in social and problem-solving skills with supervised practice in peer settings in which children receive rewards and consequences for appropriate peer interactions. It is very difficult to intervene in the peer domain, and Scout leaders, Little League coaches, and day-care personnel are typically not trained to implement effective peer interventions.

See information from CHADD and the National Resource Center on AD/HD for more expert advice on this topic.

Sources and Resources

Barkley, Russell A. (2013). *Taking charge of ADHD* (3rd ed.). New York: Guilford Press.

Children & Adults with Attention Deficit/Hyperactivity Disorder (CHADD). See articles and links related to social skills for children with ADHD on the CHADD website at www.chadd.org/Understanding-ADHD/Parents-Caregivers-of-Children-with-ADHD/Behavior-and-Social-Skills/Social-Skills-for-Children-with-ADHD.aspx.

Cohen, Cathi. (2000). *Raise your child's social IQ*. Silver Spring, MD: Advantage Books.

Committee for Children. (2008). *Second step: Social skills for early childhood-grade 8*. Committee for Children. Retrieved from www.cfchildren.org/second-step.aspx. Each grade level of this evidence-based classroom program features developmentally appropriate ways to teach core social-emotional skills such as empathy, emotion management, and problem solving, as well as self-regulation and executive function skills.

Giler, Janet Z. (2000). *Socially ADDept: A manual for parents of children with ADHD and/or learning disabilities*. Santa Barbara, CA: CES Publications.

Giler, Janet. (2011). *Socially ADDept: Teaching social skills to children with ADHD, LD, and Asperger's*. San Francisco: Jossey-Bass.

Knoff, Howard M. (n.d.). *The stop & think social skills program for schools* (preK–8). With role-playing and group activities, this nationally recognized program addresses four developmental levels and helps students learn interpersonal, survival, problem solving, and conflict resolution skills. Available through. Voyager Sopris at http://www.voyagersopris.com/curriculum/subject/school-climate/stop-think-social-skills-program

Lewis-Palmer, T. (2007). *Embedding social skills instruction throughout the day*. Retrieved from www.pbis.org/common/pbisresources/presentations/palmer0RPBS20307.ppt#1

McGinnis, Ellen, & Goldstein, Arnold. (1997). *Skillstreaming the adolescent: New strategies and perspectives for teaching prosocial skills*. Champaign, IL: Research Press.

McGinnis, Ellen, & Goldstein, Arnold. (1999). *Skillstreaming the elementary school child*. Champaign, IL: Research Press.

Mikami, Amori Yee. (2011). How you can be a friendship coach for your child with ADHD. *Attention Magazine*, *18*(1), 16–19.

National Association of School Psychologists (NASP). (2002). Fact sheet on social skills: Promoting positive behavior, academic success, and school safety. Retrieved from www.nasponline.org/resources/factsheets/socialskills_fs.aspx

National Resource Center on AD/HD. (n.d.). Psychosocial treatment for children and adolescents with ADHD. *What We Know, 7 short*. Retrieved from http://help4adhd.org/documents/WWK7s.pdf

OSEP Technical Assistance Center on Positive Behavioral Interventions and Supports (http://www.pbis.org) was established by the Office of Special Education Programs, US Department of Education, to give schools capacity-building information and technical assistance for identifying, adapting, and sustaining effective schoolwide disciplinary practices.

Sheridan, Susan M. (1995). *The tough kid social skills book*. Longmont, CO: Sopris West.

The Incredible Years programs for parents, teachers, and children reduce challenging behaviors in children and increase their social-emotional learning and self-control skills. Parents and teachers use various strategies to help children regulate their emotions and improve their social skills (www.incredibleyears.com).

Walker, H. M., McConnell, S., Holmes, D., Todis, B., Walker, J., & Golden, N. (1983). *ACCEPTS program curriculum guide: The Walker social skills curriculum.* Austin, TX: Pro-Ed Publishers.

Section 3

Instructional Strategies, Accommodations, and Supports

Contents

Please note that a lot of the content of these lists has been adapted and updated from my other books, published by Jossey-Bass/Wiley, which you may be interested in exploring for further information, tools, and strategies:

Rief, Sandra. (2003). *The ADHD book of lists: A practical guide for helping children and teens with attention deficit disorders.* San Francisco: Jossey-Bass.

Rief, Sandra. (2005). *How to reach & teach children with ADD/ADHD: Practical techniques, strategies and interventions* (2nd ed.). San Francisco: Jossey-Bass.

Rief, Sandra. (2008). *The ADD/ADHD checklist: A practical reference for parents and teachers* (2nd ed.). San Francisco: Jossey-Bass.

Rief, Sandra, & Heimburge, Julie. (2006). *How to reach & teach all children in the inclusive classroom* (2nd ed.). San Francisco: Jossey-Bass.

Rief, Sandra & Heimburge, Julie (2007). *How to reach and teach all children through balanced literacy (grades 3–8).* San Francisco: Jossey-Bass.

Rief, Sandra & Stern, Judith (2010). *The dyslexia checklist: A practical reference for parents and teachers.* San Francisco: Jossey-Bass.

3.1 Adaptations, Accommodations, Modifications: What's the Difference?

The terms *adaptations, accommodations*, and *modifications* can be confusing. First, let's clarify the meanings.

Adaptations

Adaptations are any adjustments in the curriculum, instructional components, environmental elements, or requirements or expectations of the student. Adaptations are part of what teachers do to meet the needs of diverse learners. A good teacher attempts to differentiate instruction and make adjustments to enable all students to succeed. The purpose of adaptations is to increase a student's academic achievement and social, emotional, and behavioral functioning. Adaptations in the general education curriculum, intended in federal laws to protect the rights of students with disabilities (IDEA and Section 504), are changes permissible to enable the student equal opportunity to access, results, and benefits in the least restrictive setting. Adaptations may involve adjustments or changes in the following areas:

- Materials
- Methods
- Teaching strategies
- Pacing
- Environment
- Assignments
- Task demands
- Grading
- Testing or evaluation
- Feedback
- Lesson presentation
- Reinforcement
- Student demonstration of understanding or mastery of content
- Student response opportunities
- Location
- Scheduling
- Level of support
- Degree of participation
- Time allotted
- Size or quantity of task or assignment

Adaptations include both accommodations and modifications.

Accommodations

Accommodations are adaptations that do not fundamentally change the performance standards, instructional level, or content of what the student is expected to learn. The curricular content and expectations for performance and mastery are the same as for other students in the class or grade. Accommodations are provisions that enable a student to attain the following:

- Better access to the general education curriculum
- Learn and demonstrate mastery of content
- Meet the same performance goals that other students in the classroom or grade level are expected to achieve.

Accommodations typically include adaptations or adjustments such as these:

- Extended time to complete tasks or tests
- Change of location or setting (a quiet location for working on an assignment or testing)
- Extra support or assistance (one-on-one or small group)
- Assistance with organization or time management (keeping track of materials, recording assignments, breaking down large assignments)
- Providing tools or aids to support learning (outlines, graphic organizers, study guides, assistive technology, audio books, color-highlighted textbook)
- Note-taking assistance
- Computer access or other assistive technology
- Preferential seating to enable a student to focus better during class and to receive more direct and frequent prompting, monitoring, and feedback from the teacher
- Allowing a student to dictate answers to a scribe
- Allowing a student to take a large test by doing one page at a time
- An oral reader for some tests
- Allowing a student to take a test by giving answers orally
- Providing a student with a written set of directions as a backup to orally presented information
- There are numerous accommodations listed throughout this book (behavioral, environmental, academic and instructional, homework, and others).

Modifications

Modifications are adaptations that do alter or change in some way what the student is learning (the content or part of the curriculum) or what we are measuring. They also change to some degree the performance standards—the expectations for that student compared with what is required of his or her peers in the same classroom or grade.

Examples of modifications include the following:

- Giving a student a different or alternative assignment; for example, a student may be assigned to write a single paragraph on a topic and draw an illustration rather than write a five-paragraph essay
- Working with instructional materials at a lower level than other students of that grade

- Using a reading anthology from a lower grade level rather than a grade-level text when the class is doing a unit on comparing short stories
- Providing some students with a partially filled-in graphic organizer for a science lab experiment rather than the blank one used by their classmates
- Reducing the number of words that a child needs to learn for a spelling test or testing him or her on different words
- Providing an alternate form of a test to a student
- Shortening assignments to focus on just a few key concepts
- Using a different report card format; for example, a student may receive a narrative report card rather than grades or he or she may be graded according to different standards from those used to measure the majority of students
- Allowing students in middle school or high school to have a modified class schedule; for example, they might be given an extra study hall or not be required to take a foreign language

Hamilton and Kessler (n.d.) explain, "Accommodations level the playing field for students by changing 'how' they work through the general education curriculum. Modifications go beyond that, and alter the field (game) entirely. Modifications change 'what' is learned and therefore change the content of the grade-specific curriculum."

Be Aware

Whether a support or adaptation is an accommodation or modification depends on what is being measured. For example, providing extra time on a test is a modification if the test is measuring fluency or speed, but is an accommodation if not.

For students with disabilities, necessary accommodations and modifications as per their IEPs or 504 accommodation plans are *educational rights* not favors granted by teachers or school staff. It is generally recommended that accommodations be tried whenever possible before more significant modifications in curriculum or work expectations are made. Many students with disabilities require both accommodations and modifications. For example, students with significant reading disabilities need to build reading competency through instruction and materials at an appropriate level in order to strengthen and practice skills, as well as have access to compensatory methods, tools, and supports to enable them to access grade-level curriculum.

Sources and Resources

Center for Parent Information and Resources. (2010). Supports, modifications, and accommodations for students. Retrieved from www.parentcenterhub.org/repository/accommodations/

Deschenes, Cathy, Ebeling, David, & Sprague, Jeffrey. (1994). *Adapting curriculum & instruction in inclusive classrooms*. Bloomington, IN: ISDD-CSCI.

Hamilton, Kori, & Kessler, Elizabeth. (n.d.). Accommodations and modifications: Wait, they're not the same? National Dissemination Center for Children with Disabilities (NICHY). Retrieved from http://www.gadoe.org/Curriculum-Instruction-and-Assessment/Special-Education-Services/Documents/Co-Teaching%20Modules/Module%204/27%20nichcy.org-Accommodations_and_modifications_Wait_theyre_not_the_same.pdf

Nolet, Victor, & McLaughlin, Margaret J. (2000). *Accessing the general curriculum*. Thousand Oaks, CA: Corwin Press.

3.2 Getting and Focusing Students' Attention

Before beginning instruction, teachers need to obtain students' attention and direct their focus to the task at hand. The following are classroom strategies and techniques to do so.

Auditory Techniques

- Signal auditorily through the use of music: chimes, rainstick, xylophone, playing a bar or chord on a keyboard, or a few seconds of a recorded song.
- There are various squeezy toys and other noisemakers that make a novel sound that may be a fun auditory signal. Beepers, timers, ring tones may also be used.
- Use a clap pattern. You clap a particular pattern (for example, two slow and three fast claps) and students repeat the clap pattern back to you.
- Use a clear verbal signal ("Popsicles … Freeze!" or "Everybody … Ready … " or "1, 2, 3, eyes on me").
- Use your voice to get attention, making use of effective pauses and tone variation; whispering also works.
- Use a call-and-response technique, with the teacher calling out a word or phrase and students respond with repeating the word or phrase or with a specific set response word or phrase. See Whole Brain Teaching's (www.wholebrainteaching.com) "Class … Yes!" technique and variations for getting students' attention.

Visual Techniques

- Use visual signals such as flashing the lights or raising your hand, which signals the students to raise their hands and stop talking until everyone is silent and attentive.
- Teach specific hand signals such as American Sign Language to signal students. See free downloadable posters and examples for the classroom on Rick Morris's website (www.newmanagement.com).
- Use pictures and other graphics, gestures, manipulatives, and other interesting visuals to engage students' attention and interest. If using a projector such as a document camera, project on the screen some novel object or image to grab students' attention.
- Use a dowel or other pointer to point to written material you want students to focus on.
- Use visual timers such as Time Timer (www.timetimer.com), Time Tracker (www.learningresources.com), online visual timers such as those found at Online-Stopwatch (www.online-stopwatch.com/classroom-timers), or one of the visual timer apps such as Stoplight Clock.
- Cover or remove visual distractions. Erase unnecessary information from the board, and remove visual clutter.
- Eye contact is important. Students should be facing you when you are speaking, especially when instructions are being given. Position all students so that they can see the board, screen, or chart. Always allow students to readjust their seating and signal you if their visibility is blocked. Teach students who are seated with desks in clusters and not facing you how to turn their chairs and bodies around quickly and quietly when signaled to do so.

- Try using a flashlight or laser pointer. Turn off the lights and get students to focus by illuminating objects or words with the laser or flashlight.
- Color is highly effective in getting attention. Use colored pens and bold colors to write or frame important information. Use color highlighting pens or tape and colored sticky notes. Write, circle, or underline in color key words (particularly when giving directions).
- See *Lists 2.3, 2.12, 3.5, 3.7, 4.2, 4.6, 5.3, 5.8, 5.9, 5.10, and 5.14* for more on multisensory strategies to enhance attention and focus.

The Tech Advantage

In today's classrooms we have the benefit of modern technology to capture students' attention and increase their participation. Document cameras, interactive whiteboards, and the other constantly evolving electronic and multimedia tools are highly motivating and engaging—greatly enhancing our ability to reach and teach all learners.

Arousing Students' Curiosity and Anticipation

- Ask an interesting, speculative question; show a picture; tell a little story; or read a related poem or passage to generate discussion and interest in the upcoming lesson.
- Add a bit of mystery by bringing in one or more objects relevant to the upcoming lesson in a box, bag, pillowcase, or draped with a cloth that you later reveal. This is a wonderful way to generate predictions and can lead to excellent discussions or writing activities.

Liven It Up

- Try playfulness, silliness, humor, the use of props, and a bit of theatrics to get attention and peak interest.
- Use storytelling, real-life examples, and anecdotes, particularly personal ones, such as something that happened to you as a child.
- Be an animated, enthusiastic presenter. Model excitement about the upcoming lesson.

Make It Personal

- When giving examples, use students' names or other people they know (only in a positive way and not to embarrass the student). Make the examples interesting and relevant to them.
- Activate students' prior knowledge and draw on their past experiences.

Organizing Student Thinking

- Provide an overview of the major points the students will be studying and their relationship to prior learning.
- Explain the lesson's purpose and importance. Identify the objectives, content standards being addressed, and ultimate goals or outcomes to be achieved by the end of the session or unit.

- Graphic organizers (there are numerous kinds) are excellent tools to focus attention as well as help students organize and comprehend ideas and information (*Lists 4.3, 4.6, 5.4, 5.7*).
- Post a few key points for students to be attentive to, listen for, and think about during the lesson.

Management Tips

- Walk by or stand near a distractible student. Place a hand on the student's shoulder, tap the desk, or use another cue to get his or her attention.
- Position or seat the student in a location that enables you to easily make eye contact and provide prompts and cues to get his or her attention when needed (*List 2.1*).

3.3 Maintaining Students' Attention and Participation

Sustaining students' attention requires active not passive learning. It also requires that teachers incorporate a variety of formats and activities that are woven throughout the lesson.

General Tips for Keeping Students Engaged

- Move around in the classroom, maintaining your visibility, as well as providing individual assistance (clarification, cueing and prompting, redirection) and feedback as needed.
- Use high-interest materials and teach to students' varied learning styles (*List 3.7*).
- Write key words or pictures on the board or projector while presenting.
- Use technology to enhance instruction—document cameras, interactive white-boards, video-streaming, PowerPoint, interactive software, the Internet, and tools for students such as tablets and netbooks.
- Illustrate throughout your presentation, even if you lack the skill or talent to draw well. Drawings do not have to be sophisticated or accurate. In fact, generally the sillier they are, the better, and stick figures are fine. Your efforts to illustrate vocabulary, concepts, and so forth not only focus students' attention, but help in the retention of information.
- Incorporate demonstrations, role-playing, hands-on activities, anecdotes and story-telling, and multimedia presentations into your teaching whenever possible.
- Build in several movement opportunities during the lesson.
- Reduce lag time by being prepared.
- Monitor and vary your rate, volume, and tone of voice.
- Have students write down brief notes or illustrate key points during instruction.
- Endeavor to greatly increase student responses by saying and doing something with the information being taught throughout the lesson. This can be done, for example, through frequent pair-shares. "Turn to your partner and summarize [or paraphrase or share] your understanding," or "With your partner, clarify any questions you still have about what we just discussed."
- Supplement verbal presentations with visuals, graphics, and demonstrations.
- Use a variety of graphic organizers and techniques, such as webbing, graphing, clustering, mapping, and outlining.
- Increase the amount of teacher modeling, guided practice, and immediate feedback to students.
- Use study guides, partial outlines, or other graphic tools to accompany verbal presentation. While you are presenting a lesson or giving a lecture, students fill in the missing words based on what you are saying or writing on the board or overhead. Jotting down a few words or filling in missing information in a guided format is helpful in maintaining attention.
- Cooperative learning formats (partners or small groups) are highly effective in keeping students engaged and participating during lessons. Teachers need to follow the proper structure for cooperative learning groups concerning assignment of roles, individual accountability, and other matters. This is not just group work.

Many students with ADHD do not function well in groups without clearly defined structure and expectations.

- Use motivating apps, games, and programs for specific skill building and practice that provide for frequent feedback and self-correction.
- Differentiating instruction is necessary for keeping students motivated and engaged. Offer students a choice of activities, projects, assignments, and options in how they demonstrate their learning—oral or written reports, demonstrations, or creative designs, for example.
- Differentiate instruction through use of learning centers, flexible grouping, interest groups, independent projects and study, and a variety of other instructional strategies, structures, and accommodations.
- See *List 3.8* for more on this topic.

Questioning Techniques to Increase Student Engagement and Response Opportunities

Teachers who have the most success in engaging students are those who are skilled in the art of questioning. They know how to design instruction and provide high student-response opportunities, accountability, critical and divergent thinking, and active participation, with everyone having a voice that is heard and respected.

- Format lessons to include a variety of questioning techniques that involve whole-class, small-group, partner, and individual responses.
- Before asking for a verbal response to a question, have all students jot down their best-guess answer. Then call for volunteers to verbally answer the question.
- Build in wait time in your questioning techniques so that students have the time to process the question and formulate their thoughts before responding.
- Common Core questioning, with its focus on deep critical thinking, elaboration of ideas, and being able to explain one's reasoning and support with evidence, is a difficult task for many students—particularly those with ADHD and learning disabilities. Provide extra guidance, scaffolding, and support as needed.
- Structure the lesson so that it includes the opportunity to work in pairs or small groups for maximum student involvement and attention. Use alternatives to simply calling on students one at a time. Instead, have students respond by telling their partner, writing down or drawing their response, and so forth.
- Use questioning strategies that encourage student success—for example, probing techniques, providing clues, asking students if they would like more time to think about the question.
- Expand on students' partial answers: "Tell me more." "How did you arrive at that answer?"
- Pose a question, ask for volunteers, and wait until there are several hands raised before calling on individual students to respond.
- Make use of a set of individual student cards or popsicle sticks with the names of each student written on them. Draw a card from the deck or pull a stick from the can to call on students randomly and fairly. Draw names from the discard pile as well or use two sets of class cards that you pull from. That way, students who have already been called on must remain attentive, because they know their name may be drawn again.

- It is important for teachers to incorporate many techniques that enable students to have frequent response opportunities throughout instruction. Following are some suggestions for whole-group (full-class), small-group, and partner responses that require active involvement of students.

Whole-Group and Unison Responses

- *Use choral responses.* Have students recite poems or share reading of short passages or lines from the text chorally (in unison). Singing songs or chants, reviewing such material as irregular and sight words or math facts, and whole-class response to flash cards are examples of choral responses.
- *Hand signals for whole-group responses.* Unison responses can also be obtained by having students use various hand signals—for example, thumbs up–thumbs down or open hand–closed hand responses from students indicating "yes-no," "I agree–I disagree," or any other "either-or" response.
- *Write-on tools* (other than paper and pencil). Most students (particularly those with ADHD or learning disabilities who often resist paper-and-pencil work) are more motivated to use alternatives such as colored pens and markers on individual dry erase boards. These can be used in any content area for short answer responses and enable the teacher to quickly assess students' understanding.
- *Use electronic devices and digital response tools.* Whole-group responses can be made via apps such as I Response (http://iresponseapp.com), iClicker (www1.iclicker.com), and Poll Everywhere (www.polleverywhere.com/classroom-response-system). These are all useful for formative assessments.
- *Premade response cards.* Elicit unison responses through premade response cards—for example, (1) a small set of cards with a single-hole punch which are held together by a metal ring, (2) four or five cards that are held together by a brass fastener and opened up like a fan, and (3) a single-card made of cardstock or construction paper that is divided into sections (halves, thirds, or quarters), preprinted with a choice of answers in each section of the card. Each student indicates his or her answer by placing a clothespin on the box of the card containing that choice or holding up his or her answer choice on the ringed card set. When the teacher poses the question and provides a signal ("Ready … show"), students select their answer by holding up their response card so the teacher can see. Premade response cards are very useful at any grade level or content area to integrate into whole-class questioning strategies.

Small-Group and Partner Responses

- Much of classroom instruction involves small groups of students working together. Small-group active responses take place in any cooperative learning group structure. There are countless activities, learning tasks, and projects that are best accomplished in small groups, such as creating a product together, solving a problem, brainstorming, analyzing, summarizing, conducting an experiment, studying and reviewing, reading and discussing, and others.
- Use of partners (pair-shares) is perhaps the most effective method for maximizing student engagement. Students turn to their partner for short interactions: predicting, clarifying directions, summarizing information, drilling and practicing (vocabulary, spelling words, math facts), combining ideas and resources for a joint project, taking turns reading aloud or questioning and discussing a reading passage together,

listening to and providing feedback on each other's writing, working out math problems together, checking that each other correctly recorded homework assignments in his or her daily planner, and numerous other tasks.

- Partner activities are an excellent format for keeping students with ADHD engaged and productive. When these students are partnered with well-focused, tolerant, and cooperative classmates, there is also less likelihood of behavioral or social problems than in a whole or small group. Try building in some opportunities for "standing partner" activities—enabling students to get out of their seats to work and share with their partner while standing rather than sitting.
- Here are some more partner-structured examples:
  - "Pair up with your neighbor and share your ideas about . . . ."
  - "Turn to your partner [or neighbor] and . . . ." After giving partners a chance to respond, ask for volunteers to share with the whole class: "Who would be willing to share what you or your partner thought about ... ?"
  - "Turn to your partner [or the person across from you or behind you], and discuss ... for a few minutes" or "Write down with your partner all the things you can think of that . . . ."
  - "Help each other figure out how to do this . . . ."
  - "Try answering your partner's three selected questions about this reading material."
- *Note:* For related strategies on keeping students engaged, see *Lists 2.12, 3.2, 3.4, 3.7, 3.8, 4.3* and all of the academic strategies in section 5.

3.4 Keeping Students On Task during Seatwork

Students with ADHD often have significant difficulty remaining focused and productive during independent seatwork activities because of inattention, distractibility, and poor impulse control. Weaknesses in working memory and self-monitoring also interfere with successful completion of independent classwork assignments. The following strategies are beneficial for all students but are particularly important for those with ADHD:

- Provide sufficient guided practice before having students work independently on seatwork activities.
- Be aware that if the student was not paying attention when you taught something necessary for understanding the seatwork assignment, he or she won't be able to do the work without being retaught or getting assistance.
- Check for clarity. Make sure your directions are clear and students understand them before beginning their seatwork.
- Give students a manageable amount of work that they are capable of doing independently.
- Make sure necessary supplies are available so students can work during independent time without excuses. Have extra (but less desirable) materials available for unprepared students. For example, rather than providing new pencils, have a can of old pencils or golf pencils they may borrow from.
- Keeping a small plastic pencil sharpener at their desk eliminates the excuse for students to get up and sharpen their pencil when they should be seated and working.
- Send students to their seats with a written task card or checklist of things to do. Instruct them to cross out or make a check mark as they complete each task.
- Be sure that the independent seatwork assigned is developmentally appropriate and within the student's capability of doing it successfully without assistance. Nevertheless, provide access to peer or adult assistance as needed.
- Assign study buddies or partners for clarification purposes during seatwork. When part of the class has a seatwork assignment to do while you are working with other students (say, during a guided reading group), set the expectation that students who have a question during seatwork must first ask their partner or classmates in their table group. Only if no one in the group can answer the question may the teacher be interrupted. Some teachers also assign one or more "experts" of the day for students to go to in need of help.
- Scan the classroom frequently, praising students specifically whom you observe to be on task. All students need this positive reinforcement, and it also serves as a reminder to students who tend to have difficulty in this area.
- Monitor students with ADHD frequently during seatwork time. Ask them periodically to show you what they have accomplished. Redirect them when they are off task.
- Prepare a signal to be used from the child's desk to indicate to the teacher that he or she needs help. One method is to provide a red card to prop up or a red, plastic cup

or other object which can be placed on the desk when the student needs to signal for assistance. When scanning the room, the teacher can spot the cup or card to see who needs help.

- Give other fail-proof work that the student can do in the meantime if he or she is stumped on an assignment and needs to wait for teacher attention or assistance.
- Try using a timer and beat-the-clock system to motivate completion of a reasonable amount of work for students with ADHD. Set short time intervals for each timing. For example, if it is a twenty-minute seatwork period, provide for two ten-minute timings or four five-minute timings with mini-goals set in advance (how much work must be completed during that time frame). Reward for on-task behavior and having met the work completion goal during that time interval.
- Accommodate the need for quiet, less distracting work areas during independent work through the use of study carrels, privacy boards, and optional seat or table away from the student's regular assigned desk.
- Permit the use of headphones or earplugs or other tools during seatwork as an accommodation for students who are easily distracted by sounds in the classroom environment.
- Many students with ADHD need help getting activated. Once they do get started, they are often able to do the work independently. Try to offer support getting them started on the assignment.
- Read the first paragraph or page together or watch as the student solves the first few math problems. Then, let the student continue independently.
- Provide examples of problems or other references at their desk to help with the assigned task.
- Block or mask some pages of assigned seatwork by covering up part of the page or folding the page under so smaller amounts are visible at one time.
- Cut worksheet assignments in half or smaller segments and pass out one part at a time. Blocking or cutting into segments pages of work may help reduce the frustration a student feels on seeing a paper that appears lengthy and overwhelming.
- See *Lists 2.12, 3.5, 4.1, 4.2, 4.8, and 4.10* for more strategies related to this topic.

3.5 Adaptations of Assignments and Materials

Students with ADHD (particularly those with coexisting learning disabilities) commonly need accommodations and modifications as well as extra support or tools to help them with assignments and enable them to demonstrate their learning.

Accommodations and Modifications of Assignments

- Reduce the number of paper-and-pencil tasks. Provide accommodations to bypass written output difficulties and allow students to show their mastery or understanding of subject matter through means other than writing; possibilities are demonstrations, verbal responses, oral exams, and projects.
- Modify or otherwise adjust the length of tasks. Shorten assignments or work periods.
- For written tasks, allow student to use cursive handwriting or printing (whichever is easier for the student and more legible to read) or the computer.
- Allow student to dictate responses while someone else records or transcribes them.
- Reduce the amount of required copying from the board or books. Provide a photocopy or copying assistance instead.
- Record assignments clearly for students to see and in a consistent location, such as a designated area of the board.
- Back up oral directions with written instructions.
- Provide directions that are clear and listed step-by-step with a few words and pictures if appropriate.
- Simplify complex directions.
- Monitor the student closely as he or she begins assignments to ensure understanding.
- Assist students in getting started on assignments.
- Many students with ADHD have a hard time organizing their ideas and getting started in their writing. With a sentence starter or topic sentence provided as a scaffold to begin their paragraph, they are often able to continue writing the rest of the paragraph without a problem.
- Structure assignments so that they are broken down into a series of smaller segments. Assign one part at a time.
- Check assignments midway through (or sooner) for corrective feedback.
- Break long-term assignments into segments. Provide interim due dates and help with time management and monitoring of project time lines.
- Use an individual contract or other incentive system with positive reinforcement for work completion.
- Initiate a daily report card or other individualized monitoring form between home and school. Indicate work production and completion of assignments as one of the behaviors to be monitored, evaluated, and reinforced at home and school.
- Provide extended time for completion of assignments.
- Use digitized texts.
- Adjust the reading level of the assignment.

- Provide more direct and guided instruction, with lots of support and scaffolding, before student works on the assignment independently.
- Differentiate the assignment by modifying the level of difficulty or complexity, offering choice in how students work (independently or with a partner or small group), and offering project and assignment options that draw on a range of student learning style preferences, strengths, and interests.
- When providing options to choose from, limit the number of choices in tasks, topics, and activities so as not to overwhelm the student.
- Assist the student in determining the amount of time the assignment should take to complete.
- Get the student started on assignments in class and monitor his or her progress.
- Keep in mind that it typically takes students with ADHD significantly longer than other students (often two to four times as long) to produce work. Factor that in when giving assignments for in-class work and homework.
- Modify homework as needed, being responsive to parent feedback about the battle and stress in homes surrounding homework issues.
- Provide in-school assistance getting started on homework assignments.
- Allow students options for how they get the assignment done, such as working independently or with a partner, working at their desk or on a beanbag chair.
- Provide options for how the student demonstrates his or her learning. For example, if he or she struggles with writing by hand, the student may dictate to a scribe, type, or record the work verbally on a digital recorder or on the computer using voice recognition technology.
- Assign projects that give students the opportunity to incorporate music, drama, art, construction, designing, writing, speaking, use of technology, research, and any means of creative expression.
- Provide an assignment sheet, planner, or calendar as well as teacher or peer assistance to ensure that assignments are recorded daily and taken home.
- Provide samples and models of at standard and exemplary work.
- Provide a rubric or scoring guide detailing your guidelines and expectations, including the specific criteria that will be used to evaluate students on the assignment.
- Increase the novelty of the task by turning it into a game or providing different materials for student use, for example, dry erase boards and colored markers rather than paper and pencil.
- Provide handouts that have fewer items on a page than usual and are easy to read.
- Reduce the number of problems on the page.
- Enlarge the type size and spacing on the page.
- Increase direct assistance and support. This includes peers and cross-age tutors.
- Send students text message reminders about assignments.
- See *List 3.8* on Universal Design for Learning (UDL) and differentiated instruction with regard to ensuring lesson designs that are inclusive of all students in the classroom.

Adaptations and Modifications of Materials

Use materials that increase the rate and immediacy of feedback.

- Make answer keys accessible for immediate self-correction.
- Use flashcards with answers on the back for immediate checking and correction.
- Use interactive educational software, apps, and online programs for teaching and reinforcing academic skills.
- Use computer programs and apps for practicing basic skills: spelling, word recognition, math facts, grammar, and vocabulary.
- Provide access to information and to other resources available through engaging technologies.

Note: The element of self-correction, self-pacing, and competition against oneself or the computer (not another peer) is much less threatening for children with learning difficulties and those who have low self-esteem. The immediate feedback and reward, color and sound, graphics, and novelty in the programming are highly motivational—perfect for holding the interest of children with ADHD.

Use a Recording Device

- Record directions and specific instructions for tasks so students may listen as many times as necessary.
- Record text chapters and literature that students may listen to, preferably while following along with the text.
- Record test questions for students to respond to verbally or in writing.
- Record lectures, assignments, and class reviews prior to exams.
- Download digital recordings of your lectures and organize them by date or subject matter so students may easily access important points you present in class.
- Allow students with ADHD to use their cell phone, a recorder, or other device to give personal self-reminders.
- Recommend that students use a recorder as a study tool for verbalizing information and rehearsing before performance tasks.

Structure Materials to Enhance Students' Attention and Focus

- Block sections of the page by covering it partially with a marker or folding it in such a way that only part of the print is shown at one time; another option is to cut the page into parts, such as a math worksheet with rows of problems handed out one or two rows at a time.
- Frame the material.
- Highlight, underline, circle, and draw arrows and boxes in vivid colors.
- Provide clear, clean copies of handouts that are well organized and easy to read.
- Use illustrations and graphics.
- Enlarge the type size and spacing on the page.

- Provide markers (strips of cardboard, window box frames, or index cards) to students who lose their place frequently when reading. When attention drifts, so do eyes from the page, and a tool of some type that is placed on the page can help.
- Provide an outline of the lesson.
- Rearrange the page format to simplify and reduce visual distractions.
- Provide students with materials and tools for keeping organized.
- Use bins, colored boxes, and other storage and organizational supplies for keeping clutter and unneeded material out of students' view.

Compensate for Writing Difficulties

- Permit writing directly on the page or test booklet rather than having to copy answers onto another page or answer sheet.
- Experiment with a variety of pencil grips to find one that is comfortable for the student's use.
- Have the student experiment with the use of a mechanical pencil. It might be a better option for those children who exert so much pressure while writing that the lead frequently breaks.
- Provide a clipboard to anchor papers.
- Provide access to the computer, tablet, or to a portable word processor, and allow use of these tools for their written work.
- Experiment with different-sized graph paper and lined paper. Some children with writing difficulties can write more neatly and easily within smaller or narrower lines; others do better with wider lines.
- Provide printed pages rather than requiring students to copy from the board or book onto paper.
- Permit students to write by hand in either print or cursive—whichever is easier and more legible.
- There is excellent assistive technology available, such as programs with word prediction and speech recognition, that are very helpful for students with writing difficulties. Students receiving special education services should have their assistive technology needs addressed in their IEPs.

Math Material Supports and Adaptations

- Reduce the number of problems on the page.
- Use frames, boxes, or windows to separate and space problems.
- Use graph paper to structure the placement of numerals and help with alignment and organization of problems.
- Use an assortment of colorful, concrete, manipulative materials (pattern blocks, tiles, cubes, counters, number lines, more–less than spinners, dice, beans, or cups) to teach and reinforce number concepts of whole numbers, fractions, geometry, quantity, patterning, and so forth.
- Use calculators for problem solving and for checking work after paper-and-pencil calculations.

- Allow the use of and provide students with multiplication tables and charts, a chart of formulas, and list of measurements and conversions.
- Use the many highly engaging and motivating interactive apps, software, and online programs for teaching, practicing, and reinforcing math skills.

Additional Suggestions

- Provide a second set of books for students with ADHD to keep at home.
- Use creative learning center activities, games, and hands-on, motivating materials. My books (Rief & Heimburge, 2006; 2007, and Fetzer & Rief, 2001) in the "Sources and Resources" section of this list contain a host of such activities.
- Have an array of learning materials and books that span the range of developmental levels of students in order to differentiate instruction. For example, if the class is studying inventors, have an assortment of biographies and resources on inventors available at an easy reading level through more challenging levels. Regardless of the readability level, students can learn the same general concepts and information.
- Use word walls and anchor charts for student reference.
- Provide information through digital text, which can be converted to speech and adjusted for easier reading (enlarged print, different font, and other ways).
- For more information and strategies related to this topic, see *Lists 2.12, 3.3, 3.4, 3.7, 3.8, 4.1,4.2, 4.6, 4.8, 4.10, and those throughout section* 5.

Sources and Resources

Rief, Sandra, & Heimburge, Julie. (2006). *How to reach & teach all children in the inclusive classroom* (2nd ed.). San Francisco: Jossey-Bass.

Rief, Sandra, & Heimburge, Julie. (2007). *How to reach & teach all children through balanced literacy: User-friendly strategies, tools, activities, and ready-to-use materials.* San Francisco: Jossey-Bass.

Fetzer, Nancy & Rief, Sandra (2001). *Alphabet learning center activities kit.* San Francisco: Jossey-Bass.

3.6 Testing Adaptations and Supports

As pointed out in *List 3.1*, in many cases, the same adaptation can be either an accommodation or modification, depending on what is being measured. For example, reading an exam aloud to a student is an accommodation if the test is not assessing reading ability, just content knowledge. It would be a modification if reading skill is being measured in some way.

Following is an extensive list of possible adaptations to be considered when trying to provide a fair assessment of students' learning. Included are recommendations to keep in mind when preparing exams for *all students*. Others should be considered as accommodations or modifications for students who are unable to demonstrate their comprehension or mastery of the content material under normal testing conditions and criteria.

- Prior to testing, conduct extensive reviews.
- Provide students with all handouts and test copies that are easy to read (typed, written in clear language, at least double-spaced, clean copies, and with ample margins).
- Avoid handwritten tests.
- Eliminate unnecessary words and confusing language in the test.
- State directions in clear terms and simple sentences.
- Underline or color-highlight directions or key words in the directions.
- Provide many opportunities for short-answer assessment: multiple choice, matching, and other similar questions.
- On vocabulary tests, give the definition and have the student supply the word rather than providing the word and having the student fill in the definition.
- For fill-in-the-blank tests, provide a word bank for students to select the correct word for the blanks.
- Provide students with examples of different types of test questions they will be responsible for on the exam.
- Administer frequent short quizzes throughout the teaching unit, reviewing the next day, and thus providing feedback to students on their understanding of the material. The quizzes may be graded with scores recorded or just used to help students in their learning and confidence prior to the exam.
- Read aloud the directions for the different parts of the test before students begin the exam.
- Teach students the strategies and skills for taking a variety of tests: true-false, multiple choice, fill-in-the-blank, essay, fill-in-the-bubble, and others.
- Give students the opportunity to write their own test questions in a variety of formats.
- Practice all types of testing formats, sharing and discussing test-taking strategies.
- Use more short answer testing formats (fill-in-the-blank, matching, multiple choice). Test only what has been taught.
- Provide generous workspace on the test, particularly for math tests.
- Avoid questions that are worded in a way to deliberately trick students.
- Write multiple-choice questions with choices listed vertically rather than horizontally, because it is easier to read that way.

- Use portfolio assessment: progress evaluated on individual performance and improvement as opposed to comparing with other students.
- For a change of routine, assign take-home tests on occasion.
- Reduce the weight of a single test grade. Have several shorter and more frequent quizzes rather than a lengthy unit test.
- Allow students to use graph paper or other paper to solve math problems and attach to the test rather than requiring that computation be done on the limited workspace directly on the math test. The same can apply for tests in other subjects that require written responses or showing their work to solve a problem.
- Divide a test into parts, administering each part on different days rather than rushing students to complete lengthy tests in one class period.
- Don't penalize for spelling, grammar, or other mechanics on tests that are measuring mastery of content in other areas.
- Use privacy boards at desks during test-taking time or find other means of reducing distractions when students are tested.

Individualized Testing Accommodations and Modifications

Students with disabilities may have specific testing accommodations and modifications included in their IEPs or 504 accommodation plans, such as the following:

- Read the directions aloud and provide additional clarification to students as needed.
- Administer the test in a different location individually or in a small group, for example, the resource room.
- Substitute an oral for a written test as appropriate.
- Permit the student to verbalize his or her answers to essay questions on a recording device rather than write them or in addition to writing the response. For students with writing disabilities, this alternative will provide a more accurate assessment of their understanding.
- Permit students to respond to test questions on the computer, netbook, or other tablet.
- Allow students with writing disabilities to retake the test orally after given in written form to add points to their score if they are able to demonstrate greater knowledge and mastery than shown on the written test (especially for essay questions).
- Read test items orally to students.
- Provide audio-recorded test questions so students can go back and listen to the questions as many times as needed.
- Before providing the final grade on a test, point out some test items you spot as incorrect and allow the student to try self-correcting careless errors before the scoring.
- Give reduced spelling lists for students who struggle with spelling (for example, ten to fifteen words rather than twenty). When dictating the words on the test, dictate those ten to fifteen words in any order first; then continue with the other words for the rest of the class. The students who are tested on reduced spelling lists have the option of trying the additional words being dictated for bonus points. But misspelling any of those additional words will not be counted against them on their test grade.

- Score tests for number correct out of the total number assigned per student (which can be shortened for individual students).
- Eliminate the need for students with writing difficulties to copy test questions from the board or book before answering. Allow students to directly write in the test booklet if needed.
- Seat the student near the teacher or in an optimal location for teacher monitoring and focusing.
- Permit an adult to serve as a scribe and record the student's answers if needed.
- Allow calculator and multiplication charts and tables on math tests that are assessing problem-solving skills, not computation.
- Revise the test format, as needed, for certain students depending on their special needs; you can reduce the number of items on a page, increase the spacing between items, use a simplified vocabulary, or use a larger type size.
- Color the processing signs on math tests for students who do not focus well on details and make careless errors because of inattention, for example, highlight yellow for addition, green for subtraction, and blue for multiplication.
- Permit the use of earplugs, headsets, or some other device to block out auditory distractions during testing.
- Provide for additional test-preparation opportunities.
- Permit brief breaks during testing if needed.
- Administer the test at a different time of the day than other students are being tested.
- Administer the test in shorter intervals in a few different sessions.
- Provide extended time for testing (for example, one and a half or twice the amount of time) than is allotted for the rest of the students in the class.
- Allow subtests to be administered in a different order.

Accommodations for Standardized Testing

In addition to taking classroom tests, most students will take some form of high-stakes test during their school years. An example of some testing accommodations that can be made available to students, depending on the nature and severity of their disabilities as well as the specific tests given and the adequacy of the documentation, include the following:

- Extended time
- Large-print test booklets
- Human reader (reads test or directions orally to student)
- Computer use
- Reduced number of test items on each page
- Use of scribe to write student's answers
- Audio recorder so that answers can be spoken
- Permission to write answers directly in test booklet
- Testing in another room or at another test site

- Testing in an individual or small-group setting
- Preferential seating
- Breaks between tests

Under IDEA and Section 504, students with disabilities need to be considered for testing accommodations by submitting documentation for review and following specific procedures to determine eligibility. Parents should work together with school personnel or private evaluators to apply for appropriate test accommodations if they are needed (Rief & Stern, 2010).

Source and Resource

Rief, Sandra & Stern, Judith (2010). *The dyslexia checklist: A practical reference for parents and teachers.* San Francisco: Jossey-Bass.

3.7 Accommodating Learning Style Differences and Sensory Needs

Not everyone learns in the same way. Our learning styles encompass a number of factors, such as sensory modality preferences. Some of us learn best when we can see it (show me), or hear it (tell me), and still others prefer information to be presented or practiced kinesthetically (through movement) or tactile opportunities (through touch).

Modality preferences are the sensory channels through which it may be easier for a person to learn and process information. It does not mean that one has an impairment or weakness in the other modalities but that one favors a particular means of receiving information (input) or in showing his or her understanding (output).

The following describes what is often referred to as being an auditory learner, visual learner, or tactile-kinesthetic learner. Most of us use a combination of modalities and are not just one type of learner, but we may have stronger learning and retention when information is presented and activities are designed with strategies that tap into our modality strengths and preferences. Teachers who use multisensory instruction best reach and teach all students. Every lesson should be presented using a variety of auditory, visual, and tactile-kinesthetic strategies, and choices should be offered to students as to how they access information and demonstrate their learning.

Visual Learners

This type of student learns best by doing the following:

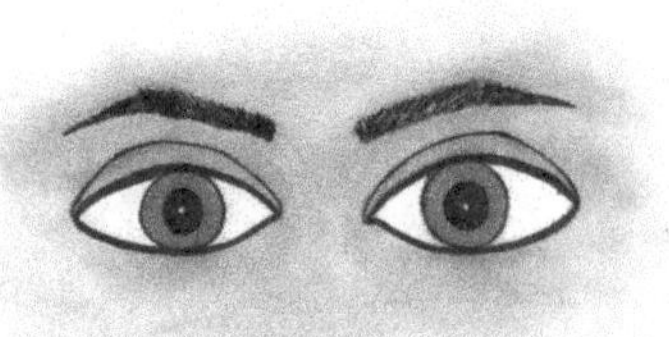

- Seeing, watching, observing, viewing, and reading
- Using visual stimulation: pictures, images, graphics, and printed words

Support visual learners by providing and encouraging the use of these tools:

- Graphic organizers
- Written directions (including pictures)
- Maps, charts, diagrams
- Handouts
- Flashcards
- Videos, DVDs, movies, multimedia presentations
- Advance organizers, framed outlines
- Modeling, demonstrating, illustrating
- Color-highlighted materials
- Interactive whiteboards
- Overhead projector and document cameras
- Dry erase, flannel, and magnetic boards
- Clustering, webbing, diagramming

- Strategic use of color (organizing and highlighting important information to remember)
- Letter cards (arrange into words), word cards (arrange into sentences), and sentence strips (arrange into paragraphs)
- Circling, underlining, drawing boxes, and using visual symbols next to important information
- Outlining the configuration of word shapes and color-coding structural elements (prefixes, syllables, suffixes, vowels) to aid visual learners with word recognition and spelling
- Prompt students visually ("Can you see what I mean?" "Look at this ... ")
- Visual cues to alert, get attention, and remind a student:
  - Tape a target behavior card on the child's desk
  - Point to a visual prompt of the routine or expectation

Auditory Learners

This type of student learns best by the doing the following:

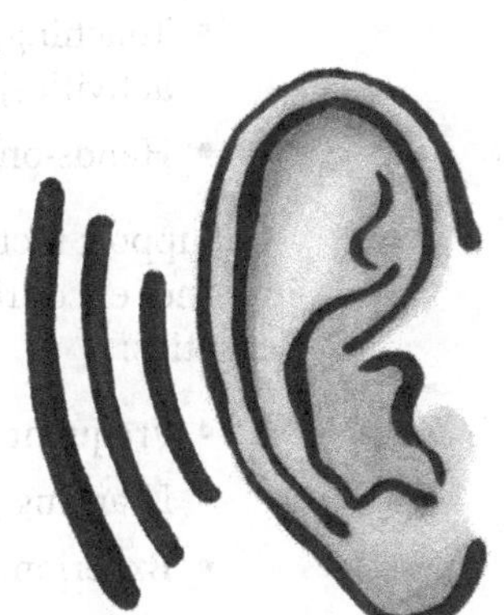

- Verbalizing, explaining, discussing, and listening
- Asking and answering questions
- Studying with a partner or small group
- Thinking out loud or self-talking

Support auditory learners by providing and encouraging the use of these tools:

- Music (rhythm, beat, and melody) to reinforce learning of information
- Rhyming, poems, songs, jingles
- Drama
- Stories
- Speeches, debates
- Recorded books
- Access to a listening post and headphones
- Text to speech technology
- Brainstorming
- Oral reports
- Word games
- Paraphrasing
- Verbal repetition
- Verbalizing through tasks (self-talk)
- Spelling bees
- Audio materials

- Phonics
- Reader's theater
- Cooperative learning (working with partners or small groups)
- Think-pair-share
- Discussions, study groups
- Reciprocal teaching
- Auditory cues to alert, get attention, and remind student:
  - A brief verbal message, such as "Listen ... this is important"
  - Nonverbal auditory signals (chimes, bell)

Tactile-Kinesthetic Learners

This type of student learns best by doing the following:

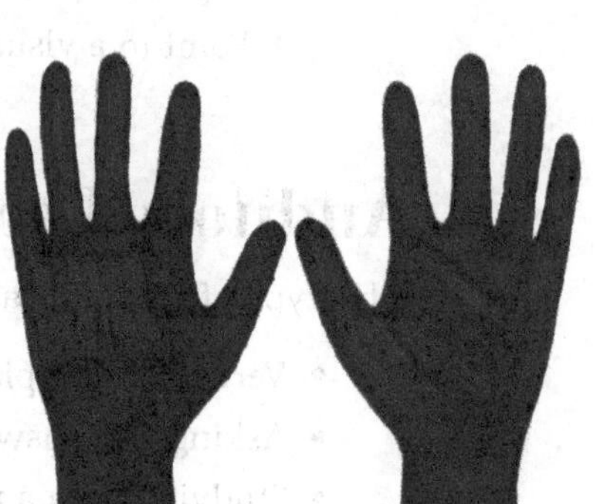

- Touching, doing, moving (physical activities)
- Hands-on learning

Support tactile-kinesthetic learners by providing and encouraging the use of these tools and activities:

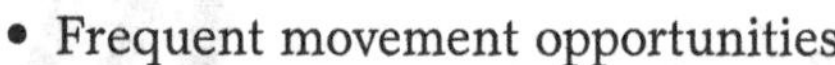

- Frequent movement opportunities
- Learning games
- Experiential learning
- Field trips
- Project-oriented, active learning
- Objects to touch (such as math manipulatives)
- Lab experiences
- Performances, role-playing, simulations
- Construction
- Arts and crafts
- Computers and other technology
- Concrete examples for abstract concepts (such as arm wrestling to demonstrate the conflict between protagonists and antagonists in a story)
- Tracing with fingers on sandpaper, carpet, and other textures or surfaces
- Studying information while in motion or physically doing something (walking, riding a bike, jumping rope, bouncing a ball, jotting down notes); even reading can be done at home with a book propped up while riding a stationary bike or walking on a treadmill
- Tactile-kinesthetic cues to alert, get attention, and remind student (such as a hand on shoulder)

Children with ADHD commonly have a greater than average need to touch and move. Giving them something to do with their hands and bodies while sitting in class can help them self-regulate, focus, and function better in the classroom. Teachers may experiment with sensory strategies and tools, such as these recommended by occupational therapists:

- Velcro adhered to the underside of the student's chair or desk—somewhere that the student can easily reach and discretely be able to rub to keep his or her hands busy
- Exercise bands placed around the front legs of a student's chair. When seated at the desk, the student places his or her feet behind the band and can push against the band, stretching it forward (Sitko, 2014). The child can also bounce legs directly on the band.
- Seating options such as a rocking chair, exercise ball, or wiggle cushions
- Chewing gum or eating something crunchy, such as apples, carrots, or pretzels (Sproat & Martin, n.d.)
- Fidget toys (also called sensory toys); see *Lists 2.6, 2.12, 2.13, and 2.16* for more on this topic and look for resources from companies such as Therapy Shoppe (www.therapyshoppe.com), National Autism Resources (www.nationalautismresources.com), and others
- Occupational therapists have the most expertise in this area.

Other Styles

Learning styles are also composed of cognitive styles, for example:

Analytic learners tend to be sequential processors who learn best by

- Working from parts to whole
- Making lists
- Following step-by-step in a process

Global learners tend to be simultaneous processors of information who learn best by

- Seeing the big picture (given examples of the end product)
- Focusing on the whole or main concepts first and then tackling the details
- Using clustering, webbing, mind mapping, and other such techniques

Environmental Factors

Environmental factors are another element of learning style. For example, some students are more productive with music in the background and others need complete quiet in order to concentrate. See *List 2.3 and 4.9* for more on this topic.

Sources and Resources

Sitko, Elizabeth Rosto. (2014). Sensory strategies for the classroom. Retrieved from http://occupational-therapy.advanceweb.com/Web-Extras/Online-Extras/Sensory-Strategies-for-the-Classroom.aspx

Sproat, Christine, & Martin, Allison. (n.d.). Strategies for use in your classroom. Retrieved from www.canyonkids.com/alerting/

3.8 Research-Based Instructional Approaches and Intervention Resources

This list describes key instructional strategies and approaches for helping students with varying learning challenges to access the curriculum and achieve grade-level standards. For students with ADHD who also have coexisting learning disabilities as well as executive function impairments, these strategies and instructional elements are particularly important for success in general education classrooms.

Universal Design for Learning (UDL)

- This is a research-based educational framework first defined by the Center for Applied Special Technology (CAST) in the 1990s for creating curriculum from the outset designed to remove barriers and provide all learners with various ways of acquiring information and knowledge, and multiple means of student engagement and expression.
- "UDL is a set of principles for curriculum development that give all individuals equal opportunities to learn. UDL provides a blueprint for creating instructional goals, methods, materials, and assessments that work for everyone—not a single, one-size-fits-all solution but rather flexible approaches that can be customized and adjusted for individual needs" (CAST, n.d.).
- See UDL information and tools from CAST (www.cast.org), the National UDL Center (www.udlcenter.org), and The IRIS Center (http://iris.peabody.vanderbilt.edu/) in the "Sources and Resources" section of this list.

Differentiated Instruction

Carol Ann Tomlinson, an educational leader in differentiated instruction, explains (2000, p.6), Curriculum tells us what to teach. Differentiation tells us how to teach the same standard to a range of learners by employing a variety of teaching and learning modes."

"Differentiation means tailoring instruction to meet individual needs. Whether teachers differentiate content, process, products, or the learning environment, the use of ongoing assessment and flexible grouping makes this a successful approach to instruction" (Tomlinson, n.d.). Similar to UDL, differentiated instruction is also based on the understanding that one size does not fit all and that teachers need to make adjustments and employ strategies to better reach and teach all of the diverse learners in the classroom.

There are numerous ways a teacher can go about differentiating the content of the lesson, learning tasks, activities, the lesson presentation, materials used, and student products. The following are some strategies that incorporate UDL and differentiated instruction:

- Multiple and flexible groupings of students
- Providing academic and instructional scaffolds, supports, and accommodations based on students' individual needs (as described in lists throughout this book)
- Providing numerous opportunities for student choices and options (projects, activities, assignments, tools, and materials) that draw on individual strengths and interests
- Designing activities that span the developmental skill and ability range of students, providing choices and levels of complexity in assignments to meet the needs of all

students in an inclusive classroom; an example of this is tiered assignments, which vary the level of difficulty, the process, or product

- Providing students with choices of where, how, and with whom they work and with choices about topics of study, ways of learning, and modes of expression
- Lessons designed and presented with different learning needs in mind, as in the following sections

Inclusive Lesson Presentations Strategies

- Clearly state the lesson's purpose and relevance and exactly what students will be learning. Indicate content standards being addressed in the lesson.
- Project an outline of the lesson for students to follow.
- Build background knowledge and use strategies that enable students to share what they already know about a topic before instructing on that topic.
- Use multisensory instruction—multimodal methods to present a lesson (*List 3.7*).
- Introduce lessons with strategies to capture students' attention, arouse their curiosity, and set the stage for learning (*List 3.2*).
- Use strategies to engage students' interest and maintain their attention and participation (*List 3.3*).
- Use questioning techniques that maximize student engagement and response opportunities (*List 3.3*).
- Structure lessons with a variety of instructional formats (whole group, small group, partner, and individual) (*List 3.3*).
- Build in opportunities for movement during the lesson (*List 3.3*).
- Use a variety of materials and adapt materials as needed for individual students (*List 3.5*).
- Provide opportunities to preview new material before it is taught in class, such as seeing an outline of the upcoming lesson and preteaching difficult academic vocabulary.
- Consider ways to provide students access to your lectures or class review sessions as an additional opportunity to listen again and supplement what they heard in class or to enable absent students to hear what they missed.
- Summarize key points and let students know what is important for them to remember.
- Pause throughout instruction to question students' understanding of concepts.
- Frequently monitor and assess students' understanding and mastery, reteaching when indicated.
- Monitor and vary your rate, volume, and tone of voice.
- Move throughout the room and provide individual assistance (clarification, cueing, prompting, redirection, and feedback) as needed.
- Use a variety of graphic organizers and techniques such as webbing, graphing, clustering, mapping, and outlining.
- Frequently review and make connections to information and concepts that have been previously taught and provide cumulative practice of previously learned skills.

- Teach thematically across the curriculum whenever possible because students better grasp the connection and learn most effectively when information is integrated and interrelated.
- Present lessons in short, brief segments and time blocks, giving students opportunities to respond in some format with high frequency throughout the lesson. For example, pause after short amounts of information are presented and have students share their understanding with a partner.
- Provide as many opportunities as possible for small-group instruction with the teacher.
- Present using models, examples, visuals, role-playing, demonstrations, and audiovisual materials.
- Consult with a special education teacher or other staff member for how to adapt instruction and teach concepts or skills in different ways.
- See lists in sections 3, 4, 5, and 7 for many related instructional strategies.

Note: Differentiated instruction is one of the best ways to provide primary tier 1 intervention under a Response to Intervention (RTI) model. See *List 6.1* as well as the section below on RTI.

Peer-Mediated Instruction and Intervention

- Two types of peer-mediated instruction and intervention are cooperative learning and classwide peer tutoring.
- Students with ADHD typically do not function well in unstructured groups, but they can be very successful with well-designed cooperative learning groups. Cooperative learning is a well-structured group format to collaboratively achieve common goals. It includes specific elements, such as positive interdependence, individual accountability, and others. The author's book *How to Reach & Teach Children with ADD/ADHD* contains a chapter on cooperative learning with a social skills lesson plan for cooperative learning groups and ideas for monitoring and intervening during cooperative group activities.
- Classwide peer-tutoring programs involve pairs of students (structured by the teacher) being taught how to tutor one another so that each tutee receives one-on-one instruction and feedback for half of the time period. After each tutee completes the assigned tasks and earns points for his or her progress, the students switch roles. The point earnings of the dyads are posted in the classroom. Because the students are rewarded as a pair, the tutor is as invested in the exercise as the tutee (Hall & Stagila, 2003).
- The Peer Assisted Learning Strategies (PALS) programs for reading and math, developed by researchers Douglas and Lynn Fuchs at Vanderbilt University, are classwide peer-tutoring programs being used successfully in many schools. See the "Sources and Resources" section in this list.

Cognitive Strategy Instruction (CSI)

- Cognitive strategy instruction (CSI) is one of the most effective ways of improving academic performance for children with learning difficulties and for helping students develop the necessary skills to be self-regulated learners. The University of Nebraska-Lincoln's Cognitive Strategy Instruction website (http://cehs.unl.edu/csi) is an outstanding resource—describing CSI and implementation of the Self-Regulated Strategy Development (SRSD) model, developed by Karen Harris and Steven Graham.

- SRSD is probably the most well-known program and has been implemented widely in many schools and validated as effective by extensive research.
- The University of Nebraska-Lincoln's website on CSI is very comprehensive and offers free online cognitive strategies for reading, writing, math, note taking, test taking, and other study skills, lesson plans, and other information for implementation.
- Some of the components in cognitive strategy instruction use these modes:
  - Introducing the strategy and discussing how it will be useful to students
  - Goal setting
  - Self-questioning
  - Use of mnemonics
  - Modeling the strategy through think-alouds
  - Helping students memorize the steps in the strategy
  - Providing guided and then independent practice
  - Monitoring student use of the strategies and providing feedback
- See *List 4.3* for more on this topic.

Response to Intervention (RTI)

- This is a multitiered instructional approach that focuses on problem prevention and early identification of students who are not progressing at the same level and rate as their peers. It typically involves three tiers of interventions for students at risk of academic failure:

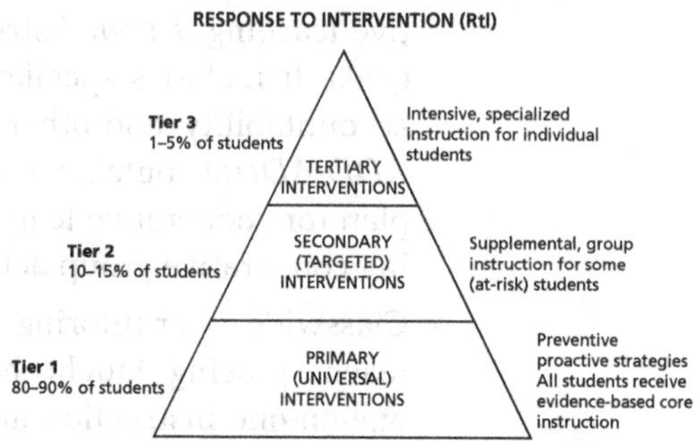

RESPONSE TO INTERVENTION (RtI)

Tier 3
1–5% of students
TERTIARY INTERVENTIONS
Intensive, specialized instruction for individual students

Tier 2
10–15% of students
SECONDARY (TARGETED) INTERVENTIONS
Supplemental, group instruction for some (at-risk) students

Tier 1
80–90% of students
PRIMARY (UNIVERSAL) INTERVENTIONS
Preventive proactive strategies All students receive evidence-based core instruction

  - Tier 1 (primary intervention) is proactive and involves evidence-based core instruction with teachers differentiating instruction and providing supports and accommodations as needed for individual students in the classroom. The classroom teacher is the provider of tier 1 intervention.
  - Tier 2 (targeted, secondary intervention) provides students who are not responding well to tier 1 intervention with additional instruction targeting the skills in need of development using an evidence-based program. It does not replace core classroom instruction but is supplemental and usually provided in small-group instruction.
  - Tier 3 (intensive, individualized) intervention is for students who are not responding adequately to tier 1 and tier 2 interventions.
- See *List 6.1* for more details on this topic. There are numerous resources on RTI, such as those listed in the "Sources and Resources" section of this list and in *List 6.1*.

Key Instructional Components for Designing Interventions for Struggling Learners

Many students with ADHD also have coexisting learning disabilities, such as dyslexia, and need targeted, more intensive academic intervention through RTI, special education, or other means. Based on an abundance of research, the key elements of instructional design for such intervention programs generally include the following:

- *Direct and explicit*. Each skill, rule, and strategy is taught clearly and directly, without assuming that the student has even the most basic foundational skills or background knowledge.
  - Introduce and focus on one new skill or strategy at a time.
  - Introduce, practice, and review skills using specific procedures.
  - Provide explicit teacher modeling.
  - Use demonstrations, graphics, manipulatives, think-alouds, and other multisensory tools and techniques.
  - Model the use of strategies through demonstration and think-alouds.
  - Have students practice using one skill or strategy multiple times before combining with other skills or strategies.
  - Provide a high degree of guided practice, frequently checking for students' understanding and giving immediate corrective feedback.
- *Systematic and structured*. Students are taught a systematic scope and sequence of skills, starting at a beginning level to ensure mastery of foundational skills and filling in holes in a student's repertoire of skills.
  - Complex tasks are broken down into simpler, more manageable ones.
  - Skills and tasks are taught step-by-step.
  - Each lesson gradually builds on previously taught skills or concepts.
  - Students are moved along at an appropriate individual pace.
  - Supports and scaffolding are provided as needed for success.
  - The scaffolds or supports are gradually reduced or eliminated as the student gains proficiency.
- *Multisensory*. Multimodal techniques are used to tap into individual learning strengths, strengthen connections, and make learning more memorable.
- *Targeted and intensive instruction* (as described in RTI). Intensifying instruction usually involves increasing the amount of instructional time for teaching and practicing the skills or by decreasing the number of students in the intervention group.
- *Frequent progress monitoring*. Use reliable, valid measures of student progress and adjust instruction accordingly (Rief & Stern, 2010; Vaughn Gross Center for Reading and Language Arts, 2010).

Sources and Resources

Universal Design for Learning

CAST UDL Lesson Builder. This is a free online tool that teaches educators to customize standards-based curriculum to meet individual learning needs. (http://www.cast.org/udl/index.html)

Center for Applied Special Technology (CAST). (2014). What is universal design for learning? Retrieved from www.cast.org/udl/index.html

IRIS Center, Vanderbilt Peabody College (http://iris.peabody.vanderbilt.edu) is a national center dedicated to improving education outcomes for all children, especially those with disabilities birth through age twenty-one. See their modules on UDL at http://iris.peabody.vanderbilt.edu/module/udl.

National Center on Accessible Instructional Materials (http://aim.cast.org/)

National Center on Universal Design for Learning (www.udlcenter.org). See their guidelines for developing lessons and units of study and curricula to reduce barriers as well as optimize levels of challenge and support to meet the needs of all learners from the beginning. The guidelines also help educators identify the barriers found in existing curricula. (www.udlcenter.org/aboutudl/udlguidelines)

Universal Design (from University of Washington). (2012). Academic accommodations for students with learning disabilities. Washington DO-IT. Retrieved from www.washington.edu/doit/Brochures/Academics/accomm_ld.html

Differentiated Instruction

Tomlinson, Carol A. (2000). Reconcilable differences: Standards-based teaching and differentiation. *Educational Leadership, 58*(1), 6–11.

Tomlinson, Carol A. (n.d.). What is differentiated instruction? Retrieved from www.readingrockets.org/article/263

There are numerous books and resources on how to differentiate instruction, including these:

Rief, Sandra, & Heimburge, Julie (2006). *How to reach and teach all children in the inclusive classroom (2nd edition)*. San Francisco: Jossey-Bass.

Rief, Sandra, & Heimburge, Julie. (2007). *How to reach & teach all children through balanced literacy*. San Francisco: Jossey-Bass.

Peer-Mediated Instruction

Hall, Tracey, & Stegila, Andrea. (2003). Peer-mediated instruction and intervention. National Center on Accessible Instructional Materials AIM Center. Retrieved from http://aim.cast.org/learn/historyarchive/backgroundpapers/peer-mediated_instruction#.U2KZEpAU-Ul

PALS (reading and math peer-assisted learning strategies) programs. Vanderbilt Kennedy Center for Research on Human Development. Retrieved from http://kc.vanderbilt.edu/pals

Cognitive Strategies

The IRIS Center (http://iris.peabody.vanderbilt.edu/module/srs/) on self-regulated strategy development (SRSD)

The University of Nebraska-Lincoln Cognitive Strategy Instruction website provides a wealth of information and strategies. (http://cehs.unl.edu/csi)

Response to Intervention and Instructional Interventions for Struggling Learners

Center on Instruction. Online course: Intensive interventions for students struggling in reading and mathematics (http://centeroninstruction.org/online-course-intensive-interventions-for-students-struggling-in-reading-and-mathematics). This free self-paced online course comes in a series of four modules based on the practice guide Intensive Interventions for Students Struggling in Reading and Mathematics. It provides research-based guidance for intensifying instruction in reading and mathematics for students with significant learning difficulties, including students with disabilities, in kindergarten through grade 12.

Center on Response to Intervention at American Institutes for Research (www.rti4success.org)

IRIS Center (http://iris.peabody.vanderbilt.edu/)

Murray, C. S., Coleman, M. A., Vaughn, S., Wanzek, J., & Roberts, G. (2012). *Designing and delivering intensive interventions: A teacher's toolkit*. Portsmouth, NH: RMC Research Corporation, Center on Instruction. Retrieved from www.centeroninstruction.org/designing-and-delivering-intensive-interventions-a-teachers-toolkit

Rief, Sandra & Stern, Judith (2010). *The dyslexia checklist: A practical reference for parents and teachers*. San Francisco: Jossey-Bass.

Rief at Pinterest: Numerous resources on RTI and other instructional interventions on author's Pinterest boards at www.pinterest.com/sandrarief.

Vaughn Gross Center for Reading and Language Arts. (2010). Response to intervention: Intervention handouts. University of Texas System/Texas Education Agency. Retrieved from www.centeroninstruction.org/files/3_Handouts.pdf

Section 4

Study Skills, Organization, and Other Executive Function Strategies

Contents

Please note that a lot of the content of these lists has been adapted and updated from my other books, published by Jossey-Bass/Wiley, which you may be interested in exploring for further information, tools, and strategies:

Rief, S. (2003). *The ADHD book of lists: A practical guide for helping children and teens with attention deficit disorders*. San Francisco: Jossey-Bass.

Rief, S. (2005). *How to reach & teach children with ADD/ADHD: Practical techniques, strategies and interventions* (2nd ed.). San Francisco: Jossey-Bass.

Rief, S. (2008). *The ADD/ADHD checklist: A practical reference for parents and teachers* (2nd ed.). San Francisco: Jossey-Bass.

Rief, Sandra, & Heimburge, Julie. (2006). *How to reach & teach all children in the inclusive classroom* (2nd ed.). San Francisco: Jossey-Bass.

Rief, Sandra & Stern, Judith (2010). *The dyslexia checklist: A practical reference for parents and teachers.* San Francisco: Jossey-Bass.

4.1 Working Memory Weaknesses and Supports

Children and teens with ADHD experience many of their most significant academic and functional difficulties as a result of working memory weaknesses. Working memory (WM) is one of the executive functions that is needed for numerous aspects of daily life and is critical to learning and performing successfully at school (*Lists 1.2, 1.4*).

Definitions and Descriptions of Working Memory

- WM has been described as our *mental workspace,* a place to hold information online, so to speak, long enough to manipulate it in order to solve a problem or complete a task (Katz, 2011).
- WM has also been described as our brain's sticky note (Alloway, 2010) or *cognitive desktop* (Kaufman, 2010), which allows a person to temporarily hold and manipulate information while engaging in other cognitive tasks.
- WM is holding in mind what you are doing: the goal that you hope to attain and the means that you intend to use to get there (Barkley, 2013).
- WM is an active and limited-capacity memory system that acquires information from short- or long-term memory, sensory input, and automatic memory, and then holds the information for a short time while a task is being performed (Baddeley, 2006; Meltzer, 2010).
- WM can be understood as an internal scratch pad. It provides us with a place to store information that we will need to use for the next step of a task, but that we do not need to store beyond that time. For those with weak working memory, it is as if their scratch pads are much smaller than expected, so that they cannot hold as much information in mind as others do. Further, the lettering on the scratch pad seems to be written in disappearing ink, so the words or images fade more quickly than for others (Cooper-Kahn & Dietzel, 2008).
- WM provides a mental jotting pad that is used to store important information in the course of our everyday lives for short amounts of time—for seconds or minutes at most (Gathercole & Alloway, 2008).

Verbal and Nonverbal Working Memory

- According to Dr. Russell Barkley (2013), WM comes in two forms that we use for holding things in mind to guide us over time to our goals:
  - *Verbal.* This type of WM uses words, for example, talking to ourselves in our mind's voice as we go about our day, writing notes to ourselves, and reciting rules to ourselves.
  - *Nonverbal.* This type of WM is largely imagery. We use visual images of our past to guide us, like a car's GPS when driving.
- Nonverbal (visual-spatial) working memory uses a kind of visual sketchpad of the brain. It allows you to envision something and to keep it in your mind's eye. Verbal (auditory) working memory taps into the sound or phonological system (Alloway, 2010; Baddeley, 2006; Meltzer, 2010).

Working Memory Deficits and ADHD

- Students with ADHD lag behind their peers significantly in their development of WM and other executive functions. Their WM ability may be a few years behind that of most of their classmates. A key challenge for students with ADHD is that school work places a heavy demand on WM, which often exceeds or overloads their limited WM capacity. This can result in a host of academic and learning problems as well as social and behavioral ones.
- Children and teens with ADHD have less ability to rely on their WMs to remember what they need to do, frequently forgetting information needed to successfully complete academic tasks.
- WM weaknesses are directly related to academic difficulties. Most common problems for students with ADHD are in the areas of reading comprehension, mathematical problem solving, and written composition. These are complex skills requiring high WM demands—being able to hold and mentally juggle large amounts of information throughout the process.
- For many children with ADHD, their impaired ability to hold events and information in mind (such as rules, past experiences, and consequences) to guide their actions interferes with their behavioral and social success.
- WM weaknesses are not exclusive to ADHD. For example, this is a significant impairment associated with learning disabilities as well. Many children with ADHD also have coexisting learning disabilities, such as dyslexia, in which case WM difficulties cause additional learning problems (for example, decoding words, reading fluency, and spelling).

Difficulties Associated with Poor Working Memory

- Difficulty following multistep directions
- Loses track of steps taken or where they are in a process
- Not remembering instructions of what to do next and may appear noncompliant (but actually forgot what to do)
- Forgets to do assigned tasks, chores, and other responsibilities
- Forgets to record assignments and bring required materials to and from school
- Forgets steps in a process (of academic tasks and classroom procedures)
- Forgets to do parts of assignments (incomplete work)
- Forgets to turn in homework (even when it is completed)
- Poor reading comprehension skills, such as pulling out the main idea, summarizing, making inferences
- Frequently needs to reread because of forgetting the information
- Struggles with the whole process of written language (for example, remembering and expressing ideas effectively in well-organized sentences, paragraphs, and essays; incomplete or off-target responses to writing prompts)
- Numerous errors in writing mechanics (forgetting to use punctuation marks or capitalization)

- Numerous errors in math computation (difficulty remembering steps of long division or other algorithms)
- Poor mental math skills and ability to solve word problems
- Poor note-taking skills
- Forgets what he or she wants to say (and may blurt out or interrupt so as not to lose that thought)
- Frequently misplaces and loses items and belongings

See *Lists 1.2, 1.5, 4.4, 5.1, 5.6 and 5.13* for more on signs and symptoms related to WM weaknesses.

Working Memory Strategies and Supports

The primary intervention for supporting individuals with WM weaknesses is providing strategies and accommodations that prevent or minimize WM demands. Teachers and parents need to be aware of how we present information, give directions, and expect children to perform tasks—making appropriate adjustments to avoid overloading their WM capacity.

Because their internal cognitive space for remembering things is limited (significantly more so than other children or teens their age), use strategies that externalize the information for them. This means placing verbal and visual reminders directly in their immediate environment where they need to use that information. Doing so frees up some of the space needed from their cognitive desktop of memory in order to more efficiently and effectively carry out the expected task or behavior.

- Give clear, simple, step-by-step directions (*Lists 2.1, 2.2, 2.4*).
- Repeat directions and have the child do so to ensure understanding.
- Provide all directions in verbal and written forms.
- Provide lots of visual and auditory cues and prompts (*Lists 2.1, 2.2, 2.3, 2.12, 2.13, 3.2, 4.5, 4.6*).
- Adapt assignments and materials to accommodate memory weaknesses (*List 3.5*).
- Make testing adaptations to accommodate memory weaknesses, such as providing word banks for fill-in-the-blank tests (*List 3.6*).
- Provide environmental supports that aid memory (*List 2.3*).
- Use graphic organizers, partial outlines, and other graphic tools to accompany verbal presentation (*Lists 3.2, 3.3*).
- Allow use of a multiplication grid and calculator during mathematical problem solving (*List 5.14*).
- Break down all assignments and tasks into a series of shorter parts and steps.
- Post visual schedules, rules, steps of procedures and routines, and task expectations. Give individual copies as well.
- Model and encourage use of to-do lists and schedules. Prompt children to refer to their list and schedule for what to do next (*Lists 4.7, 4.8*).
- Provide information using multisensory strategies (*List 3.7*).
- Use active reading strategies that involve doing something immediately after reading short amounts of material (*Lists 5.4, 5.5*).
- Break down writing assignments into the stages of the writing process (prewriting, drafting, revising, editing, publishing). Work on one stage of the process at a time

with scaffolds and supports as needed. Also, focus on one aspect involved in the writing assignment at a time. For example, during the prewrite stage, first work on brainstorming and generating ideas, then organize thoughts and information on a graphic organizer, or when it is time to revise and write a subsequent draft, do so one paragraph at a time (*Lists 5.7, 5.8, 5.9, and 5.12*).

- Use strategies that minimize students needing to wait a long time to respond to a question or be able to share what is on their mind, for example, by making frequent use of pair-shares during instruction (*Lists 2.13, 3.3*).
- Provide sticky notes for jotting down thoughts they don't want to lose while waiting to be called on to speak (*List 2.13*).
- Provide note-taking assistance because this is a very difficult skill for students with WM weaknesses—having to record notes simultaneously while listening and trying to determine the most important information presented by the teacher (*List 5.12*).
- Teach mnemonics and other memory strategies (*Lists 4.2, 4.3*).
- Use electronic tools to help students remember and to compensate for WM weaknesses.
- Provide memory aids in literacy such as lists (posted or individual copies) of word walls, high-frequency words, commonly misspelled words, examples of different parts of speech, figurative language, synonyms for overly used vocabulary words, phonics and spelling rules, anchor charts for reading comprehension, and written language (*Lists 5.3, 5.5, 5.7, 5.8, 5.9, 5.10 and 5.11*).
- Provide memory aids in math, such as posted or individual copies of multiplication tables, examples of algorithms, steps for mathematical problem solving, and math anchor charts, number lines, and manipulatives (*Lists 3.5, 5.14*).
- Provide visual references of classroom and group rules and class procedures (*Lists 2.1, 2.3*).
- Give enough practice and rehearsal of procedures so that they become routine. Behaviors that are automatic no longer require use of much working memory space (*List 2.1*).
- Chunk information presented into small amounts and have the students use it right away. For example, after a few minutes of mini-lecture on a topic, students then work with their partners or small groups responding in some way to the information (*Lists 3.3, 5.4*).
- Use instructional approaches and techniques that support students with learning challenges, including WM weaknesses (*List 3.8*).
- Use organization, time management, and homework strategies that support the needs of children and teens with poor WM (*Lists 4.5 through 4.10*).
- Consider the services of an ADHD coach to help support older students with WM difficulties keep on target (*List 7.6*).

Cognitive Working Memory Training (CWMT) Programs

Over the past decade or so there have been various brain training (cognitive training) programs developed and designed to improve working memory and other cognitive functions. Cogmed (www.cogmed.com) is a cognitive working memory training program used by many clinicians and with commercial versions for home and school use (*List 1.23*).

There have been mixed reviews of the benefit of CWMT in ADHD treatment. According to Schultz and Cook (2014, p. 30), "brain-training research is in its infancy and the results are as yet inconsistent and inconclusive." Dr. David Rabiner (2014) reviewed some of the newest research on working memory training at this time, concluding, "If one's treatment goal is to enhance working memory, CWMT may have real value. If the goal is to bring ADHD symptoms under control, however, these findings indicate that for most children with ADHD, CWMT would not currently be considered a reasonable substitute for medication and/or behavior therapy."

Sources and Resources

Alloway, Tracy P. (2010). *Improving working memory: Supporting students' learning*. Thousand Oaks, CA: Sage.

Baddeley, A. (2006). Working memory: An overview. In S. Pickering (Ed.), *Working memory and education* (pp. 3–26). Boston: Academic Press.

Barkley, Russell A. (2013, February). Understanding and improving your child's behavior. *ADDitude Magazine*'s ADHD Expert Webinar and Podcast series. Audio archive and transcript of Dr. Barkley's podcast is available at *ADDitude Magazine* at www.additudemag.com/webinars and the transcript can be retrieved from http://add-assets.com/asset/4149.pdf.

Cooper-Kahn, Joyce, & Dietzel, Laurie. (2008). *Late, lost, and unprepared: A parent's guide to helping children with executive functioning*. Bethesda, MD: Woodbine House.

Gathercole, Susan, & Alloway, Tracy Packiam. (2008). *Working memory and learning: A practical guide for teachers*. Thousand Oaks, CA: Sage Publications

Katz, Mark. (2011). Classroom strategies for improving working memory. *Attention Magazine*, *18*(1), 6–9.

Kaufman, Christopher. (2010). *Executive function in the classroom*. Baltimore, MD: Paul H. Brookes.

Meltzer, Lynn. (2010). *Promoting executive function in the classroom*. New York: Guilford Press.

Rabiner, David. (2014, March). New research casts doubt on working memory training for ADHD. *Attention Research* Update. Retrieved from www.helpforadd.com/2014/march.htm

Rief, Sandra. (2015). *Executive function: Practical applications in the classroom*. (laminated guide, expanded and updated). Port Chester, NY: National Professional Resources.

Schultz, Jerome, & Cook, Pam. (2014). Brain fitness programs: Buy? Or buyer beware? *Attention Magazine*, *21*(5), 28–31.

Stuart, Annie. What is working memory and why does it matter? Retrieved from www.ncld.org/types-learning-disabilities/executive-function-disorders/what-is-working-memory-why-does-matter/

Swanson, H. L. (1999). Instructional components that predict treatment outcomes for students with learning disabilities: Support for a combined strategy and direct instruction model. *Learning Disabilities Research and Practice*, *14*, 129–140.

4.2 Strategies to Aid Memory

List 4.1 discusses working memory, which is a key executive dysfunction in individuals with ADHD. In addition to the WM strategies and supports described in *List 4.1,* this list shares more strategies to aid memory for learning and retention of information.

Use Mnemonics

Mnemonics are memory devices or tricks that help us remember information by associating it with something familiar. Mnemonics include techniques such as acronyms, acrostics, keywords, pegwords, and more.

- Teach children to create first-letter mnemonics (acronyms and acrostics) to help them remember steps in a process or procedure, sequences, or other information.

Examples of Acronyms

- HOMES (the Great Lakes): Huron, Ontario, Michigan, Erie, and Superior
- ROY G. BIV (the seven colors in the spectrum of the rainbow): red, orange, yellow, green, blue, indigo, violet
- SCUBA: self-contained underwater breathing apparatus
- RICE (for how to treat a sprain): rest, ice, compress, elevate

Examples of Acrostics

- **D**ead **M**onsters **S**mell **B**ad (the steps for long division): divide, multiply, subtract, bring down
- **E**very **G**ood **B**oy **D**oes **F**ine (the sequence of lines in the treble clef): E, G, B, D, F
- **P**lease **E**xcuse **M**y **D**ear **A**unt **S**ally (the order for solving algebraic equations): parentheses, exponents, multiplication, division, addition, subtraction. This is also remembered by the acronym, PEMDAS.

- Many cognitive learning strategies use acronyms and acrostics, and examples can be found throughout this book (*Lists 4.3, 5.4, 5.7, 5.8, 5.9, 5.14*). There are several academic, organization, and study strategies found at the website of James Madison University's Learning Toolbox (http://coe.jmu.edu/learningtoolbox), for example, CHECK—a study skills strategy, which stands for
  - **C**hange environments (to one free from distractions).
  - **H**ave all equipment nearby.
  - **E**stablish rewards for yourself.
  - **C**reate a checklist of tasks to be done.
  - **K**eep a worry pad (if ideas popping into your head are distracting you).
- *Keyword mnemonics.* When students are learning new vocabulary words and their meanings, try using the *keyword* technique: Pair the new word with a similar-sounding word that can be visualized. For example, to learn the word "felons," which sounds like "melons" and means "criminals," visualize some melons in prison clothing marching to jail. See Vocabulary Cartoons at www.vocabularycartoons.com for books and resources that teach vocabulary words by using this technique of linking word associations that rhyme and visual associations in the form of humorous

cartoons. The keyword mnemonic is very helpful in learning vocabulary words in foreign languages as well.

- *Pegword mnemonics*. To help students remember math facts, have them try this mnemonic device: Associate each number from 0 to 9 with what is called a *pegword*—a rhyming or similar-sounding word that can be visualized concretely (for example, two-shoe, three-tree, four-door, six-sticks), and then make an association for the numbers you are trying to memorize. For example, to learn $6 \times 4 = 24$ or $4 \times 6 = 24$, one can visualize a door (4) with a pile of sticks (6) in front of it, and think: "Every day (24 hours), someone leaves a pile of sticks in front of my door." See the programs Memory Joggers (www.memoryjoggers.com) and Times Tables the Fun Way (www.citycreek.com), which teach math facts using these techniques.
- Use mnemonics to aid spelling. Have students use mnemonics to help them spell the tricky parts of words. For example, to remember there is the letter "r" after "b" in February, a student might think, "Fe**br**uary is a cold month … brrr," or "The princi**pal** is my pal" to remember which spelling to use for "principle" or "principal."
- Suggest that state or national capitals can be learned using mnemonics. For example, to remember that Springfield is the capital of Illinois, a student might think, "I can't spring out of bed when I'm ill." To remember that Amsterdam is the capital of the Netherlands, a student might think of hamsters running around in Never Never Land.

Use Music and Rhyme

- Many of us have been amazed at how very young children with limited speaking vocabularies quickly learn the lyrics to lengthy songs. Songs and rhymes are powerful vehicles for learning and remembering information.
- Raps, rhymes, jingles, and songs help in learning multiplication tables, phonics, and other information (for example, US presidents or steps in a cycle or process). Many learning songs and videos are found on YouTube, such as the several phonics songs at (www.pinterest.com/sandrarief/phonics-decoding-fluency).
- Some resources that teach through this method can be found on these websites:
  - Songs for Learning (http://songsforlearning.com/)
  - Musically Aligned (www.musicallyaligned.com)
  - Songs for Teaching (www.songsforteaching.com/index.html)
- Create your own verses of information to learn and memorize to familiar melodies such as "Row, Row, Row Your Boat" or "Twinkle, Twinkle, Little Star." This method facilitates memorization and makes learning more fun. It is how most of us learned the sequence of the alphabet and the months of the year.
- Use rhymes to help students remember rules (for example, "i before e except after c").

Try These Other Memory Strategies and Tips

- Memory is strengthened by creating meaningful links and associations. Find ways for information that is related to go together, such as by grouping the information into categories.
- Create silly stories that link information (such as a lengthy sequence of items to remember) by associating each item you want to recall with an image or action in

the story. Your stories should use vivid imagery, color, and action and be as absurd and exaggerated as possible, which makes it more memorable.

- Chunk information that needs to be remembered into small bites. Long series of numbers, such as Social Security numbers and phone numbers, are chunked for that reason.
- Emotional memory is very strong. When you can evoke an emotion while teaching something, it sticks. Storytelling is a powerful teaching tool because stories evoke emotions in the listener. When something is humorous, it also evokes emotions that make learning fun and more likely to be remembered.
- To help lock new information into long-term memory, do something interactive or reflective with the new learning, for example, talk about it, jot down notes, write an entry in a learning log or journal, draw something related, or fill out a graphic organizer.
- Play memory games, such as these:
  - *I'm Going on a Trip.* One person says, "I'm going on a trip, and in my suitcase, I'm packing a_____." The next person repeats that line and the item the previous person(s) said in correct sequence, adding a new item at the end to the list. This game gives children practice with auditory memory and sequencing skills.
  - *Concentration.* Turn up two cards out of an array of several that are facing down, and find matches. This game is good for practicing visual memory skills. This can also be done as a study technique. One of the cards in each pair is the question; the other is the answer.
  - There are a number of games that can be played at home and school, such as those suggested by Teacher Support Force (www.teacher-support-force.com/memory-activities.html) and at websites such as Kids Memory (www.kidsmemory.com/) and Play Kids Games (http://playkidsgames.com).
- Games make any learning memorable (because they tap into emotional memory). So, find ways to practice and review information taught through games.
- There are numerous examples of strategies to help students with memory weaknesses found on the author's Pinterest boards at www.pinterest.com/sandrarief/.

Provide Support for Memory Weaknesses

- See *List 4.1* for strategies, supports, and accommodations specific to helping children and teens with poor WM.
- See *Lists 4.5 through 4.10* for strategies and supports that teachers and parents can provide to help children and teens with memory weaknesses function better in the areas of organization, time management, and homework.
- See *Lists 5.3 through 5.14* for supports and accommodations in reading, math, and written language that are affected by memory weaknesses.
- Supply and use sticky notes for reminders. Encourage students to place them in strategic locations.
- Use color and pictures to aid memory.
- After directions are given, have the child repeat the directions to you or someone else, such as a peer partner.
- Provide frequent practice and review in a variety of formats.
- Avoid timed tests. Give extra time for recalling and responding.

- Provide checklists, task cards, reminders of expectations, and written directions for independent work activities.
- Have students flag, tab, or highlight important information in the text to be remembered.
- Research shows that we remember best that which we actually practice by doing and when the information and material is used immediately, such as by teaching it to someone else. Methods such as the whole brain teaching (WBT) strategy of Teach-Okay are models for doing this in the classroom. See www.wholebrainteaching.com.
- Use study strategies that aid memory, such as RCRC, which stands for the steps of the strategy: read, cover, recite, check (*List 4.3*).
- Use technology tools to compensate for memory weaknesses, such as recording information and programming reminders on personal electronic devices, use of vibrating alarms, and aids such as spell-checkers and calculators.
- Use multisensory strategies to make memories through multiple pathways in the brain. When teaching or trying to learn something, read it, say it, type it, recite it, use gestures to associate with it, move while practicing the information.
- Sing a list of names, a to-do list, or other items to remember to the melody of a well-known simple song, such as "Happy Birthday to You."
- Present information and have students practice it through multiple modalities so memory is built through multiple pathways. To better remember, read it, type it, say it, write it, hear it, feel it, taste it, smell it, and use some kind of gesture or movement together with it. Any combination using more than one of the senses makes stronger learning and better recall (*List 3.7*).
- Look for ways to help students visualize the ideas and information being taught. Images are much more memorable than words. Provide graphic cues. Illustrate while teaching and have students draw illustrations or symbols of some kind to help them remember information.
- Help students recognize and find patterns in what they are trying to remember, such as letter patterns in words to make spelling easier and noting number patterns on a one to one hundred grid.
- Link any new learning to prior knowledge. If we don't connect or process information in some meaningful way, the brain will not store that information.
- Use graphic organizers and semantic maps for helping students see how information is connected and giving a visual framework that aids memory.
- Provide frequent practice and review in different ways so that different neural networks are activated, which aids memory.
- Give students frequently opportunities to practice and rehearse what they are learning with partners or within cooperative groups. The more they talk about it, the better they remember it.

Sources and Resources

Kids Memory (www.kidsmemory.com)

The Learning Toolbox (http://coe.jmu.edu/learningtoolbox/) is James Madison University Special Education Program's website of strategies. The Learning Toolbox was developed as part of the Model Demonstration Project for Improving Postsecondary Education for Students with Mild Disabilities, a US Office of Education grant awarded to James

Madison University. The purpose of the project was to develop, implement, and evaluate the effectiveness of course-specific strategy instruction with college students who have learning disabilities and ADHD. This one-on-one instructional approach significantly helped students improve their academic performance. One of the goals of this project was to share what they have learned. This website provides a way of sharing this approach so that others might use it.

Memory Joggers (www.memoryjoggers.com)

Play Kids Games (http://playkidsgames.com)

Teacher Support Force (www.teacher-support-force.com/memory-activities.html)

Times Tables the Fun Way (www.citycreek.com)

Vocabulary Cartoons (www.vocabularycartoons.com)

4.3 Metacognitive and Other Learning Strategies

Students with ADHD benefit greatly from being taught specific learning and study strategies for school success.

Chamot and O'Malley (1994) describe learning strategies as encompassing the following types or categories:

- *Metacognitive strategies.* Planning for learning, monitoring one's own comprehension and production, and evaluating how well one has achieved a learning objective
- *Metacognitive knowledge.* Understanding one's own mental processes and approach to learning, the nature of the learning task, and the strategies that should be effective
- *Cognitive strategies.* Manipulating the material to be learned mentally (as in making images or elaborating) or physically (as in grouping items to be learned or taking notes)

Metacognitive Strategies

- Metacognition is "thinking about thinking" and involves consciously overseeing whether you are on the right track or need to make changes in your thinking or approaches.
- Metacognitive skills involve the following skills:
  - Previewing and planning for how to go about learning or studying the material
  - Organizing for the task, getting ready, and setting goals
  - Monitoring one's own attention, production, and comprehension
  - Self-assessment and evaluation of how well goals were met and learning took place
- Students with ADHD have poor self-regulation and executive functioning, which is what is involved in metacognition. These children typically lack self-awareness of what is working and not working for them and adjusting what they are doing accordingly in order to accomplish their goals.

It is important to teach metacognitive strategies, such as the following:

- Planning when, where, and how to study
- Monitoring one's comprehension during listening or reading
- Monitoring one's production (oral or written) while it is taking place
- Self-assessing how well one has accomplished a learning task
- Reflecting on what one has learned (Chamot & O'Malley, 1994)

Model and encourage students to ask themselves questions such as the following:

Self-direction

- "What is my goal?"
- "What do I need to do?"
- "What will I need?"
- "How will I do this?"
- "How much time will I need?"

Self-monitoring and self-correction

- "How am I doing?"
- "Do I need other information or resources?"
- "Do I need more support?"

Self-evaluation

- "How did I do?"
- "Did I finish on time?" (Hennessy & Soper, 2003)

Teachers use metacognitive strategies for reading comprehension and other learning when they actively involve students in activities requiring them to make connections, set goals for learning, make a plan, monitor their progress, and respond to sentence stems, such as the following:

"I'm thinking ... "

"I'm picturing or visualizing ... "

"I'm wondering ... "

"This reminds me of ... "

Here are three examples of metacognitive learning strategies:

Journal responses. There are a variety of ways to use journals to engage students in thinking, questioning, making associations, and so forth during their reading, and responding and reflecting after their reading.

- *Double entry journals.* The paper is divided into two columns. Notes are taken in the left column, citing anything of particular interest to the reader (e.g., quote, description, metaphor) along with the page number. In the right-hand column, the reader comments and records personal thoughts, interpretations, connections, and questions triggered by that section of the text.
- *Metacognitive journal and learning log.* The page is divided into two columns. The left column is labeled "What I Learned." The right column is labeled "How I Learned This." This assists students in thinking about and analyzing their own learning process. The right-hand column can state other things, as well. For example, "How This Affects Me" or "Why This Was Difficult or Easy for Me." The key is reflection and analysis of one's own learning.

Reading logs. Students can write their feelings, associations, connections, and questions in response to the reading. They may be given specific prompts to guide what is recorded in their logs. For example, "What did you learn?" "How did this make you feel?" "How did this relate to any of your own life experiences?" "What did you like or dislike about the author's style of writing?"

Think aloud. This involves externalizing and making overt the thinking processes used when reading.

- The teacher reads to students while they follow along in their books.
- While reading, the teacher models aloud the process of interacting with the text (for example, making predictions, describing what she visualizes, working through problems to figure out unknown vocabulary, and making connections).

- The teacher models how to self-monitor his or her own comprehension by stopping periodically and asking, "Is this making sense to me?"
- Students can then practice some of these strategies with partners.

Cognitive Learning Strategies (CSI)

Cognitive strategy instruction (CSI) is an explicit instructional method that is well-researched and effective for students with learning disabilities. CSI uses a highly interactive, sequenced approach consisting of guided instruction and practice leading to internalization of the strategic routine and independent performance of the task over time (Krawec & Montague, 2012).

Cognitive strategies differ from metacognitive strategies but closely overlap. Livingston (1997) explains:

> Cognitive strategies are used to help an individual achieve a particular goal (e.g., understanding a text) while metacognitive strategies are used to ensure that the goal has been reached (e.g., quizzing oneself to evaluate one's understanding of that text). Metacognitive and cognitive strategies may overlap in that the same strategy, such as questioning, could be regarded as either a cognitive or a metacognitive strategy depending on what the purpose for using that strategy may be. For example, you may use a self-questioning strategy while reading as a means of obtaining knowledge (cognitive), or as a way of monitoring what you have read (metacognitive).

Cognitive strategies typically come in the form of an acronym for students to better recall the steps of the strategy, which is explicitly taught and practiced. Following are some examples of some common cognitive learning strategies.

SQ3R

This strategy increases comprehension and retention of textbook material (expository or informational) and involves the following steps:

1. *Survey*. Briefly look through the reading assignment at the titles, chapter headings, illustrations, charts, and graphs. Skim through the assignment and read the chapter summary or end-of-chapter questions.
2. *Question*. Turn the headings and subheadings of the text into questions. For example: *Producing Antibodies* can become "How do our bodies produce antibodies?" *Organic motor fuels* can become "What are the different organic motor fuels?"
3. *Reading*. Read to find the answers to the developed questions. Identify the main ideas and jot down any questions, notes, or unknown vocabulary.
4. *Recite*. At the end of each chapter section, state the gist of what was read. *Note:* Restating or summarizing into an audio recording device is often very effective.
5. *Review*. Check recall of important information from the reading. To that end, a study guide of some kind may be created.

SQ4R

This is the same as SQ3R but includes an additional step beginning with the /r/ sound: *write*. The SQ4R procedure is survey, question, read, recite, write, and review. After a brief verbal summary of what the reading passage is about, one must write the answers to the questions (in step 2) and then review.

RCRC

This is a study strategy involving these steps (Archer & Gleason, 1989):

- Read a little bit of material. Read it more than once.
- Cover the material with your hand.
- Recite. Tell yourself what you have read.
- Check. Lift your hand and check. If you forget something important, begin again.

There are numerous cognitive learning and study strategies. The University of Nebraska-Lincoln's website on CSI shares a number of cognitive strategies for reading, writing, math, note taking, test taking, and other study skills (http://cehs.unl.edu/csi). James Madison University's Learning Toolbox (http://coe.jmu.edu/learningtoolbox/site_map.html) is another online source of cognitive strategies that are beneficial for students with ADHD.

The Self-Regulated Strategy Development Approach (SRSD) pioneered and researched by Harris and Graham, University of Kansas, has developed numerous learning strategies that are widely used, such as the following.

RAP

Schumaker, Denton, and Deshler (1984) devised a strategy for active reading and aiding comprehension, involving the following steps:

- *Read* the paragraph.
- *Ask* self to identify the main idea and two supporting details.
- *Paraphrase* or *put* the main ideas and details into one's own words.

POW + TREE

Harris, Graham, Mason, and Friedlander (2008) created these steps for writing persuasive essays. The POW and TREE go together. This and several other SRSD strategies are described on the IRIS Center website of Vanderbilt University (http://iris.peabody.vanderbilt.edu/module/pow/).

POW

- Pick an idea or opinion.
- Organize and generate notes and ideas for each part of the TREE.
- Write and say more.

TREE

- Topic sentence. Formulate a topic sentence that expresses an opinion.
- Reasons (give at least three) to support the topic sentence.
- Explanation. Explain your reason.
- Ending. Formulate a statement to summarize the topic sentence.

The following are some additional study and learning strategies:

- *Note taking.* This requires listening and simultaneously writing down major ideas and key information in a useful format so the information can later be accessed. There are a variety of note-taking techniques. One example is the Cornell note-taking method, which involves the following steps:
  - Divide a paper into two columns.
  - The first column (which is about one-fourth to one-third of the width of the paper) is where key terms, questions, additions, and corrections are written after the class period. It is used for recall of important information.
  - The right column is about three-fourths or two-thirds of the width of the paper. This is where the lecture notes are written (on the front side of the page only).
  - Students are to review their notes within twenty-four hours (preferably within three hours) after the lecture. During this time they reread and then fill in key terms, make additions, corrections, and so on in the left column.
  - In addition, space is left at the bottom of the page for a summary. Good note taking requires learning how to make abbreviations and use symbols.
- See more metacognitive and cognitive strategies in other lists throughout this book for reading (*Lists 5.3, 5.4, 5.5*), for math (*List 5.14*), and for writing (*Lists 5.7, 5.8, 5.9*).
- *See List 3.8* on research-based instructional approaches for more on this topic.

Sources and Resources

Archer, Anita, & Gleason, Mary. (1989). *Skills for school success.* North Billerica, MA: Curriculum Associates.

Chamot, A., & O'Malley, J. (1994). *The CALLA handbook: Implementing cognitive academic language learning.* Reading, MA: Addison-Wesley.

Harris, K., Graham, S., Mason, L., & Friedlander, B. (2008). *Powerful writing strategies for all students.* Baltimore, MD: Paul H. Brookes.

Hennessy, Nancy, & Soper, Sandi. (2003). Exercising executive function for efficient learning. Conference session at 54th Annual Conference of the International Dyslexia Association, San Diego, California, November 12–15.

Krawec, Jennifer, & Montague, Jennifer. (2012). *Current practice alerts: A focus on cognitive strategy, 19.* Division for Learning Disabilities and the Division for Research. Retrieved from http://s3.amazonaws.com/cmi-teaching-ld/alerts/21/uploaded_files/original_Alert19.pdf?1331403099

Livingston, Jennifer A. (1997). Metacognition: An overview. Graduate School of Education, State University of New York at Buffalo. Retrieved from http://gse.buffalo.edu/fas/shuell/cep564/metacog.htm

Schumaker, J. B., Denton, P., & Deshler, D. D. (1984). *The paraphrasing strategy.* Lawrence: The University of Kansas.

Rief, Sandra. (2005). *How to reach & teach children with ADD/ADHD: Practical techniques, strategies, and interventions* (2nd ed.). San Francisco: Jossey-Bass.

4.4 ADHD: Difficulties with Organization, Time Management, and Homework

People with ADHD experience difficulty to varying degrees with organization and time management as a direct result of their executive function impairment. For many children, teens, and adults with ADHD, these are their most significant weaknesses interfering with achievement of their goals and success at school and work. Regardless of how bright and capable the student may be, failing to meet deadlines, missing assignments, and poorly organized work affects their grades and academic achievement.

Students with ADHD typically also have major issues with homework production, which requires organization and time management and a number of other executive skills. In families of children and teens with ADHD, tears and battles over homework are common and chronic problems. With regard to homework production, teachers need to factor in that it often takes students with ADHD considerably longer than average to complete the work. What teachers anticipate should take twenty minutes to finish often takes a child with ADHD an hour or more. Homework is particularly a challenge because of the child's fatigue and frustration at the end of the day. Without the provision of home structures and supports (and often some medication), it is unlikely that much work is able to be accomplished by the end of the day or evening.

Students with ADHD often exhibit these problematic behaviors that are caused by disorganization and poor ability to judge and manage time:

- Messy desk, work area, locker, backpack, notebook, bedroom
- Cannot find, forgets to bring, or frequently loses important things (books, materials, assignments, personal belongings)
- Poor scheduling and pacing
- Lack of foresight and planning
- Lack of awareness of time passing
- Poor judgment of how much time is needed to accomplish tasks or arrive somewhere on time (factoring in the extra time for traveling and unforeseen interferences)
- Inadequately estimating how long a task will take and allotting sufficient time to complete it
- Not adequately prepared with needed materials
- Missing deadlines and due dates
- Lateness (to class, activities, appointments)
- Poor management of long-term projects and assignments (research projects, book reports)
- Procrastination
- Slow to get started and initiate the task
- Difficulty prioritizing activities and things that need to be done

Homework difficulties are also directly related to WM weaknesses as well, for example:

- Forgetting to record assignments
- Forgetting to take home books and needed supplies for homework
- Forgetting to turn in homework (even when it is completed)

It is important for parents and teachers to remember that these weaknesses are part of the child's disorder related to their underdeveloped executive functioning (*Lists 1.2, 1.4*). Punishment for weak skills caused by their neurobiological disorder is not the solution.

There are a number of strategies and supports recommended for parents and teachers to help with homework and to build important organization and time management skills (*Lists 4.5 through 4.10*).

4.5 What Parents Can Do to Help with Organization

Children with ADHD are often significantly delayed in their development of organization skills. They need to be taught strategies and encouraged to use methods that will work for them. They also need much more direct adult support and organizational assistance than most other children their age so that their impaired organizational skills don't cause them to fail at school.

Supplies and Materials

- Provide your child with a backpack and notebook or binder according to the teacher's specifications.
- It is recommended that beginning in third grade your child should use a three-ring binder with colored subject dividers and a plastic pouch for pencils and other small supplies. Students in kindergarten through second grade should use a soft pocket folder for storing their papers.
- Provide a spelling dictionary or list of common and frequently misspelled words, a multiplication chart, and any other useful reference materials for your child's notebook.
- Provide your child with plastic sleeves that can be inserted into the notebook for storing important papers that are not three-hole punched.
- Place hole-punched colored folders in the binder—for example, red for homework, blue for parent notices or papers to be left at home. When folders are attached to notebook rings, papers that are placed in the folders have less chance of being lost or falling out.
- Another technique is to use large laminated envelopes that are hole-punched and inserted in the binder for homework and assorted project papers.
- An accordion folder is an alternative to a three-ring binder for those children who find it easier to manage at school. The tabs of the accordion folder are labeled for homework assignments, work to turn in, and each subject. At school during the day, papers can be quickly placed behind the tab for that subject. Nevertheless, I recommend that papers not needed in school should be refiled in the evening into the three-ring binder maintained at home.
- Your child's planner, monthly calendar, or assignment sheet should be hole-punched and kept in the front of the notebook (or in the front or back file of an accordion folder if used instead of the three-ring binder at school).
- Provide the necessary supplies to help your child be organized at school. You will likely have to replace and replenish school supplies often. Have your child take inventory of what needs replacement or ask the teacher.
- Use of a specific bag for organizing and keeping each of your child's extracurricular activity supplies is helpful. Provide a laminated list or place the list inside of a

transparent plastic sleeve that itemizes what needs to be inside the bag (for example, equipment, shoes, uniform, or notebooks).

- Provide materials to organize their locker at school (for example, shelves, magnetic hooks, and other accessories).

The Homework Supply Kit

You can help significantly reduce time searching the house for homework supplies and materials. This is a frustrating waste of precious minutes that also causes a major break in productivity, unnecessarily pulling your child off task. This homework supply kit can be stored in anything portable—preferably a lightweight container with a lid. With this system, it does not matter where your son or daughter chooses to study. The necessary supplies can accompany your child anywhere.

These are recommended supplies (depending on the age of your child):

- Plenty of paper
- Paper clips
- Sharpened pencils with erasers
- Single-hole punch
- Pencil sharpener
- Three-hole punch
- Ruler
- Dictionary
- Crayons
- Thesaurus
- Paper hole reinforcers
- Electronic spell-checker
- Glue stick
- Self-stick notepads
- Colored pencils
- Highlighter pens
- Colored pens and markers (thick and thin points)
- Index cards
- Stapler with box of staples
- Calculator
- Clipboard

Your Child's Room and Work Area

- Help your child clear out desk drawers and shelves of work, projects, and papers that were from different school years. Together, decide on what you would like to keep and store out of the way (in colored boxes, portfolios, or large plastic zipped bags) in order to make room for current papers and projects.
- Provide your child with a corkboard and pins to hang up important papers.

- Keep trays and bins for storing supplies and materials that will remove some of the clutter from the desktop.
- Provide the necessary storage space for organizing your child's room efficiently: shelves, closet space, bins, trays, drawers.
- Label shelves and storage bins. Clear storage bins are often preferable.
- In addition to a master family calendar, provide your child with a desk calendar that serves as an overview of important dates, activities, and events.
- Use fun, creative ways to keep your child's (and family's) belongings organized and easy to locate. See examples of organized children's rooms and homework areas as well as tips and creative home organization ideas from Pinterest users at www.pinterest.com/sandrarief/home-organization-homework-areas/.

Use Visual Reminders and Memory Cues

- Dry erase boards are helpful to hang in a central location of the home for all messages and notes to family members. In addition, hang one in your child's room for important reminders and messages.
- Write notes and reminders on colored sticky notes and place on mirrors, doors, and other places your child is likely to see them.
- Encourage your child to write himself or herself notes and leave them on the pillow, by the backpack, by car keys, and so forth.
- Use electronic reminders and organizers.
- Use color strategically:
  - Provide a file with color-coded folders in which your child can keep papers stored categorically.
  - Color-coordinate by subject area—for example, notebook and book cover for history text in green, schedule with time and room number of history class highlighted in green, and the tab of the subject divider in the notebook for history is in green.
  - Color-code entries on a calendar according to category: school-related, sports, and social activities, for example.
- Take photos to use as cues or reminders for how your child's room or work area should be straightened up and organized or provide a visual checklist your child can follow.

More Organizational Tips

- Take the time to regularly help your child clean and organize his or her backpack, notebook, desk, and room. Help with sorting, filing, and discarding.
- Assist your child with cleaning and organizing by at least starting the job together or giving clear reminders for how to carry out the task, such as with a simple task card or checklist.
- Offer a reward or incentive for straightening and organizing materials, putting away belongings, and so forth.
- If using a token economy system or other behavioral incentive program at home (*Lists 2.2, 2.7, 2.9*), give points or tokens for meeting an organizational or clean-up goal.

- Label your child's materials and possessions with his or her name.
- Take digital pictures of school projects, copy school work your child did on the computer, and scan other important documents of your child's work each semester or school year for safekeeping.
- To avoid early-morning rush and stress, have your child get as much as possible organized and ready for school the night before; for example, set out the next day's outfit, prepare lunch, and load everything into the backpack. Shower or bathe in the evening.
- Have your child place his or her loaded backpack in the same spot every night.
- If organization and time management are areas of weakness for you as well as your child, consider hiring an ADHD coach (*List 7.6*).
- You may want to consider Cheryl Carter's (2011) recommendation for making a lost-and-found box for items not put in their proper place and charging family members for getting items out of the box. Carter recommends, for example, that a child can be charged with an extra chore to do so.
- According to Kutscher and Moran (2009), people use three basic organizing styles: visual, spatial-cozy, and chronological-sequential. Because everyone's brain organizes and recalls information differently, the organizational method that works for you may not be the one that works best for your child. It is recommended to learn how a given child best organizes himself or herself and use techniques that fit the child's organizational style. For more information, see their book in the "Sources and Resources" section of this list.
- See the example in the appendix of the "High School Daily Reminder Item List" of materials to pack and bring to class each day of the week (A-23).
- *See List 5.7* for ways to help your child plan and organize ideas for writing—a common difficulty for children with ADHD.
- See *List 4.6* for recommendations of what teachers can do to help students with organization.

Sources and Resources

Carter, Cheryl R. (2011). *Organize your ADD/ADHD child: A practical guide for parents.* London: Jessica Kingsley.

Cooper-Kahn, Joyce, & Dietzel, Laurie. (2008). *Late, lost, and unprepared: A parents' guide to helping children with executive functioning*. Bethesda, MD: Woodbine House.

Kutscher, Martin L., & Moran, Marcella. (2009). *Organizing the disorganized child: Simple strategies to succeed in school*. New York: Harper Studio.

Rief at Pinterest. For several tips and organizational strategies, see https://www.pinterest.com/sandrarief/home-organization-homework-areas/

4.6 What Teachers Can Do to Help with Organization

Students with ADHD often have significant difficulty with organization, a common impairment because of poor executive functioning skills (*Lists 1.2, 1.5,*). It is important that teachers recognize that disorganization is related to these children's disorder and to provide the needed support, assistance, and teaching of organization skills. Fortunately, any efforts to teach students how to be organized and in creating and maintaining an organized classroom benefits *all* students, not just those with ADHD.

Organize Student Workspace and Materials

- Require the use of a three-ring binder or notebook starting in third grade (fourth grade at the latest).
- Students in kindergarten through second grade should use a pocket folder for carrying their papers daily.
- Require all students to carry a backpack and to bring the notebook, binder, or pocket folder to and from school in their backpack every day. Starting at an early age with this expectation builds the habit by training both students and their parents to use these organizational tools daily.

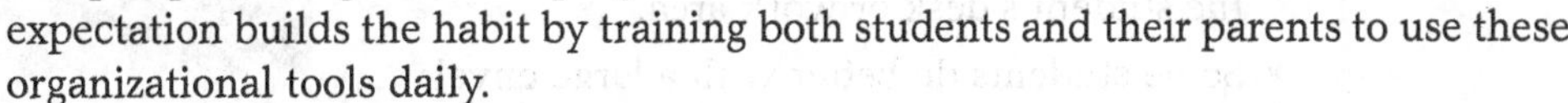

- Require the use of colored subject dividers and a pencil pouch for the notebook to include a few sharpened pencils with erasers, a plastic pencil sharpener, and other small supplies and essentials. A flat, plastic three-hole puncher that can be inserted in the rings of the notebook is also recommended.

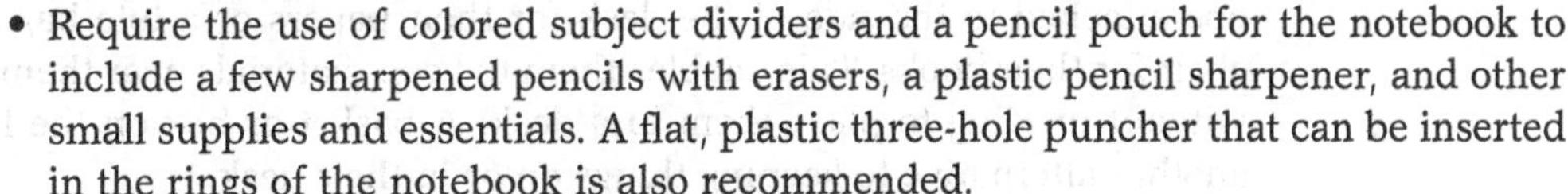

- Teach students how to keep their papers organized by placing them in the appropriate subject section of their notebooks.
- Require the use of a monthly assignment calendar or planner or a daily or weekly assignment sheet to be kept at all times at the front of the notebook. Whichever is used (calendar, student planner, or assignment sheet) it should be three-hole punched for storage in the notebook. Students should use it consistently for recording all classroom assignments and the teacher should model and monitor its use. See examples of homework assignment sheets in the appendix (A-18, A-19, and A-20).
- Students should have a consistent location in their notebook for storing homework assignments (or work to do and work to turn in). There are a variety of ways for doing so:
  - Use colored pocket folders (single pocket or double) that are three-hole punched and inserted in the notebook. For example, a red pocket folder can be labeled "homework" and contain all homework; a different colored folder may be for graded and returned papers or anything to leave at home.
  - Use large laminated envelopes that are three-hole punched and inserted into the notebook for homework, assorted project papers, and so forth.
- Encourage students to keep a supply of notebook paper handy in a consistent location of their binder.
- Provide handouts to students that are always three-hole punched in advance.

- Give the student a clipboard for anchoring papers on the desk or if doing work in a beanbag chair or other location.
- Consider attaching a pencil to the child's desk (with either string or Velcro).
- Provide bins, cans, boxes, buckets, trays, baskets, and other containers for storing materials and supplies and having them easily accessible at desks and tables or nearby when needed.
- To help students keep papers stored appropriately in the notebook, provide adhesive hole reinforcers for ripped-out papers and plastic sleeves for papers that you do not want to three-hole punch.
- Encourage students who need daily reference tools, such as the times tables chart or lists of frequently misspelled words, to keep them in a section of their notebook.
- Some students have difficulty managing the three-ring notebook system and may do better using an accordion folder. Students who are using the accordion folder should color-code and label the tabs of each section or pocket of the folder: the subjects (preferably labeled sequentially according to the daily schedule), homework to do, papers to turn in, and a place for storing the planner, for example. 
- Limit the amount of materials or clutter on the student's desk or work area.
- Some students do better with a large envelope attached to the side of the desk for their papers or a tote bag on back of the chair for their books. This enables them to keep materials near them and accessible without needing to place them in a desk. A basket or box on the floor or shelf is another alternative to keeping things on or in their desk.
- Organize the classroom with clearly labeled shelves, files, and bins so that you and the students know precisely where things belong and can easily locate (and replace) them.
- Provide a work-in-progress folder for incomplete work.

Visual Reminders and Memory Cues

- Use visual or pictorial cues for showing expected materials, daily routines, and schedules to organize for the day.
- See the example in the appendix of a "High School Daily Reminder Item List" of materials to pack and bring to class each day of the week (A-23).
- Encourage students to use sticky notes for reminders to themselves. Have them stick the notes on book covers, their lockers and planners, and other useful places.
- Use color strategically for help organizing:
  - Color coordinate by subject area to make locating subject materials quick and easy. For example, the science text is covered in yellow paper or has a yellow adhesive dot on the binding, the science notebook or lab book or folder is yellow, the schedule with the science class period and room number is highlighted in yellow, and so is the tab or divider for science in the three-ring notebook or accordion folder.

- Use one specific colored box, tray, or folder for students to place completed assignments they are turning in and another colored box, tray, or folder for unfinished work.
- Prepare important notices and handouts on colored paper, preferably color-coded for certain categories, for example, weekly or monthly newsletters in blue and spelling lists in pink.
- Use brightly colored paper for project assignments, providing details and due dates. Give the student two copies: one for the notebook and one to be posted at home.

Monitor, Support, and Motivate

- Schedule periodic desk and notebook organization time (end of day, once a week, or bimonthly). Time should be provided for cleaning out unnecessary papers and items from students' desks and filing papers in the proper sections of their notebooks. Students with ADHD may need assistance from table partners, a well-organized classmate, or adult in doing so.
- Cleaning up student work areas should be part of the daily routine between activities. Incentives such as earning table points or the class earning a minute or two toward a preferred activity at the end of the week can be provided for quick cleanups—meaning they finished the job before the timer goes off or a song played ends.
- Have random desk and notebook organization spot checks. Positively reinforce using prizes, certificates, and privileges such as "no homework tonight passes" for passing inspection of notebook and work space checks. See sample in the appendix.
- Provide bonus points or some other bonus for improved organization and reward your disorganized students who, on request, are able to quickly locate a certain book or paper in their desk or notebook.
- Provide peer or adult assistance to help disorganized students organize desks, backpacks, and binders. It helps, for example, to have another organized student or adult supervise as desk contents are dumped into a shopping bag and brought to another area with a larger area while working on this. Recycle unnecessary papers, apply adhesive paper reinforcers to ripped-out papers, refile papers in the appropriate section of the notebook, and throw away trash.
- Arrange for peer or adult assistance in locker organization as well for students with ADHD and suggest to parents to provide their child with some locker organization tools and accessories, such as shelves or magnetic hooks.
- At the end of the day, make sure that students with ADHD have necessary books or materials in their backpack to take home.
- Use the buddy system (partners A and B) to monitor each other for organization. For example, when giving instructions on where items need to be put away or papers filed, partners check each other to make sure it is done properly.
- Provide in-school help and adult assistance as needed for putting together projects, such as display boards for a research project. For example, many students with ADHD impulsively glue papers to boards without first planning for the amount of space they have on display boards. Help with the little extras that make projects look much better, such as nice lettering on the computer, cutting papers straight with a paper cutter rather than scissors, and organizing prior to mounting objects.

Organizational Assistance in Planning and Thinking

- Provide advanced organizers and study guides to help students organize their thinking about key topics of the lesson.
- Use graphic organizers. Model and guide through the use of all graphic organizers that aid comprehension and planning: sequence charts, story maps, sentence maps, webs, clusters, flowcharts, and Venn diagrams, for example. Structure writing assignments of various genres.
- Provide framed outlines for filling in missing words and phrases during instruction.
- Help students organize their ideas (prewriting, preplanning) with the use of sticky notes, whiteboards and dry erase pens, audio recorders, and questioning and prompting.
- Encourage the use of software or apps that help students plan and organize their written work. For example, the programs Inspiration and Kidspiration enable children to easily web and organize ideas and outline them. See www.inspiration.com.
- With all writing assignments, provide a scoring rubric to help the student in planning, organizing, and producing work at standard with grade-level expectations.
- See *List 5.7* for much more on this topic.

More Organizational Tips

- Encourage students to organize materials when they arrive at class each day and before dismissal at the end of the school day.
- Provide models for how to organize papers (for example, a sample paper with proper headings, margins, and spacing).
- Provide models of well-organized projects.
- Require that materials and supplies be labeled with students' names.
- Keep spare supplies available so that no time is wasted as students search or ask around to borrow from classmates. Consider "charging" students (for example, they must pay you from their class money or tokens) or fining them in some way (points) for not being prepared and needing to borrow supplies.
- Allow for natural consequences of not having materials. Do not positively reinforce students who are unprepared by giving them new, desirable materials and supplies. Instead, let students borrow only your less desirable materials. For example, many teachers keep a box of golf pencils and old pencils and erasers for this purpose.
- Many teachers have provided ideas for organizing the classroom environment and student materials on Pinterest: www.pinterest.com/sandrarief/class-organization-time-mgmt/.
- See *List 4.5* for recommendations on what parents can do to help their child with organization.

Sources and Resources

Archer, Anita, & Gleason, Mary. (1990). *Skills for school success*. North Billerica, MA: Curriculum Associates.

Dendy, Chris A. Zeigler (2011). *Teaching teens with ADD, ADHD & executive function deficits: A quick reference guide for teachers and parents, 2nd edition.* Bethesda: Woodbine House.

Kutscher, Martin L., & Moran, Marcella. (2009). *Organizing the disorganized child: Simple strategies to succeed in school.* New York: Harper Studio.

Goldberg, Donna, with Zwiebel, Jennifer. (2005). *The organized student: Teaching children the skills for success in school and beyond.* New York: Fireside.

Rief at Pinterest. For several tips and organizational strategies, see https://www.pinterest.com/sandrarief/class-organization-time-mgmt/

4.7 What Parents Can Do to Help with Time Management

Difficulty with adequately budgeting and managing time is certainly not unique to children or teens with ADHD. But for those with ADHD, time awareness and time management are often exceedingly difficult and problematic. Poor ability to measure and estimate time is characteristic of ADHD and executive function impairment (*Lists 1.2, 1.5, 4.4*).

Time Awareness

- Practice time estimation with your child. Make a game out of predicting, timing, and checking your child's time estimates for various activities.
- Have your child write start times and stop times on homework assignments for better awareness of how long it takes to do work; this is also good information to share with the teacher.
- Cue your child with time reminders such as "You have fifteen minutes to get ready before we leave the house" and set the timer.

Tools, Schedules, and Supports

- Make sure your child knows how to tell time and read a nondigital (analog) clock.
- Check that your child knows how to read calendars and schedules.
- Make sure clocks in the home are accurate.
- Watches or alarms can be set to vibrate and cue your child to be on task, be somewhere, call home, or take medication, for example. The WatchMinder (www.watchminder.com) is a good tool for school and can vibrate and alert your child silently in class with preprogrammed messages.
- There are other beneficial electronic devices with timers to help remember appointments, curfews, and keep on schedule. See suggested timers and alarm clocks in "Sources and Resources" section at the end of this list.

- Visual timers such as Time Timer (www.timetimer.com) enable your child to see the passing of time and are very beneficial for children with ADHD.
- Teach and model how to use to-do lists by writing down things that need to be done and then crossing off accomplished tasks.
- Help your child schedule the evening and estimate how long each homework assignment or other activity should take.
- Developing the habit of using a personal planner or agenda is essential. Your child should be expected to record assignments in a planner, calendar, agenda, or assignment log of some sort by the mid- to upper-elementary grades.
- Expect your child to record assignments and monitor that this is being done. Ask to see your son or daughter's assignment calendars, sheets, and planners every day. See the teacher for help in ensuring that assignments are recorded. Your child may need direct assistance from a classmate, buddy, or the teacher to be sure assignments are recorded (*Lists 4.8, 4.9, 4.10*).

- Post a large calendar or wall chart in a central location of the home for scheduling family activities and events. Encourage everyone to refer to it daily. Each family member may have his or her own color of pen for recording on the calendar.
- Help transfer important extracurricular activities and scheduling to your child's personal calendar or planner.
- Phone calls, electronic messages, and social media can easily interfere with staying on schedule and pull your child off task. If your child has a cell phone, remove it from the room while doing homework or otherwise restrict access if possible during homework time; have your child return calls, messages, or check social media during breaks.
- Help your child create a weekly schedule. For older children, a recommended time management strategy is to take a few days to track and record how they spend their time over the course of twenty-four hours. After a few days, your child should have better awareness of how much time is typically spent on routine activities: meals, sleeping, grooming, walking to class, screen time (watching television or the computer), texting or talking on the phone, recreational and social activities, and study and homework time. See the example of a "Student Weekly Planning Schedule" (A-21) in the appendix.
- With your child, schedule a time for homework. This is a priority. Some children like to come home and immediately get part or all of their homework done and out of the way. Others need a break before tackling any homework. The homework schedule should be adhered to as consistently as possible (*List 4.9*).

Managing Routines and Schedules

- Try to keep bedtime and wake-up time as consistent as possible, with predictable routines for getting ready in the morning and night. Clear reminders of the routine (for example, through the use of a checklist of sequential tasks to complete) reduce the nagging, rushing around, and negative interactions at these times of the day.
- Checklists are great tools for time management and staying on schedule. Each task that is completed on the list or chart is crossed off.
- Combine checklists and routines with a positive reinforcement system. If your child has all items completed and checked off by a certain time, he or she earns extra points or tokens as a reward.
- Help your child establish a routine for extracurricular activities as well. Include scheduled time for practice and gathering needed items (with the aid of a checklist) for that extracurricular activity.
- Help your child get in the habit of checking his or her planner and calendar a few times a day.
- Try not to overschedule your child, particularly during the school week.

Long-Term Projects

- Your assistance with time management and structuring of long-term school assignments such as book reports and science and research projects are critical to your child's success. Build in plenty of time. When scheduling, allow for unforeseen glitches and delays.

- Help your child break down longer assignments into smaller, manageable chunks with deadlines marked on the calendar for completing incremental steps of the project.
- Pay close attention to due dates and post the project requirements. Together with your child, record on a master calendar the due date of the final project and plan when to do the steps along the way (for example, going to the library, gathering resources).
- Ask the teacher for feedback and help in monitoring that your child is on track with the project. Do not assume your child is working on projects at school, even if he or she is given some time in class to do so.
- Large and long-term projects can be easily overwhelming and discouraging for your child (and you, too). Your son or daughter will likely need your assistance, as well as help at school, with pacing and monitoring time lines toward project completion.
- See *Lists 2.2, 2.3, 2.6, 2.7, 2.12, 4.2, 4.5, 4.6, 4.7, 4.8, 4.9, and 4.10* for related information and strategies.

Sources and Resources

See many time management tools and ideas from Pinterest users at www.pinterest.com/sandrarief/class-organization-time-mgmt/ and www.pinterest.com/sandrarief/time-management/.

See recommendations on alarms and timers from *ADDitude Magazine* (www.additudemag.com):

ADDitude Magazine Editors. (n.d.). Timers for ADHD children: ADDitude readers—and their attention deficit children—put three timers to the test. *ADDitude Magazine.* Retrieved from www.additudemag.com/adhd/article/6653.2.html

Sandler, Michael. (n.d.). The best ADHD tools: Alarm clocks. *ADDitude Magazine.* Retrieved from www.additudemag.com/adhd/article/901.html

There are some excellent books for helping ADHD children, teens, and adults with time management. These are three of my favorites:

Cooper-Kahn, Joyce, & Dietzel, Laurie. (2008). *Late, lost, and unprepared*. Bethesda, MD: Woodbine House.

Dendy, Chris A. Zeigler (2011). *Teaching teens with ADD, ADHD & executive function deficits: A quick reference guide for teachers and parents, 2nd edition*. Bethesda, MD: Woodbine House.

Ratey, Nancy A. (2008). *The disorganized mind: Coaching your ADHD brain to take control of your time, tasks, and talents*. New York: St. Martin's Griffin.

4.8 What Teachers Can Do to Help with Time Management

Students with ADHD often have significant difficulty with time awareness and time management. This is an executive function impairment that causes many problems at school. It is important for teachers to understand that lateness and being oblivious to deadlines and due dates is not intentional behavior or apathy but is part of the student's disorder.

Time Awareness

- Any opportunity to practice time estimation is helpful in increasing such awareness. For example, challenge your students to estimate how long it takes to walk to the office and back without running or any other task. Make a game out of predicting, timing, and checking the students' time estimates for various activities.
- Encourage self-monitoring during independent seatwork time by recording the start time on the paper. When the work period is over, record the time, regardless of how much work the student actually produced. This is helpful documentation as well with regard to how well the student is able to stay on task and work productively.
- Help students see how they spend their time in the course of twenty-four hours (eating, sleeping, in school, in extracurricular activities, and so forth) with an assignment over the course of a few days to a week. Parents will also be involved in the assignment—helping their child track time spent on his or her activities before and after school.
- Use timers. Visual timers that enable students to see the passage of time are beneficial for students with ADHD such as Time Timer (www.timetimer.com). There are many great online timers for projecting in the classroom, such as the animated online timers at Online-Stopwatch (www.online-stopwatch.com/classroom-timers/).

Assignment Sheets and Student Planners, Calendars, and Agendas

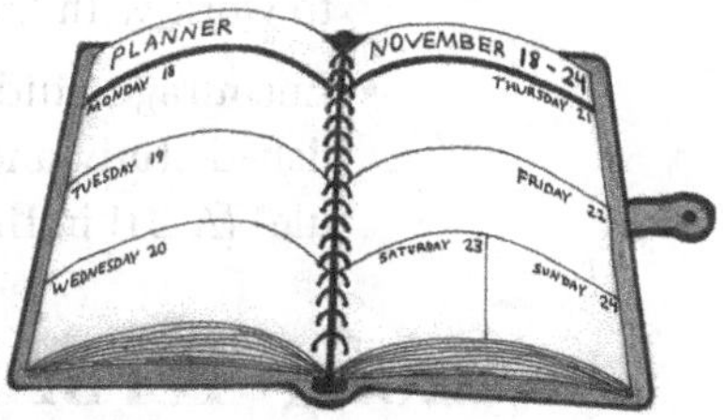

- Communicate and maintain the clear expectation that all assignments are to be recorded on whatever tool is used in your classroom: a planner, calendar, or assignment sheet. For students to build this important study skill habit, it is important that you are consistent and make recording assignments a priority.
- Model and walk students through the process of recording assignments by writing down and projecting a copy of the filled-in planner or calendar or assignment sheet. Allow time at the beginning or end of the subject period or school day to do so.
- Provide extra assistance to students who have difficulty recording assignments.
- Assign study buddies so students can help each other. These partners can be responsible for checking each other to make sure assignments are recorded on their planner or calendar. When a student is absent, the buddy can collect all handouts, notices, and assignments for the absent student.
- Partners should exchange contact information to call, text, or e-mail when the other is absent and communicate about what was missed that day in class.

- Routinely ask table partners or buddies (or groups seated together) to check each other and make sure everyone has recorded the information accurately. Some teachers have partners initial each other's planner after doing so.
- Keep a master monthly calendar posted in the classroom, recording special activities and events that are scheduled and when assignments are due.
- If students are using a daily planner or assignment sheet, also provide them with a single- or double-page monthly calendar for important dates they can see at a glance. Help them record due dates of projects, tests, class trips, and other important activities and events for the month onto the monthly calendar.
- Check and initial the assignment sheet, calendar, or planner for students who need extra monitoring and ask their parents to do so as well.
- Recommended planners for students with ADHD and LD are those with plenty of writing space for each day of the week and are as clean and distraction-free as possible. Some student planners provide very little room for recording assignments, which is problematic for many children, particularly those who have dysgraphia. (*Lists 5.6, 5.11*)
- See examples of assignment sheets in the appendix (A-18, A-19, A-20).

Schedules

- Post all schedules and refer to them throughout the day.
- Walk through the schedule each day, and point out any changes in the daily or weekly schedule or routine that will be taking place.
- With younger students, use a pictorial schedule depicting the daily routine.
- For students receiving special education or related services, write down their weekly schedule and have copies for their easy reference that they can tape to their desks, place in their notebook, or attach to the inside of their locker door.
- Keep each student's special schedule accessible so that you know the days and times they are pulled out of class or when service providers are coming to the classroom to work with the student.
- Encourage students and parents to plan a weekly schedule, including an established study and homework schedule, using the "Student Weekly Planning Schedule" (A-21) in the appendix.

Long-Term Projects

- Structure long-term assignments (book reports, research projects) by breaking them into smaller, manageable increments.
- Make sure students have access to needed materials.
- Assign incremental due dates to help structure the time line toward project completion. For example, assign separate due dates for each stage of the project: getting a topic approved, submitting an outline, listing notes or resources, turning in first draft, and so forth.
- Make sure that students pay close attention to due dates. Post those due dates and frequently refer to them as reminders.

- Make sure that parents of students with ADHD are aware of the project and due dates. Besides sending home a hard copy of the handout explaining project guidelines, time line, and scoring rubric, consider also calling home and sending an e-mail attachment with the important information as well. You may want to have parents sign a form to return to school indicating that they are aware of the assignment. Keep project information and reminders posted on your school or class website if you have one.
- Suggest to parents that they closely monitor time lines and help with pacing (for example, promptly get their child started on gathering resources).
- Monitor progress by asking to see what the student has accomplished and provide feedback along the way.
- Consider providing some of your parents of students with ADHD advanced notice about upcoming projects and reports, enabling them to get a head start, especially with planning and research.

Other Ways Teachers Can Help with Time Management

- Provide students with a course outline or syllabus.
- Assist with prioritization of activities and workload.
- Teach students how to tell time and read a nondigital clock.
- Teach students how to read calendars and schedules.
- Make sure that all due dates are presented to students both orally and visually with frequent reminders.
- Use to-do lists, modeling for the class how to write down and cross off accomplished tasks.
- Allow older students to use their electronic devices (calendars, things-to-do features, productivity apps, vibrating alarms) for time management. For students who prefer to use their electronic device for recording assignments, allow them to do so in addition to writing it down in a planner. Taking a snapshot with their smartphones of the assignments written on the board is another option.
- Provide enough time during transitions to put material away and get organized for the next activity.
- Set timers for transitions. ("You have five minutes to finish working and put away your materials.")
- Include "seated by beginning bell time" or some other similar behavior to indicate the student's punctuality on any home-to-school monitoring system such as a daily report card or monitoring form. See *Lists 2.5 and 2.9* and examples of daily report cards and monitoring forms in the appendix (A-2 through A-8).
- If tardiness is an issue with the student, try an individual contract to motivate the student to improve this behavior.
- Provide extended time as needed; consider flexibility regarding late work.
- Use frequent praise and positive reinforcement. Reward students for meeting deadlines and finishing assignments on time.

- Suggest to parents the recommendations and tips for homework and time management in *Lists 4.7 and 4.9.*
- For more strategies and information related to this topic, see *Lists 1.2, 1.5, 2.3, 3.4, 3.5, 4.2, 4.4, 4.10, 7.5, and 7.8.*

Sources and Resources

See many time management tools and ideas from Pinterest users at www.pinterest.com/sandrarief/class-organization-time-mgmt/ and www.pinterest.com/sandrarief/time-management/.

4.9 Homework Tips for Parents

Homework time is often very stressful in homes of children with ADHD. After a full day of school, having to work on and complete more assignments is very difficult and frustrating for the child and parents. To support your child through the homework process, consider these tips.

Creating the Work Environment

- Make sure your child has a quiet work space, preferably where it is easy for you to supervise and monitor work production.
- Provide your child the necessary homework supplies, materials, and organized work area (*List 4.5*).
- Limit distractions (unnecessary noise, activity, and phone calls) in your home during homework hours. Turn off the TV.
- Experiment with music softly playing while doing homework. Music may help block auditory distractions in the environment. The right music stimulates the brain and can be helpful for studying. Try various types of classical and instrumental music and other selections of your child's choice that may make studying more pleasant and increase productivity (*List 7.7*).

Developing a Homework Routine and Schedule

- Together with your child, establish a specific time and place for homework. In order to develop a homework habit, it is important to adhere to a homework schedule as closely and consistently as possible.
- Consider a variety of factors when scheduling for homework: extracurricular activities, medication effects at that time, mealtimes and bedtimes, other chores and responsibilities, your availability to supervise and monitor, and your child's individual preferences and learning styles.
- Some children prefer and are more productive if they start homework shortly after they come home from school. Others need time to play, relax first, and then start homework later. However, they should not wait until the evening to get started.
- Encourage and help your child get in the habit of putting all books, notebooks, signed notes, and other necessary materials inside the backpack before bedtime.
- Place the backpack in a consistent location (for example, by the front door) so that your child cannot miss seeing or tripping over it when leaving the house in the morning.
- See *Lists 2.12, 4.2, and 4.5.*

Preparation and Structuring

- Expect your child to have all assignments recorded. Request the teacher's help in making sure all assignments are recorded daily. Perhaps the teacher can initial or sign your child's planner or assignment sheet each day or you can use another system, such as if school policy permits to have your child use his or her cell phone or other electronic device to take a picture of the assignments written on the board, or record a message listing the homework and materials needed to him- or herself.

- Emphasize to your child the importance of not leaving school without double-checking the assignment sheet or calendar and making sure all necessary books and materials to do the homework are in the backpack.
- Have your child take the phone numbers of a few responsible classmates to call or text if there are questions about school work. Many schools help in this regard with homework hotlines, recording daily assignments on teachers' voice mail, or classroom websites where teachers post assignments online.
- Help your child look over all homework assignments for the evening and organize materials needed before beginning.
- If your child frequently forgets to bring textbooks home, ask if you can borrow another set for home. If not, consider purchasing one if you are able.
- Assist your child in dividing assignments into smaller segments that are more manageable and less overwhelming. Long-term assignments such as reports and projects particularly need to be structured into a series of shorter steps in order to complete them on time. Help do so and then be vigilant in monitoring and supporting your child through the process.
- See *Lists 2.12, 4.2, 4.5, 4.6, 4.7,4.8, and 4.10* for more on this topic.

Help during Homework

- The amount of direct assistance required during homework will depend on the complexity of the assignment, the task demands (such as amount of writing required), and the needs of your child.
- Assist your child in getting started on assignments, perhaps by reading the directions together, color-highlighting the key words in the directions, doing the first few items together, observing as your child does the next problem or item independently, and offering feedback and help if needed. Then get up and leave.
- Monitor and give feedback without doing all the work together. You want your child to attempt as much as possible independently.
- Even with younger children, try to get your child started and then check and give feedback on small segments of his or her independent work (for example, after every few problems or one row completed). Being available to help and assist as needed is wonderful, but try not to get in the habit of having your child rely on your overseeing every minute.
- As tempting as it may be, even when homework time is dragging on, do not do the work for your child.
- Have your child work a certain amount of time and then stop. Do not force him or her to spend an excessive and inappropriate amount of time on homework. If you feel your child worked enough for one night, write a note to the teacher and attach it to the homework.
- If your child struggles in writing, he or she may dictate as you write and record the responses. These accommodations to help bypass writing difficulties are reasonable for children with ADHD. Speak to the teacher (*List 5.12*).
- It is not your responsibility to correct all of your child's errors on homework or make him or her complete and turn in a perfect paper.
- As homework supervisor and coach, praise your child for being on task, getting to work, and taking responsibility. Give extra praise for accomplishment and progress.

Increasing Motivation and Work Production

- Use a timer to challenge your child to stay on task and reward work completed with relative accuracy during that time frame. Tell your child that you will come back to check his or her progress on homework when the timer rings.
- A beat-the-clock system is often effective in motivating children to complete a task before the timer goes off.
- Ask to see what your child has accomplished after a certain amount of time or to show you when a particular assignment is done. Praise and reward work on completion.
- Help your child in setting up mini-goals of work completion (for example, read a specified number of pages, finish writing one paragraph, complete a row of problems). When accomplishing the goal or task, your child is rewarded with a break and perhaps points or tokens or other reinforcers.
- Remind your child to do homework and offer incentives: "When you finish your homework, you can do . . . ."
- Allow your child a break between homework assignments. In fact, your child can reward him- or herself with a snack and a play or exercise break after completing each assignment or two.
- A contract for a larger incentive or reinforcer may be worked out as part of a plan to motivate your child to persist and follow through with homework—for example, "If you have no missing or late homework assignments this next week, you will earn . . . ."
- Avoid nagging and threatening. Instead use incentives to support and motivate your child through the difficult task of doing homework.
- Enforce consequences such as loss of points on a token economy or behavior modification system when your child fails to bring home needed assignments or materials to do the homework.
- Withhold privileges (for example, no TV or other screen time or access to the phone) until a reasonable amount of homework has been accomplished.
- Encourage your child and praise his or her efforts for trying the homework assignments.
- See *Lists 2.2, 2.4, 2.7, 2.9, 2.12, 4.1, 4.7, and 7.5* for more related strategies.

Communicating with Teachers about Homework Issues

- Let the teacher know if the homework is too confusing or difficult for your child to do (or for you to understand from the directions what is expected).
- If homework is a frequent cause of battles, tears, and frustration in your home, seek help. Make an appointment with the teacher to discuss the homework problems and request reasonable modifications and adjustments in homework assignments.
- Communicate with the teacher and try to come to an agreement about daily homework expectations. Remind the teacher that children with ADHD often take two to three times longer (or more) to complete the same amount of work as their peers and that some of the homework demands exceed your child's capacity without enormous stress.

- Let the teacher know your child's frustration and tolerance level in the evening. The teacher needs to be aware of the amount of time it takes your child to complete tasks and what efforts you are making to help at home.
- Ask for progress notes or use of a daily or weekly report card that keep you appraised as to how your child is doing.
- See *Lists 2.9, 4.10, 7.1, 7.2, 7.3, and 7.8* for more information and strategies related to this topic.

Other Ways to Help

- If your child is on medication during the school day, but cannot get through the homework once the medication effects wear off, consult with your doctor. Many children with ADHD are more successful with homework when given a small dose of medication in the late afternoon or switching to a prescription with a long-acting formula (*Lists 1.20, 1.21*).
- Many students with ADHD need homework accommodations written into a 504 plan or IEP (*Lists 6.3, 6.4, 6.5*).
- Supervise your child in placing completed work in his or her homework folder and backpack. Students with ADHD often forget to turn in their homework, even if they spent hours completing it. You may want to arrange with the teacher a system of collecting your child's homework immediately on his or her arrival at school or e-mailing homework to the teacher in the evening or before school in the morning to ensure that your child turns in the work and receives credit for doing so.
- Help your child study for tests and use effective learning strategies. Use memory strategies to increase recall and retention of material. Practice and study using a variety of multisensory formats and memory techniques (*Lists 3.7, 4.1, 4.2, 4.3*).
- If your child struggles with reading, math, or writing, see academic strategies and supports found in *Lists 5.3 through 5.14*.
- Many parents find it very difficult to help their own child with homework. If that is the case, find someone who can. Consider hiring a tutor. Often a junior or senior high school student or college student is ideal, depending on the need and age of your child. Every community has a variety of tutorial services available. Of course, check references.
- For recommended strategies teachers can use to teach skills and support students with organization, time management, and homework, see *Lists 4.6, 4.8, and 4.10.*
- Consider purchasing or obtaining assistive technology (AT), such as text-to-speech software to speed up the reading process or suggested technology supports in *List 5.12* if your child struggles in writing.

Source and Resource

Rief at Pinterest. For examples of homework areas, see https://www.pinterest.com/sandrarief/home-organization-homework-areas/

Zentall, Sydney S., & Goldstein, Sam. (1999). *Seven steps to homework success: A family guide to solving common homework problems.* Plantation, FL: Specialty Press.

4.10 Homework Tips for Teachers

Homework time is often a nightmare in homes of children with ADHD. There are many ways teachers can be supportive and build a good relationship between home and school in the process. Keep in mind how much longer it typically takes for a student with ADHD to do the work. What takes your other students about fifteen to twenty minutes to complete often takes three to four times that long for those with ADHD, even with parental supervision and direct assistance. The following are adjustments that a teacher can make to help students with ADHD succeed:

- Be responsive to parents who are reporting great frustration surrounding homework. Be willing to make adjustments so that students with ADHD spend a reasonable amount of time doing their homework. For example, shorten the assignment or reduce the amount of writing required.
- Many students with ADHD who receive medication during the school day to help them focus and stay on task are often not receiving medication benefits after school or in the evening hours. It is an unreasonable expectation that parents be able to get their child to produce at home what you were not able to get the child to produce all day at school.
- Many teachers have a practice of sending home unfinished classwork. Avoid this if possible. Of course, some in-class assignments will need to be completed at home, but try to find alternatives for your students with ADHD when possible. Provide the necessary modifications and supports so that in-school work is in-school work and homework is homework.
- Remember that homework should be a time for reviewing and practicing what students have been taught in class. Do not give assignments involving new information that parents are expected to teach their children.
- Homework should not be busywork. Make the homework relevant and purposeful so that time spent is helpful in reinforcing skills or concepts you have taught.
- Never add on homework as a punishment or negative consequence for misbehavior at school.
- Avoid unnecessary copying, recopying, or expectations for high standards of neatness for students with ADHD.
- Visually post homework assignments as well as explain them. Write the assignments in a consistent location of the classroom (corner of the board or on a chart stand, for example).
- Modify the homework for students with ADHD or learning disabilities, particularly reducing the written output required. Ask yourself, "What is the goal?" "What do I want the students to learn from the assignment?" "Can they get the concepts without having to do all the writing?" "Can they practice the skills in an easier, more motivating format?" "Can they practice the skills doing fewer problems?"
- If you have extra copies of textbooks to loan parents, do so for students who are forgetful and frequently leave the books they need at home or school.
- If writing is difficult for a student, encourage him or her to do assignments on a computer or other electronic device or give permission for specific assignments to be dictated to a parent or tutor.
- Do not excessively penalize students with ADHD for late or incomplete homework assignments. If a negative consequence is necessary, perhaps a point deduction is reasonable; a zero grade is not.

Communicate Clearly

- Read homework instructions aloud. Make sure you have explained the assignments carefully and clarified students' questions.
- If your school has homework hotlines or you use online sites for sharing information and communicating with parents and students, use them regularly. Keep information to parents and students regarding assignments up-to-date.
- Ask parents to let you know if their child is spending too much time on homework or expressing significant frustration or lack of understanding. Agree on time limits so that a child has needed free time every evening.
- Communicate regularly with parents of students who are falling behind in homework. Do not wait until the student is so far behind in completing work that catching up is almost impossible. For example, use a monitoring form indicating missing assignments or notify parents by phone, text, e-mail, or other way every *x* number of missing or incomplete assignments.
- When you assign a long-term major project or report, consider calling the parents of some students. Just because you have talked about the assignment a lot in class and provided written information does not mean the parents know a thing about it. You may call to ask parents to check the notebook for the written information about the project or volunteer to send another copy to post at home. A heads-up phone call or e-mail to parents about the assignment and letting parents know you are available for support and assistance as needed is appreciated and can make a big difference in how the student does the assignment.
- Communicate with other teachers in your team. Students who have several teachers are often assigned a number of tests, large projects, and reading assignments all at the same time from their different classes. Be sensitive to scheduling. Stagger due dates and coordinate whenever possible with other teachers to avoid the heavy stress of everything being due at the same time.
- See *Lists 7.1 and 7.3* for more on this topic.

Provide Monitoring and Support

- Students with ADHD must record their homework assignments before leaving your classroom. See *Lists 4.2, 4.6, and 4.8* for strategies and supports to ensure this is done.
- Supervise students who tend to be forgetful before they leave at the end of the day. Make sure they have their materials, books, and assignments recorded and in their backpacks.
- Assign a study buddy (or two) to your students with ADHD. Study buddies are responsible, willing classmates whom they can phone, text, or e-mail in the evening regarding homework questions or to find out what they missed on days they are absent.

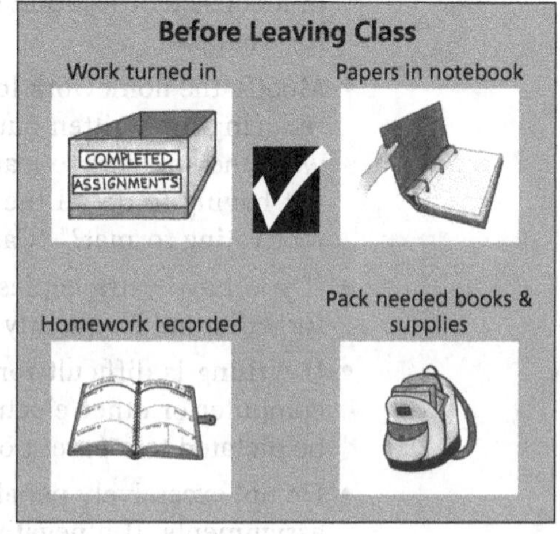

- One of the most important things you can do to help all students (and their parents) keep on top of homework, tests, and long-term projects is to require use of an assignment sheet, calendar, or planner. Then guide, walk-through, and monitor the recording of assignments. If this is a daily expectation and routine, everyone in the class will benefit.
- Check and initial students' assignment calendar, sheet, or planner every day, if needed.
- Have parents initial the assignment planner, calendar, or sheet daily. Designate a place for parents and teacher to write notes to each other—an excellent system for communication between home and school.
- Establish a system for directly collecting homework from your students with ADHD. Even when they have spent hours on homework assignments, it is very common for students with ADHD to forget to turn them in and get credit for the work they did.
- Work with your school about the possibility of having supervised study halls, homework labs or clubs, tutorials, and other assistance available for students who need it. For many students, being able to begin homework at school with support is very helpful.
- Be sure to collect homework and give some feedback when you return it. It is frustrating to students and parents to spend a lot of time on homework that the teacher never bothers to collect.
- Allow the student to e-mail homework to you to avoid lost assignments, a common problem of students with ADHD.
- For long-term projects or large tests, provide students with a written time line or checklist of intermediate deadlines to encourage appropriate pacing of the work. Allow students to turn in long-term assignments in parts as they are completed.
- Make yourself available at a specified time once or twice a week (before school, during lunch) so that students can come to you to ask homework questions or get feedback on work they have started.
- See *Lists 4.6, 4.8, and 7.8* for more related information and strategies.

Keep Things in Perspective

- It is critical for students with ADHD to participate in extracurricular activities. They need every opportunity to develop areas of strength and interest (athletics, dance, arts, music) that will be their source of self-esteem and motivation. These nonacademic, after-school activities are important to their development, and the child should have the time to participate.
- Be flexible and willing to make adjustments in the homework load, differentiating homework assignments and making accommodations as needed. For example, be flexible on giving credit for work that is turned in late and accept homework that is dictated by a student to a parent scribe (*List 3.5*).
- Keep in mind that some of your students with ADHD may work with tutors or counselors and participate in programs outside of school to boost skills as an intervention. Factor that in when assigning homework to these students as well.
- Remind parents that you do not expect to see perfectly done homework with no errors. Homework is a tool for seeing what students can do independently. It is not the parent's job to make sure that everything is correct.

Increase Motivation

- Try to make the homework assignments more interesting. One way to add interest and increase motivation to work on homework is to build in the component of student choice. For example, you can tell students to select three of the five questions to answer or choose one of the three topics offered.
- Include some homework that incorporates an element of play or fun, such as a learning game to reinforce or practice a skill.
- Allow students to create products other than written ones (for example, let students make a poster, write a song, or prepare a PowerPoint presentation) in order to show understanding of a concept.
- Write a goal for improvement in homework performance together with the student (and the parent if possible). If, for example, the child turns in less than 50 percent of homework assignments during the typical week, the initial goal might be to turn in 70 percent of weekly assignments, gradually raising the goal or performance standard to 80 percent and then 90 percent as the student achieves success.
- Write the goal into a contract or daily report card with rewards for achieving the goal. See *List 2.9* and sample DRCs in the appendix (A-2 through A-8 and A-11).
- Reward students for completed and turned in homework with extra points, tangible treats, "one free homework" pass, "one late homework without penalty" pass, special privileges, or whatever else students find positively reinforcing (*List 2.7*).
- See www.homeworkopoly.com for a tool and method to motivate students to turn in their homework.
- See *List 4.9* for how parents can help their child with homework.

Section 5

Academic Difficulties, Strategies, and Supports in Reading, Writing, and Math

Contents

Please note that a lot of the content of these lists has been adapted and updated from my other books, published by Jossey-Bass/Wiley, which you may be interested in exploring for further information, tools, and strategies:

Fetzer, Nancy & Rief, Sandra (2002). *Alphabet learning center activities kit.* San Francisco: Jossey-Bass.

Rief, S. (2003). *The ADHD book of lists: A practical guide for helping children and teens with attention deficit disorders.* San Francisco: Jossey-Bass.

Rief, S. (2005). *How to reach & teach children with ADD/ADHD: Practical techniques, strategies and interventions* (2nd ed.). San Francisco: Jossey-Bass.

Rief, S. (2008). *The ADD/ADHD checklist: A practical reference for parents and teachers* (2nd ed.). San Francisco: Jossey-Bass.

Rief, Sandra, & Heimburge, Julie. (2006). *How to reach & teach all children in the inclusive classroom* (2nd ed.). San Francisco: Jossey-Bass.

Rief, Sandra, & Heimburge, Julie. (2007). *How to reach & teach all children through balanced literacy: User-friendly strategies, tools, activities, and ready-to-use materials.* San Francisco: Jossey-Bass.

Rief, Sandra & Stern, Judith (2010). *The dyslexia checklist: A practical reference for parents and teachers.* San Francisco: Jossey-Bass.

5.1 Common Reading Problems in Children and Teens with ADHD

- Roughly 25 to 50 percent of children with ADHD also have specific learning disabilities, and reading disorders are the most common.
- According to Dr. Russell Barkley (2013), up to 35 percent of school-age children with ADHD are likely to have a reading disorder.
- Learning disabilities are neurobiologically based problems with processing information that affect one or more processes of input (taking in), integrating (organizing, sequencing, remembering), and output (expression) of the information.
- The most common of the learning disabilities is *dyslexia,* which refers to a language-based learning disability in basic reading skills and spelling. The problems of children with dyslexia most commonly stem from difficulty in processing speech sounds within words (phonological awareness) and making the connection between sounds and the written symbols—letters and patterns of letter combinations (graphemes) that represent sounds in words.

Definition of Dyslexia

- The International Dyslexia Association (2013) defines dyslexia as "a specific learning disability that is neurobiological in origin. It is characterized by difficulties with accurate and/or fluent word recognition and by poor spelling and decoding abilities. These difficulties typically result from a deficit in the phonological component of language that is often unexpected in relation to other cognitive abilities and the provision of effective classroom instruction. Secondary consequences may include problems in reading comprehension and reduced reading experience that can impede growth of vocabulary and background knowledge" (p. 3).
- Some signs of dyslexia (Rief & Stern, 2010) include the following:
  - Poor phonemic awareness and phonological processing (noticing, thinking about, and working with or manipulating the individual sounds in words); difficulties may include rhyming; identifying the beginning, middle, and ending sounds in words they hear; and recognizing, blending, and separating individual sounds within words
  - Difficulty learning the alphabet and letter-sound correspondence
  - Poor decoding skills—being able to learn and apply phonics skills and the ability to sound out individual words
  - Poor reading fluency—very slow, labored, and choppy; difficulty reading with ease, speed, and expression
  - Many inaccuracies (adding or deleting letters, sounds, or syllables from words, skipping words or lines of text when reading)
  - Sequencing errors (reading words with sounds out of order, for example, "aminal" instead of "animal," or missequencing letters or syllables in a word when spelling, such as "gril" for "girl," or confusing the order of events when summarizing a story or trying to recall the beginning, middle, and end)

- Difficulty recognizing and remembering common sight words, such as *said, from,* and *they;* may approach these like new words each time they are seen
- Poor reading comprehension
- Difficulty remembering what was read
- Very poor spelling and difficulty learning spelling strategies

- If a child is exhibiting signs of dyslexia, it is important that he or she be evaluated and receives the research-validated interventions that are known to be most effective in building deficient reading skills. See *Lists 3.8, 5.3, 5.4, 5.5,* the "Sources and Resources" section of this list, and websites on dyslexia and learning disabilities in *List 7.12.*

Other Common Reading Errors and Weaknesses in Children and Teens with ADHD

- Many individuals with ADHD do not have coexisting dyslexia or a specific reading disorder. They may appear to be strong readers, yet often do have some reading challenges.
- In spite of their reading aptitude, because of the inherent difficulties associated with inattention, distractibility, poor working memory and other executive functions, children with ADHD commonly have reading errors, inconsistencies, and spotty comprehension.
- Attention and executive function impairments have a significant effect on reading, even if the student does not have a reading disorder per se.
- Research shows that the construction of meaning from text (reading comprehension) is very much dependent on the quality of students' self-directed cognitive abilities—his or her executive functions (Gaskin, Satlow, & Pressley, 2007; Kaufman, 2010).

Inattention—Related Reading Errors and Difficulties

- Students can be drawn off task while reading and therefore miss words and important details.
- People cannot remember what has been read if they haven't paid attention to what they were reading—affecting recall and comprehension of the text.
- Maintaining attention and focusing on what they are reading, particularly when reading silently or if there are distractions in the environment, can be a challenge.
- When students' attention drifts, so do their eyes from the page, and they lose their place when reading.
- Inattention may cause them to skip not only individual words when reading but sometimes even whole lines of text without noticing.
- They may have trouble paying attention to stories and other text that is read out loud in class. When one person is reading orally, students with ADHD commonly

have a hard time following along with the rest of the class. They are frequently on the wrong page of the book and especially struggle to follow if the reader lacks fluency and expression.

- "They may be unable to sustain attention with sufficient consistency to learn letter names and/or letter-sound correspondences, resulting in an incomplete or erratic knowledge of phonics, even though the language processing skills are otherwise intact." They may also not notice all the parts of the word they are reading (such as word endings) and omit words or parts of words (Kaufman, 2010, p. 98).

Impulsivity—Related Reading Errors and Difficulties

- Children with ADHD may have the tendency to guess at unfamiliar words without taking the time to decode them (even though they have strong decoding skills) or to read words by looking at only part of the word, resulting in inaccuracies.
- Impulsive students may respond to teacher questions about the reading material too quickly—before fully thinking about the question and forming a thoughtful answer.

Working Memory–Related Errors and Difficulties

- Working memory plays a very significant role in the reading process, and limited working memory capacity can cause problems decoding accurately, reading with fluency, recall, and with comprehension of the text.
- Reading multisyllable words requires keeping part of the word (one syllable) in mind while decoding or sounding out the next syllable. Some decoding difficulties may result from working memory issues (Kaufman, 2010; Levine, 1998).
- Children who can read fluently in an automatic manner are freed from having to devote much working memory to the decoding process. Those who are slow, laborious readers use so much working memory to decode the words that they have little working memory capacity left for the act of comprehension (Kaufman, 2010; Samuels, 2006).
- Students with poor working memory forget the content of what they have read from one paragraph or page to the next. People with ADHD frequently need to reread the material numerous times for it to sink in.
- Poor working memory results in limited recall of the reading material. This affects the ability to summarize, retell accurately, and respond to reading comprehension questions.
- Kaufman (2010, p. 103) shares Dr. Mel Levine's analogy (2002): Working memory is the cognitive stewpot in which new information is mixed with prior knowledge to allow comprehension to occur. Some students have small or "leaky" working memory systems that are unable to contain the various bits and pieces of information needed for comprehension to occur.

Metacognition—Related Errors and Difficulties

- This refers to a person's ability to think about his or her own thinking, learning, and understanding. Reading comprehension requires the ability to self-monitor while reading—to be aware of and know when the text is making sense or not.
- Students with ADHD often read superficially, going through the motions but not fully engaged and thinking about whether what they are reading makes sense.
- When noticing that what they have read does not make sense, good readers then apply fix-up strategies in order to repair their comprehension and gain meaning from the text. Children with ADHD often do not do so.
- Poor metacognition affects the ability to read critically and deeply—deriving the most meaning from the text.

Other Executive Function–Related Difficulties

- Students with ADHD may have difficulty with initiation—or getting started on and keeping up the level of effort and motivation to complete reading assignments (particularly material that is dry, lengthy, and tedious to read).
- Cognitive flexibility may be an issue, causing them to have difficulty using flexible strategies, for example, to decode unfamiliar words or for applying strategies to aid their reading comprehension.
- When reading, they may not be using their internal language and self-talk to be actively engaged in the text, for example, by asking themselves questions such as these:
  - "What is the main idea?"
  - "What is the author trying to say in this paragraph?"
  - "What does this remind me of?" (making connections, reflecting as they read)
  - "What do I predict is going to happen next?"

Processing Speed–Related Errors and Difficulties

Children and teens with ADHD (particularly inattentive-type ADHD) and learning disabilities often have slower processing speeds—which is the rate at which information is processed. This has nothing to do with intelligence. It is not that someone with this problem is a "slow learner" but that he or she processes information at a slower speed, which may cause difficulties with the following:

- Automatic word recognition and reading fluency
- Keeping up with the pace of instruction
- Responding quickly to teacher questions and following along in class discussions
- Word retrieval—pulling up from memory the precise words one wants to use when speaking or writing

Related Lists

- See *Lists 2.12, 3.8, 4.1, 5.2, 5.3, 5.4, and 5.5.*

Sources and Resources

Barkley, Russell A. (2013). *Taking charge of ADHD: The complete, authoritative guide for parents* (3rd ed.). New York: Guilford Press.

Blake, Kevin. (2000). Two common reading problems experienced by many AD/HD adults. *Attention Magazine*, *6*(5), 30–36.

Gaskin, L.W., Satlow, E., & Pressley, M. (2007). Executive control of reading comprehension in elementary school. In L. Meltzer (Ed.), *Executive function in education: From theory to practice* (pp. 194–215). New York: Guilford Press.

International Dyslexia Association. (2008, March). Just the facts: Definition of dyslexia. Retrieved from www.interdys.org/ewebeditpro5/upload/Definition.pdf

International Dyslexia Association. (2013). *Dyslexia in the classroom: What every teacher needs to know*. Baltimore, MD: International Dyslexia Association (IDA).

Israel, S. E., Block, C.C., Bauserman, K. L., & Kinnucan-Welsch, K. (2005). *Metacognition in literacy learning: Theory, assessment, instruction, and professional development*. Mahwah, NJ: Lawrence Erlbaum.

Kaufman, Christopher. (2010). *Executive function in the classroom*. Baltimore, MD: Paul H. Brookes.

Levine, Mel. (1998). *Developmental variation and learning disorders*. Cambridge, MA: Educational Publishing Service.

Levine, Mel. (2002). *A mind at a time*. New York: Simon & Schuster.

Lovett, Maureen W., Lacerenza, Léa, Steinbach, Karen A., & De Palma, Maria. (2014). Development and evaluation of a research-based intervention program for children and adolescents with reading disabilities. *Interventions to Improve Reading Skills*, *40*(3), 21–29.

Lyon, G. Reid. (1999). The NICHD research program in reading development, reading disorders and reading instruction: A summary of research findings. *Keys to successful learning: A national summit on research in learning disabilities*. New York: The National Center for Learning Disabilities.

National Institute of Child Health and Human Development (NICHD). (2000). *Report of the National Reading Panel: Teaching children to read; An evidence-based assessment of the scientific literature on reading and its implications for reading instruction: Reports of the subgroups* (NIH Publication No. 00-4754). Washington, DC: US Government Printing Office.

Rief, Sandra & Stern, Judith (2010). *The dyslexia checklist: A practical reference for parents and teachers.* San Francisco: Jossey-Bass.

Samuels, S. J. (2006). Reading fluency: It's past, present, and future. In T. Rasinski, C. Blachowicz, & K. Lems (Eds.), *Fluency instruction: Research-based best practices* (pp. 7-20). New York: Guilford Press.

5.2 The Reading Process: What Good Readers Do

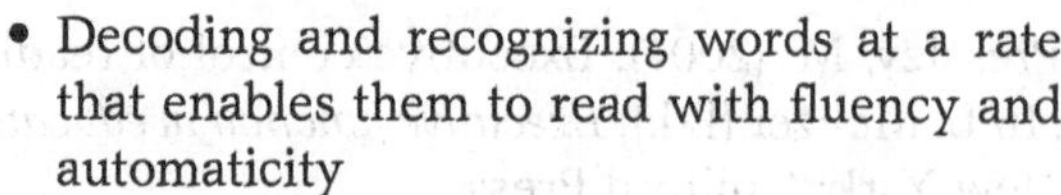

Reading is a complex process with the goal to acquire meaning from the printed word. Good readers are adept at the following:

- Decoding and recognizing words at a rate that enables them to read with fluency and automaticity
- Using all cueing systems (semantic, syntactic, and graphophonic) to figure out unfamiliar words or language
- Understanding and figuring out challenging vocabulary and word meanings
- Knowing how to read for specific purposes
- Using whatever background or prior knowledge they have about the subject to make inferences and get meaning out of what they are reading
- Making connections as they read to other material previously read, to their own life and experiences, and to other information and concepts they know ("This reminds me of . . .")
- Reflecting as they read
- Using effective metacognitive strategies to think about what they are reading and self-monitoring their comprehension and understanding
- Checking for their own comprehension and using self-correcting (fix-up) strategies when realizing they are not getting meaning or making sense of what is being read
- Constantly thinking ahead, predicting, and either confirming or changing their predictions as they read
- Self-monitoring the amount of attention and effort required when reading; aware of which parts can be read quickly by skimming and scanning and which parts require close attention, concentration, and perhaps rereading a few times for better recall and comprehension
- Understanding organization and structure for different types of text (literary and expository)
- Understanding story structure and the organization of literary text (characters, setting, problem, action, resolution to problem)
- Understanding the structures or schemas for various kinds of expository (nonfiction) text
- Knowing how to use text features and organizational and graphic aids (such as the glossary, index, table of contents, charts, graphs, headings and subheadings, graphs and diagrams) to aid comprehension
- Visualizing when they are reading (scenes, characters) and making mental images
- Distinguishing main ideas and important information from details and less important information in the text
- Critically evaluating what they are reading in whatever format it is presented (printed or digital)
- Engaging in many kinds of thinking processes while reading (such as questioning, analyzing, synthesizing, interpreting, evaluating, and reflecting)
- Focusing on the main content rather than extraneous information

- Recognizing and understanding text structures, such as cause-and-effect, problem-and-solution, and compare-and-contrast relationships
- Making inferences (reading between the lines) based on clues in the text using schema—what they already know, connections they have made, and the process of predicting and confirming
- Finding evidence in the text to support their opinions
- Knowing which strategies to use for various reading tasks and types of material
- Being able to flexibly apply and monitor a variety of effective strategies in the process of actively reading for meaning

In addition, good readers do the following:

- Self-select books of personal interest and find pleasure in reading books and other choice reading materials
- Read from a variety of fictional and nonfiction genres (such as historical fiction, biographies, fables, memoirs) and critically evaluate what they are reading in whatever format it is presented (printed or digital)

Note: As described in *Lists 1.2, 1.5, 2.12, 4.1, and 5.1* executive function impairment and attention weaknesses may cause children and teens with ADHD to have difficulty and lack proficiency with some of these skills and reading behaviors. See *Lists 3.5, 3.8, 4.1, 4.3, 5.3, 5.4, and 5.5* for strategies to help.

Source and Resource

Harvey, S., & Goudvis, A. (2000). *Strategies that work: Teaching comprehension to enhance understanding*. York, ME: Stenhouse.

5.3 Strategies for Building Word Recognition, Decoding, Fluency, and Vocabulary

- Many children with ADHD also have the coexisting learning disability—dyslexia. As described in *List 5.1,* dyslexia is characterized by poor ability to read and spell words. These children struggle with word recognition and the ability to use phonics and other skills to decode or figure out unfamiliar words. Because they read slowly and laboriously, their reading fluency (speed, flow, and accuracy) is affected and therefore impairs their reading comprehension.
- However, not all children who have poor word recognition and decoding skills and lack fluency have dyslexia. These students may have had minimal phonics and word analysis instruction and simply may not have been taught these skills and strategies sufficiently. Also, children with ADHD who do not have dyslexia may be weak in these skills because of issues related to inattention and poor working memory capacity (*List 5.1*).
- In order to become fluent readers, children must first become skilled at recognizing and decoding the printed word. They need a large enough bank of words that they can read at an automatic level without having to sound them out (for example, high-frequency words and irregular or sight words such as *said, their,* and *they*).
- These students also need direct, explicit instruction (and early intervention whenever possible) in how to break the code in reading, which involves learning and proficiency in these skills:
  - Alphabet knowledge
  - Letter-sound association for all consonants, vowels (long and short *a, e, i, o, u*), consonant blends (for example, *cl, br, st*), consonant digraphs (*ch, sh, th*), vowel digraphs and dipthongs (such as *oa, ea, ai, oi, ou*), and vowel patterns (final *e, r*-controlled)
  - Rapid blending of isolated sounds into words
  - Recognition of rhyming sound families or visual patterns in words such as *rock/stock/flock* or *right/might/flight/bright*. These are called word families or onset and rimes. *Note:* Onsets are the letters before the vowel (*r, st, fl*). Rimes are the vowel and following letters in single-syllable words (*-ock and -ight*).
  - Structural analysis of words—awareness of word parts such as root words, prefixes, and suffixes that carry meaning
  - Knowledge of syllable types and strategies for decoding multisyllabic words
- Children need to be taught strategies and cueing systems to use as they read to decode the text correctly.
  - *Semantic cues.* Determining if the word makes sense in the context of what is being read and being able to self-correct (substitute a different word if it does not make sense)
  - *Syntactic cues.* Determining if the word sounds right grammatically and being able to self-correct (substitute a different word that grammatically fits in the context of what is being read)
  - *Graphophonic cues.* Using recognition of the printed letters (graphemes) and their corresponding sounds (phonemes) to figure out unfamiliar words

Word Recognition and Decoding

- Most children learn best to read and spell when provided with explicit, systematic phonics instruction. This is a key instructional intervention for children with dyslexia. Kaufman (2010, p. 105) explains how this type of instruction is also important for children with executive function weaknesses:

  > "Word identification strategies that emphasize systematic, explicit teaching methods and that keep returning to specific skills until they are clearly mastered are far more likely to produce lasting skill development in children with executive function challenge because they make clear what is being taught and include lots of guided repetition." (*List 3.8*)

- Kaufman also explains the importance of explicitly teaching children with executive function weaknesses the practice of left-to-right sound blending. He shares the technique advocated by Beck (2006) of successive or cumulative blending in order to alleviate some of the burden from working memory when sounding out words. Here is an example of sounding out the word *trick* using this approach: The child first says /*t*/ and then /*r*/ and then combines the sounds to say /*tr*/. Then the / *i*/sound is added and the child goes back and says /*tri*/. Then the *ck* or /*k*/ sound is added and the whole word is then sounded out in sequence. That technique supports children with poor working memory having to hold on to the individual sounds in memory while working through the rest of the word.
- There are programs for teaching letter-sound associations that are multisensory and use various mnemonic strategies to make the learning more memorable and permanent (such as incorporating a kinesthetic body movement associated with the letter sound or calling attention to how the sound is formed in the mouth). Some programs to explore are Zoo-Phonics, Lindamood-Bell, and Alphabet Learning Center Activities Kit's alphabet system. See the "Sources and Resources" section of this list.
- Explicitly teach strategies for decoding words, such as breaking multiple-syllable words apart according to syllable types (closed, open, final *e*, vowel team, *r*-controlled, diphthong, consonant *-le*) and explicitly teaching prefixes and suffixes and rapid recognition of these important word parts.
- Teach strategies for pulling apart words, stretching out sounds (particularly vowel sounds), and substituting the alternate sounds that vowels or vowel combinations can make when one doesn't work. For example, in sounding out the word *health*. The *ea* can make the long *e* sound as in *sea* or the short *e* sound as in *set*. If the child reads the word with the long *e* sound and figures out that it is not a recognized word, he or she should then try the other vowel sound (short *e*).
- Sight words can be taught and practiced using a variety of multisensory strategies, color to highlight and call attention to certain letters within the word, and game formats to motivate practice and repetition. These are all beneficial techniques for helping to lock these words into memory for automatic retrieval when reading or spelling them.
- Word Sorts is another popular instructional technique for studying words and focusing on elements that are the same or different. This involves sorting words into two or three categories according to features of the word, for example, sounds within the word (sorting into long *a*/ short *a*, *ch*/*sh*, *er*/*ir*/*ur*, *ou*/*oi*) or different word endings (*-sion*/*-tion*).
- *Note:* The author's books *Alphabet Learning Center Activities Kit* (Fetzer & Rief, 2002) and *The Dyslexia Checklist* (Rief & Stern, 2010) contain numerous strategies

and motivating activities for teaching and practicing alphabet and letter-sound association, sight words, phonics, and decoding skills. Also, see the strategies posted on these Pinterest boards: www.pinterest.com/sandrarief/alphabet-letter-sounds/, www.pinterest.com/sandrarief/sight-words/, and www.pinterest.com/sandrarief/phonics-decoding-fluency/. For tips and tricks for helping children who have directionality confusion and commonly reverse letters *b* and *d* when reading or spelling, see www.pinterest.com/sandrarief/b-d-tricks-strategies/.

Instruction for Students with Dyslexia

- Students with reading disabilities who struggle with word recognition and decoding need intensive, systematic instruction in language skills. Most research-validated programs for teaching decoding skills and the recommended intervention programs for children with dyslexia, whether provided at school or privately, use curriculum that is based on Orton-Gillingham methodology. The instructional approach of these programs is as follows.
  - *Direct and explicit*. Each skill, rule of language, and strategy for reading and spelling words must be taught clearly and directly, without assuming that the student has even the most basic foundational skills or background knowledge about the English written language.
  - *Systematic and structured*. Students with dyslexia typically have gaps in their understanding of how the English written language system works. They need to be taught a systematic scope and sequence (coverage and organization) of skills, starting at a beginning level to ensure mastery of foundational skills and filling in holes in a student's repertoire of skills.
  - *Cumulative*. Each lesson and skills taught is cumulative—gradually building on previously taught skills or concepts as students are moved along step-by-step, at an appropriate individual pace.
  - *Multisensory*. Regardless of the program used, teaching children with dyslexia requires the use of multisensory techniques, which make learning more memorable. Students with dyslexia usually learn best when instruction incorporates some combination of auditory, visual, and tactile-kinesthetic input.

In addition, students with dyslexia need an intensity of instruction that is greater than that needed for students without learning problems:

- Sufficient time provided for direct skill and strategy instruction
- Numerous practice opportunities with immediate corrective feedback and reinforcement
- Instruction provided either one-on-one or in small groups of students of the same skill level
- Ongoing assessment and careful monitoring of progress
- Some of the various Orton-Gillingham-based intervention programs are Alphabetic Phonics, Orton-Gillingham, Slingerland, Barton Reading and Spelling System, Wilson Fundations and Wilson Reading, Project Read, Language!, Spalding Method, Sonday System, Go Phonics, Lexia, and Starting Over. See their websites and others in the resources listed in the "Sources and Resources" section.
- See *Lists 5.1 and 5.5* for more information on dyslexia.

Building Fluency

- Reading fluency is the ability to recognize words and read with ease, speed, accuracy, and expression.
- Because fluent readers do not need to put forth a lot of mental energy trying to figure out the words on the page, it frees them to focus their attention on comprehension and makes reading far more enjoyable and rewarding than it is for readers who labor to read word by word (Allington, 2006; Armbruster, Lehr, & Osborn, 2001).

Factors That Contribute to Fluency

- *Accuracy*. Being able to decode or recognize words correctly. Building phonics skills, word attack skills, and sight recognition of high-frequency and irregular words is necessary to improve reading accuracy.
- *Rate*. Being able to read individual words and connected text quickly. Reading speed (rate) increases with practice and rereading. Rate is measured by words correct per minute or length of time needed to complete a passage.
- *Automaticity*. Accurate, effortless, and rapid word recognition—not having to put mental effort into identifying words. Automaticity requires rapid decoding of unfamiliar words and recognizing a high number of familiar words by sight. Practice and memory play a significant part in automaticity.
- *Prosody*. Being able to read with good expression that sounds like speech (appropriate pitch, tone, phrasing, stress or emphasis, pacing, and rhythm). Prosody, which plays an important part in comprehension of text, is developed through listening to good reading models and practice.
- *Vocabulary*. Word knowledge. Knowing the meaning of a word makes it easier and quicker to read. Vocabulary development increases fluency by improving recognition of words in print.
- *Processing speed*. How quickly one processes information—for example, on seeing written words, how quickly one can convert those symbols into speech (whether one is reading silently or aloud)
- *Reading volume*. How much one reads. The more children read, the greater their exposure to words will be, facilitating vocabulary acquisition and word recognition. Struggling readers read less because it is not pleasurable; therefore, they often get less exposure to words and less practice than their grade-level peers.
- *Correct practice*. Repeated use of reading skills. Fluency is developed through many opportunities to practice skills correctly, which means reading aloud to an adult or skilled reader who can provide corrective feedback as needed.

Fluency-Building Strategies

Research shows that fluency can be developed through a variety of techniques, particularly through repeated monitored oral reading.

- *Student-adult reading*. The adult reads aloud first, providing a model of fluent reading. The student then rereads the same passage, with adult assistance and coaching as needed. For example, if the student gets stuck on a word, the adult reads the word and the child repeats it. The student rereads the passage a few times until it is read fluently with ease and expression.

- *Partner reading or buddy reading*. Partner reading can be done in various ways. One way is to pair a stronger reader with a less fluent reader. The stronger reader first reads the page or passage aloud, pointing to the words while the partner follows along. Then, the less fluent reader rereads the same passage while the stronger partner assists and coaches (gently correcting errors, after which the partner rereads the passage). In another variation, partners at the same reading level are paired in order to reread a passage or story a few times in different formats:
    - Alternating paragraphs or pages
    - Having first one partner read the whole passage, then the other
    - Having one partner read for a few minutes, then switching
    - Reading in unison while one points under the words
- *Choral reading*. This technique involves reading text aloud in unison after it is first modeled for fluent oral reading. Everyone looks at the text as it is read. There are different ways of doing choral reading in the classroom: using individual copies for rereading aloud together or providing large-size text that students can see from where they are seated. This is usually done by projecting text on a screen, for example, via a document camera, or using a big book, or writing the words of a poem, song, or passage in large print on the board or chart paper.
    - The teacher models and reads the text with fluency while sweeping a finger or marker under the words in phrases—not word by word—to match the flow of speech.
    - The material is reread; this time, students join in for choral rereading of all or parts of the text a few times.
    - For fun, teachers can vary sections of the text to be read by different groups (for example, boys and girls, left side of room and right side of room).
- *Echo reading*. The teacher reads aloud a short section of text (a single sentence, a paragraph, or a verse of a poem). Immediately, the students echo what was just read while the teacher points to or sweeps under the words. Echo reading can be done with a whole group or just an individual student. Poetry and song lyrics work well for fluency practice.
- *Recording-assisted reading*. A student reads along with an audio recording of a passage or book that has been recorded by a fluent reader. After hearing it read several times, the student reads along with the recording and practices until the text can be read fluently. Some recorded books may not be appropriate for fluency practice because they may have too many unfamiliar words or concepts.
- *Software programs*. Students use a program such as Read Naturally (www.readnaturally.com), which combines teacher modeling, repeated reading, assessment, and progress monitoring on the computer.

Additional Fluency Strategies

- *Readers theater*. Many theater scripts are excellent for fluency practice. Students practice reading their assigned parts from the script in order to perform for classmates or other audiences.
- *Practicing in order to perform*. In addition to readers theater, many other performance opportunities—for example, puppet shows, plays, choral concerts, or poetry

parties—can provide a means of getting struggling readers to practice fluency by rehearsing in preparation for performance.

- *Cross-age buddy reading.* Older students often have younger reading buddies. Reading a book with good expression provides fluency practice in preparation for reading that book to their younger buddies.
- *Timed repeated reading and charting.* Students read a short passage for one minute. The teacher determines the words correct per minute (reading rate) on that passage and the student charts or graphs the score. This procedure continues with repeated readings until the target reading rate is reached.

Remediation Challenge

- For older students with reading disabilities, fluency is probably the most difficult area to remediate because of the cumulative effect of years of minimal practice in reading words correctly.
- Lack of correct practice results in a huge deficiency in the number of words that the reader can recognize instantly by sight and a much slower reading rate than grade-level peers.
- Some fluency-building programs include Jamestown Timed Reading (www.glecoe.com), Quick Reads at (www.quickreads.org), Read Naturally (www.readnaturally.com), and The Fluency Formula Program (www.scholastic.com).
- Explore the tool BeeLine Reader (www.BeeLineReader.com) to aid easier, faster reading on computers, tablets, and smartphones. This technology applies an eye-guiding color gradient to text that helps reduce line transition errors (accidentally skipping a line or rereading the same line twice). The color gradient generated by BeeLine Reader helps guide the reader's eyes from the end of one line to the beginning of the next, which significantly reduces the chance of accidentally skipping or repeating lines. By making line transitions easier and more natural, BeeLine Reader enables the reader to transition more quickly from line to line—increasing reading speed, particularly on mobile devices.
- See author's books in the "Sources and Resources" section (Rief, 2005; Rief & Heimburge, 2007; Rief & Stern, 2010) for additional strategies and activities for strengthening reading fluency.
- See *List 7.12* for numerous motivating online resources under the category of phonics, sight words, word recognition, spelling, and fluency.

Tips for Oral Reading in the Classroom

Oral reading in the classroom is necessary but can be problematic. To discuss a text, it is naturally important that all students have read the material. However, round-robin reading, with the students taking individual turns reading aloud to the class, is generally not the most effective strategy, especially for students with reading disabilities or attention difficulties.

- Students who have reading difficulty have a hard time following along and staying on track. They may also become so fearful of being embarrassed by their poor reading skills that they spend the whole period in anxiety, trying to predict what will be their portion to read and practicing ahead. Therefore, they are not listening or following along.

- Have students first read silently before the class or group reads orally. Students (particularly older ones) who are uncomfortable reading orally should never be forced to read out loud to the class. They should be able to volunteer when they wish to read in front of the class. Buddy reading or reading in small groups is a much safer, preferable way for students to practice their oral reading.

Tips for Independent Reading

- Independent reading is also critical for building fluency, but the book must be at an appropriate level to read without support. One method of quickly determining if a book is at a child's appropriate independent level is the five-finger check described in *List 5.5*. Another method is one in twenty: select a passage from a child's chosen book to read orally. If the child makes less than one error in twenty words, the reading material is at his or her independent level.
- *Note:* Many children with attention difficulties have a hard time maintaining their focus and paying attention to the words they are reading silently. As mentioned, for these students as well as those who have an auditory processing learning disability, hearing the words (softly saying the words aloud) to themselves may help them attend to or better process what they are reading. Permit them to take their book to a quiet corner and read to themselves aloud. Another strategy is to provide a curved, hollow plastic device that is held to the ear like a telephone receiver while softly whispering the words into the other end. The device channels the voice directly to the child's ear to provide the auditory input without disturbing others. Two recommended products are Whisperphone available through www.linguisystems.com and Toobaloo available through www.superduperinc.com. It can also be constructed by fitting together two PVC plastic elbow pipes.

Vocabulary

- Although many students with ADHD and learning disabilities have a strong oral vocabulary, their poor reading skills impede their recognition and acquisition of the hundreds of new words that their classmates who are skilled readers learn through reading. Students who read a lot are exposed to complex, sophisticated words through their reading and have a stronger vocabulary than minimal readers.
- They may also have a weaker vocabulary than their peers because of poor retrieval of words from memory that restrict word usage when speaking and writing, as well as underlying language difficulties impeding comprehension of figures of speech and nuances of language (such as metaphors, idioms, puns, and words with multiple meanings).

Strategies for Vocabulary Development and Working with Words

- *Directly teaching words.* Define words for students using simple explanations and synonyms. If possible, use antonyms (opposites) as well. For example, tell students, "The word *emaciated* means really skinny—extremely thin, often from starving. It's the opposite of fat or plump." Give examples and nonexamples: "The starving kitten was weak and emaciated when they found it." "Might a child living in poverty who is undernourished be emaciated?" "Do these people look emaciated?" (Show pictures of average and heavy people.) Have students generate their own examples of the word in a sentence or with a picture.

- *Context clues.* Reading a word in the context of the rest of the sentence and surrounding sentences is an important strategy for figuring out meanings of unknown words. Have students read a word (or listen to it being read) in the context of the surrounding sentences and try to guess the meaning.
- *Semantic webs.* These are visual displays or graphic organizers for helping students learn vocabulary and understand word relationships. Write a specific vocabulary word in the center of the page. Other related words, phrases, characteristics, properties, or examples relating to that word are written around the page, radiating from the center vocabulary word (like a spider web).
- *Multiple meanings.* Provide practice in working with words with multiple meanings.
- *Teach word roots.* Many English words have Greek, Latin, or Anglo-Saxon roots. For example, *phon* is the Greek root that means sound. From that root, many words can be derived—such as telephone and phonology. Recognizing words with the same root is helpful in understanding word meanings.
- *Word lists or anchor charts.* Post lists of words, adding to them throughout the year as new words are encountered. Topics for these lists might include the following:
  - Character traits—for example, *inquisitive, stubborn, compassionate*
  - Feelings—for example, *suspicious, optimistic, discouraged*
  - Alternatives to overused words such as *said, went,* or *nice*—for example, alternatives to *said* might include *stated, responded, announced*
- *Definitions.* Teach dictionary skills. Model and provide practice in looking up words in references such as dictionaries, glossaries, and thesauri.
- *Make it visual, make it memorable.* Make illustrations, use symbols to represent ideas, label, color, highlight, or use graphic organizers to help students remember words and their associations with other words or ideas.
- *Games and word play.* Games that build vocabulary and make learning about words fun can be made or purchased. Choose games carefully or make adaptations as needed (extended or no time limits, providing assistance in reading words on the game card).
  - Crossword puzzles are excellent for building word knowledge.
  - Play commercial games that enhance vocabulary and language skills, such as Password, Jeopardy, One-Minute Wonders, Outburst, and Pictionary.
- *Mapping unknown words.* Provide activities that require students to map information for a new word. Have them write the word and sentence in which it is found in the text; record its definition, synonyms for the word, and an example or illustration; and write a sentence using the word.
- *Figurative language.* Teach these elements through a variety of activities:
  - Share idioms such as "He saw the handwriting on the wall." Explain the difference between literal and figurative meaning.
  - Find examples of metaphors to chart and illustrate. Examples: "The man is a rock." "That is a half-baked idea."
- *Precision with words.* Teach students how valuable it is to use just the right words to convey meaning most precisely. Provide activities in which students work in groups or partners to arrange an array of words along a continuum—for example, words

that describe moving from here to there: *ambled . . . strolled . . . walked . . . jogged . . . dashed.*

- Preview text and frontload or explain important or difficulty words prior to reading.
- See author's books (Rief, 2005; Rief & Heimburge, 2007; Rief & Stern, 2010) for several other recommended strategies for vocabulary development, as well as many activities across grade levels posted at www.pinterest.com/sandrarief/vocabularylanguage/.
- See *List 7.12* for suggested online vocabulary resources.

Points to Keep in Mind

- A number of students have difficulty with the language and vocabulary of books at their grade level. However, all children should have the opportunity to hear and discuss literature and expository text that is interesting, motivating, and at a challenging level.
- Although the vocabulary may be difficult, a nonproficient reader can participate equally in reading of grade-level material through shared reading, read-alouds, teacher-guided reading, listening to recorded text, and the host of reading comprehension strategies in which students collaboratively read the text (*Lists 3.5, 5.4*).
- According to Dr. Louisa Moats (2001), normally progressing students can read most of the words in their listening vocabulary by fourth or fifth grade. From then on, they learn new vocabulary—primarily by reading—at the rate of several thousand new words per year. Many poor readers must overcome a huge vocabulary deficit before they will be able to read successfully beyond the fifth-grade level.
- Because it is a challenge, many children with ADHD are reluctant readers. See *List 5.5* for strategies recommended to parents to motivate children to read and the numerous online resources and apps in *List 7.12*.

Sources and Resources

Allington, R. (2006). *What really matters for struggling readers: Designing research-based programs* (2nd ed.). Boston: Pearson Education.

Ambruster, B. B., Lehr, F., & Osborn, J. (2001, September). Put reading first: The research building blocks for teaching children to read. National Institute for Literacy. Retrieved from www.nifl.gov/parthershipforreading/publications/reading_first1.html

Beck, I. L. (2006). *Making sense of phonics: The how's and why's*. New York: Guilford Press.

Fetzer, Nancy, & Rief, Sandra. (2002). *Alphabet learning center activities kit:* San Francisco: Jossey-Bass. Book and holders and fasties alphabet charts available at www.sandrarief.com.

Kaufman, Christopher. (2010). *Executive function in the classroom*. Baltimore, MD: Paul H. Brookes.

Moats, Louisa. (2001). When older kids can't read. *Educational Leadership*, *58*, 6.

Rief, S. (2005). *How to reach & teach children with ADD/ADHD: Practical techniques, strategies and interventions* (2nd ed.). San Francisco: Jossey-Bass.

Rief, Sandra, & Heimburge, Julie. (2007). *How to reach & teach all children through balanced literacy: User-friendly strategies, tools, activities, and ready-to-use materials*. San Francisco: Jossey-Bass.

Rief, Sandra & Stern, Judith (2010). *The dyslexia checklist: A practical reference for parents and teachers*. San Francisco: Jossey-Bass.

Zoo-Phonics (www.zoo-phonics.com/home.html)

Some Reading Intervention Programs for Children and Teens with Dyslexia

Most of the following programs incorporate Orton-Gillingham approaches

- Alphabetic Phonics (http://eps.schoolspecialty.com/products/literacy/learning-differences/alphabetic-phonics/about-the-program)
- Barton Reading and Spelling System (www.bartonreading.com/)
- Go Phonics (www.gophonics.com/)
- Language! (www.voyagersopris.com/curriculum/subject/literacy/language-4th-edition)
- Lexia Learning (http://lexialearning.com/product)
- Lindamood-Bell (www.lindamoodbell.com/)
- Nessy Reading (http://www.nessy.com/us/)
- Orton-Gillingham (www.orton-gillingham.com/)
- Project Read (www.projectread.com/)
- Rewards (for grades 4–12) (www.voyagersopris.com/curriculum/subject/literacy/rewards)
- Slingerland (www.slingerland.org/)
- Sonday System (www.winsorlearning.com/site/instructional-materials/sonday-system-1/)
- Sounds in Syllables (http://www.mlti-nm.com/Sounds-In-Syllables.html)
- Spalding Method (www.spalding.org/)
- Starting Over (www.knighteducation.com/classroomProducts/default.html)
- Wilson Fundations (www.fundations.com/)
- Wilson Reading (www.wilsonlanguage.com/fs_program_wrs.htm)

5.4 Strategies for Reading Comprehension

Comprehension—getting meaning from text—is the purpose of reading. It requires the reader to actively process the text, self-monitor for understanding, and know how and when to apply various meaning-making strategies when something doesn't make sense. Key strategies for readers with ADHD are those that keep them actively engaged throughout the reading process—thinking about, questioning, and responding to the reading material in order to maintain their attention, comprehend, and recall what they have read.

All students in today's classrooms with Common Core State Standards (CCSS) are required to interact with and read complex texts carefully and deeply for meaning. They also must support their opinions and responses to reading comprehension questions by going back and finding evidence from the text. This is not an easy task for those with attention and executive function weaknesses.

A number of strategies are helpful and effective prior to reading, during reading, and after completing the reading assignment to aid with recall and comprehension.

Strategies for Before Reading

Prereading strategies are important for activating the reader's prior knowledge about the topic, building connections and comprehension of the text, and generating interest and motivation to read the material.

- Prior to reading, relate the story or reading material to the students' experiences and background knowledge through discussions, brainstorming, and charting prior knowledge ("What do we already know about ... ?").
- Set the stage and establish the purpose for what they are about to read—for example, "As you read, think about what you would do if . . . ."
- Ask them to make predictions prior to reading.
- Generate interest and increase their background knowledge and frame of reference before reading by using concrete objects and audiovisuals related to the topic of study, such as maps, music, photos, and videos.
- Provide time to preview the text (look at the cover, illustrations, thumb through to peruse chapter titles, headings, chapter questions) before reading the material. Another way to preview is to have the students listen to passages read aloud first before independently studying and rereading.
- To activate prior knowledge, students may be asked to write down everything they know about the topic in their learning log or to brainstorm and record in the first column of a KWL chart (see the "KWL" section).
- Discuss selected vocabulary that may be challenging in the text.
- Link prior knowledge to new concepts and information that will be studied using advance organizers, anticipation guides, and other prereading strategies and tools. My other books (see the "Sources and Resources" section) provide detailed information about these strategies.

Strategies for During Reading

Students need to be taught information about different kinds of text and strategies to apply during the reading process to aid comprehension. Students need to learn (through teacher modeling and guided practice) how to interact with the text while reading through strategies such as questioning, visualizing, annotating, and jotting down thoughts. They also need to be able to identify the author's purpose, audience, text structures for literary and expository text, and how to use clues the author provides and other information to infer and draw conclusions. Some of these points and strategies will be shared in more detail later in this list.

- Teach students how to paraphrase a paragraph or section, putting into his or her own words the main idea and significant details. Have students do so with a partner. Paraphrasing and stating it into a recording device is a helpful technique for independent reading.
- Teach the student how to find and pay attention to the introductory and summary paragraphs, how to find the subject and main ideas, and how to sift out the key facts and important details.
- Teach clustering, webbing, and mapping to pull out the main idea and supporting details from the text.
- Teach how to use the glossary, table of contents, index, charts, graphs, and maps, pay attention to italicized and boldface print, and other text features to get meaning from informational text.
- Give a few stopping points at strategic locations throughout the text for readers to interact with the material in some manner: to stop and question, react to, discuss, summarize, predict, clarify, or record.
- Provide a pad of sticky notes. Encourage students to jot down notes, unfamiliar words to clarify, and questions to place by items in the text they do not understand as they read, connections made, reactions to what they have read, and so forth. They can place the sticky note next to key points and main ideas for fast reference.
- Have students use specific coded symbols as they are reading and placing sticky notes in the text. The code may be, for example, a question mark for confusing parts or questions, an exclamation mark for exciting parts or for surprising parts, a star or asterisk to indicate something important, a check mark for "I understand," T-T for text-to-text connections, and so forth.
- Have students annotate or make marks directly on text pages (circling unfamiliar vocabulary, underlining words or phrases, and writing thoughts in the margins)—which is a key strategy in close reading.
- Teach story mapping: identifying the setting (time and place), characters, conflicts and problems, action and events, climax, and resolution of conflicts.
- Help children learn to self-monitor their own comprehension by asking themselves questions while reading: "What is the problem or conflict?" "What might the character do to resolve the problem?" "Why did she say that?" "What was the main point the author is trying to make in this section?" "Did I understand this?" "What were the steps for this procedure?" "What part does not make sense?" Questioning and self-questioning keep readers actively thinking about and processing the material.
- Teach and model strategies for resolving difficulties when comprehension breaks down: slowing the pace, going back and rereading, reading ahead to see if their questions are clarified later, talking with someone about their confusion, or jotting down questions to check later.
- Provide study guides to aid in looking for key information in the text.

- To help students who have difficulty staying on task, focused, and motivated while reading silently, do the following:
  - Set mini-goals in pacing their reading. Have the child read to a certain point in the text or to read for a predetermined amount of time. After reading to that point, the child is rewarded with a brief break.
  - Allow the child to subvocalize—say the words aloud softly as he or she is reading to themselves or use a Whisperphone device (*Lists 2.12, 5.3, 5.5*). This auditory feedback can assist with focus and attention to the reading material.
- Use any of the instructional strategies involving collaborative reading and analysis of the material, such as reciprocal teaching, GIST, book clubs, and buddy or partner reading. Learning and recall are greatly enhanced by the act of talking about the text. See "Other Reading Comprehension Strategies" for some of these strategies. More are described in author's other published books.
- Read Works (www.readworks.org)—a nonprofit presented by leading researchers and teachers in research-based reading comprehension instruction—provides free informational articles (grades K–12) with question sets on a wide variety of topics as well as literary passages.

Strategies for After Reading

These strategies involve the reader in deeper thinking and exploration of the reading material.

- After reading the text, students use their new insights and understanding to complete filling out charts and graphic organizers such as KWL charts and learning logs that were partially filled out during the prereading and during-reading stages.
- Have deep discussions about the concepts or events in the text or in character analysis.
- Make connections through related writing activities.
- Do further extension activities related to the theme and content of the reading to apply the learning.

Many of the strategies used during reading are also continued or completed after the reading.

Graphic Organizers

The following graphic organizers are useful for increasing comprehension and recall of text:

- *Framed outlines.* Students are given copies of a teacher-prepared outline that contains missing information for them to fill in during and after the reading.
- *Storyboards.* Divide a board or piece of paper into sections and have students draw or write story events in sequence in each box or frame.
- *Story maps.* This graphic includes essential elements of a story (setting, characters, time, place, problem or conflict, actions or happenings, and resolution).
- *Story frames.* These are sentence starters to fill in that provide a skeleton of the story or chapter. For example: "The setting of this chapter takes place ________. The character faced a problem when ___________. First he ___________. Next, ... Then __________. I predict in the next chapter ____________________."

- *Time lines*. These are used to help the student visualize chronological text and the sequence of events.
- *Plot charts*. Students fill in the following information that cycles through the plot of a story: Somebody (list the character) … wanted (goal) … but (what happened or interfered with the character achieving his or her goal) … and so (what happened next) . . . .
- *Prediction charts*. Charts that are modified as the story is being read. Based on the title and illustrations, students make initial predictions. As they read, stop and predict what will happen next. Continue questioning, predicting, and recording. Make clear to students that predictions are best guesses based on the information we know at the time and that good readers are constantly predicting when they are reading.
- *Venn diagram*. Two overlapping circles are used to display differences and similarities between characters, books, settings, topics, or events.
- *Comparison chart*. Much like a Venn diagram, this chart compares and contrasts two or more items, events, concepts, characters, and themes.
- *Flowchart*. A flowchart organizes a series of items or thoughts in logical order.
- *Webs, cluster maps, and semantic maps*. A central concept or main idea is placed in the center of related subtopics, and further details extend from each of the subtopic areas. These are used to categorize or identify related information.
- *5W chart*. After reading an article or excerpt from a text, the student identifies the 5W elements (who? what? when? where? why?) and records that information on the chart.
- *Character web*. Put the character's name in center of the web with traits and descriptions stemming from the center

Note: There are numerous other graphic organizers for main idea and supporting detail, cause and effect, sequence, classification matrices, and so forth. See the many online graphic organizers, many of them free, such as those found at Ed Helper (www .edhelper.com).

More Key Comprehension Strategies

- *Summarizing*. This is one of the most important reading comprehension skills. Sometimes the main idea is explicit and easy to find and other times it is implied or embedded in the passage. Use techniques that require students to summarize what they have read at various stopping points throughout the text. For example, students can summarize at the end of a passage with a one-sentence statement to tell to their partner and then write down the main event or two key points from the text on a sticky note at the end of chapters.
- *Narrative text structure*. Explicitly teach story grammar or story mapping so students understand the structure of the narrative (literary) text. This includes setting (time and place), characters, problems or conflicts, sequence of major events (rising actions), climax, and the resolution of conflicts or problem solution. Younger students generally focus on the main characters, setting, and story structure—beginning, middle, and end.
- *Expository or informational text structure*. Teach students how to identify the main ideas and supportive details (facts, statistics, examples) in the text. They are taught that informational text uses the structures of description (providing details or characteristics of a topic), order and sequence (outlining chronological events or

steps in which events occur as in a procedure), compare and contrast (showing similarities and differences between people, places, things, or events), problem and solution (information is given about a problem and at least one solution is presented or the issue is solved), and cause and effect (a description of a cause or reason for why something happens and the effect that follows the cause).

- *Close reading.* CCSS prioritizes students being able to think deeply about complex text and answer text-dependent questions—extracting evidence from the text to support their answers and conclusions. Through the process of close reading, students learn to do so.
  - According to Fisher (2014), close reading is "a careful and purposeful rereading of a text . . . an encounter with the text where students really focus on what the author had to say, what the author's purpose was, what the words mean, and what the structure of the text tells us." It is an approach for uncovering multiple layers of meaning (Boyles, 2012/2013).
  - The strategy involves rereading the text or portions of it a few times for specific purposes. In the second read, for example, students may explore some elements such as the organizational structure or author's word choices and language used. A third read would go deeper—critically analyzing what the author was trying to convey, making connections, and so forth.
  - Close reading is a very interactive process that may involve a variety of strategies such as discussion with partners or groups, circling unfamiliar words, color highlighting important information, and jotting down thoughts, questions, reactions, and connections on sticky notes or in the margins. Close readers are actively observing, questioning, and interacting with the text as they dig deep for clues to figure out what the author is really trying to say and gathering evidence to respond to text-dependent questions.
  - Nancy Boyles suggests four basic questions students should ask themselves in close reading: What is the author telling me here? Are there any hard or important words? What does the author want me to understand? How does the author play with language to add to meaning?

Other Reading Comprehension Strategies

Anticipation Guide

This is a series of teacher-generated statements about a topic given to students in advance of the reading. Students individually respond to the statements (with true or false) before reading about that topic. Typically, they are asked to discuss their choices briefly with partners or small groups prior to reading the passage. After reading the text material, they again discuss whether their beliefs have changed.

Directed Reading-Thinking Activity (DRTA)

Students are guided in active reading to make predictions about a passage or story. Then the passage is read (orally or silently) and at predetermined points students are asked to summarize the reading. At these points students are asked to confirm or revise their predictions and to give reasons for their decisions with evidence located and cited from the text. After a certain number of passages or pages read, the process starts again.

Imagery and Visualization

This is a technique that aids comprehension by creating mental pictures of what is being read. Students are encouraged to create an image in their mind as they read. This skill can be taught through a series of guided questioning techniques that elicit from the child vivid detailed pictures as they move through the passage. Examples of guided questions: "What do you see?" "What colors?" "Where is he sitting?" "How does it feel?" *Note:* A good resource for teaching this skill is the program by Nanci Bell entitled Visualizing and Verbalizing for Language Comprehension and Thinking.

KWL

This is a strategy used prior, during, and after the reading process. It involves a chart divided into three columns:

- The first column (*K*) indicates what is already *known* about the subject or topic. This step activates students' prior knowledge. Ideas are recorded during a class brainstorm.
- The middle column (*W*) is what the students *want* to learn or find out about the subject. This column sets the purpose for reading—to find the answers to those questions.
- The third column (*L*) is filled in on the chart as new information is *learned* from the reading or other teaching. This column is for recording "what we learned."

KWL Plus is the same as KWL, except it also adds mapping and summarization to the original KWL strategy. These two tasks incorporate the powerful tools of restructuring text and rewriting to help students process information (Ong, 2000). The information listed on the chart is mapped and organized graphically under categories of topics. Finally, a summary is written based on that graphic organization of ideas. There are other variations of the KWL strategy as well.

GIST

GIST stands for generating interaction between schemata and text (Swanson & DeLaPaz, 1998). This is a strategy used for comprehending informational text and determining the gist of the reading material:

- In cooperative groups, students read sections silently.
- When done reading a short section, the members of the group work together to write a one-sentence summary.
- All group members then record that summary sentence.
- Students continue in this fashion of reading a segment, stopping at logical points, jointly deciding on a summary sentence, and then recording on their own papers.
- Those papers can then serve as a study guide for the reading material.

Reciprocal Teaching

This approach, originally developed by Palincsar and Brown (1984, 1985), is one of the best-researched strategies available to teachers (Marzano, Pickering, & Pollock, 2001). It involves students working together in cooperative groups taking turns designing and asking questions and leading the group in the process of discussing and working through small portions of the text for comprehension purposes. Research has found that good readers spontaneously use strategies of predicting, questioning, clarifying, and summarizing. Poor readers do not self-monitor or use these strategies, which lead to understanding.

In a reciprocal teaching format, the group is lead through the process of reading a short section and (1) *questioning* about the content read to identify important information in the passage; (2) *summarizing* (Questions to help with summarizing may be asked, such as "What is this paragraph mostly about? What would be a good title for this passage?"); (3) *clarifying* anything confusing in the reading (Clarifying questions might include "Has anyone heard this expression before? What do you think it means?" "Can anyone explain this?"); and continues with (4) *predicting* what will happen in the next portion of the reading. The students proceed in this format, taking turns in the leader role as they read the next portions of the text.

Question-Answer Relationships (QAR)

Students are taught different classifications of questions: (1) right there, (2) think and search, and (3) on your own (Raphael, 1982).

1. The answers to right-there questions are stated directly in the text and simply require literal comprehension.
2. The answers to think-and-search questions are not as explicit and easy to locate but are found somewhere within the text. Answering these questions requires interpretive or inferential comprehension and reading between the lines. Finding the main idea of a passage is an example of inferential comprehension.
3. On-your-own questions are more abstract, and the answers cannot be found in the text. These questions require reading beyond the lines and involve higher-order thinking skills such as analyzing, evaluating, and creative thinking. Examples include comparing and contrasting or answering questions such as "What do you think caused... to happen?" "What other solution can you think of for that problem?"

Journal Entries

Use reflective journals, metacognitive journals, and double-entry journals (*List 4.3*).

Literature Logs

Have students record their personal reflections, summaries, and predictions.

Retelling

Review the literature students have read through storytelling, summarizing, time lines, quick writes, quick draws, audio recordings, pocket charts with colored sentence strips, plot charts, or any of the graphic organizers.

Hot Seat

A student volunteer is put on the hot seat, representing a particular character from the story. Students ask him or her questions that must be answered in the way the character would answer them.

Reader's Theater

Work on scripting a piece of literature into dialogue, then read it aloud dramatically.

Note: See author's books (2005, 2006, 2007, 2010) for additional strategies, such as fishbowl, jigsaw, guided reading, literature circles and book clubs, the PASS strategy, and several reading comprehension strategies and activities in content areas as well as several ideas for book projects and activities.

See numerous practical ideas and creative reading comprehension strategies for elementary through high school shared by teachers on Pinterest at www.pinterest.com/sandrarief/reading-comprehension/.

See *List 7.12* for websites with motivating content and activities for students that can boost reading comprehension.

Sources and Resources

Bell, Nanci. (1991). *Visualizing and verbalizing for language comprehension and thinking*. Paso Robles, CA: Academy of Reading Publications.

Boyles, Nancy. (2012/2013). Closing in on close reading. *Educational Leadership, 70*(4), 36–41. Retrieved at www.ascd.org/publications/educational-leadership/dec12/vol70/num04/Closing-in-on-Close-Reading.aspx

Burke, Beth. (n.d.). A close look at close reading: Scaffolding students with complex texts. Retrieved from http://nieonline.com/tbtimes/downloads/CCSS_reading.pdf

Fisher, Douglas. (2014). Close reading and the CCSS, part 1. Retrieved from www.mhecommoncoretoolbox.com/close-reading-and-the-ccss-part-1.html

Marzano, Robert, Pickering, Debra, & Pollock, Jane. (2001). *Classroom instruction that works: Research-based strategies for increasing student achievement*. Alexandria, VA: Association for Supervision & Curriculum Development.

Ong, Faye (Ed.). (2000). *Strategic teaching and learning: Standards-based instruction to promote content literacy in grades four through twelve*. Sacramento: California Department of Education.

Palincsar, A., & Brown, A. (1984). Reciprocal teaching of comprehension fostering and comprehension monitoring activities. *Cognition and Instruction, 1*(2), 117–175.

Palincsar, A., & Brown, A. (1985). Reciprocal teaching: Activities to promote reading with your mind. In T. L. Harris & E. J. Cooper (Eds.), *Reading, thinking, and concept development: Strategies for the classroom*. New York: The College Board.

Raphael, T. (1982). Questioning-answering strategies for children. *The Reading Teacher, 37*, 377–382.

Swanson, P. N., & DeLaPaz, S. (1998). Teaching effective comprehension strategies to students with learning and reading disabilities. *Intervention in School and Clinic, 33*, 209–218.

Note: See author's books (2005, 2006, 2007, 2010) *in the shaded box on page 272* for additional strategies, such as fishbowl, jigsaw, guided reading, literature circles and book clubs, the PASS strategy, and several reading comprehension strategies and activities in content areas as well as several ideas for book projects and activities.

5.5 Reading Tips and Strategies for Parents

As described in *List 5.1,* reading challenges are common in children and teens with ADHD, particularly for the approximately 25 to 35 percent who have the coexisting learning disability of dyslexia. There are many ways to help your child strengthen reading skills and become a more proficient, motivated reader.

- Try to read to and with your child every day. It is very beneficial to read to your child even if he or she is a fairly proficient reader. Doing so enables your child to enjoy books of interest with you of higher reading levels than he or she can read independently. Exposing your child to good literature and the various writing styles of several different authors does wonders for language and vocabulary development, building comprehension skills, and providing a model for your child of good writing.
- For independent reading, it is very important that your child find just-right books, which means books he or she can read without a struggle (with about 95 percent accuracy). The general rule of thumb for determining if a book is too hard or just right is no more than five words on the page that are too difficult for him or her to read or understand.
- Encourage your child to do independent reading with these easy-to-read books. Doing so builds confidence as well as reading fluency skills. These are the kinds of books that can be read and reread aloud (to you, younger siblings, or anyone who will listen).
- It is also fun to practice oral reading by doing so into a recording device. Children tend to enjoy doing so and playing it back to listen to their own recordings.
- Read the same book together with your child. You can do shared reading in a number of ways—for example, you read the pages on the left and your child reads the pages on the right or "You read this paragraph, and I'll read the next." You can also read small parts together in unison, with you running your finger under the words as you and your child read those lines aloud together.
- When listening to your son or daughter read, do not stop to correct or make your child sound out every single word. You can just tell them most of the words they don't know to keep the reading moving along. For some words you can coach your child in using different cueing strategies. For example, when approaching a tricky word that your child cannot figure out, prompt to pass over that word and read to the end of the sentence. Then see if your child can go back and figure out the unfamiliar word. Ask questions such as the following:
  - "Does that make sense?"
  - "Did that sound right to you?"
  - "What other word beginning with that sound would make sense here?"
  - "Does that look like another word you know?"
  - "Let's look at the first part of the word and try sounding that out." (Break the word into syllables and sound out part by part.)
  - "Are there any little words in that big word that you know?"
- Distractible children often lose their place easily while reading so provide a bookmark to help keep their place. You might also block the page partially by placing a piece of cardboard, paper, or index card over part of the page. You may also want to

try a boxed frame around a piece of colored transparent plastic to place on the book while reading. Such frames are available at HeadsUp (www.headsupnow.com).

- Help your child break down lengthy reading assignments (such as reading a chapter book and writing a book report). These types of assignments cause a lot of frustration for children with ADHD and parents. Encourage your child to read a few pages a day or a certain number of chapters per week so that the task isn't so overwhelming or left to the last minute to complete. It is important to review and talk about what has already been read to keep the previous pages fresh in mind. Try reading the book your child is reading so that you can discuss it together, have your child summarize after reading a section into a recording device, or take brief notes on the pages read.
- See Learning Ally (www.LearningAlly.org), a nonprofit supporting children and families with learning disabilities and Bookshare (www.bookshare.org). Both organizations provide wonderful services and resources for students with reading disabilities. Membership provides your child unlimited access to books, textbooks, and other material in audio format. For some, membership is free. Definitely check their websites for more information if your child has dyslexia and is a struggling reader.
- Photocopy a chapter or unit from your child's textbook to make it easier to study the text. Encourage your child to color-highlight key information and take notes directly on those photocopied pages. For example, important vocabulary and definitions can be highlighted in one color (yellow), the main ideas can be highlighted another color (orange), and so forth.
- Use some of the before-, during-, and after-reading strategies in *List 5.4* to keep your child actively engaged in the reading process and to build reading comprehension skills. Also see the "Sources and Resources" section of this list for reading comprehension and the strategies found at www.pinterest.com/sandrarief/reading-comprehension/.
- See *List 5.3* for strategies that build decoding, vocabulary skills, and reading fluency. Also, explore the strategies and activities at www.pinterest.com/sandrarief/sight-words/, www.pinterest.com/sandrarief/vocabularylanguage/, and www.pinterest.com/sandrarief/phonics-decoding-fluency/ and those found in the "Sources and Resources" section of this list.
- Try having your child use some of the metacognitive and cognitive learning strategies described in *List 4.3,* such as think-alouds, SQ3R, or the RCRC strategy while reading.
- For young children, play games and activities that strengthen phonological and phonemic awareness, alphabet skills, and help to learn letter-sound correspondence. See the many activities in author's books (2010, 2002, 2001) and the many strategies found on Pinterest at www.pinterest.com/sandrarief/alphabet-letter-sounds/ and www.pinterest.com/sandrarief/phonological-phonemic-awareness/.

Motivating Your Struggling or Reluctant Reader

- Find the right books that will capture your child's interest. Before heading to the library or book store, check some of the many lists of award-winning books, such as Children's Choice, Caldecott and Newbery winners, and numerous compiled lists of best books for children of all ages and reading levels. See www.pinterest.com/sandrarief/books-for-kids/.

- Take advantage of all the audio books that are available for listening pleasure. Try listening to an audio book as a family, for example, during a long car ride. Explore the following resources as well as your public library:
  - Audible (www.audible.com)—a division of Amazon that has thousands of audible downloadable books for kids; there are other companies that also provide the same to customers
  - Story Place (http://storyplace.org)—a children's digital bilingual (Spanish and English) library site, which includes a collection of online texts
  - Tales2Go (www.tales2go.org)—an award-winning children's mobile audio book service that streams thousands of name-brand titles from leading publishers and storytellers to mobile devices and desktops
  - Storyline Online (www.storylineonline.net)—an online video-streaming program featuring famous people reading books aloud to children; your child can also read the words along with the celebrity reader if he or she wishes
- There are several options to just reading books. Your child may be motivated to read other forms of material, such as these:
  - Joke and riddle books
  - Comic books
  - Magazines (for example, *Sports Illustrated for Kids, Ranger Rick, Cricket,* or *Kids Discover*)
  - Directions or manuals for a new game or project they want to use
  - Poetry
  - Recipes
  - Reference books with color pictures and short reading passages
  - Sheet music with lyrics of favorite songs
  - Closed-caption TV shows
- Another fun way to get your child to practice reading is through karaoke. You can find songs your child likes on YouTube that show the lyrics. It is a great family activity to sing along following the lyrics—with or without the vocals of the artist.
- Have your child participate in school book clubs, purchasing inexpensive books of choice on a regular basis.
- There are many board games, apps, and online interactive websites for kids that have fun, motivating activities. For example, *Sports Illustrated for Kids* (www.sikids.com) has activities that may be a great way to get your sports-loving, reluctant readers to read. See *List 7.12* for numerous educational websites that have digital games and fun activities that may engage your child's interest while strengthening reading skills.
- Use incentives for home reading. Create a chart of some type, placing a sticker on the chart for each book read, or have your child record the number of pages he or she reads and provide a reward when reaching a goal of a certain number of pages read.
- Check out the summer reading incentive programs such as those offered through Barnes & Noble, Scholastic Summer Challenge, Pizza Hut, or your local library.
- See the author's other books in the "Sources and Resources" section and on page 272 for more on motivating struggling and reluctant readers.

If You Suspect Your Child Has a Reading Disability (Dyslexia)

- As with ADHD, dyslexia is a brain-based disorder. Both disorders commonly coexist. The treatment for dyslexia is instructional—providing reading training by a trained professional using a multisensory structured language program with the appropriate degree of intensity to achieve results. We know the research-based instructional approaches that actually retrain the brain and strengthen the neural connections involved in reading—helping dyslexics learn to read and spell.
- If your child has signs and symptoms of dyslexia (as described in *List 5.1*), do not wait to see if your child improves with time and maturity. Waiting to intervene does not benefit a child.
- Early identification and intervention (that is, when a child is in preschool through second grade) are most effective in preventing reading problems. Research shows that with appropriate early intervention, most children who are at-risk readers can overcome many of their difficulties and increase their reading skills to an average level.
- Regardless of your child's age, diagnosing a reading disability and intervention is very important and is never too late. However, remediation is more difficult as a person gets older and must be more intensive in order to overcome years of reading failure.
- Discuss concerns with your child's teacher. Ask the teacher or the principal, special education teacher, reading specialist, school psychologist, or speech-language therapist about screening or assessment for dyslexia and reading disabilities. Be relentless if the school district is suggesting a wait-and-see approach.
- Some states have laws and protocols for specifically screening and evaluating students who are at risk of or show signs of dyslexia. Those students identified as having dyslexia are then provided specialized interventions by qualified professionals, using research-based dyslexia instructional programs and best practices. Check with your local education agency or see the website of Literate Nation.org for information about states with existing dyslexia laws.
- Other states do not specifically use the term *dyslexia* or refer to dyslexia in IEPs, 504 plans, or in discussion with parents. It is grouped under the broader term of learning disabilities (because dyslexia is one of the specific learning disabilities). Of course, parents still have the right to request evaluation and school districts are required to evaluate a child if a disability is suspected that impairs learning. See *Lists 6.1, 6.3, and 6.4*.
- Become familiar with the information in section 6 on educational rights and laws as well as the system or structure that may be in place at your child's school for providing and monitoring targeted intervention programs to students in need.
- In general, intervention programs for children with dyslexia are multisensory-structured language programs, what is often referred to as Orton-Gillingham-based programs. See *Lists 3.8, 5.1, and 5.3,* the "Sources and Resources" section in this and at the end of other lists for more on this topic.
- There are two grass-roots movements in the United States that are currently advocating for legislation and policies to dramatically improve the education of students with dyslexia and other struggling readers. This includes among other things: mandatory teacher training on dyslexia—warning signs and appropriate intervention

strategies, and mandatory early screening. For more information, see Literate Nation (http://literatenation.org) and Decoding Dyslexia (www.decodingdyslexia.net).

For more detailed information about dyslexia and strategies to help, see the book below authored by Rief and Stern (2010).

Sources and Resources

Fetzer, Nancy & Rief, Sandra (2002). *Alphabet learning center activities kit*. San Francisco: Jossey-Bass.

LD Online. (n.d.). Multisensory structured language programs: Content and principles of instruction. Retrieved from www.ldonline.org/article/6332/

Rief, Sandra (2001). *Ready ... start ... school: Nurturing and guiding your child through preschool and kindergarten*. Paramus, NJ: Prentice-Hall Press.

Rief, Sandra & Stern, Judith (2010). *The dyslexia checklist: A practical reference for parents and teachers*. San Francisco: Jossey-Bass.

Texas Education Agency. (2014, July). Dyslexia handbook: Procedures concerning dyslexia and related disorders, revised. Retrieved from www4.esc13.net/uploads/dyslexia/docs/TEA_Dyslexia_Handbook_08_04_14_Final_1.pdf

Resources on Reading Disabilities and Supports

- Dyslexia Reading Well (www.dyslexia-reading-well.com)
- Florida Center for Reading Research (www.fcrr.org)
- International Dyslexia Association (www.interdys.org/)
- LD Online (www.ldonline.org)
- Learning Disabilities Association of America (http://ldaamerica.org/)
- National Center for Learning Disabilities (www.ncld.org)
- Reading A-Z (www.readinga-z.com)
- Reading Rockets (www.readingrockets.org)
- ReadWriteThink. (www.readwritethink.org)
- See others in *Lists 5.3, 5.4, and 7.12*.

5.6 Why Writing Is a Struggle

Written language is the most common area of academic weakness in children and teens with ADHD and learning disabilities because the process is complex and places a very high demand on executive functions. Producing a writing assignment requires the integration and often simultaneous use of numerous skills and brain processes, many of which are areas of significant weakness for them. This includes, for example, planning and organization, memory, self-monitoring, cognitive flexibility, as well as skill and facility with language, spelling, and mechanical skills, speed of processing, and more. Therefore, the act of writing is often tedious, overwhelming, and aversive for students with ADHD or LD.

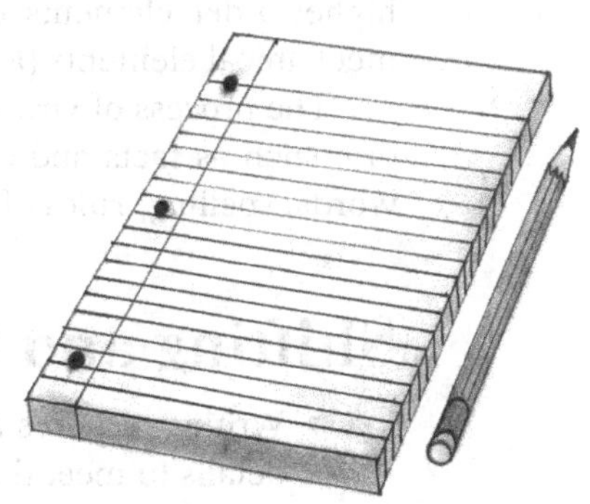

These children are often verbal and knowledgeable but struggle to show what they know on paper because of their impairments in the following areas.

Planning and Organization

Writing requires being able to generate, plan, and organize ideas. When given a written assignment, students with ADHD often get stuck here. They do not know what to write about, how to organize and begin, or how to narrow down and focus on a topic.

- Writing requires taking the time to first think carefully about what one wants to communicate and planning what and how to write it before actually beginning to write.
- There is a specific organizational structure for different types of writing (for example, persuasive essays, response to literature, narrative account) that students need to know and follow.

Attention and Inhibition

Resisting distractions, staying focused, and sustaining attention through the difficult task of written composition is a major challenge for many students with ADHD, causing minimal written production and output. Because of inattention, the student may be unaware of all the components of the writing task assigned. Inattention to details also results in many errors in spelling, capitalization, and punctuation.

Working Memory and Retrieval

Working memory is necessary in order to hold onto and juggle the many different thoughts the writer wants to express while manipulating those ideas and transcribing simultaneously onto paper. It involves these skills:

- Holding onto the big ideas as well as the supporting details while constructing a written piece
- Remembering the goal and purpose of the writing assignment, the structure of the writing genre, and intended audience

- Keeping in mind the language choices and mechanics (vocabulary, grammar, sentence structure, spelling, punctuation) and sequencing of ideas while recording ideas in written format
- Maintaining focus on the train of thought so the flow of the writing will not veer off course

Those with working memory deficits lack the cognitive work space to focus on the higher-order elements of text generation while simultaneously attending to lower-end mechanical elements (Kaufman, 2010; McCutchen, 2006).

The process of writing also requires the retrieval of information from long-term memory, such as facts and experiences and other prior knowledge, and recall of vocabulary words, spelling, rules of grammar, and mechanics (capitalization and punctuation).

Shifting and Cognitive Flexibility

- Writing requires being able to shift flexibly from the major themes to the relevant details to meet the demands of the writing task (Meltzer, 2010).
- Constructing and transcribing what one wants to communicate requires constantly shifting back and forth between the big picture and the relevant details. Writers are flexibly making revisions as they write (such as changing wording and moving ideas around).

Self-Monitoring

Fluent writing and successful completion of writing assignments requires the following self-monitoring skills:

- Awareness of the writing assignment requirements, how much time they have for completing the assignment, what resources or information needs to be obtained for doing so, and other such things
- Keeping the intended audience in mind and writing to that audience with a clear purpose
- Following and referring back to the specific structure of a writing genre to make sure the parts of the organizational structure (for example, for a five-paragraph essay) are all included
- Knowing how to read one's own work critically in order to make revisions and develop ideas
- Checking one's work to see that teacher expectations and performance standards are being met

Speed of Written Output and Production

Some students with ADHD rush through writing assignments, producing illegible work with many careless errors. Others with ADHD write excruciatingly slowly. Although they know the answers and can verbally express their thoughts and ideas articulately, they are unable to put more than a few words or sentences down on paper. Needless to say, this is extremely frustrating. Part of the problem with speed of output may be because of the following issues:

- Impulsivity
- Difficulty sustaining attention to task
- Difficulty maintaining the mental energy required in written expression
- Graphomotor dysfunction
- Slow processing speed
- Just wanting to be done with a very tedious and difficult task

Language

Writing requires the ability to do the following:

- Express thoughts in a logical, fluid, and coherent manner
- Use the most precise vocabulary and word knowledge to express oneself and communicate to the reader effectively
- Use figurative language (such as similes and metaphors) and descriptive, colorful vocabulary to make the piece of writing more interesting
- Use proper grammar and sentence structure

Graphomotor Skills

Many children with ADHD or LD have impairments in graphomotor skills (and have *dysgraphia*), which affect the physical task of writing (handwriting) and organization of print on the page. They often have trouble with the following:

- Writing neatly on or within the given lines
- Spacing and organizing their writing on the page
- Copying from the board or book onto paper
- Using fine-motor skills, causing the act of handwriting to be very inefficient, fatiguing, and frustrating; it can affect, for example, pencil grip, pressure exerted, and legibility
- Executing print or cursive or typing with precision or speed

Spelling

- Children with ADHD may be poor spellers because of inattention to visual detail and not noticing and therefore not able to recall the letters, sequence, or visual patterns within words. Working memory difficulties affect spelling—keeping in mind the letter sounds and sequence for the word while getting it down on paper. Impulsivity and inattention also make these children more prone to careless spelling errors.
- Children and teens with coexisting dyslexia have more significant spelling errors as a result of phonemic awareness and phonological processing difficulties (*Lists 5.1, 5.3, 7.12*).

Steps of the Writing Process and Potential Problems

Prewrite

This very important step of the writing process is where planning and organization takes place—before beginning the actual writing. This initial stage is where students with ADHD often get stuck, many of whom having difficulty analyzing the task, brainstorming and gathering ideas and information, deciding what to write about and narrowing down a topic, and organizing and sequencing ideas and information. *See List 5.7* for prewriting strategies and supports.

Draft

Writing a draft involves turning ideas from the planning stage into written sentences, adding details, and elaborating. This is the composition stage, which can be very difficult for students with ADHD and learning disabilities. Weaknesses in working memory and retrieval, language usage, self-monitoring (or metacognitive awareness), and slow processing or production speed can impair the ADHD or LD writer's efficiency in turning prewriting plans into a viable first draft. Some children are also immobilized when ideas don't flow or they don't know how to spell a certain word. *See List 5.8* for drafting and composition strategies and supports.

Revise

Once an initial draft is completed, good writers understand that a number of changes will be needed before a writing project is in its final form. Revising requires the ability to self-monitor one's work, reread it carefully, and identify ways to improve flow and sequence, language usage, and clarity. These are difficult tasks for children and teens with ADHD or learning disabilities. When writing is a struggle and a first draft has finally been produced, these students often resist making revisions and want to submit their initial draft. *See List 5.9* for strategies and supports to use during the revision process.

Edit

Editing is the proofreading stage of writing. Noticing and identifying grammatical, spelling, and mechanical (capitalization and punctuation) errors and then fixing them are tedious tasks requiring attention to detail and close self-monitoring. It is unrealistic to expect students with ADHD or learning disabilities to edit their work without help (such as adult or peer editing or use of assistive technology). *See Lists 5.9 and 5.12* for editing strategies and supports.

Publish

The last stage of the writing process is completing and sharing the final product. When a student feels proud of a piece of writing and shares it, this part of the process is rewarding.

Sources and Resources

Kaufman, Christopher. (2010). *Executive function in the classroom*. Baltimore, MD: Paul H. Brookes.

Levine, Mel. (1998). *Developmental variation and learning disorders*. Cambridge, MA: Educational Publishing Services.

McCutchen, D. (2006). Cognitive factors in the development of children's writing. In C. A. MacArthur, S. Graham, & J. Fitzgerald (Eds.), *Handbook of writing research* (pp. 115–130). New York: Guilford Press.

Meltzer, Lynn. (2010). *Promoting executive function in the classroom*. New York: Guilford Press.

Misunderstood Minds. (2002). Writing basics, difficulties, responses. WGBH Educational Foundation. Retrieved from www.pbs.org/wgbh/misunderstoodminds

5.7 Strategies to Help with Prewriting: Planning and Organization

Prewriting is a critical stage of the writing process involving the generation, planning, and organization of ideas and deciding what and how to express ideas before beginning to write. This is a significant challenge for children with ADHD because of the high executive function demands. The prewriting techniques in this checklist are designed to stimulate ideas, topic selection, and effective planning and also provide much-needed structure, organization, and motivation to write.

Prewriting Techniques in the Classroom

- *Brainstorming.* Sessions are no more than three to five minutes and focused. Given a general theme or topic, students call out whatever comes to mind related to that topic while someone records all responses from the class.
- *Quick writes.* Students have a few minutes to write down everything that they can think of related to a given topic, which can be single words or phrases or simple pictures or symbols to represent ideas. Model the same uninterrupted writing or drawing on a topic of your choice to demonstrate the process to students.
- *Writing topic folders.* Students maintain a folder, card file, or notebook of possible ideas for writing topics. These might include hobbies, places visited, jobs they have done, personal interests, colorful and interesting people they know, pets, special field trips or activities, observations, wonderings, and so forth. The writing folder can also be in the form of a personal collage. Students can use words and pictures cut out of magazines and travel brochures or sources and laminate the folder when done.
- *Capture ideas electronically.* There are a number of apps for capturing, sorting, and storing ideas, for example, Popplet, Springpad, and Evernote. Visually gathering and organizing ideas and topics of interest can also be done on Pinterest.
- *Telling personal stories.* In small groups or with partners, students tell personal stories in response to prompts—for example, "Tell about a time you or someone you knew got lost." After sharing in their groups, students fill out graphic organizers or outlines of their story.
- *Writing prompts.* A stimulus is provided, such as a story, quote, picture, news article, video, or song, to prompt writing.
- *Sample topic sentences.* For students who continue to struggle to find ideas, providing a choice of topic sentences or a story starter (a sentence or two to introduce a topic) might be helpful.
- *Looking at reference books.* Students can browse many kinds of books in order to gather ideas for writing topics (for example, mysteries of nature, music, sports, fashion).
- *Verbalizing ideas into a recording device.* Some students benefit from talking into a digital recorder and then transcribing their ideas.
- *Sharing exemplary and at-standard pieces of writing.* To help students generate ideas of their own as well as understand the structure of a particular genre, read them some good examples. Read aloud (and project on an overhead or document camera) some pieces of student writing and then discuss them.

- *Talk them through*. Help students who are stuck in picking a topic by sharing ideas aloud, jotting them down for them, and helping them narrow down and choose.
- *Modeled writing*. Model the process of brainstorming, organizing, and recording ideas.
- *Frames*. Providing frames helps struggling writers get started and guides them in planning. Example: "I remember my first day of ______ when I was ___ years old. I felt ______________."
- *Explicitly teach strategies* for analyzing the writing prompt or assignment, thinking and gathering ideas, and planning and organizing prior to allowing students to start writing.

Once students have selected the topic, model the process of jotting down main ideas and related details in some format that can then be manipulated easily—moving ideas around and organizing them.

- A helpful technique is to have the student write main ideas and supporting details on separate index cards, sticky notes, or sentence strips. That makes it easier to spread out and group, organize, and sequence those thoughts and ideas. Color-coding related ideas and information is also helpful.
- This technique of capturing ideas (words, phrases, pictures) on a word document or on the student's electronic devices and moving them around and organizing that way is also helpful in the planning and prewriting stage.
- Sandler (2005) recommends that in the prewriting stage, students can use their learning style preference for representing and organizing ideas. Visual learners, for example, can draw pictures to represent main and secondary points to move around on the table. Kinesthetic learners who think best by feeling things can use pieces of a game board to represent each of their ideas to move around, and auditory learners can dictate ideas into a digital recorder, download data into a computer, and move ideas around.

Using Planning Forms and Visual Organizers

- *Graphic organizers*. These are among the most effective ways to help writers generate their ideas as well as formulate and organize their thoughts. The following are some examples of graphic organizers; others are found in *List 5.4*.
  - *Clustering*. Write the main idea in a box or rectangle in the center of the page and surround the main idea box with bubbles containing the supporting ideas.
  - *Mind mapping*. Draw a circle at the center of a page. Write the topic inside the center circle and write related ideas on lines stemming from the circle. This technique is also called *webbing* and the graphic is called a *web*.
  - *Apps and software organizers*. There is excellent software for creating mind maps, diagrams, and other visual organizers to aid in the prewriting process that are easy and motivating for children to use. Two recommended programs are Inspiration and Kidspiration from www.inspiration.com. Inspiration also has an outlining feature built in. Categories listed in the graphic web format are automatically placed in outline form with the press of a button. Older students may find these programs useful for mind mapping or just capturing ideas quickly: Mindjet MindManager, Microsoft OneNote, FreeMind, and Evernote.

- *Story maps*. These are used in planning the critical elements to be included when writing a story: setting, characters, problem, action, and resolution.

- There are many websites with downloadable graphic organizers, such as Houghton Mifflin's Education Place (www.eduplace.com) and those at Ed Helper.com (http://edhelper.com/teachers/General_graphic_organizers.htm). The linear organizers—those that provide the specific step-by-step structure (for example, the introduction, three main ideas and supporting details, and a conclusion)—are often the most beneficial.
- *Other idea development tools and resources*. See the excellent resources and tips for teaching idea development at Writing Fix (http://writingfix.com/6_traits/idea_development.htm), a website sponsored by Nevada educators Corbett and Dena Harrison and the Northern Nevada Writing Project.

Thinking and Questioning

- Provide a prewriting checklist that lists specific questions students need to ask themselves at this stage of the writing process. These help the writer think through, plan, and organize prior to drafting. Such questioning can be done independently, but it is also recommended that they engage in this questioning process with someone else (a peer or partner or with parent or teacher) and during guided writing.
- When creating a prewriting checklist, teachers may want to select a few questions, such as these:
  - Who is my target audience?
  - What is my purpose for this writing: to persuade, inform, entertain, or something else?
  - What do I already know about this topic?
  - Can I write enough about my selected topic?
  - Which writing genre am I going to use?
  - In what style or voice will I write?
  - What are some words, ideas, or phrases related to my topic?
- Prewriting checklists may be divided into specific questions for the beginning, middle, and end of the piece of writing.

Beginning (Opening)

- How will I introduce the subject or topic?
- What kind of hook can I use in the introduction to capture the audience's attention and interest?
- What will be the main idea about my subject?

Middle (Body)

- What interesting details and examples might I use?
- What will be my flow and sequence of ideas?
- Where should I research and gather interesting information about my topic?

Ending (Conclusion)

- What is the message I want to share with readers?
- What would be an interesting, snappy, or exciting ending?

Mnemonic Strategies

There are a few cognitive strategies in the form of an acronym that help students remember prewrite steps:

- PLEASE (Meltzer, 2010; Welch, 1992)
  - **P**ick a topic. **L**ist your ideas about the topic. **E**valuate your list. **A**ctivate the paragraph with a topic sentence. **S**upply supporting sentences. **E**valuate your list.
- BOTEC—This is a prewrite strategy originally found in Essay Express (Research ILD & FableVision, 2005) and adapted by Kaufman (2010):
  - **B**rainstorming, **O**rganizing (or Ordering), **T**opic (or Thesis), **E**vidence (or Examples), **C**onclusion
- The POW and TREE strategies by Karen Harris and Steve Graham (1989; Harris, Graham, & Mason, 2002) are among the research-validated writing strategies that are part of the Self-Regulated Strategy Development (SRSD) model:
  - POW (for all writing assignments): **P**ick my idea. **O**rganize my notes. **W**rite and say more.
  - TREE (for opinion papers): **T**opic sentence, **R**easons (three or more), **E**xplain reasons, **E**nding. (See *List 4.3*)

Other Recommended Instructional Techniques in the Prewriting Stage

See Nancy Fetzer's website (www.nancyfetzer.com) for demonstrations of exemplary instructional techniques in a whole-class setting that include modeling aloud the thinking process, use of graphic organizers to structure thinking and planning, mnemonic strategies (total physical response and gestures, acronyms to remember steps and writing components), oral rehearsal of what students plan to say prior to writing, and other research-based and engaging techniques.

Tips for Parents for Helping Their Children Think of Writing Topics

- Look through family albums together and reminisce about people and events. Talk about happenings in your child's life (humorous incidents, scary moments, milestones) that your son or daughter may not remember. Share family stories and discuss current events.
- Ask leading questions that encourage your child to open up and share his or her feelings, fears, dreams, aspirations, or likes and dislikes.
- Provide books, reference materials, and access to the library, the Internet, and other resources.
- Talking about the writing assignment with your child helps to organize thoughts and clarify his or her thinking before getting started on the actual writing.

- Encourage your child to keep a journal or digital file for jotting down thoughts or questions he or she is pondering; observations; things that have happened to him or her that caused embarrassment, fear, joy, or other strong feelings; reactions to events in the news; and connections he or she has made between movies seen, books read, music heard, and his or her own life. These are all possible topics for future essays, personal narratives, and other writing assignments.
- For research projects, help your child find and choose a topic that is not too broad or too narrow to write about and begin the research process as early as possible.
- When your child is researching a topic, remind him or her of the importance of writing down the source so he or she can later cite it. If cutting and pasting from the Internet, show your child how to always copy the URL as well.
- See *Lists 4.1, 4.2, 4.3, 4.5, 4.6, 5.6, and 5.12* for more information and related strategies.

Sources and Resources

Graham, S., & Harris, K. R. (1989). Improving learning disabled students' skills at composing essays: Self-instructional strategy training. *Exceptional Children*, *56*, 201–214.

Harris, Karen R., & Graham, Steve. (1996). *Making the writing process work: Strategies for composition and self-regulation*. Cambridge, MA: Brookline.

Harris, Karen, Graham, Steve, & Mason, Linda. (2002). POW plus TREE equals powerful opinion essays: Improving writing in the early grades. *CASLNews*, *6*, 1–4.

Kaufman, Christopher. (2010). *Executive function in the classroom*. Baltimore, MD: Paul H. Brookes.

Meltzer, Lynn. (2010). *Promoting executive function in the classroom*. New York: Guildford Press.

ResearchILD & Fable Vision. (2005). *Essay express: Strategies for successful essay writing* [Computer software]. Boston: Fable Vision.

Sandler, Michael. (2005). Personal best: Term paper time. *ADDitude Magazine*, *6*(2), 47–48.

Welch, M. (1992). The PLEASE strategy: A metacognitive learning strategy for improving the paragraph writing of students with mild disabilities. *Learning Disability Quarterly*, *15*, 119–128.

5.8 Strategies for Building Skills in Written Expression

Written expression is the most common academic area of difficulty among students with ADHD. Several brain processes and skills are involved and used simultaneously (for example, language, attention, memory, sequencing, organization, planning, self-monitoring, and critical thinking) when composing a written piece of work (*List 5.6*).

Students are expected to meet grade-level standards in several writing formats and genres, such as persuasive essays, personal narratives, summaries, and reports, and teachers have the challenge of differentiating instruction to writers of varying levels. The teaching of writing requires knowing how to scaffold the instruction and provide the necessary structures and supports to students who need more help in the writing process. Even students with significant writing difficulties are able to meet writing standards when they receive explicit teaching, modeling, and guided practice of writing skills and strategies.

Teach the craft of writing and composing by using some of these approaches:

- *Modeled writing*. Demonstrate the use of strategies, enabling students to witness the thinking and self-questioning processes that are used while composing. Speak aloud what you are thinking (metacognition) while creating a draft of some piece of writing—for example, a beginning paragraph with an interesting lead. Project your writing on a screen so that students can follow the process.
- *Explicit instruction in paragraph construction*. Good writers need to be proficient in constructing various (such as procedural, descriptive, compare and contrast, how-to, and narrative) types of paragraphs.
- *Student examples*. Have student volunteers share parts of what they are writing to provide examples for the class. Student sharing in front of the whole class should be done only by volunteers (unless the work is in its final form).
- *Guided writing*. Work with students in groups that are differentiated in various ways, such as skill level or degree of assistance needed, topic chosen, or stage of the writing process students are at. Some students in the class may be writing a single cohesive paragraph and others are composing multiple paragraphs.
- *Sensory descriptions*. Teach students through modeling by sharing descriptive examples from literature, helping the reader to feel, hear, see, taste, and smell through words.
- *Sentence starters*. Provide a list of sentence starters that students can use to help them remember to include important points, such as evidence and support for their statements in their writing (for example, "This was demonstrated when . . . .").
- *Topic sentences*. Help students who have difficulty getting started by providing a list of possible sentence starters or topic sentences.
- *Frames*. Provide writing frames for scaffolding or support. Example: "The author, ____________ (*insert name*), wrote a/an ____________ (*insert genre*) titled ____________________ (*title*), which took place ________________ (*where and when*)."
- *Genre structures*. Explicitly teach, model, and illustrate the structure and format for each genre used, for example, informational reports with a topic, main ideas (usually three), supporting details, and a conclusion, or a summary structure that includes an introduction, body, and conclusion.

- *Rubrics*. Provide rubrics (scoring guides) with all writing assignments. Rubrics explain the performance standards for the assignment and what is expected for elements such as content, organization, mechanics, or neatness in order to meet or exceed grade-level standards. Rubrics are particularly helpful for students with writing difficulties and their parents, teachers, and tutors because they explain exactly what is expected in the assignment and describe the criteria for proficiency.
  - Rubrics typically use a scale of 1 to 4 or 1 to 5 (for example, 1 = novice, 2 = apprentice, 3 = practitioner, 4 = expert).
  - Teachers can create their own rubric that is specific to an assignment or use generic ones for a specific genre. Rubrics can also be found on the Internet—for example, at www.rubistar.4teachers.org.
- *Monitoring*. Provide support for children with ADHD, who often take much longer to complete writing assignments than other students. Getting them started early, notifying parents of the requirements, and jointly monitoring throughout the assignment are very helpful.
- *Instructional programs*. There are some excellent commercial programs that explicitly teach students written composition skills through a structured approach with multisensory tools. Such programs scaffold learning through step-by-step approaches, graphic organizers, color coding, and other means in order to enhance the craft of writing. Some recommended resources are Empowering Writers by Mariconda and Auray (www.empoweringwriters.com), Step Up to Writing by Maureen Auman (www.voyagersopris.com), and Nancy Fetzer's Writing Curriculum (www.nancyfetzer.com).

Teaching Sentence Structure and Expanded Word Choices

- Teach sentence structure and build sentence-writing skills. Children need to understand that all complete sentences have (1) a subject (a noun: a person, place, or thing) that tells who or what is doing something and (2) a predicate (a verb or prepositional phrases) that tell about the subject.
- Teach children to write interesting, expanded sentences. Start with a simple sentence (for example, *The puppy cried.*). Have them dress it up by adding or substituting descriptive adjectives and adverbs, more powerful verbs, and prepositional phrases. (When? Where? How? Why?) Example: *The frightened puppy whimpered and whined as it hid, shaking, under the sofa during the thunderstorm.*
- Teach students to use descriptive language that will enhance their writing style. Generate class and individual lists of descriptive and figurative language found in literature or poetry:
  - *Metaphors* (comparisons such as "The room is an oven" or "His temper is an unpredictable thunderstorm")
  - *Similes* (comparisons using the word *like* or *as,* such as "helpless as a newborn baby")
  - *Onomatopoeia* (words that echo sounds, such as *sizzle, crack, pop*).
- Post lists and provide desk or notebook copies for reference of transition or linking words and phrases:
  - Words that signal sequence: *first of all, furthermore, later*

- Words that signal comparison and contrast of two or more things: *nevertheless, conversely*
- Words that signal cause and effect: *consequently, as a result*
- Words that indicate an author's point of view: *I suggest, I believe*

See many examples of such lists at www.pinterest.com/sandrarief/vocabularylanguage/.

Teaching Students to Compose a Draft

- Help students with writing by teaching them to prepare effectively. When students write their initial draft, a graphic organizer or planning sheet filled out at the prewriting stage should be their guide. They should already know their audience, genre structure, topic, point of view, sequence (for a narrative piece), or main idea and supporting details (for an informational piece).
- Have students write their rough drafts in pencil or erasable pen or have them draft electronically on a computer or other word processor, such as an AlphaSmart (*Lists 5.11, 5.12*).
- If students are typing drafts, show them how to save each successive draft with a new date or draft number and how to back up their work. Handwritten drafts should also always be dated.
- Provide a scribe for students who have trouble getting their thoughts written down.
- Encourage students not to worry about spelling or mechanics at this stage of initial drafting—as long as they can read their own work.
- Students with ADHD may get stuck on the introductory paragraph and may do better if, after the initial planning, they write some of the other paragraphs first. They can work on an introductory paragraph and conclusion later.
- When assigning an essay, particularly in response to questions or a prompt, ensure that students understand what is being asked and what needs to be addressed in their essay. First, carefully read and analyze the prompt or question.
- See online supports such as Essay Information (http://essayinfo.com/essays), which provides explicit instructions and information for writing different types of essays, such as paragraph, argumentative, persuasive, response, comparison, and narrative.
- For several strategies and activities for composition across grade levels, see Rief and Heimburge (2007) and www.pinterest.com/sandrarief/writing-strategies-activities.

Teaching Self-Monitoring

Written expression requires considerable self-monitoring. Writers should put themselves in the place of their potential readers and keep asking themselves questions such as "Does this make sense?" "Is this clear?" "Do my ideas flow logically?" "Am I using the best choice of words?"

- Provide students with a checklist of self-monitoring questions to use as a guide while composing, for example, "What kind of hook can I use to capture the reader's attention?"
- Teach students to use learning strategies such as OSWALD and WRITE, which provide steps to follow in composing an essay:

- OSWALD (from James Madison University's Learning Toolbox at http://coe.jmu.edu/learningtoolbox/oswald.html):
  - Outline the major points and details that you want to include in your paper.
  - Say the outline aloud. Read the outline over to see the relationship between ideas. As you read the outline, think of the main ideas that are most important to your paper.
  - Write an introduction, a paragraph introducing your paper. Include the main ideas that you chose when you read the outline aloud.
  - Add connecting ideas. Write sentences to connect ideas from one paragraph to another. Think of words that help show the relationship between ideas (for example, *therefore, after*).
  - Look over the connections. Reread your paper, starting with the introduction. Make sure that each paragraph is connected to the introduction and to the other paragraphs.
  - Draft the conclusion. Based on your introduction and the ideas presented in the body of your paper, write an ending that wraps up the ideas.
- WRITE (Harris & Graham, 2005; Harris, Graham, Mason, Friedlander, & Reid, 2007):
  - Work from your plan to develop your thesis statement. Start with an attention getter.
  - Remember your goals (mature vocabulary, organization, varied sentence types, maintaining topic control).
  - Include a transition word for each paragraph.
  - Try to use different kinds of sentences.
  - Use Exciting, interesting words.

Sources and Resources

Auman, M. (2008). *Step up to writing*. Dallas: Voyager Sopris Learning.

ERIC/OSEP. (2002). Strengthening the second "R": Helping students with disabilities prepare well-written compositions. *Special Education, 10*.

Fetzer, N. (2013). *Nancy Fetzer's writing curriculum*. Murrieta, CA: Nancy Fetzer's Literacy Connections. (for grades K–1, 2–3, and 4–6)

Harris, K., & Graham, S. (1999). Programmatic intervention research: Illustrations from the evolution of self-regulated strategy development. *Learning Disability Quarterly, 22*, 251–262.

Harris, K. R., & Graham, S. (2005). *Writing better: Effective strategies for teaching students with learning difficulties*. Baltimore, MD: Paul H. Brookes.

Harris, K. R., Graham, S., Mason, L. H., Friedlander, B., & Reid, R. (2007). *Powerful writing strategies for all students*. Baltimore, MD: Paul H. Brookes.

Mariconda, B., & Auray, D. P. (2005). *The comprehensive expository writing guide: All the skills you need to teach good writing* (2nd ed.). Trumbull, CT: Empowering Writers.

Rief, S. and Heimburge, J. (2007). *How to reach and teach all children through balanced literacy: User-friendly strategies, tools, activities, and ready-to-use materials.* San Francisco: Jossey-Bass.

Online Writing Resources

The Writing Center at The University of North Carolina at Chapel Hill has free handouts on a variety of writing topics (http://writingcenter.unc.edu/handouts/). They share tips and strategies on all aspects of the writing process. They also have online strategy demonstrations that can be seen on YouTube at their UNCWritingCenter YouTube Channel (www.youtube.com/user/UNCWritingCenter).

Project WRITE (www.kc.vanderbilt.edu/projectwrite/). On this website you can access lesson plans and support materials for story and persuasive writing strategies designed to improve the writing and self-regulation behaviors of students in grades 1 through 3. Lesson plans and support materials are provided for working individually with students having difficulties with behavior and writing and for classwide self-regulated strategy instruction in inclusive classrooms.

IRIS Center for Training Enhancements at Vanderbilt University (http://iris.peabody.vanderbilt.edu/). A free, online interactive tutorial is available that includes all stages of instruction and video clips. Under the Learning Strategy modules, there is one entitled "Improving Writing Performance: A Strategy for Writing Expository Essays" (http://iris.peabody.vanderbilt.edu/module/pow/).

See other online resources in the other writing lists in this section as well as in *List 7.12*.

5.9 Strategies for Revising and Editing

For children and teens with ADHD, this stage of the writing process (revising, proofreading, and making corrections) is the one that generally meets with the most resistance.

Revising written work involves adding or deleting information, resequencing the order of sentences and paragraphs, and choosing words that better communicate your meaning. Revision requires self-monitoring and critically evaluating one's own work, as well as the motivation to put forth the effort in rewriting subsequent drafts until complete. This is very difficult and tedious for students with ADHD or learning disabilities. For many, once they have struggled to complete the first draft, they consider their written work as done.

Editing involves proofreading for errors in grammar, mechanics, and spelling and then polishing the final product. Students with ADHD are typically very weak in editing skills because it requires focused attention to details and close self-monitoring. It is unrealistic to expect they will be able to adequately proofread for their own errors and fix them without direct help, such as teacher, parent, or peer editing or assistive technology supports.

Strategies for Helping Students with Revision

- Encourage students to write rough drafts on every other line of the paper to make it easier to revise and edit.
- Allow students to compose on a computer, laptop, AlphaSmart, netbook, or tablet with a word processing app. Composing on an electronic device with word processing capabilities is ideal for revising subsequent drafts more easily and for organization and management of written work.
- Model and demonstrate the steps for revising—one step at a time.
- Provide checklists to help students self-monitor during the revision process. Select some (not all) of the following questions in creating a list appropriate to the developmental level of the child:
  - Does my introduction capture the attention of my readers?
  - Did I develop my ideas logically?
  - Have I given enough information?
  - Does everything make sense?
  - Did I stick to my topic?
  - Have I presented my ideas clearly and in the right order?
  - Have I given details and examples for each main idea?
  - Do I need to insert, move around, or delete any ideas?
  - Have I used interesting descriptive words?
  - Do my paragraphs have a beginning, middle, and end?
  - Have I replaced overused words?
  - Did I write an interesting, powerful conclusion?

- Have students read their drafts to a peer in order to obtain feedback. The partner listens, asks questions, indicates when more information is needed, and makes other suggestions. Parents can also provide feedback in order to help their child learn to make appropriate revisions. Information can be inserted with carets (^) or on sticky notes next to where it will be added.
- When a student is revising a composition, suggest that he or she address one aspect of the writing at a time. For example, a student could focus first on clarity, flow, and sequence, then read for sentence variety and descriptive language, and next for overused words.
- Teach the skill of combining sentences and encourage this technique when students are revising. Example: *The day was hot and sunny. The girls ate ice cream cones. They played and rode their bikes*. These three sentences can be combined: *The girls ate ice cream cones, played, and rode their bikes on the hot, sunny day*.
- During the revision process, have students identify sentences that can be improved. Encourage them to find boring, simple sentences and embellish them.
- When listening to a child read an initial draft, provide positive feedback by describing something you like about the piece, acknowledging the student's growth in a specific skill, or recognizing the student's effort. Ask probing questions when something is unclear and more information is needed.
- If revising is overwhelming for the student, consider providing a scribe. Let children dictate the changes they want to make and have the scribe record those changes on the paper.
- Teach the revision mnemonic of *ARMS*: **A**dd sentences, details, examples, and descriptive words. **R**emove unneeded words and sentences. **M**ove the placement of words, phrases, sentences, or paragraphs. **S**ubstitute words or sentences for others (for example, more powerful verbs).

Strategies for Helping Students with Editing

- Provide direct instruction and guided practice in the proper use of mechanics (punctuation and capitalization).
- Have students use peer editing as well as adult assistance. A peer or adult partner can point out run-on or incomplete sentences, missing or incorrect capitalization or punctuation, and misspelled words.
- Teach students how to use editing tools and options (thesaurus, spell-checker, cut and paste) on word processing programs or apps.
- Even though self-editing is hard, encourage it by having students read aloud their work and identify what doesn't look or sound right.
- When self-editing, have students circle (or code) words that they think are misspelled. Later, with assistance as needed, they can go back and check the spelling.
- There are many spelling and grammar checking apps, software, and online programs that are very helpful in the editing process. Ghotit (www.ghotit.com), for example, is one such program designed especially for people with dyslexia. Besides those built into word processing programs, there are various editing apps, such as Hemingway and Proofread Text Editor, and spell-check apps available. Talking hand-held spell-checkers, such as Children's Talking Dictionary and Spell Corrector by Franklin Electronics, are helpful as well.

- Teach editing symbols (insert, delete, capitalize, new paragraph). Provide reference charts that show those symbols.
- After modeling how to jointly edit a piece of writing for the whole class, have students work with partners to check each other's work.
- Have students use colored pencils as they edit for one thing at a time. For example, have them check each sentence and underline the final punctuation in red, capital letters in blue.
- Provide an editing checklist to help students proofread their own work for capitalization, sentence structure, and mechanical errors. Following is a list of possible questions to include in a proofreading checklist:
    - Did I use complete sentences?
    - Did I begin all sentences with capital letters?
    - Did I end sentences with a final punctuation mark (., ?, !)?
    - Have I capitalized all proper nouns?
    - Have I checked spelling?
    - Have I indented my paragraphs?
    - Are verb tenses consistent?
    - Are there run-on sentences?
    - Is my paper neat and organized?

Other Tips for Helping Students with Their Writing

- Conduct teacher-student writing conferences in which students respond to their own writing. ("My best sentence is __________." "A simile or metaphor I used was __________.") The student reflects on his or her own work. Student and teacher share what they like about the writing.
- Have students evaluate where they have improved and skills to target for continued improvement. ("My writing has improved in __________ [sentence structure, paragraphing, organization, punctuation, spelling]. I plan to work on __________.")
- Provide a rubric with all writing assignments. Show models of work that is at standard and that exceeds the standard.
- Teach students who are drafting on a computer how to find overused words that they might want to replace. With the control-F function, they can type in the word and quickly find it throughout the document so that it can be replaced.
- Use the track changes and comment features in Microsoft Word. Another reader (parent, teacher, peer) can make comments and note suggested changes in the file of a draft that a student has written on a computer.
- See *List 5.12* for more on assistive technology that helps in the revision and editing processes and resources listed within and at the end of *Lists 5.6 through 5.12.*

Learning Strategies

Strategies that incorporate mnemonic techniques to remember steps of a strategy and apply them independently are powerful for students with ADHD and learning disabilities. Here are four learning strategies for revision and editing:

- *COPS* is an error-monitoring strategy (Schumaker et al., 1981). A writer reads through his or her work four times, each time checking the writing for one of the four components in the following list and correcting errors.

  Capitalize. Have I capitalized the first word of each sentence and all proper nouns?

  Overall. How is the overall appearance (spacing, indentation, neatness)?

  Punctuation. Have I put in commas, semicolons, and end punctuation?

  Spelling. Have I spelled the words correctly?

- *SCOPE* is a learning strategy for proofreading from Learning Toolbox at James Madison University (http://coe.jmu.edu/learningtoolbox). The student reads the paper five times, each time looking for a different type of error.
  Spelling. Reread your paper for misspelled words. Use a spelling checker. Try writing misspelled words in different ways to see if one looks right. Use a dictionary to find correct spellings.
  Capitalization. Reread your paper to make sure all words are correctly capitalized.
  Order of words. Read your paper aloud. Point to each word as you say it to make sure that no words have been omitted, added, or mixed up.
  Punctuation. Reread your paper to check for correct punctuation.
  Express complete thoughts. Reread each sentence aloud to make sure that sentences are grammatically correct. (Each sentence should have a complete thought, there should be no run-on sentences, and all parts of the sentence should agree.) The sentences should sound right.

- *SPORTS* (Meltzer et al., 2006) is an acronym for editing written work for these elements:

  Sentence structure

  Punctuation

  Organization

  Repetition

  Tenses

  Spelling

- Sandler (2005) recommends that in the editing process, students read their work aloud and ask themselves these three Cs:

  C—Clear (Are my points clear and understandable?)

  C—Concise (Am I wordy or repetitive?)

  C—Clean (Are there grammar, spelling, or typo errors to clean up?)

Sources and Resources

Harris, K. R., & Graham, S. (2005). *Writing better: Effective strategies for teaching students with learning difficulties*. Baltimore, MD: Paul H. Brookes.

Harris, K. R., Graham, S., Mason, L. H., Friedlander, B., & Reid, R. (2007). *Powerful writing strategies for all students*. Baltimore, MD: Paul H. Brookes.

Meltzer, L., Roditi, B., Steinberg, J., Biddle, K., Taber, S., Caron, K., et al. (2006). *Strategies for success: Classroom teaching techniques for students with learning problems* (2nd ed.). Austin, TX: PRO-ED.

Sandler, Michael. (2005). Personal best: Term paper time. *ADDitude Magazine*, *6*(2), 47–48.

Schumaker, J. B., Deshler, D. D., Nolan, S., Clark, F. L., Alley, G. R., & Warner, M. M. (1981). *Error monitoring: A learning strategy for improving academic performance of LD adolescents* (Research Report No. 32). Lawrence: University of Kansas, Institute for Research on Learning Disabilities.

5.10 Spelling: Challenges, Strategies, and Supports

Accurate spelling requires good phonological processing and phonics skills, which are areas of significant weakness for students with dyslexia. Because ADHD and dyslexia are common coexisting disorders, many children and teens with ADHD have these phonological and language-based processing difficulties, which make spelling a struggle.

- Students with ADHD who do not have coexisting dyslexia may have spelling difficulties related to inattention (noticing features of the word), impulsivity (writing the word without thinking through each of the letters or checking to see if it looks accurate), and weaknesses in working memory (holding the word in mind while sounding out and recording it).
- Spelling taxes a child's memory (working memory and long-term) and is complicated by the ease or difficulty the child has in writing the letters legibly and in the proper order (International Dyslexia Association, 2008).
- Inaccurate spelling can have a negative impact on the way a written product is judged.
- When students are weak spellers, their written work suffers. Instead of using words they may not know how to spell, they may limit the vocabulary they use, reducing the quality and quantity of their writing.
- When students struggle with spelling, they have less mental energy to focus on what they want to say and how to organize their thoughts when writing.
- To become competent spellers, students must master a sequence of skills and progress through developmental stages of spelling, which takes longer and requires more intensive instruction for students with dyslexia.
- Students with spelling disabilities need to have effective instruction to learn to spell as well as accommodations and modifications to help them compensate for their weaknesses.

Spelling Instruction

- A systematic, sequential approach is the most effective form of spelling instruction for most students but is a necessity for those with dyslexia. Effective spelling instruction encompasses the following:
    - *Multisensory*. Students learn by seeing, hearing, saying, and writing the words.
    - *Sequential and incremental*. Instruction moves in order from simple concepts and skills to more complex ones.
    - *Cumulative*. Students are engaged in ongoing review of previous concepts and words.
    - *Individualized*. Instruction is customized because students vary in their spelling acquisition skills and level of performance.
    - *Explicit*. Students are taught specific spelling rules rather than being expected to figure out spelling patterns on their own (*List 3.8*).
- Use developmental spelling inventories and assessment tools to determine the extent of a student's spelling knowledge as well as missing skills to guide instruction.

- Provide systematic phonics training to students who are deficient in this skill and are poor spellers. The majority of words in the English language are phonetically regular and can be decoded and spelled correctly with phonetic knowledge and strategy application.
- Although there are exceptions and irregular words in the English language, the English spelling system is not unpredictable. Even students with severe spelling disabilities can become much more competent spellers when they are explicitly taught letter-sound correspondences and letter patterns from simple to the more complex, the six basic syllable types of English, some of the rules such as when to double consonants, and meaningful word parts (prefixes and suffixes).
- Many English words are derived from other languages (such as Latin, Greek, Old English), resulting in letter combinations that may be unfamiliar to students. Learning about the origin of words is also helpful in improving skills in reading, vocabulary, and spelling.
- Introduce words on the board or projector. As a class, ask students to look at the configuration or shape of the word. Have them also look for little words within the word and any mnemonic clues that would be helpful in remembering how to spell the word. Write the word in syllables in different colored pens. Discuss its meaning and use it in context.
- Teach students to look for patterns in words by using phonograms, word families, and onsets and rimes. Color-highlight patterns within the words.
- Use word sorts to provide opportunities for students to discover common patterns. For example, students would place *stopping, sitting,* and *cutting* in one column (doubling the consonant before adding *-ing*), while *reading, playing,* and *sorting* would go in another column. Have students state the spelling rules for each column.
- The high-frequency irregular words that students are expected to spell correctly in their written work should be posted in a highly visible location. In addition, student desk or notebook copies can be provided for reference.
- Maintain a word wall in the classroom that includes content-area words, high-frequency words, and other words deemed important listed under each letter of the alphabet.
- Use mnemonics whenever possible to help students remember and learn memory strategies to apply in the future.
  - Examples: *friend*: I am a friEND to the END; *church*: You are (U/R) in church.
  - Create pictures using words. (For example, write *look* with the *o*'s drawn as eyes; write *clown* and then draw a funny hat on top.)
- Use choral, unison techniques for practicing the spelling of nonphonetic words. Practice irregular nonphonetic words by creative techniques to help in recall. For example, make up a chant, clap out the letters in the words, spell the words using American Sign Language, or use voice inflections to help call attention to certain letters (for example, emphasizing the tricky letters in a louder voice).
- Post an example of a picture association for different phonograms for student reference—for example, a picture of an eagle for *ea,* a picture of a house for *ou,* and a train or snail for *ai.*
- Provide many peer tutoring and partner spelling opportunities, such as quizzing and practicing together in fun ways.

- Have several resources readily available for student access, such as dictionaries, electronic spell-checkers, and lists of commonly used words
- Teach the "look, say, write" method of practice: "Look at the word and trace it with your finger or your pencil. Say the word. Spell it out loud while you copy it. Now, write the word without looking. Check it against the one you traced. Did you write it correctly? If you made a mistake, fix it now, and think of a way to remember the correct spelling."
- Modify spelling lists for students with spelling disabilities, as needed.
- Make up word skeletons. Example: __ __ s __ r __ __ e __ t for the word *instrument*. The child needs to fill in the missing letters.
- Make a set of flash cards and study each of the words with a partner or parent. Put aside the cards of the words that were missed and restudy them.
- There are irregular, high frequency words that are best to learn a few at a time; practice writing them frequently in multisensory ways.

Motivating, Multisensory Techniques for Practicing Spelling Words

Using Fun Materials and Tactile Strategies

- Dip a clean paintbrush in water and write words on the tabletop or chalkboard.
- Write words in the air using a stiff arm and large muscle movements while sounding the words out (sky writing).
- Use the rainbow technique of tracing over each word at least three different times in different colors (pencils, crayons, chalk, or markers). Then, without looking, write the word from memory.
- Write words in a flat tray or box of colored sand or salt using one or two fingers.
- Write words in glue or liquid starch on pieces of cardboard. Then sprinkle any powdery material, glitter, yarn, beans, macaroni, sequins, or other material to create textured, three-dimensional spelling words. Substances such as sand, salt, and glitter are good to use for students who benefit from tracing the words with their fingers. *Note*: The act of tracing with fingers on a texture helps make a sensory imprint on the brain that increases memory and retention.
- Write words in a sandbox with a stick.
- Dictate the words and have the child write them on a dry erase board.
- Pair with another student and write words on each other's back with a finger, with the receiver identifying the word by feel.
- While sitting on the carpet, practice writing the words directly on the carpet with two fingers using large muscle movements.
- Practice writing words on individual chalkboards (or dry erase boards) with colored chalk (or colored dry erase pens).
- Finger-paint words using shaving cream on tabletops. Or use pudding, whipped cream, or frosting on waxed paper or paper plates.
- Type each of the words in a variety of fonts, colors, and sizes.

- Write the words using alphabet manipulatives and tactile letters. Examples are magnetic letters, sponge letters, alphabet stamps, alphabet cereal, letter tiles, and linking letter cubes.
- Practice writing words with a glitter pen, a neon gel pen on black paper, or other special pen.
- Use a flashlight in a darkened room or laser pen to "write" the words on a wall.
- Write words forming the letters with clay or Wikki Stix (www.wikkistix.com).

Using Song and Movement

- Pair movement while spelling words aloud: clapping to each letter, bouncing a ball, using a yo-yo, jumping rope, or jumping on a trampoline are some of the many possibilities.
- Tap out the sounds or syllables in words using a pencil on a desk, fingertips to the desk or other arm, or spell words while tapping with one hand down the other arm, from shoulder to hand.
- Chant the spelling of words that are irregular and hard to sound out phonetically.
- Use kinesthetic cues for letters and sounds and act out those motions or refer to those cues when segmenting words to spell. Various programs for teaching letter and sound associations include body movements as a kinesthetic cue for each sound or calling attention to the mouth and tongue positions and how sounds are formed and feel. Sing spelling words to common tunes or melodies.
- Spell words standing up for consonant letters and sitting down for vowels.

Using Color and Visual Highlighting

- Color-code tricky letters (silent letters) in hard-to-spell words.
- Write the words by syllables in different colors.
- Write silent letters (ghost letters) using a white pen.
- After taking a pretest, color the known part of a word (correctly spelled letters) in one color. By the time the word is spelled correctly with further trials, the whole word should be written in color.
- Write all the vowels of the word in red.
- Color-code key elements and features of the word (for example, prefixes and suffixes, final *e*).
- Write out each of the words. Circle the silent letters and underline the vowels.
- Underline misspelled letters or trouble spots in words.

Other Techniques for Learning and Practicing Words

- Trace words with a pencil while spelling the word. Then trace with an eraser. Get up and do a brief physical activity, such as five jumping jacks. Now write the word and check it for accuracy.
- Practice using the copy, write, cover, check method (CWCC).
- See the "Sources and Resources" section of this list for more on spelling instruction for students with spelling disabilities, including author's books (2007, 2010) and Pinterest boards https://www.pinterest.com/sandrarief/spelling-word-work.

Sources and Resources

Carreker, S. (2011). Teaching spelling. In J. R. Birsh (Ed.), *Multisensory teaching of basic language skills* (3rd ed.). Baltimore, MD: Paul H. Brookes.

Henry, M. K. (2010). *Unlocking literacy: Effective decoding and spelling instruction* (2nd ed.). Baltimore, MD: Paul H. Brookes.

International Dyslexia Association. (2008). Just the facts: Testing and evaluation. Retrieved from www.interdys.org/ewebeditpro5/upload/TestingandEvaluation.pdf

International Dyslexia Association. (2011). Just the facts: Spelling. Retrieved from www.interdys.org/ewebeditpro5/upload/SpellingRev.2011.pdf

Moats, L. C. (2010) *Speech to print: Language essentials for teachers* (2nd ed.). Baltimore, MD: Paul H. Brookes.

Rief, Sandra, & Heimburge, Julie. (2007). *How to reach & teach all children through balanced literacy: User-friendly strategies, tools, activities, and ready-to-use materials*. San Francisco: Jossey-Bass.

Rief, Sandra & Stern, Judith (2010). *The dyslexia checklist: A practical reference for parents and teachers*. San Francisco: Jossey-Bass.

For more creative spelling, phonics, and sight word strategies (for reading and writing), see www.pinterest.com/sandrarief/spelling-word-work/, www.pinterest.com/sandrarief/phonics-decoding-fluency/, and www.pinterest.com/sandrarief/sight-words/.

5.11 Improving Handwriting and the Legibility of Written Work

Struggles with handwriting and written organization interfere with production and being able to show what you know. Paper-and-pencil tasks are a source of great frustration for many children with ADHD. When the physical act of writing is so tedious and the results of these efforts are messy and illegible, it is no wonder that children with ADHD often hate to write and resist doing so.

- If you observe a child struggling with the physical task of writing (correct letter formation, pencil grip, speed, and legibility), share concerns with school staff and consider consulting with an occupational therapist. An evaluation and perhaps services from an occupational therapist or other specialist may be needed. Accommodations and supports, such as use of assistive technology to compensate for or alleviate some of the writing struggle, are also generally necessary.
- Many children with ADHD also have the learning disability referred to as *dysgraphia*—a disability in handwriting. Children with dysgraphia may have difficulty with orthographic coding, which is the ability to store written words in working memory while the letters in the words are analyzed (in order to spell them). They may also have difficulty with planning the sequential finger movements to form the letters when handwriting (International Dyslexia Association, 2012).

Signs of dysgraphia include the following (Jones, 2003; NCLD, 2014):

- Inconsistencies: mixtures of print and cursive; upper and lower case; irregular sizes, shapes, or slants of letters
- Unfinished words or letters, omitted words
- Inconsistent position on page with respect to lines and margins
- Cramped or unusual grip, especially holding the writing instrument very close to the paper or holding the thumb over two fingers and writing from the wrist
- Strange wrist, body, or paper position
- Talking to self while writing or carefully watching the hand that is writing
- Inability to write or draw in a line or within margins
- Slow or labored copying or writing even if it is neat and legible
- Content that does not reflect the student's other language skills
- Inefficient speed in copying
- Poor fluency of letter formation
- Fatigue while writing
- Lack of automatic letter formation

Because more emphasis has been placed on communicating in writing with technology, less has been placed on teaching and learning handwriting. This is reflected in the Common Core State Standards (CCSS). Standards for legible manuscript writing are included for kindergarten and grade 1, but beyond that, individual states are given the option of including handwriting in the curriculum at higher grades. Several states have done so (Universal Publishing editors, 2012).

- Research supports the benefits of teaching and learning handwriting skills, besides the obvious.
- MRI studies show that the practice of writing by hand helps with learning letters and shapes, can improve idea composition and expression, and may aid fine-motor-skill development (Bounds, 2010).

Handwriting Tips, Strategies, and Programs

- Group letters by similarity of formation (for example, *l/t/i; a/c/d; v/w*) when teaching and practicing how to write them.
- After first tracing over letters, have the child write a few independently, and then circle his or her best effort.
- One highly recommended program for teaching print and cursive to children, especially those with writing difficulties, is Handwriting without Tears, developed by an occupational therapist Jan Olsen (www.hwtears.com). The program uses multisensory techniques and mnemonic cues for helping children learn proper letter formation; it also structures the sequence of letters introduced by clusters. For example, cursive *o, w, b,* and *v* are taught together as the "tow-truck letters" because of their special high endings.
- Another highly recommended handwriting program is Living Letters (by EduClime) (www.educlime.com). This program uses multisensory techniques, associative stories, special colored writing paper (sky, grass, earth), magnetic tracer sets, and other unique and motivating tools.
- Provide visual cues such as a starting dot and numbered arrows as a guide for the correct letter formation (direction and sequence of strokes).
- There are pencil grips of different shapes, materials, and designs that can make it easier if a child struggles to hold and manipulate a pencil. Experiment with different kinds. See www.therapro.com, www.therapyshoppe.com, and other companies that carry such products.
- Try self-drying clay around the pencil to mold to the size and shape of the child's fingers and grip.
- Try mechanical pencils for students who frequently break their pencil tips from applying too much pressure. Although mechanical pencil tips can also break easily, at least the student doesn't need to sharpen his or her pencil frequently throughout the day—pulling the student off task.
- Share how studies have proven that teachers tend to give students the benefit of the doubt and grade higher if their papers are neat rather than sloppy or hard to read.
- Provide sufficient time to write in order to avoid time pressures.
- Set realistic, mutually agreed-on expectations for neatness.
- Some children find it easier to write using narrow-ruled paper with a shorter line height; others do better using paper with wider-ruled lines.
- Teach placing an index finger between words (finger spacing) to help children who run their words together without spacing.
- If using a pen, provide ones with erasable ink.
- Remind the child to anchor his or her paper with the nonwriting hand or arm to keep it from moving while writing.

- If the student's paper is frequently sliding around, try attaching the paper to a clipboard.
- Provide a strip or chart of alphabet letters (manuscript or cursive) on the student's desk for reference for letter formation. Draw directional arrows on the letters the child finds confusing and difficult to write.

Tactile-Kinesthetic Techniques to Motivate Letter Formation

- Make a gel bag by placing some hair gel in a plastic bag with a zipper lock. With a permanent marker, write each letter for practice on the outside of the bag. While tracing the letter, the child feels the interesting texture of the gel inside the bag, especially when the gel or ooze bag has been refrigerated.
- Color-code the strokes of a letter on the outside of the gel bag. The first phase of the stroke can be one color and the second phase can be another color. Arrows can be drawn indicating the directions of the letter formation as well.
- Practice correct letter formation by tracing with their finger letters written with directionality arrows on a variety of textures (puff paint, which is a fabric paint with a 3-D effect when it dries, or sandpaper, for example). Have the child also practice writing the letters with two fingers in a colored salt or sand tray or on the carpet. The sensory input through the fingers helps in recalling the letter formation.
- Provide guided practice by modeling letter formation in large movements, talking through the steps while writing the letter in color.
- Write letters in the air with large muscle movements while giving a verbal prompt. Holding the child's wrist, write in large strokes in the air while talking through the strokes. For example, with the letter *B,* give the following instruction: "Start at the top. Straight line down. Back to the top. Sideways smile. Another sideways smile." Then repeat without guiding the child's hand but observe that the formation is correct.
- There are several apps that teach and provide motivating practice in letter formation, such as Touch and Write (by Fizzbrain), ABC Cursive Writing (by Deep Pocket Series), iCanWrite (by Fiendsoft), iWriteWords (by gdiplus), and Wet-Dry-Try Suite (part of the Handwriting without Tears program). Touch and Write, for example, is a fun app in which children practice writing (print or cursive) using several different writing textures (such as, shaving cream, grape jelly) on a variety of paper options.
- To view several motivating strategies for teaching, practicing, and enhancing handwriting and fine-motor skills, see the many posted at www.pinterest.com/sandrarief/handwriting-fine-motor-skills/. For ideas to help with letter formation of commonly confused letters *b* and *d,* see www.pinterest.com/sandrarief/b-d-tricks-strategies/.

Additional Tips

- Provide a lot of practice at home and school when children are learning how to print or write in cursive. Observe carefully as the child practices and intervene immediately when you notice errors in letter formation. Gently correct if you observe the child making the strokes incorrectly (for example, bottom-to-top rather than top-to-bottom or circles formed clockwise rather than counterclockwise).

- Teachers can provide parents with a model of how the letters are being taught in class and any verbal prompts so there is consistency between home and school in teaching handwriting.
- Provide prompts for correct letter formation and directionality by placing a green dot indicating the starting point for the stroke and arrows showing the direction to write the strokes of the letters.
- Provide frequent practice and corrective feedback using short trace-and-copy activities.
- Allow students for whom cursive is a struggle to print.
- Encourage appropriate sitting, posture, and anchoring of paper when writing.
- Add variety for motivational purposes, using different sizes, shapes, textures, and colors of paper and assorted writing instruments. Also, have students write on individual chalkboards with colored chalk or dry erase boards with colored pens.
- Provide a slant board for better wrist position. You can make one by covering an old three-ring notebook completely with contact paper. The child then places his or her paper on the slant board when writing.
- Teach and post your expectations—for example, writing on one side of the paper only, draft papers written on every other line, math papers with two or three line spaces between problems, heading on upper-right section of paper.
- Post and provide individual copies of handwriting checklists for students to self-monitor their own written work for legibility. This list could contain questions (depending on age and developmental level and grade-level standards):
  - Are my letters resting on the line?
  - Do tall letters reach the top line and do short letters reach the middle line?
  - Do I have space between words?
  - Are my letters the right size (not too small, not too large)?
  - Am I writing within the lines?
  - Are my words in lowercase unless there is supposed to be a capital?
  - Am I consistent in my letters: all print or all cursive, not mixed?
  - Have I stayed within the margins of the paper?
- For more tips, strategies, and assistive technology to help alleviate or bypass some of the struggle with handwriting, speed of output, and legibility of written work, see *List 5.12* and author's other books listed on page 272.
- For a number of helpful resources on dysgraphia and helping children who struggle to write, see those by educational therapist Regina Richards, including her book for children entitled *Eli, the Boy Who Hated to Write* (2008).

Sources and Resources

Bounds, Gwendolyn. (2010). How handwriting trains the brain: Forming letters is key to learning, memory, ideas. *Wall Street Journal* (Oct. 5). Retrieved from http://online.wsj.com/article/SB10001424052748704631504575531932754922518.html

International Dyslexia Association. (2012). Just the facts: Understanding dysgraphia. Retrieved from www.interdys.org/ewebeditpro5/upload/UnderstandingDysgraphiaFactSheet3.14.12.pdf

Jones, Susan. (2003). Accommodations for students with handwriting problems. *The Resource, 18*(1), 6–12.

National Center for Learning Disabilities (NCLD). (2014). What is dysgraphia? Retrieved from http://ncld.org/types-learning-disabilities/dysgraphia/what-is-dysgraphia

Richards, Regina, & Richards, Eli. (2008). *Eli, the boy who hated to write* (2nd ed.). Riverside, CA: RET Center Press.

Richards, Regina. (2005). *When writing's a problem: Understanding dysgraphia and helpful hints for reluctant writers* (4th ed.). Riverside, CA: RET Center Press.

Spear-Swerling, Louise. (2006). The importance of teaching handwriting. LD Online .org. Retrieved from www.ldonline.org/spearswerling/The_Importance_of_Teaching_Handwriting

Universal Publishing editors. (2012, Jan.). Handwriting and the Common Core State Standards. Universal Publishing Writing is Learning blog. Retrieved from www.upub.net/Handwriting-and-the-Common-Core-State-Standards-News.html

5.12 Strategies to Bypass and Accommodate Writing Difficulties

For Teachers

- It commonly takes children with ADHD significantly longer than others their age or grade to produce written work. An assignment that takes most students twenty minutes or so to complete may take hours for a child with ADHD. So, keep that in mind when giving written assignments and homework to these students and when sending home incomplete work.
- Assign reasonable amounts of homework and writing assignments.
- Make adjustments in order to accept modified homework that requires reduced amounts of writing. Discuss the adjustments ahead of time with students and parents.
- When writing in class is required, allow students to take extra time as needed, particularly on essay questions for written assessments.
- Substitute nonwritten, hands-on assignments and oral presentations for written assignments.
- Give students options and choices that do not require writing but may involve investigating, building, drawing, simulating, telling, demonstrating, and so on.
- Reduce the need to copy from the board or book. Provide photocopies of notes or share notes digitally with students. Another option is to let students access notes via the interactive whiteboard or take snapshots from the board or book on their smartphone or other personal devices to download later.
- Enlarge the space for doing written work on math papers, tests, and worksheets.
- Stress the accuracy and quality of writing, not the volume.
- Permit students to dictate responses and have someone else (an adult, classmate, or cross-age tutor) be a scribe and write down what the student says.
- Allow oral responses for assignments and tests when appropriate.
- Follow written exams with an oral exam and average the two grades for students who may know the correct answers but cannot show their understanding adequately on a written exam.
- Allow students to print or use cursive handwriting or type when appropriate—whichever is easier, quicker, and more legible.
- Provide in-class time to get started on assignments.
- Provide note-taking assistance. Assign students who need assistance a buddy to take notes, share, and compare. Encourage students to take their own notes but allow them to supplement their own notes with more detailed, organized copies from the note taker.
- Provide partial outlines or frames in which the student fills in the missing information while listening to lectures.
- Provide tools such as highlighting tape, paper with wide and narrow lines, various types of pens and pencils, and different shapes of pencil grips.
- Allow the student to use of audio recorders instead of writing for summarizing learning, responding to questions, planning and recording ideas, and instructions.

- Teach keyboarding and word processing skills or suggest that students learn by using a software, app, or online program at home.
- Help the student get started writing by talking or prompting through the first few sentences or so. Have the student dictate while an adult writes the first few sentences to get the student started.
- On writing assignments, grade content and mechanics separately.
- Provide graphic organizers or other structural aids for written assignments.
- If a child struggles to hold a pencil, have him or her try a pencil grip to make it easier. Pencil grips in different shapes, materials, and designs are available.
- Have students try a mechanical pencil if they frequently break pencil tips from applying too much pressure.
- Set realistic, mutually agreed-on expectations for neatness.
- If a student's paper frequently slides around, attach the paper to a clipboard.
- Post your expectations for how assignments should appear (for example, writing on one side of the paper only, draft papers written on alternate lines, math papers with two or three line spaces between problems).
- Provide visual cues such as starting dots and numbered arrows in order to support correct letter formation (direction and sequence of strokes).
- See *Lists 5.7, 5.8, 5.9, 5.10, and 5.11* for additional accommodations at different stages of the writing process.
- See other related supports and accommodations in *Lists 3.5, 3.6, 3.7, 4.1, 4.9, and 4.10.*

Use of Assistive Tools and Technology

Many writing difficulties that students with ADHD and LD experience can be alleviated significantly with assistive technology, which is now affordable and accessible. An assistive technology device is any item, piece of equipment, or product system used to increase, maintain, or improve the functional capabilities of individuals with a disability.

- Students with ADHD who qualify for assistive technology under IDEA or Section 504 have that fact documented in their IEP or 504 accommodation plan (*Lists 6.4, 6.5*). This includes tools and training in their use. Assistive technology equipment or services designated in their plan are provided by the school district.
- Allow the use of electronic spell-checkers, dictionaries, thesauri, and other electronic tools if helpful.
- Use quality programs that are designed with features to support the writing process such as Write: Outloud, Co-Writer 4000, Draft: Builder, and SOLO (www.donjohnston.com), Inspiration and Kidspiration (www.inspiration.com), and Read and Write Gold (www.texthelp.com).
- Provide or allow the use of a desktop or laptop computer, a portable word processor (such as NEO), or a tablet, netbook, or other electronic device with word processing capability.
- Some software programs are designed specifically for those with reading and writing disabilities. They have features such as speech recognition, word prediction, text-to-speech, and audible spell-check. A few of the companies that carry such software are TextHelp, Kurzweil Educational Systems, BrightEye Technology, Quillsoft, and Don Johnston.

- Other lists in this book addressing reading, writing, math, and homework also contain strategies and accommodations to help students with writing difficulties.

Word Processing

- The use of word processing has revolutionized the way we write. To be freed from the task of handwriting and to be able to easily save drafts of work, revise by cutting and pasting, edit with tools such as spell-check and grammar-check, and produce easy-to-read copies are satisfying to both writer and reader.
- Knowing that it is relatively easy to revise, reorganize, replace vocabulary, and correct spelling and grammar enables writers to focus on the content and produce better writing. Learning how to use word processing with proficiency needs to be a priority for students with writing disabilities.

Typing and Keyboarding Software, Online Programs, and Apps

To get the most out of word processing, learning how to type quickly and accurately is very beneficial. Even though today's students are commonly very proficient with messaging and typing on their electronic devices, learning proper keyboarding skills and being able to type without looking at a keyboard is still beneficial.

Some software and online programs as well as apps for learning or practicing keyboarding and typing include the following:

- Typing Instructor Deluxe or Typing Instructor for Kids Platinum (Individual Software)
- Type to Learn (Sunburst)
- Disney's Adventures in Typing with Timon & Pumba (Disney Interactive)
- Read Write and Type (Talking Fingers)
- JumpStart Typing (Knowledge Adventure)
- Mavis Beacon Teaches Typing (The Learning Company)
- Look and Learn Keyboard Typing System and iColorType (KeyWrite)
- UltraKey (Bytes of Learning, Inc.)
- Dance Mat Typing (BBC UK Schools)
- Burning Fingers (itunesapple.com)

Word Predictors and Spelling Checkers

- Word predictors analyze words as they are typed and try to predict the words that the user is most likely to want from a dictionary or lexicon of words. As the writer types a letter of the alphabet, the program offers a list of the most common words beginning with that letter. If the first letter does not bring up the right word, more choices are offered when a second letter is typed. Some programs speak the words from the list out loud to help the writer select the desired word.
- Spelling checkers are very helpful for writers with spelling difficulties. Many software or online programs that are designed for struggling readers and writers have word prediction and spell-checking functions with an audio component (Co-Writer, Write:OutLoud, Read & Write GOLD, WordQ, and SpeakQ). The word choices are read aloud from the computer to make it easier for the user to identify the appropriate word.

- Ghotit Context Spellchecker Service (www.ghotit.com) is a set of services designed specifically for dyslexic adults and children or others with significant spelling disabilities whose spelling and typing errors are too far from the correct spelling of the word or out of context to benefit from regular spelling checkers.

Speech-to-Text Software

- Speech recognition technology, such as Dragon Naturally Speaking (by Nuance), enables users to dictate and have their oral language automatically converted into print.
- Speech-to-text technology can be very beneficial for those who struggle to get their ideas down in writing or who need to type and find doing so slow and tedious. It can be very useful in the writing process, but it does have its glitches.
- Harris (2014) points out that the skill of dictation is not as easy as it seems. Students must organize what they are going to say before they speak it and then need to edit what they have dictated, which as discussed in *Lists 5.6 and 5.9,* is not an easy task for children or teens with ADHD.
- Sometimes there are many errors that need to be corrected because the program does not recognize or misinterprets what the speaker has dictated, which is frustrating for the user.
- As voice-recognition technology continues to improve, this may be the most efficient way for struggling writers to independently output what they want to say in writing.

Text-to-Speech Software

- Text-to-speech software enables the user to see the print (digitized text) highlighted as they hear it being read aloud. Some examples of text-to-speech software include Read & Write Gold, ClaroRead Plus, Kurzweil 3000, Write:OutLoud and Read:OutLoud, and ReadPlease.
- Programs with these text-to-speech features can be very helpful for individuals with ADHD or learning disabilities, particularly during the revision and editing stages of writing.

Apps to Support the Writing Process

- There are several apps that are helpful throughout the writing process. See those in *List 5.7* that include organization, note-taking, and mind-mapping apps. See Hatton and Hatton's (n.d.) recommendations and those recommended for children with ADHD at Learning Works for Kids (http://learningworksforkids.com).

Sources and Resources

Harris, Zara. (2014). To write or to type? *Attention Magazine*, *21*(2), 18–21.

Hatton, Darla, & Hatton, Kaila. (n.d.). Apps for students with dysgraphia and writing difficulties. National Center for Learning Disabilities (NCLD). Retrieved from www.ncld.org/students-disabilities/assistive-technology-education/apps-students-ld-dysgraphia-writing-difficulties

There are also new assistive technology tools being reviewed frequently at *ADDitude Magazine* (www.additudemag.com) that may support struggling writers.

5.13 Math Difficulties Related to ADHD and Learning Disabilities

Although many students with ADHD and learning disabilities (LD) have strong mathematical aptitude, many others have significant weaknesses and struggle with math computation and problem solving. Mathematics involves multiple processes and brain functions, some of which may be areas of weakness for students with ADHD or LD.

- Math difficulties may be because of ADHD-related weaknesses such as inattention, poor organization and planning, working memory, and self-monitoring. Others may result from a learning disability, for example, sequential processing, visual-spatial-motor, and language.
- About 20 to 26 percent of students with ADHD have a specific math disability (Aro, 2014; DeRuvo, 2009; Mayes & Calhoun, 2006). Learning disabilities related to math are called *dyscalculia*.

Attention Weaknesses

Attention weaknesses may affect the following:

- Noticing operational signs in math problems (for example, being aware that the plus sign changes to minus sign and need to switch from adding to subtracting)
- Paying attention to other details (for example, decimal points and other symbols)
- Checking one's work, finding errors in computation, and self-correcting
- Losing place while working on a math problem
- Being able to sustain the focus and mental effort necessary to complete the problems with accuracy
- Having problems with attention resulting in numerous careless errors and inconsistent performance, even when the student is skilled at solving the math problems

Memory Weaknesses

- Working memory is heavily taxed in math computation and problem solving—having to hold multiple pieces of information in mind during the process. Rapid retrieval of information from long-term memory is also involved.

Memory weaknesses may affect the following:

- The learning and acquisition of basic math facts
- Being able to recall math facts and retrieve those facts quickly and automatically
- Computing multistep problems (forgetful of sequence and recalling where they are in the process)
- Recalling rules, procedures, algorithms, teacher instruction, and directions

Other Executive Skill Weaknesses

Executive function weaknesses involving planning, organizing, inhibition, cognitive flexibility, and self-monitoring may affect the following:

- Planning and organizing strategies and steps for solving a problem
- Previewing the problem, thinking ahead, and planning before beginning
- Awareness if something is not working or making sense (for example, the answer is not close to the estimate) and shifting or readjusting to try another strategy
- Time awareness in pacing and working the problems given
- Self-monitoring their performance, persevering when strategies need to be changed or calculations need to be reworked, checking for errors and self-correcting

Sequencing Weaknesses

Sequential processing difficulties may cause problems:

- Being able to do algebra and other step-by-step equations involving following an order of operations
- Executing any multistep procedure
- Being able to do skip counting (3, 6, 9, 12, 15 . . . ; and counting by multiples of other numbers)
- Recognizing and following patterns

Visual-Motor, Fine-Motor, and Spatial-Organization Weaknesses

Weaknesses in these areas may affect the following:

- Copying problems from the board or book onto paper
- Aligning numbers, decimal points, and so forth accurately on paper
- Writing and computing within the minimal amount of given space on the page, spacing between problems, and leaving enough room to compute and record answers
- Remembering and using correct directionality for solving math problems (for example, beginning with the column to the right and moving right to left, regrouping accurately)
- Recognizing and not confusing similar-looking symbols (such as + and × signs, numerals in sequence such as 203 and 302, and geometric shapes)
- Speed of writing down problems and answers—either too fast and illegible or too slow and cannot keep up or complete assignments and tests
- These difficulties result in numerous errors and the need for frequent erasing and correction, causing the student much frustration.

Language Weaknesses

Linguistic or language weaknesses may affect the following:

- Understanding and relating to the numerous abstract terms in math
- Difficulty with processing the language of mathematics

- Solving word problems (interpreting and understanding what is being asked, separating relevant from irrelevant information provided)
- Following directions

Written Expression Weaknesses

- Because writing is infused in all curricular areas in today's classrooms, students are generally expected to write about their thinking processes and how they solved problems. Consequently, a student who may be strong with numbers and mathematical problem solving but struggles in written expression may do poorly in math class as a result of language and writing difficulties.

Related Lists

- See *List 5.14* for math strategies and interventions.

Sources and Resources

Aro, Lisa. (2014). When things don't add up. *ADDitude Magazine*, *14*(4), 51–53.

DeRuvo, Silvia L. (2009). *Strategies for teaching adolescents with ADHD (Grades 6–12)*. San Francisco: Jossey-Bass.

Mayes, S. D., & Calhoun, S. I. (2006). Frequency of reading, math and writing difficulties in children with clinical disorders. *Learning and Individual Differences*, *16*, 145–157.

Misunderstood Minds. (n.d.). Difficulty with mathematics.. Retrieved from www.pbs.org/wgbh/misunderstoodminds/mathdiffs.html

Nicholls, C. J. (2001). The link between AD/HD and learning disabilities in mathematics. CHADD 13th Annual Conference, Anaheim, California, October 17–21.

5.14 Math Strategies and Interventions

As described in *List 5.13,* students with ADHD and learning disabilities often have academic difficulties in math computation and problem solving related to their executive function and processing weaknesses. Fortunately, there are a number of ways that teachers and parents can help them strengthen skills and improve mathematical performance.

Strategies for Increasing Focus and Attention

- Color-highlight or underline key words and vocabulary in word problems: shared, doubled, product, average, larger, slower, difference, altogether, equal parts, and so on.
- Color-dot the ones (units) column to remind students the direction of where to begin computation.
- Color-highlight processing signs so that students who are inattentive will notice the change in operational signs on a page. For example, color addition signs yellow, subtraction signs pink, and so forth.
- Color-highlight place value. For example, given the number 16,432,781, write the hundreds (781) in green, the thousands (432) in orange, and the millions (16) in blue.
- Reduce the number of problems on a page.
- Block part of the page while the student is working on problems or fold the paper under to reveal just one or two rows at a time.
- Cut up a page of problems into strips or rows and give one strip one at a time to students.
- Allow students to stand up and stretch or take a break of some kind after completing a certain number of problems and checking them for accuracy.
- See *Lists 2.12 and 3.5* for more on this topic.

Strategies and Supports for Memory and Recall of Math Facts and Procedures

- Make multiplication charts and tables readily available for reference to accommodate students who have difficulty memorizing and reliably recalling math facts.
- Free up students' working memory load by providing or having them first write down the steps of an algorithm or procedure.
- List steps and procedures to multistep problems and algorithms. Post clear numbered steps or give students a desk copy model of steps for solving problems.
- Keep sample math problems on the board and have students keep them in a notebook for reference.
- Post anchor charts in the classroom as clear visual reminders of math processes and strategies taught. See examples at www.pinterest.com/sandrarief/math-strategies-activities.

- Use mnemonic devices (memory clues, images, and associations) to help students remember math facts, sequential steps and procedures, and abstract math concepts and vocabulary.
- Make use of rhymes, chants, raps, or songs to help students memorize the multiplication tables. Children can make up their own or use those commercially available.
- Use mnemonics, such as *D*ead *M*onsters *S*mell *B*ad, for learning the steps of long division (*d*ivide, *m*ultiply, *s*ubtract, *b*ring down) or *I V*iew *X*rays (1, V, X for recalling Roman numerals one, five, and ten). There are a variety of such math mnemonics at Educational World (see the "Sources and Resources" section of this list).
- Some mnemonic programs are available that use picture associations and clever stories to help master multiplication facts as well. Three such programs are Time Tables the Fun Way: A Picture Method of Learning the Multiplication Facts (www.citycreek.com), Memory Joggers (www.memoryjoggers.com), and Semple Math (www.semplemath.com)
- Teach children to look for patterns to help them learn their math facts. One recommended program is Teach Your Child the Multiplication Tables with Dazzling Patterns, Grids and Tricks! (www.TeaCHildMath.com).
- Once students know multiples of up to the five times tables, teach the nine times table. Recognizing and recalling the commutative property of multiplication (for example, $3 \times 7 = 7 \times 3$) significantly reduces the stress and feeling that there are so many facts to learn. Actually, there will only be six more facts left to memorize: 6×6, 6×7, 6×8, 7×7, 7×8, and 8×8.
- Practice one sequence of multiples at a time (the two or three times tables, for example) in a variety of multisensory formats until the child achieves mastery.
- Encourage students to keep a card file of specific math skills, concepts, rules, and algorithms taught, along with specific examples of each on the card for reference.
- Practice and review facts in frequent, brief sessions (five minutes per session a few times each day). This can be done at home in a fun, relaxed manner.
- Daily timings of basic facts can be great practice and motivation if students compete against themselves, not their classmates. Have students chart their own progress and mastery. Do not display this information for the whole class to see.
- Teach the different finger tricks available for learning ×6, ×7, ×8, and ×9 tables. Some are demonstrated on YouTube videos. See examples at www.pinterest.com/sandrarief/math-strategies-activities/.
- See *Lists 4.1 and 4.2* for more on this topic.

Strategies to Compensate for Spatial-Organization and Perceptual-Motor Difficulties

- Encourage students to write and solve their computation problems on graph paper rather than notebook paper. Experiment with graph paper of varying square and grid sizes.
- Turning notebook paper sideways (with the lines running vertically rather than horizontally) makes it much easier for students to keep numbers aligned in columns and reduces careless errors.

- Reduce the requirement of copying problems from the board or book by photocopying the page or writing out the problems on paper for students who need this help.
- Provide a large work space on tests. If necessary, rewrite test items on another paper with lots of room for computation.
- Provide lots of space on the page between problems and the bottom of the page.
- See *Lists 5.11 and 5.12* for more on this topic.

Self-Monitoring and Metacognitive Strategies

- Model how to first read problems (particularly word problems) and plan a strategy for solving them before beginning the work.
- Teach how to estimate and determine whether a given answer is reasonable.
- Have students keep a journal of their thinking, reasoning, questions, and understanding of math concepts. Also, have them write their understanding about mathematical concepts before and after the unit is taught.
- Model talking out loud while reasoning and thinking about a mathematical problem. Encourage students to do the same, externalizing their thinking and verbalizing while solving problems. Listen to students as they think out loud and correct gaps in their comprehension when possible.
- Teach students to think about what they are being asked to figure out in the problem and state it in their own words.
- Help students self-monitor their productivity and accuracy by having them record the number of math problems they completed accurately during a set period of class time. Have them keep a log and graph of this information for added benefit.
- Meltzer (2010) shares the importance of using a consistent, reliable, and systematic strategy for students to check their work on math word problems. The strategy she describes encourages students to ask themselves these questions:
  - Did I **read** the question carefully?
  - Did I **circle** the key words and relevant numbers?
  - Did I **estimate** the answer?
  - Did I **calculate** correctly?
  - Did I **compare** my estimate to my answer? Is my answer reasonable?
- Meltzer suggests creating a mnemonic to remember these questions, such as "Ravenous Chickens Eat Crunchy Cheerios."
- See *Lists 4.1, 4.2, and 4.3* for more on this topic.

Instructional and Assessment Strategies and Modifications

Make the abstract more concrete.

- Provide many kinds of manipulatives to help students visualize and work out math problems. Cubes, chips, tiles, counters, beans, base-ten blocks, and number lines are some of the many possibilities.

- Introduce mathematical concepts with demonstrations using real-life examples and motivating situations. For example, cut a sandwich into 5 equal parts to share in a small group (1/5 per student) or first count the total and then equally divide a bag of candy among a number of students (32 pieces divided by 5 kids = 6 each with 2 left over).

Teach, model, and practice problem-solving strategies.

- Model and encourage the use of drawing, diagramming, and labeling in the problem-solving process.
- Work problems on the board or document camera using color to make the steps and processes visually clear.
  - Teach key words that indicate the process. For example, the words *product, times, doubled,* and *tripled* all indicate multiplication. The words *average, quotient, equal parts, sharing,* and *divisible by* all indicate division.
  - Teach and model a variety of problem-solving strategies: read the problem out loud at least twice before beginning, finding clue words, looking for a pattern, constructing a table, making an organized list, using objects, drawing a picture, working backward, making a model, eliminating possibilities, and guessing and checking, among others.
  - Always build in time during the lesson for students to share how they solved the problem and emphasize the variety of ways, not just one method, to solve them.

Use adaptive assessment strategies and supports.

- Allow extra time on math tests so students are not rushed and make careless errors.
- Avoid the anxiety of timed tests and drills, especially those posted for all students in the class to see, and extend the amount of time permitted for certain students as passing.
- Grade by number of correct problems over the number assigned (which could be different for students receiving modified homework or classwork).
- Provide frequent checks for accuracy and immediate feedback whenever possible. This reduces the frustration of having to erase and fix a number of problems done incorrectly. Set a certain number of problems to complete (for example, one row only or three to four problems) and then check students before they are permitted to continue. Student partners can also compare answers after working every few problems on their own. If they don't agree on any of the answers after reworking the problem together, those students can then ask other classmates or the teacher.

Provide other supportive instructional strategies.

- Reduce the number of problems assigned (half-page, evens only, odds only).
- Allow and encourage students to use calculators, particularly for checking their work.
- Increase the amount of practice and review. Make sets of practice and review problems (a few per page) with answers on the back for independent practice.
- Provide many opportunities for using math in the context of real-life situations: using money,

balancing a checkbook, determining mileage on a fantasy road trip, comparison shopping, and paying for a meal, with tax and tip, for example. See Rief and Heimburge (2006) for more than eighty such survival math activities that are appropriate for students in grades 3 through 8.

Use cooperative learning structures and formats in math instruction.

- *Partners.* Working in pairs, one works a problem while the other coaches. Roles are reversed. Then, after a couple of problems are completed, partners pair up with another set of pairs and compare answers.
- *Groups or teams.* Teams of four work a problem together and check each other's understanding on one or more problems. Then the team breaks into two pairs who continue to work together to solve the next couple of problems. Students then continue independently working similar problems and comparing answers with each other.

Increase students' motivation.

- Play team math games in class.
- Let students choose one or two problems that they get to cross out or eliminate from their math homework assignment.
- Try the strategy of letting a student who is busy on task working on the in-class math assignment to roll a die. Whatever number comes up on the die is the number of *fewer* math problems the student has to do that night for the homework assignment. See the blog "Keeping Students on Task During Seatwork" describing this strategy at www.sandrarief.com/2012/08/15/great-strategy-for-motivating-on-task-behavior.
- Use electronic games for drill and practice of math skills. These programs have the benefit of being adjusted for speed and level of difficulty. They also provide immediate feedback and are fun, nonthreatening, and motivating for children.
- There are many sources of engaging, motivating online games and programs, such as FunBrain.com, Math-Play.com, CoolMath4Kids.com, Fuel the Brain.com, Math Cats.com, Mr.Nussbaum.com, IXL.com, Mathletics.com, AAAmath.com, Webmath.com, and others. See *List 7.12* for these and other resources.
- There are numerous math ideas shared by creative teachers for grades K–12 found at my math Pinterest board. See www.pinterest.com/sandrarief/math-strategies-activities/.
- See *Lists 3.3, 3.5, 3.6, 3.7, 4.1, and 4.2* for more related information and strategies.

Tips for Parents

- Practice functional math skills (measurement, time concepts, counting money and change) as much as possible at home. These are critical skills that teachers often do not have enough time to teach until mastery. Parents can include their child in activities such as cooking, baking, constructing, sewing, gardening, and home improvements, which are great ways to teach and reinforce functional math skills and fun to do together.
- Motivate the practice of skills through the use of games. Although there are many electronic math games that children can play by themselves, they do not compare to the benefits derived from the face-to-face interaction of playing board, card, and dice games together as a family.

- Many board games and card games such as Battleship, Mastermind, Othello, Chess, Dominos, Uno, Crazy 8s, Rummy, and War are great for sharpening a host of skills (for example, counting, arithmetic, problem solving, logic, sequencing, spatial relations, mental math, probability, and strategic thinking) while having fun.
- See author's blog, "Fun Ways to Boost Your Child's Math Skills This Summer and Beyond" for numerous math games and puzzles, real-life math applications, and online math resources at www.sandrarief.com/2013/07/23/fun-ways-to-boost-your-childs-math-skills-this-summer-and-beyond.
- For suggested math apps that are beneficial for children with ADHD, see Learning Works for Kids (www.learningworksforkids.com).

Sources and Resources

Education World. Links to several math mneumonics. Retrieved from www.educationworld.com/a_curr/archives/mnemonics.shtml

Francis, Eugenia. (n.d.). *Teach your child the multiplication tables, fast, fun & easy: With dazzling patterns, grids and tricks* (2nd ed.). CreateSpace Independent Publishing Platform. Retrieved from www.teachildmath.com/

Meltzer, Lynn. (2010). *Promoting executive function in the classroom.* New York: Guilford Press.

PBS. (2002). Misunderstood minds: Math strategies. WGBH Educational Foundation. Retrieved from www.pbs.org/wgbh/misunderstoodminds/mathstrats.html

Polloway, Edward A., Patton, James R., Serna, Loretta, & Bailey, Jenevie W. (2012). *Strategies for teaching learners with special needs* (10th ed.). Upper Saddle River, NJ: Pearson.

Rief, Sandra, & Heimburge, Julie. (2006). *How to reach & teach all children in the inclusive classroom* (2nd ed.). San Francisco: Jossey-Bass.

Rief, Sandra. (2013). Fun and free interactive online math games. Retrieved from www.sandrarief.com/2013/06/28/fun-interactive-online-math-games

Rodriguez, Judy, & Rodriguez, Dave. 2013 *Time tables the fun way: A picture method of learning the multiplication facts (3rd edition).* Minneapolis: City Creek Press.

Semple, Janice L. *Semple math: A complete basic skills mathematics program.* Attleboro Falls, MA: Semple Math. Retrieved from www.semplemath.com/

Yates, Donnalyn. *Memory joggers.* Irvine, CA: Memory Joggers. Retrieved from www.memoryjoggers.com

Section 6

Educational Rights and Systems of Support at School

Contents

Please note that a lot of the content of these lists has been adapted and updated from my other books, published by Jossey-Bass/Wiley, which you may be interested in exploring for further information, tools, and strategies:

Rief, S. (2003). *The ADHD book of lists: A practical guide for helping children and teens with attention deficit disorders*. San Francisco: Jossey-Bass.

Rief, S. (2005). *How to reach & teach children with ADD/ADHD: Practical techniques, strategies and interventions* (2nd ed.). San Francisco: Jossey-Bass.

Rief, S. (2008). *The ADD/ADHD checklist: A practical reference for parents and teachers* (2nd ed.). San Francisco: Jossey-Bass.

Rief, Sandra & Stern, Judith (2010). *The dyslexia checklist: A practical reference for parents and teachers*. San Francisco: Jossey-Bass.

6.1 Response to Intervention (RTI)

What is RTI?

- A schoolwide process that provides systematic, research-based instruction and a continuum of intervention tiers to struggling learners
- A single, integrated system of instruction and intervention aimed at improving educational outcomes for all students and guided by data on student outcomes from frequent progress-monitoring measures
- The practice of providing high-quality instruction and research-based interventions matched to students' needs, using individual students' response to those interventions to make a range of educational decisions—including some that are part of the process of determining whether a student qualifies for special education under the specific learning disabilities category
- An approach intended to eliminate a wait-to-fail situation before struggling students are provided the help they need to succeed in school
- Included in federal special education law, IDEA 2004, as part of the effort to direct schools to address students' problems earlier, before a referral to special education is needed
- A process intended to enable more students to have their needs adequately met in general education, which would in turn reduce the number of students requiring special education
- A framework for structuring early intervening services (EIS) under IDEA 2004 and offers an alternative to the traditional discrepancy model between IQ and achievement as a means of identifying students with learning disabilities who qualify for special education

Essential Components of RTI

- High-quality, research-based instruction for all students, differentiated to match their learning needs
- Universal screening of all students early in the school year and repeated during the year to identify students at risk for academic or behavioral failure
- Implementation of scientifically proven interventions to address students' learning problems
- Administration of interventions by highly qualified personnel
- Interventions delivered with fidelity (in accordance with the programs' instructions and protocol)
- Multiple, increasingly intense tiers of intervention
- Continuous monitoring of students' performance and response to interventions
- Educational decisions about individual students based on solid assessment data and monitoring of student progress
- Parental involvement and team-based decision making in regard to a student's educational needs.

The Three-Tiered Model of Intervention

School districts vary in their implementation of tiered intervention models. Most common is the three-tiered model of academic and behavioral supports and interventions, represented as a pyramid divided into three sections: the largest section and bottom part of the pyramid (about 80 to 90 percent of students) represents tier 1; a smaller section in the middle of the pyramid (about 10 to 15 percent) represents tier 2; and the small part at the top (about 1 to 5 percent) represents tier 3.

Tier 1: Primary (Universal) Intervention

- Tier 1 focuses on taking a proactive approach, aiming to prevent problems by identifying at-risk students and catching students in need of support before they fail.
- High-quality, research-based instruction in the core curriculum and effective management and behavioral supports are provided by classroom teachers. These are referred to as *primary* or *universal* interventions.
- The effective strategies and differentiated instruction provided at this tier should allow approximately 80 to 90 percent of students to achieve academically and function successfully.
- Screening, regular assessment, progress monitoring, and group interventions are provided for all students.
- Identified at-risk students receive additional instruction within the general education classroom for a period of time, during which progress is closely monitored, data are collected, and the need for tier 2 intervention is determined.

Tier 2: Secondary (Targeted) Intervention

- Tier 2 involves more intense, targeted interventions to strengthen the skills of students who do not responding adequately with tier 1 support.

- Research-based interventions are provided in addition to core instruction in the general curriculum, usually in small groups. This supplemental instruction does not replace the classroom curriculum.
- Tier 2 intervention is also referred to as *secondary* intervention.
- Tier 2 will be the appropriate level of support for approximately 10 to 15 percent of the school population for boosting their skills.
- Tier 2 interventions are applied for a limited time (generally no more than ten weeks), during which students' progress is frequently monitored in order to gauge the effectiveness of the intervention and determine whether tier 3 intervention is needed.

Tier 3: Tertiary (Intensive) Intervention

- In tier 3, intensive, individualized interventions target the skill deficits of students who do not adequately respond to intervention in tiers 1 and 2.
- Students at tier 3 receive the most minutes of instruction, delivered by teachers who are well trained to implement the intensive, intervention programs.
- Tier 3 is also referred to as *tertiary* intervention.
- Tier 3 is the stage at which children are considered for special education.
- In some school districts, tier 3 is when referral for special education and evaluation takes place. (Documented evidence of lack of response to intervention at tiers 1 and 2 is a component of the evaluation.) For students who are found to be eligible for special education, tier 3 intervention would include special education services.
- In other districts, a more intensive, individualized tier 3 intervention is provided within general education, generally delivered by reading specialists or other specialists. Referral and evaluation for special education follows if the student does not make adequate progress. In these districts, special education is tier 4.

RTI and IDEA 2004

- When the Individuals with Disabilities Education Act (IDEA) was reauthorized in 2004, it changed the way that school districts are permitted to evaluate and identify students with learning disabilities. It is important to note that students with ADHD who have coexisting learning disabilities may qualify for special education if meeting the eligibility criteria under the specific learning disability (SLD) category, as well as the other health impaired (OHI) category.
- Traditionally, a formula that quantified the discrepancy between a student's IQ and his or her achievement was used to determine whether a student had a learning disability and qualified for special education.
- There had been problems with the IQ-achievement discrepancy formula and concerns about requiring its use in the diagnosis of learning disabilities and determination of eligibility for special education. Many people felt strongly that the discrepancy formula was not a reliable means of diagnosing a learning disability and was also resulting in too many students having to a wait to fail before they were able to qualify for needed services.
- IDEA 2004 changed this. It enabled schools to use RTI (the student's response or lack thereof to interventions) as part of the evaluation process in determining whether a student has specific learning disabilities and is eligible for special education.

- The law stresses the need to use instructional practices in general education that are supported by research and that focus on prevention of problems. Early intervening services (EIS) are to be provided to help students who are not yet identified as eligible for special education but who require additional academic or behavioral support.
- IDEA 2004 allows school districts to use up to 15 percent of their federal special education funds for EIS for students in need of academic or behavioral support and intervention who have not yet been identified as needing special education. RTI is a perfect vehicle for providing these early intervening services.
- According to IDEA 2004, a student who consistently performs below state-approved grade-level standards on scientifically validated interventions and who fails to respond successfully to additional supports and interventions of increasing intensity may be determined to have a learning disability.
- In 2006, the US Department of Education issued the final regulations that provided clarification and guidance to states and school districts about how to implement IDEA 2004 and RTI.
- The regulations specify the following:
  - Schools must provide early intervention to struggling learners in general education delivered by highly qualified personnel.
  - Data-based documentation of repeated assessments at reasonable intervals must be collected and used to guide educational decisions through a problem-solving approach.
  - The RTI process is encouraged (in lieu of the IQ-achievement discrepancy formula) as one component of a comprehensive evaluation for the purpose of identifying students with learning disabilities and determining eligibility for special education.
  - To identify whether a student has a learning disability, it must be determined that the low achievement is not because of the student's lack of appropriate instruction in general education.
  - If frequent monitoring of progress and data-based documentation shows that a student is still not making adequate progress after receiving research-based instruction and intervention, a referral for evaluation is appropriate.

Benefits of RTI

When implemented effectively, RTI has many benefits, particularly for those with coexisting dyslexia or other learning disabilities. RTI can do the following:

- Significantly reduce academic failure and behavioral problems, increasing the success of many students within general education
- Reduce inappropriate or unnecessary special education referrals and placements
- Increase the quality of instruction and the use of research-validated practices in general education classrooms
- Reduce the time that a student waits before receiving additional instructional assistance
- Prevent reading disabilities and subsequent years of school failure and loss of self-esteem by providing scientifically based instruction and early intervention

- Ensure that general education assumes responsibility for all children (including those with disabilities) and provides the degree of support and intervention that individual students need for success. No longer should a struggling reader need to qualify for special education in order to receive effective reading instruction to improve skills, nor do children need to wait until they lag behind grade-level peers so that even with intensive remediation, they cannot catch up.
- Prevent some children with dyslexia and other learning disabilities from requiring special education because the research-based instruction and supports within general education sufficiently meet their needs
- Reduce some unnecessary and time-consuming testing from the evaluation process

Potential Disadvantages of RTI for Students with Dyslexia or Other Learning Disabilities

There are also some potential problems and disadvantages with RTI, particularly in determining if a student has a specific learning disability and is eligible for special education. Parents and educators need to know these facts:

- The law does not address how children should be evaluated when they do not respond to the interventions.
- There is ambiguity about the components of a comprehensive evaluation under this model (as opposed to the traditional discrepancy model) for determining the presence of learning disabilities.
- The effectiveness of a school's implementation of RTI requires the designated staff (well trained in the research-based methods) for providing the intervention programs. Not every school will have the availability of these highly qualified personnel to implement the interventions, so the success of the RTI model will vary from school to school.
- There are no time lines in the law for how long students should receive interventions in RTI tiers before they are referred for evaluation.

Important Information for Parents and Schools

- Be aware that the law specifies that a referral for special education and a comprehensive evaluation may be made at any time. If a disability is suspected, regardless of the tier, parents and teachers or other school personnel may refer the student for a special education evaluation.
- Parents need to be informed of their rights to request such a referral for evaluation, regardless of where the student is in the RTI process. Parents should also be provided with written notice of IDEA procedural safeguards.
- RTI is meant to be a collaborative process. Parents should be fully included and involved in all decision making (intervention options and course of action for their child).
- There should be close communication regarding the child's progress and documentation of all steps taken.
- For more information and recommendations from the RTI Network on what schools should do to avoid the risk of litigation because parents find they are being denied or delayed in having their child evaluated for special education, see Martin (n.d.).

RTI and PBIS

RTI as described in this list and *List 3.8* addresses the tiered academic and instructional interventions and supports provided in schools to students in need. The Positive Behavioral Interventions and Supports (PBIS) model described in *Lists 2.9 and 2.17* is the three-tiered system of RTI for implementing behavioral interventions at increasingly more intensive levels, depending on students' needs. Both RTI or PBIS are very beneficial for students with ADHD and others with academic and behavioral challenges.

Note: The information in this list and others in this section regarding educational laws and policies is meant as a general guide for parents and educators. Check and clarify with experts from your local and state education agencies.

Sources and Resources

Center on Instruction (www.centeroninstruction.org)

Center on Response to Intervention at American Institutes for Research (www.rti4success.org/)

Horowitz, S. H. (2013). Response to Intervention (RTI): Tiers without tears. Retrieved from http://www.ncld.org.php53-22.ord1-1.websitetestlink.com/new-on-ldorg/blogs/research-roundup-tiers-without-tears-[updated]

IRIS Center Peabody College Vanderbilt University (http://iris.peabody.vanderbilt.edu/)

Klatz, Mary Beth. (2006). Response to Intervention (RTI): A primer for parents. National Association for School Psychologists. Retrieved from www.nasponline.org/resources/factsheets/rtiprimer.aspx

Martín, Jose L. (n.d.). Legal implications of Response to Intervention and special education identification. RTI Action Network. Retrieved from www.rtinetwork.org/learn/ld/legal-implications-of-response-to-intervention-and-special-education-identification

National Center for Learning Disabilities. (n.d.). A parent resource for RTI. Retrieved from www.ncld.org/parents-child-disabilities

Pinterest links on RTI (www.pinterest.com/sandrarief/response-to-intervention-rti/)

Pinterest links on PBIS (www.pinterest.com/sandrarief/pbis-schoolwide-positive-behavior-support/)

Positive Behavioral Interventions and Supports. US Department of Education's Office of Special Education Programs (OSEP) Technical Assistance Center on PBIS (www.pbis.org)

RTI Action Network (www.rtinetwork.org)

RTI Central (www.rtictrl.org)

RTI Classification Tool and Resource Locator (RTI CTRL) (www.rtictrl.org)

6.2 The Student Support Team (SST) Process

Most schools have a team process for assisting teachers in devising instructional and behavioral strategies and supports for students experiencing difficulties in general education. This process and team is referred to by many names:

- SST can stand for "student support team," "student study team," or "student success team."
- In some districts the team is called the "SAT" (student assistance team), "SIT" (student intervention team), "IST" (instructional support team), or "TAT" (teacher assistance team).
- In others it may be called the "consultation team," "child guidance team," "child study team," "multidisciplinary intervention team," and so forth.
- More recently, the SST may be called the "RTI team" (Response to Intervention team).
- As with RTI (*List 6.1*), the SST (or whatever name the district chooses to use) is part of a schoolwide general education process for problem solving issues with and supporting students in need of additional assistance.
- The intent of the SST process is to enable individual students who are struggling and their classroom teachers to receive support and intervention that will hopefully be effective in adequately addressing the student's needs in the general education program. It also serves as protocol in many districts for examining student needs and trying to resolve issues as part of the prereferral to the special education process.
- SSTs have been in place in most schools for a number of years. RTI is built on the SST process but takes it further. RTI is typically a stronger, more accountable system for ensuring that students not succeeding in the general education classroom are identified, provided research-based interventions, their progress closely monitored with objective data, and given more intensive help if response to the intervention is not sufficient (*List 6.1*).
- RTI provides for a "well-defined, step-by-step method of problem-solving and troubleshooting to identify precisely where students are experiencing frustration and failure and a procedure for collecting data that allows for prompt decision making about what to do next to accelerate students' learning" (Horowitz, 2013, p. 1). With many schools now implementing RTI, the SST process may be incorporated into the RTI process—structured and operating differently than it did in the past. RTI may have replaced the SST, absorbed it under the new RTI structure, or the school may have both teams and processes in place.
- The SST process and protocol varies from district to district and school to school. In any case, every school should have a regular process and forum for teachers to be able to meet with a team in order to share their concerns about certain students and receive input and support on developing and monitoring a targeted plan of interventions to help that student.
- The SST meetings, which meet on a regularly scheduled basis, should be designed to efficiently discuss, strategize appropriate interventions, monitor progress, and follow up with further action for those particular students on the agenda.

Depending on the staff available at the school (and their schedules), the members of the team vary. For example, the team might include the following:

- The school psychologist, school counselor, special educator (resource teacher), school nurse, administrator, and classroom teacher(s)
- Other specialists (speech and language therapist, adapted PE teacher, occupational therapist) may not be in attendance at all team meetings but participate when the team will be discussing a student with issues involving language or motor skills.
- School social worker, reading or other subject area specialist, and others with various areas of expertise
- Minimally, the team should include the teacher requesting the meeting and at least another two or three of the people noted in this list.

The Role of Parents

- Parents are generally requested to attend the SST meeting because parent input is extremely important and helpful in the problem-solving and strategy-planning process.
- Parents may be asked to share about their child's functioning at home and school, his or her areas of strength and interest, and what they perceive as their child's difficulties and needs. Parents will be asked if any of the behaviors of concern observed at school are also observed at home or other settings.
- Any information that parents are willing to supply to assist in determining an appropriate plan of action for the child is very helpful. Parents may be asked what they have found to be effective in motivating and reinforcing their child.
- Regardless of whether a parent is able to attend the meeting, schools should share a summary of the meeting and plan of action.
- If parents are not attending the SST meeting, it is recommended that the school obtain their input by phone interview or sending home a parent input form prior to the meeting.
- If parents inquire about an evaluation for special education, they may be asked if they are willing to first discuss their concerns at an SST meeting (which should be scheduled very quickly and timely).
- It is important to understand that parents have the right to directly request a formal assessment for special education and related services under IDEA or Section 504 without the requirement of first going through the SST or RTI process (*Lists 6.1, 6.3, 6.4, 6.5*).
- Sometimes schools will initiate the IEP evaluation process and still concurrently schedule the SST meeting to discuss and document what has already been tried and the effectiveness of those strategies and interventions.

The Role of the School

Note: The SST process is sometimes perceived as the gatekeeper to special education because teachers may view the process as extra hoops to jump through before a child is referred. Perhaps in some schools this is the case. But this collaborative team problem-solving process is not intended to significantly delay appropriate referrals to special education.

The SST and the RTI process when implemented well and functioning as it should is a highly effective method for early intervention, providing much needed support to struggling students and their teachers.

The benefits to the school include the following:

- Provides teacher with access to a group of colleagues who share information and expertise in order to help the teacher better meet the individual needs of students
- Assists the teacher in problem solving, strategizing, and developing a plan of appropriate classroom interventions
- Facilitates student access to additional school-based interventions and perhaps community-based supports and interventions (as needed)
- Provides teachers with an expanded toolbox or repertoire of instructional and behavioral strategies and adaptations that are useful not only for the targeted student but also others with similar learning and behavioral challenges in their classroom
- Provides the necessary prereferral intervention documentation if a formal referral for special education is required
- Enhances the home-school partnership in efforts to collaboratively address student needs
- Schools may have more than one team in a building, particularly those with a large population or high percentage of students in need of support. To be effective, schools must be creative in finding ways to meet more frequently and consistently, as well as expand on the resources and personnel in the building who can contribute and participate in the SST. For example:
  - Establishing a few teams in the building with different members of support staff, administration, and teachers assigned to each team
  - Using a layered or tiered SST process and structure; for example, students are first discussed and a plan of action with strategies is designed in grade-level teacher teams, cluster teams, or house teams; if problems are not resolved at this level, then a schoolwide level SST is scheduled with parents and other SST members

The Role of Teachers

It is very helpful for teachers to follow through on preliminary steps prior to the SST meeting:

- Implement some strategies and interventions to address the areas of concern and document effectiveness
- Communicate with previous teachers
- Review the cumulative records and student data
- Collect work samples
- Share concerns and action taken with appropriate SST members at the informal level as appropriate
- Establish communication with parents—notifying them of observations, concerns, attempts to assist, and so on

With prereferral steps taken, then the SST meeting is more productive. The team is in a position to recommend next-step interventions. Teachers should be prepared when meeting with the team to do the following:

- Describe the student's strengths, interests, and positive traits
- Identify and clearly describe their areas of concern about the student's functioning (academic, behavioral, social-emotional)
- Share data and documentation regarding the student's areas of weakness and strategies and supports that have been tried so far

Additional Points

- Recommendations for referrals for special education or an ADHD evaluation are best initiated through the SST or RTI team.
- If it appears that a student may have ADHD, the teacher and other members of the team who know and interact with the child are able to share observations about the child's functioning in various school settings with parents. The SST or RTI meeting is often the perfect forum to share information, strategies, and resources with parents and recommend any screening or evaluation when indicated (*List1.17*).
- For the SST or RTI process to be effective, it has to be a priority in the school. Administrators must make all efforts to resolve scheduling issues by providing coverage for classroom teachers if the meetings take place during school hours.
- A good SST action plan for a child with ADHD can be similar to a 504 plan. After assessing and determining eligibility, many 504 accommodation plans involve basically rewriting the SST interventions and strategies that have been effective and adding any other agreed-on accommodations, supports, and information onto a district 504 form (*List 6.5*).
- For an action plan to be effective (whether it is one generated at an SST or RTI meeting, a 504 plan, or an IEP) there must be close monitoring and follow-up for accountability. The best of plans fail if we do not revisit the plan, assess how effective it is, and make changes as needed.

Sources and Resources

Horowitz, S. H. (2013). Response to intervention (RTI): Tiers without tears. Retrieved from www.ncld.org/students-disabilities/rti-parent-school-relationship/response-intervention-tiers-without-tears

National Center for Learning Disabilities. (n.d.). Pre-referral services. Parent guide to IDEA. Retrieved from http://ncld.org/parents-child-disabilities/idea-guide/chapter-1-pre-referral-services

6.3 Educational Rights for Students with ADHD

Note: The information in this list and others in this section regarding educational laws and policies are meant as a general guide for parents and educators. Check and clarify with experts from your local and state education agencies.

There are two main laws protecting students with disabilities, including ADHD:

- Individuals with Disabilities Education Act (known as IDEA or IDEA 2004)
- Section 504 of the Rehabilitation Act of 1973 (known as Section 504)

Another law that protects individuals with disabilities is The Americans with Disabilities Act (ADA), a federal civil rights law that was amended in 2008 and went into effect in 2009. The Americans with Disabilities Amendments Act of 2008 (ADAA), made significant changes that affected students with ADHD in that it expanded the eligibility criteria under Section 504.

- *IDEA* is the federal law in the United States governing how states and public agencies provide early intervention, special education, and related services to children with disabilities. It was reauthorized by Congress in 2004, and the final regulations by the US Department of Education clarifying how the law is to be implemented by state and local education agencies were issued in 2006.
- *Section 504* is a civil rights statute that prohibits discrimination against individuals with disabilities and is enforced by the US Office of Civil Rights.

Both IDEA and Section 504 require school districts to provide students with disabilities with the following:

- A free appropriate public education (FAPE) in the least restrictive environment (LRE) with their nondisabled peers to the maximum extent appropriate to their needs
- Supports (adaptations, accommodations, modifications) to enable the student to participate and learn in the general education program
- The opportunity to participate in extracurricular and nonacademic activities
- A free, nondiscriminatory evaluation
- Procedural due process

There are different criteria for eligibility, services, and supports available, and procedures and safeguards for implementing the laws. Therefore, it is important for parents, educators, clinicians, and advocates to be well aware of the variations between IDEA and Section 504 and fully informed about their respective advantages and disadvantages.

IDEA 2004

- IDEA applies to students known or suspected of having a disability and specifies what the public school system is required to provide to such students and their parents or guardians.

- IDEA provides for special education and related services to students who meet the eligibility criteria under one of thirteen separate disability categories. Students with ADHD most commonly and appropriately fall under the IDEA disability category of other health impaired (OHI).

Other Health Impaired (OHI) Eligibility Criteria

- The child has a chronic or acute health problem. (ADD and ADHD are chronic health problems that are specifically listed in IDEA among a number of others, such as diabetes, epilepsy, and Tourette syndrome.)
- This health problem causes "limited strength, vitality, or alertness" in the educational environment. This includes limited alertness to educational tasks because of heightened alertness to environmental stimuli.
- This disabling condition results in an adverse effect on the child's educational performance to the extent that special education is needed. *Note*: The adverse effect on educational performance is not limited to academics. It can include impairments in other aspects of school functioning, such as behavior, as well.

More OHI Eligibility Information

- The requirements for determining an OHI vary from state to state.
- Some states and school districts will require a physician's medical diagnosis or confirmation of ADD or ADHD.
- Some states do not require a medical diagnosis or physician's statement in determining that a child has an attention deficit disorder for educational purposes.
- Check with your local school district regarding specific requirements for an OHI diagnosis.
- The school's multidisciplinary team will gather relevant information, and determine through their evaluation process and school-based assessment if the student meets OHI criteria.
- See *Lists 1.15, 1.16, 1.18, and 6.4* for more information related to this topic.

More Key Features of IDEA

- The IEP must incorporate important considerations regarding the students' strengths, participation in district and state assessments, and special factors, such as behavioral factors and needs, proficiency in English, and language needs.
- When disciplinary actions are being considered involving removal of the student to the degree that it is considered a "change of placement," there must first be a "manifestation determination review" by the IEP team. The results of this review determine the disciplinary action the school district is permitted to impose on the student. See List 6.6 for what constitutes a "change of placement" and more detailed information on this topic.
- Under IDEA, students who qualify for special education and related services receive an IEP that must meet these conditions:
  - Tailored to meet the unique needs of the student
  - Developed by a multidisciplinary team, which includes the child's parents
  - Be the guide for every educational decision made for the student
  - Reviewed by the team annually

- Children found eligible under IDEA are entitled to the specially designed instruction at no cost to parents, including special education programs, related services, modifications, and accommodations the IEP team determines are needed for educational benefit.
- The IEP is a detailed plan. It specifies the programs, supports, services, and supplementary aids that are to be provided and requires measurable annual goals and reports on progress.
- At all stages, parents are an integral part of the process and team, and the IEP does not go into effect until parents sign and thereby agree to the plan.
- The IEP process begins when a student is referred for evaluation because of a suspected disability, and a process of formal evaluation is initiated to determine eligibility for special education and related services.
- IDEA 2004 requires that the evaluation obtain accurate information about the student's academic, developmental, and functional skills.
- See *Lists 6.4 and 6.6* for more on IDEA and IEPs.

Keep the Following in Mind Regarding IDEA and Students with ADHD

- Some students with ADHD qualify for special education and related services under other disability categories besides OHI. Some meet eligibility criteria under the category of specific learning disability (SLD) and some may qualify under the emotional disturbance (ED) category. If a student has learning disabilities or behavioral or emotional needs, those should all be addressed in the IEP regardless of the category under which he or she is found eligible.
- IDEA 2004 makes it clear that eligibility for special education is not based on academic impairment alone. The student is not required to have failing grades or test scores to qualify for special education and related services. Students are eligible for a free appropriate public education even though the child has not failed or been retained in a course or grade and is advancing from grade to grade.
- Chris Dendy (2011) points out the important fact that students with ADHD may be passing classes primarily because of medication or herculean efforts of the student, parent, or tutors. If those supports are withdrawn, academic performance may decline significantly. Educators need to take that into consideration.
- Other factors related to the disorder that are impairing the student's educational performance to a significant degree (social, behavioral, executive function–related difficulties) must be considered as well when determining eligibility.

Section 504 of the Rehabilitation Act of 1973

Section 504 protects the rights of people with disabilities against discrimination and applies to any agency that receives federal funding, which includes all public schools, charter schools, and many private schools.

- Children with ADHD who may not be eligible for services under IDEA (and do not qualify for special education) are often able to receive accommodations, supports, and related services in school under a Section 504 plan.

- As noted earlier, Section 504 has different criteria for eligibility, procedures, safeguards, and services available to children than IDEA.
- Section 504 protects students if they fit the following criteria:
  - The student is regarded or has a record of having a physical or mental impairment.
  - The physical or mental impairment substantially limits one or more major life activities, which includes activities such as learning, concentrating, reading, and thinking. *Note*: As with IDEA, this does not necessarily mean poor grades or academic achievement. Other factors, for example, low rate of work production, significant disorganization, off-task behavior, and social or behavioral issues can indicate the substantial negative impact of the disorder on their learning and school functioning.

Section 504 entitles eligible students to the following:

- Reasonable accommodations in the educational program
- Commensurate opportunities to learn as nondisabled peers
- Appropriate interventions within the general education program

Additional points to consider about Section 504:

- The implementation of the plan is primarily the responsibility of the general education school staff.
- The 504 plan could also involve modification of nonacademic times or school environments, for example, cafeteria, recess, and playground.
- Supports under Section 504 might also include the provision of various services (counseling, health services, assistive technology, organizational training and assistance, and speech therapy, for example).

The 504 process differs from an IEP in these ways:

- Is simpler—less bureaucracy and regulations
- Is generally easier to evaluate and determine eligibility
- Requires much less with regard to procedures, paperwork, and so forth

Note: Children who qualify under IDEA eligibility criteria are automatically covered by Section 504 protections. However, the reverse is not true. Even though students found to be ineligible for special education services under IDEA *may* be found eligible under Section 504, they are *not automatically* covered.

504 Accommodations

Section 504 plans should include some accommodations that are deemed most important so the student can have equal opportunity to be successful at school. See *List 6.5* for examples of some common 504 accommodations as well as many more found in lists throughout this book (in sections 2, 3, 4, and 5).

The Americans with Disabilities Act (ADA) and Section 504

- ADA often overlaps and complements Section 504. Although the definitions of an individual with a disability in ADA and Section 504 are identical, ADA is a statute that has broader application than Section 504. This means ADA and its regulations apply to Section 504 (Dendy, 2011).
- ADA was amended in 2008, and is called the Americans with Disabilities Act Amendments Act (or ADAAA).
- ADAAA expanded major life activities to include reading, concentrating, thinking, communicating, and neurological and brain functions.
- ADAAA also provided for a broader and more inclusive interpretation of "substantially limits" that affects determining if a student has a disability under Section 504.
- ADAAA also added that "mitigating measures" that offset the effects of an impairment (such as medication, assistive technology, or accommodations and services) cannot be used in determining whether a student has a disability.
- See *List 6.5* for more on this topic.

Which Is More Advantageous for Students with ADHD—IDEA or Section 504?

- This is a decision that the team (parents and school personnel) must make considering eligibility criteria and the specific needs of the individual student.
- For students with ADHD who have more significant and complex school difficulties, IDEA (and receiving an IEP) is usually preferable for the following reasons:
  - An IEP provides more protections (procedural safeguards, monitoring, accountability, and regulations) with regard to evaluation, frequency of review, parent participation, disciplinary action, and other factors.
  - Specific and measurable goals addressing the student's areas of need are written in the IEP and regularly monitored for progress.
  - There is a much wider range of program options, services, and supports available.
  - IDEA provides funding for programs and services. The school district receives funds for students being served with an IEP. Section 504 is nonfunded and the school district receives no financial assistance for implementation.
- Generally speaking, an IEP carries more weight and is taken more seriously by school staff.
- For students who have milder impairments and do not need special education, a 504 plan is a faster, easier procedure for obtaining accommodations and supports. They can be highly effective for those students whose educational needs can be addressed through adjustments, modifications, and accommodations in the general curriculum and classroom.
- See *Lists 6.4, 6.5, 6.6, and 7.12* for more detailed information on Section 504, IDEA, the special education and IEP process, and other related topics.

Sources and Resources

ADDitude Magazine has a section in every issue on "Your Legal Rights," which provides expert advice and answers to questions about ADHD and the law.

CHADD and *ADDitude Magazine* both have free webinars from experts on a variety of topics, including educational rights of students with ADHD.

Cohen, Matthew. (2009). *A guide to special education advocacy: What parents, clinicians, and advocates need to know*. London: Jessica Kingsley.

Children and Adults with Attention-Deficit/Hyperactivity Disorder (CHADD). (2012). *Educational rights for children with attention-deficit/hyperactivity disorder (ADHD): A primer for parents* (4th ed.) (in both English and Spanish). Retrieved from www.help4adhd.org/documents/NRC_Bilingual_Educational_Rights_Guide_2012.pdf

Dendy, Chris A. Zeigler (2011). *Teaching teens with ADD, ADHD & executive function deficits* (2nd ed.). Bethesda, MD: Woodbine House.

Durheim, Mary, & Dendy, Chris A. Zeigler (2006). *CHADD educator's manual*. Landover, MD: CHADD.

CHADD and the National Resource Center on ADHD information on this topic can be found at these sites:

www.help4adhd.org/en/education/rights
www.help4adhd.org/en/education/rights/504
www.help4adhd.org/en/education/rights/idea
www.help4adhd.org/en/education/rights/iepfav

See other resources at the end of *Lists 6.4, 6.5, and 6.6,* as well as those in *List 7.7*.

Other Organizations and Resources That Address Educational Rights for Children with Disabilities

Center for Parent Information and Resources (CPIR) (http://www.parentcenterhub.org/resources/). This website now contains the information formerly available at National Dissemination Center for Children with Disabilities (NICHCY) and Technical Assistance Alliance for Parent Centers (taalliance.org), which no longer exist.

Council for Exceptional Children (www.cec.sped.org)

Council of Parent Attorneys and Advocates (www.copaa.org)

Family and Advocates Partnership for Education (www.fape.org)

IDEA Partnership (www.ideapartnership.org)

Individuals with Disabilities Act (IDEA) (www.ed.gov/offices/OSERS/IDEA/regs.html)

LD Online (www.ldonline.org)

Learning Disabilities Association of America (http://ldaamerica.org/)

Matt Cohen and Associates (https://mattcohenandassociates.com)

National Association of State Directors of Special Education (www.nasdse.org)

National Center for Learning Disabilities (www.ncld.org)

Parent Advocacy Coalition for Educational Rights (PACER Center) (www.pacer.org)

US Department of Education (on IDEA 2004) (http://idea.ed.gov)

Wrightslaw (www.wrightslaw.com)

6.4 Federal Law IDEA and Special Education

Note: The information in this list and others in this section regarding educational laws and policies are meant as a general guide for parents and educators. Check and clarify with experts from your local and state education agencies.

IDEA is the federal special education law that protects the educational rights of students with disabilities and governs special education. This law has been in effect since 1975, but it has been amended by Congress numerous times over the years. IDEA was reauthorized in 2004 and became effective the following year.

The US Department of Education provides clarification to states and school districts about how to implement IDEA. Some clarifying regulations were issued in 2006 and others at the end of 2008.

Some of the information in this list and the others in this book section related to educational laws may change when new IDEA amendments and regulations take place. This list is meant as a brief overview for reference. It is recommended to obtain more information about the current law and regulations from your state and local school district and other sources (such as those listed in the "Sources and Resources" section of this list).

Basic Information about Special Education Law (IDEA 2004)

- IDEA requires school districts to provide children with disabilities with a free and appropriate public education (FAPE), which means provision of special education and related services necessary for the child to benefit from his or her education.
- The FAPE is to be delivered in the least restrictive setting (LRE). This means that students should be educated and included to the maximum extent appropriate to their individual needs with their typically developing peers.
- An IEP, tailored to the specific needs of the individual student, must be developed for each student who is classified with a disability and who meets eligibility criteria for special education and related services.
- All decisions related to the child's education are to be guided by the IEP, developed by the school's multidisciplinary team, which includes the parents as full participants and members of the team.
- IDEA includes rules and requirements for special education and providing specially designed instruction and related services to meet the individual needs of qualifying children with disabilities at no cost to parents.
- There are thirteen categories of disabilities under which a student who meets the eligibility criteria may qualify for special education and related services. Students with ADHD most commonly are found eligible under the category of other health impaired (OHI). Those with coexisting learning disabilities often qualify under the category of specific learning disabilities (SLD), and some with emotional and behavioral disorders may qualify under the category of emotional disturbance (ED).
- To determine eligibility, the school district must provide a nondiscriminatory comprehensive evaluation, which includes information obtained about the student's developmental and functional skills as well as academics.
- IDEA requires that the disability adversely affect the student's educational performance (that it impairs learning or other areas of functioning) in order for the student to qualify for special education. *The law does not require that a student has*

failed courses or has been retained in a course or a grade in order to be eligible for special education and related services.

- The IEP that is developed by the multidisciplinary team must address all of the identified areas of need. So, if a student with ADHD is found eligible under OHI, SLD, or ED, the IEP should include goals, supports, and accommodations that address the child's identified learning, behavioral, and functional needs.
- IDEA provides a broad array of protections for children with disabilities and their parents. There are a number of rules, regulations, procedural safeguards, and time lines that govern the referral and IEP processes. There are rules and regulations regarding how disputes between parents and the school district are to be handled with regard to the referral, evaluation or any part of the IEP process or placement. Many state laws and rules go beyond the requirement of IDEA. Parents should become familiar with disability laws in their own state because there is some variance among states.
- RTI was introduced in IDEA 2004 as an early intervention within general education—providing at-risk and struggling students with high-quality, research-based interventions to hopefully prevent the need for special education.
- Up to 15 percent of a school district's special education budget may be spent on "early intervening services" (EIS) such as those provided through RTI (*List 6.1*).
- IDEA 2004 created significant changes to how children with suspected learning disabilities are able to be evaluated and found eligible for special education. See "Specific Learning Disabilities Criteria" later in this list as well as in List 6.3. on eligibility criteria under the specific learning disabilities category as well as *List 6.3*.
- There are extensive rules and procedures regarding how schools should promote positive behavioral strategies and interventions (as a preventive measure to avoid behavioral problems) and for how to respond when children with a disability requires disciplinary action for more serious behaviors and breaking of school rules (*Lists 2.17, 6.6*).
- Parents have many rights under the law:
  - Access to their child's educational records, including all testing results
  - Notification of any proposed change in programs or services
  - Revoking consent at any time to their child's participation in special education
  - Due process and other ways to resolve disputes when in disagreement with the school
- To avoid litigation, the law gives parents and schools the right to request an impartial hearing and for a resolution session, which is an alternative to mediation, prior to a due process hearing. Parents have a right to file a due process complaint with their local school district when issues cannot be resolved. An impartial hearing officer hears these cases.
- IDEA requires provision of services and supports for the child to benefit from his or her education, not to maximize the child's potential.
- Special education is a service, not a place, which may include many settings (the regular classroom, a resource room, a special education class placement, or alternative setting). Most students with ADHD with IEPs are served in the general education classroom for at least most of the school day. Placement is a team decision, based on the student's needs.

Related Services

IDEA provides eligible students with related services that are developmental and corrective and other supportive services necessary for them to benefit from special education. These services include, but are not limited to the following:

- Speech-language pathology
- Occupational therapy
- Counseling services
- Psychological services
- Transportation
- Medical services
- School health services
- Parent training and counseling
- Social work services in schools

Referral and Evaluation

- Parents or school personnel may refer a child, requesting an evaluation to determine eligibility for special education and related services.
- Requests for evaluation should be made in writing to the school or district (usually to the principal or director of special education). A referral may be made by parents, school personnel, school district staff, or other persons with knowledge about a student.
- Once a referral is made, the school staff determines whether it believes an evaluation is needed based on a review of the child's functioning and school performance. If so, parents are given written notification of the referral, proposed testing, time lines, and other information. Parents must give informed and written consent to any testing.
- The assessment plan developed by the school's multidisciplinary team must address all areas of suspected disability.
- After parents or guardians are informed of their rights and consent to the assessment plan, the child receives a comprehensive evaluation by the multidisciplinary team of school professionals.
- A variety of nondiscriminatory assessment tools and strategies must be used to gather relevant functional, developmental, and academic information about the child, including information provided by the parent. This information may include among other things any independent educational evaluations by competent professionals that the parents provide.
- The school evaluation must be conducted by qualified professionals who are competent to administer and interpret the results of the particular tests given.
- IDEA 2004 added the requirement that the evaluation is to be conducted in the "language and form most likely to yield accurate information."
- Under IDEA 2004 schools are given sixty calendar days to complete the evaluation from the date parents give their written consent (unless the state law provides otherwise).

- The RTI process and efforts to provide early intervening services may cause issues with regard to the time line for evaluation. See *List 6.1* for more on this topic, as well as the "Sources and Resources" section of this list.
- When more intensive interventions are being implemented as part of the RTI process and EIS, generally there is agreement among parents and teachers to delay opening the sixty-day time line for evaluation. As discussed in *List 6.1,* parents have the right to request an evaluation at any time—even within an RTI system.
- IEPs are to be reviewed annually (or sooner if needed).
- Reevaluation occurs every three years unless the parent and school district agree that a reevaluation is not necessary at this time.
- If there is disagreement about whether a child needs an evaluation, parents or the district have a right to a due process hearing.

Individualized Education Programs (IEPs)

If the student is found to have a qualifying disability that is causing an adverse educational impact to the degree that special education and related services are needed, the IEP is then developed by the IEP team.

IEP Team Members

Writing the IEP is a joint collaborative effort by the IEP team, composed minimally of the following people:

- The child's parents or guardians
- Not fewer than one regular education teacher of the child (if the child is, or may be, participating in the regular education environment)
- Not fewer than one special education teacher or provider of the child
- An individual (usually the school psychologist) who can interpret the instructional implications of the evaluation results
- A local school representative who is qualified to provide or supervise the provision of special education to the child and is knowledgeable about the general education curriculum and about the availability of resources
- Others (at the discretion of the parent or agency) who have knowledge or special expertise regarding the child
- The student with the disability, when appropriate

IEP Contents

IDEA has very specific requirements as to the content of the IEP:

- A statement identifying the child's disability or disabilities
- Present levels of educational performance (academic, developmental, and functional) provided in each area of need, which should be described in such a way that it is a baseline for measuring and determining progress over time
- A statement of how the child's disability affects his or her learning, participation, and progress in the general education curriculum

- Measurable annual goals designed to enable the student to be involved in and make progress in the general education curriculum and meet other needs resulting from the disability
- A description of how the child's progress toward meeting the annual goals will be measured and when periodic reports on the child's progress toward goals will be provided
- A statement of the special education and related services, supplementary aids and services, and any program modifications or supports to be provided to the child or on behalf of the child (such as support for the classroom teacher)
- The extent (if any) to which the child will not participate with nondisabled children in the regular class and other school activities
- A statement of any individual accommodations or modifications that are necessary to measure the academic achievement and functional performance of the child on state and district-wide assessments
- The starting date, frequency, duration, and location of services of all special education, related services, and supplementary aids and supports
- A statement of the assistive technology and assistive technology services the child needs to benefit from his or her education
- Transition goals and services that must be in place no later than by the time the student is sixteen years of age—that is education and training goals to help students with disabilities make a transition to work or further education and independent living after high school (*List 7.5*).

Other Things Regarding IEPs

- When developing an IEP, the team needs to consider the student's strengths, not just deficits, and parent concerns and input about the student's functioning at home and school.
- The team needs to discuss and consider special factors depending on the needs of the child, for example, if the child's behaviors are interfering with his or her learning or the learning of others.
- Parents must be kept informed of their child's progress on IEP goals during the year.

Eligibility for Students with ADHD under OHI or SLD Categories

Most students with ADHD who will qualify for special education will meet eligibility criteria under the disability category of OHI.

OHI Eligibility Criteria

- The child has a chronic or acute health problem. (ADD and ADHD are chronic health problems that are specifically listed in IDEA.)
- The health problem causes "limited strength, vitality, or alertness" in the educational environment, which includes limited alertness to educational tasks because of heightened alertness to environmental stimuli.

- This health problem results in an adverse effect on the child's educational performance to the extent that special education is needed.

Some states and school districts require a medical diagnosis of ADHD and a physician's statement of such to qualify a student under OHI; others do not require it. The following is what the law says about the requirement of a medical evaluation for the purposes of determining a child has a disability, such as ADHD:

> - For educational purposes, local school district policy determines whether a medical evaluation is required. The school may require an evaluation, in which case it must pay for it. Alternatively, the school district may utilize its multidisciplinary team, including a psychologist or other professional qualified to diagnose AD/HD, to make the determination for educational purposes (Cohen, n-d).
> - Under 34 CFR §300.306(c)(1)(i), in interpreting evaluation data for the purpose of determining whether the child is a child with a disability under Part B of the IDEA and the educational needs of the child, the group of qualified professionals and the parent must draw upon information from a variety of sources, including aptitude and achievement tests, parent input, and teacher recommendations, as well as information about the child's physical condition, social or cultural background, and adaptive behavior.
> - Under 34 CFR §300.306(c)(1)(ii), the public agency must ensure that information obtained from all of these sources is documented and carefully considered. There is nothing in the IDEA or the Part B regulations that would prevent a public agency from obtaining a medical diagnosis prior to determining whether the child has a particular disability and the educational needs of the child. Also, there is nothing in the IDEA or the Part B regulations that would prohibit a State from requiring that a medical diagnosis be obtained for purposes of determining whether a child has a particular disability, such as attention deficit disorder/attention deficit hyperactivity disorder or autism, provided the medical diagnosis is obtained at public expense and at no cost to the parents and is not used as the sole criterion for determining an appropriate educational program for the child (US Department of Education, 2011b).

Note: See Question B-2 at this government source below (2011b) for more on this topic.

- See *List 6.3* for more details and information on how students with ADHD may be found eligible for special education and related services under OHI.

Specific Learning Disabilities (SLD) Eligibility Criteria

Many children with ADHD have coexisting learning disabilities (approximately 25 to 50 percent), and those students may meet eligibility criteria under the category of specific learning disability (SLD).

IDEA 2004 and the regulations issued by the Department of Education in 2006 and 2008 changed the way schools can identify students with learning disabilities and find them eligible for special education and related services. According to the law, a state needs to do the following:

- Must not require the use of a severe discrepancy between intellectual ability and achievement for determining whether a child has a specific learning disability
- Must permit the use of a process based on the child's response to scientific, research-based intervention
- May permit the use of other alternative research-based procedures for determining whether a child has a specific learning disability, as defined in 34 CFR 300.8(c)(10)

- RTI was given as an option for states and school districts to use (instead of the traditional discrepancy formula between IQ test scores and achievement test scores) as part of the process for determining whether a child has an SLD and is eligible for special education (*List 6.1*).
- In addition to an RTI option, the 2006 regulations also gave school districts the option of determining a learning disability based on a pattern of strengths and weaknesses in performance, achievement, or both, relative to the age, state-appropriate grade-level standards, or intellectual development. (This is an alternative research-based procedure.)
- Another part of the criteria is that the child does not achieve adequately for his or her age or to meet state-approved grade-level standards in one or more of the following areas, when provided with learning experiences and appropriate instruction:
  - Oral expression
  - Listening comprehension
  - Written expression
  - Basic reading skills
  - Reading fluency skills
  - Reading comprehension
  - Mathematics calculation
  - Mathematics problem solving
- See the US Department of Education, Office of Special Education Programs document "Identification of Specific Learning Disabilities" (in the "Sources and Resources" section) for complete details on this topic.
- See *List 6.3* for more information on IDEA and a comparison of Section 504 and IDEA with regard to advantages and disadvantages for students with ADHD.
- See *List 6.1* for the importance of RTI as of IDEA 2004 and its impact on struggling students.
- See *List 6.6* for information about manifestation determination reviews and disciplinary safeguards for students with ADHD or other disabilities under the law.

Sources and Resources

Center on Response to Intervention at American Institutes for Research (www.rti4success.org/related-rti-topics/special-education)

CHADD and *ADDitude Magazine* have wonderful webinars from experts on a variety of topics, including educational rights of students with ADHD.

Cohen, Matthew. (2009). *A guide to special education advocacy: What parents, clinicians and advocates need to know*. London: Jessica Kingsley.

Cohen, Matthew. (n-p). The child advocate AD/HD under IDEA. *Child Advocate*. Retrieved from www.childadvocate.net/adhd_and_idea.htm

Dendy, Chris A. Zeigler (2011). *Teaching teens with ADD, ADHD & executive function deficits*, 2nd edition. Bethesda, MD: Woodbine House

Durheim, Mary, & Dendy, Chris A. Zeigler (2006). *CHADD educator's manual*. Landover, MD: CHADD.

CHADD and the National Resource Center on ADHD information on this topic can be found at these sites:
www.help4adhd.org/en/education/rights

www.help4adhd.org/en/education/rights/504
www.help4adhd.org/en/education/rights/idea
www.help4adhd.org/en/education/rights/iepfav

Children and Adults with Attention-Deficit/Hyperactivity Disorder (CHADD). (2012). *Educational rights for children with attention-deficit/hyperactivity disorder (ADHD): A primer for parents* (4th ed.) (in both English and Spanish). Retrieved from www.help4adhd.org/documents/NRC_Bilingual_Educational_Rights_Guide_2012.pdf

IRIS Center Peabody College Vanderbilt University (http://iris.peabody.vanderbilt.edu/)

Klatz, Mary Beth. (2006). Response to intervention (RTI): A primer for parents. National Association for School Psychologists. NASP Resources. Retrieved from www.nasponline.org/resources/factsheets/rtiprimer.aspx

National Center for Learning Disabilities (www.ncld.org)

Positive Behavioral Interventions and Supports (US Department of Education's Office of Special Education Programs [OSEP] Technical Assistance Center on PBIS) (www.pbis.org)

RTI Action Network (www.rtinetwork.org)

RTI Central (www.rtictrl.org)

US Department of Education. (2011a). Building the legacy: IDEA 2004. Identification of specific learning disabilities. Retrieved from http://idea.ed.gov/explore/view/p/%2Croot%2Cdynamic%2CTopicalBrief%2C23%2C

US Department of Education. (2011b). Building the legacy: IDEA 2004 Q & A: Questions and answers on IEPs, evaluations, and reevaluations. Retrieved from http://idea.ed.gov/explore/view/p/,root,dynamic,QaCorner,3,

Other Organizations and Resources on IDEA, Special Education, and Educational Rights for Children with Disabilities

Center for Parent Information and Resources (CPIR) (www.parentcenterhub.org/resources/). This website now contains the information that was formerly available at National Dissemination Center for Children with Disabilities (NICHCY) and Technical Assistance Alliance for Parent Centers (talliance.org), which no longer exist.

Council for Exceptional Children (www.cec.sped.org)

Council of Parent Attorneys and Advocates (www.copaa.org)

Family and Advocates Partnership for Education (www.fape.org)

Federation for Children with Special Needs (http://fcsn.org)

IDEA Partnership (www.ideapartnership.org)

Individuals with Disabilities Act (IDEA) (www.ed.gov/offices/OSERS/IDEA/regs.html)

LD Online (www.ldonline.org)

Learning Disabilities Association of America (http://ldaamerica.org/)

Matt Cohen and Associates (https://mattcohenandassociates.com)

National Association of State Directors of Special Education (www.nasdse.org)

National Center for Learning Disabilities (www.ncld.org)

Parent Advocacy Coalition for Educational Rights (PACER Center) (www.pacer.org)

US Department of Education. (n.d.). OSEP building the legacy: IDEA 2004. Retrieved from http://idea.ed.gov

Wrightslaw (www.wrightslaw.com)

6.5 Section 504 Law and How It Applies to Students with ADHD

Note: The information in this list and others in this section regarding educational laws and policies are meant as a general guide for parents and educators. Check and clarify with experts from your local and state education agencies.

Section 504 of the Rehabilitation Act of 1973 is one of the federal laws that protect the rights of children and teens with disabilities (including ADHD). Students with ADHD may be eligible for Section 504 accommodations and supports if they meet eligibility criteria. Many students with ADHD are served under 504 plans.

When a child with ADHD is evaluated under IDEA (*Lists 6.3, 6.4*) and does not qualify for special education and related services under IDEA, often that child is found eligible to receive accommodations, supports, supplementary, and related aids or services, depending on need, under a Section 504 plan. Parents and teachers of students with ADHD need to be familiar with both IDEA and Section 504.

What Is Section 504?

- Section 504 of the Rehabilitation Act of 1973 (known as *Section 504*) is a federal civil rights statute that prohibits discrimination against people with disabilities.
- This civil rights law protects the rights of individuals with disabilities in programs and activities that receive federal financial aid and is enforced by the US Office of Civil Rights (OCR).
- It applies to any agency that receives federal funding, which includes all public schools and many charter, private schools, technical schools, colleges, and others.
- Children who qualify for services under IDEA eligibility criteria are automatically covered under Section 504. However, the reverse is not true.
- Whereas IDEA is federally funded, Section 504 is not. School districts or agencies receive no financial assistance for implementing it.
- Even though there is no funding for providing services required under Section 504, the OCR can withhold federal funds to any programs or agencies (for example, school districts) that do not comply.
- Section 504 provides protection for qualifying students with disabilities at school, requiring schools to provide them with needed accommodations and services so that they can receive an education to the extent as those students without a disability.
- Section 504 is intended to level the playing field for students with disabilities so that their needs are met as adequately as those of nondisabled students.

Many of the same protections under Section 504 are also mandated under IDEA:

- A free and appropriate public education (FAPE) to every qualified person with a disability, provided in the least restrictive environment (LRE) with their nondisabled peers to the maximum extent appropriate to their individual needs
- Supports (adaptations, accommodations, modifications, related and supplementary aids and services), based on their educational needs, to enable each student an equal opportunity to participate and learn in the general education program

- Equal opportunity to participate in all academic, nonacademic, and extracurricular activities the school has to offer
- A free, nondiscriminatory evaluation
- Procedural due process
- A plan to support the student in general education

Section 504 also differs considerably from IDEA in educational provisions and protections for students (criteria for eligibility, procedures, safeguards, and so forth). See *Lists 6.3, 6.4, and 6.6,* as well as the "Sources and Resources" section of this list.

Section 504 Eligibility Criteria

- Eligibility for protections under Section 504 is based on the existence of an identified physical or mental condition or impairment that "substantially limits a major life activity." See examples of major life activities under Changes to Section 504 as of ADA Amendments Act of 2008.
- Section 504 defines an individual with a disability as any person who (1) has a physical or mental impairment, (2) has a record of, or (3) is regarded as having such an impairment.

What Is the Americans with Disabilities Act (ADA) Amendments Act of 2008 (ADAAA)?

- Another US law that protects individuals with disabilities is the Americans with Disabilities Act (ADA), a civil rights law that was amended in 2008 and called the ADA Amendments Act of 2008 (ADAAA).
- These amendments made significant changes to ADA of 1990. Because these two civil rights statutes (Section 504 and ADAAA) are interpreted together, these 2008 amendments also apply to Section 504's rules, definition of who has a disability, eligibility criteria, and other factors.
- These changes under ADAAA have a direct impact on Section 504 and how it affects students with ADHD.

Changes to Section 504 as of ADA Amendments Act of 2008 (ADAAA)

There have been significant changes to Section 504 eligibility criteria as of the ADAAA:

- "Major life activity" has been expanded to include additional examples of major life activities, such as reading, concentrating, thinking, communicating, interacting with others, and major bodily functions. These include neurological and brain functions.
- Language was added: "An impairment that is episodic or in remission is a disability if it would substantially limit a major life activity when active." So the limitation of a major life activity doesn't need to be constant.
- "Mitigating measures" can no longer be used when evaluating whether a person has a disability (except for the use of contact lenses or glasses that correct a vision problem). Mitigating measures, which offset the effects of an impairment include,

among other things, medication, hearing aids, and learning adaptations (such as assistive technology or accommodations).

- Schools must now evaluate under Section 504 without considering the impact of these mitigating measures (for example, a student's use of medication, recorded books, reading assistance, or extra time on tests) in determining whether a student has a disability.
- These changes broadened the definition of *disability* and enable more people with disabilities to be found eligible for protections under this civil antidiscrimination law, including students with ADHD.

Important Information about Section 504

- Students with disabilities (including ADHD) are not automatically covered under Section 504. As with IDEA, there must be a substantial negative impact of the disorder on the student's learning and school functioning in order to be found eligible for a 504 accommodation plan. This is a school team determination after assessment whether or not the student's disability is causing a substantial negative impact.
- As with IDEA, under Section 504 a student does not need to have failing grades or low academic achievement to show the disability is substantially limiting learning or other major life function. Other factors, such as a low rate of work production, significant disorganization, or social or behavioral issues can indicate the substantial negative impact in the school environment.
- Section 504 entitles eligible students to reasonable accommodations in the educational program, commensurate opportunities to learn as nondisabled peers, and appropriate interventions within the general education program.
- The implementation of the plan is primarily the responsibility of the general education school staff.
- The 504 plan could also involve modification of nonacademic times, such as the lunchroom, recess, and physical education.
- Supports under Section 504 might also include the provision of such services as counseling, health, organizational assistance, and assistive technology.
- In contrast to the IEP, the 504 process is simpler, has less bureaucracy and fewer regulations, is generally easier to evaluate and determine eligibility, and requires much less with regard to procedures, paperwork, and so forth.

504 Accommodations

Section 504 plans include some accommodations that are deemed most important for a student to have an equal opportunity to be successful at school. They do not include everything that might be helpful for a student, just reasonable supports that generally the teacher is to provide. Lists throughout this book, particularly the academic, behavioral, instructional, environmental, and other executive function–related topics (such as in organization, time management, and working memory) in sections 2 through 5 have many possible accommodations and supports that can be included as needed for a student with ADHD. Following are a few examples of some possible 504 plan accommodations:

- Preferential seating (near the teacher or a good role model, away from distractions)
- Breaking long-term projects and work assignments into shorter tasks

- Audio recordings of books
- Reduced homework assignments
- Extended time on tests
- Receiving a copy of class notes from a designated note taker
- Cueing and prompting before transitions and changes of activity
- Frequent breaks and opportunities for movement
- Assistance with organization of materials and work space
- Assistive technology, such as access to a computer or portable word processor for written work and a calculator for math computation
- A peer buddy to clarify directions
- A peer tutor
- Use of daily and weekly notes or a monitoring form between home and school for communication about school performance

Sources and Resources

CHADD, *ADDitude Magazine,* and other ADHD organizations and resources often provide webinars (many of them free) from experts on a variety of topics, including educational rights of students with ADHD.

Children and Adults with Attention-Deficit/Hyperactivity Disorder (CHADD). (2012). *Educational rights for children with attention-deficit/hyperactivity disorder (ADHD): A primer for parents* (4th ed.) (in both English and Spanish). Retrieved from www.help4adhd.org/documents/NRC_Bilingual_Educational_Rights_Guide_2012.pdf

Cohen, Matthew. (2009). *A guide to special education advocacy: What parents, clinicians and advocates need to know*. London: Jessica Kingsley.

Dendy, Chris A. Zeigler (2011). *Teaching teens with ADD, ADHD & executive function deficits, second edition*. Bethesda, MD: Woodbine House.

Durheim, Mary. (n.d.). A parent's guide to section 504 in public schools. Retrieved from www.greatschools.org/special-education/legal-rights/868-section-504

Durheim, Mary, & Dendy, Chris A. Zeigler (2006). *CHADD educator's manual*. Landover, MD: CHADD.

Rief, Sandra (2010). *Section 504: Classroom accommodations*. Port Chester, NY: National Professional Resources. (laminated guide)

The National Resource Center on ADHD (help4adhd) is an excellent source of information on Section 504, IDEA, and the educational rights of students with ADHD. See www.help4adhd.org/en/education/rights/504 and www.help4adhd.org/en/education/rights/WWK4.

Zirkel, Perry A. (2009). What does the law say? New section 504 student eligibility standards. *Teaching Exceptional Children, 41*(4), 68–71.

Other Organizations and Resources for Information on Section 504

See those listed at the end of *List 6.4* under "Other Organizations and Resources on IDEA, Special Education, and Educational Rights for Children with Disabilities," which also provides more information regarding Section 504.

6.6 Disciplining Students with Disabilities under IDEA

Note: The information in this list and others in this section regarding educational laws and policies are meant as a general guide for parents and educators. Check and clarify with experts from your local and state education agencies.

IDEA addresses the disciplinary action schools are allowed to take when a child with disabilities violates a local code of student conduct. There are protections for students with disabilities when certain criteria are met under the law. Because students with ADHD often have behavior difficulties resulting in disciplinary action, such as school suspensions, it is important for parents and school personnel to be aware of and understand this section of the law.

This list is a summary of what is current regarding IDEA's regulations on discipline. It is highly recommended to read more in depth information directly from the law in Part B of IDEA from §§300.530 through 300.536, and in sources such as those listed in the "Sources and Resources" section of this list. Also, because codes of conduct vary, parents should be familiar with policies of their child's school district with regard to codes of conduct and consequences for breaking them.

Note: The law refers to school districts as local education agencies (LEA). *Schools, school districts,* and *LEAs* are terms used interchangeably in this book.

Removal from School (Suspensions and Expulsions)

The following applies to children with disabilities:

- A child may be removed to an appropriate interim alternative educational setting, another setting, or suspension for not more than ten school days in a row—to the extent applied to children without disabilities. During a removal of up to ten school days in one school year, schools do not need to provide the child with special education services as long as they also do not provide educational services to children without disabilities who are similarly removed.
- Schools have the authority to make additional removals of the child as long as it is not for more than ten school days in a row in a school year and if those removals do not constitute a "change of placement."
- A change of placement means the removal is for more than ten consecutive school days or if the child has had a series of removals that constitute a pattern (which is determined on a case-by-case basis by the school district).
- A pattern of removals exists in these circumstances:
  - The series of removals total more than ten school days in a school year.
  - The child's behavior is substantially similar to the child's behavior in previous incidents that resulted in the series of removals.
  - Additional factors exist, such as the length of each removal, the total amount of time the child has been removed, and the proximity of the removals to one another.
- The parent may request a due process hearing if there is disagreement with the LEA about the removal of a student.

- On the date when the decision is made to make a removal that constitutes a change of placement because of a child's violation of a code of student conduct, the parents must be notified by the school district of that decision and provided with the procedural safeguard notice.

What Is a Manifestation Determination Review?

- This is a formal review by the LEA, the parent, and relevant members of the child's IEP team that needs to take place no later than ten school days from the time the school makes the decision to change a student's placement. The LEA must reach a manifestation determination within those ten school days.
- The purpose of the manifestation review is to determine whether or not the child's conduct that resulted in the recommendation for suspension or expulsion (1) was caused by or substantially linked to his or her disability or (2) was a direct result of the school district's failure to implement the child's IEP.
- The manifestation determination review team makes its decision based on a review of all relevant information in the student's file, including the child's IEP, any teacher observations, and any relevant information provided by the parents. In making its determination the review team should consider factors such as the child's school program, environmental factors; the child's home factors; the child's mental, physical, and developmental challenges; and the child's discipline history.
- If the team determines that the behavior resulting in violating the code of conduct was a direct result of the school's failure to implement the child's IEP, it must take immediate steps to remedy those deficiencies.
- If the team finds the child's misconduct was because of or had a direct and substantial relationship to his or her disability, then the team needs to immediately conduct a functional behavioral assessment (FBA) if one had not already been conducted and to write a behavioral intervention plan (BIP), unless one already exists. If the BIP does already exist, then the team needs to review and modify it, as needed.
- Placement for the student with disabilities when the review does determine that one of these two conditions occurred requires that the child be returned to the placement from which he or she was removed except when (1) the behavioral infraction involved special circumstances of weapons, drugs, or serious bodily injury or (2) the parents and school agree to change the child's placement as part of the modification of the BIP.
- When the manifestation review finds that the behavior resulting in removal was not a direct result of the LEA's failure to implement the child's IEP, and the violation of the code of conduct is not substantially linked to the child's disability, then school personnel have the authority to apply the same disciplinary procedures as would be applied to a child without disabilities (although any special education and related services that is required must still be provided).

What Is a Functional Behavior Assessment (FBA)?

- FBA is a problem-solving process for determining the causes and functions of a student's problem behavior, the settings or environments most likely for those specific behaviors to occur, and the consequences that result from the misbehaviors

"An FBA is a structured method for gathering data about the circumstances and consequences of the child's behavior to identify patterns or causes of the behavior" (Cohen, 2009, p. 183).

- "FBA is the process of gathering and analyzing information about a student's behavior and accompanying circumstances in order to determine the purpose or intent of the actions. This investigation is designed to help educators: determine the appropriateness of the present educational placement and services, and whether changes would help the student display more acceptable behavior; identify positive interventions that would reduce the undesirable behavior; and identify appropriate behaviors to be substituted in the place of the inappropriate ones." (McIntyre, 2014).
- An FBA requires examining the antecedents (conditions that exist or events that may be identified as triggers to the problem behaviors). Antecedents involve any number of factors (for example, environmental, physical, performance and skill demands, teacher-student interactions) that precede the problem behavior. By identifying the antecedents, they may then be adjusted to prevent or reduce the reoccurrence of the misbehavior in the future (see *List 2.11*).
- The FBA also looks at the consequences that occur (positive and negative) as a result of the misbehavior. *Note*: When problematic behaviors occur repeatedly, something is reinforcing or sustaining that behavior. In other words, the consequences (for example, classmates' laughter and attention, being sent out of the classroom) are actually meeting a function or need of that student (such as, for attention, for escaping an unpleasant task) and reinforcing the problem behavior. The data gathered from the FBA can help in determining whether the reactions to the behavior are improving the behavior or making it worse.
- By observing and examining these factors in the classroom and other school settings, a BIP is then developed specific to that student.
- See *Lists 2.9, 2.11, and 2.17* for more related information.

What Is a Behavioral Intervention Plan (BIP)?

- Once the IEP team has conducted the FBA, the information is used to develop a behavioral intervention plan that specifies what behaviors are being targeted for change and how that will be carried out.
- The BIP is designed with a focus on using proactive strategies and interventions to avoid and reduce the likelihood of problematic behavior, teaching the student appropriate strategies and skills.
- The team also identifies positive reinforcers (rewards) to use with the student in the implementation of a behavioral plan that are meaningful and motivating to the individual student (*List 2.7*).
- Corrective consequences appropriate to the student's disability are included in the plan and need to be implemented by those adults responsible for disciplining the student (*List 2.1*).
- The BIP is a very clear plan to address the problem behavior(s). It contains specific information, such as previously implemented interventions and whether they were or were not effective in changing the behavior, a description of the behavior(s) to be targeted, the function of the behavior, what behaviors will be taught to the student to replace the inappropriate behaviors, who will be involved in the interventions,

procedures to be followed, how behavioral changes will be measured, a schedule for doing so, and so forth.

- As one of the leading special education law experts, attorney Matt Cohen (2009, p. 185) points out, "In developing behavioral intervention strategies, it is critical to recognize that many students may lack the emotional, behavioral, or social skill that is necessary to display the desired behavior. The student may require training or assistance in developing the skill, whether through provision of specified skills training, counseling, modeling of behavior, participation in groups with other students to role play or practice the behavior, and/or ongoing constructive feedback and support from staff."
- See *List 2.9* for more on FBAs and BIPS.

Case-by-Case Determination

- School personnel may consider any unique circumstances on a case-by-case basis when determining whether a change of placement is appropriate for a child with a disability who violates a code of student conduct.

Services for Students with a Change of Placement

A child with a disability who is removed from his or her current placement (long-term suspension or expulsion) must get the following:

- Continue to receive educational services so as to enable the child to continue to participate in the general education curriculum, although in another setting, and to progress toward meeting the goals set out in his or her IEP.
- Receive, as appropriate, an FBA and behavioral intervention services and modifications that are designed to address the behavior violation so that it does not recur.

What Are "Special Circumstances" under the Law?

School personnel may remove a student to an interim alternative educational setting for not more than forty-five school days without regard to whether the behavior is determined to be a manifestation of the child's disability if the child does one of the following:

- Carries a weapon to or possesses a weapon at school, on school premises, or to or at a school function under the jurisdiction of a state or local education agency
- Knowingly possesses or uses illegal drugs or sells or solicits the sale of a controlled substance while at school, on school premises, or at a school function under the jurisdiction of a state or local education agency
- Has inflicted serious bodily injury on another person while at school, on school premises, or at a school function under the jurisdiction of a state or local education agency

Note: There is more clarification directly in the law regarding the definition of serious bodily injury and dangerous weapons.

The Right to Due Process and Appeal

- The parent of a child with a disability who disagrees with any decision regarding placement or the manifestation determination or a school district that believes that maintaining the current placement of the child is likely to result in injury to the child or others may appeal the decision by requesting a hearing.
- Whenever a hearing is requested, the parents or the LEA involved in the dispute must have an opportunity for an impartial due process hearing.
- The state or LEA is responsible for arranging the expedited due process hearing, which must occur within twenty school days of the date the complaint requesting the hearing is filed.
- Resolving disputes through alternative means is recommended when possible, such as through a resolution meeting or mediation.

Protections for Students Who Do Not Have IEPs

The discipline procedures under IDEA 2004 also contain the provision of a "basis of knowledge" that would apply under certain circumstances for a child who has not been determined to be eligible for special education and related services. If that child engaged in behavior that violated a code of student conduct, he or she may be protected under this section of the law if the situation was such that the LEA had knowledge that the student was a child with a disability before the behavior that resulted in the disciplinary action occurred. This basis of knowledge would apply under the following circumstances:

- The parent of the child expressed concern in writing to supervisory or administrative school district personnel or a teacher of the child expressed concern that the child is in need of special education and related services.
- The parent of the child requested an evaluation of the child.
- The teacher of the child or other school personnel expressed specific concerns about a pattern of behavior demonstrated by the child directly to the director of special education or to other supervisory personnel of the LEA.

This would not apply if the parent has not allowed an evaluation, has refused services, or if the child has been evaluated and determined to not be a child with a disability.

Sources and Resources

Center for Effective Collaboration and Practice (http://cecp.air.org/fba/)

Center for Parent Information and Resources (CPIR) (www.parentcenterhub.org/resources/)

Center on Response to Intervention at American Institutes for Research (www.rti4success.org/related-rti-topics/special-education)

CHADD and the National Resource Center on ADHD (www.help4adhd.org)

CHADD and *ADDitude Magazine* have wonderful webinars from experts on a variety of topics, including educational rights of students with ADHD.

Children and Adults with Attention-Deficit/Hyperactivity Disorder (CHADD). (2012). *Educational rights for children with attention-deficit/hyperactivity disorder (ADHD): A primer for parents* (4th ed.) (in both English and Spanish). Retrieved from www.help4adhd.org/documents/NRC_Bilingual_Educational_Rights_Guide_2012.pdf

Cohen, Matthew. (2009). *A guide to special education advocacy: What parents, clinicians and advocates need to know*. London: Jessica Kingsley.

Cohen, Matthew. (2013). The *Child Advocate* AD/HD under IDEA. *The Child Advocate*. Retrieved from www.childadvocate.net/adhd_and_idea.htm

Council for Exceptional Children (www.cec.sped.org)

Council of Parent Attorneys and Advocates (www.copaa.org)

Dendy, Chris A. Zeigler (2011). *Teaching teens with ADD, ADHD & executive function deficits, Second Edition*. Bethesda, MD: Woodbine House.

Durheim, Mary, & Dendy, Chris A. Zeigler (2006). *CHADD educator's manual*. Landover, MD: CHADD.

Family and Advocates Partnership for Education (www.fape.org)

Federation for Children with Special Needs (http://fcsn.org)

IDEA and US Department of Education (http://idea.ed.gov/). Federal site for information about the Individuals with Disabilities Education Act (IDEA).

IDEA Partnership (funded by the US Department of Education Office of Special Education Programs) informs families and educators about IDEA and strategies to improve educational outcomes for students with disabilities (www.ideapartnership.org).

Individuals with Disabilities Act (IDEA) (www.ed.gov/offices/OSERS/IDEA/regs.html)

IRIS Center Peabody College Vanderbilt University (http://iris.peabody.vanderbilt.edu/)

LD Online (www.ldonline.org)

Learning Disabilities Association of America (http://ldaamerica.org/)

Matt Cohen and Associates (https://mattcohenandassociates.com)

McIntyre, Tom. (2014). Functional behavioral assessments (FBA). Retrieved from www.behavioradvisor.com/FBA.html

National Association of State Directors of Special Education (www.nasdse.org)

National Center for Learning Disabilities (www.ncld.org)

Parent Advocacy Coalition for Educational Rights (PACER Center) (www.pacer.org)

Positive Behavioral Interventions and Supports (US Department of Education's Office of Special Education Programs [OSEP] Technical Assistance Center on PBIS) (www.pbis.org)

US Department of Education, OSEP. (n.d.). Building the legacy: IDEA 2004. Retrieved from http://idea.ed.gov

Wrightslaw (www.wrightslaw.com)

Section 7

Understanding, Supporting, and Improving Outcomes for Children and Teens with ADHD

Contents

Please note that a lot of the content of these lists has been adapted and updated from my other books, published by Jossey-Bass/Wiley, which you may be interested in exploring for further information, tools, and strategies:

Rief, S. (2003). *The ADHD book of lists: A practical guide for helping children and teens with attention deficit disorders*. San Francisco: Jossey-Bass.

Rief, S. (2005). *How to reach & teach children with ADD/ADHD: Practical techniques, strategies and interventions* (2nd ed.). San Francisco: Jossey-Bass.

Rief, S. (2008). *The ADD/ADHD checklist: A practical reference for parents and teachers* (2nd ed.). San Francisco: Jossey-Bass.

Rief, Sandra, & Heimburge, Julie. (2006). *How to reach & teach all children in the inclusive classroom* (2nd ed.). San Francisco: Jossey-Bass.

Rief, Sandra & Stern, Judith (2010). *The Dyslexia Checklist: A Practical Reference for Parents and Teachers*. San Francisco: Jossey-Bass.

7.1 The Necessity of a Team Approach

The success of children and teens with ADHD is dependent on team effort. It is critical that in the diagnostic process as well as in any treatment and intervention provided to have teamwork, collaboration, and close communication among all parties: home, school, physician, and other service providers.

The Diagnostic Process

- Parents provide information regarding their child's history (medical, school, family) and behaviors (past and present) through interviews, rating forms, and questionnaires.
- Classroom teachers and other school personnel directly working with the student or observing the child's functioning in various school settings provide their observations and data regarding the student's symptoms and school functioning.
- A qualified, licensed physician, psychologist, or other medical or mental health professional evaluates the child for ADHD using the information and data provided by parents or other caregivers and the school.
- Eligibility for special education, related services, and accommodations may be conducted by the school's multidisciplinary assessment team, which may involve a number of school district professionals: school psychologist, special educator or other learning specialist, speech-language therapist, school nurse, occupational therapist, or others.
- For more information on the diagnostic process, see *Lists 1.14 through 1.18 and 6.3–6.5.*

The Treatment Plan

- The most effective approach in treating ADHD is multimodal, involving a number of interventions from a variety of different professionals and service providers (at school and outside of school). For more on multimodal treatment, see *Lists 1.19, 1.20, 1.21, 1.22, 7.6, 7.7.*
- School interventions are generally provided through a variety of school professionals and other resources that may include general and special education teachers, school counselor, social worker, psychologist, nurse, speech-language therapist, adapted physical education, occupational therapist, administrators, aides (instructional, guidance, management), other staff and school mentors, tutors, and volunteers (peer, cross-age, parent, community).
- Medical intervention, which is often part of the treatment for ADHD, may be provided by pediatricians, family practitioners, child psychiatrists, neurologists, or other licensed professionals who are able to prescribe medication.
- It is important for the child or teen to participate in activities that build on his or her interests and strengths and provide an emotional and physical outlet. This may involve the support of athletic coaches, youth group leaders, scout leaders, mentors, or instructors working with the child or teen in extracurricular activities.
- The child or teen may be involved in other treatments and interventions to address specific needs, among them, counseling or behavior therapy, social skills training, private academic tutoring, and ADHD coaching.

- Parent training groups may be provided by various community professionals or other trained facilitators in behavior management and positive discipline strategies.
- A multidisciplinary team of school professionals will be involved in the development and monitoring of supports and intervention for students in need. This may mean the school's SST or RTI team (*Lists 6.1, 6.2*), or the IEP team for students being evaluated for, or receiving special education and related services. A multidisciplinary team will be involved in any IEP or 504 accommodation plan. If the student is receiving special education, then the school's special education service providers will be involved in the implementation of all aspects of the child's IEP (*Lists 6.3, 6.4, 6.5*).
- Support groups for parents of children and teens with ADHD such as CHADD (Children and Adults with Attention Deficit/Hyperactivity Disorder; www.chadd.org) are composed of a number of people in the community, both parents and professionals, who can serve as a resource and support, a very helpful intervention for parents.

More about the Team Approach

- A child or teen taking medication requires close and ongoing monitoring and communication among the teachers, parents, and physician. If there is a school nurse, he or she is often the liaison in this communication process regarding medication management (*List 1.21*).
- Most K–12 students with ADHD require close communication and monitoring between home and school to be successful. Teachers need to keep parents well informed about work assignments, upcoming tests, and projects; how the student is performing and keeping up with daily work; as well as behavior and other issues. Parents need to communicate with teachers regarding how the student is functioning at home, the child's stress level, and other issues. In addition, parents need to stay on top of monitoring that homework is being done and following through with any home-school plans (for example, to aid and reinforce behavior, work production, and organization skills). See *Lists 2.9, 2.17, 4.9, 4.10, 7.2, 7.3,* and home-school communication and monitoring forms (A-2, A-3, A-4, A-5, A-6, A-7, A-8, A-18, A-19, A-20) in the appendix.
- Most students with ADHD will be educated in general education classrooms. Some receive special education services, whereas others do not. Collaboration and consultation between special education and classroom teachers regarding effective strategies and accommodations is very helpful in addressing the child's needs.
- The child or teen must be included in the team effort. Once students are old enough, they need to learn about ADHD and understand the reason for the treatments and interventions. If they are taking medication, they need to understand what it does and does not do. Teens need to be involved and take an active role in their treatment plan. See the "Sources and Resources" section of this list for some suggested books written for children and teens with ADHD.
- It is the parent who is ultimately the director or case manager of his or her child's ADHD team of support, coordinating and monitoring the efforts of the team. To ensure that those involved in the child's interventions and treatment are kept informed and updated, parents generally need to oversee that communication is taking place. To make sure that intervention plans are being implemented as designed, parents should be actively involved and monitoring. See the "Sources

and Resources" section of this list for how to help parents of children with ADHD better take on this role of case manager.

- For more related topics (parent advocacy, communication tips, and relationship building between home and school), see *Lists 7.2 and 7.3.*

Sources and Resources

For Parents as Case Managers

Torres, Dulce, Gill, Maureen, & Taylor-Klaus, Elaine. (2013). The parent's role makes a difference, part one in parents as case managers: A road for ADHD management. *Attention Magazine, 20*(5), 14–21.

Resources for Children and Teens about ADHD

There are lists with several books for children and teens with ADHD, such as those found at these sites:

http://add.about.com/od/adhdresources/a/kidbooks.htm
www.addvance.com/bookstore/children.html
www.addwarehouse.com/shopsite_sc/store/html/children.html

Two excellent books for kids that I recommend:

Dendy, Chris A. Zeigler & Zeigler, Alex. (2003) *A bird's-eye view of life with ADD and ADHD: Advice from young survivors*, 2nd edition. Cedar Bluff, AL: Cherish the Children

Quinn, Patricia, & Stern, Judith. (2009). *Putting on the brakes: Understanding and taking control of your ADD or ADHD* (2nd ed.). Washington, DC: Magination Press.

7.2 Advocacy Tips for Parents

To best advocate for your child, it is essential to become knowledgeable about ADHD, your child's educational needs, and effective strategies, supports, and interventions. You must educate yourself to understand as much as you can about the disorder and research-validated treatments for ADHD.

It is very important to be aware of your child's educational rights under the law and how to communicate with school personnel and navigate within the school system to ensure your child obtains the necessary help for school success. Parents must also learn to do so, as well, with medical and mental health systems and providers involved in their child's care.

None of this is easy. It is time consuming and difficult, but no one is more invested in a child's well-being than you, the parent or guardian. Seek help and guidance. There are many resources to help you. Be confident in your ability and try not to get discouraged. Parents and guardians who are experienced advocating for their child with school and health care systems have acquired their skills out of necessity, over time, and do not give up.

Know Your Child's Educational Rights

- Your child has many educational rights under federal law that are found in the lists in section 6 of this book and in the "Sources and Resources" section at the end of those lists.
- Learn about your child's rights under federal and state laws to a free, appropriate public education, eligibility criteria, procedures, and all of the protections and provisions for students who qualify under IDEA and Section 504 (*Lists 6.3, 6.4, 6.5*).
- Parents have a right to request an evaluation of their child at no charge to them if there is a known or suspected disability they feel is affecting their child's school performance and functioning.
- "A full and comprehensive evaluation is the cornerstone of ensuring that the local school district meets your child's needs. A parent can only advocate for the needs of his or her child if those needs are properly identified and articulated" (Tudisco, 2007, p. 13).
- Schools generally have multidisciplinary teams that may be called a student support team (SST) or something similar and may have a response to intervention (RTI) process in their building (*Lists 6.1, 6.2*). Schools generally request that parents proceed through the school's SST or RTI process before testing for special education is done. This is appropriate and generally recommended. Parents need to know, however, that under the law, referrals to the school district for an evaluation may be made at any time and without the requirement of first completing an SST or RTI process.
- When an IEP process is initiated, there is paperwork from the school district that you will receive regarding procedures, the assessment plan, and your due process rights under the law. If you have any questions, it is important to read the paperwork and ask questions before signing.
- After testing, there will be an IEP meeting at which time the results of the evaluation will be shared with you and other members of the team. Ask for clarification on any of the test data, interpretations, or recommendations you have questions about.
- If your child qualifies for special education or related services, an IEP will be written with specific goals and objectives to address your child's areas of need. You are an

integral part of the team in planning your child's special education program and goals. Be prepared for that IEP meeting in order to give your input and ensure your satisfaction with the goals, objectives, and accommodations designed to address the needs of your child.

- Most students with ADHD who qualify for special education will be in the general education classroom with special supports and services. But, if the team's recommendation is to place your child outside the general education classroom, ask to observe those special education classes or placement. You will want to make sure the program or placement is appropriate. You do not have to accept any services, programs, or placements. Know that you also have the right to discontinue any services or programs at any time.
- Your child might not qualify or need special education programs or services but may be eligible for and benefit from a 504 accommodation plan. If your child receives a 504 plan, be prepared to share the accommodations and supports that you feel are necessary for your child to learn and succeed in school.
- Be aware that there are provisions in the laws for due process and other less adversarial ways of resolving conflicts between parents and the school district.
- Parents have the right to an independent educational evaluation if they disagree with the school district's evaluation.
- There are also disciplinary rights under the law for students with disabilities (*List 6.6*).
- See *Lists 6.1 through 6.6*, and resources listed in the "Sources and Resources" section of those lists and in *List 7.12* for much more on this topic.

Be an Effective Advocate at Team Meetings

- Parents can easily feel uncomfortable at school team meetings discussing their child. These team meetings may involve several members of the school or district staff, and they can feel intimidating. It can also be painful to hear and talk about your child's difficulties.
- Try to enter such meetings with an open mind, cooperative attitude, and problem-solving approach. Be willing to share your opinions, feelings, observations, suggestions, and any information about your child or the rest of the family that may help with planning and intervention.
- Do not be embarrassed to ask questions and request that any unfamiliar language (educational jargon) be explained. Ask for clarification on anything you do not understand. If you need a more thorough explanation of the test results and recommendations, make sure it is provided.
- Be open to what the other team members have to say, but make sure that your concerns are expressed as well. Speak up if you feel that your point of view has not been heard.
- Take notes during meetings. In addition, it is helpful if you come to meetings prepared with a few notes to yourself regarding items you wish to share, discuss, or ask about.
- You are welcome to bring someone with you to meetings. It is most helpful if both parents can attend school meetings together, even if parents are divorced but share custody. Schools frequently work with sensitive family situations and do what they can to communicate and work effectively with parents and guardians.

- Understanding the disorder and how it is impairing your child's school functioning are critical to be able to effectively advocate for his or her needs when sharing at meetings.
- To be an effective advocate for your child, prepare for meetings by trying to learn about the following:
  - How your child is functioning in the classroom and other school settings
  - In what areas your child is struggling—academic, social-emotional, and behavioral
  - The kinds of supports and accommodations that may be helpful and available
  - The goals on your child's IEP (if he or she has one) in order to check that they are being worked on and your child is making progress on those goals.

Maintain Good Records

- Keep a file on your child that includes all copies of testing, reports, IEPs and 504 plans, report cards, health records, immunization, and other important data.
- Include in the file a log of communication with the school and other professionals working with your child:
  - Dates of doctor appointments and medication logs
  - Summaries of conversations and meetings, notification of disciplinary actions and referrals your child received at school, interventions promised to be put into effect, and so forth
- Having the information in a file that is readily accessible will likely come in handy at some time.

More Tips

Robert M. Tudisco, an expert in ADHD and the law, offers this excellent advice (2007):

- "Create a paper trail, and follow up every meeting with a letter that paraphrases your understanding of what took place at the meeting." (p. 14) "Know what you want going in. Define your position early and provide a clinical basis for why it is necessary." (p. 14)
- "Diplomacy will get you everywhere. How parties communicate with each other determines 85 to 90 percent of the process (Tudisco, 2007, p. 14)."

List 7.3 provides communication tips for parents when interfacing with teachers and other school district staff. Here are additional positive communication recommendations from the book, *The Dyslexia Checklist* (Rief & Stern, 2010):

- Regularly monitor your child's school programs and plans as well as his or her progress. Keep in mind that if something is not working, it can always be changed. Communicate your concerns and attempt to solve problems using a cooperative team approach. The best way is to maintain close communication with the school to monitor growth and progress and implement changes and modifications as needed.
- Keep a record of your attempts to reach school or district staff members. If you are unable to get through to someone in a timely manner, contact the supervisor.
- Sometimes there is a fine line between being a steady advocate and being a pest. Ask for what is appropriate. Avoid demands that may be unreasonable. Choose words carefully and avoid antagonism. Many requests can be framed in such a way that they invite discussion rather than refusal.

- Keep in mind that your child is one student in the school. Monitor the way you may be coming across.
- Listen carefully to what teachers have to say. They are often real advocates for your child. If not, maintaining positive communication and providing helpful information may establish a better working relationship.
- Create a good working relationship. Try to see yourself as part of the team. You are asking your child's teachers and school to go the extra mile for your child. Offer your own help and cooperation. It's not only about the letter of the law.
- Remember that the law may ensure that requirements are met, but your tone and manner can help create a strong, positive relationship or an adversarial one with a school. Staff members are more likely to work with you when they feel supported and appreciated.

Know When You Need Additional Support or Services

- Hiring a private consultant to provide an evaluation of your child's learning needs is an important step if your child is unable to get one through the school system or if you believe more information is needed. Clinics, hospitals, and private evaluators in your area should be considered if you decide to have a private evaluation.
- If your child is working privately with a tutor, educational therapist, ADHD coach, or other professional, you may want to bring that person to the school to participate in meetings with the school team.
- Special education advocates, educational consultants, or mental health professionals who have worked with your child may also be helpful supports during a meeting.
- You may want to consider hiring a legal advocate who specializes in education law if you have had a history of difficulty in dealing with the school or district or if you believe that your child is not receiving the educational services to which he or she is entitled (Rief & Stern, 2010).

Ensure the Right Care from Doctors and Other Professionals

- If through your health care plan you are limited as to which doctors your child may see for an ADHD evaluation, be sure that the physician is aware of and follows American Psychiatric Association (APA) and American Academy of Pediatrics (AAP) guidelines in the diagnostic and treatment process (*Lists 1.3, 1.14, 1.15*).
- When seeking professionals in your community, be assertive in checking their qualifications. Look for experience and expertise in treating children with ADHD and coexisting conditions. Be sure you feel comfortable and confident with the clinicians treating your child. They should take the time to listen, address your concerns, and answer your questions and those of your child. If the doctor does not appear committed to a team approach and communicating with you and the school, find someone else (*List 1.14*).
- You will be the case manager, coordinating the efforts and communicating with the various professionals working with and treating your child. It is in your hands to facilitate the necessary communication among parties. For example, if your child is

receiving medication, make sure that the doctor obtains feedback from the school as to the medication effects on symptoms, functioning, and any apparent side effects (*List 1.21*).

Sources and Resources

CHADD has a great deal of resources for parent advocacy (www.chadd.org/Advocacy.aspx) and CHADD's Parent to Parent training program.

Cohen, Matthew. (2009). *A guide to special education advocacy: What parents, clinicians, and advocates need to know*. Philadelphia: Jessica Kingsley.

Jensen, Peter S. (2004). *Making the system work for your child with ADHD*. New York: Guilford Press.

Rief, Sandra & Stern, Judith (2010). *The Dyslexia Checklist: A Practical Reference for Parents and Teachers*. San Francisco: Jossey-Bass.

Tudisco, Robert M. (2007). The four ATES of effective student advocacy: Evaluate, educate, communicate, and advocate. *Attention Magazine, 14*(3), 12–17.

Your state's Parent Training and Information Center (www.parentcenterhub.org/find-your-center/)

7.3 Parent and Teacher Communication and Relations

Tips for Teachers

Establishing open lines of communication between home and school is critical to the success of students with ADHD.

- To build rapport and a positive relationship with parents, make every effort to learn about and recognize the student's individual strengths, interests, and positive characteristics.
- Be able to speak to parents about their child's areas of strength and competence as well as concerns.
- Much closer, frequent, ongoing communication is needed with parents of students with ADHD than is generally necessary with other parents. Determine with parents what system will work best: phone calls, text messages, e-mail, daily or weekly notes, logs, or something else.
- Make yourself easily accessible and let parents know when and how they can best reach you.
- When contacting parents, be prepared to describe how the student is functioning (academically, behaviorally, socially).
- If you are calling a parent to share concerns, always try to have something positive to share with them as well and end on a positive note.
- Be careful not to judge or blame parents and never make assumptions.
- State your observations objectively about the student's performance without labeling the behavior, for example, as "lazy" or "apathetic."
- Ask parents about strategies that have been effective in the past, what they have found to be helpful at home, and their suggestions.
- Show empathy and listen carefully.
- Never recommend to parents that they should medicate their child. Redirect medication questions to their child's physician or the school nurse. If the student has been diagnosed with ADHD and is taking medication, your observations and feedback about the child's functioning during the school day is very important.
- If you note positive or negative changes in a student's behavior and performance, for example, better able to stay on task and complete work, more attentive, notably better self-control, increase or decrease in outbursts and emotional responses, or lethargy, report these observations to parents. Parents need your feedback to share with treating physicians.
- You may suspect that a student has been placed on medication, had a change of prescription, or did not take his or her medication (based on the child's change in behavior, positive or negative). Do not wait for the student's parents to inform you of changes in treatment; they may be waiting to see if you noticed anything different or significant enough to contact them.
- When observing such changes, communicate with parents—for example, "I noticed that Jared had three really good days so far this week. He has been very focused and completed 90 percent of his work. I'm so pleased." Or "I don't know why, but Kelli has been weepy and not wanting to participate in class the past two days. She didn't want to go out for recess either, which is very unusual for her."

- To build a positive relationship with parents, communicate in these ways:
  - In a manner that is respectful and nonjudgmental
  - That you welcome their partnership and all collaborative efforts (school, home, other professionals at school and in the community)
  - Your acknowledgment that they are the experts on their son or daughter
  - That you value their input and any information or insights they can share with you
  - Your sincere interest in understanding their child's needs
  - Your willingness to put forth the extra time and effort to help their child be successful

- See *List 1.21* for sharing your feedback with parents when a child is on medication.
- See *List 4.10* on communicating with parents about homework issues.
- See *Lists 1.17 and 6.2* for communicating concerns and recommending possible evaluation for students who are not as yet diagnosed with ADHD.

Tips for Parents

- Your level of involvement with the school significantly increases when you have a child with any disability or special needs. As a parent of a child with ADHD, you will need to communicate with school staff to a far greater degree than is necessary for most children.
- Most teachers want to help their students succeed in their class and are willing to put forth the extra time and effort to do so. This is especially true when they have a positive, friendly relationship with parents and feel respected and supported by them.
- Let teachers know you are interested, available, and accessible and want to do what is needed to help your child.
- At the beginning of the school year (within the first few weeks), meet with your child's teachers, share information about your child, and establish the best means of communication (phone, e-mail, text, communication notes or a journal between home and school, or other method).
- Ask for suggestions on how you can best help and ways to work together effectively.
- Besides informing teachers early in the year about your child's challenges and needs, be sure to share about your child's strengths and interests and some strategies that have been most successful in the past.
- Some parents find it helpful to provide teachers at the beginning of the year with a brief letter or form with written information introducing their child.
- Communicate closely, openly, and frequently with classroom teachers. Find out as much as you can about how your child is functioning at school and ways you can support him or her at home.
- Keep in mind what is reasonable when making requests. Take into consideration the challenges of teachers trying to meet the individual needs of a classroom of students—a few to several of whom may also have various learning, behavioral, or social-emotional difficulties, requiring the teacher's extra time, attention, and effort.

- When teachers share their perspective about your child or school situations, even if you disagree or find what teachers say upsetting, try to remain calm and polite. After listening carefully, ask specific questions for clarification, and then focus the discussion on solutions to problems.
- Keep discussions constructive and respectful.
- Dr. Edward (Ned) Hallowell (2007, p. 21) offers this expert advice: "Coming fully armed with information and demanding a course of action tends to set up conflict. A more successful approach, and one that generates empathy and mutual respect, is to approach the teacher and the school in a spirit of cooperation." He also suggests that when sharing information about ADHD and your child's needs, "unwrap that information as it is appropriate. Some of it should be shared immediately, so that teachers can get to know your child's needs, but some of it should be shared later, after you have established a strong relationship. A teacher will be more inclined to make the effort to learn about ADHD and your child's needs if she is happily involved and doesn't feel threatened."
- Try to ensure that your son or daughter is coming to school ready to learn: adequate sleep, prepared with books, materials, and homework, and having received medication if it is prescribed.
- Often the best way to establish a positive relationship with the school is to be a helpful, involved parent who volunteers time and service to the school. There are countless ways that schools can use the direct or indirect services of parents. All schools seek parent involvement in the classroom or on various school committees, programs, and projects. Become more involved in the school community and get to know staff members.
- Let teachers or other staff members who are making an effort on behalf of your child know that you are appreciative. It is generally the little things that make a difference in showing your appreciation: a thank-you note, a positive comment or message to the teacher or administrator, a positive e-mail to teacher with a copy to the principal.
- You might wish to provide the teacher or school professional library with a donation of a book or other resources and information about ADHD. Much of the teacher training and public awareness regarding ADHD has been a direct result of parents' strong efforts (individually, as a small group of parents and interested professionals, and through organizations such as CHADD) to educate others about the needs of their children.
- Your child's school success may require the use of tools, such as timers and assignment notebooks, and purchase of items to be used as rewards for achieving goals in a behavioral plan. This can be expensive for a teacher so consider offering to purchase such items the teacher needs to help your child.
- For related topics regarding communicating, advocating for your child, and working effectively and productively with schools, see *Lists 7.1 and 7.2*.

Sources and Resources

Hallam, Susan. (2008). Help teachers help your child. *ADDitude Magazine, 8*(5), 52–53.

Hallowell, Edward. (2007). Dr. Ned Hallowell on building rapport with teachers. *ADDitude Magazine, 7*(3), 21. Retrieved from www.additudemag.com/adhd/article/2494.html

7.4 ADHD in Young Children (Ages Three to Five)

- Most children with ADHD are not diagnosed until the elementary school grades. With very young children it is harder to distinguish between what is normal rambunctious, inattentive, and uninhibited behavior from what is abnormal and symptomatic of ADHD. Inattention and high activity level are typical behaviors of preschoolers, but of course, most do not have ADHD.
- Although most children are not diagnosed with ADHD until they are six years or older, those youngsters exhibiting very significant difficulties with ADHD symptoms are now being identified at a younger age, enabling them to receive earlier intervention. Recent and ongoing research as well as the American Academy of Pediatrics' (2011) revised guidelines for the diagnosis, evaluation, and treatment of ADHD address ADHD in preschool-age children and how to best treat the disorder in this population.
- Early identification of ADHD or any related developmental problems and early intervention can make a huge positive difference in the life of the child and family. It can significantly minimize the social, behavioral, or learning difficulties the child experiences as a result of the disorder and prevent a lot of struggle down the road.

Developmental Signs and Symptoms of ADHD in Young Children

- Teeter (1998) summarized the research regarding key characteristics of ADHD during the preschool stage, some of which include the following:
  - Parental stress is at its zenith.
  - Often difficult to toilet train
  - Impulsive responding
  - Hyperactivity during structured activities
  - Inattention and distractibility to tasks are high.
  - Shifts from one activity to another
  - Peer rejection is common.
- Mahone (2014) describes these additional symptoms of ADHD that are common in preschool children:
  - Dislikes or avoids activities that require paying attention for more than a minute or two (such as playing with a toy or listening to a story)
  - Talks a lot more and makes more noise than typical of other children the same age
  - Nearly always restless
  - Has gotten into dangerous situations because of fearlessness and has been injured because of moving too fast or running when not supposed to
  - Aggressive with playmates
- Schusteff (2007, p. 49) explains that with ADHD in preschoolers, "the tipping point in diagnosis is usually a matter of degree." These kids are much more extreme in their behaviors than the average three-year-old.
  - It is common for the child to also have other developmental delays, for example, in speech and language, motor skills, or academic readiness skills (such as learning and remembering ABCs, numbers, shapes, or letter-sound associations).

- If a child is diagnosed with ADHD in the preschool or kindergarten years, the symptoms are typically quite severe and are persistent over time and across settings. The child sadly experiences many behavioral, social, and interpersonal difficulties. It is not uncommon for these children to be kicked out of one or more early childhood programs—often because of aggressive and oppositional behavior. These children are at high risk for many more problems down the road, so early intervention is critical.
- If a child has ADHD, the preschool or kindergarten teacher will find the behaviors to be very problematic and excessive in comparison to other children. It is appropriate for the teacher to share observations and concerns with parents and support staff and implement strategies and supports to address the needs of the child. Almost all of the teaching and parenting techniques recommended throughout this book are applicable and effective for children in this age bracket as well.

What the Research Shows

PATS Study (2006)

- The first long-term comprehensive study of ADHD treatment in this population was the Preschool ADHD Treatment Study (PATS), sponsored by the National Institute of Mental Health, conducted by researchers at six sites. The study included more than three hundred preschoolers with severe ADHD symptoms, ages three to five.
- All children and their parents first participated in a ten-week behavioral therapy and training course in behavior modification techniques, such as consistent use of positive and negative consequences. More than a third of those children were treated successfully with behavior modification and did not proceed to the medication stage of the study.
- The children who did not improve after the behavior therapy course were included in the medication part of the study. They were given low doses of methylphenidate (stimulant medication), monitored very closely, and compared to those taking a placebo. Although most of the children tolerated the drug well, 11 percent had to drop out of the study as a result of intolerable side effects.
- The findings were that those children taking the medication had a more marked reduction of their ADHD symptoms compared to children taking a placebo.
- The conclusions of this 2006 PATS study was that preschoolers with severe ADHD benefit when treated with behavior modification only or a combination of behavior modification and low doses of methylphenidate. Although medication was found to be generally effective and safe, preschoolers appear to be more prone to side effects than older children and need close monitoring for side effects (National Institutes of Health National Institute of Mental Health [NIMH], 2006).

PATS Study (Six-Year Follow-Up)

- There was a six-year follow-up to the PATS study (Riddle et al., 2012). Approximately 70 percent of the original children participated in the follow-up study and most all still met criteria for ADHD.
- Conclusions were that ADHD in preschoolers is a relatively stable diagnosis over a six-year period. The course is generally chronic, with high symptom severity and impairment in very young children with moderate-to-severe ADHD, despite treatment with medication. Development of more effective ADHD intervention strategies is needed for this age group.

Other Research

- There is a lot of other research taking place with young children to learn more about the developmental course of ADHD and better interventions for the disorder from a young age.
- We know that there are developmental brain differences from an early age that are driving some of the behaviors that we see (Mahone et al., 2011).

Diagnosis and Intervention

- Parents should discuss concerns with their pediatrician or other developmental specialist and their child's preschool or kindergarten teacher.
- When ADHD symptoms exceed what seems normal for other children their age, and when symptoms are persistent and observable in different settings (such as home and the preschool or day-care environments), an evaluation is recommended.
- ADHD and other developmental issues are best identified early so intervention (parent training, behavior modification at home and school, medication in some cases, and speech-language therapy, occupational therapy, or other services needed) can be started.
- A wait-and-see approach may not be in the child's best interest. When a child has ADHD, behaviors that affect social and academic performance generally do not improve by just providing more time to mature. Other interventions will be necessary to specifically target their areas of weakness and build their skills. Early intervention is always the most beneficial for children with disabilities and special needs.
- Wolraich (2007) describes the recommended interventions for preschool children who exhibit symptoms of ADHD:
  - Begin with a parent training program: a group program, such as the CHADD-sponsored Parent to Parent program (see www.chadd.org) or an individual program for more intense training, such as the Parent Child Interaction Training, which works with the child and parent or other caregiver together to improve overall behavior and to reduce parenting stress. (www.pcit.org). The child does not need a diagnosis of ADHD for parents to participate in these programs and learn the skills (*Lists 1.14, 1.19, 1.22*).
  - If parent training does not sufficiently address the problems, parents should have their child evaluated by their pediatrician (if the doctor is knowledgeable about ADHD in young children) or other clinician, such as a child psychiatrist, child psychologist, or developmental behavioral pediatrician.
  - Based on the evaluation, parents can consider a more intense behavior modification program, treatment with stimulant medication, or a combination of both.
- *Lists 1.3 and 1.15* discuss what is involved in an evaluation for ADHD and the diagnostic criteria. The American Academy of Pediatrics wrote and published new clinical practice guidelines for the diagnosis, evaluation, and treatment of ADHD in children and adolescents (AAP, 2011) taking into account what was learned from the research about the benefits of diagnosing and treating children with ADHD who are younger than six.

- The new AAP guidelines included for the first time these recommendations for treating children with ADHD under six years old:
  - The primary care clinician should prescribe evidence-based parent- or teacher-administered behavior therapy as the first line of treatment and may prescribe methylphenidate if the behavior interventions do not provide significant improvement and there is moderate to severe continuing disturbance in the child's function.
  - When behavior therapy is not available, the clinician needs to weigh the risks of starting medication at an early age against the harm of delaying diagnosis and treatment (*Lists 1.15, 1.20*).

Other Preschool-Kindergarten Interventions

Child Find

There is a component of IDEA that requires states and local education agencies (school districts) to identify, locate, and evaluate all children with disabilities. It begins with a review or screening of available information about the child suspected of having a disability. When screening indicates the possibility of an educational disability, the child is evaluated in relevant areas. When results indicate that a child is disabled and in need of special education services, an individualized plan is developed. Young children found eligible for special education or related services receive those educational interventions at no cost to parents. Check with your local office of special education. (See *List 6.3* on educational rights.)

Mark Katz (2009a) reviewed two excellent intervention programs for young children with ADHD.

First Step to Success

This program, developed under the direction of Hill Walker, is recognized nationally as an effective early intervention for reducing aggression in children who display such behaviors during their early school years. Researchers also are finding this program helpful in young children who exhibit symptoms of ADHD. The preschool version of the First Step program is a home-school intervention for teaching sharing, cooperation, following rules, and other social skills. It is proven to reduce serious behavior problems, such as aggression and opposition-defiance, and improve school readiness and interpersonal skills. For more information, see First Steps to Success Preschool Edition by Voyager Sopris Learning at www.firststeptosuccess.org or www.voyagersopris.com.

Tools of the Mind

This program teaches preschoolers how to use different mental tools to gain greater control of their social, emotional, and cognitive behaviors. (Katz, 2013). A 2007 study conducted by neuroscientist Adele Diamond showed that children enrolled in preschool classrooms using Tools of the Mind improved in their ability to resist distractions and temptations (inhibitory control), mentally hold information in mind (working memory), and flexibly adjust to change (cognitive flexibility). According to Katz (2009b, p. 7), "Tools of the Mind is currently being implemented in more than 450 preschool and kindergarten regular education and special education classrooms throughout the United States. Schools are finding the program compatible with Response to Intervention" (*List 6.1*). For more information, see www.toolsofthemind.org.

Strategies and Tips for Parents

- The same principles of parenting, effective behavior management, and problem prevention described in the section 2 lists of this book and others apply to parents of young children with ADHD as well.
- It is highly recommended to start early in seeking help from specialists to learn how to cope with and manage your young child's challenging behaviors and more difficult temperaments. There are many resources available to help you learn how to do so: parenting classes, behavior management training, counseling, parent support groups such as CHADD, books and DVDs, and other materials (*Lists 1.22, 2.17, 7.12*).
- Play games and engage your child in activities that require him or her to practice self-control (such as Red Light Green Light, or Freeze!), and to teach important social skills such as waiting, listening, taking turns, and following directions (*Lists 2.13, 7.12*). Also, see the "Sources and Resources" section of this list for some books of strategies, activities, and interventions for young children with ADHD.
- It is important to provide the necessary structure and manage the environmental factors to help your child be successful by anticipating potential problems and planning accordingly. For example, it is important to childproof your home for safety (*Lists 2.3, 2.13*).
- Many children, not just those with ADHD, have difficulty adjusting to a classroom environment, the hours away from home, the structure and expectations of their preschool or kindergarten teacher, and relating to the other children. Sometimes it just takes time for them to make the adjustment and feel comfortable in the new environment. It is often the case that some of the behaviors that were problematic at the beginning of the year diminish and are no longer a significant issue once the children have learned the routine and structure, bonded with their teacher, and matured somewhat.
- It is difficult for many parents to decide whether or not their child is ready to start kindergarten or wait another year (particularly those with late birthdays). Be aware that boys are typically later in their development than girls, and children with ADHD are developmentally behind their peers in self-regulation and executive skills.
- It helps if you can visit the kindergarten classes at the school and speak with teachers to have a better feel for the environment and expectations. Seek advice from your pediatrician or others to make the most informed decision. Your gut feeling after doing your research is probably the best decision (Rief, 2001).

Strategies and Tips for Preschool and Kindergarten Teachers

- In preschool and kindergarten, every behavioral expectation and social skill must be taught. Teachers need to explain and model each desired behavior and practice until all students know precisely what is expected from them, including how to line up, stand in line, walk in line, move to groups and learning centers, sit on the rug or at the table, raise a hand to get the teacher's attention, and use indoor voices.
- Teachers need to model, role-play, and have children practice expectations—for example, "Show me what to do when you have something you want to say." "Who wants to show us how we get our lunch boxes and line up for lunch?"
- Literature that has manners and appropriate behavior as a theme, such as sharing and being a good friend, is helpful in teaching behavioral expectations and

social skills. So are puppets, music, games, visual display, role-playing, and other such means.

- Behavior management techniques for children with ADHD in preschool and kindergarten are similar to those in higher grades: visual prompting and cueing, a high degree of feedback, proximity control, group positive reinforcement systems, corrective consequences that are applied consistently, and individualized behavioral plans and supports (*Lists 2.1, 2.3, 2.4, 2.8, 2.10, 2.11, 2.12, 2.13, 2.15, 2.17*).
- *Quiet space*. Sometimes children with ADHD are on sensory overload and can become agitated or disruptive. It is important to allow them time and space to settle, regroup, and get away from some of the overstimulation. It helps to have an area that is designed for this purpose, with calming music they can listen to with earphones, pillows, and stuffed animals, for example. Teachers may ask, "Do you need to move ... ?" "Is there a better place to do your work?" Or they can redirect the child to a quieter, calmer area by whispering to him or her, "Go to the pillow area and read [look at] a book" (*Lists 2.3, 2.13, 2.15*).
- *Diversionary tactics*. The perceptive teacher will watch for signs of children beginning to get restless or agitated and try diverting their attention (for example, "Sara, come help me turn the pages of this book") to redirect their behavior. Most young children love to be the teacher's helper. They can be given a task such as wiping down tables, putting up chairs, or passing out papers (*List 2.15*).
- *Positive attention*. As with older children, the best way to manage is through watching for positive behaviors and recognizing children for what they are doing right. "I see how nicely Coby and Jason are taking turns. Thank you for working so cooperatively." Besides specific praise from teachers, positive recognition and appreciation from peers is important as well: "Let's give a big round of applause to ... " (children clap finger-to-finger in a large circular movement). "Let's give ourselves a pat on the back" (children reach over and pat themselves on the back). "Let's give the silent cheer for ... " (*List 2.1*).
- *Check for specific behaviors*. Ask, "Are your eyes on me?" "Are your ears open and on full power?" "Where should you be sitting right now?" "Are we sitting 'criss-cross applesauce'?"
- *Visual prompts*. Use these for all behavioral expectations. For example, make class charts with pictures depicting the behaviors you want students to demonstrate. Point to and refer to those visuals frequently. Keep your camera handy and take photos of children who are sitting appropriately or raising their hand to speak, for example, and use those photos as reminders of appropriate behaviors. (See examples of visual prompts at the end of the appendix.)
- *Environmental structuring*. Children with ADHD often have difficulty knowing and understanding their physical boundaries. They tend to invade other people's space and react adversely to being crowded or bumped into. They are helped by having concrete visual structuring of their space, such as with colored duct tape to indicate their boundaries on the carpet area or at tables. Also, placing them in the front or back of line (not in the middle) can avoid some problems when walking in lines (*List 2.3*).
- Some children need individualized behavior modification charts or daily report cards for working to improve one or two specific behaviors, such as staying in their assigned place or keeping hands and feet to themselves. (See *Lists 2.5 and 2.9*.)
- Young children need to be reinforced frequently; short time frames of appropriate behavior can earn the child a star, a smiley face, a sticker on a chart, or other reward.

Prepare and reassure children who are easily frustrated with tasks. For example, "Which do you think will be easier: the cutting or the gluing?" "I know you can do this, but if you need help ... "

- Refer the child to your school team to share concerns about the student's development or functioning. The child can be screened for vision or hearing, speech-language, learning, motor skills, or other areas of concern, and evaluated if indicated (*Lists 1.17, 6.1, 6.2*).

Sources and Resources

American Academy of Pediatrics (AAP). (2011). ADHD: Clinical practice guidelines for the diagnosis, evaluation, and treatment of attention-deficit/hyperactivity disorder in children and adolescents. *Pediatrics, 128*(5), 1007–1022.

DuPaul, George, & Kern, Lee. (2011). *Young children with ADHD: Early identification and intervention*. Washington, DC: American Psychological Association.

Jones, Clare B. (1991). *Sourcebook for children with attention deficit disorder: A management guide for early childhood professionals and parents*. Tucson, AZ: Communications Skill Builders.

Katz, Mark. (2009a). First step to success: An early intervention for children with symptoms of AD/HD. *Attention Magazine, 16*(4) 8–9.

Katz, Mark. (2009b). Tools of the mind: Helping children develop self-regulation. *Attention Magazine, 16*(3), 6–7.

Katz, Mark. (2013). Interventions at the point of performance: The power of play. *Attention Magazine, 20*(5), 6–7.

Lougy, Richard, DeRuvo, Silvia, & Rosenthal, David. (2007). *Teaching young children with ADHD*. Thousand Oaks, CA: Corwin Press.

Mahone, E. Mark (2012, Nov.). ADHD in preschool children. CHADD Webinar recording retrieved at: http://www.chadd.org/Support/Ask-the-Expert-Online-Chats/Ask-the-Expert-Chat-Transcripts.aspx

National Institutes of Mental Health. (2006, Oct.). Preschoolers with ADHD improve with low doses of medication. Retrieved from www.nimh.nih.gov/news/science-news/2006/preschoolers-with-adhd-improve-with-low-doses-of-medication.shtml

Reimers, Cathy, & Brunger, Bruce. (1999). *ADHD in the young child: Driven to redirection*. Plantation, FL: Specialty Press.

Riddle, M., Yershova, K., Lazzaretto, D., et al. (2012, Dec.). The preschool attention-deficit/hyperactivity disorder treatment study 6-year follow-up. *Journal of the American Academy of Child & Adolescent Psychiatry*. Retrieved from www.jaacap.com/article/S0890-8567(12)00993.8/abstract

Rief, Sandra. (2001). *Ready, start, school: Nurturing and guiding your child through preschool and kindergarten*. Paramus, NJ: Prentice-Hall.

Schusteff, Arlene. (2007). Preschoolers and ADHD. *ADDitude Magazine, 7*(3), 49–51.

Severson, H., Feil, E., Stiller, B., Kavanaugh, K., Golly, A., & Walker, H. (n.d.). First steps to success. Voyager Sopris Learning. Retrieved from www.voyagersopris.com/curriculum/subject/school-climate/first-step-to-success

Teeter, Phyllis A. (1998). *Interventions for AD/HD: Treatment in developmental context*. New York: Guilford Press.

Wolraich, Mark L. (2007). Preschoolers and AD/HD. *Attention Magazine, 14*(3), 9–10.

7.5 ADHD in Middle School and High School

- For most children with ADHD the symptoms continue into adolescence to varying degrees. Some symptoms may diminish, but other problems may emerge or intensify during middle school and high school. Many preteens and teens find these years to be the most difficult and stressful for them and their families.
- Hyperactivity in adolescence generally manifests more as restlessness rather than the overt hyperactivity seen in younger children.
- Impulsivity can be more problematic during the teen years. Poor self-control and lack of inhibition in adolescence is associated with many risk factors, including significantly more than average traffic violations, accidents, teen pregnancies, as well as conduct that results in conflict with school authorities, parents, and law enforcement (*List 1.6*).
- Many children with ADHD who were able to cope and stay afloat academically in elementary school find themselves overwhelmed and unable to do so with the heavy workload of middle and secondary school.
- Many students with ADHD are not diagnosed until the middle or high school years. This is particularly common for those who have the predominantly inattentive presentation of the disorder.
- Adolescents with ADHD may appear mature physically and grown up, but looks are deceiving. They are typically far less mature behaviorally and emotionally than their same-age peers. They do not act their age because they have a developmental delay of approximately 30 percent in their self-regulation and executive skills. A fifteen-year-old with ADHD will likely behave like a ten- or eleven-year-old in some respects and a twelve-year-old may behave more like an eight- or nine-year-old because of this developmental lag. Do not let their intelligence and physical maturity mislead you (*Lists 1.2, 1.4*).
- Although they may be of an age when the expectation is to demonstrate more independence, responsibility, and self-control, the reality is that preteens and teens with ADHD take longer to exhibit those behaviors. They need more adult monitoring, supervision, and direct supports than their peers.
- Executive function weaknesses typically become much more problematic in middle and high school, impairing academic performance for many students with ADHD. Academic tasks and teacher expectations involve a much higher demand than in elementary school for organization, planning, time management, working memory, and other executive skills (*Lists 1.2, 1.5, 4.1, 4.4, 5.1, 5.6, 5.13*).

Other issues and factors for teens and preteens with ADHD include the following:

- Poor study skills (work habits, note taking, test taking)
- Managing multiple teachers' behavioral expectations, classroom procedures, and work requirements
- Social difficulties, such as being the victim of teasing, bullying, and social isolation, which can be devastating at this age
- Desire for peer approval, coupled with impulsivity and not stopping to think before they act, resulting in inappropriate conduct that gets them into trouble
- Besides these special challenges related to their ADHD, adolescents must also cope with the normal stresses and anxieties of other kids this age, such as changes and transitions to a new school when entering middle or high school; dealing with

several teachers, each with his or her own teaching style, expectations, and requirements; physical changes; the desire for independence; and enormous social and peer pressures and need to be accepted and fit in.

- Students in these grades often complain about school being boring, and they do not see the connection between what is taught in school and their own lives. Instruction at this level must be meaningful, relevant, challenging, motivating, and designed for active participation and engagement. It also needs to tap into students' interests and strengths (*Lists 3.2, 3.3, 3.7, 3.8*).
- It is very important for parents and teachers to be aware that at least two-thirds of children and teens with ADHD have or will develop at least one other coexisting disorder, for example, anxiety disorder, oppositional defiant disorder, conduct disorder, or sleep disorder. Any coexisting disorder, which may develop in middle or high school, needs to be diagnosed before the proper treatment can occur. The preteen or teen needs the support and treatment for these or other conditions or disorders from medical and mental health professionals.
- Learning disabilities, such as dyslexia, is a very common coexisting disorder. Approximately 25 to 50 percent of children and teens with ADHD also have a learning disability. These students need the educational interventions (specialized instruction and related services, as well as academic supports and accommodations) to do well in school. Many students with ADHD are never evaluated for learning disabilities, and many with known learning disabilities have undiagnosed ADHD. It should always be suspected that a child or teen with ADHD who is struggling in learning (reading, writing, or math) also has learning disabilities and should be evaluated to determine their learning and academic needs. See *Lists 1.6, 1.8, 1.18, 6.4*.
- It is very important to reevaluate when other conditions are suspected or current treatment is not working well and implement whatever interventions may be necessary at this time: academic assistance, medical treatment or adjustment in medication, counseling, or something else.
- Students of this age still benefit from incentive systems, daily report cards, contracts, and other forms of home and school monitoring plans (*List 2.9 and charts A-4, A-6, A-8, A-11*).
- Adolescents with ADHD need help from parents and teachers:
  - Awareness and understanding of ADHD and strategies to help them deal with their challenges
  - Reasonable and realistic expectations
  - Use of a positive discipline approach rather than punishment as the primary mode of dealing with behavior
  - Monitoring and supervision (although they may complain bitterly)
  - Open channels of communication with mutual problem solving and involvement in decision making
  - Lots of encouragement and support
  - A plan to prepare them for whatever their goals are once they graduate high school.
  - See *List 7.8* for more on this topic.
- Preteens and teens should be educated about ADHD to understand the disorder and ways to better manage the symptoms. If they receive medication, they need to

know what medication does and does not do. It is encouraging when they learn that so many highly successful people in every walk of life have ADHD and the disorder does not limit their potential.

- As students with ADHD enter the middle and high school grades, they need to learn to advocate for themselves and how to politely request help when needed. Parents still need to take an active role monitoring and communicating with teachers but it is important for students of this age to speak directly with their teachers about their needs and the kinds of supports or accommodations they think will help them learn and perform better in their classrooms. Teachers are generally impressed when students care enough about wanting to do well in their classes that they ask for help when needed.
- One of the advantages in high school is the availability of more options in scheduling. Sometimes the best intervention is a change of classes or teachers. Other times, rescheduling a class with the same teacher but at a more optimal time of day makes a difference. For example, if the teen fatigues in the afternoon and is most alert and energetic in the morning, scheduling the hardest classes in the morning would help.
- Parents of adolescents with ADHD need to be vigilant in monitoring their child's performance in his or her classes and not wait until regular progress reports, by which time the student may be too far behind to get caught up. Teachers may be asked to send more frequent progress reports or keep parents informed by e-mail or other communication systems throughout the grading period.
- Teens with ADHD generally need an adult at school who serves officially or unofficially as a case manager to monitor progress, advise, and intervene in school situations. For students with IEPs, the special education teacher is often the case manager. Sometimes a guidance counselor, homeroom teacher, or other staff member serves this function.
- Some middle and high schools have in place supportive interventions available to students in need, such as mentors, homework and organization assistance, study skills and learning strategies classes, and tutoring. Students with ADHD would benefit from such school supports as well as the opportunity to participate in clubs, sports, and electives to build on their interests and showcase their areas of strength.
- These are years when it is very difficult for parents and teachers to find that proper balance: how to teach children to assume responsibility for their own learning and behavioral choices and how to intervene as we guide and support them to success.
- ADHD in adolescent girls typically manifests differently than in boys. See *List 1.12* for information about ADHD in girls.
- The bulk of strategies and interventions for ADHD (instructional, environmental, organizational, and behavioral) recommended throughout this book are effective and appropriate for adolescents as well.

Tips for Parents

- When your child is transitioning from elementary to middle school or from middle to high school, it helps to have a dry run before school starts to walk around the campus, see where the classes are located, and practice quickly opening and closing their combination locks.
- Drivers with ADHD have more speeding citations and accidents in which they were at fault than other drivers. Be aware that your ADHD teen may be of driving age but

is developmentally less mature. It is recommended to have firm guidelines and an agreement between you and your son or daughter regarding your driving expectations once they get their license. A driving contract to help enforce rules, encourage responsibility, and keep everyone safe may be helpful, such as the one *ADDitude Magazine* shares as an example (see the link in "Sources and Resources" below).

- Consider hiring a tutor, learning specialist, or an ADHD coach to help your son or daughter keep up with school assignments and improve academic and executive skills. This can be a very helpful support for your teen and alleviates some of the burden from you. In adolescence parental micromanagement is typically resented and becomes the source of conflict between the teen and parents. Having someone else involved in keeping your child on track and following through with school assignments can help not only toward your child's school success but also your relationship. (See *List 7.6* on ADHD coaching.)
- "Parents play an important role in preparing their child for, and guiding them through, the middle school transition. Relatively simple steps such as establishing a homework management plan, monitoring friendship patterns, and facilitating positive social interactions can make a big difference in the development process" (Evans, Serpell, & White, 2005, p. 31).
- Kids with ADHD need a lot of reminders from parents, but how they are given can make a difference in how those reminders are accepted by the preteen or teen. Guare, Dawson, and Guare (2013) recommend to avoid nagging and send your teens reminders that are more indirect such as a note, voice mail, or text message reminder.
- "If your child has a 504 Plan, maintaining that plan throughout high school is a critical element in keeping your high school student with ADHD academically on track" (Lepre, 2008, 46). Lepre also recommends that parents meet not only with the teen's teachers early in the year, but also to meet with and develop a working relationship with the guidance counselor, who is the "link between the school and your adolescent" (p. 46).
- Chris Dendy (2002, p. 17), author of several books on ADHD in teenagers, recommends these actions parents can take to influence a successful outcome for your teen: "seeking accommodations at school, fine-tuning medication, using positive parenting practices, providing supervision, avoiding hostile interactions and harsh punishments, avoiding nagging and personal attacks, and last and perhaps most importantly, believing in your child!"

Transition Plans

- In the effort to improve postsecondary results for students with disabilities, IDEA added new provisions in transition planning for high school students with IEPs when it was reauthorized by Congress in 2004.
- "A transition plan is the section of the Individualized Education Program (IEP) that outlines transition goals and services for the student. The transition plan is based on a high school student's individual needs, strengths, skills, and interests. Transition planning is used to identify and develop goals which need to be accomplished during the current school year to assist the student in meeting his or her post-high school goals" (Stanberry, n.d., p.1).
- By the time a student is sixteen years old (although it may occur sooner), plans for transition services are required under IDEA 2004 to become part of the IEP.

The IEP team looks at what the student intends to do after high school—perhaps get a higher education or enter the work world. Transition plans address needs such as preparation for college entrance examinations, consideration of career choices, development of extracurricular interests, and job training possibilities (Rief & Stern, 2010).

- Transition planning and services include the following new requirements:
  - Appropriate measurable postsecondary goals based on age-appropriate transition assessments related to training, education, employment, and, when appropriate, independent living skills
  - Goals that reflect the student's strengths, preferences, and interests (not just the student's deficits)
  - A process designed to be results oriented and focus on improving the academic and functional achievement of the student to facilitate movement from school to postschool activities
  - A statement of the transition services needed to help the student reach those goals, which includes courses of study
  - See the "Sources and Resources" section in List 6.4 for *Lists* on IDEA and special education for more information on transition plans.
- High school students with ADHD who have IEPs and parents should be actively involved as part of the IEP team in developing their ITP in order for the transition plan to be most meaningful and motivating for them.

Sources and Resources

ADDitude Magazine editors. Driving contract. *ADDitude Magazine*. Retrieved from www.additudemag.com/adhd-web/article/579.html

www.greatschools.org/special-education/health/873.transition-planning-for-students-with-ieps.gs

Dendy, Chris A. Zeigler (June 2002) Finding the joy—Parenting teenagers with AD/HD. CHADD: *Attention Magazine*, *8*(6), 15–20.

Evans, Steven W., Serpell, Zewelanji, & White, Casey. (2005). The transition to middle school: Preparing for challenge and success. *Attention Magazine, 12*(3) 29–31.

Guare, Richard, Dawson, Peg, & Guare, Colin. (2013). Get your teen ready for life. *ADDitude Magazine, 15*(4), 26–29. Excerpted from their book, *Smart but scattered teens* (2013). New York: Guilford Press.

Lepre, Susan. (2008). Ten steps to academic success. *Attention Magazine, 15*(4), 46–47.

Rief, Sandra & Stern, Judith (2010). *The Dyslexia Checklist: A Practical Reference for Parents and Teachers*. San Francisco: Jossey-Bass.

Stanberry, Kristin. (n.d.). *Transition planning for students with IEPs*. Retrieved from http://www.greatschools.org/special-education/health/873-transition-planning-for-students-with-ieps.gs

Some Other Recommended Resources for Parents and Teachers of Teens with ADHD

Barkley, Russell A., Robin, Arthur L., & Benton, Christine M. (2013). *Your defiant teen: Ten steps to resolve conflict and rebuild your relationship* (2nd ed.). New York: Guilford Press.

Brown, Thomas E. (2014). *Smart but stuck: Emotions in teens and adults with ADHD*. San Francisco: Jossey-Bass.

DeRuvo, Silvia L. (2009). *Strategies for teaching adolescents with ADHD: Effective classroom techniques across the content areas*. San Francisco: Jossey-Bass.

Dendy, Chris A. & Zeigler, Alex. (2003). *A bird's-eye view of life with ADD and AD/HD: Advice from young survivors*. Cedar Bluff, Alabama: Cherish the Children.

Dendy, Chris A. Zeigler (2011). *Teaching teens with ADD, ADHD & executive function deficits, 2nd edition*. Bethesda, MD: Woodbine House.

Dendy, Chris A. Zeiger (2013) *Teenagers with ADD and ADHD—A parent's guide*. Bethesda, MD.

Ellison, Phyllis Anne Teeter. (2000). Strategies for adolescents with AD/HD: Goal setting and increasing independence. *The CHADD information and resource guide to AD/HD*. Landover, MD: CHADD.

Fowler, Mary. (2001). *Maybe you know my teen*. New York: Broadway Books.

Guare, Richard, & Dawson, Peg. (2013). *Smart but scattered teens: The executive skills program for helping teens reach their potential*. New York: Guilford Press.

Nadeau, Kathleen. (1998). *Help 4 ADD @ high school*. Silver Spring, MD: Advantage Books.

Parker, Harvey. (1999). *Put yourself in their shoes: Understanding teenagers with ADHD*. Plantation, FL: Specialty Press.

Robin, Arthur L., & Barkley, Russell A. (1999). *ADHD in adolescents: Diagnosis and treatment*. New York: Guilford Press.

Snyder, Marlene, & Hamphill, Rae. (2000). Parents of teen drivers with AD/HD: Proceed with caution. *The CHADD information and resource guide to AD/HD*. Landover, MD: CHADD.

7.6 ADHD Coaching

Many people have been helped by coaches of various kinds, such as business and executive coaches, athletic coaches, weight-loss coaches, and life coaches. One of the interventions that many adults and teens with ADHD are finding helpful as part of the multimodal treatment plan (*Lists 1.19, 1.23*) is ADHD coaching.

What Is ADHD Coaching?

- ADHD coaching is a field that emerged around the mid-1990s that uses life skills and academic coaching strategies as well as knowledge of ADHD and the impact of executive function impairments to support ADHD clients in reaching their goals.
- ADHD coaching is a service in which a trained coach assists the client (typically an adolescent or adult) with structured and realistic goal setting and supportive strategies to achieve those personal goals, helping them understand and manage their ADHD symptoms.
- A coach is not a therapist, psychologist, or tutor. The coach's role is to work with the ADHD client with a focus on specific, practical actions—providing encouragement, feedback, and accountability.
- "Coaching occurs when one person (the coach) provides objective feedback and guidance in an organized and methodical fashion to help another person (the client) address a problem or achieve identified goals" (CHADD National Resource Center on AD/HD (n.d.)).
- "ADHD coaching is a specialized type of life coaching that addresses the common challenges ADHD can often bring, particularly in the areas related to scheduling, goal setting, confidence building, organizing, focusing, prioritizing, and persisting at tasks. In addition, ADHD coaching can help in the development of effective self-advocacy skills" (Low, 2010).
- According to Nancy Ratey, a leader in the field, "AD/HD coaching is a personalized service tailored to a person's individual needs. The coach works with clients on problem areas and daily issues caused by AD/HD, such as time management, procrastination, prioritization, and impulsivity. The coach is not there to hold a client's hand. The coach is there to be on the sidelines helping the client to remember his or her pitfalls and learn ways to self-initiate change" (Goodman, 2008, p. 10).
- ADHD coaches are change agents—assisting their ADHD client to identify and set realistic goals, develop systems and strategies to manage their ADHD symptoms, and succeed in achieving their goals.
- Coaching does not work for everyone, and for anyone to make changes in his or her behavior or learn and apply new skills, it takes time. For coaching to be an effective intervention the individual must want to make changes and be ready and willing to engage in the coaching process.
- Because there is no licensure required of coaches, check that the person is experienced and well trained by a reputable coaching program or organization, such as one of those in the "Sources and Resources" section of this list. ADHD coaches for adolescents should also be experienced and skilled working with youth.

- ADHD coaches assist their clients in understanding ADHD and its impact on their life while developing skills and strategies that draw on their strengths and aim to bypass their weaknesses.

How ADHD Coaches Work with Preteens, Teens, and College Students

- Jodi Sleeper-Triplett, another leader in the ADHD coaching field explains:
  - "Coaching offers young people with ADHD a supportive structure through which they can explore life options, learn new skills, and start to be more independent while in a safe space. Coaching provides a sounding board, a source for ideas, and a safety net that all help the young person with ADHD try new ways of operating, go after what he or she wants, collect him- or herself when things go differently than planned, and then try again, each time growing a little wiser and a little more confident" (Sleeper-Triplett, 2010, p. 23).
  - "By providing coaching to teens, coaches have an opportunity to help bridge the gap between childhood and adulthood while simultaneously helping parents to step back and allow the maturation process to proceed at a pace that is right for their teen" (Sleeper-Triplett, 2013, p. 26).
- Coaches work with young ADHD clients to improve academic performance by addressing specific skills (for example, organization, time management, prioritizing, self-awareness, talking to teachers about their needs and other self-advocacy skills, planning and breaking down long-term projects and assignments, and keeping the student on track and accountable for following through with planned actions.
- Coaching students also involves regular coaching sessions that can be conducted in whichever formats are most convenient and preferred, such as face-to-face meetings (directly or through Skype or other video or webcam format) or by phone. Check-ins between sessions take place frequently and are done through phone calls, e-mails, or text messages.
- See Plumer and Stoner (2005) and Dawson (2013) for information on applying coaching strategies and techniques at school for students with ADHD-related issues. This is not the same as getting a professional ADHD coach, but may be of particular interest as a school-based intervention and support.

Research

- Until 2010 the evidence of ADHD coaching benefits had been strictly anecdotal. Many people reported the positive effects of ADHD coaching on their lives, but there was little if any research evidence that coaching helps teens improve their functioning or skills.
- The first large-scale study on the effectiveness of coaching on the academic and social performance of college students with ADHD was conducted by a faculty team from Wayne State University in Detroit, Michigan.
- One hundred twenty-seven students from eight universities and two community colleges from a variety of geographic regions across the United States participated in the twenty-seven-month study. This study examined the effects on college students with ADHD who received Edge ADHD coaching sessions, which are based on the JST model for ADHD youth coaching. The results of the study were that students

who received this ADHD coaching were able to formulate goals more realistically and consistently work toward achieving them, manage their time more effectively, and stick with tasks even when they found them challenging. In addition, students reported that coaching helped them to feel less stress, greater empowerment, increased confidence, and have more balanced lives, as well as other improvements. For more information, see Field, Parker, Sawilowsky, and Rolands (2010) in the "Sources and Resources" section of this list or the pdf of the summary or full report at http://edgefoundation.org/information/research

Professional Coaching Organizations and Training Programs

These organizations have a directory of ADHD coaches with information on trained individuals who provide this service. Also, check CHADD's professional directory (www.chadd.org) and *ADDitude Magazine*'s directory (http://directory.additudemag.com).

ADD Coach Academy (www.addcoachacademy.com)

ADHD Coaches Organization (www.adhdcoaches.org)

Edge Foundation (http://edgefoundation.org)

Institute for the Advancement of ADHD Coaching (http://adhdcoaches.org/circle/iaacadhd-coach-certification/)

International Coach Federation (http://coachfederation.org)

JST Coaching (www.jstcoach.com)

Professional Association of ADHD Coaches (www.paaccoaches.org)

Sources and Resources

ADDA Subcommittee on ADD Coaching. (2002). Nancy Ratey & Peter Jaksa (Eds.), *The ADDA guiding principles for coaching individuals with attention deficit disorder*. Retrieved from www.nancyratey.com/adhdcoaching/adda-coachingprinciples

Dawson, Peg. (2013). Coaching: A versatile strategy for addressing executive skill weaknesses. *Attention Magazine, 20*(6), 22–25.

Field, Sharon, Parker, David, Sawilowsky, Shlomo, & Rolands, Laura. (2010, Aug. 31). *Quantifying the effectiveness of coaching for college students with attention deficit/hyperactivity disorder: Final report to the Edge Foundation*. Detroit, MI: College of Education, Wayne State University.

Goodman, Bryan. (2008). Everything you ever wanted to know about ADHD coaching (but were too busy to ask): Ask the Expert interview with Nancy Ratey. *Attention Magazine, 15*(5), 10–13.

Low, Keath. (2010, Dec. 8). The benefits of ADHD coaching: Coaching improves executive functioning for college students with ADHD. About.com. Retrieved from http://add.about.com/od/treatmentoptions/a/The-Benefits-Of-Adhd-Coaching.htm

National Resource Center on AD/HD. (2003). Coaching for adults with AD/HD. *What We Know, 18*. Retrieved from www.help4adhd.org/documents/WWK18.pdf

National Resource Center on AD/HD. (n.d.). Introduction to coaching. Retrieved from www.help4adhd.org/en/living/coaching

Plumer, P. J., & Stoner, G. (2005). The relative effects of classwide peer tutoring and peer coaching on the positive social behaviors of children with ADHD. *Journal of Attention Disorders, 9,* 290–300.

Ratey, Nancy. (2008a). Complete guide to ADHD coaching. *ADDitude Magazine*. Retrieved from www.additudemad.com/adhd/article/3619.html

Ratey, Nancy A. (2008b). *The disorganized mind: Coaching your ADHD brain to take control of your time, tasks, and talents*. New York: St. Martin's Press.

Sleeper-Triplett, Jodi. (2010). Empowering youth with ADHD. *Attention Magazine, 17*(5), 22–25.

Sleeper-Triplett, Jodi. (2013). Is ADHD coaching right for my teen? *Attention Magazine, 20*(6), 26–29.

Additional Books and Resources on Coaching Students with ADHD (Youth and Young Adults)

Dawson, P., & Guare, R. (2013). *Coaching students with executive skills deficits*. New York: Guilford Press

McCarthy, Laura Flynn. (n.d.). What you need to know about ADHD coaching. *ADDitude Magazine*. Retrieved from www.additudemag.com/adhd/article/4002.html

Quinn, Patricia O., Ratey, Nancy A., & Maitland, Theresa L. (2000). *Coaching college students with AD/HD: Issues and answers*. Bethesda, MD: Advantage Books.

Sleeper-Triplett, Jodi. (2010). *Empowering youth with ADHD: Your guide to coaching adolescents and young adults for coaches, parents, and professionals*. Plantation, FL: Specialty Press/A.D.D. Warehouse.

7.7 Healthy, Fun, and Therapeutic Ways to Help Manage ADHD Symptoms

In the past couple of decades we have learned a lot more about healthy, positive ways to reduce stress, strengthen attention and focus, and enhance our physical and emotional well-being. Science supports what most of us intuitively know: the importance of exercise and sports, art and music, or other positive outlets to channel one's energy and emotions, the value of relaxation, calming, focusing, and stress-reduction strategies, being outdoors in nature, and the joy of laughter and play. Research is now showing the specific benefits for those with ADHD.

Meditation Practices and Mindfulness

Meditation and practices involving attention to one's breathing have been used for centuries. Recent research has been looking at the positive effects of such practices on people (mostly adults and teens, but also younger children) with ADHD.

- The first study of mindfulness or "mindful awareness" training in adults and teens with ADHD was conducted at UCLA's Mindful Awareness Research Center (MARC) (http://marc.ucla.edu), which was led by Lidia Zylowska, a co-developer of UCLA's Mindful Awareness Program for ADHD (MAP).
- UCLA's study involved an eight-week program in mindfulness meditation in twenty-four adults and eight teens with ADHD. Results were promising.

Mindfulness is described as the following:

- Experiencing life from moment to moment with full awareness and acceptance and a practice that teaches us to pay greater attention to our internal and external experience (http://marc.ucla.edu).
- "It is a skill that can be developed through a type of meditation that is about little more than focused attention—our mind becomes lost in thought, and we bring it back. The art of mindfulness is noticing our mind wandering, and guiding it back to real life and to a sense of balance, without giving ourselves a hard time for having wandered off in the first place" (Bertin, 2011a, p. 17).
- The practice of mindful awareness can guide students to improve relationships, create relaxation and calmness, soothe the self, increase memory, enhance focus, reduce stress, manage reactions and emotions, increase self-acceptance, and feel more at ease with test taking (UCLA's MARC website http://marc.ucla.edu/).

According to Zylowska in an interview with ADDitude editors (2010), and her book (2012), reviewed by Katz (2012):

- Mindful awareness practice improves a person's ability to control or regulate his or her attention and emotional state. It has the benefit of reducing stress and anxiety levels. People who learn mindful awareness skills are better able to resist distractions, manage emotions, and notice an impulse arising without acting on it.
- Through mindfulness people with ADHD develop the ability to not only be aware of their attention, but to monitor and remember where it goes. The ability to notice where our attention wanders actually increases our ability to redirect it to where we want it to be.

- The practice involves sitting down in a quiet, comfortable place and spending initially five minutes focusing on the sensation of breathing in and out and how it feels when your stomach rises and falls. When finding yourself thinking of something else, to refocus your attention on breathing. With practice and increasing gradually the length of time doing so, a person learns to inhibit distractions, recognize when his or her mind drifts, and refocus.

More about meditation and mindfulness:

- The University of Massachusetts also has a Center for Mindfulness. They have been doing research for a number of years on mindfulness, particularly with patients in their stress-reduction program. See www.umassmed.edu/cfm/.
- There is a nonprofit organization, founded by Susan Kaiser Greenland, called Inner Kids Foundation (http://innerkids.org) that teaches meditation practices in schools.
- Listen to Dr. Mark Bertin's webinar through the A.D.D. Resource Center at http://www.addrc.org/add-and-mindfulness_audio/ for a good overview on mindfulness and ADHD.
- For more information and resources on this topic, see those in the "Sources and Resources" section at the end of this list.

Breathing and Progressive Relaxation Techniques with Children

- Teach children how to take conscious deep breaths to relax while listening to the sound of the air coming in and out. Show them how to inhale deeply (preferably through the nose) and slowly exhale through the mouth. The abdomen rises and expands during inhaling.
- Students can do relaxation breathing in their chairs, seated on the floor cross-legged with eyes closed, lying down, or even standing. Breathing exercises in yoga can be taught to children, too.
- Teach progressive muscle relaxation by isolating different body parts and then tightening and relaxing them. For example, while they are lying on the floor, instruct them to tighten or squeeze their toes on the left foot while taking a deep breath in and then relax the toes with a slow breath out. Continue to do the same tightening and relaxing muscles up the left leg (calf muscles, knee, thigh). Proceed in this fashion to the right side of the lower body, to the abdomen and upper body, each arm, hands and fingers, chest, neck, jaw, and face.
- Teach children that when their bodies are relaxed, they are better able to think and plan. Help them understand that when they are nervous, stressed, and angry, there is a tensing of certain body parts that they should be able to feel. Once they learn to recognize when their fists clench, jaws tighten, and stomachs harden, there are strategies that can help reduce the tension and give them better self-control, such as by breathing deeply and sending their breaths consciously to relax body parts.
- Help guide children to visualize that with each breath they take in, their body becomes filled slowly with a soothing color, aroma, sound, light, warmth, or other pleasant, comfortable feeling. For example, ask students to think of a color that makes them feel comfortable, peaceful, and relaxed. Then practice with closed eyes, breathing in that color and sending it (blowing it) throughout the body—the color going down their throat, into the neck and chest, down to the stomach, and so on.

Yoga and Other Controlled Exercises

Yoga has many health and psychological benefits, among them stress reduction and heightening one's focus and self-awareness. Learning and practicing yoga may help children quiet themselves in order to feel calm, relaxed, and better able to concentrate.

Organizations and Resources for Teaching Yoga and Mindfulness to Children

- Little Flower Yoga (http://littlefloweryoga.com)
- YoKid (http://yokid.org)
- Yoga Kids (http://yogakids.com/)
- Yoga 4 Classrooms (www.yoga4classrooms.com)
- In addition to finding yoga classes for children in your community, there are many good books and DVDs books that teach yoga postures and slow movement games and exercises for children, a few of which include those in the "Sources and Resources" section at the end of this list by Cohen Harper (2013), Flynn (2013), Goldberg (2013), and Wenig (2003).

Other

- Controlled exercises, such as those taught through Brain Gym (www.braingym.com) or others recommended by an occupational therapist may be useful to teach children with ADHD as well.

Guided Imagery and Visualization

- The ability to visualize colorful, vivid images with rich imagination and detailed action is a natural skill of childhood. These same skills have been found useful in empowering people to help overcome obstacles in their lives. Visualization techniques are used to improve memory and learning, facilitate healing, and strengthen other important skills, such as studying, social skills, coping, and creative expression.
- Teach children to visualize themselves in situations where they are achieving and being successful. For example, prior to taking a test, they can visualize themselves in detail: focused, well prepared, and working diligently taking the test. Encourage them to see themselves persistently and carefully reading each item, pacing themselves, and confidently answering questions. They can imagine feeling relaxed, not nervous or anxious. Have students picture themselves finishing the test and going back to check for careless errors.
- Many resources use these techniques for self-help and management, for example, Imagery for Kids: Discovering Your Special Place (2004) and The Power of Your Child's Imagination (2009) by Charlotte Reznick (www.imageryforkids.com) combines gentle music and a guided journey. Ready, Set, R.E.L.A.X. (1997) by Jeffrey Allen and Roger Klein is a program designed to help reduce children's stress and anxiety by progressive muscle relaxation, guided visualization, and positive self-talk (www.readysetrelax.com).
- According to Reznick (n.d.), "From preschoolers to adolescents, guided imagery can build confidence and self-esteem, as well as help children develop their

own inner resources, and learn to express feelings they generally are not able to verbalize. Imagery has been specifically helpful in such areas as developing positive social skills and study habits, overcoming school phobia, calming hyperactivity, developing empathy and sensitivity, increasing creative expression, and much more."

Exercise and Physical Activity

We are all aware of the health benefits of exercise. Scientific evidence shows that physical activity can improve brain function as well.

- Exercise stimulates the central nervous system by increasing blood flow and oxygen to the brain.
- Exercise strengthens muscles, improves coordination, builds stamina, elevates mood, and is a positive outlet for excess energy. It has many benefits for a person's physical and mental health, learning, and overall well-being.
- Research indicates that exercise results in the growth of new nerve cells and increases in the levels of certain brain chemicals (Lara, 2012; van Prag, 2009; Wendt, 2011).

Exercise and ADHD

- Exercise is particularly beneficial for children and adults with ADHD because it has been shown to increase focus and alertness and boost memory and other cognitive skills.
- Studies suggest a link between physical activity and behavior and academic performance of children with ADHD. Research shows that exercise improves the attention system by increasing the levels of the brain chemicals dopamine and norepinephrine. Exercise has beneficial effects on other areas of the brain as well. Regular physical activity boosts the functioning and performance of children and adults with ADHD (Ratey, 2008).
- A study by Verret, Guay, Berthiaume, Gardiner, and Béliveau (2012) showed that doing moderate to vigorous intensity exercise forty-five minutes a day, three times a week, for ten weeks improved cognitive function and behavior in children with ADHD (Lara, 2012).
- According to Ratey (2008), for those with ADHD, highly structured exercise that requires complex movements such as martial arts, gymnastics, ballet, figure skating, or rock climbing have a greater positive impact than aerobic exercise alone.
- Sports, dance, and other such physical activities are not only fun but also teach and provide opportunities to practice focused attention, self-discipline, and self-control.

What Type of Physical Activity Is Best for Kids with ADHD?

It is clear how important it is to get kids with ADHD involved in a sport or other physical activity. The key is finding the one or ones that are right for the individual child.

- Some children with ADHD have difficulty in team sports, especially those that have a lot of down time and require having to wait patiently for their turn to participate, such as baseball. Poor social skills, low frustration tolerance, distractibility, and lack of self-control can cause problems in a team sport. Unfortunately, poor performance in a team sport can lead to ridicule and social rejection of a child with an already fragile self-esteem.

- Many children with ADHD do best in individual sports, such as swimming, diving, martial arts, gymnastics, wrestling, track and field, tennis, skating, horseback riding, golf, or fencing. Of the martial arts, Tae Kwon Do is reported to be particularly beneficial for kids with ADHD.
- It is most important to find a sport or other physical activity that the child is interested in pursuing and has the motivation required to put forth the effort and stick to it.
- Although team sports are not the best for some children with ADHD, others do fine or excel in them. Team activities are great ways to learn and practice social skills such as cooperation, taking turns, as well as following directions and other important skills that are often weak in children with ADHD (*List 2.17*).

Parents and Teachers Should Consider

- Exercise in the morning, such as a before-school jogging program or aerobic workout, may increase a child's academic and behavioral performance.
- Recess is an important time of the day for students with ADHD, and loss of recess as a negative consequence should be avoided.
- Movement breaks and exercise activities incorporated throughout the school day are important for all students, especially those with ADHD.
- When a child is showing signs of agitation, frustration, or anger, a quick exercise break can help regulate those emotions and avoid escalating behavior.
- Exercise before sitting down to do homework is helpful for many children with ADHD.
- Use exercise breaks between activities at home and school. For example, encourage short breaks to shoot baskets, dance, jump on a trampoline, or whatever else the child enjoys as rewards for accomplishing mini-goals.
- See *Lists 2.3, 2.4, 2.15, 2.16, 3.3, 3.4, 3.5, 3.7, and 4.9* for more on this topic.

Green Time

- A few studies have shown that exposure to green, outdoor settings can be beneficial for children with ADHD, with improved symptoms, particularly in attention.
- "Studies show that kids with ADHD who spend time outdoors in a green setting—a tree-lined street, park, or grassy backyard—feel calmer and more focused than those who spend hours at the computer or on an asphalt playground" (Taylor, 2008, p. 30).
- Based on their studies, researchers Kuo and Taylor (2004) recommend that children with ADHD play outdoors before starting on homework or any activity that requires attention.
- It is suggested that parents do activities together with their child that are out in nature, such as a family hike or bike ride or going to the park together. Finding an outdoor activity that the child loves and making it part of a regular routine may be helpful.
- Letting students work under a tree or play a game on an open field or other natural setting may also have benefits back in the classroom.

More Fun and Play and Laughter

- Play is the work of childhood and important for people of all ages. There are different types of play, all of which are beneficial when balanced. According to Learning Works for Kids (http://learningworksforkids.com/), children's play should include a balance of social play (with friends, siblings, parents, teammates), active (physical) play, creative play (which involves exploration, innovation, and imagination), digital play (which can involve apps, digital games, tablets, or other digital technologies), and free play with no predetermined rules (Katz, 2013).
- Many games stimulate and strengthen thinking and reasoning, imagination, problem solving, social skills, memory, coordination, focused attention, and lots of other skills (*Lists 2.12, 2.13, 5.3, 5.10, 5.14, 7.12*).
- Laughter is one of the best ways to release stress and feel good. The chemicals released in the body through laughter reduce pain and tension. So take time to play together, have fun, and laugh!

Music

Music is well known to have many positive benefits in addition to pleasure and enjoyment. Music can be helpful for relaxation, soothing away worries, and bringing a sense of inner peace. Music also stimulates and activates the brain. Brain imaging shows how music lights up certain brain regions.

- Many people find that they are better able to focus and are more motivated and productive when listening to music. Neuroscience is learning more and more about the effects of auditory stimulation on the brain, and music therapy is being used to help heal the brain as well (for example, in people with traumatic brain injuries, Alzheimer's, and autism).
- "For children with ADHD music therapy bolsters attention and focus, reduces hyperactivity, and strengthens social skills." The rhythm and structure of music may be helpful in regulating the ADHD brain. It can be used as a tool to help train the brain for stronger focus and self-control (Rodgers, 2012, p. 47).
- Many teachers find that playing classical music, soothing environmental sounds, and instrumental arrangements contribute to better learning, attention, and behavior. Different forms of music have been found to be effective in increasing the ability to focus, soothe, and relax to boost learning, creativity, and critical-thinking skills.
- Environmental sounds (of a rain forest, oceans, or waterfalls, for example) and classical music (such as Debussy's *Claire de Lune* and Vivaldi's *Four Seasons*) have a calming effect. Examples of contemporary artists whose music is calming are Kitaro, George Winston, Steven Halpern, Enya, Hillary Stagg, Zamfir, Moby, Peter Kater, and Jim Chappell.
- Certain kinds of instrumental music arrangements and rhythmic patterns are believed to have calming and focusing effects, such as those with sixty beats per minute, the same tempo as a resting heart rate. Gary Lamb's music (www.garylamb.com) and REI Institute (www.reiinstitute.com) are two sources for such music.
- "Research shows that pleasurable music increases dopamine levels in the brain. This neurotransmitter—responsible for regulating attention, working memory, and motivation—is in low supply in ADHD brains" (Rodgers, 2012, p. 47).
- Listening to energizing music can help children and teens with ADHD when they are cognitively fatigued or have low energy for tasks.

- Encourage and provide the opportunity for children to learn how to play musical instruments. The discipline of learning and practicing an instrument can be difficult, but if the child learns how to play an instrument and enjoys doing so, it will be a gift for life.
- Experiment with different kinds of music at home and in the classroom. Creating a playlist of songs for specific routines can be very helpful. For example, create a home morning playlist with a few songs that correlate with the schedule. Morning songs can be upbeat and energizing, and an evening playlist can have songs correlating with the getting ready for bed routine, ending with songs that are slow tempo and relaxing. Certain songs played in the classroom can signal to students it is time for cleaning up, lining up, and other transitions (*Lists 2.1, 2.10*).

Art

Any opportunity to give children creative outlets that they find pleasurable is well worth pursuing. Many children with ADHD and learning disabilities have artistic strengths and talent. Drawing, painting, sculpting, photography, and other forms of visual art expression can have very beneficial effects. Painting, drawing, and sculpting are a great hands-on treatment for calming mind and body.

The visual arts are a means of self-expression and enable one to express graphically what may be difficult to do verbally, such as talking about feelings and emotions. Art therapy is based on the premise that self-expression can be used to address emotional problems, develop interpersonal skills, manage behavior, reduce stress, and increase self-awareness. Different parts of the brain are engaged when painting, drawing, and sculpting, for example, those involved in motor skills, attention, and working memory (Nelson, n.d.).

It may be helpful for parents and teachers to give a child a piece of clay to manipulate or paper and crayons when seeing signs of agitation, frustration, or anger. Working with artistic materials can be a simple and pleasurable way to help a child calm down and regain control.

Sources and Resources

ADDitude editors. (2006). The natural remedy for ADD: An interview with Dr. Frances Kuo. *ADDitude Magazine, 6*(4), 14–15.

ADDitude editors. (2010). Breathing lessons: Meditative powers. *ADDitude Magazine, 11*(2), 41–42.

Barrow, Karen. (2010). Dose of nature. *ADDitude Magazine, 11*(2), 38–40.

Bertin, Mark (2011a). Mindfulness and managing ADHD. *Attention Magazine, 18*(3), 16-17.

Bertin, Mark. (2011b). *The family ADHD solution*. New York: Palgrave Macmillan.

Bertin, Mark. (2014). ADD/ADHD and mindfulness - audio presentation. By A.D.D. Resource Center. Retrieved from http://www.addrc.org/add-and-mindfulness_audio/

Cohen Harper, Jennifer. (2013). *Little flower yoga for kids: A yoga and mindfulness program to help your child improve attention and emotional balance*. Oakland, CA: New Harbinger Publications.

Flynn, Lisa. (2013). *Yoga for children: 200+ yoga poses, breathing exercises, and meditations for healthier, happier, more resilient children*. Avon, MA: Adams Media.

Goldberg, Louise. (2013). *Yoga therapy for children with autism and special needs*. New York: W. W. Norton.

Halperin, Jeffrey M., Yoon, Carol A., & Rozon, Maria. (2011). Play together: Having fun while helping your child with ADHD. *Attention Magazine, 18*(3), 20–23.

Jackson, Maggie. (2008). Brain training. *ADDitude Magazine, 9*(2), 39–43.

Kaiser Greenland, Susan. (2010). *The mindful child*. New York: Atria Books. Retrieved from www.susankaisergreenland.com/book.html

Katz, Mark. (2012). Mindfulness and adult ADHD. *Attention Magazine, 19*(3), 7–8.

Katz, Mark. (2013). CHADD's promising practices: Learning works for kids: A healthy and balanced play diet. *Attention Magazine, 20*(4), 6–7.

Kuo, F. E., & Taylor, A. F. (2004). A potential natural treatments for attention-deficit/hyperactivity disorder: Evidence from a national study. *American Journal of Public Health, 94*(9), 1580–1586.

Lara, Michael. (2012). The exercise prescription for ADHD. *Attention Magazine, 19*(3), 22–25.

Mulrine, Christopher F., Prater, Mary Ann, & Jenkins, Amelia. (2008). *Teaching exceptional children, 40*(5) 16–22.

Nelson, Stacey. (n.d.). Art therapy: Controlling symptoms with creativity. *ADDitude Magazine*. Retrieved from www.additudemag.com/adhd/article/10114.html

Ratey, John J. (2008). The exercise solution. *ADDitude Magazine, 8*(4), 36–39.

Ratey, John J., with Hagerman, Eric. (2008). *Spark: The revolutionary new science of exercise and the brain*. New York: Little, Brown.

Rodgers, Anni Layne. (2012). Your child's brain on music. *ADDitude Magazine, 12*(4), 47–50.

Taylor, John F. (2008). Let the games begin. *ADDitude Magazine, 8*(5), 30–31.

van Prag, H. (2009). Exercise and the brain: Something to chew on. *Trends in Neurosciences, 32*(5), 283–290.

Verret, C., Guay, M. C., Berthiaume, C., Gardiner, P., & Béliveau, L. (2012). A physical activity program improves behavior and cognitive functions in children with ADHD: An exploratory study. *Journal of Attention Disorders, 16*(1), 71–80.

Wendt, Michael. (2011). Linking fitness and academic readiness. *Attention Magazine, 18*(3), 28–29.

Wenig, Marsha. (2003). *YogaKids: Educating the whole child through yoga*. New York: Stewart, Tabori and Chang.

Zylowska, Lidia. (2012). *The mindfulness prescription for adult ADHD: An 8-step program for strengthening attention, managing emotions, and achieving your goals*. Trumpeter Books.

7.8 What Kids with ADHD Need from Parents and Teachers

What Children and Teens Need from Parents

- Their unconditional love and acceptance and to hear and feel frequently how much they are loved and appreciated
- To know they are not deficient in the eyes of their parents—that the focus is on their strengths, not weaknesses
- Reasonable and realistic expectations
- Empathy, tolerance, and forgiveness
- Positive attention and feedback
- Support and encouragement
- Clear limits and structure
- Fair, clear, and reasonable rules and expectations
- Monitoring, supervision, and follow-through
- Positive and proactive rather than reactive discipline
- Consistency and logical, reasonable consequences
- Predictability of schedules and routines
- Lots of reminders and prompts without nagging, criticism, or sarcasm
- Praise and recognition for what they are doing right
- To hear the words: "That was a good choice you made." "Thank you for … " "I'm proud of you." "I have confidence in you." "I'm here for you."
- To be able to let down their guard at home and express their needs, thoughts, and emotions openly
- To feel they have choices and are involved in some decision making
- Help in understanding and labeling their feelings ("I'm frustrated [or disappointed or worried].")
- To have their feelings validated by parents' active listening
- For parents to focus on important issues and downplay less critical ones
- An emphasis on their own personal best efforts and self-improvement
- Help with coping skills and feelings of anxiety, frustration, or anger
- Modeling and practicing calm, rational, problem solving
- To know that it is okay to make mistakes and for parents to acknowledge when they make mistakes themselves
- Buffering from unnecessary stress and frustration
- Preparation for changes and allowing time to adapt and adjust
- Fun and good humor
- Escape valve outlets
- Numerous opportunities to develop their areas of strength, pursue their interests, and participate in extracurricular and enrichment activities
- Special time with parents, not contingent on anything, just time to talk and have fun together, building and strengthening the relationship

- Help with organization, time management, and study skills
- Structuring of their work environment, tasks, and materials
- Help getting started with chores, assignments, and projects
- Help with planning, following schedules, and keeping on target with deadlines and responsibilities
- Parents' involvement and close communication with the school
- Parents to become knowledgeable about ADHD so that they will be well equipped to manage, support, and advocate effectively on their behalf
- The support, intervention, and treatments known (proven by research) to be most effective in managing the symptoms of ADHD
- Their belief in the child and optimism about the future

What Students with ADHD Need from Teachers

- A positive classroom environment that is welcoming, organized, inclusive, and well managed
- To feel safe and comfortable in the classroom environment, knowing that they will be treated with dignity and respect, and not ever deliberately criticized, embarrassed, or humiliated in front of their peers
- A classroom that is well structured with clear expectations and well-practiced procedures and with predictability of schedules and routines
- Instruction and materials that motivate, engage their interest, and keep them actively involved, therefore minimizing boredom and frustration (the sources of many behavior problems in the classroom)
- Clearly defined and enforced rules and consequences
- Structuring of their work environment, tasks, and materials
- Assistance through transitions
- Assistance in helping to focus and maintain attention
- Discreet cueing, prompting, and reminders
- Help and training with organization, time management, and study skills
- Learning-style and environmental accommodations
- Extra time to process information and perform tasks
- Creative, interesting, and challenging curriculum
- Choices, options, and flexibility
- Differentiated instruction
- Teaching strategies that build on their strengths and help bypass their weaknesses
- More frequent reinforcement and powerful rewards than are often needed by other students
- Variety, variety, variety
- Positive attention from teachers and peers
- Ongoing support, encouragement, and coaching for skills in which they are weak
- An emphasis on their own personal best efforts and self-improvement rather than on competition against one another

- The opportunity to participate in school activities that showcase their areas of strength (art, music, PE, creative electives) to their peers
- A school plan (IEP or 504 if eligible) or informal supports and interventions that may involve a plan developed by the SST or through the RTI process that is implemented and monitored for effectiveness
- Teachers who embody the following qualities:
  - Balance of firmness and flexibility (willing to make accommodations)
  - Kindness
  - Tolerance and a positive attitude
  - Fairness
  - Authority (clearly in control of the classroom)
  - Good communication and problem-solving skills
- Teachers who do the following:
  - Understand ADHD
  - Maintain high expectations, yet provide support to enable students to achieve those expectations and standards
  - Model self-control and the ability to stay calm (not react out of anger)
  - Make adjustments and modifications in homework and other performance demands as needed
  - Show they have a sense of humor and truly enjoy teaching
  - Make learning fun
  - Encourage and motivate students by seeing past the behaviors to the whole child
  - Believe the child belongs in his or her classroom and will do what it takes to help the student succeed

7.9 What Parents of Children with ADHD Need

Parenting a child with ADHD is generally more challenging and far more stressful than parenting a child without the disorder.

- Many people, not understanding the struggles of children with ADHD and their families, can be very judgmental. They may unfairly assume the child's lack of self-control and problem behaviors are because of poor parenting and lack of discipline.
- Parents of children with ADHD need to cope with not only the many challenges that other parents do not face but also the admonishments and unsolicited advice of relatives and others who simply do not understand the disorder.
- As a parent of child with ADHD (particularly if your son or daughter has severe ADHD symptoms), you may feel overwhelmed, exhausted, isolated, or shunned by other parents and at a loss of what to do to best help your child. Try not to get discouraged and know that you are not alone. There are many other parents who do understand and are happy to help and offer support. There is much that can be done to help your child be happy and successful and to get support for yourself, as well.

Become Educated about ADHD

- Fortunately, there is a wealth of resources available about ADHD, with reliable information and expert advice. The more you know and understand about the disorder, school laws, educational rights, research-validated treatments, and practical strategies for success, the better. This knowledge will give you confidence, hope, and skills to make life easier for your child and family.
- There are many ways to learn about ADHD:
  - Attend conferences such as a national or regional CHADD conferences or those sponsored by other organizations with speakers on ADHD.
  - Read extensively.
  - Listen to podcasts or webinars by expert speakers on ADHD-related topics (such as those sponsored by CHADD (www.chadd.org), The National Resource Center on AD/HD (www.help4adhd.org), the Attention Deficit Disorder Association (http://add.org), *ADDitude Magazine* (www.additudemag.com), and others such as the Learning Disability Association (http://ldaamerica.org).
- CHADD's Parent to Parent Family Training on ADHD is highly regarded and effective. The fourteen-hour program (seven two-hour sessions) was developed by Linda Smith, Beth Kaplanek, and Mary Durheim, parents who lived the experience but who also have had access to the best researchers and practitioners in the country. The Parent to Parent program is provided by instructors who have family members with ADHD and have been certified to provide the training in their community. The training can also be received online with a choice of two formats. There is an online webinar in which participants interact with the trainer and other class members. There is also an on-demand class, in which participants can have access for three months to the prerecorded training sessions and materials.
- Joining CHADD is the best investment you can make in your ADHD education. The benefits of membership are numerous. By taking advantage of the conferences, speakers, publications, parent training, and networking opportunities,

you will gain the confidence, skills, and knowledge you need to make informed decisions and best advocate for your child's needs. For more information, go to www.chadd.org/Training-Events/Parent-to-Parent-Program/Family-Training-on-ADHD-In-Your-Community.aspx.

Professional Help

- If you are having personal problems with stress and coping, seek counseling. It is very common for families of children with ADHD to need counseling at some point. Marital strife and family issues are common when there is a child in the family with any disability or special needs. There are often conflicts between parents with regard to the ADHD child and issues related to the financial burden of getting a child the needed help and treatments. It is important that any counselor or therapist you may turn to for help is knowledgeable about ADHD and related issues (*Lists 1.19, 1.22*).
- As case managers of your child's team of support (*Lists 7.1, 7.2*), it is important to find professionals with whom you feel comfortable and confident that they have the knowledge and expertise in helping children with ADHD and coexisting conditions. Other parents of children with ADHD are often the best sources for referrals to professionals in the community. Your local CHADD chapter is a good place to find other parents in your community able to recommend clinicians (counselors, physicians, psychologists) experienced and skilled in treating ADHD.
- You need the support of teachers: their accessibility and willingness to communicate regularly and work with you in partnership, their sensitivity and responsiveness to issues you report (such as the battle with homework or social problems), and of course, their flexibility, understanding, and commitment to helping your child succeed. Find ways to best build a collaborative relationship, working on common target goals with your child's teacher and other school staff who interact with your son or daughter (*Lists 2.5, 4.10, 7.3, 7.8*).

Network with Other Parents

- Probably the best support and source of comfort and hope you can find is through connecting with and networking with other parents of children with ADHD. Find out information about your local chapter of CHADD (www.chadd.org) or LDA (Learning Disabilities Association of America) (http://ldaamerica.org). These organizations are wonderful sources of information, support, and networking with other parents in your community who have children with ADHD, learning disabilities, or both (*Lists 1.19, 7.12*).
- Local chapters of these national organizations typically have monthly meetings with opportunities for parents to network and share with other parents and to hear speakers (generally local professionals with expertise in ADHD). It is worth your time to attend some meetings or other events if available in your community.
- There are online opportunities to network with other parents as well (for example, through chats and community forums of the national organizations and *ADDitude Magazine* (www.additudemag.com or http://addconnect.com). The online community forums are a great way to ask questions and get answers from ADHD experts and other individuals who may have had the same experiences as you.
- Many communities offer support groups and networking for parents in addition to the national organizations (for example, through schools, individual therapists' practices, hospitals, and agencies).

Be Kind to Yourself

- Do not neglect your own needs.
- Find some time for yourself and for participating in activities that give you pleasure.
- Enjoy your family and focus on the positive.
- Be confident in your parenting and don't beat yourself up over things you wish you knew earlier or had done differently.
- Be optimistic about your child's future!

7.10 ADHD and Gifted (Dual Exceptionalities)

Twice exceptional or dual exceptional (also referred to as *2e*) students are those who are gifted and also have a disability such as ADHD, dyslexia or another learning disability, or Asperger's syndrome. Some children with ADHD have multiple exceptionalities. For example, they are gifted and have ADHD and dyslexia. These children have very high potential in one or more areas and significant learning challenges in others. A twice exceptional student might, for example, be very advanced in math and well below grade level in reading. Because of lack of awareness, understanding, and appropriate diagnosis, students with dual exceptionalities may fall through the cracks and not receive appropriate services.

Gifted Students

- The federal government's educational definition of gifted and talented students are those "who give evidence of high achievement capability in areas such as intellectual, creative, artistic, or leadership capacity, or in specific academic fields, and who need services or activities not ordinarily provided by the school in order to fully develop those capabilities" (No Child Left Behind Act, 2004).
- States and districts vary in their criteria for identifying gifted students and how to deliver special services, programs, and activities to children meeting eligibility criteria.
- "Most identification happens in schools and is for the purpose of selecting students to participate in the school's gifted program. There are no nation-wide or even state-wide standards for identification. Each school district makes a determination about which and how many students it is able to service within its programs based on its definitions, philosophy, and resources." (National Society for the Gifted and Talented, n.d.)
- "There is a vast disparity in programs and services across and within states, leaving many high-ability students without the supports they need to achieve at high levels, which is a disservice to them and to the nation" (National Association for Gifted Children, n.d.).

Special Challenges for Twice Exceptional Students

- *Being misunderstood.* Disorders such as ADHD or dyslexia have nothing to do with IQ. Children may be highly intelligent yet have significant learning difficulties. Because they are bright, their underachievement is unfairly attributed to their being lazy or apathetic.
- *Emotional issues.* Twice exceptional students may be at risk for anxiety or low self-esteem that arise from the frustration of coping with their learning and executive function challenges and trying to live up to high expectations (often their own) to excel academically.
- *Being identified as gifted.* Twice exceptional students' disability may mask their giftedness. They may not be evaluated because average academic performance prevents them from being considered candidates for gifted programs. Others may be evaluated but not identified as gifted because of poor test-taking skills.

- *Having their disorder diagnosed and treated.* Many gifted children use their intelligence to compensate for their learning difficulties. They may go years without being diagnosed (sometimes into adulthood). Their giftedness masks their disability, but compensating for their disability on their own may take an emotional toll.
- *Receiving appropriate educational programming or services.* Twice exceptional students may not receive the intellectually challenging curriculum or enrichment they need. Also, they are far less likely to be found eligible for special education programs, related services, or accommodations, particularly when they compensate and perform at grade level.

According to Shari Gent in her interview for CHADD's *Attention* (Goodman, 2008, p. 10):

> - Gifted children with AD/HD score with greater variability among subtests on standardized tests of cognitive ability than either gifted children without AD/HD or typical children.
> - Classwork of the gifted child with AD/HD is more variable than the typical child with AD/HD. The gifted child with AD/HD will have more high performing moments.
> - Gifted children with AD/HD are more likely than the typical child with AD/HD to excel in one subject area and to have a greater knowledge of strategies. Most have a high ability to conceptualize, but poor cognitive efficiency. They are great at understanding ideas or the big picture but have difficulty managing the details and demonstrating their knowledge quickly and accurately. Therefore they seem intelligent but cannot perform.

What Twice Exceptional Students Need

- Proper evaluation and diagnosis
- Enriching experiences beyond the basic school curriculum
- Acceleration in areas of strength (being allowed to move quickly through basic content curriculum that they have already mastered, providing extra time to work on challenging projects of interest)
- A mentor to encourage and guide them
- Teamwork among school and district staff and parents who are working to meet their unique educational needs
- Opportunities to develop their strengths and interests
- The same opportunities that other gifted students receive
- Accommodations for their special needs (They may be successful in gifted programs and advanced placement classes if they are given supports and accommodations, such as assistive technology.)
- Advocacy by parents and teachers

Tips for Parents and Teachers of Twice Exceptional Students

- Be alert to signs of dual or multiple exceptionalities; don't be thrown off by highly discrepant abilities.
- Share observations with each other. Refer students for appropriate diagnostic assessments.

- Seek opportunities to nurture students' talents and showcase their strengths.
- Address emotional and self-esteem issues that arise; provide encouragement and support.

Sources and Resources

Goodman, Bryan, with Gent, Shari. (2008). Twice exceptional students. *Attention Magazine, 15*(4), 10–13.

National Association for Gifted Children. (n.d.). Gifted education in the U.S. Retrieved from: http://www.nagc.org/resources-publications/resources/gifted-education-us

National Society for the Gifted and Talented (NSGT). (n.d.). Giftedness defined. Retrieved from www.nsgt.org/giftedness-defined/

No Child Left Behind Act, Pub. L. No. 107.110, Title IX, Part A, Definitions §22 (2002); §7802, 20 U.S.C.; §22 (2004).

For more information on this topic, see these resources:

Association for the Education of Gifted Underachieving Students (www.aegus1.org). Note: There are several articles at this website that may be of interest.

Smart Kids with Learning Disabilities (www.smartkidswithld.org)

Twice Exceptional Newsletter (Glen Ellyn Media) (www.2enewsletter.com)

Uniquely Gifted Resources for Gifted Children with Special Needs (www.uniquelygifted.org)

7.11 Do's and Don'ts for Parents and Teachers

- **Don't** expect a child to be able to do things that developmentally he or she is not yet able to do.
- **Do** remember that children with ADHD are delayed in their development of executive functions, which means they may be a few years behind their peers in their ability to control their impulses, regulate their emotions, plan, organize, manage time, and other executive skills (*Lists 1.2, 1.4, 4.1, 4.4*).
- **Don't** assume when a child does not listen and follow directions that he or she is deliberately noncompliant.
- **Do** remember that attention, working memory, and difficulty stopping one activity to do something else (some of the EF weaknesses of children with ADHD) are more likely the reason, and you may need to use other strategies to improve this behavior (*Lists 2.4, 2.12, 2.13, 4.2*).
- **Don't** overly focus your radar on the child's misbehaviors.
- **Do** consciously make an effort to notice and pay attention to the child when he or she is behaving appropriately. In other words, catch the child being good and reinforce that positive behavior with your praise and attention (*Lists 2.1, 2.2*).
- **Don't** forget or overlook how essential it is to cultivate and nurture the child's areas of strength and interest.
- **Do** involve the child in as many opportunities as possible to build on his or her talents, interests, and passions. Help the child gain confidence and competence through those activities in life that give him or her joy.
- **Don't** try to control what no one has control over—someone else's behavior.
- **Do** work on what you can take control over: your own responses to the child's behavior, your own education and knowledge about ADHD and effective behavioral strategies, and the structuring, management, and discipline practices you choose to employ (*List 2.14*).
- **Don't** give up on using behavior modification techniques.
- **Do** know that these behavioral interventions, although not easy to implement and follow through with consistently, can be very helpful. Use of incentive systems and behavioral programs (for example, charts, tokens, and rewards) for improving a child's behavior is an important part of managing ADHD at home and school. If you are using a system that is no longer working, realize that you need to revamp and revise the program or technique from time to time to maintain the interest and motivation of children with ADHD. For example, change the reward menu options or chart design. It is well worth the time and effort (*Lists 2.1, 2.2, 2.6, 2.7, 2.8, 2.9, 2.12, 2.13*).
- **Don't** respond or dole out negative consequences for a child's misbehavior when you are in an angry, emotional state.
- **Do** wait until you have had a chance to calm down, regain your composure, and have the ability to think through an appropriate response before acting (*Lists 2.14, 2.15, 2.16*).
- **Don't** believe all that you hear or read about ADHD. There is a lot of inaccurate and erroneous information about ADHD on the Internet and other media.
- **Do** seek out information about ADHD and treatments that are proven effective; come from reputable, reliable sources; and are based on evidence from scientific research (*Lists 1.4, 1.19, 1.20, 1.22, 1.23,* and within many other lists within this book).

Additional Do's and Don'ts for Parents

- **Don't** keep your child's ADHD a secret from those who spend much time with him or her (for example, babysitters, teachers, coaches, relatives, close family friends).
- **Do** inform those people so they better understand your child and his or her ADHD-related behaviors. It is helpful to share, as well, some key strategies you find effective in preventing or minimizing some of the challenging behaviors.
- **Don't** bypass the classroom teacher by going directly to the school administrator with issues or concerns.
- **Do** grant a teacher the professional courtesy and respect to first go to him or her to share your concerns, discuss problems, and try to resolve them together before bringing the issues or concerns to the administrator.
- **Don't** be overly demanding of teachers with regard to the individual attention and degree of accommodations you expect for your child.
- **Do** understand the teacher's responsibility to all students in the classroom. Keep in mind what is reasonable when making requests.
- **Don't** doubt your parenting abilities or be hard on yourself for what might have or have not taken place so far.
- **Do** know that it is never too late to learn, make changes, and move ahead. You are not to blame for your child's ADHD or for not acting on what you did not yet know.
- **Don't** think you are alone and have no other parents to talk to who understand your child's and family's challenges.
- **Do** know that there are many ways to connect and network with other parents of children with ADHD, which is very beneficial and a wonderful source of support. There are various parent groups for children with ADHD depending on the community. Throughout the United States there are local chapters of CHADD. Go to the national website at www.chadd.org to find your local CHADD chapter. Attend at least a few of their meetings. There are often local professionals who speak on ADHD-related topics and parents share and learn from each other.
- **Don't** neglect yourself or your own needs (for good physical and mental health, nurturing, respite, and support).
- **Do** take time for yourself. Seek help. Find ways to recharge and fulfill your own personal needs. This is important for everyone—especially parents who live with the daily stress that is so common in families of children with ADHD or other disabilities. You are best able to parent and care for your family when you are happy and healthy.
- See *Lists 1.13, 7.1, 7.2, 7.3, and 7.8* for more information related to this topic.

Additional Do's and Don'ts for Teachers

- **Don't** be afraid to ask questions and seek advice and support when you have concerns about a student or need help or guidance.
- **Do** involve your support staff for assistance, consult with your special education teachers, and use the problem-solving approach through your school's SST or RTI teams (*Lists 6.1, 6.2*).
- **Don't** neglect to do everything you can to forge a collaborative relationship with parents.

- **Do** invite partnership and teamwork with parents:
  - Welcome them to visit the school and observe their child in the classroom (assuming this does not conflict with school policy).
  - Communicate with them frequently and regularly and make a plan for working together such as using a daily report card on specific goals (*Lists 2.5, 2.9,* and the appendix).
  - Let parents know that you care very much about their son or daughter and are willing to go the extra mile to help their child succeed.
  - Try the other strategies suggested in *Lists 4.6, 4.8, 4.10, 7.1, and 7.3.*
- **Don't** listen to previous teachers who are eager to share the negative traits and characteristics of their students to you.
- **Do** assume the best of the child. Allow each student to start the year with a fresh, clean slate.
- **Don't** get discouraged when plans or strategies are not working with a student.
- **Do** be tenacious and relentless in trying other strategies and revising the plan. If plan A stops working, there is always plan B, C, D, and so forth.
- **Don't** work alone.
- **Do** find buddies, share with colleagues, and collaborate.
- **Don't** worry about others who may feel it is unfair to make accommodations or modifications for certain students.
- **Do** make the accommodations and other adaptations needed for individual students to succeed. Fairness is equal opportunity to learn and be successful and trying to give each student what he or she needs for that to happen. It does not mean giving every student the same thing.
- **Don't** underestimate how important you are in the life of your students with ADHD.
- **Do** know that all that you do to help these students achieve success—your extra time and energy, positive mind-set and efforts, and positive relationship you build with them—makes a huge difference for those students and their families.

7.12 Recommended Websites and Resources

The following websites are listed alphabetically by category.

US National Organizations, Nonprofits, and Government-Supported Information about ADHD and Learning Disabilities

American Academy of Child and Adolescent Psychiatry (www.aacap.org) (search ADHD)

American Academy of Pediatrics (www.aap.org) (search ADHD)

American Psychological Association (www.apa.org) (search ADHD)

Attention Deficit Disorder Association (ADDA) (www.add.org)

Centers for Disease Control and Prevention (www.cdc.gov) (search ADHD)

Children & Adults with Attention Deficit-Hyperactivity Disorder (CHADD) (www.chadd.org)

Council for Exceptional Children (CEC) (www.cec.sped.org)

Council for Learning Disabilities (www.cldinternational.org)

Division for Learning Disabilities (http://teachingLD.org www.dldcec.org)

International Dyslexia Association (IDA) (www.interdys.org)

Learning Disabilities Association of America (LDA) (www.ldanatl.org)

Learning Disabilities: Information and Resources (www.ldonline.org)

National Alliance on Mental Illness (www.nami.org) (search ADHD)

National Association of School Psychologists (www.nasponline.org) (search ADHD)

National Center for Learning Disabilities (NCLD) (www.ncld.org)

National Institute of Child Health & Child Development (www.nichd.nih.gov) (search ADHD)

National Institute of Mental Health (www.nimh.nih.gov) (search ADHD)

National Resource Center for AD/HD (a program of CHADD) (www.help4adhd.org)

National Research Center on Learning Disabilities (www.nrcld.org)

Other Information and Resources on ADHD and Related Topics

About.com (on ADD/ADHD) (http://add.about.com/ADD)

ADDitude Magazine (www.additudemag.com/)

ADDvance (http://addvance.com) (website of Patricia Quinn and Kathleen Nadeau for information on girls and women with ADHD)

A.D.D. Warehouse (www.addwarehouse.com)

ADHD Shared Focus (www.adhdsharedfocus.com) and ADHD and You (www.adhdandyou.com) (for parents and guardians, educators, and students; sponsored by Shire Pharmaceuticals)

Attention (CHADD's publication) (www.chadd.org)

Attention Deficit Disorder Resources (www.addresources.org/)

Dr. Russell Barkley's official site for information about ADHD (www.russellbarkley.net)

Center for Children and Families (http://ccf.buffalo.edu/resources_downloads.php) (ADHD fact sheets, treatment programs, and assessment instruments for parents, teachers, mental health professionals, and students)

Centre for ADHD Awareness, Canada (CADDAC) (www.caddac.ca)

Health Central (www.healthcentral.com/adhd)

Healthy Place (www.healthyplace.com/) (search ADHD)

Help for ADD (www.helpforadd.com) (David Rabiner's site; subscribers receive a free monthly report called *Attention Research Update* summarizing some of the latest research on ADHD.)

Inside ADHD (www.InsideADHD.org) (supported by Shire Pharmaceuticals)

Kids Health (www.kidshealth.org) (search ADHD) (sponsored by Nemours Center for Children's Health Media Nemours Foundation)

Kids in the House (www.kidsinthehouse.com) (a parenting resource, contains thousands of videos on parenting including videos under ADD/ADHD by Ned Hallowell, Robert Brooks, and Jerome Schultz)

Learning Works for Kids (http://learningworksforkids.com/adhd/) (information on apps and games for ADHD)

Mayo Clinic (www.mayoclinic.org) (search ADHD)

Medical News Today (www.medicalnewstoday.com/categories/adhd)

National Federation of Families for Children's Mental Health (www.ffcmh.org/)

University of Maryland Medical Center (http://umm.edu/health/medical/reports/articles/attention-deficit-hyperactivity-disorder)

*My website (www.sandrarief.com) as well the websites of many other authors and experts on ADHD also share information and tools for managing ADHD. There are national organizations and online resources for other disabilities and disorders that commonly coexist with ADHD. Other countries in Latin America, Europe, and elsewhere also have ADHD support groups and organizations.

Resources for Managing Behavior and Self-Regulation Interventions

Association for Positive Behavior Support (www.apbs.org)

Behavior Advisor (www.BEHAVIORAdvisor.com) (website of Thomas McIntyre)

Center for Children and Families (www.ccf.buffalo.edu/resources_downloads.php) (twelve-page packet of daily report cards developed by William Pelham Jr. et al. and lots of other resources)

Direct behavior ratings (www.directbehaviorratings.org) (University of Connecticut)

Free printable behavior charts (www.FreePrintableBehaviorCharts.com)

Intervention Central (www.interventioncentral.org) (Jim Wright's website)

New Management (www.newmanagement.com) (Rick Morris's website)

Pinterest (www.pinterest.com/sandrarief/class-behavior-management/ and www.pinterest.com/sandrarief/self-regulation/) (numerous practical strategies on classroom behavior management and self-regulation)

Positive Behavioral Interventions and Supports (www.pbis.org) (US Department of Education Office of Special Education Program's Technical Assistance Center of PBIS)

Special Connections (www.specialconnections.ku.edu) (University of Kansas's site for research-validated strategies to help students with special needs in general education classrooms)

Whole Brain Teaching (http://wholebrainteaching.com/) (Chris Biffle's website)

Why Try program (www.whytry.org) (social-emotional learning program)

*See the many other websites listed in section 2 of this book for behavioral strategies, supports, tools, and interventions.

Research-Based Resources Related to Teaching and Learning

American Institutes for Research: The Access Center (www.air.org/project/access-center-improving-outcomes-all-students-k-8) (The Access Center was a national technical assistance center funded by the Office of Special Education Programs [OSEP] within the Department of Education. The purpose of the Access Center was to improve access to the general education curriculum for students with disabilities at the elementary and middle school levels.)

Center on Instruction for K-8 interventions (www.centeroninstruction.org) (one of five national content centers funded by the US Department of Education to support the sixteen regional comprehensive centers as they helped state education leaders raise student achievement, close achievement gaps, and improve teaching and learning for all students in their state)

Cognitive Strategy Instruction at University of Nebraska Lincoln (www.unl.edu/csi)

Evidence-Based Intervention Network (http://ebi.missouri.edu/) (The EBI Network at University of Missouri has been developed to provide guidance in the selection and implementation of evidence-based interventions in the classroom setting.)

Florida Center for Reading Research (www.fcrr.org) (The Florida Center for Reading Research [FCRR] is a multidisciplinary research center at Florida State University. FCRR explores all aspects of reading research—basic research into literacy-related skills for typically developing readers and those who struggle, studies of effective prevention and intervention, and psychometric work on formative assessment.)

Intervention Central (www.interventioncentral.org) (lots of instructional interventions and strategies)

IRIS Center (http://iris.peabody.vanderbilt.edu) (provides free online interactive resources that translate research about educating students with disabilities into practice)

KU Center for Research on Learning (www.ku-crl.org) (the University of Kansas Center for Research on Learning)

Learning Toolbox (http://coe.jmu.edu/LearningToolbox) (James Madison University Learning Toolbox: cognitive, mnemonic-based learning strategies)

National Center for Accelerating Student Learning (http://kc.vanderbilt.edu/casl)

Reading Rockets (www.readingrockets.org) (a national multimedia literacy initiative offering information and resources on how young kids learn to read, why so many struggle, and how caring adults can help)

Read Write Think (www.readwritethink.org) (affiliated with International Reading Association)

Rubistar (http://rubistar.4teachers.org) (a free tool for helping teachers make rubrics)

Teach-nology (www.teach-nology.com) (free rubrics, premade lessons by grade level, and lots of other resources for teachers)

What Works Clearinghouse (www.whatworks.ed.gov) (of the Institute for Education Sciences in the US Department of Education)

See the many other resources on effective instructional and learning practices in lists throughout sections 3, 4, and 5.

Resources Regarding Special Education, IEPs, Disability Rights, and RTI

Center for Parent Information and Resources' Library (www.parentcenterhub.org/resources) (The National Dissemination Center for Children with Disabilities [NICHCY] no longer exists but all of their publications as well as training curriculum on IDEA 2004 that was formerly available at www.nichcy.org is now available at www.parentcenterhub.org.)

Council of Parent Attorneys & Advocates (www.copaa.org)

Federation for Children with Special Needs (www.fcsn.org)

IDEA (http://idea.ed.gov/explore/home) (US Department of Education, Office of Special Education Programs' [OSEP's] IDEA website).

National Association of School Psychologists (NASP) (www.nasponline.org)

National Center on Response to Intervention (www.rti4success.org)

Office of Special Education and Rehabilitated Services (www.ed.gov/offices/OSERS)

Wrightslaw (www.wrightslaw.com) (regarding students with disabilities' rights under IDEA and Section 504)

See additional resources listed in *Lists 6.1 through 6.6.* Many of the ADHD and LD organizations and resources listed previously in this list also have information on these topics.

Fun and Educational Websites and More

Here are some educational websites, many of them free, that parents and teachers may find helpful in motivating children to learn and practice academic skills.

ABC Teach (www.abcteach.com/) (preK–8 grade materials and creative activities; over five thousand free documents available, including printable worksheets, interactive activities, and more)

Brain Pop (www.brainpop.com/) (provides wonderful animated videos about a wide range of topics children will encounter in school. There's also BrainPop Jr. and BrainPop Free Stuff [www.brainpop.com/free_stuff/], free educational movies, and lots of games and activities for kids.)

Discover Education (www.discoveryeducation.com) (has great, free games, interactives, and resources for students [and parents])

Fuel the Brain (www.fuelthebrain.com/) (provides numerous free or inexpensive games, interactives, and printables to help enhance and practice elementary skills in math, science, and language arts)

Fun Brain (www.funbrain.com/) (published by Family Education Network; a great site of free educational games, online books, and comics; for kids preschool–8; offers more than one hundred fun, interactive games that develop skills in math, reading, and literacy)

Internet4Classrooms (www.internet4classrooms.com/) (packed full of free K–12 games, activities, and other free resources; huge lists of linked resources can be accessed by grade level or subject)

Mr. Nussbaum (www.mrnussbaum.com) (provides lots of free interactive games, research themes, activities for K–8, and teacher tools)

Positive Engagement Project (PEP) (http://pepnonprofit.org) (provides lots of K–6 free learning games and strategies)

Power My Learning (http://powermylearning.com/) (links to hundreds of high-quality educational games and activities that are organized by subject area and by grade level; accounts are free)

ReadWriteThink (www.readwritethink.org/bright-ideas/) (has a lot of engaging activities, projects, and games at each grade level for teachers or parents to use with children)

Scholastic (www.scholastic.com/kids/stacks/index.asp) (free interactive games and activities)

Sheppard Software (www.sheppardsoftware.com) (lots of free, interactive, educational games designed for kids in grades K–5 in math, grammar, geography, science, health, art, and more)

Sports Illustrated for Kids (www.sikids.com/) (interactive website with articles on sports-related topics and lots of games; great way to get your sports-loving, reluctant readers to read)

Starfall (www.starfall.com) (a wonderful site to teach children reading using a systematic phonics approach in conjunction with phonemic awareness practice; for children as young as toddlers until about second grade or so)

Story Place (www.storyplace.org/) (a children's digital Spanish and English bilingual library site, which includes a collection of online texts and fun interactive activities for elementary kids)

Teacher Resources for Parents (http://teacherresourcesforparents.com/) (provides parents with fun and practical ways to enrich their children and better prepare them for school)

Turtle Diary (www.turtlediary.com/) (has an extensive range of online educational games and activities geared for kids preK–2; lots of the games and resources are for free, but paid membership gives full access)

Math

AAA Math (www.aaamath.com/) (a free site for thousands of interactive arithmetic lessons for kids K–8; unlimited practice is available on each topic; immediate feedback prevents practicing and learning incorrect methods)

Cool Math 4 Kids (www.coolmath4kids.com/) (lots of games, puzzles, brain benders, and fun ways to practice math skills)

Dreambox Learning Math (www.dreambox.com) (combines a rigorous math curriculum with fun online lessons that adjust to the way your child learns)

Fun Brain (www.funbrain.com/math/index.html and www.funbrain.com/kidscenter.html) (lots of free math games)

IXL (www.ixl.com/) (for students K–8; a math-practice website with unlimited practice questions on hundreds of topics for each grade level; the questions also adapt to your child's ability, increasing in difficulty as they improve; the system measures how much time your child spends on any particular skill once he or she completes a skill)

Math Card Wars (http://letsplaymath.net/2006/12/29/the-game-that-is-worth-1000-worksheets/)

Math Cats (www.mathcats.com/) (has lots of math games, quizzes, interactive projects, and more for elementary school students)

Mathletics (www.mathletics.com/) (a motivating online math program for home and school)

Math-Play (www.math-play.com/) (a site of free online math games by grade level, content, and game type)

PBS Kids (http://pbskids.org/games/math.html) (preK–1 math)

Pinterest (http://pinterest.com/sandrarief/math-strategies-activities/) (lots of math strategies and activities)

Sheppard Software (www.sheppardsoftware.com/math.htm) (free online interactive math games)

Ten Marks (www.tenmarks.com/summer/signup) (online math program)

Webmath (http://webmath.com/) (a math-help website that generates answers to specific math questions and problems, as entered by a user, at any particular moment; the math answers are generated and displayed real-time, at the moment a web user types in his or her math problem and clicks "solve"; in addition to the answers, Webmath also shows the student how to arrive at the answer)

See *List 5.14* for more fun math strategies.

Phonics, Sight Words, Word Recognition, Spelling, and Reading Fluency

FunFonix (www.funfonix.com) (free phonics games and activities)

Giggle Poetry (www.gigglepoetry.com) (has hundreds of funny poems for children to read and rate)

Pinterest (www.pinterest.com/sandrarief/) (See the numerous activities, strategies, and games found under the categories of sight words, phonics-decoding-fluency, and spelling and word work.)

Poetry 4 Kids: Ken Nesbitt's Children's Poetry Playground (www.poetry4kids.com) (funny poems, books, games, contests, lessons, discussion forums, great rhyming dictionary, streaming audio, and more)

Reading Rockets (www.readingrockets.org) (national multimedia literacy initiative offering information and resources on how young kids learn to read, why so many struggle, and how caring adults can help)

Starfall (www.starfall.com/) (alphabet, letter-sound association, beginning reading)

Teaching Heart (www.teachingheart.net/readerstheater.htm) (has readers theater scripts, which are little plays for grades K–3; it's a fun way to get kids to practice reading with expression and fluency)

Many of these sites (for example, Fun Brain, Fuel the Brain, Turtle Diary, Power My Learning, PEP Nonprofit) also have games and activities for phonics, word recognition, sight words, and spelling.

See *Lists 5.3, 5.5, and 5.10* for more related strategies.

Reading Comprehension

PEP (http://pepnonprofit.org) (See their downloads for Comprehension Shuffle and Primary Comprehension Shuffle.)

Pinterest (http://pinterest.com/sandrarief/reading-comprehension/—reading-comprehension board and http://pinterest.com/sandrarief/inferences-summarizing/)

ReadWorks (www.readworks.org/) (free website with more than one thousand nonfiction passages and comprehension questions to go with them; excellent resource for building and practicing reading comprehension skills)

See *List 5.4* for more reading comprehension strategies.

Audio Books

Audible (www.audible.com/) (has thousands of audible downloadable books for kids; a division of Amazon)

Audio Bookshelf (www.audiobookshelf.com)

Bookshare (www.bookshare.org)

Learning Ally (www.learningally.org) (formerly Recordings for the Blind and Dyslexic; both Bookshare and Learning Ally provide access to free digitized books for eligible students with reading disabilities)

Recorded Books (www.recordedbooks.com)

Storyline Online (www.storylineonline.net/) (an online video-streaming program featuring famous people, for example, James Earl Jones and Betty White, reading books aloud to children)

Tales2Go (www.tales2go.com/) (an award-winning kids' mobile audio book service that streams thousands of name-brand titles from leading publishers and storytellers to mobile devices and desktops in the classroom and beyond)

Tumble Books (www.tumblebooks.com)

Lists of Recommended Books for Kids by Categories and Ages

Children's Choice (www.reading.org/Resources/Booklists/ChildrensChoices.aspx) (Children's Choices Reading Lists: International Reading Association's winners of children's choice books)

Pinterest (http://pinterest.com/sandrarief/books-for-kids/) (contains numerous lists of books by categories that will motivate children of all ages)

Reading Rockets (www.readingrockets.org/books/summer/)

Writing

Many of these websites (such as ReadWriteThink, FunBrain, and Internet4Classrooms) have wonderful writing activities as well as games for building skills in components of writing (spelling, grammar, vocabulary).

Can Teach (www.canteach.ca/elementary/prompts.html) (extensive list of writing prompts and journal ideas)

Pinterest (http://pinterest.com/sandrarief/writing-strategies-activities/) (lots of writing strategies and activities) and (http://pinterest.com/sandrarief/handwriting-fine-motor-skills/) (fun, motivating ways to learn and practice handwriting and fine-motor skills)

Writing Fix (www.writingfix.com/) (features interactive writing activities, tools, games, and so on for building stronger writing skills in writers of any age)

See *Lists 5.7 through 5.12* for related strategies, assistive technology, and other resources for struggling or reluctant writers.

Vocabulary

Dictionary (http://dictionary.reference.com/) (online dictionary)

Fun Brain (www.funbrain.com/words.html) (vocabulary games and activities for children at different levels)

Picture Dictionary (www.pdictionary.com/) (online picture dictionary)

Thesaurus (http://thesaurus.com/) (online thesaurus)

Vocabulary (www.vocabulary.com/) (free vocabulary education site with interactive games, puzzles, and activities at different levels of difficult; great source for learning new words and how they are used)

See *List 5.3*.

Science and Social Studies

Animal Discovery (http://animaldiscovery.com) (links to animal facts, games, and more)

Arkive (www.arkive.org/) (Explore fifteen thousand of the world's endangered species. With over one hundred thousand photos and videos, discover what these animals, plants, and fungi look like, what makes them special, and why we should protect them.)

Discovery Education (www.discoveryeducation.com) (Parents, students, and teachers can access educational videos, free printables, free worksheets, free lesson plans, and more.)

E School News (www.eschoolnews.com/2013/04/07/ten-of-the-best-virtual-field-trips/3/) (This article on ten of the best virtual field trips has links to lots of cool places to explore online, for example, www.whitehouse.gov/about/inside-white-house/interactive-tour [the White House] or to see a 360-degree view of the seven wonders of the world [www.panoramas.dk/7.wonders].)

Global Trek (http://teacher.scholastic.com/activities/globaltrek/) (created for kids to explore the world from their computer; they are asked to choose from a list of countries and will be asked to keep a travel journal to write about different topics during their online trip)

Inner Body (www.innerbody.com/image/digeov.html) (a site to learn about human anatomy, with interactive pictures and descriptions of thousands of objects in the body)

NASA (www.nasa.gov/audience/forstudents/5.8/index.html, www.nasa.gov/audience/forkids/kidsclub/flash/index.html, and http://quest.nasa.gov/) (NASA's sites of interactive learning activities, challenges, games, information for kids) and (http://mars.jpl.nasa.gov/participate/funzone/) (NASA's Mars for Kids; great interactive website for kids to explore Mars)

National Geographic for Kids (http://kids.nationalgeographic.com/kids) (lots of free videos, and short one-page articles on many interesting topics; great resource to get kids to read nonfiction and build comprehension)

Educational Apps for Kids

IGameMm.com (http://igamemom.com/best-educational-apps-for-kids/) (This site is great for reviews of educational apps for kids.)

Learning Works for Kids (http://learningworksforkids.com/apps/?skill=alternative-learners_adhd) (reviews of recommended Apps for kids with ADHD)

Pinterest (http://pinterest.com/sandrarief/technology/) (lots of lists of recommended educational apps)

Reading Rockets (www.readingrockets.org/teaching/reading101/literacyapps/) (list of top educational literacy apps)

Appendix

Charts, Forms, and Visual Prompts

Appendix materials are also available online at www.wiley.com/go/adhdbol2. The password is the last five digits of the book's ISBN, which is 37754.

Thanks to: Itzik Rief, Julie Heimburge, Abigail Roldan, Janet Poulos, Amanda Gerber, Alison Finberg, and Earl Chen for creating and sharing some of the charts found in this appendix.

CLASSROOM PROCEDURES
What Do You Expect Students to Do When ...?

- they need to sharpen a pencil ______
- they don't have paper or other needed supplies ______
- they finish work early ______
- they have a question during instruction ______
- they need to go to the restroom ______
- they want to throw something in the trash ______
- they have a question during independent work ______
- they need a drink of water ______
- there are class interruptions (e.g., announcements on the intercom) ______
- they enter the classroom at the beginning of day (period) ______
- they enter the classroom after recess, PE, or lunch ______
- they prepare to leave the classroom at end of the day (period) ______
- moving into or changing groups ______
- the bell rings ______
- they are late or tardy ______
- they return after being absent ______
- listening to and responding to questions ______
- you signal for attention ______
- working cooperatively (partner or small group) ______
- turning in papers, passing papers, exchanging papers ______
- moving about the room ______
- lining up ______
- working at learning centers or stations ______

Procedures and routines to teach immediately: signaling and getting their attention and quieting class, entering class and dismissal, how to and where to keep materials and belongings, preparing for class and homework assignments (e.g., paper headings, recording assignments in planner or assignment calendar)

____________'S DAILY REPORT

Date______________

	stays seated		on task		follows directions	
Times or Subjects	No More than __ Warning(s)		No More than __ Warning(s)		No More than __ Warning(s)	
	+	–	+	–	+	–
	+	–	+	–	+	–
	+	–	+	–	+	–
	+	–	+	–	+	–
	+	–	+	–	+	–
	+	–	+	–	+	–
	+	–	+	–	+	–
	+	–	+	–	+	–
	+	–	+	–	+	–
	+	–	+	–	+	–
	+	–	+	–	+	–

My goal is to earn at least ___ pluses (+) by the end of the day (or ___ percent showing great behavior and effort).

If I meet my goal, I will earn a reward or privilege of:

____
Teacher signature

____
Parent or guardian signature

Daily Behavior Report for ________________

	Stays in Assigned Place	Uses Class Time Effectively	Respectful to Adults and Classmates
Morning	☺ Keep trying	☺ Keep trying	☺ Keep trying
Recess			☺ Keep trying
Afternoon	☺ Keep trying	☺ Keep trying	☺ Keep trying
Specials	☺ Keep trying	☺ Keep trying	☺ Keep trying

Notes:

Daily Behavior Report for ________________

	Stays in Assigned Place	Uses Class Time Effectively	Respectful to Adults and Classmates
Morning	☺ Keep trying	☺ Keep trying	☺ Keep trying
Recess			☺ Keep trying
Afternoon	☺ Keep trying	☺ Keep trying	☺ Keep trying
Specials	☺ Keep trying	☺ Keep trying	☺ Keep trying

Notes:

DAILY OR WEEKLY REPORT CARD

Name: ______________________ **Week of:** ______________ **Daily Goal:** _________ **Points (total for day)**

Period	MONDAY		TUESDAY		WEDNESDAY		THURSDAY		FRIDAY	
	Conduct	Classwork	Conduct	Classwork	Conduct	Classwork	Conduct	Classwork	Conduct	Classwork
1										
2										
3										
4										
5										
6										
7										
Total points →										
Any teacher comments										
	Parent or guardian signature		Parent or guardian signature		Parent or guardian signature		Parent or guardian signature		Parent or guardian signature	

CONDUCT: - *Was respectful to adults and classmates* - *Followed teacher directions* - *Raised hand to speak (didn't blurt out or interrupt)* - *Stayed in assigned place (received permission to leave seat)*

CLASSWORK: - *Participated in lessons and activities* - *Started on assignments right away* - *Came to class prepared (with homework and materials)* - *Stayed on task with little redirection*

Teacher directions: Please enter a conduct score (0–4 points) and a classwork score (0–4 points) at the end of the class period. Base your score on how many of the four specific conduct and classwork behaviors the student demonstrated in your class that day.

Reward or Privilege earned for meeting daily goal: ____________________
Reward or Privilege earned for a successful week (a minimum of __ days of meeting the daily goal): ____________
Parents or guardians, please sign nightly and have your son or daughter return the form to school each day. It is your child's responsibility to bring the form from class to class and to bring this report to and from school daily.

MY BEHAVIOR REPORT

Name: ____________ Teacher: ____________ Week of: ________

BEHAVIOR	MONDAY			TUESDAY			WEDNESDAY			THURSDAY			FRIDAY		
	Before recess	After recess	After lunch	Before recess	After recess	After lunch	Before recess	After recess	After lunch	Before recess	After recess	After lunch	Before recess	After recess	After lunch
I followed the rules and my teacher's directions.															
I did my work.															

Parent or guardian signature ____________

______ smileys per day earns ____________

____

______ smileys per week earns

____

____

Yes, I did!

Daily Performance Record

NAME: ______________________________ DATE: ____________

SUBJECT	BEHAVIOR	TURNED IN HOMEWORK	PREPARED FOR CLASS	USED CLASS TIME EFECTIVELY
Teacher ________	Good Average Poor	YES NO	YES NO	Yes Somewhat NO
Teacher ________	Good Average Poor	YES NO	YES NO	Yes Somewhat NO
Teacher ________	Good Average Poor	YES NO	YES NO	Yes Somewhat NO
Teacher ________	Good Average Poor	YES NO	YES NO	Yes Somewhat NO
Teacher ________	Good Average Poor	YES NO	YES NO	Yes Somewhat NO
Teacher ________	Good Average Poor	YES NO	YES NO	Yes Somewhat NO

Please sign and return ______________________________ ____________

Parent or guardian signature Date

Name: Date:

Subject or Time	Stays in Seat	Follows Directions	Completes Assignment
Language Arts			
Reading Intervention			
Writing			
Music/ Computers			
Science/Social Studies			
Math Warm Up			
Math			
Total:	☺	☺	☺

Goal is______ ☺ per day to earn a happy day reward.

I earned______ ☺ today.

______ happy days a **week** earns:

Parent or guardian signature:

Extra notes:

Name: Date:

Subject or Time	Stays in Seat	Follows Directions	Completes Assignment
Total:	☺	☺	☺

Goal is______ ☺ per day to earn a happy day reward.

I earned ☺ today.

______ happy days a **week** earns:

Parent or guardian signature:

Extra notes:

MIDDLE SCHOOL DAILY REPORT

STUDENT NAME ____________________ DATE ___________

Teachers: Please write Y ("yes") or N ("no") by each behavior at end of class and sign or initial. You may also write comments.

1st Period **Comments and Signature or Initials**

________ ON TIME TO CLASS
________ HOMEWORK TURNED IN
________ USED CLASS TIME PRODUCTIVELY
________ FOLLOWED CLASS RULES (no more than two warnings)

2nd Period **Comments and Signature or Initials**

________ ON TIME TO CLASS
________ HOMEWORK TURNED IN
________ USED CLASS TIME PRODUCTIVELY
________ FOLLOWED CLASS RULES (no more than two warnings)

3rd Period **Comments and Signature or Initials**

________ ON TIME TO CLASS
________ HOMEWORK TURNED IN
________ USED CLASS TIME PRODUCTIVELY
________ FOLLOWED CLASS RULES (no more than two warnings)

4th Period **Comments and Signature or Initials**

________ ON TIME TO CLASS
________ HOMEWORK TURNED IN
________ USED CLASS TIME PRODUCTIVELY
________ FOLLOWED CLASS RULES (no more than two warnings)

5th Period **Comments and Signature or Initials**

________ ON TIME TO CLASS
________ HOMEWORK TURNED IN
________ USED CLASS TIME PRODUCTIVELY
________ FOLLOWED CLASS RULES (no more than two warnings)

6th Period **Comments and Signature or Initials**

________ ON TIME TO CLASS
________ HOMEWORK TURNED IN
________ USED CLASS TIME PRODUCTIVELY
________ FOLLOWED CLASS RULES (no more than two warnings)

7th Period **Comments and Signature or Initials**

________ ON TIME TO CLASS
________ HOMEWORK TURNED IN
________ USED CLASS TIME PRODUCTIVELY
________ FOLLOWED CLASS RULES (no more than two warnings)

Total number of yeses received today ________.

A minimum of ___ yeses are required in order to earn agreed-on reward or privilege.

A successful day of meeting the goal will result in ______________________________

Student Signature __________________ Parent or guardian Signature ______________

CONNECT THE DOTS CHART

INDIVIDUAL OR CLASS ____________

DATE STARTED ____________

DATE FINISHED ____________

REWARD ____________

HOW TO USE THE CHART

1. Select a class or individual goal (e.g., all homework turned in).
2. If you meet the goal, color in and connect to the next dot.
3. When the chart is filled (all dots are colored), the reward is earned.

RACE TO THE GOAL CHART

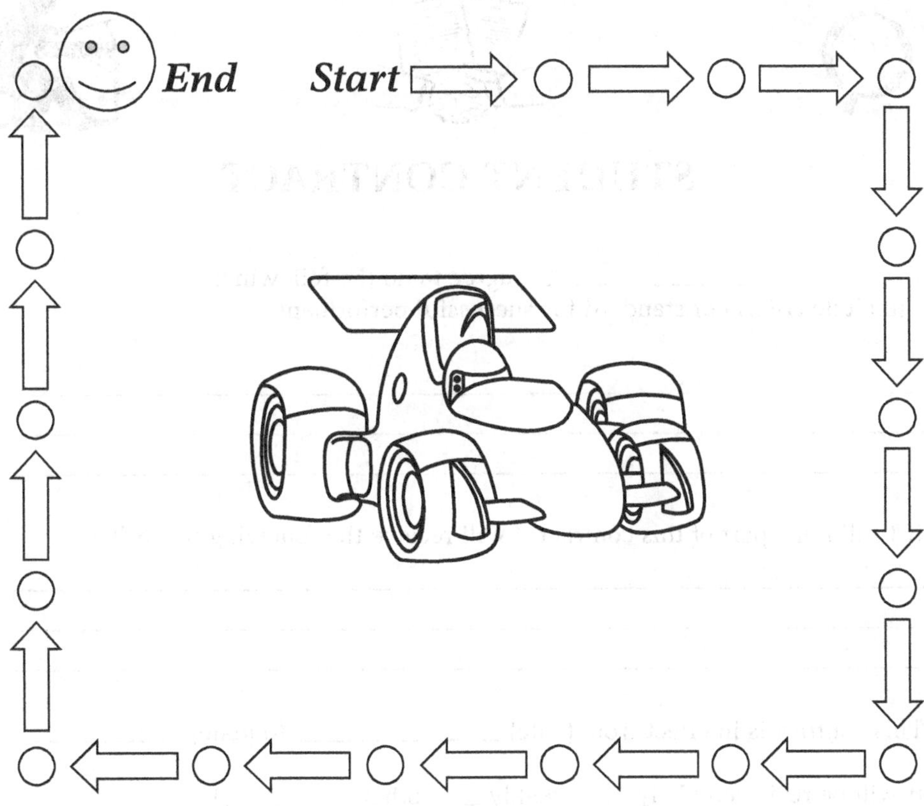

Individual or Class Goal: ____________

____

Date Started: ____________

Date Finished: ____________

Reward: ____________

____

____

How to Use the Chart

1. Select a class or individual student goal (e.g., followed class rules with no more than two reminders).
2. At designated time frames (e.g., before lunch, end of day), a dot is colored in if the target behavioral goal was met.
3. When chart is filled (all dots are colored), the reward is earned.

STUDENT CONTRACT

I, ______________________________, agree to do the following:
(include criteria or standard for successful performance.)

____

____

____

If I fulfill my part of this contract, I will receive the following reward(s):

____

____

____

This contract is in effect from (date) ______________ to (date) ____________ .

It will be reviewed (daily_____ weekly_____ other__________).

Signed:

______________________	______________________	______________________
Student	**Teacher**	**Parent**

Student–Generated Progress Report

The following is a short progress report for today/this week. Your child has evaluated himself/herself. My initials appear next to the evaluation for each section if I am in agreement.

Behavior in Class

________________ **Exceptional, splendid, excellent!**

________________ **Good**

________________ **So-so (had some difficulty)**

________________ **Needs to improve**

Homework

________________ **Wow! Everything's done!**

________________ **Good. Almost everything is done.**

________________ **Help! I need to catch up.**

Class work

________________ **Quality stuff!**

________________ **Pretty good**

________________ **Could be better**

Notebook

________________ **Neat!**

________________ **Okay**

________________ **Messy**

Student signature ________________________________

Parent or guardian signature ________________________________

Date ________________________________

HOME NOTE

Today we ______________________________

____

I learned ______________________________

____

I had fun ______________________________

____

I need to work on ______________________________

____

____

Date ______________

Student ______________

RESPONSE COST CHART

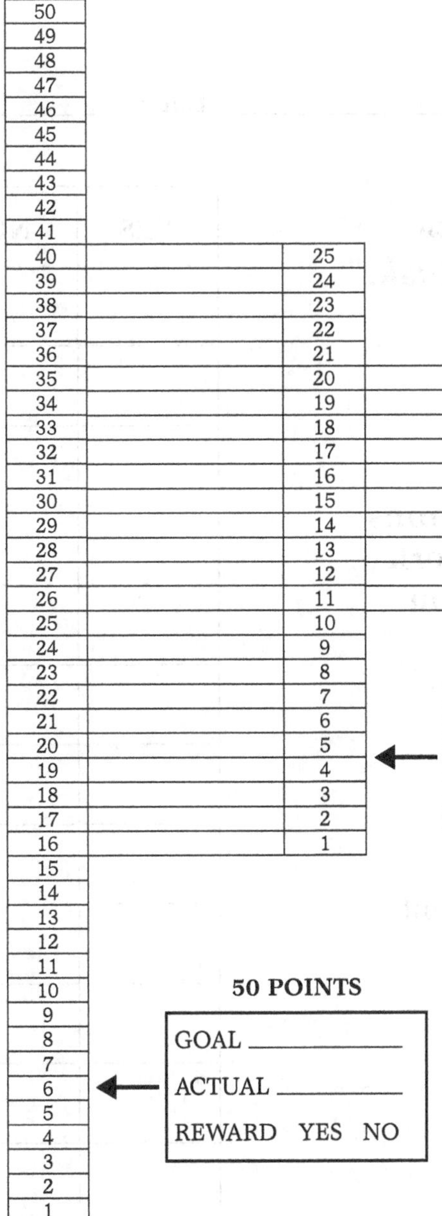

10 POINTS

GOAL ______

ACTUAL ______

REWARD YES NO

25 POINTS

GOAL ______

ACTUAL ______

REWARD YES NO

50 POINTS

GOAL ______

ACTUAL ______

REWARD YES NO

Note If the baseline frequency of the behavior does not fit in one of the 3-point columns above, use the 50-point column and adjust from there. For example, if you need 30, start from the 30 box and deduct points from there.

1. Select a problematic behavior to monitor (e.g., blurting or calling out, getting into arguments or fights, teasing, out of seat without permission).
2. Record the frequency of the behavior during a few days to a week and get a daily average (baseline).
3. Use one of above point columns as appropriate, based on the average number of occurrences of that behavior per day (50, 25, or 10).
4. Cross out 1 point (starting at 50, 25, or 10) each time the behavior occurs.
5. Start with achievable goal. For example. for the 25 column, mark the goal as 5 (which indicates a 20 percent improvement).
6. If the student has 5 or more remaining points, reward is earned. Circle the "yes."
7. Raise the goal for success until behavior has improved to a manageable level.

SELF-MONITORING FORM

Name: ______________________ **Period:** ______________ **Date:** ____________

Whenever you hear the signal*, check √yourself: *"I was focused and on task."*

Mark the YES or NO box in the columns on the right. Continue doing your work and mark "yes" or "no" each time you hear the sound.

*<u>Note to parents and teachers:</u>
Set a digital timer to make a sound at short regular or random intervals while your child or student is doing independent work (class work or homework).

YES	NO

Teacher Signature ______________________________ (if used at school)

NAME: ______________________________ DATE: ____________________

STUDENT GOAL SHEET

My goal for the day or week is:

____

____

____

This is my plan for reaching my goal:

1. ____
2. ____
3. ____

My reward for meeting the goal: ____________________________

____

____________ **I met my goal.** ____________ **I didn't meet it yet.**

Something I will work on tomorrow or next week is: ______

____

____

Name: ____________________________

Date: ______________________________ Goal for +s ___________

Turn in folder	+	−
Hang up jacket	+	−
Hang up backpack	+	−
Clean up area	+	−
Hands to self	+	−
Raise hand	+	−
Be at right place during centers	+	−
Walk in hall	+	−
Line up for recess quietly	+	−
Come in from recess quietly	+	−
Put on jacket or pack it up	+	−
Pack up folder	+	−
Show +/− sheet to teacher	+	−

How many +? ____________________

Did I reach my goal? 

HOMEWORK ASSIGNMENTS

WEEK OF __________

Teacher signature __________ **Parent or guardian signature** ____________

ASSIGNMENT	CLASS/ TEACHER	ASSIGNED DATE	DUE DATE

HOMEWORK ASSIGNMENT LOG

Week of: ___________

Teacher signature: _____________ **Parent or guardian signature:** _____________

Date	Subject	*Assignment*	
		Materials	Due date:
			Date turned in:
		Assignment	
		Materials	Due date:
			Date turned in:
		Assignment	
		Materials	Due date:
			Date turned in:
		Assignment	
		Materials	Due date:
			Date turned in:
		Assignment	
		Materials	Due date:
			Date turned in:

Homework Tracking Sheet

Name: ______________________ Date: ______________________

Class	Completed Classroom Assignments?		Homework	Upcoming Projects or Exams	Teacher Initials
	Yes	No			
Period 1	**Yes or No**			Date:	
Period 2	**Yes or No**			Date:	
Period 3	**Yes or No**			Date:	
Period 4	**Yes or No**			Date:	
Period 5	**Yes or No**			Date:	
Period 6	**Yes or No**			Date:	

Parent or guardian signature: ______________

MISSING ASSIGNMENTS OR NEEDS TO COMPLETE

Period 1: ______________________

Period 2: ______________________

Period 3: ______________________

Period 4: ______________________

Period 5: ______________________

Period 6: ______________________

STUDENT WEEKLY PLANNING SCHEDULE

Student name ____________________ **Parent or guardian signature** ____________________

Time	Monday	Tuesday	Wednesday	Thursday	Friday	Saturday	Sunday
3:00-4:00							
4:00-5:00							
5:00-6:00							
6:00-7:00							
7:00-8:00							
8:00-9:00							
9:00-10:00							

THINGS TO DO TODAY

DATE ____________________ **COMPLETED**

1. ____________________ ☐
2. ____________________ ☐
3. ____________________ ☐
4. ____________________ ☐
5. ____________________ ☐
6. ____________________ ☐
7. ____________________ ☐
8. ____________________ ☐
9. ____________________ ☐
10. ____________________ ☐
11. ____________________ ☐
12. ____________________ ☐

High School Daily Reminder Item List Name: ___________________

This piece of paper contains a list of items that you should bring to school every day (or on specific days). The list is unique to your class schedule. Do not lose this piece of paper!

Everyday	Student planner and calendar School uniform (polo, khakis, belt) Backpack Writing utensils
Period 1 - Pre-calculus	Textbook Notebook Calculator Daily homework
Period 2 - US History	Textbook (Mondays and Fridays only) Notebook Planner
Period 3 - Chemistry	Textbook Notebook Colored Folder Organizer Homework Lab coat (Wednesday only) Goggles (Wednesday only)
Period 4 - British Literature	Book (varies throughout quarter) Notebook Writing journal
Period 5 - Art 3	Sketchbook Notebook Camera (Thursdays only)
Period 6 - PE	PE uniform (T-shirt, shorts)
Period 7 - Elective - Finance	Notebook Laptop (Thursdays only)

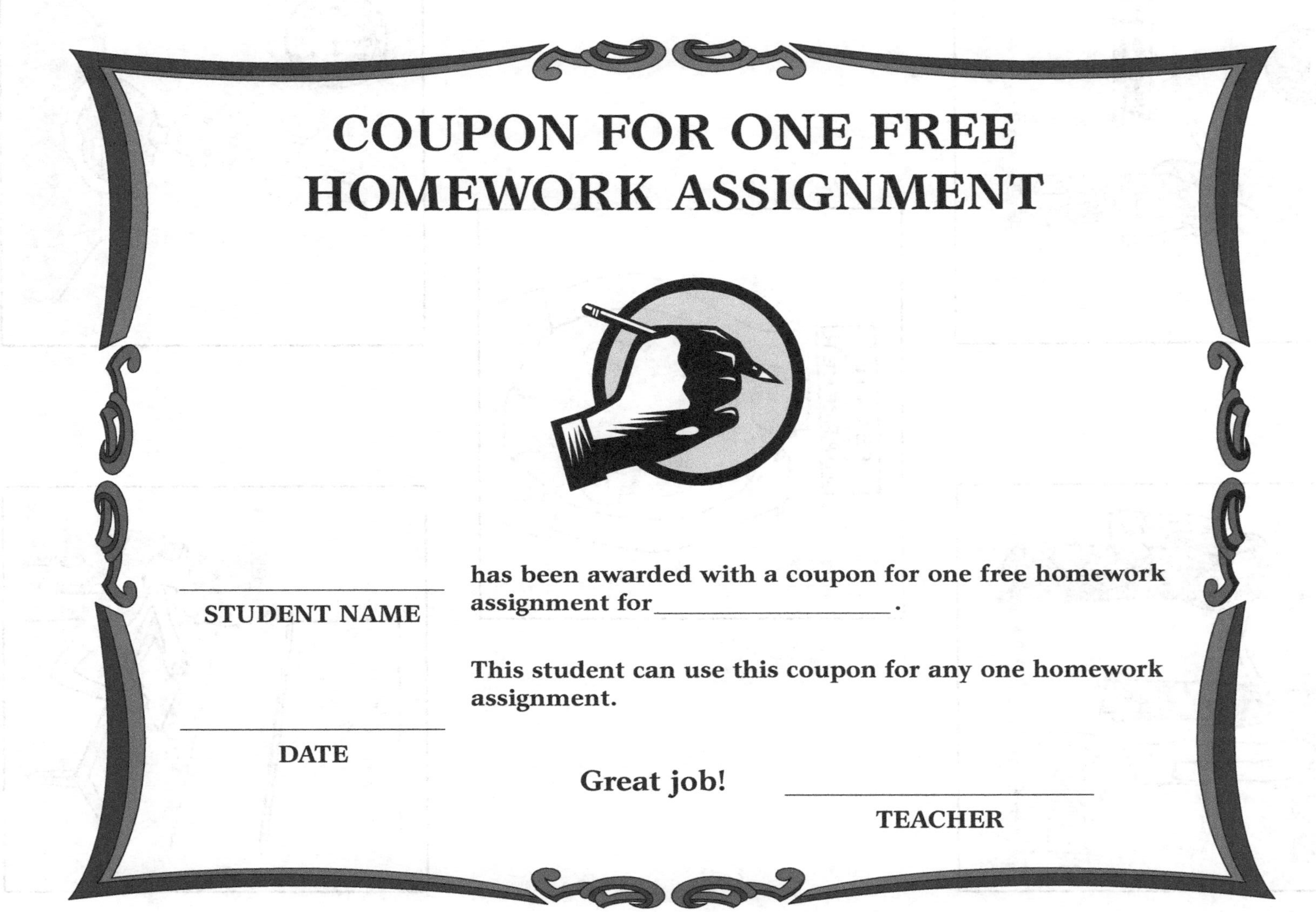

COUPON FOR ONE FREE HOMEWORK ASSIGNMENT

____
STUDENT NAME

has been awarded with a coupon for one free homework assignment for _______________.

This student can use this coupon for any one homework assignment.

____
DATE

Great job!

____
TEACHER

COAT/HAT RACK
BILLY
LUNCHES

HOMEWORK BIN

PENCIL
SHARPENER

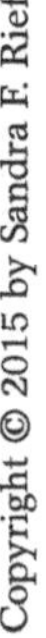

Warmup Activity
① 392
x 21
② Name as many countries in Europe that you can think of.

RING
RING

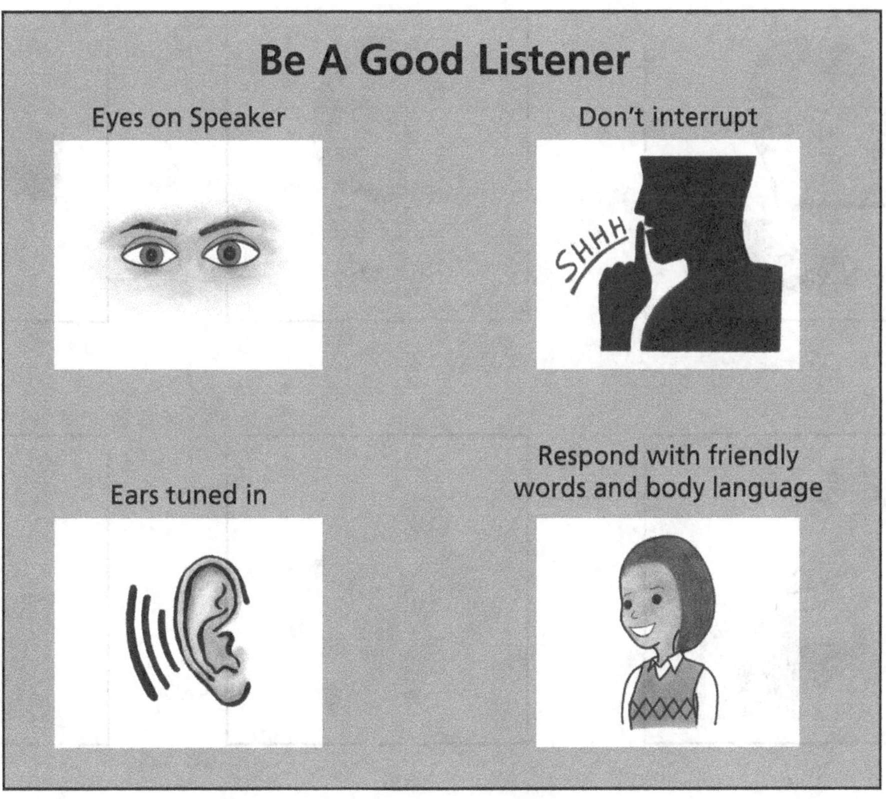
Be A Good Listener
Eyes on Speaker
Don't interrupt
SHHH
Ears tuned in
Respond with friendly words and body language

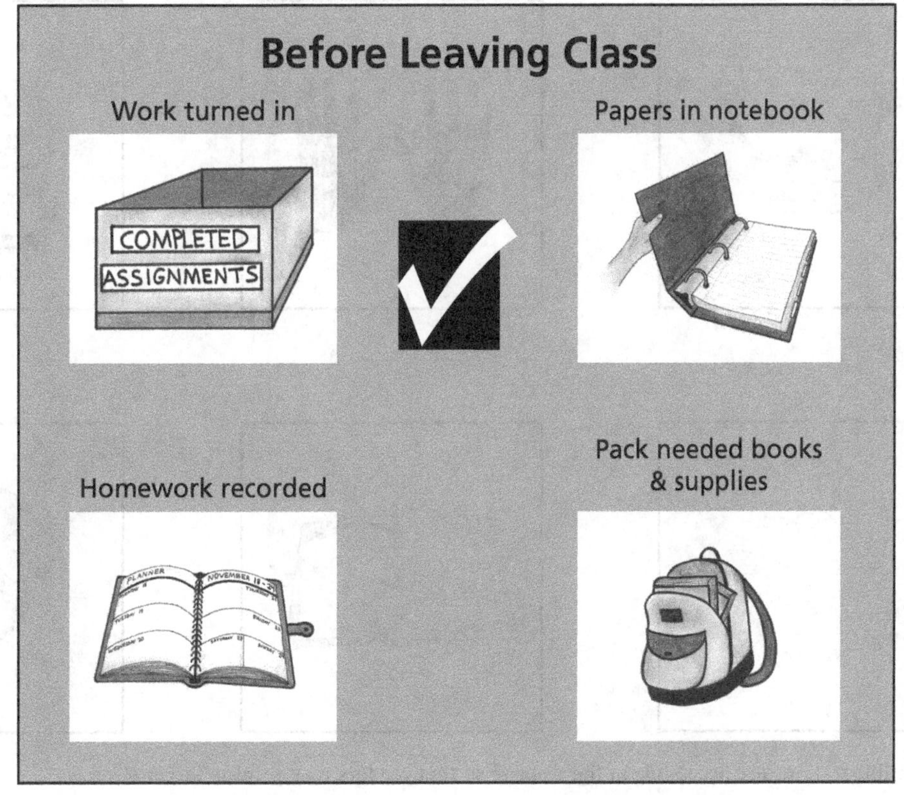
Before Leaving Class
Work turned in
COMPLETED
ASSIGNMENTS
Papers in notebook
Homework recorded
Pack needed books & supplies

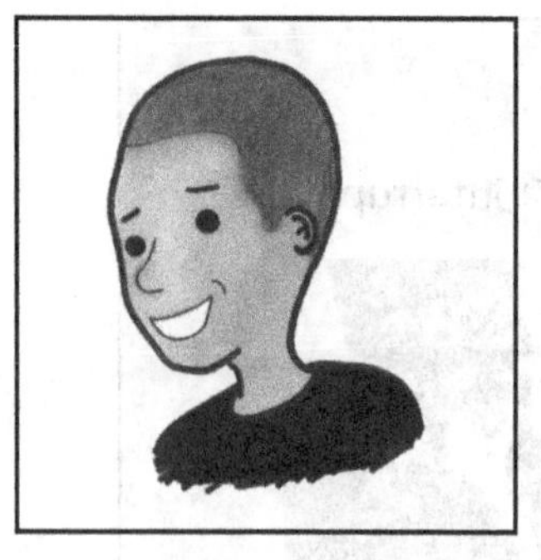

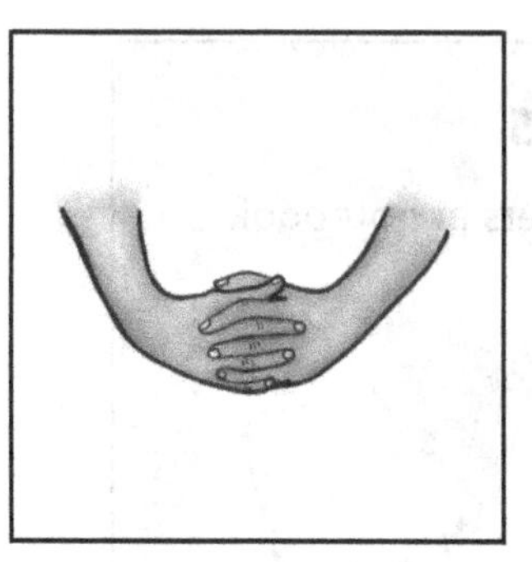

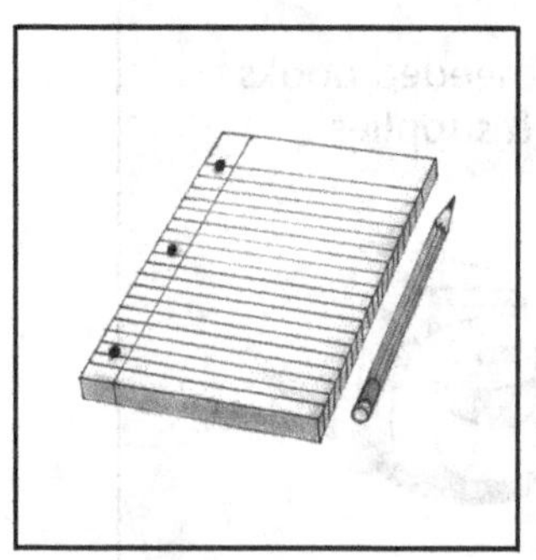

These illustrations are accessible at the website so that readers may print in larger sizes.

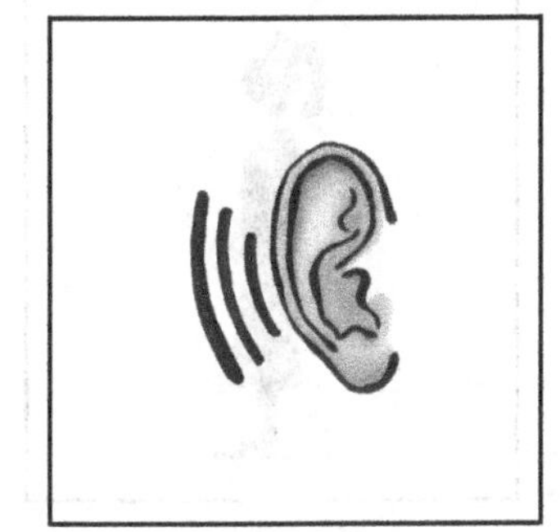

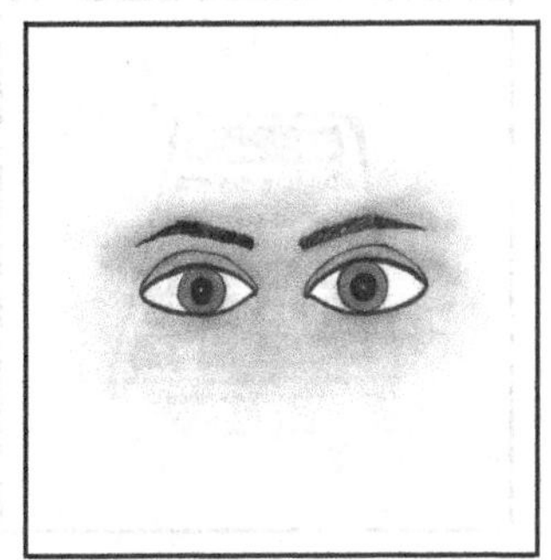

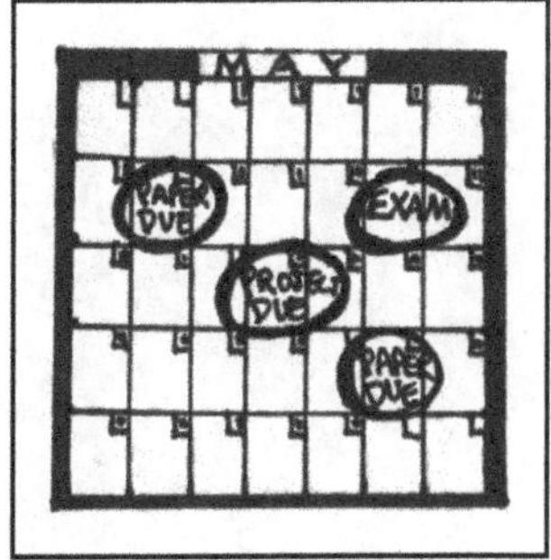

These illustrations are accessible at the website so that readers may print in larger sizes.

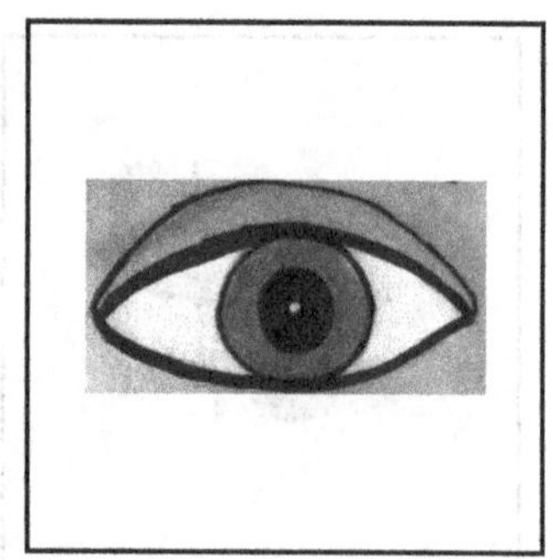

These illustrations are accessible at the website so that readers may print in larger sizes.

Index

B

C

D

E

F

G

H

I

J

K

L

M

N

O

P

Q

R

S

T

U

V

W